April 1988

To Joy -

One of the best

I've ever had - in public and private life - I hope this serves as a pleasant reminder of your visit to Fresno -

With affection & admiration -

Karen Humphrey.

FRESNO
Valley of Abundance

Linda M.C. Abbott PhD.
Author

Produced by:
H. Markus & Co.
Fine Printing

Special Acknowledgements

This book could not have been produced without the superb cooperation and combined talents of hundreds of people and organizations.

Special acknowledgements must go to the following individuals and groups who played such a key role in the production of this book.

TO: **Linda Abbott** — for her many miles of travel, numerous interviews, and countless hours of research and writing, which provided the narrative for this book.

TO: **Ernie Hergenroeder** — for his creative designs and layout leading to the production and presentation of the book.

TO: **Fresno County & City Chamber of Commerce Staff** who helped prepare, edit and proof this book.

TO: **Joseph Frisina, Jr.** who served as lead photographer for many of the pictures taken specifically for this book.

TO: **The Fresno Camera Club** and its **President Dan Sniffin** whose members furnished many beautiful photographs for this book.

TO: **Harry Markus, Lynn Levy** and **Roger Hampton** for their professional expertise in the pre-production and printing of this book.

TO: **Arsen** and **Renee Apkarian** whose professional assistance in typography was invaluable.

TO: The many **patrons** whose financial support was essential for the production of a book of this quality.

TO: **Russ Sloan** who secured the financial patrons and oversaw the complete production of this book.

TO: **The officers and Board of the Fresno County and City Chamber of Commerce** who had the vision and dedication to undertake the production of such a book for the education and enjoyment of thousands of Fresno residents, visitors, and interested parties.

Thank you all,
The Fresno County and City
Chamber of Commerce

Publisher: Fresno County and City Chamber of Commerce
Publication Coordinator: Russ Sloan
Produced by: H. Markus and Co. Fine Printing
Staff for Fresno: Valley of Abundance
Author: Linda M.C. Abbott, PhD.
Design and Layout Artist: Ernie Hergenroeder
Assistant Pasteup and Layout: Elizabeth Woods-McAfee
Corporate Profiles: Communications staff of the Fresno County and City Chamber of Commerce
Editing: Sharon Stochler
Proofreaders: Blanche Milhahn, Frances White, Michale Lehman
Corporate Sponsor Coordinator: Russ Sloan

Published in 1988
Printed in the United States of America
First Edition

Library of Congress Cataloging-in-Publication Data
Abbott, PhD., Linda M.C.
Fresno: Valley of Abundance

Bibliography: p. 236
Includes Index

1. Fresno (CA) - History
2. Fresno (CA) - Description
3. Fresno (CA) - Quality of Life

1. Title II. Title: Fresno: Valley of Abundance

ISBN 0-945347-00-6

Contributing Photography Acknowledgements

Judy M. Baker
Bob Barnes
CSUF Information Office
Steve Dzerigian
Joseph Frisina, Jr.
Russell Fey
Fresno City and County Historical Society
Fresno Gateway Magazine
Hans Halberstadt
Wayne Jackson
Byron Miksch, Jr.
Clair Nelson
Hartt Porteous
Walt Puhn
Galen Rowell
Dan Sniffin
Schoenwald-Oba Morgensen-Pohll-Miller, Inc.
State Center Community College Information Office
Warren Sucaringen
Anna Woodward
Scott Zimmerman

Contents

FOREWARD

Chapter 1 *A Central California Lifestyle* 1
Fresno Overview, Churches, Residential Lifestyle

Chapter 2 *A Heritage of the Soil* 19
Early Residents and Growth

Chapter 3 *Newcomers — People and Business* 41
Fresno's Ethnic Roots and Diversity,
Emerging New Businesses

Chapter 4 *The Economic Base* 56
Agriculture, Business, Industry, Finance and Development

Chapter 5 *The Service Sectors* 95
Health, Education, Law and Other Professions

Chapter 6 *Network in Action* 137
Government, Transportation, and Communications

Chapter 7 *Recreation and Cultural Arts* 159
National Parks, Scenic Attractions, Arts, Music,
Museums and the Zoo

Chapter 8 *Community Spirit* 183
Philanthropy, Sports, Convention Center, the Fair,
Area Parks and Attractions

Chapter 9 *Around the County* 197
Profiling Fresno County's Incorporated Cities

Chapter 10 *Vistas of Tomorrow* 219
Economic Development, Planning for Growth,
Ideas for the Future

Acknowledgements 233

Approaching A Century of Leadership 234

Patrons 235

Bibliography 236

Index 236

Fresno Fast Facts

History:
Fresno is the Spanish name for "ash" which, like so many Spanish place names throughout California, is a legacy of the era of Mexican rule. The original Fresno County seat (1856-1875) was located at the town of Millerton on the San Joaquin River, an area now flooded behind the Friant Dam. The original County Court House was moved and has been preserved as a historic building-museum at the dam site. With the coming of the railroad, the populace voted to move the county seat 25 miles south to a wilderness point on the new Central Pacific line. That site developed into present-day downtown Fresno, a city incorporated on October 27, 1885.

Quick Facts

Population	Area (as of 1-1-87)	Elevation
Metro 415,000	299 Sq. Mi.	- - - - -
City 297,000	95 Sq. Mi.	328 ft. AMSL
County 588,345	6,000 Sq. Mi.	14,254 (max.)

	Housing Units	Assessed Value
City	117,380	$ 8.314 million
County	221,045	$19.788 million

Location:
The only place in the nation just 90 minutes from three National Parks, Fresno is in the center of the Central San Joaquin Valley.

Trade area:
The Retail Trade Area covers five counties and a population of 1.207 million persons. The Wholesale Trade Area covers eight counties and a population of 2.038 million persons.

Local Government:
The City of Fresno has a council-manager form of government with seven elected councilmen, one of whom is the elected mayor. Council employs a chief administrative officer. Fresno County is divided into five supervisorial districts; a chief administrative office serves the elected Board of Supervisors.

Transportation:
Fresno, designated a U.S. Port-of-Entry, is a hub of transportation facilities of all kinds, connecting Central California to destinations throughout the world.

With one private and two municipal airports, Fresno provides facilities for both private and commercial aviation. PSA, Continental, Sky West, American Eagle, United Express, United and Delta operate regularly scheduled flights from the Fresno Air Terminal. Both Santa Fe and Southern Pacific Railroads have extensive freight terminal facilities here and service Amtrak passenger trains. Greyhound has a terminal in Fresno, in addition to Fresno Transit providing local service. Dozens of trucking firms provide service of every description to all parts of the country.

Automobile Registration:
An application for a California driver's license should be completed within 10 days of becoming a permanent resident of California. Car license and registration is required 20 days after entry to the state. For California automobile registration and driver's license information, contact the State Department of Motor Vehicles, 655 W. Olive, Fresno, CA., 93728 or call (209) 445-5469.

Agriculture
Fresno County is the nation's number one farm county, averaging over $2 billion dollars a year in production of nearly 200 commercial crops.

Fresno County Cities Population
(as of 1-1-87)

Clovis	42,000
Coalinga	7,825
Firebaugh	3,910
Fowler	3,020
Huron	3,660
Kerman	4,240
Kingsburg	6,025
Uninc	161,700
Mendota	6,800
Orange Cove	4,580
Parlier	6,600
Reedley	13,750
Sanger	14,700
San Joaquin	2,050
Selma	13,500

Distances from Fresno:

Destination	Miles
Bakersfield	108
Carmel	164
Kings Canyon National Park	55
Los Angeles	222
Monterey	150
Sacramento	171
San Luis Obispo	139
San Francisco	184
Sequoia National Park	85
Yosemite	92

Climatological Chart (30 YR. AVG.)

	Daily Max.	Daily Min.	Normal Rainfall	Sunshine %
JAN.	54.2	37.4	1.82	46
FEB.	61.2	40.9	1.64	80
MAR.	66.5	43.7	1.67	94
APR.	74.1	47.5	.98	94
MAY	82.5	53.2	.35	95
JUN.	91.2	59.4	.10	93
JULY	98.7	64.7	.01	96
AUG.	96.7	63.1	.01	98
SEPT.	89.9	58.2	.17	97
OCT.	79.0	50.5	.54	86
NOV.	66.0	42.4	1.02	49
DEC.	54.9	37.8	1.55	46
AVG.	76.2	49.9	9.86	83

Crop Values (1986)

Field Crops	$483,687,000
Seed Crops	47,064,000
Vegetable Crops	368,120,000
Fruit and Nut Crops	775,104,600
Nursery Products	10,331,000
Livestock and Poultry	297,384,000
Livestock and Poultry Products	134,338,000
Apiary	6,065,000
Timber Harvest	3,628,000
Total	$2,125,721,600

Employment: ('86 estimates)

1. Agricultural	53,500
2. Construction	11,700
3. Manufacturing	20,800
4. Transportation & Public Utilities	10,300
5. Wholesale & Retail Trade	50,300
6. Finance, Insurance, Real Estate	13,700
7. Services	44,000
8. Government	43,600

FOREWORD

In 1985 the City of Fresno celebrated its centennial with great fanfare. This celebration gave the community an excellent opportunity to look back with pride on the unusual growth and development which the City and County of Fresno have enjoyed. Stopping in this way to take inventory on our progress also gave us a good opportunity to assess the future and to plan logically for it.

Blessed with a temperate climate, fertile land and abundant water, it is not surprising that Fresno County has maintained its image as a bright spot in California. Even during the great depression of the '30s, Fresno drew nationwide attention for being an economic oasis. Land costs are 75 to 85 percent lower in Fresno County than in California's coastal communities, housing is 35 to 40 percent less costly, prime office space costs one-third to one-half what it would in other parts of the state, and the wage scale of an abundant and quality labor force is commensurately lower than elsewhere in the state. These are some of the economic values which have contributed to making Fresno County the most productive agricultural county in the nation for many years.

It is quite common to find brochures and pamphlets that cite the business and agricultural statistics which make Fresno so unique. Also, pictures such as those found in this beautiful book support the statistical record. However, there is one ingredient that almost defies written or pictorial description which I feel is a most important factor enabling Fresno County to be a star performer year after year. It is the quality of life that is enjoyed by all people who choose to live here. It is infectious. Once you have experienced it and have been able to compare it with other communities you become addicted to it. In fact, very often people will turn down a promotion within a larger corporation if it means moving out of the Fresno area. Also, it is common for some even to leave their employer if a move to a large metropolitan area is necessary. One might ask why this quality of life is so unique and how it translates into prosperity for people and businesses who choose to locate here. I believe this is an easy question to answer.

In the last several years Fresno County, while maintaining its preeminence in agriculture, has attracted businesses without ties to agriculture. Because of its central location within easy reach of California's ever growing population, Fresno County has been selected by major firms in a variety of industries for their regional operations. Insurance, plastics, data processing and heavy manufacturing firms have all made significant commitments to Fresno. The Internal Revenue Service has established its major facility for the western states in Fresno. In addition to the economic advantages, many human enhancements contribute strongly to the quality of life in Fresno. With a population of approximately 600,000, Fresno County by some standards could be regarded as large. This population easily supports a highly ranked education system including the renowned Fresno campus of California State University. Fresno also enjoys quality art, history and science museums and a delightful symphony orchestra.

By examining the population from another perspective, one can readily understand the rural and small town feel which the various communities making up Fresno County transmit in the form of enjoyable living. Fresno is really a community of communities bound together strongly by mutual interests.

Lewis S. Eaton, Chairman of Guarantee Savings and former president of the Fresno County and City Chamber of Commerce, is one of Fresno's most influential citizens. As the first recipient of the chamber's most prestigious Leon S. Peters Award, Mr. Eaton brings a lifelong Fresno perspective to his commentary.

Mr. Eaton has been a key leader in community affairs, including the Fresno Zoo, Arts Center, the Fresno Metropolitan Museum, Rotary Playland, Channel 18 Public Television, Woodward Park, Fresno Community Hospital, Fresno Board of Education, and Fresno State University, as well as a host of civic, educational, corporate, and public service-oriented groups, associations, and foundations.

Heavy commuter traffic does not exist here, and most people live within an easy 15 minute drive to work.

At Fresno's back door is one of the most spectacular recreation areas in the United States. The snow-capped Sierra Nevada rising to heights exceeding 14,000 feet and three of the nation's major national parks, Yosemite, Sequoia and Kings Canyon, are within sight and a short drive away. Even those who love the seashore can find beaches within a couple of hours by automobile. These all make for a wide range of options for the recreation minded.

In summary, Fresno County is a multifaceted area with a multitude of selling features. It is large enough to support a solid range of commercial and cultural opportunities, yet small enough to provide a comfortable and very affordable quality of life.

Much of the credit for helping Fresno coordinate an orderly growth process over many years must go to the Fresno County and City Chamber of Commerce. It has won awards for its performance and quality publications, and is responsible for the creation of this book. There is no better place to start in your quest for information about Fresno than at the Chamber. I encourage you to inquire, and I know you will be rewarded.

Lewis S. Eaton

Once there was a desert, a land harder than the miners and cattlemen who — lured by the freedom of riches — dared to cross it. One thinks of Moses, leading the people of Israel to a promised land that hardly looked promising to them then, parched and journey-spent. Here a desert has bloomed too, transformed into a garden of the sun, the most bountiful land in the world. Where only thorns and brush once grew, the harvest yields now feed the nation and much of the world as well. Two billion dollars a year, over 200 different crops — some harvested several times a year, 47 of California's 50 most important crops — the superlatives are staggering!

Imagine a valley so vast that it stretches from the sun-browned coastal mountains to the snowy Sierra peaks, a valley with gold, and black gold, and the white gold of cotton as well. Imagine a place where business starts with agribusiness and includes the most sophisticated transactions made anywhere, where culture starts with agriculture and transcends the human condition in myriad forms of beauty and delight, echoing the rhythms and patterns of the seasons and the soil. Several nations in one, several regions coexisting peacefully, citrus and grapes, nuts and melons, figs and potatoes, snow peas and corn: the productivity of the ever fertile valley and of its earnest, hardworking people is a legend of our time.

Once desperadoes roamed wild and free, outlaws inspired wonderful stories. Today, the frontier spirit still shows in the "can-do" culture of the West. You can feel the steel in the people's resolve — the spirit that forced blooms from the desert, gold from the mountains and fortunes from some accidentally dried grapes. It is a spirit to be reckoned with.

Individual effort makes a difference here, in the best tradition of frontier. One man saved a beautiful building to be the home of his dream museum. Another man organized his friends and neighbors to bring children from troubled Ireland and the Middle East to Fresno for safe, peaceful vacations. Another spurred his Rotary Club to raise funds for ambulances for remote Mexican villages and then, not satisfied, drove them there. One woman's gift for hospice care brought comfort to many. Over and over the personal touch matters; the individual counts.

And in this family, football and fund-raiser town, the group counts too. When a small Fresno boy needed a liver transplant, his neighbors led a parade that raised the money. The local newspaper carried daily progress reports from his hospital bed in Texas to the anxious new friends he had left

1: A Central Valley Lifestyle

Woodward Lake By Grupe Development Company

SANDALWOOD DEVELOPMENT CORP.

COMMITMENT TO AFFORDABILITY

Bob Barnes

Steven C. Hall, President of Sandalwood Development Corporation, has built everything from apartments to condominiums to residential subdivisions in Fresno. And throughout every project, he has kept one perspective first and foremost in his work: commitment to affordability.

Hall realizes that every time he creates a new home, he is contributing to one of the special qualities of life in Fresno, the sense of community, of a neighborhood that is as strong as it is diverse.

A native Californian, Hall is well aware of what a difference that feeling can make, for he has lived in such varied locales as Patterson, San Jose, Lodi and San Diego. He is now a Fresno resident.

"Fresno is unique among the major metropolitan areas of California," said Hall. "It is a city where economic growth and the maintenance of affordable housing go hand-in-hand. Often we have heard of other communities that sacrifice one for the other."

That special quality about Fresno has been a beacon to Sandalwood's commitment to affordability, for it reflects upon the other facets of the area: educational facilities recognized nationwide for their outstanding advancements, the focus on family which fosters the strong sense of community and the subtle blending of rural and urban life-styles.

Sandalwood Development was incorporated in 1981 by Hall, who is the sole stockholder. A graduate of the California State University system with a Bachelor of Arts, he worked at Wells Fargo Bank for eight years specializing in construction lending, marketing and administration. He has also served as the senior loan officer for the Bank of Fresno, an independent bank.

The company, which is sole stockholder of Sandalwood Construction Company, Inc. and Sandalwood Realty Corporation, currently has a 70-unit Planned Unit Development underway in the northeast area of Fresno called Millbrook Place. In addition, 70 percent of Phase I of a single family, semi-custom subdivision of Sandalwood Homes has been completed. Located in the northeast section of town, another 40 units will be available in the spring of 1988 with the opening of Phase II. A 12-unit apartment complex near the Fresno Airport is being built along with an 81-unit residential subdivision in Hanford.

In each project, Hall's commitment to affordability is as visible as his involvement in the community. For example, he serves as the Vice President of the Building Industry Association of the San Joaquin Valley.

"The B.I.A. has always been committed to maintaining affordable housing in the Fresno area," Hall said, "and because of that commitment, I am involved and I believe in the work of the association. In the end, we are all working for the same goal, affordable housing, and that benefits the consumer, the community and our quality of life."

at home. When the college football team (undefeated in 1985) takes to the road, a red-clad wave of loyal fans follows, taking the Fresno spirit along. When Passport Fresno showcased the city's 77 ethnic groups, nearly 80,000 people came to celebrate, to learn and to understand their neighbors.

Fresno is also a city with a sense of humor. When Carol Burnett's comedy mini-series, "Fresno," was filmed and shown here, the city gave itself a party to remember. Vintage limousines carried the party-goers to a star-studded reception in the elegant "Met" Museum. The street was covered with red carpet, and a brass band played as the revelers strolled to the private showing. For all its sophisticated pleasures — wines, skiing, galleries, museums, ethnic restaurants of every nation, boutiques and tennis clubs, Fresno is a family town of solid folks — a little luckier than most, perhaps, to live carefree, productive lives in the Valley of Abundance.

A city with many faces, Fresno is the finance, retail, education, health, law and cultural center of the great San Joaquin Valley.

CSUF Information Office

Head coach Jim Sweeney intently scans the sideline as Red Wave fans cheer on their Bulldogs.

Bob Barnes

But beyond that, Hall noted the B.I.A.'s involvement in helping pass school bonds, restoring the historic Meux Home and building the castle at Storyland in Roeding Park as examples of commitment that benefit other areas of the community.

Steven C. Hall has seen what making a commitment can do, and his commitment to affordable housing as with the B.I.A.'s, has helped create the sense of community that helps make Fresno so unique.

Hartt Porteous

A powerful Caterpillar tractor plows the fertile valley soil at the base of the towering Sierras.

Hartt Porteous

Morning light reflects off the rugged Sierra mountain terrain.

Minutes from awe-inspiring Yosemite, Sequoia and Kings Canyon National Parks, it is also but a short stop from the rugged Big Sur coast. Halfway between Los Angeles and San Francisco, Fresno is the warehouse and distribution center of the state. Proud of its history and eager to take on the challenge of the future, Fresno is the symbol of the new American culture. Formed of brightly colored strands of ethnic diversity, linked by love of the land and gratitude for beauty, the culture blends the contemporary, casual West Coast lifestyle with the solid virtues of the faith- and family-oriented Midwest. As Ellis Island's promise shone brightly for 19th century immigrants, so Fresno welcomes the world today. In this fast-growing metropolis, respect for the heritage of the soil and a willingness to work are still the only required passports for success.

Hartt Porteous

Fresno's people believe in the effectiveness of work — hard, rewarding work, bringing solutions where only problems existed. Their faith shows in big ideas: a community-wide planning conference called Vision 90, a Ronald McDonald House for parents of hospitalized children, a Fourth of July celebration that helps fund a hospice. Faith in work also shows in the small, meaningful touches: a volunteer spirit that coaches kids' teams, reads to nursing home residents, packs sandwiches for the needy. Harmony, diversity, caring and vitality all characterize this boom town which is so big and so small all at once.

But underlying it all is the rhythm of the seasons and the land, the rich, fertile, sustaining, everlasting lushness of the world's richest soil. Fruit hangs heavy on the trees; vines are burdened with grapes; hearts are filled with gratitude for a life so good. Welcome to Fresno, Valley of Abundance!

FRESNO'S CHURCHES

Newcomers to the Central Valley often remark on the enduring middle-American values that shape individual and family life in this garden of the sun. In large measure, the value structure which is prevalent in the Fresno area is attributable to its roots. Sunk deep in agrarian culture, the roots of Fresno's people have an unmistakable spiritual element, a heritage of generations of trust: trust in the soil, trust in the seasons, trust in the dignity of human labor, trust in the guidance of a higher power.

The architectural reflection of this heritage of trust is found throughout the metropolitan area in Fresno's

Wayne Jackson

approximately 400 churches, two synagogues, Buddhist temple and gathering place for the university-based Moslem community. Most Christian denominations are represented, as are both the Conservative and Reform Jewish traditions. A number of church buildings, particularly those whose congregations represent distinct ethnic groups, are architectural gems. The West Fresno Buddhist Temple is an outstandingly beautiful building of historical importance, as are Saint Alphonsus Catholic Church and several of the Armenian churches.

The City Parks and Recreation Department lists 38 churches having special historical, architectural or ethnic significance. The city arranges tours of these churches from time to time for visiting groups, and the city's Creative Activities for You (CAFY) selections often include programs featuring ethnic dinners prepared by members of local congregations. Armenian, Chinese, Japanese, Indian, Black, Mexican, Greek, Danish, Volga German and Serbian churches are found in Fresno; several of the groups have more than one congregation.

The older and ethnic churches are not the only attractive buildings designed for religious purposes in Fresno. North Fruit Street features a tent-topped contemporary Lutheran church, and Clovis is home to an attractive facility of the Church of Jesus Christ of Latter Day Saints. On Herndon Avenue there are several contemporary Protestant churches; the massive grey stone walls of Saint Anthony of Padua Catholic Church grace Bullard Avenue.

(Continued on page 7)

Picture at top captures fall leaves on courthouse grounds. Picture at bottom is of Temple Beth Israel Synagogue.

THE PEOPLES CHURCH

A STRONG CHURCH FAMILY

PASTOR G.L. JOHNSON

A vital part of the Fresno community since 1955, Peoples Church has come to be known as a very representative cross section of the people of the central San Joaquin Valley.

As newcomers to Fresno soon find this to be one of the friendliest cities in California, they also experience the warmth of loving welcome as they meet the church family that is The Peoples Church.

As Fresno has grown, The Peoples Church has continued to grow and welcome people from all ethnic and socioeconomic backgrounds.

A Bible teaching church, led by the dedicated guidance of Pastor G.L. Johnson, this church family is strongly committed to serving the Lord, the people of its community and this generation around the world. It can be truthfully said that the sun never sets upon the mission influence of The Peoples Church family.

Out of concern for the people of the Fresno community, The Peoples Church maintains a Contact phone-in assistance ministry for those who simply need someone to talk with or need referral to other agencies for help. Hundreds of calls are also made to individuals within the Fresno community who might otherwise not have social contact due to their physical limitations. Hospital and convalescent home visitations occur daily as a ministry of the pastoral staff and congregation.

The church family continues to be actively involved in the ongoing ministries of the Fresno Rescue Mission, the Evangel Home for Women of Fresno and the sharing of Bible studies in the Fresno jail. The church also offers free individual family and marriage counseling. And, in cooperation with several churches, The Peoples Church family is a cosponsor of the Fresno Christian School, which is a kindergarten through twelfth grade system.

Parents are reassured by the beautiful nursery facilities and well-trained nursery staff. Families and single parents with preschoolers, elementary age children or youth find Peoples to be a church that provides loving care to their children while instructing them in Biblical values and principles on which to base a Godly and successful life-style.

College and career adults through senior adults enjoy excellent Bible learning opportunities as well as some of the finest, friendliest times of fellowship and fun anywhere.

The music ministry of The Peoples Church offers a wide opportunity for participation and worship. The Cathedral Choir, the handbell choir, children's choirs, High School/College choir, mixed ensemble, male quartet, ladies ensemble, Lightstream and Psalms of Praise minister in jails, in convalescent homes, in special Christmas and Easter presentations, in the church worship services and in missionary outreach around the world.

Offering worship and Sunday School opportunities for every age on Sunday mornings at 9:15 and 10:45, and a worship service at 6:00 p.m. Sunday evening, a mid-week Family Night service at 7:00 p.m. on Wednesdays, and multiple Bible studies and activities for all ages throughout the week, the people of The Peoples Church prayerfully seek to be a positive influence on the quality of life for the Fresno community.

Pictured below - Fresno's Buddhist Temple.

Throughout the city, stained glass and soaring steel attest to the hopes, prayers and vision of the city's communities of faith. In each congregation, faith takes form in myriad individual and corporate actions. Many area churches, such as Wesley United Methodist, are actively involved in service to the refugee community. Many congregations sponsor camps and youth organizations which have both spiritual and social aims. Northwest Church hosts a fun-filled summer church school which draws nearly 700 delighted youngsters!

Area churches in Fresno as in many other communities have joined together to bring their combined strength to bear on persistent social problems. Evangelicals for Social Action, a national outreach organization, has a chapter in Fresno which is supported by 14 area churches. Evangelicals for Social Action informs the Christian community of social needs and creates channels to facilitate the meeting of those needs. Among these channels are crisis relief, educational forums, a furniture bank, bus trips for seniors and a church services network known as Love, Inc. One of 50 chapters, the Fresno group also operates a program called Christian Gleaners where church groups are organized to gather excess produce from fields and packers and distribute it to agencies which feed the poor.

Similarly, Fresno Metropolitan Ministry seeks to inform the community and organize people for responsible social action. With financial support from 30 congregations and in-kind support from twice that number, Metro Ministry each year sets an ambitious agenda at its planning retreat. The efforts of this group have given birth to a number of creative problem-solving programs. A health awareness and training videotape project enables low-income women and their physicians to tell their health stories to their peers. Metro's adopt-a-home project links area churches with convalescent homes for mutual awareness, sharing and support. Metro is active in working for improved human relations throughout the community as it attempts to break down barriers of race, age and income. It tackles the problems of unemployment and inadequate health care, and has an excellent program of theological education for lay people. All are part of a day's work for this vital, caring organization.

In prayer, in contemplation, and in loving action, Fresno's faithful contribute to the solid, enduring spirit of an exceptionally blessed community.

RESIDENTIAL LIFESTYLES

A. Leo Wilson Photo

Fresno's active housing market is typical of high-growth areas. The Fresno Board of Realtors reports a membership of 1,700 agents, approximately 800 of whom are brokers. Operating out of nearly 600 real estate offices, the brokers, the 112 affiliate offices and a sizeable number of non-member real estate agents find a stable source of employment in the Fresno area.

In the greater Fresno area, a total of 4,657 residential units, valued at $386,620,985, were sold in the twelve months prior to April, 1987. The majority of these — 1,015 units — were three-bedroom homes; approximately equal numbers of smaller and larger units (about 250 each) sold in that period. Sales of three-bedroom homes are up 23.8 percent over the previous year; sales of four-bedroom homes are up 19.3 percent, and sales of homes with five bedrooms increased by 75 percent. Total residential properties sales in April 1987 increased 19 percent over the preceding April, indicating that the most substantial growth is in sale of larger homes.

City of Fresno building permits support this interpretation. Multiple family unit permits issued in 1986 totaled 1,912, far fewer than the 3,786 issued in 1985 or the 3,647 permits issued in 1984. In the same period, single family unit building permits jumped to 1,552, from 1,137 in 1985 and 1,047 in 1984. Valuation nearly doubled in single family building permits, going from $56,464,777 in 1984 to $95,907,471 in 1986. At the same time, valuation in multiple family building permits decreased by nearly half, dropping from $81,843,074 in 1984 to $46,278,483 in 1986. Clearly, the trend is toward single family homes of at least three bedrooms.

(Continued on page 10)

LEO WILSON CONSTRUCTION

QUALITY AND DISTINCTIVE ELEGANCE

Maybe it's because Leo Wilson grew up in the San Joaquin Valley that he takes a particular pride in helping to guide and shape it. Whatever the reason, his effect is evident.

Leo attended the Porterville public schools, and graduated from California State University, Fresno, with a degree in business administration. Upon graduation, he started selling residential lots in the northwest Fresno area. While selling, he was also learning . . . what people wanted and looked for in homes and lots. He also discovered many residential needs and wishes *not* being met by the properties available. So in 1966 he began his building career in Equity Homes, a partnership. In 1977 he formed Wilson Construction, Ltd., to address the demand he perceived.

It became obvious rather soon that in order to build-in the kind of features and quality he felt belonged in his homes, Leo would have to affect the economies of multi-unit construction. And there seemed to be no reason why these same economies couldn't benefit from individually designed custom homes, too. It was this philosophy that spawned the success of Wilson Construction.

Today Wilson Construction has an administrative staff of 14, its own design department . . . and to make sure things get done just so . . . a full time finish crew on payroll. The goal is consistent quality, and the goal is being met.

"We are committed to the future of the Fresno area," explained Leo. "Our Dominion project just east of Woodward Park is an example of what we see for the years ahead. 520 acres of rolling land that offer a unique setting for an entire community. There will be an appropriate home style for every lifestyle and family situation, an array of single family homes, detached and patio as well as townhouses and apartments. There are first homes for beginning families, custom home lots up to 1/3 acre, and smaller units for couples whose children have grown and moved out, all within a community that offers virtually every possible amenity. The Dominion will even have its own commercial service center elementary school site."

"Six residental villages will comprise the project . . . each with its own park . . . all linked by jogging and bike paths through greenways. It's a ten year plan that will eventually contain 2,500 units and a population of approximately 6,000. I think it's the most exciting concept in Central California." While The Dominion is the newest and most visible facet of Wilson Construction, previous projects have attracted equal interest and met with equal success.

The common thread through all Wilson developments is the dedication to quality and the distinctive elegance of his designs. It's a reputation that's been growing for 20 years and has cast Leo into a leadership role in both industry and community. He's a member of Rotary International and an active supporter of California State University, Fresno. Leo has served many times as president of the Building Industry Association.

In Leo's case, leader also implies innovator. He has many Fresno firsts to his credit: the city's first Planned Unit Development, the first custom neighborhood of large homes, Fresno's first condo and first residential development with a man-made lake, and Fresno's first Gold Nugget Award for land planning and design (the Royal Coach Estates project).

Leo A. Wilson, builder, planner, leader, innovator and shaper of Fresno's future.

A. Leo Wilson Photo

A. Leo Wilson Photo

ST. ANTHONY OF PADUA

AN ACTIVE CATHOLIC PARISH

The Roman Catholic Church has been in Fresno since the first days of the city. The bishop of the Diocese of Fresno, Joseph J. Madera, resides here, presiding over 86 parishes in the eight central counties of California.

There are thirteen parishes in the City of Fresno, one of the youngest and largest being St. Anthony of Padua. The neo-Gothic Church was designed by architects Nargis and Darden and built by Tri-Central Construction Company in 1968.

St. Anthony's elementary school (K-8) celebrated its 25th anniversary in the Fall of 1987. In 1986 the U.S. Department of Education honored St. Anthony's with the "Excellence in Education" Award. The school is currently doubling its enrollment, one grade at a time, under the leadership of Principal Dan Makley.

There are four other Catholic elementary schools in Fresno. The pride of the Catholic school system is San Joaquin Memorial High School, founded in 1945, and staffed by the Christian Brothers and the Sisters of the Holy Cross. It has a reputation as a college prep school with high academic standards. Situated on a beautiful sprawling campus in the heart of town, it has been home to thousands of loyal alumni, both men and women, who are grateful for the Christian formation that was theirs at San Joaquin Memorial.

St. Anthony's parish is bustling with activity. The youth program is especially vibrant under the leadership of Tom Neumeier. There are six Sunday Masses each weekend enhanced by the music of a professional liturgical staff. Holy Cross Sister Doreen Marie heads a small army of volunteers and works extensively in religious education, especially with those who are considering entering the Church.

Young Father Robert Jaramillo is kept busy with St. Anthony's Young Adults and the Businessman's Breakfast Meetings, among his many other duties.

Parishioners are proud of St. Anthony's, especially the "old-timers" who built a school and church and then a *new* church within the span of a few short years. Most of this activity took place under the leadership of former pastor Msgr. Patrick Flood. The Parish Council, the Finance Council, the School Board, and the Parents Club give the parish its vision and direction. There are 24 other parish organizations, comprising some 1900 Catholic men and women.

The current pastor, Monsignor E. James Petersen, is active in both civic and diocesan affairs but loves the life of the parish most of all. He is a promoter of Catholic schools and of education in general.

When you visit Fresno, stop by St. Anthony's and see for yourself why people love it.

San Joaquin Memorial High School offers high quality educational opportunities as a private college prep school and is staffed by the Christian Brothers and the Sisters of the Holy Cross.

Anchoring a corner of downtown Fresno, the Bank of America building assumes a low profile as the more historic Helm building rises in the background.

Bob Barnes

Demographic data provides ample support for Fresno's family-town image. In the four county Fresno market area, only 20.3 percent of the people live alone. Two-person households account for 31.3 percent of the population. Three- to four-person households account for the largest segment — 34.2 percent, and 14.1 percent of Fresno residents live in households of five or more persons.

Income levels reflect some of Fresno's unusual characteristics. The largest category, with effective buying income under $15,000 (1986) consists of 112,400 households which include refugees, seasonal laborers and students. The second largest category, 87,610 households with effective buying income over $35,000, consists of the rapidly growing, highly educated professional and managerial upscale market. The remaining two categories consist of 82,370 households with effective buying income of $15,000 to $24,949, and 62,280 households with effective buying income of $25,000 to $34,999.

The Bank of America has compiled comparative statistics for Fresno and the State of California for 1984 which show mid-scale households of 31.3 percent in Fresno and 34 percent for the state; upscale households of 15.6 percent for Fresno and 20 percent for the state, and mass households of 53.2 percent for Fresno and 46 percent for the state as a whole. Fresno's owner-occupied percentage for 1980 stood at 54.9 percent compared with 52 percent statewide. Its percentage of professional and managerial residents was 26.3 percent, slightly lower than the state figure of 28.4 percent. In 1980, 39.8 percent of Fresno residents were college educated, compared with 42 percent in the state as a whole. When one takes into account the influx of thousands of Asian refugees each year, the seasonal agricultural labor force and the dependence of the region on agriculture, these modest variations from state averages can be readily understood.

Fresno's active housing market is evidenced by the volume of lending which takes place in the city. In April of 1987, for example, Security Pacific had the highest dollar value in real estate activity — $21,770,000 in 142 loans processed that month. Guarantee Savings posted the largest number of loans that month, with 205; their dollar value was $17,126,000. Bank of America was third in both number of loans — 109, and dollar value — $14,226,000. Great Western, Great American, All Valley Mortgage, Financial Savings, Glen Fed Mortgage and Commonwealth Mortgage followed with between 56 and 87 loans processed in the month.

(Continued on page 13)

Bob Barnes

The Holy Trinity Armenian Apostolic Church in downtown Fresno stands as a beautiful active symbol of historic church architecture.

Fresno High School's classic architecture represents but one of Fresno's seven high schools.

Duncan Water Gardens is one of Fresno's most beautiful and unique settings developed by Dick and Jackie Duncan for the enjoyment of visitors and area residents.

Wayne Jackson

Hartt Porteous

Woodward Park is the host site for the beautiful Shin Zen Japanese Gardens located in north Fresno.

Bob Barnes

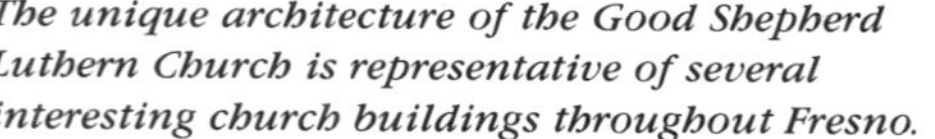

The unique architecture of the Good Shepherd Luthern Church is representative of several interesting church buildings throughout Fresno.

GRUPE DEVELOPMENT COMPANY

THE PLANNED COMMUNITY IN FRESNO

As consumer trends in the mid-80's turned towards amenities that helped complement a more active life-style and fuller utilization of leisure time, home shoppers began to seek an environment to fit their needs. Their search signaled Fresno's readiness for the introduction of a planned community.

What, one asks, is a planned community?

Bill Jirsa, vice president of Grupe Development Company, developers of Woodward Lake, the first planned community in the Fresno area, said, "A true planned community includes five essential elements: the size to offer an appealing diversity of homes in a varied price range; all appropriate amenities to bring needed day-to-day services to the homeowners; the opportunity to select and maintain aesthetic surroundings and a desired life-style; a variety of recreational amenities; and, what I call a 'sense of arrival."

The size of the Woodward Lake project allowed the developer to incorporate a wide variety of economic and life-style choices into the planned community. Woodward Lake consists of more than 400 acres centered around a 56 acre private lake. Single family homes are planned and built in several compatible neighborhoods within the larger community. With this large scale planned community concept, Woodward Lake also brings needed day-to-day services to residents. A school, child care facility, church and neighborhood shopping center are all provided in the plan.

The next element, the opportunity to select and maintain a desired life-style, is one of the major appeals for homeowners at Woodward Lake. By actively participating in the Homeowner's Association of Woodward Lake, people have a say in how the planned community is run and how it looks.

The protective covenants of Woodward Lake provide for an architectural control committee. The committee reviews and approves all building and landscape plans. The process serves as one of the checks and balances to ensure that both property and aesthetic values can be enhanced and a chosen life-style maintained.

Recreational amenities essential to a planned community abound at Woodward Lake. The lake itself provides boating, fishing and a stunning visual setting. The Community Center is used extensively by members for social events. The recreation complex includes a white sand beach, a community boat dock, a junior Olympic sized pool, tennis courts, a basket ball court and a large deck and open lawn area. Aerobic programs, community picnics, tennis tournaments, biking and jogging are also available.

The final element, the "sense of arrival", is one of the most desirable elements created by the planned community, according to Jirsa. "Driving past the entry sign and through the gate at Woodward Lake, residents get that special feeling of arrival. I'm home!"

The Grupe Company has been developing water-oriented planned communities throughout the western United States since 1966. The first homes constructed by the company and several selected builders at Woodward Lake were offered for sale in July, 1985. In just two years, more than 450 lots and homes have been sold. This response to living on or near a lovely lake, especially in Fresno, is indicative of the tremendous popularity of the planned community development at Woodward Lake.

NORTHWEST CHURCH

COME W.I.N. WITH US

Northwest Church lies situated on seven beautiful acres of Fresno on the northwest corner of West and Barstow. The congregation is comprised of over 1500 faithful. In addition to the two regular Sunday worship services, the other services offered include Bible study for the young and old, youth group events, a Christian singles group and a couples fellowship.

Parishioners can participate in the choir, community outreach programs, home and hospital visitations, prayer

These figures translate into jobs for real estate agents and business for the banking industry. But the deeper meaning behind them is homes — homes for new families moving into Fresno, homes for families moving up, retirement homes for golden years in the Golden State.

In north Fresno, the second most active housing market is the starter category. These are homes in the $70,000 to $110,000 range, selling to first-time buyers. Such families tend to make their housing choices based on convenience to

Clair E. Nelsen

Clair E. Nelsen

work and retail centers, flexibility of the home to meet the needs of a growing family, and affordability. Lots for these homes are generally between 4,000 and 8,000 square feet, and most of the homes are production units.

The most active north Fresno market is that of upgrade homes; about 900 of these are sold each year at prices ranging from $120,000 to $160,000. Single family home lot sizes in this category are from 8,500 to 12,000 square feet, and the semi-custom units are from 1,750 to 2,600 square groups, teaching and other opportunities.

Northwest's physical plant includes the main sanctuary and office building, the small chapel, the Northwest Christian Growth Center and the "Annex."

The Education Building is probably the most widely-used facility in the complex. Hosting both church and community functions, this facility is an area of constant activities, which include Sunday morning adult and children's classes, Awana and Bethel on Wednesday nights, and junior/senior high school functions among others.

The northwest corner of the education building houses the Library/Media center. With over 7,000 books, it is the largest collection of its kind in the valley. Cassettes, video tapes, records and children's materials complement the fine collection of written texts.

The Northwest School System is a private, Christian, nonprofit enterprise which uses the education building extensively during the week. The church supplies space and utilities, while tuitions and private donations support the actual program.

In addition to all the programs provided at Northwest on a regular basis, there are a number of special events, most of them seasonal, in which the church body participates. Examples include special Easter services, periodic church picnics and socials, "Five Daze of Fun" for young children during the summer, the Harvest Dinner in November and a Christmas Candlelight service in December.

The congregation also supports ministry programs abroad. "Sunday Live With Bufe," a challenging spiritual talk show hosted by Northwest Pastor Bufe Karraker, can be heard every Sunday morning from 6:30 a.m. to 7:00 a.m. on KMJ-Newstalk 58.

"On behalf of the entire congregation, I want to personally welcome you to Northwest Church," says Pastor Karraker. "We are delighted that you have taken the time to investigate what we're doing, and we pray that you will give us the opportunity to minister to you. If we can help you in any way, we would love to do just that."

Reverend Bufe Karraker robustly leads his Northwest congregation in song during Christmas services.

When Pastor Karraker says "we can help," he means he and his pastoral staff including: Jerry Klippert, Assistant Pastor; Michele Evans, Director of Christian Education; Dave Shroyer, Minister of Music; Mike Reinhold, Youth Pastor and Mitch Ribera, College/Career Pastor.

Northwest Church blends a strong music program with sound biblical teaching to reach thousands of Fresnans annually. It is a church that has made a conscious effort of outreach throughout the community and strives to be a meaningful part of its peoples daily lives.

The church enthusiastically Welcomes In Newcomers. Northwest's motto says, "Come 'W.I.N.' with us!" Newcomers are invited for coffee and doughnuts and an informal getting acquainted period every Sunday morning from 9:45 a.m.-10:30 a.m. in the church library.

This residence in North Fresno symbolizes the grace and beauty of the many lovely custom homes being built as the city expands to the north.

feet in size. People are attracted to this housing category by prestige, school district location and appropriate size for active families.

The move-up market, at $150,000 to $220,000, is highly varied. It includes semi-custom family homes, zero-lot line homes and zero-lot line attached homes. Most are located on one-quarter to one-half acre lots. The luxury home market, targeted for mature families and empty-nesters, includes custom homes ranging from $200,000 to $500,000 situated on one-half to two acre lots arranged for privacy and view. The luxury home selection is exceptionally varied, from country ranchettes — complete with horse barns, to river bluff condominiums. Home amenities in these mid- and upper-market homes include swimming pools, spas, semitropical landscape design and tennis courts. Some have tropical fish ponds, putting greens, stables and other custom comforts.

Hartt Porteous

KIRKWOOD'S DESIGN GALLERY

FINE FURNITURE FOR THREE GENERATIONS

Kirkwood's Design Gallery has quite a history here in Fresno. Established in 1900, this quality furniture store can look back over three generations of ownership, and three generations of growth and continued success. Together with his partner, Richard Doyle, Bruce Kirkwood has built Kirkwood's Design Gallery into something his grandfather would be proud of. When Bruce Kirkwood's grandfather, Harry, first opened the doors of his store back at the turn of the century, he wanted to keep his customers happy, and he hoped to sell a lot of furniture. That is just what he did. It wasn't long before he had

Dan Sniffin

Typical homes in the Sunnyside area rest on large spacious lots with mature landscaping and definitely reflect a country atmosphere.

opened a second and a third store right here in Fresno. Bruce Kirkwood's father, Ray, joined his father in the furniture business in 1924. Then in the 1930's Ray's father and brother, Dewey, closed two of the stores here in Fresno to take the furniture business up to Oakland. They left Ray in charge of the one Fresno store. Ray's business thrived for many years in downtown Fresno on Fulton and Inyo Streets. Then in February of 1963, Kirkwood's Wayside Furniture, as it was known then, moved into its brand new building on Cedar at Clinton, the same location it has today. Back in 1963 there were a total of three salespeople, and selling furniture is just what they did. Then in July of 1971, Bruce Kirkwood became the owner. He made the decision to emphasize design along with furniture sales, and Kirkwood's Wayside Furniture soon became Kirkwood's Design Gallery. Richard Doyle joined the company as Bruce Kirkwood's partner in February of 1973. Today Kirkwood's Design Gallery is one fine furniture store with 24,000 square feet of showroom and six professional designers on staff.

Kirkwood's has been serving the Fresno area for a long time, and one major reason for its staying power is the fact that through the years Kirkwood's has kept right in step with the vastly changing styles. Inside Kirkwood's beautiful showroom, you will find the latest in contemporary furniture styles and accessories. The professional design staff is very aware that furniture styles are constantly changing just as fashion is constantly changing. When a Kirkwood's designer shows a customer the latest in furniture design, it will most assuredly be just that. Kirkwood's Design Gallery has a history of its own, and is very aware that though some styles of furniture may be centuries old, they are timeless in their ability to please. Kirkwood's carries a beautiful selection of traditional furniture for the more conservative and classic look. Whether it is traditional or contemporary, Kirkwood's carries only top-of-the-line merchandise from such well-known manufacturers as Henredon, whose fine craftsmanship and quality materials set them high above most others in the industry. Kirkwood's also carries Statton, known for their solid cherrywood furniture, exquisite Chapman lamps from all over the world, and beautiful etchings from England, hand watercolored in our country.

Browsing through Kirkwood's Design Gallery will please anyone. There are many vignettes centered around various themes of color and style. The vignettes not only show off Kirkwood's beautiful furniture and accessories, but they are also a wonderful display of the design staff's talent. Kirkwood's has so much to offer its customers. Tucked away in a corner of Kirkwood's showroom is the design center. There a customer will find thousands and thousands of samples of fabric, draperies, carpeting, and wallpaper. Planning the interior of a home is an art. The talent and knowledge of Kirkwood's professional designers enable them to help a customer turn his home into a work of art.

Today Kirkwood's Design Gallery still holds to the original intention of its founding father. With its tremendously talented and service-oriented staff and with its large inventory of competitively priced, high quality merchandise, Kirkwood's Design Gallery is keeping its customers happy and selling a lot of furniture.

These amenities are important for busy contemporary families, and their widespread availability is an indicator of Fresno's metropolitan, up-to-the-minute status. But there's another side to the city's lifestyle, too, one that is reminiscent of a simpler, more relaxed time. In the urban setting, homes — no matter how elegant — don't exist in isolation. Neighborhoods are important in Fresno. Each has its own tone and character, a distinctive quality that sets it apart. The strength of Fresno's neighborhood spirit has been the foundation of the successful Neighborhood Watch program for crime prevention, as well as the focus for block parties, carnivals and extravaganzas of holiday decorating.

Sunnyside, in the southeast corner of the community, has an elegant atmosphere. Rambling houses are set in spacious yards which often include tennis courts, pools and dry-docked sailboats. Further in on the south side, Huntington Boulevard still shows signs of its grand history. Its early century, two-story mansions are graced with tall palms. Early morning joggers beat paths upon the wide grass median, bringing the boulevard to life. A family neighborhood now, Huntington boasts block parties and festive holiday decorations which bring admirers from all over town.

VALLEY COMMUNITY CHURCH

A PRACTICAL AND SPIRITUAL MINISTRY

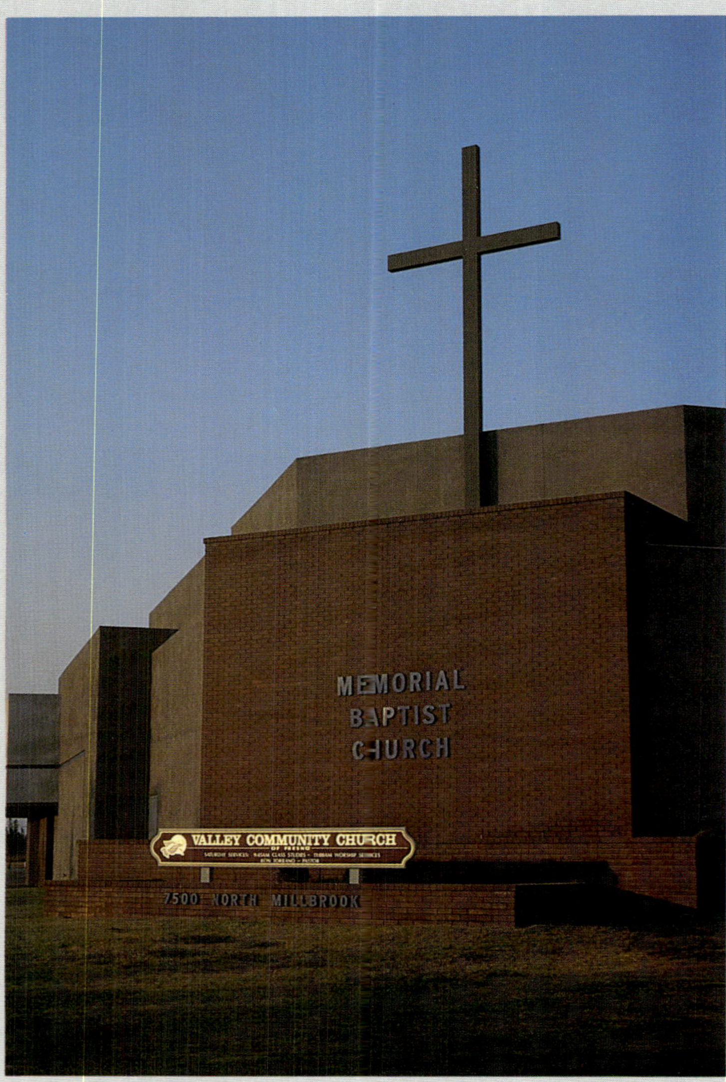

PASTOR RON TORRANO

Friendly people. Fresno is full of friendly people who really care about each other! That's a comment you hear all over town, all over the county — from out-of-towners, and from people who have lived here for years. And it's that feeling of unconditional friendship — a willingness to do whatever it takes to foster an atmosphere of community togetherness — that identifies Valley Community Church as a vital representation of Fresno itself.

Valley Community Church is actually the outgrowth of a dream shared by a handful of Fresno business people and their families, who felt there was room in our community for a non-denominational church founded solely on the premise that people are more able to see the benefits of getting to know Jesus Christ if they are free of the negative religious encumbrances of heavy institutional christianity. In such a setting the result is the experience of a positive Christian lifestyle.

And so "religion" is not an issue at Valley Community. Saturday morning Christian education classes and praise/worship services are relaxed and informal. Church-sponsored seminars and workshops are based on "practicing what we preach". The purpose is to share the joy of the Christian experience, and help each other apply Christian principles to their daily lives.

By way of example, the church facilities are not a monument to people's ability to erect magnificent buildings. Instead, the church shares buildings and grounds with Memorial Baptist Church at Millbrook and Alluvial. By renting the extremely adequate, modern facilities, Valley Community helps support another Fresno church, while offering its people all the beauty and convenience of the church home Memorial Baptist provides. The arrangement makes eminent sense from both a practical and spiritual standpoint.

And it's that comfortable blending of the practical and spiritual that they see as the key to their ministry. Head pastor, Ron Torrano, strongly encourages home Bible studies as a means of translating God's word into everyday applications. Getting together and sharing in small groups within the home, says Torrano, is a manifestation of our Bible-based Christian philosophy that brings church anbd community into a single sphere of understanding. It's no accident that a warm, responsive church like Valley Community is thriving in a friendly, close-knit community like Fresno.

Dan Sniffin

Huntington Boulevard

Stately homes grace a wide boulevard in southeast Fresno showcasing an era of elegance still very much treasured in Fresno.

Nearer the city center, the Tower District has a Bohemian main street and avenues of neat, New England college town homes. To the west, Fig Garden clings to its country ways, eschewing sidewalks and street lights. Many of Fresno's loveliest homes line Fig Garden's narrow streets; its homeowners' association is one of the most active in the city. It is here that the Christmas Tree Lane tradition began in the war years when a few giant pines and firs were strung with lights in memory of lost servicemen. Each year, thousands of cars creep along Van Ness to marvel at the miles of holiday lights and decorations.

Dan Sniffin

Christmas Tree Lane

In an area teeming with beautiful pines and stately eucalyptus trees, the residents in Old Fig Garden are a rich blend of custom built homes and lush landscaped properties.

Dan Sniffin

The residents who live in the Woodward Lake community find a leisurely lifestyle accentuated by the accessibility to the water for fun and relaxation.

Woodward Lake By Grupe Development Company

On the fast-growing north side of town, the sense of neighborhood is more tentative as residents from other towns and other parts of Fresno begin to establish new roots. Neighborhood schools and parent-teacher organizations give a sense of common purpose, as do Neighborhood Watch programs and Halloween parties. In communities set apart by security gates, and in the neighborhoods of beautifully landscaped luxury homes, golf and other leisure activities bring neighbors together. Around Woodward Lakes, it might be a neighbor's sailboat or a strange breed of dog out walking with its owner — whatever the excuse for breaking the ice, Fresno's friendly people soon become acquainted. It is, after all, home.

The old Fresno Water Tower has become Fresno's most recognized architectural symbol. Built in 1894 the tower held 250,000 gallons of water until it became inactive in 1963. Listed on the National Register of Historic Places, the water tower became a key on-site location shot during the 1986 Carol Burnett television mini-series entitled "Fresno."

A Heritage of the Soil

CHAPTER 2

Hartt Porteous

One of nature's oldest living creations, the giant sequoia rises some 274 feet majestically into the Sierra sky.

Fresno City & County Historical Society

A turn of the century Indian woman working in front of her dwelling using utensils and methods passed down for generations.

Fresno County spans the midsection of California's Central Valley, the heart of the most fertile agricultural land in the United States. Blessed with accessible pure water, above and below the surface, with deposits of oil and natural gas to the west and minerals to the east, the Central Valley has been a paradise of opportunity for generations of immigrants.

The Valley is bounded by the rugged Sierra Nevada to the east, the gentle Coast Range to the west, the Cascades to the north and the Tehachapi Mountains to the south. It is 450 miles long and 50 to 60 miles wide, and was shaped in the depths of the ocean to be sculpted by glaciers, rivers and streams over eons. Its peaceful towns and productive croplands give no hint of the Valley's geologically violent origins almost 185 million years ago. At that time the bottom of the Pacific Ocean thrust suddenly and cataclysmically beneath the crust of the North American continent, inundating all of what is now identified as the Golden State.

In the following ages, volcanic activity exposed the granite peaks of the Sierra Nevada. Debris flowed down to form the San Joaquin Valley floor and came to a halt forming the gentle slopes of the Coast Range — a geological nicety that protected the Valley from future intrusions by the Pacific Ocean.

Trapped organic material, the sediments of the Valley floor, became oil and gas deposits beneath the western regions, while gradual erosion exposed mineral deposits high in the mountains to the east. Glaciers sculpted the cliffs and precipices of Yosemite. The paths of these glaciers are visible today in the courses of the rivers and streams that carry water to the Valley below. Giant Sequoias rose to 400 feet in the mountains, and the foothills were covered with oak and several varieties of pine.

As abundant water became available, the Valley became a broad, fertile prairie of dense, tall grasses with enormous numbers of Valley Oaks on the eastern slopes. Spruce, fir, pine, willow, poplar and ash thrived — Fresno is the Spanish word for ash. Flowers, wild berries, grapes and swamp grasses filled the Valley floor. Countless species of animals made their homes in the midst of this abundance.

At a time when much of the earth was either arid desert or tropical jungle, the San Joaquin Valley was a fertile wonderland.

THE FIRST RESIDENTS

Long after the glaciers had receded, the first humans arrived in the Valley, drawn by the climate, the wild beauty of the terrain, and the abundance of game. The Yokut Indians settled on the plains, while the Monache — distant cousins of the Paiute — established settlements in the river headlands. Both communities followed hunting and gathering patterns. They used bows and arrows and traps for game, and harpoons and weighted nets in the streams and lakes. They were well nourished, having a wide variety of nuts, berries and roots to supplement their catches.

Available records show that the lifestyle of the Yokut and Monache was peaceful and unhurried. They created beautiful pottery and baskets, and wove sturdy grasses into rafts for use on the waterways. They enjoyed grand feasts, and had a well-developed mythology. Their interest in the spiritual dimension of life is revealed by the wide variety of sweathouse rituals which were important to these primitive cultures. Games of chance and skill provided entertainment and opportunity for athletic competition. They established a trade and barter network with other Central California tribes to obtain such luxuries as acorns, obsidian and seafood.

This peaceful way of life was shattered in 1769 with the first incursion of the Spanish military from the coastal missions. A century later the Gold Rush, which exposed them to foreign customs and modern conveniences, completed the destruction of their simple ways. Fire, flood and disease combined with the cultural invasion to effectively destroy the good life of the Valley's original inhabitants.

The Spanish incursion is represented best by the California Missions, which were established along the California coastline, about a day's horseback ride from one another, by the Franciscans. A northern extension of the culture of the Spanish conquistadores of Mexico, these missions were established to bring the Spanish concept of civilization to the California natives.

The Spaniards introduced new methods of agriculture and architecture along with Christianity. Converts were needed in ever increasing numbers to till the land and raise adobe structures. When the Indians chose to return to their villages, the Spanish sent troops to bring the reluctant "new believers" back to the missions. The Indians retaliated by pillaging Spanish coastal settlements, but their ranks were rapidly decimated by disease and superior Spanish weaponry.

For a time, the Franciscans considered establishing mission outposts in the interior. An expedition led by Lieutenant Gabriel Moraga visited what is now Fresno County in 1805 and again in 1806, exploring the foothill area for a suitable mission site. While traveling through Merced County, Moraga's soldiers startled swarms of lovely yellow butterflies, which inspired them to name the area Mariposa, the Spanish term for butterfly. Political instability in Spain and Mexico during the period discouraged expansion of the mission chain, and interest in the interior region subsided briefly.

In the 1820s and '30s, fur traders from the north and east discovered an abundant supply of beaver and otter along the waters of the San Joaquin River. In one decade as many as 400 English, French and American trappers plied their trade in the Valley, seriously depleting the numbers of these animals. Among the trappers was one Jedediah Strong Smith, whose carefully written journals were published following his death. He praised the Valley's abundant timber supply and vast grazing lands, and predicted that prosperous farms would one day be spread throughout the San Joaquin countryside. Kit Carson's recollections of an 1829 trip into the area are similar: "Plenty of grasses for the horses, and huge herds of elk, deer, and antelope for the hunting." Other explorers from the east were discovering the scenic attractions of Central California. In 1833 an expedition led by Captain Benjamin Bonneville crossed the Sierra from the Utah salt flats, and reported the first sightings of Yosemite Valley and the giant redwoods.

The pristine quiet of the high mountains was soon shattered by the raucous cries accompaning the frenzied rush for gold. In January of 1848 a crew representing Captain John Sutter, a Swiss imigrant businessman, discovered gold while searching for a sawmill site. By May the rush was on, despite Sutter's efforts to maintain secrecy. Government expeditions, military outposts, trading centers, saloons and squatters followed hard upon the miners. The

Hartt Porteous

A weathered archway beckons the early settlers into the religious confines of a Spanish mission.

(Continued on page 23)

THE FARMER'S MARKET

A FRESNO TRADITION FOR FOUR DECADES

With the sun perfectly surrounded by the windmill's circular framework, the key ingredients of wind, water, power, and sunshine are all captured in this unique picture.

Hartt Porteous

The Farmer's Market, in downtown Fresno, is a valley landmark built in 1948. Since that time, the pentagon-shaped center has undergone a series of changes, including a name change in 1952 to the Plaza Shopping Center. In 1979, the name was again changed back to The Farmer's Market and a major renovation was begun.

The 44,000 plus square foot enclosed mall includes seventeen ethnic restaurants, banquet rooms seating 48-250 people, plus book and furniture stores, bakery, candy, card and flower shops, health foods, fresh produce and much more. The bright, airy Farmer's Market interior was designed with a common "sidewalk cafe" dining area for all the restaurants, highlighted with a profusion of indoor vegetation, oak tables, cushioned wicker chairs, and umbrellas suspended from the ceiling. Accented in striking shades of deep green, blue and burgundy, the mall interior provides an extremely pleasant atmosphere for diners and shoppers. The center — open daily Monday through Saturday — is truly an oasis in the busy heart of the downtown area.

Shoppers, downtown business persons, office workers, and anyone attending an event at the Fresno Convention Center will find the center's location convenient. Just off Freeway 41 at Tulare Street, The Farmer's Market has several entrances and a large parking lot.

Diners can choose from the following restaurants: Alternative, Bob's Hobo House, Castillio's, Cheesecake & Stuff, Country Fair Cinnamon Rolls, Dai Ichi, House of Kebob, India's Palace, Le Cafe, Manila Cafe, Mr. T's Hofbrau, Rice Bowl, Richie's Good Burger/Good Dog, Rossi's, Round-Up B-B-Q, Yogurt Mill and Zorba The Greek. Shoppers will enjoy the wares of these merchants: Anand Art, Blum's Candy, Creative Thoughts, Flower Deli, Grandma Buffalo's Outrageous Chocolate Chip Cookies, Joie's Health Food Center, J and P Produce, Movie Connection, Rapid Print Etc., Sadler's Oak Furniture and Ye Olde Book Shoppe.

This historic photo depicts a "brush house" used by Hispanics and Vaqueros on the Valley Plains.

Fresno City & County Historical Society

Preserved still is Fresno County's original courthouse, located in Millerton overlooking Millerton Lake.

Walt Puhn

best evidence of permanent residence in Fresno County sets the date at about 1850, the year California became a state, although land grant filings are recorded a bit earlier.

Prospectors came from Peru, China, Australia and New England in the first wave of multi-ethnic California settlement. The mining towns of Coarsegold and Fine Gold sprang up in Fresno County. They were named for the type of sand and gravel (placers) at the sites. Here, as elsewhere, ten years of dreams, hard work and occasional "strikes" followed. Some discouraged miners, including a portion of the many Chinese who arrived in the 1850s, turned to other business pursuits. Hotels, supply stores and ferries appeared on the scene, some licensed by the new Fresno County government established in 1856. Military encampments were the forerunners of permanent settlements in the flatlands of the Central Valley. An early Fresno County "subdivision" is recorded at Fort Washington in 1850, near the site of a present day golf course of the same name.

On the west side of Fresno County, numerous small communities appeared. Immigrants from Mexico, Spain and Chile settled along the old road to Los Angeles, which was quite passable even in the early 1800s. Farmers cultivated the fertile bottomland around Posa Chine near present day Coalinga. This region was exceptionally lush before the severe floods of 1862-63.

Equally severe floodings in 1867-68 and the diminishing access to readily available gold slowed the mining fever in the eastern hills. As mining activity dwindled, cattle ranching and lumber harvesting took over. But sporadic mining development continued through the 1850s, engaging at one time more than 300 Chinese immigrants at scattered sites along the San Joaquin River. Private and government services multiplied during the peak period of mining. Mail service was initiated in 1858 by the Butterfield Overland Mail Company. The railroad replaced the Stockton to Los Angeles stage in 1872. Fort Miller was built in 1851 to protect settlers against Indian attacks. The Fort Miller hospital dining room was used as the first school room in the Millerton district. The fort was abandoned in 1864, as the Civil War was ending. Its blockhouse was moved to Fresno's Roeding Park for preservation when construction of Friant Dam in the 1940s necessitated flooding the historic site.

The town of Millerton, which grew up around the fort, holds the distinction of being the first seat of Fresno County. Except for Ira McCray's Oak Hotel, Millerton never had an

(Continued on page 26)

PRODUCERS DAIRY

A 54 YEAR OLD TRADITION

Part of the Producer's Dairy fleet showcasing its local heritage and touting the endorsement of Hopalong Cassidy, one of America's all time great western film heroes.

Producers Dairy was incorporated on December 22, 1932 by a group of ambitious men wanting to package quality milk products in the local Fresno community. In 1949, Larry Shehadey purchased a major interest in the company and became general manager in 1951. His primary objective was to have the highest quality dairy products in the valley. The same year, Producers opened the present plant at 144 E. Belmont, and installed the first half gallon and quart size single service packaging machines in the Central Valley. This was the most modern and acceptable package of its time and contributed to the growth of Producers in the early fifties. Producers was also the first dairy plant to have a 100% refrigerated delivery fleet in 1951 thus assuring a good, cold product arrived on the grocers' shelves.

In 1959, Mr. Shehadey built an ultra-modern milking parlor for the dairy herd at 4260 W. Madison, with an air conditioned viewing room for school children and the local community to watch the cow milking process. Over 20,000 people a year have viewed this modern milking operation.

In 1972, the Bar 20 Dairy Farms, as the milking operation is called, opened another ultra modern and larger operation west of Fresno on Whitesbridge Road. At this facility, 2,500 cows can be milked twice daily.

While Producers does not obtain all of its milk from the dairy's own farms, they were developed as a means of maintaining better control over the quality of milk from the farm. The element of high quality, fresh milk is basic with Producers and this is continued throught the processing operation.

With strict quality controls from "Moo to You," Producers has been able to produce, process and distribute the highest quality, freshest dairy products available in the Central Valley.

Producers' modern processing plant has been continuously updated with the latest, most modern equipment available for both processing and sanitizing. Most recently the addition of an in-plant plastic bottle Blow Mold Machine for Producers' "Space-Saving" bottle has increased further the quality and efficiency of the processing operation. A new refrigerated cold storage box has been added to take care of the future business expansion for Producers Dairy.

Producers offers a complete line of dairy products including Jersey Extra Rich, Homogenized Milk, Low Fat Milk, Non-Fat Milk, Chocolate Milk, Buttermilk, Acidophilus Low Fat Milk, Half and Half, Sour Cream, Cottage Cheese and many other items such as Pure Orange Juice and Fruit Ades. Producers Dairy also offers a complete line of ice cream products and ice cream novelties to better serve customers.

After 54 years of service to the valley community, Producers Dairy is proud to be one of the few remaining locally owned independent businesses. Producers' area of distribution now extends from Bakersfield in the South Valley, to Stockton in the North Central Valley, from Santa Maria in the South Central Coast Region, north through the Monterey Peninsula area, including Santa Cruz, north to Pescadero. Producers Dairy is on the move.

Larry Shehadey on the right and son, Richard Shehadey, to the left, have been a most effective father and son team, bringing quality dairy products to area residents for over 50 years.

The presence of PG & E is easily discernible by its stately multi-storied silhouette in downtown Fresno.

PG & E

A RICH, PIONEER HISTORY

Pacific Gas and Electric Company's roots are closely interwoven with California's colorful agricultural history, especially in the fertile San Joaquin Valley. The utility has been an active member of the Fresno business community providing gas service to customers almost from the very day PG & E was created — October 1905.

PG & E's presence in the city of Fresno and Fresno County was expanded in 1930, when San Joaquin Light and Power Corporation was acquired. By welding together independent utilities, PG & E gained a number of gas and electric experts, many of them hydroelectric power pioneers. Such was the case in the Fresno area with the acquisition of San Joaquin Light and Power.

Albert Graves Wishon helped the valley become the state's agricultural heartland. He was one of the first to bring electricity to central California farms.

When Wishon became manager of the San Joaquin Light and Power Company in Fresno in 1902 one of his priorities was working with farmers.

When the farmers balked at the cost of replacing their wind, gasoline and steam-powered equipment with electric motors, Wishon borrowed $25,000 and offered them motors on a nothing-down, five-years-to-pay contract. He ran out of electric motors in two days.

At the same time, Wishon aggressively built new power plants and extended power lines into rural areas where no lines had gone before. PG & E and its predecessor companies have been instrumental in turning the San Joaquin into one of the world's greatest breadbaskets.

San Joaquin Light and Power Company in 1923 erected a 10-story corporate headquarters in downtown Fresno at a cost of $1,000,000. When San Joaquin Light and Power Company merged into the PG & E system, the downtown landmark and prominent feature on Fresno's skyline became the headquarters of PG & E's San Joaquin Division and Fresno District. The division was one of 13 operating divisions which evolved as the PG & E system was established in the 48-county northern and central California service territory. The company's operations organization went unchanged until PG & E implemented a reorganization plan effective January 1, 1985.

On that date PG & E merged the San Joaquin Division with company's Stockton Division, forming the new San Joaquin Valley Region. The new region was subsequently aligned into five divisions, one of which is Fresno Division, which is headed by Division Manager B.R. (Skip) Kirchner. The division encompasses most of Fresno and Kings Counties, plus a portion of Tulare County. There is a workforce of 800 employees responsible for delivering natural gas to 170,500 customers and power to 287,000 electric customers.

Although the gas and electric utility business has become a high-tech industry and PG & E is a national industry leader in that trend, Kirchner says the investor-owned utility has not lost sight of the role of its 30,000 employees nor of the company's heritage of serving its customers needs.

"Dedicated career employees are the backbone of PG & E," said Kirchner. "One important purpose of the reorganization plan was to shift much of the decision-making process out into the divisions closer to the customers."

The Fresno area pioneer names are deeply entrenched in PG & E's history. Names such as Wishon, Balch, Courtright and Kerchkhoff live on in the form of hydroelectric power plants, reservoirs and other PG & E facilities in the foothills and the Sierra Nevada east of Fresno.

aura of permanence. Floods hastened its decline; the town never fully recovered from the devasting flood of 1867. During this period, the sparsely populated settlements on the Valley floor were growing. In 1872, the Southern Pacific Railroad decided to locate a station in Fresno, a decision that marked Fresno as the center of the county's future growth.

The 1857 California State Register's record of Fresno County's formation lists 316 voters and 1300 Indians, along with considerable livestock and a few carefully-noted doctors and lawyers. In summarizing the condition of the county's agriculture, the Registrar noted that the few fruit trees appeared to thrive "remarkably well," a hint of prosperity to come. By 1874, with encouragement from the railroad, the county seat was moved to Fresno and the Millerton era drew to a close. By 1885, the new county seat had all the earmarks of a proper Victorian city. Its citizens preferred the pleasures of home, school and church to the entertainments of rambunctious Millerton and its environs.

Cattle ranching, one of the county's primary economic activities, developed to satisfy the miners' prodigious demand for meat. Prices soared quickly from $4 to $34 a head, but dropped to $1.50 a head when a severe drought caused many ranchers to unload their herds, glutting the market. Pork and lamb supplemented the available beef; some flocks reached 40,000 head. Ranching on a smaller scale continued on long after the demand from the mines diminished, and a lumber industry developed to furnish material for the settlers' homes. More significant by far than either of these enterprises, however, was the emergence of agriculture in the Valley.

Farming was hard going in those early days. All planting and harvesting were done by hand, often with the land-owner working alongside hired Indian and Chinese laborers.

An early photo capturing the tallying of the grape harvest as the vineyard worker fills still another box.

(Continued on page 27)

No pesticides or fertilizers were available to guarantee the success of the crops, and without irrigation the farmers had to depend on rain and an occasional flood. In 1868, A. Y. Easterby began to experiment with a system of irrigation canals on his 5,000 acres. During the three years that followed, his efforts resulted in the creation of the Fresno Canal and Irrigation Company, some astonishingly high yields of wheat and cotton, and — as elsewhere in the west — a number of hostile confrontations with cattlemen. It was the old fight: the incompatibility of planned agriculture and the open range. Small farmers, or those too far from the Fresno Canal and Irrigation Company's original ditches, relied on a windmills and wells for their water supply.

In the town of Fresno, the Southern Pacific sold parcels of land adjacent to the tracks for $60 to $250; a few shopkeepers snapped them up, anticipating Fresno's growth as a commercial and shipping center. Railroad passenger service brought new residents, who were treated to a ceremonious welcome and a display of prize agricultural products as an encouragement to settle. The influx of newcomers kept housing at a premium, and a healthy competition developed in the hotel business. Saloons opened, watched over by hastily-founded temperance organizations. Dry goods stores, butcher and blacksmith shops, livery stables, a flour mill, banks and even several milliner's shops came along at the same time.

Several newspapers were in print and in competition, including The *Expositor* and the *Fresno Weekly Democrat*. A school district was established and a hospital built. Water was still in the private domain, as were the gas and telephone services launched in the next decade. A public library got off to a good start with several sizeable donations, and social clubs encouraged the expansion of cultural and literary activities. Dances were popular, and travelling circuses, boxing matches, horse races, and theater and opera performances drew large crowds.

In spite of these delights of civilization, a host of problems plagued early county residents. Fires, floods, earthquakes, a tornado and several years of scorching heat challenged the ability of the townspeople to carry on their daily lives. Coping with these natural disasters called for organization. This, together with the pressing need for street, sewer, police and fire services, gave impetus to an incorporation movement. In 1885, despite the merchants' reluctance about higher taxes, the City of Fresno was chartered.

The city's population nearly tripled in the next decade, as the California boom peaked, transforming the pioneer town. Construction proceeded a block at a time, with each new commercial section more ornate than the last. Modern Renaissance vied with Chateau Revival. Electric lighting illuminated the streets, impressing visitors (recruited by the newly-founded Board of Trade) as they rode through the city in horse-drawn streetcars. Fire and police services were initiated, the court house was expanded and a high school was established. Public parks and fountains complemented stately Victorian homes along tree-lined streets. Citizens had their choice of two magnificent opera houses — the Grady and the Barton — seating up to 1600 people. In their leisure

This classic photo depicts an early Fresno farmer tying his vines in the midst of his vineyard.

hours they enjoyed dances, attended events at the fairgrounds and participated in cultural and intellectual clubs. Picnics and hayrides attracted residents of all ages.

Fresno's comfortable lifestyle was founded on astonishingly productive agriculture. The discovery in the 1880s that wine grapes grew extremely well in the hot dry summer days and cool, arid nights was monumental. The grapes matured quickly to a ripe sweetness, yielding close to 50 times the profit per acre that could be made from wheat. In the ten years between 1889 and 1899, fruit and vineyard acreage tripled, and Fresno County skyrocketed from the 25th to the fourth most productive agricultural county in the nation.

The raisin grape industry, now the mainstay of a large portion of the county's agriculture, was launched when a clever farmer turned disaster into opportunity. Francis Eisen's grapes dried on the vine in the hot summer of 1875. Instead of taking the loss, he packaged them as an imported delicacy and successfully marketed them in San Francisco. Perhaps as a result, four San Francisco school teachers became early investors in the Hedge Row, a substantial Fresno raisin vineyard. Overall, there was a ten-fold increase in raisin production between 1882-1884, and another nine-fold increase by 1887. In 1892, A. B. Butler had the largest vineyard in the state, covering a square mile and producing more than 1,000 tons of raisins a year. M. Theo Kearney, whose home is now administered as a historical site museum by the Fresno Historical Society, created a structure for price stability when he successfully organized a raisin growers' cooperative in 1898.

A historic farm photo shows thousands of grape trays lying in the bright San Joaquin sun in the traditional raisin-making process.

The valley's early irrigation ditches and canals not only brought life-giving water to crops, but shows this young couple partaking of its recreational opportunity.

Irrigation was becoming more reliable during this period as well. The installation of two of the world's first irrigation stations — pump-driven wells — marked the beginning of public irrigation districts, bringing water to the fields at a mere three cents an acre.

Processing plants and packing houses were established, some operated on site by the larger growers. Manufacture of farm implements added an important new element to the economic mix, and several new inventions drew attention to Fresno's practical flair. Products from Valley dairies were of such high quality that some competed in the San Francisco market. County life was enriched by the traditions and crops of immigrants from many parts of the world. In the case of the Armenians, their desire to recreate the taste of their favorite Adriatic figs resulted in the introduction of an important cash crop to the Valley.

This rapid development was not without problems. Water rights disputes accompanied every phase of agricultural expansion; at one time the Fresno Canal Company was spending more money to defend itself against lawsuits than it had spent to construct its entire distribution system. Land was the subject of nearly as many disagreements. The Southern Pacific followed a practice of encouraging settlers to use its land and then forcibly evicting them when it was ready to put a rail line through. Railroad freight rates caused considerable consternation because the Southern Pacific enjoyed monopoly status.

Other sources of aggravation to early residents were insects, transients and the eccentricities of frontier justice.

From the wrong side of the county's frontier justice came a number of colorful characters who are part of local legends. Perhaps the best known is Joaquin Murietta, who came to California from Sonora, Mexico, in the heady days of the Gold Rush. Following a series of outrages to his honor and his family, he became an outlaw, tracking down and killing, one by one, the individuals who had wronged him. He so terrorized the countryside that the state legislature commissioned the California Rangers to capture or kill him. They fulfilled their commission in an 1853 showdown.

The east side of the county had its share of charlatans and outlaws too. Travelers on the Yosemite stage could count themselves fortunate if they escaped the highwaymen. In the towns, Chinese gang warfare threatened the peace of all. Crime was as democratic in gender as in geography; county records show the arrest of female shoplifters in 1895. Arsonists, fraudulent bunco operators and waves of political corruption challenged the civil order.

During this period, bankruptcies and foreclosures echoed the country's depression. The national Pullman porters' walkout struck the railroad-dependent county particularly hard.

Determined and hardy, the people responded successfully to each emergency. Bicycle relay teams got the mail through; wagon caravans substituted for the train; and the electorate rallied behind reform candidates. The crops kept coming in, and at the turn of the century Fresno was ready to move forward with confidence.

The San Joaquin River playing host to another fisherman as it lazily crosses the valley floor.

Clair E. Nelsen

(Continued on page 30)

PEPSI COLA SAN JOAQUIN BOTTLING CO.

COMMUNITY LEADER SINCE 1894

An early historic photo (1894) of the bottling works which over the years has evolved into one of the most prosperous soft drink companies in America.

Back in 1894 Jacob Richter started his first bottling plant in Fresno on the corner of Broadway and Mono Streets. Jacob knew "soda pop" when he started the "Jacob Richter Soda Works," and so his business prospered. What he didn't know was that he was starting what was to become one of the largest and most successful soft drink companies in the country: the Pepsi Cola San Joaquin Bottling Company, which today employs 580 people throughout the San Joaquin Valley and Central Coast area.

But Jacob never made a single drop of Pepsi in his "Soda Works." It wasn't that he had anything against it; it just wasn't invented yet. In fact, it was 40 years later that Jacob's sons, Elmer, Roy and Jack, decided to bottle and sell the new drink that was then sweeping the country, PEPSI COLA! In 1943, the company officially became the Pepsi Cola Bottling Company of Fresno.

This 1943 photo shows yet another stage of Pepsi's growth locally.

It was in 1957, after Roy had retired and Elmer became president, that the company outgrew the Broadway bottling plant. Elmer's sons, Bud and King, closed down the old "Soda Works" and moved into a big, modern new plant on south Maple Avenue near Jensen Avenue.

It was there, under the direction of Bud and King, that the company experienced its most dramatic growth and became the leading soft drink bottler and distributor in the valley. This was partly accomplished by the acquisition of neighboring Pepsi franchises, which now cover 13 counties in Central California. In 1977, the firm was purchased by the Liggett Group which later was acquired by Grand Metropolitan based in England. Shortly thereafter, the company changed its name to Pepsi Cola San Joaquin Bottling Company to better reflect the scope of the operation and moved into a new bigger, ultramodern plant on North Avenue.

The company's multi-million dollar bottling plant houses one of the most modern high-speed soft drink production and distribution facilities in the United States. The facility produces bottled products not only for the Fresno area but for ten counties in Central California. Branch distribution facilities are also located in Visalia, Merced, Modesto and Stockton. Last year the Pepsi Cola Bottling Company of Salinas was purchased and now the company bottles and distributes products in Monterey, San Benito and Santa Cruz counties, too.

These expansion programs followed months of research, analysis and planning in order to develop one of the most

Ever growing, the Pepsi plant seen here in 1958 depicts yet another stage of development.

Pepsi headquarters today showcased in new state of the art facilities.

This aerial view depicts the magnitude of the new facilities for the Pepsi Cola San Joaquin Bottling Company.

productive and cost-effective soft drink production and distribution operations in the country.

Through all these years of change, growth and progress, the company has taken pride in its strong community support — a trademark of the firm since the day it was founded by Jacob Richter. Company president Ron Dorrell said, "It has always been the philosophy of this company to become deeply involved in community functions and affairs, particularly high school and college activities and other youth programs. First and foremost, we are in the 'people business.' And this goes beyond our manner of dealing with our customers to include our way of dealing with our employees." Pepsi Cola San Joaquin Bottling Company is proud to be a contributing part of the San Joaquin Valley and the Central Coast.

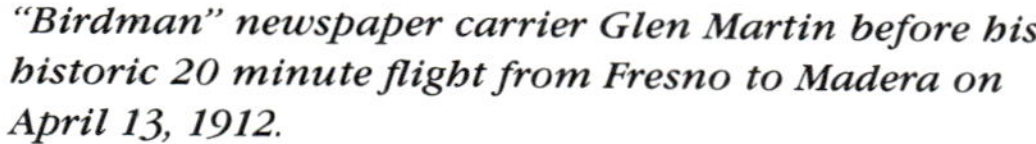

"Birdman" newspaper carrier Glen Martin before his historic 20 minute flight from Fresno to Madera on April 13, 1912.

1900-1920

The new century found Fresno at 4.13 square miles, the home of 12,470 within the city limits and 34,862 in the county. That population doubled by 1910, with new ethnic groups contributing to the central California cultural mosaic. The city was expanding rapidly to the north and east, with business and residences designed by several of the era's finest architects — notably Julia Morgan, Greene & Greene, and Bernard Maybeck.

To service these widespread areas, the city, in 1901, sold a 50-year franchise for electric streetcar service to a firm which became the Fresno Traction Company in 1903. By 1913, it served an area extending from the San Joaquin River beach and Pinedale on the north to Sunnyside on the southeast. Service was so good, the company claimed, that cars left downtown Fresno for the fairgrounds every seven minutes during the county's first air show in 1910. Half the population flocked to get their first glimpse of human flight, a mere seven years after the Wright brothers' successful flight of a powerful airplane at Kitty Hawk, North Carolina. The show's sponsor, the Chamber of Commerce, had great expectations that flight would be useful in facilitating business communications. Their hopes were realized with the beginning of air mail service to Fresno. By 1912, planes were even delivering newspapers to the smaller communities surrounding Fresno. On the ground, automobiles and taxi cabs competed with the Traction Company for customers and space on the narrow streets.

City government struggled to keep abreast of change. Reform mayors were elected to replace the ward bosses who were dominating local politics. The process of solidifying governmental authority in Fresno was a slow one. The ten-year delay in the city's original incorporation reflected the independent spirit of the early residents, and that spirit was not easily broken. Citizens preferred to see Fresno as a service and entertainment center rather than as a source of restrictive regulation.

This resistance to government can be partly explained by the composition of the population. With a citizenry made up of unreconstructed Confederates, immigrants who had escaped from various totalitarian countries and business owners who despised taxation, the civic force necessary to move toward a strong government was slow to develop. The issue was ultimately forced by several factors: the divisive power of political parties, the corrupting influence of an exceptionally strong railroad interest, the devastation wreaked by fire and flood and the challenge to order resulting from the presence of large numbers of young single men in the community. Still, the voters felt that the best government was no government at all, and they indicated this preference at every opportunity. They restricted the county supervisor's role to providing roads and limited the powers of the city fathers as well. It appears that the populace was still caught up in the romantic mythology of highwaymen and outlaw folk heroes and that residents saw the function of police as purely reactive rather than preventive.

What governmental progress took place in the early decades of the century was prompted by the demands of rapid growth. In 1916 the city Board of Trustees established the Fresno City Planning Commission, one of the first in the state. A new city hall housed government offices. It shared the urban skyline with Gottschalk's department store, the first federal building in Fresno, the Brix Building, the Fresno Hotel, the Rowell Building and the Burnett Sanitarium. In the city center, Court House Park provided a gathering place for bandstand music, gossip and courting. Nursery owner Frederick Roeding donated 72 acres on the outskirts of the city for a municipal park which would later be home to the highly regarded Fresno Zoo.

The city's population in this period included some 9,725 school age children, only half of whom were in school. Their educational needs were served by 62 teachers brought to the city from training institutions elsewhere. The need for teachers and the desire to train them locally to better meet local needs led to the establishment of Fresno Normal School in 1911. It shared a campus with the state's first junior college, opened in 1910.

At the turn of the century, livestock and grapes were the county's most important commodities. Wheat had succumbed to competition from the midwest and from overseas as crop yield declined. The area's population tripled between 1900 and 1920 as the second in a series of foreign immigration waves reached the county. Many of these immigrants settled on small farms of fewer than 50 acres; these farms accounted for 85 percent of farms started in the period. The trend to small farms was stimulated by the passage of the Federal Reclamation Act in 1902 which provided funds for irrigation dams and canals. By making surface waters readily available, it encouraged farm development — particularly on the west side. Its acreage limitation provisions, however, would prove troublesome in years to come.

Some of the west side acreage, as elsewhere in the Valley, was devoted to the production of cotton. This crop, introduced to the Valley early in the century, was destined to become the county's number one row crop. The increasing importance of cotton stimulated related developments such as the construction in 1918 of the area's first cotton gin and drying mill. The completion of a reliable highway linking the Valley to San Francisco and Los Angeles facilitated the delivery of cotton to market.

Early in the century, a number of growers' cooperatives were formed to market the bounty of the Central Valley. Sun Maid Growers and the California Fruit Growers Exchange — which promoted its "Sunkist" products aggressively — were two of the major cooperatives in those early years. The Danish Creamery Association, the oldest processing cooperative in the nation, was established in this period. Agricultural development was so phenomenal that an average of more than 150,000 acres per year were placed under irrigation for farming purposes each year between 1909 and 1919.

Fresnans' lives extended beyond the fields, however. Summertime auto excursions to Yosemite, the mountain lakes of Shaver and Huntington, the coast, or just to the banks of the San Joaquin River, were common. In town, the new Kinema and Liberty theaters provided a lively supplement to the touring stage shows at the Empire and White theaters and the Municipal Auditorium. Zapps Park drew thousands to its lake, zoo, roller coaster and swimming pool. Sports enthusiasts could cheer their favorite teams at the new baseball park. Cultural and civic groups often included picnics and dances in their schedules, and a symphony group was organized in 1910.

The Great War cast a pall on recreational pursuits. The city's patriotism was evident as it exceeded its enlistment quota. Some 1500 residents served in the armed forces, 165 of them giving their lives in action in France. When peace was declared, 25,000 residents turned out to celebrate the end of a painful period.

Hay baling via steam power. Note the size of the spoked wheel dwarfing the farmer next to it as wife and children wait in the horse and buggy.

Turn of the century lumber operations show three stalwart lumberjacks surrounded by their teams of oxen and fallen tree.

1920-1940

World War I disrupted international trade, providing a short-lived stimulus to some crops, such as wheat and olives. But hard times were ahead; post-war Prohibition dealt a severe blow to the grape industry. Raisin prices collapsed in the mid-20s, and money and credit tightened as some related businesses began to suffer. The added shock of the Depression was too much for many farmers to bear; foreclosures were frequent. Oil and cotton were still in demand, however, and their investors came through these trials relatively unscathed. The cotton industry reached a plateau of stability in 1925, when the state legislature passed a law limiting production to the Acala variety. This was an effort to discourage hybridization, thus ensuring uniform quality cotton.

The State Water Plan's completion in 1929 further boosted area agriculture by improving access to the surface water supply and eliminating problems caused by overdraft pumping of underground water. Another important step in developing a reliable water system was taken in 1935 when the Bureau of Reclamation initiated the Central Valley Project.

On the east side of the county, the land was yielding still further riches. The Sugar Pine Lumber Company in Pinedale, just north of Fresno, was producing some 100 million board feet of lumber a year. Lumber came down from the mountains on railroad cars, and the Fresno Traction Company's street cars brought workers from the city to the Pinedale plant. Flumes were used to transport 20,000 board feet of lumber a day from Shaver Lake to the mill. The Sanger Lumber Company and the Hume-Bennett Lumber Company were also active, but their wide-scale destruction of important Giant Sequoia stands is a blot on the industry's record. The pine, fir and cedar stands in eastern Fresno County were greatly depleted during this period. Several of the lumber companies experienced management difficulties and were forced to close down when the Depression caused a precipitous decline in the demand for lumber. The Sugar Pine Lumber Company site was used briefly as an internment camp during World War II and later served the Army Signal Corps.

In addition to lumbering activity in the county's eastern foothills, there were extensive mining operations in the region. In the hundred years after the Gold Rush, $905 million worth of minerals were extracted; 58 different minerals have been discovered in Fresno County. British investment fueled copper production in the Clovis area, and magnesite was being extracted in Piedra. Rivers are the key to much of this activity — from gold and quartz mining to asphalt and concrete production Four million tons of aggregate produced by area plants was used in the construction of Friant Dam. Some of the gravel operations in the region have reclaimed enough gold to completely cover operating costs.

With the railway line in the background, this historic photo shows the horse-drawn Fresno scraper at work in nearby Fowler, California.

An unusual black granite of exceptional hardness and quality is quarried in this country only in Fresno County, although it can be found in parts of Africa and India. Tungsten mines were operated in the rough high country. On the low west side, diatomite was mined and an asbestos industry flourished until the dangers of asbestos became known in the 1970s. Most significant in terms of its sustained contribution to the area's economy has been the Craycroft Brick Company, founded in 1887 and still in operation under fifth generation management. Craycroft produces tile for roofing and ornamental purposes, in addition to many types of bricks.

While agriculture, mining and the lumber industry were advancing in the rural areas, important business developments were taking place in town. Fresno Agricultural Works, later Fresno Ag Hardware, was becoming a significant business. It had been founded in 1876 by James Porteous, known throughout the world for his inventions. His Fresno Scraper, used for construction and irrigation on nearly every continent, was used in building the Panama Canal. Joining Porteous' thriving hardware and implement business on the Fresno commercial scene were The Fresno Bee, still the region's leading newspaper, the Sun Maid Raisin Corporation plant and a new Gottschalk's department store. The Roma and Cribari wineries were established, as were the Vendo Company and Duncan Ceramics. Several elegant new hotels, supermarkets and a new hospital — Saint Agnes — were built. The skyline was being transformed into that of a major urban center; the Mattei, Patterson, Pacific Southwest and San Joaquin Light and Power buildings as well as the Tower Theater in a new shopping district were all added in the 1920s.

The rising popularity of the automobile and the advent of the bus brought commuters from residential areas into the city center. The resulting traffic jams were eased somewhat in 1926 by the installation of traffic lights on the main thoroughfares. The city's limited network of developed roads was not equal to such heavy use, and in 1919 voters passed a major bond issue for road improvement. At $4.5 million it was the largest road bond ever voted in the state — an indication of Fresno residents' recognition of the importance of transportation to the county's economy.

Voters were less enthusiastic about public operation of power and lighting, and defeated a bond to purchase the existing utility company in the 1930s. Pacific Gas and Electric Company bought the local power and light company after the vote and promptly lowered the rates substantially. Even without the responsibility of providing electric service, city government had an awesome task. The

(Continued on page 35)

The Duncan Ceramics headquarters building is a showcase housing a local success story. Once a business operated out of a garage, it now has a worldwide clientele.

ELECTRIC MOTOR SHOP, INC.

SERVING THE VALLEY FOR 74 YEARS

Owner Frank Caglia on the right is flanked by his two sons, Franklin J. Caglia, far left, and Richard M. Caglia. Standing to the right of the Caglia family is a massive electric motor, typifying the scale of their operational diversity.

Fresno's Electric Motor Shop opened in 1913 as Central State Electric and has been in continuous operation since then serving the valley's industrial, commercial, agricultural and farming needs.

For nearly all of these years, Frank Caglia has been a part of the Electric Motor Shop. He came to the United States with his parents, an 8-year-old immigrant impressed and a bit overwhelmed by New York's Ellis Island. He remembers noticing the fruit stands, and being told by his father that the family would be journeying to a place where he could have all the fruit he might ever want. As a 10th-grade parochial school student in Fresno, he was recommended for a job by a local priest, Father Murphy, and began his career in 1929 with the Electric Motor Shop. In 1944, he became a part owner of the business, increasing his share in 1955. Two years later, he purchased the remaining share of the business and became sole owner. Working seven days a week, he guided the firm to its present size. Its 70 year-round employees provide a variety of services, including electric motor rewinding, motor and generator repair, electrical contracting, industrial and commercial electrical wiring. The company distributes v-belts and pulleys, motors and controls, and has one of the largest stocks of used motors in the area. Its service region covers the entire San Joaquin Valley, where its fleet of red trucks are a familiar sight.

An ancillary company, Electric Motor & Supply Co., carries industrial electrical supplies, including wiring devices, motor controls, switchboards, transformers and microswitches. Located at 250 Broadway, at the corner of Monterey and Broadway, the company provides a range of products complementing the Electric Motor Shop's services. In addition to these business interests, Frank Caglia has an interest in two waste disposal companies. One of the companies, IWS, offers commercial and industrial waste disposal systems, one to five yard containers, and compaction equipment and services. The other company, Orange Avenue Disposal, has a glass and paper recycling center, and provides shredding services for confidential material. In an ambitious project dubbed "Operation Christmas Tree," Caglia had a 52-foot tree installed by crane in place atop the company's landfill, and it was lighted each Christmas for several years before it died. A replacement tree plays an important role in Caglia's vision of the future. An original oil painting in the Electric Motor Shop depicts a lovely, flower-strewn landscape, with sheep contentedly feeding near the chapel Caglia has in mind for the mountain top, a gift of gratitude to the priests, Sisters of the Holy Cross, and all other religious orders, and to the many friends who have enriched the lives of his entire family.

Not only the future, but the best of the past, is a vital part of everyday life for Frank Caglia. File cabinets at the Electric Motor Shop are topped with marvelous Remington bronzes, reflecting the energy and excitement of the old West. Local history is very special to Mr. Caglia, as well, and his eye for quality, determination and generosity have preserved a number of outstanding area landmarks. The old Fresno arch proudly announces "The best little city in the USA," and has been carefully rebuilt and restored at Caglia's direction. Best known to valley people, however, is Caglia's success in preserving and restoring the beautiful Warnors Theater. The centerpiece of this exquisite theater, and the reason for Caglia's compelling interest, is the magnificent Robert Mortan organ, capable of producing a sound equivalent to a full 100-piece orchestra. Caglia remembers falling in love with the organ when he first heard it on opening day in 1929. To this day, he carries with him in the jeep a 1956 tape of Paul Carson playing the Warnors Organ. With his keen sense of heritage, vision of a better future and a strong personal appreciation for those who guided his path, Frank Caglia and Electric Motor Shop are among the best examples anywhere of the promise of the American dream.

This 1885 photo shows the stately Barton Opera House and Armory Hall located at Fresno and Fulton Streets.

added pressure of the post-war boom spurred the adoption of a commission form of government in 1920. Each of the five commissioners headed a separate department. By 1922 the Planning Commission had completed much of the city's zoning work. Despite some evidence of intrigue in the government office, the city's 60,000 residents enjoyed the benefits of most essential public services by that year. By 1929, Fresno — with 90,000 residents — was the tenth largest city in the state.

Many of these 90,000 residents were Dust Bowl immigrants. They joined the influx of Filipino and Mexican workers who responded to the county's fluctuating labor needs. During the Depression, social service organizations were hard pressed to meet the needs of an expanding jobless population. The Community Chest, the Salvation Army and municipal and newspaper employees rallied with food, toys, clothing and shelter for the needy.

Even in hard times, exciting developments kept alive the hope of better days to come. Charles Lindbergh visited Fresno in 1930 — one of several notables joining in the dedication of Chandler Field. State Senator Wilbur F. Chandler had given his field to the city for a municipal airport in 1929 — he had allowed pilots to use it between harvest and planting for several years before this. With city ownership, hangars, a control tower and paved runways could provide proper support for the flights.

Sports were a source of entertainment and inspiration during these turbulent times. The West Coast Relays began in Fresno in 1927, and many world records were set. In 1933, the city's Young Corbett won the World Welterweight title. Residents enjoyed spectator sports, golf on the new Fort Washington and Riverside courses, "talkies" at local theaters and dancing to the music of the Big Bands. A lovely Christmas tradition was started after World War I when homes on Van Ness Avenue displayed decorations to honor a deceased serviceman; thousands enjoy Christmas Tree Lane each December. William Saroyan's writing was beginning

Bob Barnes

Chandler Field located in West Fresno now serves a number of small aircraft helping take the traffic pressure off Fresno's main air terminal.

to draw attention to his Fresno home. The Fresno Historical Society undertook the monumental task of documenting Valley history; this was an extension of the important work done by the World War I History Committee. With Prohibition, the city lost its reputation as a wide open center of fast living. Women won the vote and enjoyed new conveniences on the home front. As the nation recovered from the Depression, Fresno took its place as an important urban center with a sophisticated population.

1940 to 1960

Fresnans felt the mounting tension, months before the country was plunged into World War II. National Guard units drew eager volunteers. When the call for enlistment came, 25,000 residents entered active service, and many more contributed through auxiliary activities. The influx of large numbers of military personnel — about 60,000 — to the three military bases around the city created a housing shortage of significant proportions. The military presence stimulated the development of USO clubs as well as entertainment establishments of a more questionable character.

Chandler Field was initially designated as a bomber base, but a larger area to the east was found to be more suitable for the establishment of Hammer Field. During the war, the federal government purchased more than 1,000 acres of land in the county. Much of this land was deeded to the city at the end of the war for the development of Fresno Air Terminal. In the 1950s, the California Air National Guard leased 53 acres; today its base occupies 100 acres. Both military and municipal monies have been used in a continuing effort to expand and improve the airport.

The end of the war ushered in another era of rapid growth, as the needs of the city grew well beyond the capacity of Chandler Field. A new municipal airport was built, and the first commercial flights took off in 1947, just a year after the opening of the country's first private residential airport — Sierra Sky Park. Fresno's connection with the rest of the state got a tremendous boost when construction began for Freeway 99, designed to link Los Angeles and Sacramento with Fresno as midpoint.

Fresno boasted three radio stations by 1944, and residents could tune in to network television programs as early as 1953. The war proved to be as much a stimulus to agriculture as to transportation and communication. Fresno had a corner on the raisin market when that fruit was being promoted as a substitute for rationed sugar; it was sole supplier of raisins to the Allies.

Water supply became more reliable with the construction of two major dams — Friant in 1944 and Pine Flat in 1954. Friant Dam, with a capacity of half a million acre feet of water, created Millerton Lake. Pine Flat Dam, approved for the Kings River in 1940, met with bureaucratic snags which delayed its completion for 15 years. Mechanization was transforming agriculture. Hand picking of cotton, for example, was nearly nonexistent after 1940. Where hand cultivation was still necessary the shortage of labor due to war-related jobs led to the importation of Mexican seasonal workers through the bracero program, which was in operation until 1964.

Unrestricted wartime growth led to annexation struggles and other challenges for the city government. A new firehouse was built, as were parks and recreation centers. The pride of the city fathers, however, was a new city hall of contemporary design. It was featured in a 1944 display of modern architecture at the Museum of Modern Art in New York City. Streetcars were replaced by a grid of city streets and roads, financed in part by the new city sales tax reluctantly approved by voters in 1948.

Easy transportation lured developers to outlying areas; this was a time of rapid expansion to the north and east. Manchester, the first large suburban shopping center, opened five miles north of downtown in 1955. In 1956 Fig Garden, the first neighborhood shopping center, opened even further north. Development followed Blackstone Avenue north and Shaw Avenue to the Clovis city limits in the northeast, where major airport development was taking place. Fearing abandonment of the city center, business leaders encouraged the city to engage the planning firm of Victor Gruen and Associates to develop an 85-acre superblock projection for the inner city. Momentum was growing for improving this central area. Following a particularly challenging newspaper series on the issue in 1956, the Fresno-Clovis Area Planning Commission prepared a general plan which led to the creation of a redevelopment agency.

Hartt Porteous

Pine Flat Dam constructed in 1954 is an asset to the agricultural, energy consuming, and recreational communities.

(Continued on page 38)

SCHOENWALD-OBA-MOGENSEN-POHLL-MILLER, INC.

ARCHITECTS & ENGINEERS ENHANCING THE CITY'S APPEARANCE

Resplendent in its nighttime aura, Fresno County's Courthouse is one of the many proud architectural achievements of SOMPM, Inc.

One of the oldest, largest and most prestigious architecture and engineering firms in Fresno is SCHOENWALD-OBA-MOGENSEN-POHLL-MILLER, INC. Founded in 1956, this midsize organization has enhanced the quality of life in Fresno through numerous facilities designed for both private and public use. In addition to a large staff of architects and designers, SOMPM, Inc. provides its clients services in the key engineering disciplines performed by licensed professional structural, civil, electrical and mechanical engineers. In order to remain progressive in the fields of architecture and engineering, SOMPM, Inc. is continually adapting new techniques and principles which are made possible through scientific advancements. The firm has aggressively adopted the latest advances in computer technology and in computer aided design and drafting (CAD), which have proven to be superior in the design process and in the overall coordination of construction documents.

Throughout its history and growth, SOMPM, Inc. has attempted to maintain variety in its practice, believing that diversity of experience enriches a practice. This variety has given the firm valuable expertise in industrial-commercial, governmental-public, educational, medical and health care, religious facilities and in areas of recreation. For over a quarter century, SOMPM, Inc. has successfully rendered professional services to hundreds of clients, and a number of these structures are easily identifiable on Fresno's horizon. In the area of government and public facilities, they include the Fresno County Courthouse, the Fresno County Sheriff's building, the main branch of the United States Postal Service

An interior view of judicial facilities within Fresno County's courthouse.

and the Fresno City Police Headquarters. The major local clients this firm has served in the industrial-commercial area include the Sun Maid Raisin Growers, PPG Industries, Rockwell Manufacturing Company, McClatchy Newspapers, Dow Chemical Company, Container Corporation of America, Coca-Cola Bottling Company, Pacific Gas and Electric Company and the Bostitch Company. Education is also one of the firms major areas of expertise, and in addition to numerous elementary and secondary educational facilities, SOMPM, Inc. masterplanned and designed all of the new structures on the Fresno City College campus.

Fresno's outstanding zoo ranks as one of California's premier zoos and is located within Roeding Park. (Pictured to the right)

Through the years, SOMPM, Inc. has been honored with numerous design awards. Several of their facilities have been selected by major manufacturers to be featured in national marketing programs. Although it is impossible to list the thousands of facilities that this firm has completed throughout the Western United States, their primary commitment has been to the design of quality environments which enhance the lifestyle of Fresno. SOMPM, Inc. will continue to thrive as a responsive, progressive and creative organization serving the community, and looks forward to the excitement of meeting the challenges created by technological advancements.

Pictured to the right is the Arts Center at Fresno City College, which is another stunning example of the design work of SOMPM, Inc.

This paved the way for a period of urban renovation.

In 1958, a survey conducted by Columbia University named Fresno as one of the ten best places in the nation in which to raise a family. This was undoubtedly due to the city's responsiveness to the problems created by rapid growth and to the outstanding business, cultural and recreational opportunities of the area.

Although the commission form of government had been responsible for much progress in the city (there was even a woman commissioner in 1955), by this time it was an anachronism. In 1957 the city embarked upon its current city manager-council form of government, with the mayor serving in a primarily ceremonial capacity.

Under the new system, bonds were passed for police station construction and for the development of new parks and playgrounds. The Zoological Society spearheaded the effort to establish Roeding Park Zoo. Development quickly spread to include a Playland built through the generosity of local Rotarians. Baseball and ice hockey teams were formed, as was a championship women's softball team.

The Fresno County Free Library moved into its new home in 1958 and continues to provide support for the educational, cultural and recreational reading interests of the community. Rapid population growth — 30,000 residents were added between 1940 and 1950 alone — mandated expansion of school services. In 1944, 136 elementary schools, 17 secondary schools and 3 junior colleges comprised the 349 school districts authorized over the county's history. Something had to be done.

Chaffee–Fresno Zoo

The Fresno Board of Education began a consolidation process shortly after moving into new district headquarters in 1950. In 1945 the Fresno City District and the Fresno High School District merged to form the Fresno Unified School District. Bullard High School opened ten years later to serve the northern portion of the city. That same year saw the dedication of the new campus of Fresno State University, which had outgrown its earlier home — now occupied by Fresno City College.

Fresno headed into the '60s with vigor.

1960 to 1985

In Fresno, as in the rest of the country, the '60s ushered in an era of social turmoil and change. Civil rights marchers joined Dr. Martin Luther King, Jr., at a rally in Ratcliff Stadium in 1964. Consumers, inspired by Caesar Chavez, boycotted table grapes to call attention to the plight of migrant farm workers. High school students rode buses to distant corners of the city to experience integrated classrooms, and environmental groups moved to acquire and preserve portions of the area's spectacular wilderness.

Activism of a different sort characterized city government. Downtown merchants supported aggressive urban redevelopment in an effort to slow the tide of fringe area expansion. With the help of the Downtown Association, city government was successful in preventing special interests from developing the city haphazardly in all directions. Under a controversial authority financing arrangement, a huge $10 million Convention Center complex was opened in 1966, together with the first multilevel downtown parking structures. The center joined the 22-story Del Webb Hotel and office complex opened in 1964, and a new state office complex, in revitalizing the city's downtown area. A new police headquarters symbolized that department's transformation from a reactive, understaffed force at the turn of the century into a high-tech, prevention-oriented operation. Its outstanding search and rescue operations contributed to a fine reputation.

Although all inner city improvements made during this period were important in revitalizing the downtown area, one gained national recognition for its creativity and high quality. In September 1964, the six-block Fulton Street pedestrian mall became Fresno's downtown showpiece. Fountains, sculpture, gardens, shaded seating areas,

This turn of the century photo taken in 1900 shows the stately architecture of the old Fresno County Courthouse.

children's playgrounds and thriving businesses drew shoppers and visitors to the heart of the city. Its success catapulted Fresno into the ranks of an "All-American City." Downtown development was recognized by the National Municipal League and publicized by Look Magazine, leading to Fresno's selection to participate in the 1967 Model Cities Program. In 1969, a new challenge to downtown business appeared as Fashion Fair Mall opened on Shaw Avenue in north Fresno.

Freeway 41 opened in 1981 making transit to and from the inner city rapid and safe. Neighborhood shopping centers proliferated as the bedroom suburbs of the north grew, and service industries and professional offices followed the flow northward.

Of the many changes and developments in this period, by far the most controversial was the replacement of Fresno's 91-year-old landmark Court House. Progress won out over preservation in a lengthy battle, but the building's cupola and statues of Justice were preserved when the building fell to the demolition crew. The lessons learned in that preservation effort were promptly applied to protect other important buildings, notably the Meux Home and the Fresno Bee building, both of which found new life as museums. The historic administration building on the Fresno City College campus was temporarily saved from demolition by serving as home to the California Agricultural Museum.

The cultural scene was enlivened not only by the dedication of these important museums, but also by the opening of the Fresno Arts Center in Radio Park. On a sadder note, Fresno's premier writer, the world-reknowned William Saroyan, died in 1981. His memory is kept alive in his beloved home town through educational efforts and displays. The Convention Center's theater proudly bears his name.

The 1970s brought a host of aggravations to the citizens of Fresno as they endured the long gasoline lines, high unemployment rates, shortages, bankruptcies and skyrocketing utility bills plaguing much of the nation. The influx of refugees from Southeast Asia taxed the city's social service agencies to the limit. It was a tough time for agriculture, the county's economic base. West side growers were embroiled in legal battles with the Interior Department over the interpretation of reclamation laws which seriously disadvantaged larger operations. Greece entered the Common Market, causing considerable damage to the Fresno raisin industry's competitve position on the international market.

Water, always a concern in the Central Valley, was the source of difficulties as the issue of draining brackish irrigation water surfaced. The Westlands Water District was formed in 1967 to deliver federal water to west side growers, following authorization in 1960 of the San Luis Project, which served a 100-mile area from Los Banos to Kettleman City. West side water concerns were cleared up at least temporarily by passage of the Reclamation Reform Act in 1982.

The problem of special governmental service districts had grown out of hand by this time; there were 150 such districts — all administered by the Board of Supervisors — in 1963. In that year, the California State Legislature established the Local Agency Formation Committee (LAFCO) to maintain order in the designation of special districts, to prevent urban sprawl and to preserve prime agricultural land for farming purposes.

As Fresno's first century drew to a close, a seasoned government and business community gave direction and structure to a city which was emerging as a California pacesetter. The decision by the federal government to locate an Internal Revenue Service Center in Fresno boosted employment and brought new vigor to the economy. The influx of new, hardworking ethnic groups helped keep the American dream alive.

Fresno State basketball plays to sellout crowds, even before its 1983 National Invitational Tournament championship.

The mosaic of peoples making up Fresno had special reason to celebrate. The Fresno State Bulldogs basketball team, coached by Boyd Grant, thrust Fresno into the national spotlight by winning the National Invitational Tournament championship in New York in 1983. Red-clad crowds filled the streets in a spontaneous celebration of local affection and pride. Just one year previously, to the delight of sports enthusiasts, the university's football team took the California Bowl title for Coach Jim Sweeney. At the top in sports and recreation, and with a renewed economy and the projection of long-range growth and prosperity, Fresno entered its second century secure, proud and just a little bit boistrous.

NEW YORK LIFE

A FINANCIAL SERVICES TEAM YOU CAN COUNT ON

Thomas W. Sommers, CLU, ChFC

John E. Horstmann, CLU

Ronald F. Karabian, CLU

Herman Kong, CLU, ChFC

Nishan Kochian

Dennis M. Stubblefield, CLU

Rod W. Stubblefield, CLU

Stuart Arakelian

George E. Alexander, CLU ChFC

Tou Chang

Mary Napoletano

For over 70 years New York Life men and women have been personally involved helping valley families and businesses with financial and estate planning. New York Life has enjoyed great success in the San Joaquin Valley and believes in reinvesting in the community it serves. The company's leaders have been active in their communities, churches and charitable groups. As a result, the Fresno organization is building on New York Life's 142 year record of living up to the commitment of helping people "get the most out of life."

Valley people have responded by consistently turning to New York Life for the placement of a long list of financial products. New York Life is a lot more than insurance. Through NYLIFE Securities Corporation - the financial products and services organization of New York Life - they provide opportunities to put money to work in new ways, to enhance financial planning for the future. Clients can select employee benefit products, mutual funds, disability and life insurance, partnership investments, 401k voluntary plans and IRA and TSA plans. New York Life is proud to be one of the largest providers of financial services in California with over 633,000 clients. New York Life agents and registered representatives are all full-time professionals with the training, experience and dedication it takes to make a difference.

New York Life's Fresno office is located at 1180 East Shaw Court.

Hartt Porteous

Newcomers—People and Business

CHAPTER 3

When the United States of America celebrated the 100th birthday of the Statue of Liberty in 1986, the nation paused to consider the significance of ethnicity in its history. In 1987, the 200th anniversary of the American Constitution, there is reason to think again about the common cultural ties that have grown in America to create one nation from many peoples — "One Nation under God." Two themes, diversity and common purpose, are woven into the history of the nation, the history of California and into the history of Fresno, the city and the county.

Less than 400 years ago the first white settlers planted the seeds of European culture on these shores. Wave after wave of immigrants have come seeking freedom from political oppression, freedom of religion and the promise of a better future for themselves and their children. America has indeed become a microcosm of world culture, a grand experiment in "E Pluribus Unum," the melding of people from many cultures into one. Americans are united in the pursuit of the "American Dream." Consider that only a few hundred years ago the ancestors of every American lived elsewhere, even the forebearers of the people we now identify as Native Americans.

The first immigrants came primarily from southern and eastern Europe. Lady Liberty symbolized their hopes and dreams. It was natural for the newly arrived to live, work, worship and marry within their own cultures, thus giving birth to the great ethnic neighborhoods of the northeastern cities. If Lady Liberty symbolized the land of promise to the immigrants, it also symbolized the ethnic differences political candidates would be wise to acknowledge. Astute office seekers, the savvy ones, frequently included a pilgrimage to Europe, a fact-finding journey, in their lexicon of accomplishments to better ensure the ethnic vote upon their return. Today the nation's power axis has shifted decidedly to the southwest. Knowledgeable politicians journey to Rio or Seoul rather than to Europe, a sign of responsiveness to the transformation of the nation's cultural composition, the economic and political consequences of which are only beginning to emerge. The European orientation of national policy is coming under scrutiny as the burgeoning Hispanic and Asian populations of the California-Florida sunbelt focus increasing attention on Latin America and on the countries of the Pacific Rim.

California has been home to a greater diversity of European people than has any other state, with citizens from Ireland, Italy, Scotland, England, France, The Netherlands, Germany, Denmark and Portugal numbered in the vast human melting pot that is California's heritage. But the mixture is changing rapidly. It is predicted that Hispanics and Asians will account for nearly 70 percent of California's population growth between 1985 and 1990. These groups, together with Blacks and other minorities, will comprise 53 percent of the state's population by the year 2010. Hispanics and non-Hispanic whites will be nearly equal in proportion by 2030, approximately 38 percent each, while the Asian population is estimated to reach more than 15 percent by

Japanese women and children are poised to start a friendly tug of war.

(Continued on page 44)

CHIHUAHUA, INC

FRESHLY BAKED TORTILLAS

Fidencio Villegas on the left, and Frank Villegas on the right, stand before their beautiful new building complex in West Fresno.

The gentle sound of Mariachi music wafts through the air; the warm, earthy scent of fresh tortillas stirs a nostalgic longing, as the Chihuahua Mercado brings a bit of Mexico's magic to downtown Fresno. Centerpiece of the Mercado, the Chihuahua Tortilleria, was founded in 1947 by the Villegas family. Second-generation management, Fidencio and Frank Villegas, assumed control of the business in 1962, operating it as a general partnership. In 1977, the business entered a new phase with its incorporation, and in 1984, the colorful, expansive Mercado at Fresno and F Streets was opened.

Chihuahua, Inc. has grown to be one of the largest Hispanic-owned corporations in the San Joaquin Valley, and is the largest of the more than 30 tortilla manufacturers in central California. Area consumers have voted Chihuahua the best by taste test, giving the company 55 percent of market share in the region. The company has 26 distribution routes bringing its products to more than 500 customers. New expansion has taken the products into the Salinas area, and into Sacramento as well. San Jose, like Sacramento, has a large Hispanic population, offering potential for expansion into that area.

With plant operation currently at 45-55 percent of capacity, Chihuahua can easily accommodate more growth. Chihuahua has already been approved as a supplier to all northern California Safeways, Nob Hill, Luckys and future Save Marts. Chihuahua also supplies Ruiz Mexican Foods, a local Mexican frozen food manufacturer, with flour and corn tortillas which are used in burrito and taquito preparation.

The manufacture and delivery of Chihuahua's products accounts for 75 percent of its total sales. Each year, more than 26 million corn and flour tortillas are produced at Chihuahua, to be sold within a 100 mile radius of Fresno. In addition to corn and flour tortillas, Chihuahua produces tortilla chips, pastries, spices, taco and tostada shells and chicharrones (pork rinds).

Supplying the company's more than 500 customers with these specialty products keeps over 200 full-time employees busy working two shifts, five days a week, year-round. Historically, May through September are the busiest months of the year, second only to the annual Christmas peak in volume. Expansion goals of the company include adding a third shift for around-the-clock, seven day-a-week production, and stabilizing the demand for consistency year-round.

Chihuahua's keen sense of future position is indicated by its recent installation of a quarter-of-a-million dollar wastewater treatment plant. This state-of-the-art addition, responsive to recently enacted governmental regulations, will help ensure the company's continued dominance of this specialty food market in the central valley.

The Mercado is more than a tortilla manufacturing plant. It also contains a retail grocery store, delicatessen and plaza, cocktail bar and leased office and shop space. On a 243,000 square foot lot, the Mercado covers a total of 59,000 square feet, with 30,000 taken up with production and warehouse space. Rental area occupies 4,500 square feet, and halls, corridors and the conference room are an additional 2,500 square feet.

Driving into the parking lot, the visitor notices Spanish-language signage, and upon entering, hears the phones answered with a cheerful !Buenos Dias! With the thoughtful touches of music, color, authentic architecture and the ever-present scent of freshly baked tortillas, the delightful ambience of old Mexico is re-created to add charm and interest in the midst of downtown Fresno.

that year. Projections indicate the labor force of California will be 27 percent Hispanic and 12 percent Asian by the year 2000.

The combination of immigration and intrastate relocation have made Fresno the fastest growing among California's ten largest cities. People from many diverse countries have found Fresno a good place to live. A 1908 news photograph shows a group of 16 Fresno school children, each from a different culture. Africans, Swedes, Basques, Russians and Japanese worked with the French, Portuguese, Italians, Irish and other ethnic groups to build a secure and prosperous life for their families in Fresno. And that tradition continues today.

Indeed, Fresno is an intricate composite of cultures. Nearly every issue of the *Fresno Bee* pictures civic leaders from a variety of national and ethnic backgrounds. In a naturalization ceremony near the time of the 200th anniversary of the U.S. Constitution, 99 valley residents from 38 countries became citizens of the United States, thereby adding greater luster to the cultural mosaic that is Fresno.

THE MEANING OF ETHNICITY

Although many Americans are now three or four generations removed from their ancestral homelands, ethnic identification is a source of pride and personal understanding for many. Even though ethnic identification is optional in the United States, many people go beyond mild curiosity about their familial roots to delve wholeheartedly into their culture of origin. They cherish customs, foods, religious traditions and languages they would be hard-pressed to justify logically or economically. Nevertheless, a sense of heritage and distinctiveness of culture prompts 85 percent of Americans to identify with at least one ethnic group. Apparently the common bonds formed among those who share an ethnic heritage give comfort and a feeling of acceptance in a sometimes cold and impersonal world.

The 1980 census report gives a useful summary of many of the 106 different ethnic groups making up the population of the United States. The 35 largest of these are shown below. A second figure shows the ten countries from which the most people emigrated to the United States in 1984.

A valley couple wears authentic European garb to mark their heritage at a local festival.

While ethnicity is fluid, changing as groups form, merge and dissolve, the 1980 census "snapshot" of the nation's mix is an illuminating depiction of the many allegiances and affections of Americans. Whether drawn together by race, religion, geography, language, tradition, folklore or by an externally-imposed stamp of distinctiveness, many Americans are acknowledging and celebrating their origins. The nation is enriched by the diversity of its citizens.

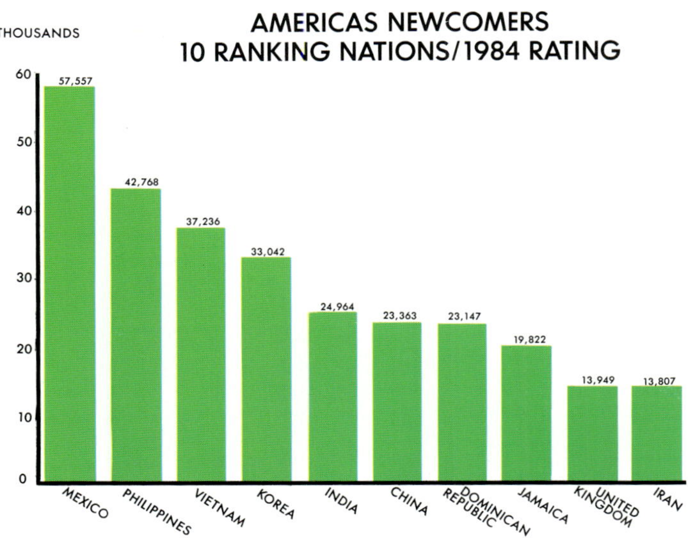

THE AMERICAN PEOPLE IMMIGRANT HOMELANDS 1984

Dutch	2%
American Indian	3%
Mexican	3%
Polish	3%
Scottish	4%
Italian	4%
French	5%
Other	6%
Afro-American	9%
Irish	18%
German	2[illegible]%
English	22%

TOTAL POPULATION
226.5 MILLION

Source: U.S. Immigration and Nationalization Service, adopted by Educational Extension Systems, Washington, DC in its 1987 Ethnic Cultures of America Calendar.

(Continued on page 46)

SAN JOAQUIN BUSINESS SERVICES GROUP, INC.

AID FOR THE ENTREPRENEUR

Members of the SJBSG Board of Directors as pictured from the right are Mike Carpenter, Roger Palomino, Frank Edwards (retired), Bob Perkins, Bill Stewart, Joe Williams, Tom Hunt and Pete Wilson — not pictured — Gene Geist, Gail Griego

San Joaquin Business Services Group, Inc. is a newly formed corporation operating as a Minority Enterprise Small Business Investment Company (MESBIC) licensed and regulated by the Small Business Administration (license approval is currently pending with the SBA).

The purpose of this venture capital investment company is to assist entrepreneurs who have been denied the opportunity to own and operate a business because of social or economic disadvantage.

With an initial capitalization of $1 million and an additional leveraged of $3 million from the SBA, venture capital in the form of loans and debt or equity securities is available to small independent businesses, both new and already established.

An integral service that is also provided is management assistance. Business evaluations are furnished; business plans are coordinated; loan packages are prepared; seminars are provided; and other appropriate supportive services are given.

Mr. Joe Williams, President

Incorporated in April, 1987, SJBSG has a nine-member board of directors with a diverse background. Dr. Bill Stewart, Chancellor of the State Center Community College district serves as the Chairman and Mr. Joe Williams, Executive Director of the Fresno County Economic Opportunities Commission, serves as the President.

Joe Williams (right) is pictured here with Board members Luisa Medina and Frank Edwards in the midst of the Executive Plaza building, a multi-million dollar acquisition to be used for the enhancement of downtown, minority businesses and human services programs.

A farmer pauses in his labors against the background of a wealth of the valley's king cotton and cloudless San Joaquin sky.

AMERICA'S COMMON CULTURE

America's common culture is woven from threads of dozens of distinctive cultures. While there are irregularities in the resulting fabric, the pursuit of liberty, justice and dignity unifies the whole. Secretary of Education William J. Bennett summarized what he believes are the three central principles of America's enduring and resilient national culture.

Foremost among these principles, said Bennett, is the democratic ethic. It recognizes the inherent worth of each individual, the equality of persons, and the human rights accorded to every citizen. This emphasis on worth encourages the full development of each individual's potential. The stress on human rights and the equality of persons promotes tolerance and mutual respect among people of differing traditions and beliefs.

A second in this set of fundamental principles, according to Bennett, is the work ethic. From the very beginning of the nation, Americans have stressed the virtue of hard work. They believe that hard work will be rewarded. Because the work ethic emphasizes individual effort, our political system — like our economic system — depends more on individual opportunity than on conflict among groups. America's heroes, whether in the political, industrial or cultural arena, tend to be those who embody the ideals of rugged individualism and personal excellence, giving the best effort to all tasks.

The third and final element in Bennett's assessment of our national values is the importance of the Judeo-Christian religious tradition. The themes of respect for others, standards for individual behavior, obligation to serve others, and a commitment to decency which are part of this heritage,have shaped our common culture. According to Bennett, a moral resolve to abide by these standards prevents the development of a culture of selfishness and bigotry.

These common cultural elements, said Bennett, are rooted in the moral imagination of Americans from every walk of life. They are transmitted through the educational system, learned in the family and debated openly in the ongoing public discussion of current issues. American lives are permeated by the principles of decency, enterprise and human worth, and the life of the society is enlightened and ennobled by a cultural consensus which promotes acceptance of diversity, transforming it into an alloy of resilient strength.

THE PEOPLE OF FRESNO

Fresno's people form a mosaic on the move, a bright array of colors and patterns, each part making a contribution to the vibrant California lifestyle. This fascinating cultural mixture has been the subject of a great deal of study. Research conducted in 1977 by the anthropology department of California State University, Fresno, identified some 70 ethnic groups in Fresno County — each with its own religion, language or cultural heritage. Drawn by the warm climate, rich soil, mountains, streams and rivers, people from nearly every nation and walk of life have come to central California. Tilling the soil, trading with their neighbors, and resolving common difficulties, they laid the foundation for today's enviable quality of life.

The Valley's first inhabitants, the Yokut and Monache Indians, lived peacefully on the Valley floor and in the foothills until newcomers with an alien concept called progress spelled their doom. The Indians had raised abundant food crops and had established far-ranging trade networks, harbingers of the civilization to come.

Fresno City & County Historical Society

A chubby-cheeked infant reposes at the entrance of a Monache or Western Mono Indian dwelling in this 1896 photo.

Occasional explorers, soldiers, and missionaries of various European and American ancestries passed through the San Joaquin Valley from the late 18th century on, but none settled to stay until the first Mexican ranchers brought their herds on to the broad, westside grasslands during the 1800s. They put down roots in the Valley's first towns where Coalinga and Mendota are today. Other Hispanic settlers spread across the Valley with their horses, sheep and cattle. One, Jose Castro, built a substantial estate stretching many miles along the banks of the San Joaquin. These early settlers are the source of the names of many of the Valley's rivers and cities, and their influence continued strong until the mid-1800s. The treaty of Guadalupe Hildago in 1848, ending the Mexican-U.S. War, gave the United States the area which now comprises the states of California, Texas and Arizona, in lieu of reparations in gold. It wasn't long before miners of Mexican heritage were subjected to burdensome taxation on their mining activities and most of them returned to Mexico.

Those who remained found merchandising a profitable alternative, and others operated ferry boats on the San Joaquin River, sold horses, established blacksmith shops and became active in civic affairs. When Asian laborers were excluded by legislative fiat at the turn of the century, Mexican agricultural workers were suddenly in demand, swelling the Hispanic population. Hispanic struggles grew and reached a high point during the Great Depression of the 1930s. This began to change after World War II when heroism of thousands of Americans of Hispanic heritage had been documented in the carnage of Asia and Europe. The GI Bill afforded many the chance to attend college and enter the professional strata of the Valley's culture. Even though the Valley has been the site of various labor disputes since World War II, there is no disputing the increasing assimilation of those of Hispanic heritage into the political and cultural leadership of the valley. Hispanics from Fresno County have played important roles in national government in the presidencies of Richard Nixon and Ronald Reagan.

Although history has no record of hostile encounters between Mexican and Chinese laborers, the well-being of one culture often improved at the expense of the other. When Chinese laborers were abundant, Mexican workers were at a disadvantage and paid lower wages. When political sentiment led to the exclusion of Chinese immigrants, Mexican workers were once again in high demand. The Chinese overcame many difficulties, but the fact that they prospered adds luster to their accomplishments as Americans. Their industriousness must be credited for much of the progress in the Central Valley. From making the bricks for the first county buildings to leadership in medical and cultural activities, people of Chinese heritage have contributed much to our quality of life. In 1874, 200 Chinese celebrated the establishment of Fresno as the county seat. In 1985 the Chinese population had grown to 6,000, making it the fourth largest population of Americans of Chinese heritage in the State of California.

Progress is equally telling for Blacks who have settled in the Central Valley. The first Black visited Fresno County in 1845 as part of General Fremont's expedition; he served without rank or pay. A few years later, when Ira McCray's Oak Hotel was the center of social life in Millerton, a Black servant was the hotel's manager and cook. Jane Derman, the county's first Black businesswoman, established a bakery and

Many a valley immigrant first found themselves employed picking grapes, just as this worker is pictured in the Papagni vineyards.

Bob Barnes

(Continued on page 49)

CAPRI SUN, INC.

FRESNO IS #1 WITH CAPRI SUN

Fresno rates high among industry officials as a good place to live and work. Among those sold on Fresno is the German owned beverage firm Capri Sun, Inc.

Hans-Peter Wild of the family-owned Wild Co. of Heidelberg, West Germany says the start-up of the plant in Fresno was the smoothest of any of the company's plants in more than 40 countries. He says Fresno has a "very capable and dedicated workforce" and a supportive community. Nearly all of the 45 employees at Capri Sun in Fresno were hired through the Private Industry Council.

Capri Sun manufacturers fruit drinks in the remodeled Market Wholesale building on South Orange Avenue in Fresno. Fresno was chosen as an ideal location because it's located between the Los Angeles and San Francisco major markets, and because it is a center for much of the fruit that the company uses in its fruit drinks.

Capri Sun has another plant located in Granite City, Illinois. It handles the market east of the Mississippi while Fresno furnishes the product for the western United States. Capri Sun in the United States is wholly owned by the Wild Co., which licenses the product throughout the world. Capri Sun's corporate headquarters is located in San Mateo, California.

The Wild Co. was founded 54 years ago by Rudolf Wild in Germany and manufactures fruit juice drinks, prepares and distributes fruit products throughout Europe for bakery and dairy uses and builds the equipment used in processing the products sold. Capri Sun was first marketed in the United States in 1979 and was an immediate success.

Capri Sun is available in nine flavors with another to be added this year. All the drinks are packaged in foil pouches. The pouch is made of triple laminated foil that provides flexibility as well as strength for the consumer.

The ingredient base for Capri Sun is imported from Germany in a "flavor-pack" concentrate containing natural essences and flavors from fruits gathered around the world. Fruit juice from local valley crops comprises ten percent of the product.

"The heart and soul of the brand comes from Germany," says Chris Mottern, president of Capri Sun, Inc. "It's part of the Wild heritage."

Capri Sun orange drink rolls through the production line.

MOTION DESIGNS

THREE FRIENDS PARLAYED A TRAGEDY INTO AN INNOVATIVE SUCCESSFUL BUSINESS

Scott Zimmerman

In 1978 a devastating hang gliding accident left sports enthusiast Marilyn Hamilton on the side of a mountain paralyzed from the waist down. Unwilling to give up her active life-style and totally disappointed with her conventional "dinosaur" stainless steel wheelchair, she turned to two friends for help.

Jim Okamoto and Don Helman, hang gliding enthusiasts, were at the time beginning to design and manufacture hang gliders. Marilyn asked them if they could build her a better wheelchair using the same aerospace technology they were mastering.

The result of their efforts was the introduction of the ultralight rigid frame . . . Quickie wheelchair, in 1980. Interest mushroomed among wheelchair sports enthusiasts who yearned for mobility coupled with maximum performance.

Next, Jim, Don and Marilyn tackled the challenge of offering the same performance and lightweight mobility, with the additional convenience of adjustable bolt-on accessories, to a larger share of wheelchair users.

Sales exploded, in 1984, with the introduction of the first modular frame, ultralight, 26-pound wheelchair. This new

laundry next to the hotel. Black cowboys herded cattle for area ranchers, and by the 1880s there were two Black churches in the county.

The exemplary service of Blacks in World War II helped pave the way to greater understanding and harmony in Fresno. The civil rights activities of the 1960s led to increased interaction of children of all races in the schools, and to greater understanding among parents. Black leadership is a dynamic force in Fresno City, exemplified by a Black city manager, mayor protem, along with a cadre of Black professionals in both the public and private sectors. The values and traditions of Fresno's Black community enrich the life of the whole community.

The exclusion of Chinese laborers by the Chinese Exclusion Act of 1882 benefited Japanese laborers as well as Mexicans. In Fresno County, as in much of the nation, however, the story of the Japanese is largely one of overcoming obstacles.

In spite of W.W. II hysteria, Japanese American community leaders encouraged their people to continue to demonstrate their tremendous courage and loyal citizenship in the face of a variety of adversities. In spite of the displacement endured by many Japanese Americans during W.W. II, numerous Japanese returned to their Fresno County homes to once again resume their productive, private and civic lives.

Japanese Americans hold a wide variety of influential positions in Valley agriculture, as well as in businesses and professions. The beautiful Buddhist Temple in downtown Fresno serves as a cultural, social and religious center for many Japanese Americans.

The European community of the county is an amalgam of ethnic groups, many of whom are intensely loyal to their cultural heritage. Important economic and cultural contributions have been made by people who came to the generation chair, Quickie 2, could be conveniently folded and the wheels easily removed by using quick release pins. Demand for Quickie products soared as consumers realized they could have it all . . . lightweight, high performance, adjustable features and compact portability. What an exciting alternative to a wheelchair industry that had been stagnant for 30 years!

Motion Designs has continued to expand its product line to include Quick 'N Easy, an innovative lightweight, non-corrosive aluminum shower/commode chair, and the new economical Quickie Rx and Breezy models. Quickie Rx and Breezy substantially broaden Motion Designs' market by appealing to the largest, most competitive segment of wheelchair users, many who depend on federal, state or private insurance reimbursements.

Along with product line expansion, Motion Designs has concentrated its sales force on specific markets. The Quickie product line is sold through a highly trained sales team focused on the rehabilitation market. Breezy, a standardized, economical wheelchair, is sold through a much broader range of medical supply dealers.

One of the most unique design features of Quickie wheelchairs is the modular frame concept. This design allows the chair to easily grow in length and width, or be modified by merely changing components, perfect for children and others with changing physical needs.

Motion Designs never looks back or stops designing. An originator of many industry firsts, in 1984, Motion Designs was recognized for its entrepreneurial spirit by being selected Western Regional Small Business of the Year.

To complement the company's commitment to stay on the leading edge in the research and development of innovative new products, Motion Designs formed a new division, Quickie Performance, in 1986. Quickie Performance manufactures and distributes high quality, high performance wheelchair components and accessories. This division also offers a wide variety of racing and sports components. Keeping a pulse on new technologies involved in the sport of wheelchair racing provides Motion Designs a valuable resource for ongoing product development.

In the six years Motion Designs has been in business, its biggest mistake has been in underestimating building size needed to handle it's phenomenal growth. The firm has grown out of a 400 sq. ft. garage, as well as 5,000, 17,000, 50,000 and 100,000 sq. ft. facilities. Construction of an additional 43,000 sq. ft. to its manufacturing facility in Fresno, California, was completed in July of this year.

This trio turned tragedy into an American success story. Shown here are Don Helman and Jim Okamoto (standing) and Marilyn Hamilton seated in the wheelchair that revolutionized the industry.

county in small groups, bringing their language, their religions, and their way of life to enrich the community.

Fresno's significant Armenian population is a case in point. From a small family of settlers in 1881, their number has grown until it stands at more than 20,000. An indication of the important role played by Armenians in the state is the election of George Deukmejian to serve as governor. Fresno's Armenian churches maintain traditions going back to the 4th century, and Armenian cultural organizations serve as reminders of a time when local groups were closed to Armenians.

Fresno celebrates its Pulitzer Prize-winning novelist and playwright, William Saroyan; the convention center theater is named in his honor. Armenians have made their mark in journalism, sculpture, music, industry and politics in Fresno, and many have attained international fame. The foresight of the late Leon S. Peters, one of the most highly respected businessmen of the community, is commemorated each year through the award of the Leon S. Peters Medal in memory of this outstanding community leader.

Much of the reputation of Fresno's Armenian citizens, however, derives from their prodigious accomplishments in agriculture. In their first 50 years in the county, Armenians acquired 40 percent of the county's acreage in raisins; they made up one-quarter of its growers. Armenians introduced Casaba and Persian melons, bleached raisins, new grape varieties and commercial pistachio crops, and led the way in fresh and dried fruit packing and shipping. Armenians continue to influence the life of the Valley in important ways.

Portuguese and Basques were recruited by early county colonists for their skill in dairy farming and sheep herding. Like most other ethnic groups, they found the Valley a congenial place to live. Many settled here to raise their families, and their influence continues to be felt in the county. The city of Kerman holds an annual Portuguese festival, and many Fresno-area families have a Sunday tradition of dining at the abundant tables of the several Basque hotels.

Swedes, Danes and Norwegians settled in small communities around the Valley. Kingsburg capitalizes on its Swedish origins, and although its population is now less than one-third Swedish, the entire community enters enthusiastically into its annual ethnic celebrations.

The Volga Germans came to Fresno by way of Russia, escaping the persecution that came to them following the overthrow of Catherine the Great, who had invited them to her country. At the turn of the century, Fresno boasted a number of German language churches and a clean, neat downtown area known as "Rooshian Town." An estimated 100,000 Volga Germans now reside in the San Joaquin Valley, adding their skills and industry to agriculture and the life of the county.

This Volga German immigrant couple pose on their farm with their pet dog in the early 1940s.

On the street corners, in the shopping malls, in the office, the factory and the school, the people of Fresno are a mosaic on the move. They celebrate the beauty of their diversity in many ways. At St. Alphonsus Church, for example, the common faith of the multi-ethnic congregation was the theme of the 75th anniversary celebration in 1983. For each of the six weeks preceding the anniversary, a member of a different ethnic group was featured during Sunday masses. At the anniversary festival, members, guests and local dignitaries enjoyed a potpourri of delicious desserts from around the world.

In 1986, Fresno was the site of the 14th annual conference of the National Association of Ethnic Studies. Scholars from colleges and universities around the country enjoyed folkloric dance at their banquet, and went about their deliberations in meeting rooms graced by the city's centennial photo-mural display, "A Century of New Neighbors."

Many of Fresno's ethnic groups came to this country to escape persecution, seeking a chance to rebuild their lives in peace. Like the Volga Germans, Armenians and others before them, Fresno's newest immigrants are part of that tradition. The protracted war in Vietnam displaced thousands of Asian people. Refugee groups from several Southeast Asian nations have made their way to the promise of the valley, which is like their homelands in many ways. Fresno is home to 2,000 Vietnamese, 2,500 Laotians and hundreds of Cambodians. Their communities have strong leaders, and if the eagerness of their children to learn is any indicator, Fresno has gained another jewel in its multicultural crown.

Far outnumbering these national groups, however, is the latest influx of Southeast Asian immigrants — the Hmong. In just five years, these highland people from Laos have added more than 15,000 people to the county's population. Several thousand more are expected to settle in the area by 1990. The Hmong people depended on agriculture for their livelihood, so the rich valley land is a natural home for them. Adults and children alike are quickly learning American customs and language. The women have formed cooperatives to market their exceptional p'an-dau needlework, and the children flock to schools to learn how to live in their new homeland. *(Continued on page 54)*

A recent Southeast Asian immigrant displays a sample of the beautiful handicraft which has already generated considerable acclaim.

FLEMING FOODS

A COMPANY ON THE MOVE

Fleming Companies, Inc. is a wholesale food distributor supplying complete product lines and operational services to over 4,400 affiliated retailers in 33 states.

Fleming Foods, a Forbes 100 company, selected Fresno as the home for a major distribution center because of the city's rapid growth and direct access to other important west coast markets. The company's Fresno operation has succeeded in positioning Fleming for continued growth, and its progress can be attributed to the area's motivated, skilled workforce and the commitment and cooperation of involved civic leaders.

For over 50 years, Fleming has pioneered the development of strong voluntary groups throughout America. Now Fleming has established California's first voluntary group, IGA. As a part of the Independent Grocers Alliance, independent retailers join forces to achieve the clout of a big chain operation, with its tremendous potential for building sales and profits.

Fleming's operating policy is unusual in that great latitude is given to division presidents, a reflection of the company's faith in the instincts of its leading entrepreneurs. In a tribute to the success of that philosophy, Fleming's distribution centers in Fresno and Fremont jointly won the prestigious IGA President's Cup for "The Greatest IGA Development in 1986." Defeating 40 other competitors, they showed a 30.9 percent increase in IGA retail sales in 1986.

Generally considered to be the second-largest wholesale grocery company in the United States, Fleming focuses its attention exclusively on food acquisition and distribution. Established in 1915, the company has grown through a careful, thoughtful acquisition policy.

Fleming's twin operational thrusts of product lines and support services have been responsible for exceptional growth. Fleming supplies a broad selection of grocery produce, meat, frozen food, dairy products, deli foods, general merchandise and associated products. In addition, its affiliated retailers have access to a broad array of support services, including retail operations, consulting, merchandising, advertising, accounting, retail electronic services, scanning support, store development, leasing, retail training, retail shelf management, financing and choices of suggested retail price zones.

Fleming's emphasis on quality and service is reflected in the corporate mission statement: The principal business of Fleming Companies is the procurement, distribution and retailing of food and related products and services to achieve a fair and growing reward for all stockholders in an environment that gives promise of realizing company and individual goals.

Bob Barnes

STARS TO GO, INC.

CONVENIENT VIDEO RENTALS

The Fresno Stars To Go team led by Jim Dailey (far left) played a significant role in the company's growth and development nationwide.

Most people are aware of the blossoming home video entertainment industry. However, many do not realize that the convenience store near their home in Fresno has the best selection in town. A pioneer and leader in the video explosion is Stars To Go, Inc., a Fresno-born company, dedicated to excellence in rentals through convenience stores.

Founded in 1984, it is a major video distribution company in the United States. Employing in excess of 100 people in Fresno and over 600 people nationwide, it operates video centers in major convenience store chains (such as Circle K and 7-Eleven.)

When it was determined video rentals would be a viable, profitable business, the major chains searched for a vendor with an established video program to ease their entry into the market. Stars To Go with its unique computerized distribution system was ready to meet the challenge. The company has a unique relationship with the large convenience store chains operating video centers in selected stores under long-term agreements. In three short years it has grown to over 5,000 video centers in 44 states.

All Stars To Go video centers have the proprietary STARTRACKER™ point of sale computer system. The system uses barcode technology which makes each rental transaction efficient and accurate. This user-friendly computer allows the customer to check out a movie in less than one minute.

The information recorded in the video center computer is transmitted each evening to Fresno via telephone lines. The rental data is recorded in the company's large data center providing unique management information concerning each store. The ability to collect information from all parts of the United States gives the company a competitive edge in managing its operations.

Each video center is stocked with over 200 movies. New movies released by studios are sent to the stores immediately so that the latest hits are available for rent. Movies in the store have to be rotated frequently so titles in the store are always changing. The company's unique movie rotation technique is driven by the company's computer system which allows it to track what's renting in each store, so the right movies are selected from the distribution center inventory and sent to the store.

The company's four regional operations centers are responsible for installing and managing the video centers. The movies, fixtures, supplies and the STARTRACKER are installed and the store employees trained. A customer service representative is assigned to each store and visits it weekly to deliver the movies, assist in training store employees and merchandise the store.

Stars To Go continues to expand and grow. To improve its distribution system, the company is installing an automated warehouse. The new facility, located in Memphis, Tennessee, will allow the company to expand its store base to in excess of 15,000 outlets. The distribution facility will be driven by a computer system through the Fresno data center.

Stars To Go is now well positioned to continue its planned expansion. The long-term opportunities available to the company are tremendous. At Stars, the sky's the limit!

NEWCOMERS IN THE BUSINESS WORLD

As new cultural groups have subtly — and sometimes markedly — changed the county's complexion, so new businesses have altered its economic mix, benefiting all the county's residents.

Fresno County, long the leading farm county in the United States, is becoming a center for manufacturing and distribution as well. In many ways, metropolitan Fresno is emerging as an important regional center, central California's hub for transportation, media, medical facilities and business services. One indicator of the changing economic mix in the county is the changing pattern of personal income source. Farm-related personal income grew $30,556,000 between 1983 and 1984, from $436,555,000 to $467,111,000. Non-farm income gained $337,330,000 during that same period, increasing from $3,610,361,000 to $3,947,691,000. In manufacturing alone, personal income in the county grew $42,775,000 in that year.

The Fresno Economic Development Corporation (EDC) estimates that in the three-year period from 1983 to 1986, 900 of the 1,000 new jobs they helped create in the county were in manufacturing. These jobs are the result of both new business development and the relocation of existing businesses — typically from crowded, expensive urban centers like Los Angeles and San Francisco, or through westward expansion of eastern concerns. New manufacturing jobs have been created in a wide variety of companies: paper products, food processing, waste-to-energy plants, construction products/materials, industrial fasteners, flexible ducting, closed-circuit television components, electronic marketing service, metal products, electronic typography, pallet manufacture, glass products, Telex machine manufacture and wholesale distribution.

The labor market as a whole grew by a healthy 71.25 percent between 1966 and 1986, but that growth was far from evenly distributed. Of the ten industry sectors listed, five took major steps forward during this period: finance, insurance and real estate services, construction, government and retail. The finance, insurance and real estate labor market showed a whopping 191.49 percent growth in that period; services were close behind with a 150.68 percent increase. With overall growth at 71.25 percent, these leaders took a disproportionate gain in labor market share. Finance, insurance and real estate increased by 2.27 percent, while the service sector scored a 5.66 percent gain.

A closer look at the most recent decade for which figures are available, 1976-1986, shows a 25.26 percent overall labor market growth, led by service, finance, insurance and real estate, and retail. These sectors, which had the highest percentage gains, added 34,600 jobs during the decade.

During the 1976-86 decade, another subtle economic shift was taking place in the county. While the wholesale sector was slipping somewhat in comparison with the general economic picture for labor market share, the retail sector made significant gains. These patterns of growth, taken together, suggest an important diversification of the county's economy. Fresno is becoming a multifaceted metropolitan economic center with a service area that encompasses central California; its economic impact is felt worldwide.

The Economic Development Corporation's listing of the eight industrial firms moving into Fresno County in 1985-86 provides a good overview of this diversification. Capri Sun, a natural fruit drink which originated in Germany, is now produced in a 100,000 square foot plant in Fresno, the west coast headquarters of this international corporation. The Fonda Group, a New Jersey-based manufacturer of paper plates and other disposable food service items, relocated from Santa Clara to a 138,000 square foot factory in Fresno. Cresco, a distributor of restaurant equipment, opened in 1986 in its 45,000 square foot warehouse in Fresno. Pella Windows distributes to six counties from its regional center in a 15,000 square foot building in Fresno. The Connecticut-based firm of Ulbrich Stainless Steel is building a west coast service center in the Fresno Air Terminal area; it will occupy a 24,000 square foot building. Also near the airport is the new 11,000 square foot main office of Mendelson-Zeller, a food brokerage subsidiary of Campbell Soup Company.

Outside the city of Fresno, several new firms add to the county's diversified manufacturing base. Western Kraft, Inc., a manufacturer of corrugated products, has located its 100,000 square foot plant in Sanger. The Japanese-owned International Seasonings soup manufacturing company has built a 100,000 square foot plant in the Malaga area. Post Technology, a bay area manufacturer of Telex equipment, has a 5,000 square foot plant in Kerman. In addition, the corporate offices for United Express — California's largest commuter airline — have been relocated from Chico to Fresno. The company's offices occupy 105,000 square feet at Fresno Air Terminal.

These eight industrial firms and two corporate offices occupy a total of 535,000 square feet of space and have brought 561 new jobs to the county's economy. EDC's work continues; there are 1,000 new inquiries under examination at this time.

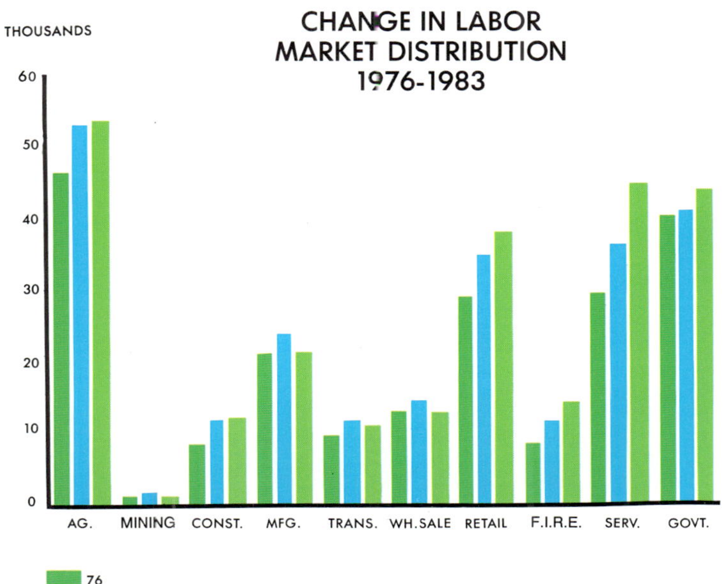

Fresno's central location, inexpensive real estate, ample work force and excellent transportation and infrastructure have attracted a wide variety of manufacturing and distribution companies. A listing of some of the products manufactured by the more than 500 plants in the county gives a sense of the diversification so important to the region's long-range economic health.

PRODUCTS MANUFACTURED IN FRESNO COUNTY

Knit Products
Sewing Thread
Leisure Clothing
Ladies' Sportswear
Women's Fashion Accessories
Tents and Awnings
Containers
Furniture
Metal Office Accessories
Partitions
Office Products
Disposable Hospital Products
Foam Trays
Insulation
Pharmaceuticals
Cleaning Chemicals
Electrical Heating Elements
Rubber Parts
Plastic Bags
Envelopes and Packaging
Flat Glass
Telecommunications Equipment
Electrical Auto Parts
Ceramics
Concrete Block and Pipe
Insulated Wire
Castings
Pop-up Roasting Thermometers
Pruning Shears
Garden Tools
Prescription Safety Glasses
Rollbars
Aluminum Windows and Doors
Steel Tanks
Propane Equipment
Chrome Wheels
Irrigation Sprinklers
Irrigation Equipment
Drip Irrigation
Cotton Ginning Parts
Grape Harvesters
Road Maintenance Equipment
Packaging Equipment
Pumps
Insulation Blowers
Spray Machines
Ag Chemicals
Filters
Digital Scales
Vending Machines
Flexible Air Duct
Mirrors
Bricks, Adobe
Truck Parts
Hydraulic Cylinders
Truck Doors
Truck Trailers
Boats
Valves
Wheelchairs
Industrial Fasteners
Water Well TV Systems

Bob Barnes

Guardian Industries, a major plate glass manufacturer, represents but one of the many diversified industries within Fresno County.

Positive, aggressive action by city and county government has made these companies feel welcome. Fresno was one of the first cities in the state to designate an Enterprise Zone — a well-defined area where state income tax reductions and other incentives encourage private investment and stimulate employment opportunities. These incentives are designed to encourage the development of new industries and entice existing businesses into relocating, as well as to facilitate expansion and diversification of businesses and industries already located within the Enterprise Zone. California state incentives for firms located in the Enterprise Zone include:

- Tax credits for hiring qualified disadvantaged individuals enrolled in job training programs
- Tax credits to qualified employees working in the Enterprise Zone
- Tax credits for sales or use tax incurred in connection with purchase of qualified property used in the zone
- Expensing of tangible, depreciable property (up to $10,000 annually) in the year of acquisition
- Net operating loss carryover for 15 years
- Deduction of interest income derived from loans to Enterprise Zone businesses

In addition to these state incentives, city Enterprise Zone incentives include:

- Permit and inspection fee reduction
- Streamlined permit and plan processing
- Industrial development bond fee reduction
- Adoption of urban renewal plans
- Urban service extension
- Job training programs
- Property marketing assistance
- Infrastructure development
- Business license fee waivers
- Targeted small business loan and economic development funds

The ten square mile Enterprise Zone shown on the map comprises a substantial industrial and commercial area, including approximately 3,000 acres designated for industrial development. Essential support services are in place, freeway and rail access is exceptional, and there is an abundant supply of workers. These factors provide the necessary raw ingredients for unusually productive and profitable economic development.

The effectiveness of positive incentives such as the Enterprise Zone in the stimulation of business growth can be seen from a review of city tax revenue growth. Business license tax revenues grew nearly fivefold over a ten-year period.

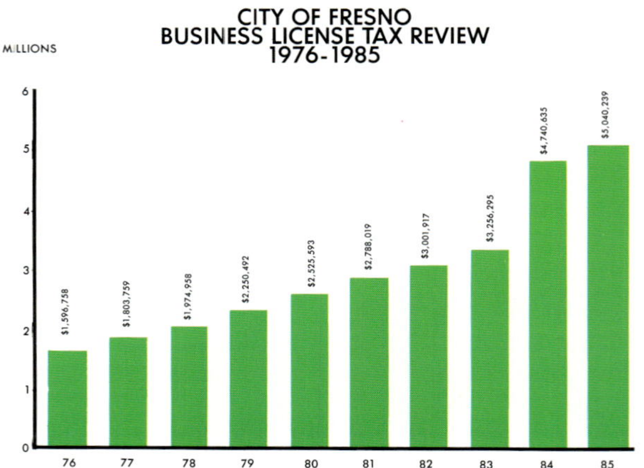

FRESNO Enterprise Zone

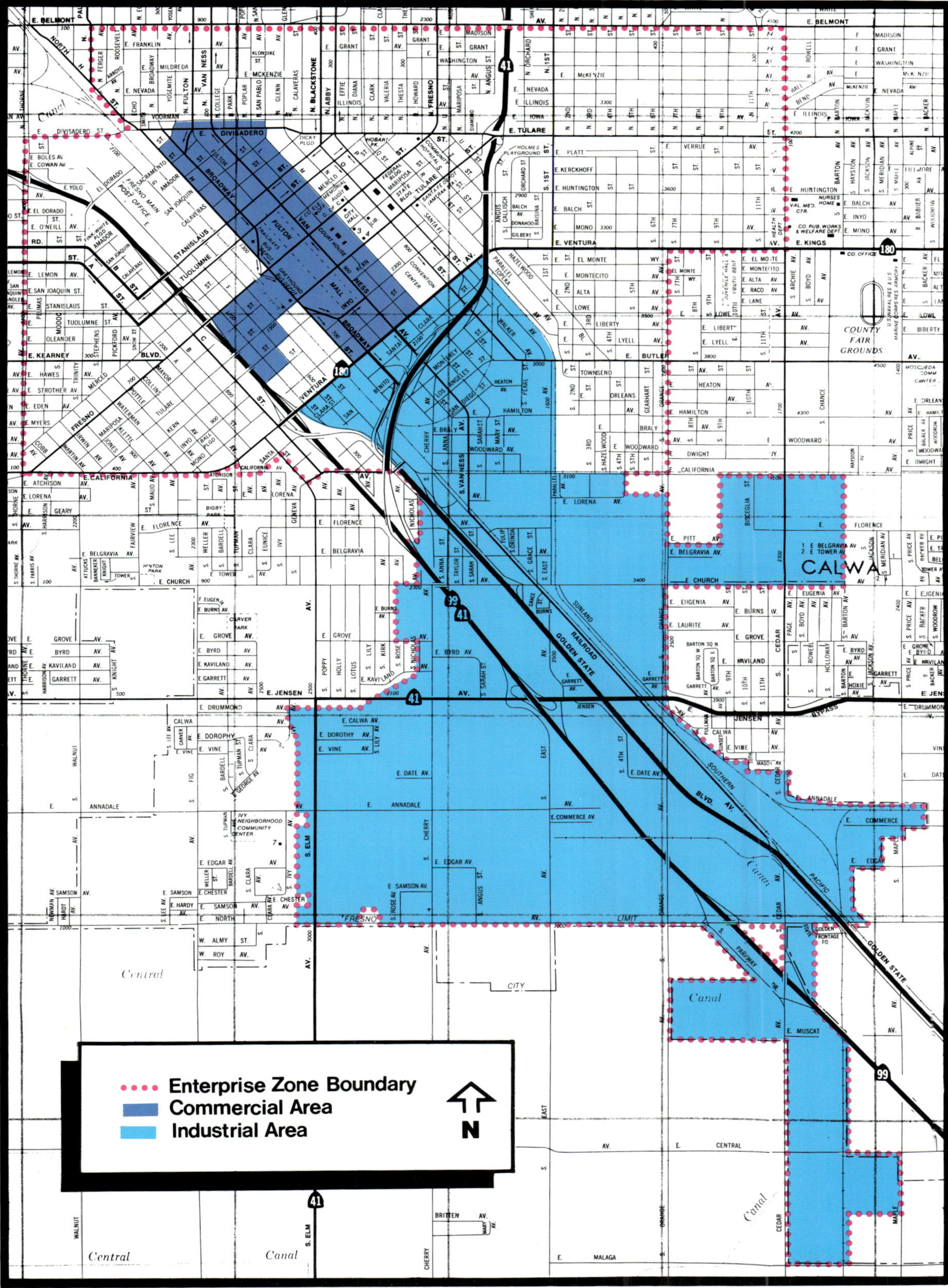

The City of Fresno's enterprise zone includes both commercial and industrial areas which qualify for significant state income tax benefits and local development incentives.

City of Fresno Office of Economic Development

While some distortion of these figures is attributable to city annexation during the period in question (the city grew from 55.77 square miles in 1976 to 93.90 square miles in 1985), real economic growth is nonetheless visible. That growth, as we have seen, has occurred in part through diversification. In the fiscal year ending June 30, 1987, there were 2,500 new business licenses issued in Fresno; this brought the total number of businesses in the city to 28,200. The vast majority — 20,000 — of businesses are retail. Professions such as law and medicine account for 3,000 business licenses, while the remaining 5,200 are distributed across manufacturing and services enterprises.

With the cooperation of city and county governments and the "can do" attitude of skilled economic development professionals, Fresno seems destined to continue to grow in ways which will enhance the outstanding quality of life for which the city is known.

The Economic Base

CHAPTER 4

Located in the heart of pro-business California, Fresno is ideally situated for economic growth and development. According to the State Department of Commerce, California — and the Central Valley in particular — are optimum choices for relocating or expanding businesses. Over the last ten years, while many states have suffered declines in manufacturing, California has increased its share of the nation's manufacturing base by 25 percent. The golden state is number one in the nation in tourism, agriculture, aerospace and biotechnology. It is home base for 41 of the companies comprising the *Fortune* 500, and for 101 of those selected by *Inc Magazine* as the 500 most dynamic companies in the nation. Nearly 1500 companies have chosen to invest over a half million dollars in locating and expanding in California since 1983.

California's attractive climate of government-business cooperation means lower taxes, reform of inhibiting regulations, a strong program of capital improvement and an impressive agenda of state initiatives. In the latter category are Rural Renaissance, Small Business Revitalization, Industrial Development Bonds, the creation of the California Economic Development Corporation and the initiation of several Enterprise Zones, with Fresno selected to be among the first.

The California work force is productive, with both absenteeism and work stoppages below the national average. Overall, in spite of wage rates only eight percent higher than the national average, California workers produce 16 percent more. The state has a high percentage of well-educated workers. More research laboratories are located in California than anywhere else in the nation, and more degrees are conferred in California than in any other state. Fifty-three percent of the state's general fund was spent on education in 1985, a 35 percent increase over the previous three years. With half the state's 320,000 high school graduates going on to college each year, California's supply of well-prepared workers seems assured.

California's consumer market is the largest in the nation, although the state accounts for only ten percent of the country's population. Consumers in other western states and in neighboring Mexico and Canada add another 71 million to the region's burgeoning market, consuming a sizeable portion of the $500 billion in goods and services produced in the state each year. Foreign trade is an increasingly important market for California business. In 1984, the state did $81.5 billion in foreign trade. Much of that activity was with Asian countries; California leads the nation in trade with Pacific Rim nations. That trade amounted to $64 billion in 1984, including approximately $25 billion with Japan alone. Foreign investment is building the state's economy as well. Of the 183 foreign-owned banking operations in California, 94 are owned by Pacific Rim country interests.

Fresno City and County are very much a part of this economic boom. Considering the ample, well educated, hardworking labor force, Enterprise Zone and other business incentives, plus the low land costs, modest housing prices — all combined in a setting of unsurpassed natural beauty, with all the conveniences of a sophisticated metropolis, it's no wonder Fresno appears year after year at or near the top of the state's "fastest growing" list.

Fresno's rapid growth has had ramifications in a number of businesses and industries. During the late 1970s, for example, the number of housing units in the metropolitan area rose by 17,000; the average yearly gain was 3,900. In the City of Fresno, the average housing unit gain for each year from 1978 to 1982 was 2,200. Clovis gained an average of 500 units each year during that time. It is expected that the area's 156,700 households will increase to 163,000 by the year 1990. Much of that increase will take place in the Woodward Park plan area in the northern part of the city. It is predicted that this area will gain 56,000 residents by the year 2000, whereas the inner city Roosevelt area is expected to increase by only 2,000 new residents. Clovis will be the second-fastest growing area, gaining 33,200 new residents by the turn of the century. Seventy percent of the county's total valuation growth in the mid-1980s has occurred in the Fresno-Clovis metropolitan area.

Commercial growth is following the pattern set by residential development. Shaw Avenue, running westward toward Highway 99, is lined with retail, office and commercial centers. Over the last decade, much of the city's high rise development has been north of the city. That trend seems to be shifting; however, lower land and tenant costs — combined with Enterprise Zone incentives — are attracting developers to the city's central core once again.

At least five factors have contributed to the rapid growth of the Fresno metropolitan area. In addition to favorable land prices and low to moderate labor costs, the city has gained a greater population base through a vigorous annexation policy. In January, 1986, the city covered 94.60 square miles, equivalent to 32 percent of the Fresno-Clovis metropolitan area. This area is 32 times the size of the city at the time of its incorporation in 1885, and three and one-third times its size in 1960. From 1885 to 1970, the annual average gain in city size was one-half square mile; for each year from 1970 to 1986 that figure was three and one-third square miles. The direction of this growth has been almost exclusively northward and eastward. Since 1960, however, there has been growth along the western fringe of the metropolitan area; significant concentrations of population have grown up recently across Highway 99.

A fourth factor in Fresno's rapid population increase, in addition to land, labor and annexation, is the immigration of Southeast Asian refugees. They have been arriving in Fresno steadily since 1981, contributing to Fresno's steeper than normal population growth curve. While Fresno has consistently ranked about eighth in population size among California cities, it has jumped from 111th most populous city in the nation in 1950 to 61st most populous in 1985. Refugee immigration is expected to remain at its current level until approximately 1990, with secondary immigration adding to the growth of the Fresno metropolitan area. Taken together, these five factors of low land cost, available and affordable labor, annexation policy, refugee immigration and attractive climate have combined to push the City of Fresno into prominence as one of the boom towns of the '80s.

Fresno County is the trade, financial, commercial, health service and education center for Central California. It is a transportation hub, with air, motor and rail services connecting the Central Valley to all points in the nation, as well as to overseas markets. The county is bisected from east to west by State Highway 180, and by two major north-south highways: State Highway 99 and Interstate Highway 5. Fresno is an inland port of entry, with air, rail, motor carrier and bus services readily available.

The county's $2 billion gross annual agricultural income keeps it in the number one position world-wide in agri-business productivity. This activity is highly diversified, with over 200 crops grown in four distinct regions of the county. The southwest is known for oil and for extensive cattle and sheep ranches. The west side has vast acreage in melons, cotton, alfalfa, barley, rice, wheat and vegetables. The mild climate of the eastern county foothills is ideal for citrus and other tree fruits. East and south of the city, grapes, nuts and fruit crops predominate. Scattered throughout the city are processing plants, cotton gins, packing houses and wineries. The agricultural abundance produced in the county provides a solid foundation for the entire economy.

While agriculture and agribusiness are the cornerstones, the economy of Fresno County is undergoing considerable diversification. Tourism is a growth industry. The spectacular national parks of the Sierras, along with the year-round recreation areas of the mountain and foothill lakes are attracting increasing numbers of people from other states and countries. Drawn by low land and labor costs, and by the gentle climate and scenic beauty of the region, businesses of many kinds are making their homes in Fresno.

Harvesting Granny Smith apples at H.P. Metzler Farms

BUSINESS AND INDUSTRY

Fresno County, long the nation's leader in agribusiness, is becoming a center for manufacturing and distribution. The area's central location, excellent transportation and infrastructure, inexpensive real estate and ample, productive work force all contribute to the increasing diversification of the economic base. Food processors, paper converters, distributors and light manufacturers have discovered that by locating in Fresno they can be on the West Coast without being in the high rent district.

Fresno's regional market area contained 344,700 households in 1984; this figure is expected to rise to 390,00 by 1990, an increase of 13.2 percent. In 1984, 33,630 households had base incomes of over $50,000, and 87,610 were in the over $35,000 bracket. The market area has traditionally been dependent on agriculture and related business. Fresno County has been first in the nation in crop production value since 1950. Of the 50 most important crops produced in California, 47 are grown in the Fresno area.

Government employment has been an important factor in the economy since Fresno's incorporation and its designation as the county seat. In addition to city and county governments, state offices — including those of the state university, and federal offices — including the new Internal Revenue Service Center, have provided government jobs for many area residents.

Retail trade has played a part in the economy since Gold Rush days, when the needs of miners and ranchers were served by commercial establishment along trails and railroad lines. The first merchants served local needs exclusively, but as the region's capacity for productivity became apparent, market expansion was inevitable. Today Fresno County is a leading exporter, not only of agricultural products, but of a wide variety of manufactured items as well. Commercial centers serve the entire Central California region. Its market size has spurred the development of a multitude of specialty shops and markets to tempt every taste.

Offices house a wide range of businesses, from financial and real estate services to legal and medical services. While there are small to medium-sized office complexes scattered throughout the metropolitan area, large office complexes are found primarily in the heart of the city. *(Continued on page 61)*

H.P. METZLER & SONS

A FAMILY COMMITMENT TO QUALITY

H.P. Metzler & Son's SUNMET label is really more than just a "label." It's a way of doing business that has been around for nearly a century. Today's SUNMET line of fresh products evolved the way all good things do: through perseverance and the dedication of a family to do all things well. It began with Peter Metzler, who immigrated to America with his Russian family in 1890. They settled in the fertile San Joaquin Valley of Central California, and built their "home place" near Del Rey — a stone's throw from Fresno. Their home place is still active to this day, and is referred to as "Ranch One" in the farming operation.

Peter, who was five when his foot touched American soil, began farming tree fruit and grape holdings as he grew into manhood. In time, he made his mark on the community, becoming bank founder, horticultural leader, and a man who many in the industry sought for guidance. Henry, Peter's only son, began his involvement in the family plot in 1932, and was to remain there until the late 40's, when he struck out on his own. Henry, like his father before him, was to become a moving force within his industry and community.

Eventually, Henry was blessed with two sons, Ronald and Dennis. In 1959, Henry and Ronald struck a partnership, thus beginning H.P. METZLER & SONS. In 1976, Dennis purchased Henry's interest, and the fourth Metzler generation has been operating the company ever since.

H. P. Metzler & Son's orchard and vineyard holding—41 separate ranches - stretch over a 180-mile corridor in the lush Central Valley of California, from Bakersfield (120 miles north of Los Angeles), Northward to Madera (20 miles north of Fresno). Other "plots" are on the drawing board for future cultivation. H. P. Metzler & Sons farms several thousand acres of apples, peaches, plums, nectarines, table grapes, nuts and citrus.

The company is the largest peach shipper in California and one of the largest in the country. Nearly 30 varieties of peaches are grown, packed and shipped under the SUNMET label. The popular O'Henry (named in honor of Henry Metzler) is California's leading variety.

From blossom to box, it's "kid-gloved" treatment by all involved. Each and every member of the Metzler farming family is proud of the SUNMET pack, and strives daily to maintain the highest quality.

The Metzler family has made a serious, long-range commitment to a relative newcomer in U.S. apple orcharding — the Granny Smith. H. P. Metzler & Sons is the largest Granny Smith apple grower and shipper in the northern hemisphere. Granny Smiths have somewhat of a history. Their discovery is not competely documented, but some reports indicate a certain Mrs. Marie Smith saw a shiny green apple on one of her trees that matured later than the other fruit. She planted the seeds from that apple, and the rest is history. Others report the same Mrs. Smith discarded some crabapples in her back yard, and from those seeds grew the Granny Smith. Whatever the truth of their discovery is, millions of people now enjoy Granny Smith apples shipped by the Metzlers.

Under the SUNMET label, the Metzler family looks forward to bringing other families goodies for generations to come.

H.P. Metzler has been the major grower of Granny Smith apples in the United States.

Nectarine processing at the H.P. Metzler facility

Industry is a comparatively new force in the economy, although a few industries have been part of the local scene for nearly a century. New industrial warehouses and business parks can be found in the Fresno Air Terminal area, north of Herndon Avenue, at Highway City along Highway 99, north of Pinedale, and in the city's Enterprise Zone. There are some constraints on the development of heavy industry in the area, chiefly environmental concerns and distance. Recognizing these constraints, business and industry recruitment efforts have focused on light manufacturing, food processing and the service sector. The area's strong educational and cultural base, as well as its mild climate and scenic beauty, serve as powerful enticements to companies seeking a western home.

Since 1964, employment in all areas except mining has grown; mining employment has been steady over the period. The total number of employees in Fresno County in 1964 was 133,900; by 1985 that figure was 244,400. In 1987, 255,500 people in Fresno County were employed.

While much of the area's economic vitality is a direct result of the $2 billion income produced by county agriculture each year, the bulk of county employment is actually in non-agricultural sectors. As farming has become increasingly mechanized and capital intensive, non-agricultural jobs have attracted more workers. While agricultural employment has grown by 15,500 employees or 41 percent in the period since 1964, employment in other sectors has doubled from the 1964 figure of 96,400.

Non-agricultural employment is fairly evenly distributed among government, retail and service sectors, with much smaller proportions in finance and real estate, construction and mining, transportation, wholesale, utilities and durable and non-durable goods. The marketing department of *The Fresno Bee* provides a visualization of this distribution:

Fresno County Non-Agriculture Employment by Industry

Past 12 Months, October 1986

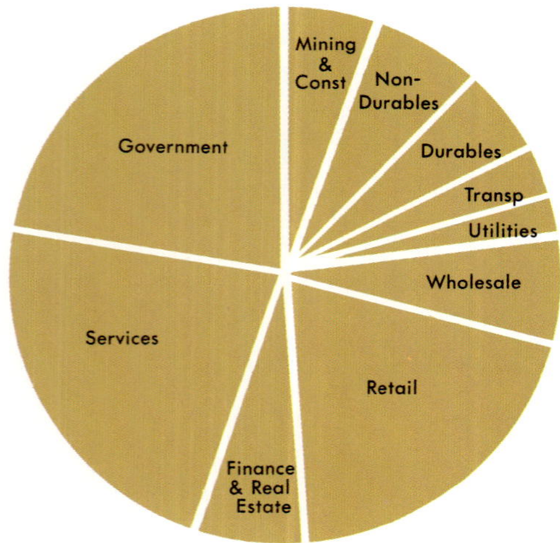

The employment picture reflects the more than 500 manufacturing plants and even more service firms located in the metropolitan area. In the manufacturing sector, there are three firms which each employ more than 1,000 workers.

FRESNO COUNTY TOTAL EMPLOYMENT

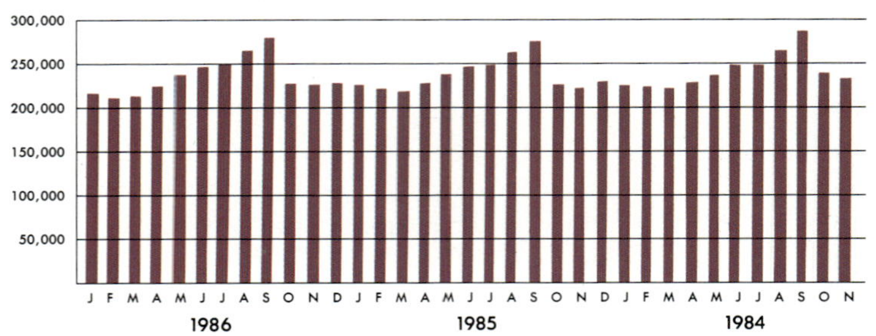

These are Vendo, one of the area's oldest companies, which manufactures vending machines and metal products; Pacific Bell, a telecommunications corporation; and Zacky Farms, a large poultry processing company. Pepsi Cola, Freuhauf Corporation (truck body manufacturing), Bayly Corporation (Western jeans) and Champion Parts Rebuilders (rebuilt auto parts) each employ between 450 and 1000 workers.

Manufacturing firms which employ between 250 and 450 workers include P.P.G. Industries, a manufacturer of flat primary and tempered glass products; Duncan Enterprises, well known for its ceramic glazes and craft items; Rug Doctor, which manufactures carpet cleaners; and several agriculture related manufacturers. In the latter category are Harris Ranch Beef Company, Ranchers Cotton Oil, Producers Cotton Oil, Lyons Magnus (pie fillings and preserves) and Fleming Foods (grocery wholesale and frozen foods).

The non-manufacturing employment picture is equally diverse. Community Hospitals of Central California and the Internal Revenue Service each employ more than 3,000 workers. The city government of Fresno is close behind, with more than 2,250. Saint Agnes Medical Center employs more than 1,800 area residents, and another 1,600 plus work at California State University, Fresno. Valley Medical Center provides work for 1,400 employees. Gottschalk's Department Stores, Pacific Bell and Bank of America each employ between 1,000 and 1,250 persons; Pacific Gas and Electric employs just over 800 workers. Firms employing between 400 and 800 include State Center Community Colleges, McClatchy Newspapers, Boyle Engineering, the Equitable Life Assurance Society Western Regional Service Center and Guarantee Savings (Glenfed). With substantial employment widely dispersed among health care, government, education, finance, communications and the professions, the non-manufacturing sector of the region's economy is well positioned for continued steady growth.

Nearly all the standard industrial code classifications are represented in the Fresno area. A look at the Industrial Directory published by the Chamber of Commerce reveals 39 listings in Agricultural Processing, four in oil and gas extraction, and more than 450 manufacturers, as well as sizeable communication and wholesale trade groupings.

The recent vigorous growth and diversity in business and industry is due in large measure to the work of the Fresno Economic Development Corporation. Before its establishment, recruitment of business and industry had

(Continued on page 64)

PEABODY FLOWAY

QUALITY VERTICAL PUMPS

Peabody Floway is a company with over a half century of experience in the manufacturing of vertical pumps for commercial, industrial, municipal and agricultural applications.

Since Peabody Floway's establishment in 1934 as Fiese & Firstenberger Manufacturing, Inc., the company has continually combined theory with practice to produce a quality line of engineered products.

Like Fresno, Floway has continued to grow and flourish. After World War II, the company underwent a number of corporate changes which allowed Floway to concentrate on the development and production of the vertical turbine pump. In 1957, the trademark — Floway — came into existence. Through progressive engineering, designing, and manufacturing techniques, the vertical turbine became a highly versatile pump with many applications in various fields. Continued growth brought about the name Floway Pumps, Inc. in 1965, adding a sense of identity and unity of purpose to the company. A merger with Peabody International in 1975 met the current needs and concerns of both firms; an interest in the environment, pollution, and safety issues, and helped Floway achieve world-wide recognition as a quality producer of vertical turbine pumping units. In 1986, Peabody Floway became a subsidiary of the Pullman Company. This Fortune 500 company has progressive ideas and leadership that will help lead Floway into the next era of success in the pumping industry.

Peabody Floway's main manufacturing plant, located in southwest Fresno, consists of approximately 200,000 square feet of production and storage area and is located on over 20 acres. Floway's organization of 165 management, engineering, sales, production and administrative support persons combine to produce thousands of reliable pumping units every year. Branch offices and warehouses in Fresno, California and Houston, Texas; as well as an extensive network of over 200 experienced representatives and distributors, have been created to distribute our products domestically and internationally.

Locally, our valley's farmers are an essential element in the future prosperity of Fresno and the nation. Their needs continue to be served by Peabody Floway, while the company has successfully expanded into other fields of application. Among these are the areas of fire pumps, radioactive waste, municipal, and industrial applications. Floway pumps can be found in numerous locations around the world; from Latin America and the Middle East, to sites including Chicago's O'Hare International Airport, where the majority of the jet fuel pumps were manufactured by Floway. In Iceland, our geothermal units allow hot underground water to be brought to the earth's surface, heating homes and buildings in the cities of Reyhjavik and Akureyrar.

Within our own community of Fresno, Peabody Floway enjoys participating in special events, contributing to Fresno's increasing quality of life. Company sponsored events, such as the March of Dimes Walk-a-thon, have proved to be worthwhile activities that Floway employees can participate in as a group. Both on the job and off, the Floway family pulls together within the community of Fresno, working to improve their quality of life.

INTERNATIONAL BUSINESS MACHINES

PEOPLE COUNT AT IBM

International Business Machines is known as one of the world's most successful organizations. IBM's business is providing information processing systems, equipment and services. Products range from typewriters and copiers to state-of-the-art circuits and chips that drive the most powerful computers. IBM develops, manufactures, markets and services computer systems from the Personal Computer to the large-scale IBM 3090. But what it all comes down to is people, approximately 400,000 in more than 130 countries.

In Fresno, IBM employs over 100 people. Each and every one of them is treated as an individual. At IBM, people are the most important asset. The very character of the company is shaped by three basic beliefs. First, respect for the individual. IBM cares about the dignity and rights of each person in the organization. Second, IBM strives to give the best customer service of any company in the world. Third, excellence is cultivated. These are not empty words — they are the foundation of a value system that touches all the company does.

IBM has been doing business in Fresno since 1948 and has enjoyed a steady business growth. In 1986 and 1987, the Fresno Branch Office ranked as one of the top offices in the company. The local IBM team includes Customer and Systems Engineers, Marketing Representatives and administrative personnel. Their mission is to market and support all IBM products.

Many IBM Fresno employees are long-term residents of the area and take special pride in the many contributions their company has made to the community over the years. IBM'ers contribute money and time to programs that make Fresno a better place to live and work. The company supports the United Way and makes selective corporate grants to individual social service organizations. In addition, IBM employees who are active in social service organizations may sponsor an IBM Fund for a Community Service Grant for a specific project. Under the IBM Service Leave Program, the company grants participating employees a one year leave with full pay and benefits to work for a social service agency.

Over the years IBM Fresno has contributed over $750,000 in grants and equipment to local service agencies and schools.

In addition to selective corporate donations to local organizations, IBM matches on a 2 for 1 basis employees' contributions to the arts, education and hospitals.

IBM is proud to be part of an exciting community and will continue its contribution to make Fresno a better place for all.

been a function of the largely volunteer Chamber of Commerce. Recruitment efforts in the 1970s were funded by both the city and county. The passage of Proposition 13 in 1978 prompted the Chamber of Commerce to forego both city and county grants. For a time it attempted to carry on the economic development function without funds, but it quickly became apparent that this approach was not practicable.

Economic development became a priority toward the end of the 1970s as population growth continued to outpace business development. The Chamber of Commerce joined with the county and the cities of Fresno and Clovis to seek solutions to the staffing and funding problems plaguing economic development. Using the San Diego EDC as a model, they founded the Economic Development Corporation in 198. The EDC is a subsidiary of the chamber, but has its own board and independent funding. It is charged with marketing the Fresno area to business and industry, and with facilitating the relocation and expansion of existing businesses.

In spite of its infancy, the EDC has made significant progress. It has compiled an impressive record of serving the many and various economic interests of the Fresno area with sensitivity and impartiality.

Fifty percent of the EDC's budget is allocated for marketing, with 25 percent budgeted for client services. An additional ten percent goes to fund research, while the remaining 15 percent covers administrative costs. The EDC responds to more than 500 inquiries annually, and sponsors an intensive, widespread marketing campaign to inform the international business community of the advantages of Fresno. In addition, the EDC assists new businesses with referrals for training, financing and development needs. It sponsors a major annual event, Preview Fresno, which is a multi-faceted promotional festival designed to introduce visiting executives to the climate, lifestyle and services available to relocating and expanding businesses in the Fresno area. Guests are treated to hosted tours of potential business sites, aerial city tours, and a variety of specialized informational tours. An exhibit hall features dozens of local business and service agency representatives eager to tell the Fresno story. The 1987 event, with the theme "Fresno County Has a New Wrinkle," featured the famous television Dancing Raisins.

Although Preview Fresno includes plenty of fun, it is serious business. With Preview Fresno and its other promotional efforts, the EDC has compiled an impressive track record of representing the best Fresno has to offer. Additional support and funding from the metropolitan area and cities throughout the county will enable the EDC to continue and expand its important work.

Retail shops in the Fulton Mall are easily accessible to the many city, county, state and federal workers employed in the downtown area.

RETAIL TRADE

Retail activity in Central California is at least 300 years old. The earliest settlers, Yokut and Monache Indians, established a network of trade routes across the valley, exchanging local produce for sea shells and preserved seafoods. When the '49ers flocked to California, tradesmen were hot on their heels, providing all the necessities of life from saddles to soap. Millerton boasted a bakery right beside its famous Oak Hotel. The area's first merchants served the needs of all comers, from miners to soldiers, Indians to homesteaders. Railroad expansion and the relocation of the county seat to Fresno brought an influx of trade establishments to the blossoming city, with new businesses opening at a dizzying pace.

Some of those early businesses are still part of the Fresno economic scene; they reflect the best traditions in retailing. One of Fresno's oldest businesses, Fresno Agricultural Works

(Continued on page 66)

GOTTSCHALKS

THE FAVORITE STORE OF VALLEY FAMILIES FOR 83 YEARS

Gottschalks stores are noted for their attractive appearance and friendly atmosphere.

Founded 83 years ago in Fresno, Gottschalks has grown to be the dominate fashion department store in each of the markets it serves. The Company's customer base consists of approximately two million people in an area that stretches through the rich Central Valley and growing Central Coast regions of California.

Since 1904, Gottschalks has enjoyed continued growth, with a sales volume exceeding 125 million in 1986. Gottschalks now has four stores in Fresno, two in Modesto and Bakersfield, plus units in Merced, Visalia, Santa Maria, San Luis Obispo, Woodland and Stockton. The Company also operates 19 specialty shops under the names Village East and Petites West. The Village East stores cater to fashions for the larger woman, and the Petites West stores feature clothing for the 5′ 4″ and under customer.

This recent expansion was made possible when, in April of 1986, Gottschalks completed a very successful initial public offering of common stock, and became a publicly held Company listed on The New York Stock Exchange. Proceeds from the offering were used to help finance the growth strategy of the Company. Strong shareholder acceptance escalated the stock strongly from the initial offering, and, after doubling in value, split two for one in the Spring of 1987.

Continuing this growth pattern, Gottschalks will open in regional malls in Chico and Clovis in 1988, and other sites are being considered as they become available.

A 140,000 square foot Distribution Center, centrally located in Fresno, plays an important role in the operation of the Company. This facility receives and marks all merchandise, and then makes distribution to all Gottschalks stores via their own truck fleet.

For merchandise and expense control, Gottschalks has developed one of the best data information centers in the United States for a Company its size. All of the stores are linked to the Computer Center, headquartered in Fresno. Point of sale terminals are tied in to the main computer and give the Company the ability to pull up instantaneous read-outs of sales in each of its stores. Inventories, payroll and many other accounting functions are also integrated into the system. The data center is a 24 hour a day operation.

Gottschalks believes in participating in the growth of the communities in which it serves. For the past 83 years, the Company has made it a strong policy to return part of its efforts to the community. Executives and associates take an active role in local cultural, charitable and community service organizations. Its eight officers alone, currently serve on no less than 25 Fresno civic organizations as directors, officers or chairpeople.

Under the leadership of Joe Levy, Chairman, and Gerald Blum, President, both grand nephews of the founder, the Company has aggressive plans for continued growth in the years to come . . . always keeping in sight Gottschalks original philosophy, "Keep giving our customers the best in fashion, quality, values and service."

This Gottschalks store at Manchester reflects the contemporary styling being used by Gottschalks for their new store additions throughout Central California.

— now Fresno Ag Hardware — was established in 1876 to manufacture and sell wagons and carriages. Farm implements, including the world-renowned Fresno Scraper, were soon added to the inventory. The company offered tractors, irrigation pumps and a full line of farm hardware implements.

In 1904, Gottschalks, the valley's leading department store chain, began what has become a long tradition of responding to the needs of area consumers. Gottschalks originally employed 28 workers in one downtown store; it now provides jobs for more than 2,000 individuals in an increasing number of outlets throughout the Central Valley. In 1986, the firm went public with an offering on the New York Stock Exchange — another milestone for Fresno's homegrown retail leader.

As successive waves of immigrants settled in the Central Valley, their people added their characteristic flavors to the retail scene. The valley's newest group, the Hmong, are no exception. More than 30 Hmong-owned businesses are among the newest additions to Fresno's thriving retail community. From oriental foods and interpreting services to auto mechanics and used car sales, the Hmong, like other immigrant groups before them, are adding to the valley's vigorous economy.

Not surprisingly, California leads the nation in retail sales. Generally speaking, it is growing at a faster rate than the Western and Pacific states as a group. Its retail growth has been consistently stronger than that of the Midwestern and Southern states since 1985. Fresno, as the retail center of Central California, shares in California's retail boom. Like Los Angeles, Fresno is accessible by many major highways. Throngs of shoppers from its four county area (population 1.01 million) flock to Fresno's malls and central city retail complex. Tourists passing through on their way to the national parks add to retail revenue, as do conventioneers who come to Fresno for the many conferences, trade shows and conventions held here each year. The average vacationer, whether from inside or outside the state, spends an estimated $600 to $800 — a healthy addition to the local economy.

Retail trade has been a major force in the nation's economy. New patterns of consumer behavior are emerging: American adults, both men and women, spend an average of six hours each week shopping. According to the *Wall Street Journal*, 70 percent of these shoppers visit regional malls at least once a week. Most people shop at neighborhood shopping centers twice a week. On the average, Americans shop at grocery stores at least twice a week. More men are shopping than ever before, and that trend is likely to continue. Teen-age boys have become extremely fashion conscious; they make up a sizeable proportion of mall shoppers, with 27 percent purchasing designer clothing on a regular basis. Shopping has taken on a recreational tone, and serves as a form of personal expression. Cars have sprouted bumper stickers reading "Born to Shop" and "When the Going Gets Tough, the Tough Go Shopping." While

FASHION FAIR MALL

WHERE GOOD THINGS HAPPEN

Shoppers can take full advantage of a wide variety of eating establishments in the Food Fair section of the mall.

For glamour, excitement, delicious food and the best people-watching anywhere, the choice is clearly Fashion Fair. For nearly twenty years, the people of Fresno have made Fashion Fair one of the most popular leisure and recreational choices in town, as well as their first choice for shopping. The spacious, carpeted and air conditioned mall provides a tempting indoor course for health-conscious walkers: 3 times around, from Penneys to Weinstocks, is an even mile. Babys nap in strollers under leafy plants as their parents and sitters nibble on giant cookies and contemplate their next purchase. Strollers enjoy the art shows, flower shows, cooking demonstrations, antique exhibits and varied educational displays regularly scheduled in the mall.

Fashion Fair's 119 stores include four major department stores, or anchors. Macy's the largest at 176,410 square feet, is at the western end of the shopping center, with Weinstock's, the second largest department store, at 154,052 square feet, at the eastern end. J.C. Penney, at 153,769 square feet, and Gottschalks, at 76,650 square feet, are centered along landscaped, carpeted hallways. The mall's lush greenery, together with its beautiful skylights, creates a garden-like atmosphere, complemented by the many comfortable seating areas thoughtfully spaced throughout the mall. The thousands of tiny lights arranged in neat rows overhead are converted each year to red bulbs for the Christmas season, creating a fantasy land environment for holiday shoppers.

Retail trade employment in Fresno County has grown from 35,900 in 1984 to 38,600 in 1987. This figure is expected to rise even more sharply as new discount department stores and regional malls open in 1987-88. The Target store, for example employs up to 250 people at each of its two new Fresno facilities. Statewide, the chain has 20,000 employees and an annual payroll in excess of $125 million. Salaries for retail clerks in the county average an affordable $3.77 per hour, according to the Chamber of Commerce's 1987 Wage and Salary Survey. The ten to 15 percent of retail employees at the supervisory and managerial level boost the economic impact of retail sector employment. As of October 1986, wholesale trades in Fresno County employed 12,500 workers, an increase of 3.3 percent over the previous year. Wholesale and retail trade employees together account for roughly 25 percent of the county's non-agricultural workers. Even though retailing participates to some extent in the boom/bust cycles which characterize other parts of the economy, it nevertheless provides a stable base of both full-time and part-time employment. Even in the worst of times, people continue to spend money to meet their needs and desires. Each new manufacturing job in the county creates between three and four new retail and service jobs, and every retail employment dollar supports area agriculture, manufacturing and service industries. Retail trade is an integral part of the economic picture of the Fresno area.

The integration of retail trade with other sectors of the economy is apparent in the location of the primary shopping centers. Fresno's downtown area, for example, is not only a

Parking is provided for 4,949 cars, and the mall's convenient hours attract shoppers from throughout California's Central Valley. The mall is open seven days a week, with extended hour during the Christmas season. Weekday hours are from 10:00 a.m. to 9:00 p.m. the wide variety of stores in the mall is designed to accomodate a broad range of tastes, and to offer complete family shopping. Whether the need is for footwear, specialty food gift packages, designer furs or posters, Fashion Fair has a shop that's certain to please.

Opened in 1976, the mall was expanded and completely remodeled in 1981, and again in 1983, when Macy's and a new wing of stores were added. Included in the new wing is the convenient and popular Food Fair, featuring 12 different eateries with taste treats ranging from stuffed potatoes to seafood. The completely enclosed mall has five entrances in addition to its department store entrances, providing ready access to all 917,679 square feet of shopping pleasure. In addition to the 119 stores in the enclosed mall area, there are six free-standing businesses located on the perimeter of the parking lot, including four banks and two full-service restaurants.

Fashion Fair, the valley's premier shopping center, is owned by the MaceRich Company of Santa Monica, California. The MaceRich Company owns and/or operates 22 malls and 19 community centers with more than 20.6 million square feet of gross leaseable area, spread throughout 15 states. In California alone, the company's portfolio includes 11 malls and 5 community centers with 11.8 million square feet in gross leasable area.

When the residential areas of Fresno began to grow northward in the 1950's, planners made room for convenient, accessible shopping centers to meet the needs of a burgeoning population. By all accounts, the approval of Fashion Fair was one of the most successful decisions of local government. From recovering cardiac patients to green-haired teens, with many a serious shopper in between, there's room for all in this bustling, mini-metropolis: Fashion Fair mall.

The spacious, carpeted and air-conditioned mall provides a tempting indoor course for health conscious walkers.

center of commerce, finance and government, but also the home of Fulton Mall, the first downtown pedestrian shopping mall to be created in the nation. With its curving walkways, outstanding public art, fountains, children's play areas, department stores and diversified specialty shops, the mall became a national model for design excellence and shopper convenience. Although it has been eclipsed by outlying centers more convenient to the city's northern population expansion, the Fulton Mall holds promise as an urban retail park serving the government, financial, legal and commercial workers who inhabit the center city each working day.

Fresno's first neighborhood shopping center opened in 1948 at Divisidero and U Streets. Since that time, nearly 100 regional, community and neighborhood centers have been developed to serve the needs of Fresno's growing metropolitan population. Shopping centers have largely followed the northward path of residential development. Manchester Mall opened in the mid-1950s five miles north of downtown; it now includes 91 stores. Fashion Fair opened still farther north in 1970 with J. C. Penney, Gottschalks and Weinstocks department stores as anchors. It expanded a decade later to encompass Macys and many additional small retail outlets and restaurants. Major regional centers are nearing completion in Clovis, to the northeast, and in the Woodward Park area.

Fountains, sculptures and tasteful landscaping punctuate downtown Fresno's Fulton Mall.

(Continued on page 70)

MANCHESTER CENTER

A GREAT PLACE TO SHOP

Manchester's attractive two-tiered mall offers a wide variety of shopping opportunities for area residents.

There are few places in the San Joaquin Valley as convenient and pleasant for shopping as Manchester Center. Located at the corner of Blackstone and Shields Avenue, Manchester Center is the only two level mall in Fresno. Retail space exceeds 900,000 square feet, with 90 stores.

Manchester Center continues to expand for customer convenience, making it a truly delightful place to browse or shop. With three major anchor stores, Gottschalks, Sears and the all new Home Express, plus unique speciality shops, banks, bakeries and nine restaurants, shoppers will more than likely find everything they need in one convenient stop.

The shopping center offers a Tram/Shuttle service for its customers, making it more convenient to shop Manchester Center. The Tram/Shuttle service also provides security throughout the parking lot to insure customer safety.

At Manchester Center shoppers are sure to find something for everyone in the family. Whether it is new shoes for dad, a new prom dress for sister, a birthday present for junior or a diamond necklace for mom, there are so many fine and distinct shops available, the choices are many. The comfortable, year around temperature is certainly a plus, and the warm friendly attitude of those who work in the various shops, makes one feel relaxed and comfortable while doing what some consider a rather tedious task - shopping. For those who enjoy shopping, it gives an added pleasure in knowing that everything is so centrally located.

Manchester Center continues to grow to meet its customers demands and looks forward to prosperous years ahead in the great San Joaquin Valley.

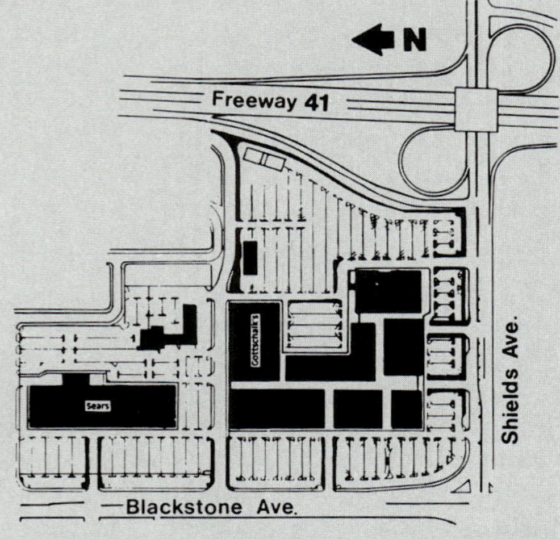

Take Freeway 41 to Shields Ave. Exit

Seventy-six percent of the metropolitan area's shopping centers are located north of Shields Avenue, which is itself five miles north of the city center.

The 40 neighborhood centers in the metropolitan area are built around supermarkets. These are surrounded by smaller establishments such as drug stores, barber and beauty shops, clothing stores, cleaners and laundromats. Eight additional neighborhood centers lack the supermarket anchor but provide important retail service outlets. Fresno's ten community shopping centers, which are larger than the neighborhood centers, include all the kinds of stores found in neighborhood centers and are likely to offer restaurants, clothing stores, small department stores, offices and variety stores in addition. The area's three regional centers include all these features as well as major department stores, banks, restaurants and specialty shops. In addition to the neighborhood, community and regional centers, Fresno has 22 arterial centers which feature home furnishings, specialty stores, jewelry and gift shops and clothing stores, in addition to restaurants.

City planning guidelines recommend one neighborhood center for every 6,000 residents, and call for a minimum of three miles between regional centers and two miles between community centers. Fresno's rapid urban development, particularly in the northern and southeastern areas of the city, has spurred shopping center development. For most Fresno residents, life's necessities and conveniences are available — almost literally — just around the corner. In January, 1986, the city's Development Department listed nearly 2,000 retail establishments in 82 active shopping centers serving the needs of the community. Not included in these figures are the numerous isolated small business establishments or the temporary retail outlets, from trade shows to corner farmer's markets, which add color and variety to the retail scene.

From the Saturday morning produce merchant to the specialty shops framing the Macy's and Gottschalks stores, a substantial portion of the area's retail merchants are small businesses employing fewer than 100 employees per store. The small business sector is one of the fastest growing segments of the local and national economy. Of the 3,138 retail businesses in the county in 1984, all but 24 had fewer than 100 employees. While the major department stores anchor shopping centers, it is the specialty shops, with their unique merchandise offerings, which build the centers' regional appeal. The competitiveness of the retail trade is evident in small business, for specialty shops are where new ideas and products are tested. Small business offers an affordable opportunity for the new entrepreneur. Almost as soon as a new grocery or dry goods store announces a site, smaller retail establishments open in the surrounding space.

In Clovis, Selma and other cities of the county, small businesses have contributed heavily to the local economy and have taken the lead in downtown restoration. Their work in developing an attractive Main Street image has combined the best of vintage exterior charm and up-to-the-minute contemporary products and services. In Fresno, the community's major business advocate — the Chamber of Commerce — has long had a strong small business flavor. Over the years, many of the area's small businesses have been members of the Chamber of Commerce. Recognizing the significance of smaller retail establishments to the vitality of the community, the chamber recently opened the Small Business Resource Center to provide information and support for this important segment of the economy.

Small business is expected to contribute heavily to projected growth in the retail economy. Retail will continue to be one of the fastest-growing sectors of the national economy for the remainder of the 1980s, and Fresno's retail trade establishments are strong participants in this trend. The city's reputation as a major retail trade, wholesale and distribution center complements and reinforces its importance as a regional center for government, health and social services, entertainment and education.

Specialty shops make up many of Fresno's smaller retailers.

FIG GARDEN VILLAGE

A TRULY UNIQUE SHOPPING CENTER

Fig Garden Village rotates its colorful flags on a seasonal basis.

Around the turn of the century, Francis J. Bullard began farming 7,200 acres south of the San Joaquin River. About ten years later, his son, E.J., and local developer J.C. Forkner began to develop the 12,000 acres that came to be known as the Fig Gardens.

The property at the northern boundary of Old Fig Garden was owned by George Sherman, whose home was where The Drug Store now stands. Sherman farmed his land first in grain and later in peaches and grapes. But, ironically, never in figs.

Sherman's daughter, Ellen, married Allen L. Funch, Sr. In the early 1950's, the Funches, parents of Fig Garden Village's present owner, Allen L. Funch, Jr., envisioned a new kind of shopping center at Shaw and Palm Avenues, with quality specialty stores, preferably owner-operated.

Their vision was realized and today the Village boasts 50 commercial establishments, including retail stores, restaurants, banks, a movie theater and a U.S. Post Office branch.

There have been many improvements since the first stores opened in 1956. The Village has evolved into a truly unique shopping center.

In 1982, an ambitious landscaping project began. The effort received community recognition and Fig Garden Village won Fresno's first Envy Award of Excellence in 1986 for outstanding beauty and environmental commitment. The back parking lot was resurfaced, landscaped and improved by a lighting system in 1986 and the Village won the Western United States competition of the Illuminating Engineers Society.

Another feature distinguishing Fig Garden Village from other shopping centers is the tradition of flying colorful banners. Forty-five of them are flown from tall poles. They are changed every two months to reflect a seasonal theme and they include

AGRICULTURE

Farms are the building blocks of the Fresno economy. Its finance, health, service, business, industrial, educational and governmental sectors all owe their vitality — if not their existence — to the consistently outstanding productivity of area farms. From the wheat and cattle ranches of the mid-1800s to the more than 200 specialized crops produced in the county today, the valley's exceptionally fertile soil, benign climate and hardworking people are the foundation of the diversified, resilient and healthy economy of the Central Valley.

Year after year, Fresno County ranks as the leading agricultural county in the nation. If it were a state, Fresno County's gross agricultural return of $2,125,721,600 in 1986 would place it 28th, between Mississippi and Tennessee, in gross agricultural receipts. The county's 3,825,779 acres — 5,978 square miles — support approximately 7,400 farms. These farms take up 2,072,188 acres, which is 54 percent of the county's land. Farms range in size from the weekend farmer's 20 acres to the sprawling corporate ranching operations involving thousands of west side acres.

But the role of agriculture in the economy of Fresno County is far more significant than the gross receipts or number of farms would indicate. The income from agriculture remains primarily in the county, turning over anywhere from three to seven times. Using a conservative standard multiplier, the overall economic impact of farming is to generate approximately $7,500,000,000 annually to the county's economy.

Similarly, the employment of 7,400 farm owners is but a small part of the farm labor story. Although much of the area's farm work is seasonal in nature, the agricultural segment nevertheless accounts for a steady one-sixth of all county employment. Agriculture related employment, from processing to packaging manufacture, equipment repair to insurance provision, involves a much larger percentage of the area's total employment picture. Agriculture serves as a barometer of the condition of other employment sectors; it is said to be "last in, first out" of a recession. Sensing this, urban party-goers will occasionally pause to note and bemoan an inopportune rain or exceptionally warm January. County residents are connected to the land and its bounty in countless ways.

Fresno agriculture is significant not only for the county, but also for the nation and the world. Cotton, for example, is the leading agricultural export product of the entire state. Three-fourths of this cotton is sold abroad. Fresno County, a coat-of-arms representing the family of the owner, Allen L. Funch, Jr.

While tradition remains important in Fig Garden Village, it is also considered essential to look ahead to the future. Fig Garden Village was the first shopping center in Fresno to take advantage of an electronic message board to communicate with shoppers and passers by.

The Fig Garden Village Merchants Association publishes a monthly newspaper, The Villager, which is available in all the stores and is mailed to nearly 40,000 homes. The Villager provides news of events in Fig Garden Village and surrounding neighborhoods and stories about the cultural happenings involving the community as a whole.

Fig Garden Village is committed to helping the community it serves with financial assistance or in cooperative efforts. The Village has lent its support to many important enterprises. Contributions have been made to the Leon S. Peters Business Building at California State University, Fresno, the Fresno Metropolitan Museum and the Hospice of Fresno. There is also a Fig Garden Village Gallery at the Fresno Arts Center and Museum.

One special association has been with the school, Bullard Project T.A.L.E.N.T., which was "adopted" by the Village in February, 1986. Youngsters from the school have been able to display their talents and promote the school by means of musical performances and a Halloween costume parade. The Village has supported student projects with advertising and publicity.

Village management strives to maintain its heritage of community involvement and friendly service, while taking full advantage of new developments for the benefit of its patrons.

Fig Garden Village received the Leadership Fresno's 1986 prestigious Envy Award for superb landscaping enhancing their retail environment.

with nearly 40 percent of the state's cotton production, contributes 76 percent of the cotton destined for export. Gross cotton lint and cotton seed receipts for the county exceeded $356 million in 1984; $270 million of this was export income.

Almonds, the county's leading horticultural export crop, is almost exclusively a California crop. Fresno County is responsible for over ten percent of the state's almond production. More than half of the almonds grown in the county in 1984 were exported, yielding an income of $23.5 million. Cotton, almonds and other Fresno County agricultural exports are delivered to such faraway places as England, Hong Kong, Costa Rica, New Zealand and Saudi Arabia.

An overview of Fresno County agriculture in 1986 gives us a picture of a vital, ever-changing industry. Gross production of field crops, although down $62,144,000 from the previous year, stood at $483,687,000. Safflower acreage increased, as did sugar beet acreage, while wheat acres declined slightly. Cotton, the county's number one crop in 1985, dropped to second place in 1986 due to a reduction of 90,000 acres as well as a drop in yield per acre.

Seed crop production value increased 16.7 percent over 1985. Alfalfa seed showed a 16 percent gain, while vegetable seed jumped by 161.9 percent; both gains were due to additional acreage. Other seed crops include barley and cotton.

Vegetable crop production was up 7.2 percent in 1986, with several crops showing gains. Broccoli posted a 39.9 percent gain, while iceberg head lettuce increased by 42.7 percent. Bell peppers increased by an impressive 81.3 percent, while sweet potatoes gained 39 percent and tomatoes were up 9.7 percent. Garlic, however, was down 48.4 percent from the previous year. Overall, gross receipts for market varieties jumped from $5,905,000 in 1985 to $25,308,000 in 1986. Processing varieties showed an even more impressive gain, from $5,662,000 in 1985 to $103,785,000 in 1986. These gains can be attributed to increases in both acreage and yield.

Over all, the value of fruit and nut crops climbed 13.2 percent from 1985 to 1986. Although the gross value of peaches dropped by 8.9 percent, almonds, grapes, raisins and plums all increased markedly in the period. Grapes, ranked the number two county crop in value in both 1984 and 1985, took over first place in 1986 with an overall value of more than $400 million!

RIVERBEND INTERNATIONAL CORP.

A DIVERSIFIED AGRICULTURAL — FOOD COMPANY

Aerial view of Riverbend's corporate headquarters from which their global activities are directed.

Many of the county's other crops showed substantial increases between 1985 and 1986. Gross production value of all nursery products increased by about one-third. Poultry production increases kept the livestock and poultry category on the positive side in spite of a 7,000-head decrease in cattle moving through area feed lots. Turkeys also showed a small increase in gross value for the year, as did all apiary products and pollination services. Livestock and poultry products posted mixed returns. Eggs showed increases in both production and value. Milk production was up, but that was offset by lower returns. Timber harvest showed the most substantial negative trend of all reported crops: it was down 30.2 percent in value from 1985.

An overview of the county's ten leading crops for 1985 and 1986 is to the right. The overall stability of Fresno County agricultural distribution is indicated by a comparison with 1976 rankings.

Now a $2 billion a year industry, Fresno County agriculture has made remarkable, steady gains over the past 20 years. Despite a downturn in the period of 1980 to 1982, the overall trend has been substantial, strong and positive.

Two crops, cotton and grapes, vie for the number one

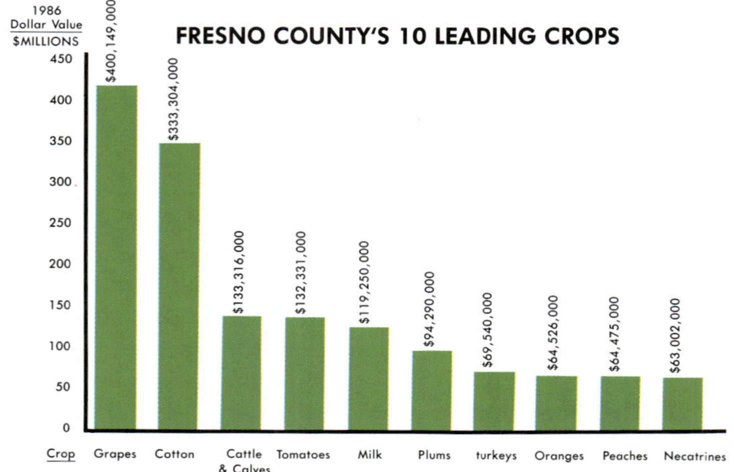

Riverbend International Corporation is a fully integrated, diversified agricultural-food company which operates throughout the southwest while its marketing programs extend throughout North America, South America, the Pacific Basin, Europe and the Mid-East. These global activities are directed from the corporate headquarters, located in eastern Fresno county at the foot of the Sierra Nevada. Riverbend's integrated operations include resource development, farming, fresh fruit and vegetable packing, food processing and marketing.

Food production is basic to all food companies and this is why farming is the foundation of the company's business. From the San Joaquin, in Central California, down through Southern California, the California desert, Arizona and Texas. Riverbend is involved in over 20,000 acres of production agriculture. On this land grow the finest varieties of citrus including navel and Valencia oranges, lemons, tangerines and grapefruit.

Additionally, it produces premium summer fruits such as peaches, plums, nectarines, grapes and other specialties like pomegranates, persimmons and Asian pears. Complementing the fruit production, vegetables are grown in abundance including different varieties of tomatoes, peppers and squash.

Preparing the produce for market is the next step and to fresh-pack these commodities, Riverbend operates six packing lines which are located through the region. These packing lines are built with state-of-the art technology including computer driven electronic sorting and grading systems. Each sophisticated installation is designed to handle several different commodities and this versatility insures the company operational efficiency and productivity.

Riverbend's processing division complements the fresh packing operations. Each of the company's processing plants is designed to be versatile and to yield the maximum commercial potential of the fruit. Therefore each facility processes all varieties of citrus fruits. After extracting the juice from the fruit, it can then be processed into single strength or frozen concentrate form. In addition to fruit juices, other commercial by-products are extracted from the fruit including all essential oils, aromas, essences and peel products. Simultaneous to citrus operation in the spring and summer months, tomatoes are processed into tomato paste. The ability to concurrently process citrus and tomatoes at the same plant is unique in the United States and essential to keep the company's operation competitive in the world market.

The final step in the process is marketing and this is the heart of Riverbend International. The company's marketing plan encompasses all aspects of international food trade. Throughout the years, its success has earned it a worldwide reputation as a reliable supplier of high quality, large volume perishable commodities. Using the latest in communications technology, and information from its European office and the company's worldwide network of agents and distributors, Riverbend's marketing team constantly monitors domestic and global market conditions in search of worldwide profit opportunities. From this data they build a global marketing plan which targets domestic profit opportunities through sales to national and regional chain store outlets as well as foreign transactions with major worldwide producers.

Another critical aspect of Riverbend's business strategy is the utilization of various technical assistance and management contracts the company maintains throughout the world. Covering all phases of food production, fresh commodity handling, food processing and international marketing activities, the operations further strengthen the company's position in the global agricultural and food economy.

As one of the few publicly traded agricultural-food companies, Riverbend stands as a leader. Its growth in worldwide food production, handling, processing and marketing contributes to Fresno County's preeminence as the world's leading agricultural county.

FRESNO COUNTY'S 10 LEADING COMMODITIES

Crop	1976 Rank	1985 Rank	1986 Rank
Grapes	2	2	1
Cotton	1	1	2
Cattle & Calves	3	3	3
Tomatoes	5	4	4
Milk	4	5	5
Plums	9	6	6
Turkeys	11	8	7
Oranges	10	9	8
Peaches	13	7	9
Nectarines	12	10	10

position from year to year. "King Cotton" led the valley in 1984 and 1985, but grapes stole the limelight in 1986. Together these two crops account for more than one-third of total crop value. The significance of grapes and cotton to the overall economic health of Fresno County indicates the need for a closer look at these two vastly different, but equally important, valley crops.

THE GRAPE INDUSTRY

Although the origin of grapes is lost in antiquity, there is evidence of their presence in the Bronze Age, around 4000 B.C. The Old Testament lists grapes among the fruits Adam and Eve cultivated, and depicts Noah as planting grapevines after the flood. And Pliny mentions 50 different wines made by the Romans from 91 varieties of grapes!

In modern times, grape growing is the world's biggest fruit industry. Grapes are grown in every one of the United States. Only apples exceed grapes in fruit crop production. In the northeastern part of the country, such varieties as Concord, Niagara and Delaware are used for wine, jellies, pies, juice and puddings. California grapes are selected for fresh consumption more often than those from any other

(Continued on page 76)

PACIFIC AGRICULTURAL SERVICES, INC.

A COMPANY CHARACTERIZED BY DIVERSITY

Bob Mandolesi (left) and Gary Mathias review a site plan for a future Herndon Avenue office project.

Pacific Agricultural Services, Inc. and its subsidiaries and affiliates combine to form one of the West's most diverse and innovative enterprises. As a full service farm management company, Pacific Ag farms in excess of 18,000 acres of permanent crops. The company's farm management business stretches from California to Arizona and encompasses a number of crops including pistachios, kiwis, jojoba, figs and fresh table grapes. Pacific Ag was a pioneer in the pistachio business, planting the first commercial grove. The company leads the industry in many of the crops it farms. The total value for real property under management is estimated at $150 million.

Pacific Agricultural Services, Inc. was also a pioneer in the irrigation business, installing one of the first drip irrigation systems in Fresno County.

Through it principals and predecessors, the company has years of experience in the propagation of tree nursery stock, the development of agricultural properties, the design and installation of irrigation systems and the brokerage of agricultural and commercial real estate.

Pacific Real Estate, a subsidiary of Pacific Agricultural Services, Inc., is licensed as a California Real Estate Broker and offers both agricultural and commercial land to investors through the operation of two separate divisions. Both divisions are characterized by strong land acquisition teams.

The agricultural division of Pacific Real Estate exclusively represents Southern Pacific Land Company, the largest land owner of intensive farming in the western United States, with land holdings exceeding 3 million acres. The ag real estate division offers clients an added advantage - the experience and expertise of the parent company. Experts are on hand to evaluate property listed for sale. In addition, the division offers full service farm management to meet the needs of absentee owners or investors. The company ranks among the top ten farm management organizations in California.

A full service commercial brokerage division complements Pacific Real Estate's agricultural concerns. The division specializes in the sale and lease of commercial office buildings, developable raw land, apartments, and industrial land and buildings. Site selection services are available for major companies wishing to relocate to the San Joaquin Valley. The professionals at Pacific Real Estate are willing to further assist companies on their relocation to Fresno and they are well-equipped to do this because they are knowledgeable about the community. Pacific Real Estate is proud of employing longtime residents of the valley and believes the company is secured by its community roots.

Pacific Ag's and Pacific Real Estate's employees contribute to the community they believe in. The company is proud to support the Bulldog Foundation, The Boy Scouts of America, The Fresno County and City Chamber of Commerce, The California Bowl, and the Association of Retarded Citizens (ARC).

Pacific Agricultural Services, Inc. and its subsidiaries have experienced rapid growth in many segments of their operations and are well equipped to serve the needs of residents and of individuals wishing to become part of this thriving community.

Ag sales personnel Allen Bennett (left) and Dennis Monahan inspecting one of Pacific Real Estate's listings.

state. In fact, about 97 percent of the country's fresh grapes come from California, with the remaining three percent grown in Arizona. About 85 percent of America's raisin grapes are grown in California, too, and 85 percent of these are grown in Fresno County. The proportions of raisin, table and wine grapes produced in the county in 1985 and 1986 are shown in the table below.

Bearing Acreage	**1985**	**1986**
Raisin Varieties	169,373	168,195
Table Varieties	8,310	8,726
Wine Varieties	37,850	37,535
Total Acreage	215,533	214,456
Total Value	$337,107,000	$400,149,000

Although bearing acreage dropped slightly from both wine and raisin varieties, crop value increased 18.7 percent overall between 1985 and 1986. Gross value increased 18.6 percent for raisins, 25.9 percent for raisins packed fresh, and 72 percent for crushed raisins. Table varieties showed an increase of 40.3 percent in gross value.

In the mid-1980s, raisins are a thriving industry in Fresno County, with about 300,000 tons processed in the area annually. Approximately 6,000 growers and 19 packers produce the crop, which is shipped to both domestic and foreign markets. The popular Sun-Maid television commercial featuring singing raisins dancing to the tune of "I Heard It Through the Grapevine" can now be seen in both England and Germany.

About 90 percent of the total raisin crop is the natural seedless variety produced from Thompsons. Sun drying evaporates the moisture and imparts the characteristic dark color and flavor most people associate with raisins. Golden seedless raisins also start as Thompson Seedless grapes, but they are dried indoors to retain their light color. Muscats, with their distinctive fruity flavor, Zante Currants and Sultanas are newer varieties of the ever popular raisin.

Because the drying process greatly reduces the fruit's bulk, it takes about four and one-half pounds of grapes to produce just one pound of raisins. Convenient, nutritious and easy to store, raisins are available and enjoyed worldwide for snacking and baking. In addition to the plain ordinary raisin, the fruit is now appearing with chocolate or yogurt coating, or mixed with such other foods as nuts and seeds. Raisins are at home anywhere, from the camper's backpack to the most elegant dessert table.

Thompson Seedless, the most popular raisin grape, is also the workhorse of the table grape industry. Aside from the month of April, fresh table grapes are picked from the vines of Fresno County every month of the year. Along with Thompson Seedless, there are about a dozen other table grape varieties which thrive in the San Joaquin Valley. All are produced with irrigation, for grapes mature during the hot summer days when little rain falls in Central California.

Painstaking cultivation, harvesting and packing practices result in flats of perfectly sweet, perfectly ripe and uniformly colored clusters ready for cool storage and shipment to neighborhood stores across the nation. Green, red and flashing black, California's beautiful and nutritious table grapes are steadily gaining popularity. In the decade between 1972 and 1982, grape consumption increased 196 percent, while overall fruit consumption gained a mere 17 percent. Per capita consumption stood at six pounds in 1986, and is expected to increase as people become more conscious of eating natural foods.

While California takes justifiable pride in its highly productive raisin and table grape industries, it would take both crops combined to match the tonnage of grapes used annually by the wine industry. Again, the versatile Thompson Seedless plays a starring role. It is often used for blending, as well as for making brandy and in the production of sparkling wines and champagnes. Other familiar varieties have given their names to the distinctive wines produced from their fruit: Cabernet, Petite Sirah, Reisling or Gewurtztraminer. For sheer product volume, Fresno County stands alone — even in wine-conscious California. All the Napa Valley wineries together don't crush as much as one of Fresno's wineries. As home to a number of important wineries, Fresno County plays a significant role in this traditional and increasingly popular use of the grape.

Fresno County grapes are also used in canning. Here again, the all-purpose Thompson Seedless excels. Its distinctive color, texture and flavor are familiar to fruit cocktail fans. Eleven million cases of fruit cocktail are canned in California each year, with grapes from Fresno County as an important ingredient. From the freshest table grapes to the most convenient preserved treats, Fresno County grapes do yeoman service for health and taste conscious Americans.

LYLES DIVERSIFIED, INC.

STRENGTH THROUGH DIVERSIFICATION

A Kaweah Construction project on the Kern River.

"Strength through Diversification" is the motto adopted when Lyles Diversified, Inc. became a holding company for its two construction companies, numerous real estate development enterprises, and manufacturing interests. Among those associated under the parent company, but with independent operations and management, are four companies important to the economy and development of Fresno and the San Joaquin Valley.

W.M. LYLES CO., a pipeline and utility construction firm organized in 1945, employs several hundred persons annually. With headquarters in Fresno, it has division offices in Bakersfield, Camarillo, Fresno, Sacramento, and Visalia. Recent job projects nearing completion are the utilities for the Avenal prison at $11,300,000 and the Corcoran prison at $10,000,000. Curtis A. Thornton is President and C.E.O.

KING COTTON

When California's early settlers needed clothing, they turned to cotton — a choice that has been made throughout history. Cotton has been found by archaeologists in ancient Mexico and in the palaces of Persian rulers of 600 B.C., and it is frequently mentioned in the Bible. As evidenced by its place in the latest Paris fashions, cotton has persistent, universal appeal as a fiber for clothing.

Cotton was first grown in California in about 1760 on mission land. The crop received a tremendous boost when Eli Whitney invented the cotton gin in 1793. Later, Teddy Roosevelt's concern about the country's continued ability to grow cotton in wartime led to the establishment of a number of experimental stations. In 1902, Dr. T. H. Kearney went to Egypt on behalf of a valley station to study varieties of cotton grown in that country. By the 1920s, a full-fledged cotton boom was on. At about that time, researchers identified a strain of cotton — the Acala — which was well adapted to the San Joaquin Valley climate. Completion of a highway to the ports of San Francisco and Los Angeles opened up a larger market, and the industry began a period of rapid growth.

Cotton continues to be California's leading agricultural export. Three-quarters of the bales produced in 1984 were

A sampling of the quality product line from Pelco.

KAWEAH CONSTRUCTION CO., a general engineering firm founded in 1952, is headquartered in Visalia but operates throughout the valley. Recent jobs include a $20,800,000 dam and powerhouse project in Kern County and a $11,200,000 waste water plant in Manteca. Albert J. Perini is President and C.E.O.

BUCKNER, INC., a manufacturer of irrigation products for 75 years, was acquired in 1984. Located at 4381 N. Brawley Avenue in Fresno, it builds quality irrigation products for the heavy turf, agricultural and residential markets. In addition to many residential and commercial customers, over 8000 golf courses nationwide and around the world use Buckner products. Vince Nolletti is President and C.E.O.

In 1987 a partnership was formed to be known as PELCO, continuing the 30-year operations of a pioneer designer and manufacturer of closed circuit television security/surveillance systems in use world-wide. It is the world's second largest producer of closed circuit television equipment. It is newly relocated in the Clovis Municipal Industrial Park in a just completed 80,000 square foot plant. David McDonald is the President and C.E.O.

Lyles Diversified, Inc.is a privately held family corporation headed by William M. Lyles as president and C.E.O. Since 1945, its operational philosophy includes objectives of high quality and reputation in any area or field in which it chooses to operate. It aims for respected relationships with its employees, customers and suppliers.

Buckner produces a wide variety of sprinkler products and accessories.

The corporation recognizes that it has an obligation to the community's civic and cultural life and growth. Personnel are encouraged to participate in and provide leadership for community activities and goals. The firms which operate in the Lyles Diversified, Inc. group share this philosophy. With their tremendous potential, look for their names, not only in Fresno, but throughout the San Joaquin Valley and wider markets.

sold overseas. In 1985, Fresno County was the highest producing cotton county in the state, with a gross return of $394,608,000 which represents 36.26 percent of the state's total gross returns on cotton. In 1986, cotton was edged out by grapes as the county's number one crop, but it still brought in a very impressive $333,304,000.

The six-county San Joaquin Valley area grows about 25 percent of the nation's cotton, and is the exclusive producer of the Acala variety. Quality control is assured through a grower-industry board. Since 1966, the Cotton Research and Promotion Act has authorized the collection of $1 per bale from growers for research and promotion, thus keeping the industry competitive in the lucrative and expanding textile market.

Acala cotton is well adapted to the valley's climate, and researchers have developed strains which are resistant to wilt and other soil-borne diseases. The Acala staple is exceptionally long and has a tensile strength greater than that of some steel! The valley's dry summers ensure a cotton product of whitest purity, without the greying attributable to rain. Fresno's strong, white, long staple cotton is a premium product which is in demand around the world. It is especially useful in wash-and-wear fabrics, and is sometimes blended with cotton of lesser quality for mass production. Seventy-five percent of the valley's cotton crop is sold prior to harvest to markets throughout the nation and abroad. Because of its premium quality and its usefulness in blends, it has never made economic sense to open cotton mills in the valley. It would be impracticable to import the necessary quantities of other varieties of cotton, or to establish mills which would compete with the long-established mills of the East and South.

AUTOMATED OFFICE SYSTEMS

SPECIALIZING IN BUSINESS COPIERS AND TELECOPIERS

The new 10,000 square foot office building is centrally located to meet the expanding needs of its customers.

Automated Office Systems was founded in 1977 by Thomas C. McGowan, when he became the central valley distributor for A.B. Dick copy and duplicating products. In 1981, the current A.O.S. name was established to reflect the increased diversity of the business and its product line. The A.B. Dick name, however, has been part of the Fresno community since 1947, when the office was first opened. AOS has built an enviable reputation on that 40 year history by providing quality

While fabric mills may be impractical in Fresno, cotton gins and cotton seed processing plants are very important factors in the region's economy. There are approximately 40 cotton gins in the Central Valley. In these gins, cotton seed is separated from fiber as the cotton passes through a series of saws. In the gin press, the fiber is wrapped and strapped into 500-pound bales containing 480 net pounds of cotton. The average yield of cotton per acre in the valley is two and a quarter bales, and about 700,000 bales of cotton are produced in the county each year. Each bale must pass rigorous inspection by a government classing office. The valley's Acala consistently tests pure. This reliability means that it brings between four and five cents a bale more in price. The practical value of a bale of cotton is illustrated by what can be done with it: one bale of cotton can produce 1,200 pillowcases, or 3,000 diapers, or 800 dress shirts!

In the last few years cotton seed, a by-product of the ginning process, has come into its own as an important crop. Early in this century, seed crushing technology improved, transportation became more reliable and new uses for cotton seed and cottonseed oil were developed. Of the several primary products which come from cotton seed processing, oil is by far the most valuable. It accounts for roughly half of the product value, and is used primarily in foods, for cooking oils, in salad dressings, in margarine or in packing oils. Cake and meal products from cotton seed are used for flour, fertilizer and animal feeds. Other products derived from crude cotton oil include soaps, glycerine and fatty acids. Cotton hulls are used for livestock feed, fertilizer and synthetic rubber. Linters produce pulp for viscose, cellulose, felts, yarns, cellulose acetate and absorbent cotton. The product list is extensive and still growing.

Cotton lint, like cotton seed, is a versatile product. Its naturally attractive characteristics — wet strength, softness, absorbency, durability and performance — are being improved through testing and experimentation. As long as King Cotton, humankind's first fiber, is in use, the San Joaquin Valley — and Fresno County — will be producing much of the very best.

OTHER CROPS

During the summer months, while cotton is ripening, cottonseed mills press safflower seed, producing yet another high quality, healthful domestic vegetable oil. This versatility is typical of the year-round productivity of Fresno

AOS has built an enviable reputation by offering the finest equipment available in the world.

Thomas C. McCown, owner and founder of AOS.

products and professional support.

Automated Office Systems specializes in business copiers and telecopiers, such as facsimile machines. The copier and FAX product lines feature Ricoh, an industry leader, with a well established reputation for quality engineering and performance. They also represent A.B. Dick Company with a full line of offset duplicating machines, long established as the workhorse of the quick printing business. Mr. McGowan strongly believes that the foundation for continued success lies in representing the finest equipment available in the world.

A.O.S. occupies a new 10,000 square foot building designed for its own use. The modern office complex and service facility is centrally located in the north section of Fresno, where customers can conveniently view a complete range of equipment in operation. The service and parts department has been substantially expanded and employs over 14 factory trained technicians. A complete stock of parts and supplies is on hand at all times, ready to support the business. Mr. McGowan feels the new building will enable the company to offer an even greater range of products and services, and allow them to keep pace with the expanding needs of the community. Sales offices are also located in Merced and Visalia to ensure prompt, efficient coverage of the market.

The professional staff consists of over 25 full-time employees including sales, technical and office support staff. Each staff member is trained to meet customer needs quickly and efficiently. The sales department can analyze the copier needs of an individual business, and formulate a solid business recommendation and plan of action. The factory trained service technicians provide the necessary technical support to keep clients' copiers in operation.

Automated Office Systems is locally owned and managed, with a personal commitment to its customers and the community. Many customers have a long affiliation with AOS, and represent a wide range of businesses including agriculture, insurance, education, health care, real estate, finance and the professions. AOS employees are involved in the communities in which they live, and many occupy leadership positions in a wide variety of industry, civic, philanthropic and arts organizations in the greater Fresno area. Automated Office Systems is committed to outstanding customer service and improving the community in which its people live and work.

County agriculture. Some crops, like alfalfa, can be harvested all year. The county produces around 700,000 tons of alfalfa each year, with as many as seven harvests in a year — a non-stop festival of fertility. Every day of every week of every year, things are being planted and harvested in Fresno County.

Within the San Joaquin Valley there are marked regional differences in soil and climate, resulting in varying types of agriculture. A drive from the foothills takes one from east side citrus and cow-calf operations through vegetable and nut farms to the cotton, sheep, cattle, cantaloupe and sugar beets of the west side. Many roads in the area pass through vineyards and neat rows of nut trees. A springtime drive through the flowering almonds and freshening vines is an inspirational experience.

Part of the area's beauty and diversity is attributable to the many nationalities which have made the fertile valley their home. Armenians introduced grapes and figs. Chinese cooks grew a wide variety of vegetables for their rancher employers. The Volga Germans brought potatoes; the Portuguese brought dairy cattle. This venerable tradition continues with the valley's newest immigrant group, the Hmong. On small plots or large farms, they work diligently to produce the snow peas, cherry tomatoes and other vegetables and staples familiar to their palates. Thus their transition to a new culture is eased, as has been the transition of immigrant groups down through the years.

Agriculture in Fresno County still includes picturesque family plots and roadside vegetable stands. But the real story of modern farming is business — big business. The $2

Valley safflowers produce a high quality healthful vegetable oil.

The Security Bank Building is a towering landmark in the downtown financial center.

billion annual gross income brought into the area by agriculture turns over between three and seven times, supporting enterprises as diverse as equipment repair shops, pallet manufacturers and insurers.

Along the way, agricultural dollars are expended on the purchase of daily necessities, recreation, health maintenance and charitable contributions. This interrelationship keeps the county committed, if only for its own self interest, to the well-being of its farmers.

Farming in Fresno County is both labor and capital intensive. Costs, risks and income levels are all significantly higher than in other areas of the nation. A 20-acre vineyard, for example, may generate $30,000 a year. But out of that $30,000 come annual cash costs of about $16,000 in addition to land expense. A farmer in Fresno can generate more off a 40-acre plot than his counterpart in the Midwest realizes from 500 acres, particularly if his 40 acres are planted in citrus or other tree fruit. But these are high risk crops, and timing is critical in ensuring their productivity. There is only a short "window" for harvesting at optimum ripeness.

Most farmers must thread their way through an intricate network of federal restrictions and subsidies; they generally borrow heavily to meet expenses. A typical farm takes out loans equivalent to 75 percent of the crop's gross value, a figure which adds up to some $1.5 billion per year in county-wide farm indebtedness. In addition to direct bank lending, gins and packing houses may borrow and advance monies to growers. This kind of loan is included in the $1.5 billion figure.

Because of the high stakes involved, farming has taken on all the attributes of big business — from computerized payroll and equipment maintenance schedules to the development of sophisticated marketing strategies. Always the backbone of the region's lifestyle, farming forms the foundation for its financial industry as well.

A REGIONAL BANKING CENTER

Fresno County's robust economy relies heavily on readily available financial expertise and loan funding sources. The area's multi-billion dollar economy is served by numerous commercial banks and savings and loan associations, with more than 120 branches conveniently located throughout the metropolitan area. While Fresno's largest home-grown financial institution, Guarantee Savings, has merged with Glenfed Inc., the city is still home to the parent companies of two smaller institutions. Western Commercial, the holding company for Fresno Bank of Commerce, Merced Bank of Commerce and Western Commercial Mortgage, and Fresno Bancorp, the parent company for Bank of Fresno and Sequoia Bank, are both located in Fresno.

The attractiveness of the Fresno market for banking activity is illustrated by both deposit growth and competition in the establishment of new branch offices. In 1984, for example, 18 new bank branch offices were established in Fresno — two thirds of the total number of branches operated by Bank of America, an area leader, in that year. In that same year, savings and loan institutions opened a total of 13 offices in the Fresno area. Fifteen new branches were opened on Shaw Avenue between 1979 and 1984, bringing to 46 the number of financial institutions located along that retail and administrative strip.

While the overall growth rate for all financial institutions in the area during the 1979 to 1984 period was 7.9 percent, certain segments showed exceptional strength. Three local independent banks led the "all others" category to a 16.7 percent growth rate, far ahead of the industry leaders, and Wells Fargo experienced a strong average annual growth rate of 15.1 percent. Taken together, banks averaged a growth rate of 7.0 percent, while savings and loans averaged 8.9 percent. In the latter category, the Fresno-based Guarantee Savings posted the lion's share of the increase.

Guarantee Savings, founded in 1919, is a local success story which will soon become a historical note as the 41-branch association merges with Glenfed, Inc. of Southern California. The effects of banking deregulation are being felt strongly in Fresno as the pace of mergers and acquisitions quickens. In one week of 1987, three different Fresno-based financial institutions were involved in merger votes. In addition to Glenfed and Guarantee, California Valley Bank shareholders voted to become part of Phoenix's Valley National Corporation, and Bank of Fresno's parent company, Fresno Bancorp, agreed to merge with Sanger's Sequoia Community Bank. Given the frequency of mergers — which is likely to accelerate with the approach of 1991, the year when full interstate banking becomes effective — any listing of banks is quickly obsolete. However, the tally made in 1985 by the Fresno Economic Development Corporation provides a picture of the range and diversity of banks active in the Fresno area at that time.

(Continued on page 84)

GUARANTEE SAVINGS

SERVING THE VALLEY'S FINANCIAL NEEDS SINCE 1919

This antique vehicle is a highly recognized trademark of Guarantee Savings.

MAX automated teller machines in 46 locations around the valley make banking easier.

Guarantee Savings' commitment to both customer service and community involvement has contributed greatly to its growth through the years. Since its founding in 1919, Guarantee's assets have increased to nearly $3 billion, ranking it in the Fortune 500 of U.S. service corporations.

With a full range of consumer and business services available, Guarantee remains a leader in the local financial services industry. Nearly two out of every five families in Fresno County have some sort of banking relationship with Guarantee Savings. In Fresno County, 26% of all local consumer and commercial deposits are in accounts at Guarantee.

Historically, Guarantee has been an innovator in the San Joaquin Valley banking industry. Guarantee's mobile branch, introduced in 1968, was the first of its kind on the West Coast. Each business day, it traveled to Valley communities to build a customer base outside of Fresno. Over the years, the mobile branch stops were replaced by full-service branches, and it was retired from service in 1975.

The introduction of Guarantee's Money Machine in the early 1970s marked the first time a California savings and loan offered its customers 24-hour access to their deposit accounts. The Money Machines were forerunners of the more sophisticated MAX automated teller machines which are now available at 46 locations throughout the Valley. In 1980, Guarantee became the first to open extended-hour branches inside local supermarkets, and in 1985, introduced drive-up ATMs to provide additional convenience to its customers.

In 1973, Guarantee Financial Corporation of California (GFCC) was formed as a holding company for Guarantee Savings. GFCC then diversified into other areas of the financial services industry including leasing, insurance, real estate development, data processing, and appraisal services. GESCO, now the nation's fourth-largest provider of data processing services to the savings and loan industry, was created as a subsidiary in 1968. Another subsidiary, Guarantee Financial Real Estate, is currently the largest residential real estate brokerage firm in Fresno County. With three offices and more than 80 agents, this division has consistently performed with top sales figures in the Fresno market.

In October 1987, GFCC merged with GLENFED, Inc., parent company of Glendale Federal Savings and Loan Association. With 217 branches in California and Florida and assets exceeding $22 billion, Glendale Federal is the nation's fifth largest savings and loan.

Throughout its history, Guarantee has emphasized quality customer service as a key to its success. The company is widely recognized as a progressive institution which maintains the friendly, efficient attitude of the original Fresno Guarantee Building-Loan Association founded in 1919.

BANK OF AMERICA

A FRESNO CORPORATE CITIZEN FOR 71 YEARS

Pictured are two of twenty-two convenient Bank of America retail branches within Fresno County.

Bank of America first came to Fresno 71 years ago, when, as the Bank of Italy, it bought the Fresno National Bank. In 1916, A.P. Giannini, the bank's legendary founder, recognized the potential of the San Joaquin Valley. He began establishing valley branches; first in Merced and then, four months later on October 21, 1916, in Fresno.

Announcing his move to Fresno, Giannini called the valley, "a great undeveloped field . . . and that is the reason we are here." He went on to say, "Fresno is as much our home as San Francisco, and we are going to do all that is possible in financial aid for businessmen and farmers."

Now, 71 years later, the valley is no longer an "undeveloped field," and Bank of America's presence here has grown with the county. The bank has remained as dedicated as was its founder to providing all possible financial aid to Fresno's industries and its citizens. The association between Bank of America and Fresno has been a long and close one, remaining strong through bad times and good.

One of the bank's current billboard ads carries the slogan, "Never Far from Where You Are." That is an apt slogan for Fresno City and County since within these boundaries Bank of America operates 22 retail branches, most of which have at least one Versateller automated teller machine available. Additionally, there are more than 10 other B of A offices in the area fulfilling administrative or service functions.

Operating this extensive banking network here in Fresno are approximately 950 employees, making Bank of America one of the city's largest employers.

Although A.P. Giannini pledged "all possible in financial aid for the businessmen and farmers," Bank of America has not limited financial aid to business and agriculture. From the beginning, the bank played a large role in local municipal financing. Since 1916, B of A has helped originate and underwrite notes and bonds in Fresno County totaling $566,666,472. These loans helped finance new schools and hospitals, improvements in water and sanitation services, redevelopment and housing projects and many other worthwhile community purposes.

From 1981 to 1985 BankAmerica Corporation, through its BankAmerica Foundation, has awarded $324,000 in grants for community programs supporting health and human services, neighborhood improvement, education, the environment, culture and the arts.

Today Bank of America's management still feels as Mr. Giannini felt when he said, "Fresno is as much our home as San Francisco."

FIRST INTERSTATE BANK

SERVING GREATER FRESNO OVER 30 YEARS

First Interstate Bank of California has been serving the banking needs of Greater Fresno for more than 30 years.

Four offices serve bank customers in Fresno. They are: Fresno Main, 1177 Van Ness Ave.; Manchester Mall Office, 3720 N. Blackstone Ave.; Tower Office, 750 E. Olive Ave., and First and Herndon Office, 7088 N. First St. Customers are also served by the bank's Fresno Commercial Loan Center in the Fresno Main Office and a Home Loan Center at Suite 126, 1300 E. Shaw Ave.

Leo C. Lutz, vice president and manager of the Fresno Main Office, has been a First Interstate Bank employee for 24 years. He has been working in the Fresno area for more than eight years. He has been manager of Fresno Main the past three years after serving as the area's corporate credit officer for five years.

Lutz said the bank's primary focus in Fresno is to finance local business, agri-business and provide various commercial and consumer services. He added that bank personnel at the four offices are well-established in the community and are knowledgable in dealing with the banking needs of Fresno residents.

First Interstate Bank of California has 319 offices statewide and is the principal subsidiary of First Interstate Bancorp, the nation's largest retail banking organization with more than 1,100 domestic offices in 18 states and international banking offices in 36 locations. First Interstate Banks operate under franchise agreements in Colorado, Hawaii, Indiana, Iowa, Montana, New Mexico, North Dakota, Wisconsin and Wyoming.

First Interstate Bank of California is the 12th largest bank in the nation and the fourth largest bank in the state. It has assets in excess of $20 billion and more than $170 billion in deposits.

The First Interstate Bank building adds a solid presence to downtown Fresno.

Bank of America maintained 16 branches in the city in 1985, with deposits of $744.6 million, holding 18.4 percent of the market share. Guarantee Savings had deposits of $965.2 million in 14 branches at that time and held the largest share of the market — 23.9 percent. Security Pacific, with 14 branches, had the third largest market share, 8.2 percent, with $332.8 million in deposits. Other banks in Fresno with several branches in 1985 included American National — two branches, Wells Fargo with four, Lloyds Bank of California — four branches, Central Bank with five, Crocker National — five branches, First Interstate Bank with four, First Bank — three branches. Regency Bank and Fresno Bank of Commerce each had two branches in 1985, and the following banks were represented with one branch each: Union Bank, Western Family Bank, Valley National Bank of Arizona, Bank of California, Community First Bank, Sumitomo Bank of California and California Valley Bank. The savings and loan associations provided service through a total of 45 branches.

Fresno's banking institutions provide a significant base of stable employment in the community. Bank of America leads with a staff of approximately 1,000. Guarantee Savings is second at 600 to 700 employees, and Security Pacific follows with a staff of about 400. Wells Fargo employs 100 area residents, and Imperial Savings provides jobs for nearly the same number. But bank employment is significant for reasons other than volume. In Fresno, as in other communities, bank management provides important community leadership. Several of Fresno's visionary bankers have been instrumental in bringing to fruition such ambitious projects as the Fresno Metropolitan Museum. Year after year, much of the leadership for Fresno's arts, education, social service and civic institutions comes from the city's bankers.

Fresno's robust financial climate can best be understood by placing the city in its context as a regional center, an important part of the complex financial picture of the entire state. In 1984, Fresno's total bank deposits were $1,928.1 million; combined deposits for all financial institutions were $3,570.1 million. In June of 1986, the total deposits for 35 institutions was $4,036 million. Between December of 1985 and December of 1986, total deposits in the state for state-chartered banks increased by 13.8 percent to a total of $78,848. Total assets for state-chartered banks in California increased to $92,402 billion over the period. Nine of the state's top ten banks (ranked by asset size) had branches in Fresno in 1986; the sole exception was City National Bank. These nine banks control 78.63 percent of the assets of all California commercial banks.

(Continued on page 86)

WELLS FARGO

A LOCAL FIXTURE SINCE 1872

Wells Fargo headquarters for their valley division is located in downtown Fresno.

Wells Fargo, one of the most famous and colorful names in the annals of American business, began operations as a banking and express company in gold rush San Francisco in 1852. Providing a broad array of services to pioneer westerners — including the operation of stagecoach lines, the safekeeping of gold and the delivery of the U.S. Mail — Wells Fargo played a key role in the growth and development of the American West.

Today, Wells Fargo Bank, a direct descendant of the pioneer firm, is one of the nation's largest financial institutions. The bank is the principal subsidiary of Wells Fargo & Company. In 1986, the company acquired Crocker National Corporation, another important California pioneer financial institution whose roots extend back to 1870.

Wells Fargo's history in Fresno and Fresno County goes back more than 100 years to pioneer days. Wells Fargo had an agency in the city of Fresno, for instance, as early as 1872. The area was an important center of pioneer railroad activity, and stagelines carrying Wells Fargo express provided important transportation links to the rail lines.

Wells Fargo eventually "rode the rails" from coast to coast in its express activities, and helped in the development of refrigerated railroad cars, which made possible the transportation of California agricultural products to other parts of the country.

Today, Fresno continues to represent an important area of activity for Wells Fargo. Wells Fargo employs approximately 350 people in Fresno. The bank has six branch offices in Fresno, which provide a full range of banking services, as well as a regional commercial banking office which focuses on the financial needs of the area's business communmity.

Several other Wells Fargo operations are also located in Fresno. They include the administration for the bank's Valley Division regional commercial banking offices, and a unit of Wells Fargo's agricultural field staff, a recognition of the area's importance in California's agricultural industry.

Wells Fargo believes that as a bank it has special opportunities to play a key role in the growth and development of the communities it serves.

One of the ways in which Wells Fargo participates in community activities is through grants from the Wells Fargo Foundation to worthwhile community organizations.

On January 1, 1986, there were 285 state-chartered banks in California, with 1,696 branch offices and 87 free-standing Automated Teller Machine (ATM) facilities. By December 31, 1986, those figures had increased to 287 state-chartered banks, 1,700 branch offices and 213 ATMs, an indication of the competitiveness of convenience and service in banking facilities. At the end of 1986, there were 114 agencies and branch offices in the state representing 100 foreign banking corporations. Over the six year period from 1981 through 1986, state-chartered banks experienced a net gain of 19.6 percent. During that same period, branch offices gained 10.7 percent while agencies of foreign banks held relatively stable with a 1.1 percent decrease. During 1985, five national banks opened for business, and an additional ten national banks were approved in the state.

California continues to be the second-largest center of international banking in the United States. Twenty-five of California's full-service state-chartered banks are operated as subsidiaries of foreign banks. The market share of assets held by these banks increased from 24.1 percent in 1977 to 36.4 percent in 1986. A grand total of $61,659,647,000 in assets is controlled by agencies and branches of 107 banks representing 28 countries of origin. Pacific Rim nations are heavily represented in banking, as they are in other businesses around the state.

CREDIT UNIONS

The credit union is becoming an increasingly popular financial tool in the Fresno area. The idea of cooperative investment and savings originated in Europe in the late 19th century. Credit unions now comprise a $166 billion asset industry in the United States; there are 16,000 credit unions with a total of 54 million members. While banks are growing at approximately 15 to 18 percent annually, credit unions are gaining assets at an impressive annual rate of 27 percent.

Credit union membership is generally based on employment in a given industry or at a certain level in government, but membership privileges are often extended to relatives of qualified members. The Educational Employees Credit Union in Fresno, for example, finds that for each qualified new member, an average of five family members eventually join the EECU. The EECU, chartered by the state in 1934, originally restricted membership to teachers. Members later voted to extend membership privileges to all employees of the state's schools systems, from preschool aides to university landscape gardeners.

The EECU members have access to a full range of financial services at this largest credit union in the county. One of the top 20 credit unions in the state, the EECU in mid-1987 had assets of $227 million; its membership at that time was 40,000. With an impressive 40 percent annual growth rate, the EECU is the 82nd largest credit union in the nation. In the volatile bank merger environment of the mid-1980s, the EECU has become for a time the largest locally controlled financial institution of any type in the region. The Sequoia Chapter of the California Credit Union League, one of 26 chapters in the state, has 41 credit unions serving 115,000 members. At the end of 1986, the Sequoia Chapter's assets totalled a respectable $650 million.

Other active credit unions in Fresno include those for federal employees, county employees, electrical workers and members of the United Food and Commercial Workers Union Local. The larger credit unions compete with regional banking, and the smaller provide a sense of cooperative financial management. All provide a service of growing importance in the changing world of finance.

STOCKS AND BONDS

The full range of investment services is readily available in Fresno. Like any financial center, the city has an active brokerage industry. The 150 to 200 licensed investment brokers and dealers represent a good cross section of brokerage houses. These include eight of the nation's leading SEC investment firms: Paine Webber; Shearson, Lehman Brothers; Dean Whitter; E.F. Hutton; Prudential-Bache; Sutro & Company; Bateman Eichler Hill Richards; and Merrill Lynch.

Fresno is home to a wide variety of firms included in the stock exchange. Local public companies represent all economic sectors. Representative firms are Gottschalks in retail, Vendo in manufacturing, Guarantee Savings in finance, and Riverbend Farms in agriculture. Such things as corporate expansion, new product development, research and marketing innovations are frequently financed through stock offerings.

Municipalities throughout the nation also use the tools of public finance to meet their obligations and expand their services. Fresno is no exception. City and county bonds have from time to time added to available investment options. International investors are attracted to Fresno by agribusiness and the dependable, economical work force. New and expanding companies are attracting investment dollars into the area from both domestic and foreign sources, adding to the vigorous economic climate. As a regional financial center and the home of a large number of mature investment houses, Fresno provides reliable, professional full-range investment services to meet the needs of the ever-expanding underwriting sector.

An indirect result of Fresno's status as Central California's financial center has been the explosive growth of the accounting business. The city has branch offices of four national firms: Touche Ross & Co., Arthur Young & Co. Peat Marwick Main, and Ernst & Whinney, as well as a multitude of small regional and local firms. Several of the major firms have offices throughout the metropolitan area and branch centers up and down the Central Valley. Accounting is a substantial local employer. There are more than 700 CPAs in the Fresno chapter of the California State Society of Certified Public Accountants. With their allied support and managerial staff, these financial sector employees contribute substance and expertise to the local economy.

(Continued on page 88)

SHEARSON LEHMAN BROTHERS

"MINDS OVER MONEY"

Shearson Lehman Brothers has become one of the San Joaquin Valley's leading financial institutions in only 12 years. The Shearson-Fresno office is approaching $300,000,000 in assets which are being managed by Financial Consultants for our valley clients.

Our philosophy of applying intellect, imagination and determination to the needs of our clients, that is, "Minds Over Money", reflects the uniqueness of our culture and how we do business. It has also helped us to become one of the most profitable firms on Wall Street.

Shearson Lehman's principal activities include securities and commodities trading as principal and agent, securities underwriting and investment banking and financial advisory services, private client service, and asset management and real estate services. By 1988 Shearson anticipates that it will be the largest member firm on the NYSE in terms of capital. With 310 offices in the United States and 22 international branches, Shearson is understandably proud of its ties with American Express and most recently with Nippon Life Insurance Company of Japan.

Our worldwide capital markets include equity (stock) trading, corporate and municipal bonds, U.S. Government and agency securities, money market instruments including commercial paper, certificates of deposit, etc., real estate mortgages and mortgage related securities, futures and commodities markets. Research at Shearson is broad based and international with experts in New York, London, Hong Kong and Tokyo.

Serving the individual investors who tend to be affluent, serious and increasingly sophisticated in their approach to investing has been responsible for a large portion of the companys growth. Asset management is the key to our success. We view our clients as individuals, each possessing unique needs and investment goals.

While we recognize that they are for the most part, busy people with limited time to devote to investing, we ask them to spend sufficient time initially to assure that any investment program undertaken is appropriate. In 1986, we adopted our customized Personal Review Outline or "PRO" analysis procedure to reflect tax reform and to give us yet greater insights into each client's needs, goals, and capacity for risk. This free analysis forms the basis for informed collaboration between the investor and our Financial Consultants.

Our unique way of working has made us number one in mergers and acquisitions, and has made us the world's leading market maker in securities. Assets in our clients accounts have more than tripled over the past three years. "We look back with pride and forward with confidence", says Harry Gaykian, Senior Vice President and Resident Manager of the Fresno branch. History has shown that every great organization has its time. "This is ours."

Pictured below: Harry Gaykian, Sr. Vice President and resident manager of Shearson Lehman Brothers in Fresno.

The IRS Center in Fresno collected more than $90 billion in 1986 from taxpayers in California and Hawaii.

THE INSURANCE INDUSTRY

Nowhere is Fresno's prominence in financial services more evident than in the burgeoning of the insurance industry in the city. All along Shaw Avenue one finds attractive office complexes housing a wide variety of insurance carriers, from small family firms to sales offices and regional headquarters of some of the major companies in the industry. The Equitable has recently relocated its regional office from the Bay area to Fresno, and Western Plan Services, Inc., will soon follow suit. Both companies cite the prohibitive labor, land and housing costs on the coast as the impetus for their relocation, and praise the lower costs, dedicated workers, quality of life and readily available vendor support they have found in Fresno. One executive recently expressed the feelings of many when he remarked on the impressive work ethic of Fresno residents of many different ethnic groups. The high quality of the part-time employee market and the work commitment of the area's re-entry women are other factors enticing financial service industries to the Fresno area.

Insurance firms in Fresno tend to be involved in the community. A portion of insurance premium dollars is reinvested locally, providing a stable source of funding for community development. Some companies hold a stake in the area's economic foundation, agriculture, through farm loans and partnerships. Insurance company employees become visible community leaders, serving on boards and committees and volunteering in support of numerous worthy causes.

Insurance firms play a significant role in the economy as employers. While New York Life has more active agents than other firms, their offices are not consolidated. In terms of scale, The Equitable's regional office is the major force among Fresno insurance companies, with upwards of 600 employees. Allstate employs nearly 300 Fresnans, and several companies hire between 150 and 200 residents: Liberty Mutual, Fireman's Fund, Aetna, Industrial Indemnity and Blue Cross in the medical insurance field. Most of the area's larger insurers are in the group health, property and casualty areas. Many others have large sales forces, but they are scattered throughout the metropolitan area in 500 to 600 offices of three or four persons each. In the last few years, the third party payor companies and medical insurance groups have undergone dramatic growth. Health Plan of America, Summa Health Plan and Travelers Health Network are part of the recent insurance industry growth spurt in the Fresno area.

Like many professions, the insurance industry has an association for the benefit and advancement of members. Fresno Life Underwriters is 450 members strong and represents more than 60 companies, from industry leaders to the smallest family operations. A vital component of the financial sector, these insurance professionals provide a wide of range of needed services, supporting the health of the economy as a whole.

THE INTERNAL REVENUE SERVICE CENTER

Across the nation, cities like Denver, San Francisco and Philadelphia have high financial profiles due to the presence of a U.S. Mint. While Fresno cannot claim to "make" money, it certainly collects a lot of it; the Internal Revenue Service Center in Fresno in 1986 collected more than $90 billion in taxes from individuals and businesses in California and Hawaii.

The IRS selected Fresno as its Western regional processing center; Fresno is one of ten such centers nationwide. In July of 1970, a task force of 20 IRS employees arrived in Fresno to begin the process of assembling a work force capable of handling the 18 million tax returns the center now processes each year. With 6,200 permanent and temporary employees during the peak filing season, the IRS can claim the largest work force in one location of any company or government agency in Fresno.

As one might expect, the establishment of the IRS regional processing center in Fresno has had a strong positive effect on the area's economy. When the decision was made to move to Fresno, the city's population was 200,000. That figure has doubled, due at least in part to the impact of the service center. The $112.7 million operating budget of the IRS includes $89.5 million for salaries and travel expenses. The employment of so many people at the IRS has impacted other service industries. The U.S. Postal Service, for example, has had to expand to accommodate the volume of mail generated by the center. It has added facilities and hired an additional 1,600 employees. The acquisition of optical character readers, necessary for maximum speed processing of the high volume of mail generated by the IRS, attracted more business to the city. As a result of the government's decision to locate the IRS center in Fresno, the city has become a major mail processing center.

The center's physical presence is as substantial as its economic impact. The IRS center occupies over 520,000 square feet of office space, the equivalent of 12 acres — or 12 football fields. Two offsite warehouses and two offsite offices, including one in nearby Tulare, comprise an additional 219,500 square feet of space. The location of the center in the southeast sector of the city has been a factor in building momentum for freeway access to that area. In many direct and indirect ways, the IRS has become one of Fresno's most important and highly regarded assets.

(Continued on page 90)

FIRST AMERICAN TITLE INSURANCE CO.

ONE OF THE OLDEST AND LARGEST FIRMS

First American Title Insurance Company, whose principal business is the issuance of title insurance and related services, is one of the nation's oldest and largest title insurance firms. From 1889 to 1957, First American had one office in Santa Ana, California. Today, over 400 branch offices and over 2,500 agents reach across the nation and overseas.

First American's beginnings in Fresno date back to 1937, when a title firm named Home Title Company was founded. Board members held their first meeting on May 4.

Home Title brought Fresno County business to First American in 1964 through an underwriting agreement effective June 1. In 1969, Philip Wilson, president and general manager of Home Title for 26 years, received board approval to pursue negotiations for a merger with First American. Home Title's name was changed to First American Title Company of Fresno in 1973.

The first office location, 2032 Mariposa Street, housed a staff of 60 people. In the late 60s, the main office moved to 1310 M Street, which underwent major remodeling in 1976. An adjoining house was acquired, and records were moved there temporarily while the interior of the office building was gutted.

A company official from Santa Ana arrived during the renovation and was dismayed to find the entire front of the building gone. But by the end of the day, the gaping hole was covered as a pre-built section of red brick and white vertical siding was installed and the building was transformed into an early American edifice. Employees and customers celebrated with an open house early in 1977.

Also in 1977, Ken Purcell joined the Fresno operation as vice president-manager. He began his title career in 1961 in Santa Ana — location of First American's national headquarters, and was a sales manager there and in Reno before starting a branch office in Colorado Springs, Colo. After five years in Colorado, he transferred to Fresno.

In 1979, First American Title Company of Fresno became a branch office of the parent firm. Today, in addition to the main office, the Fresno branch has two other offices in Fresno at 5043-B North Palm and 1177 East Shaw. The branch employs 34 people.

First American is a success story unequalled in the title insurance business. The company has maintained a stable financial structure with 1986 assets of more than $297 million. Though one of the nation's largest title insurers, its founding family continues to direct operations. Its service philosophy stays intact.

First American stock was first traded publicly in 1964. Today, the company's stock is listed on the NASDAQ National Market System.

The year 1987 marked the 98th year of title insurance service for First American, which operates through a network of more than 2,900 offices or agents in all 50 states. It also provides title services abroad in Guam, Mexico, Puerto Rico, the Virgin Islands and England.

GUARDIAN INDUSTRIES

FROM SAND TO FINISHED PRODUCT

Glass production at Guardian can be as much as 500 tons per day.

In 1978 Guardian Industries constructed a new $40 million float glass manufacturing plant on a 55 acre site in Kingsburg, near Fresno. The facility serves Guardian's customers in the Western United States and has the capacity to produce 500 tons of glass per day. The plant size is in excess of one-half million square feet and includes a horizontal continuous line to fabricate tempered glass.

Guardian sought this location to complement its existing U.S. glass manufacturing facilities in Michigan, "The Fresno area was clearly the ideal location" according to company officials. "The transportation network is well established, and the work force is committed. The people were what sold us."

Guardian, headquartered in Northville, Michigan, is privately owned and is a leading manufacturer and fabricator of flat glass products used in construction and transportation applications. The company operates five float glass production lines and one rolled glass manufacturing line in the U.S., and two float glass lines and a rolled glass line in Europe, and recently announced a third European facility. Extensive glass fabricating activities are conducted at facilities in the U.S., Canada and Europe. Other building materials manufactured by Guardian include a broad line of fiberglass insulation products. The company also serves the amateur photography market nationwide through a network of regional photo processing facilities. Guardian is committed to using the most modern technology available. Over 70 percent of the company's investment in property, plant and equipment is less than five years old. By continually upgrading equipment and utilizing the most modern technology, Guardian industries has become one of the most efficient and quality oriented glass producers in the world.

COMMERCIAL REAL ESTATE AND DEVELOPMENT

Fresno's rapid growth has created a vigorous business climate for the construction industry. Overall, building in the county is headed into its fourth largest year. Commercial and industrial construction is steady, with a boom in the new business office space and single family residential markets. The Dun & Bradstreet report on building permit values for the nation's 200 largest cities during the first quarter of 1987 gave Fresno a very respectable position. In a listing that included Miami at the high gain end — with an increase of 1,154 percent, and Odessa, Texas at the low end with an 85.7 percent decrease, Fresno held 69th place, posting a building permit value gain of 25.1 percent over first quarter 1986. This accomplishment is made more impressive by comparison with national averages; the country as a whole experienced a 2.4 percent decline in building permits issued for the quarter.

A comparison of county-wide building permits and valuations prepared by the marketing department of *The Fresno Bee* showed overall gains of 17 percent in dwelling permits, 11.3 percent in auxiliary home structure permits, and a 60 percent increase in commercial permits for the three-month period ending in April 1987 over the same period the previous year. In the month of April alone, commercial permits were up 30 percent, from 89 in April of 1986 to 117 in April of 1987.

GRUBB & ELLIS

LEADER IN THE COMMERCIAL REAL ESTATE BUSINESS

Dan K. Pollard, Vice President and District Manager of Grubb and Ellis in Fresno.

Established in 1984, the Fresno commercial real estate offices of Grubb & Ellis serve the entire San Joaquin Valley. The firm's 30 Fresno-area sales professionals are part of the largest independent real estate firm in the nation, third largest overall. Grubb & Ellis, a publicly held company, provides specialized, knowledgeable services in all areas of commercial real estate.

wide. The industry grew from 10,500 employees in 1984 to 11,100 in 1985; that figure increased to 12,000 in 1986 and to 12,800 in 1987. These figures translate to gains of 8.1 and 6.7 percent for the two most recent years. The industry has experienced a remarkable recovery from the slump of the early 1980s, when employment dropped from 11,200 to 9,500 in 1981 and still further to 8,100 in 1982.

There is ample room for continued robust development in both commercial and industrial sectors in the Fresno area. There are approximately 7,200 acres now vacant which are zoned for light and heavy industry; parcel sizes range from one-half acre to more than ten acres. There are a few parcels of up to 100 acres available for development. The metropolitan area includes 18 industrial parks or districts with level terrain and good drainage. Piling is not required, and water mains of from six to 12 inches are already in place, as are sewer lines of up to 60 inches. City and county planning departments, as well as the Fresno Economic Development Corporation, have compiled detailed data on available sites. In addition, there is an area designated as an Enterprise Zone. Fresno is one of the first cities selected by the state to use this designation. A number of tax advantages are available to businesses locating within the Enterprise Zone.

Fresno builders and developers take pains to distinguish their various complexes to make them attractive to investors and businesses. Fresno is the originator of the garden office concept wherein wide-windowed office complexes are built surrounding an atrium or garden area. This adds greatly to the ambience of the office complex, as well-landscaped gardens complement beautifully decorated office spaces. This architectural innovation has been picked up by designers in other areas, adding to Fresno's reputation as a leader. A new twist to this concept is found in the Channing Court complex on West Shaw Avenue. There, the garden office idea has been extended vertically in a multi-level adaptation of the plan. The multi-story garden office concept is an idea whose time has come; it is a harmonious marriage of aesthetic charm and intensive urban space utilization.

A number of Fresno's most prolific developers seem to have an interest in creating beautiful buildings. Several new structures are showplaces of contemporary design and beauty combined with practicality. From the Civic Center Square downtown to the stunning law, real estate, banking

Office Properties specialists rely on comprehensive computerized data banks for information on local as well as national trends. Statistics on proposed new office projects, potential vacancies, market rates, lease terms, vacancy rates, absorption studies, corporate profits, building costs and employment statistics can help pinpoint potentially profitable opportunities in the office marketplace.

As one of the largest and most experienced retail brokerage operations in the U.S., Grubb & Ellis professionals are able to provide leasing and sales information pertinent to a wide range of retail projects, from free-standing, single tenant locations to regional centers. The firm's market knowledge provides reliable guidance in site selection, land assemblage, project marketing, and the leasing and sale of retail properties.

Fresno's growth in industrial properties is in part due to the expertise of firms such as Grubb & Ellis, where industrial specialists keep pace with vital market information. Clients have access to the most current and comprehensive demographic data, as well as employee statistics, vacancy rates, feasibility studies and tenant profiles.

The professional staff at Grubb & Ellis, aware of the growing complexities of agricultural land transactions, formed an agricultural division to meet the needs of agricultural investors. Serving the San Joaquin Valley, the agricultural center of the world, the division focuses on major agribusinesses with interest in diversification, divestiture or expansion of their agricultural real estate holdings. The firm's attention to land sales recognizes the significance of land transactions as the foundation of all real estate, and focuses on marketing four types of land use: large land parcels for investment, tracts for land development, land for residential housing and in-fill parcels.

Investment properties receive special attention at Grubb & Ellis, too. Its clients have access to the only computerized system displaying available investment properties nationwide. In addition, specialists at Grubb & Ellis maintain a computerized registry of potential investors and detailed listings of 14 major categories of top institutional investors.

A portion of the Grubb and Ellis team shown from left to right are: Mark Saito, Norman Bishop, Lisa McCleerey and Daniel Koontz.

Broker specialization in property types and market areas allows more comprehensive understanding of the requirements of both buyers and sellers, and helps to develop innovative, successful, market strategies. Standardized investment listing and sales presentation packages allow rapid preparation and presentation of property descriptions for prospective purchasers. Continually updated investment analysis programs and informative quarterly publications, such as the "Investor Outlook," keep investors alert to current issues and potential trends. In these and many other innovative ways, Grubb & Ellis professionals make a significant contribution to the quality of the life and commerce in greater Fresno.

and professional office complexes on Shaw Avenue and in Fig Garden, the community boasts an increasing number of well-designed office complexes strategically located throughout the metropolitan area. Landscaping and the use of sculpture add to the impact and appeal of many of these buildings. With such beautiful and convenient office space available, it is no wonder that businesses continue to choose Fresno as their regional headquarters, adding their leadership to Fresno's growing economy.

LAND USE AND DEVELOPMENT

There is a growing thoughtfulness in Fresno regarding the promotion of growth and economic development. This concern stems from a realization of the fragility of the environment and of its irreplaceable contribution to the good life so treasured by the people of the San Joaquin Valley. In the light of increasing threats of traffic congestion, air pollution and urban sprawl, the voice of concern has taken on an urgent tone.

There is ample precedent for protecting the environment and taking a cautious approach to development. When the San Joaquin Valley "desert" was brought to life through irrigation, many of the Sierra's resources — in addition to precious water — made the abundant lifestyle of early Fresno possible. Timber, gold and hydroelectric power all played important roles in the development of the fledgling town. At the same time, groups of concerned citizens championed the cause of the Giant Sequoias, guarding them from the loggers' saws.

Early civic leaders almost universally demonstrated commitment to the future quality of life by donating parklands, preserves and other outdoor recreation sites. From the earliest days following incorporation to the most recent recommendations of the Chamber of Commerce, recognition of Fresno's dependence on the land is a clear theme of city history. There is throughout the urgent message that the beauty and abundance of the county is a treasure to be carefully protected, a gift for which all are to be stewards.

To its credit, the City of Fresno has long been on record demonstrating concern for management of growth and development. Chief among the concerns expressed over the decades has been the desire to provide adequate services to an expanding population while preserving prime agri-

(Continued on page 94)

BUILDERS CONCRETE AND RIVER ROCK PRODUCTS

THE FOUNDATION OF FRESNO'S BUILDING INDUSTRY

Brightly colored Builders Concrete trucks parked adjacent to huge conveyor belts.

Builders Concrete and River Rock Products were established 35 years ago by Donald M. Underdown, a transplanted Canadian. Underdown happened to be traveling through the San Joaquin Valley in 1945 and stopped for a "few days" when he decided he liked the area.

Underdown, like his father and grandfather before him, had worked in the construction business in Great Britain, Canada and also in Southern California.

His first venture into construction in Fresno was the road paving business. He soon realized the need and the opportunity to get into the aggregate business, which he did back in 1949.

This small start eventually grew to become River Rock Products and included a small asphalt plant. In 1952 Builders Concrete was born, beginning with one mixer truck and tons of hope.

Today River Rock Products and Builders Concrete remain family owned and operated. The companies are Fresno's only locally owned complete rock facility. The new plants located on the San Joaquin River include new asphalt and concrete operations. They produce the majority of the asphalt paving materials and ready-mix concrete for the construction industry in the Fresno area.

River Rock Products produces approximately one million tons of aggregate annually. Its asphalt plant is the largest between San Francisco and Los Angeles.

River Rock being stockpiled at its San Joaquin River plant site.

Builders Concrete runs a fleet of over thirty brightly painted mixer trucks. Its new batch plant is the only one in the Fresno area to earn a Certificate of Merit from the National Ready-MIx Concrete Association.

River Rock Products and Builders Concrete hope to continue to contribute to Fresno's construction needs for many years to come.

Logging in the Sierra is carefully monitored in an effort to assure an ongoing source of supply.

cultural land and maintaining a desirable quality of life for both current residents and future generations.

Sporadic attempts were made to give the city's early development a coherent pattern; they met with mixed success. A strong, organized and ultimately more productive chain of events was set in motion in 1958 when a private consulting firm, Victor Gruen and Associates, was hired by the city. The firm presented a plan in 1959 which provided the impetus for the creation of the downtown Fulton Mall and the Convention Center complex, for expansion of government offices in the Civic Center area, and for the Mariposa project of medical and professional offices. The Fresno-Clovis Area General Plan had been adopted by both cities and the county government in 1958.

These developments were followed in 1960 by adoption of a uniform zoning ordinance covering Fresno, Clovis and Fresno County. In addition, modern construction codes and uniform street improvement standards were adopted. The city approved a metropolitan Flood Control Ordinance and a number of redevelopment plans.

Although the city did not implement a number of the recommendations of the Gruen Plan, its courage in creating a downtown mall and its subsequent adoption of codes to guide development appear to have been important factors influencing the federal government to designate Fresno as a Model City. Monies from the Model Cities program were instrumental to the city in improving housing and recreational facilities.

Fresno City and County adopted a comprehensive General Plan in 1964. This was followed in 1969 by the creation of the Council of Fresno County Governments. This organization was charged with the task of providing intergovernmental, comprehensive regional plans, with an emphasis on highway planning. While this mandate has yet to be completely fulfilled, a number of impressive strides have been made. A few years earlier, the Local Agency Formation Commission had been given the task of finding ways to encourage orderly development of local government agencies and to discourage urban sprawl — a tall order! These cooperative efforts drew national attention, culminating in the awarding of the title of All-American City to Fresno by *Look* magazine.

In the 1970s, this spirit of farsighted planning faced difficult challenges. A downturn in the national economy was reflected in local government revenue shortfalls, and planning fell upon hard times. In 1982, the City Council reorganized and tightened its structure. The Department of Planning and Inspection was consolidated with the Department of Housing and Community Development to create one Development Department. Similar consolidation and cost cutting moves took place in the county government as well. On the positive side, efficiency should be improved by the provision of streamlined service to the building industry.

Early in the 1980s it became apparent that population forecasts for the area were seriously underestimated. Representatives from Fresno County and the cities of Fresno and Clovis reviewed the General Plan in 1982, seeking to come up with a realistic population projection. They settled on a projection of a county population of 840,000 by the year 2000.

The General Plan was updated in 1984 in the light of this projection. The revision process incorporated four basic objectives: (1) policy analysis and direction for planning issues before the city council, (2) comprehensive services delivery planning for an expanded urban area, (3) protection of prime agricultural land through integration of higher density population patterns, and (4) responsiveness to recommendations developed through Fresno's community planning process. The updated General Plan must also provide for adequate response to the mandates of the state. Far more than earlier versions, this revised plan makes explicit a concern for environmental issues, indicating a new level of maturity and sophistication in the planning process.

In addition to the mandated environmental issues of seismic safety, open space and conservation, the plan devotes attention to noise control, water resources and air quality. The Revised Plan is a model of creative incentive development designed to encourage private sector investment in the older areas of the city. Infill of vacant areas, rehabilitation, flexibility in allowing mixed usage and recycling of older buildings are among the strategies available. Overall, the Revised Plan represents a renewed dedication to the orderly management of growth.

The plan presents a comparative analysis of three population growth and physical expansion areas within the Urban Boundary line, including an anticipated facility need and cost presentation. In newer areas, as well as in undeveloped portions of the Community Plan area, higher density residential use is encouraged to maximize service efficiency. In addition, the Revised Plan details more fully the Multi-Use Center Concept first set forth in the 1974 General Plan.

The Fresno County Plaza Building, located in downtown Fresno, is the county's largest government office complex.

The Service Sector

CHAPTER 5

The afternoon sun casts long shadows over downtown Fresno.

For more than one hundred years, Fresno has been the service hub of Central California. Residents of surrounding cities and towns look to Fresno for facilities and expertise in law, medicine, education and the allied professions. From the humble one-room schools and the official county hospital of 1870 — which cost Dr. Lewis Leach a whopping $350 to build — have evolved contemporary educational and medical enterprises, the equal of any in the nation. Frontier posse justice has been replaced with an imposing multi-story courthouse, helicopter patrolled traffic and 911 telephone emergency access.

Even though citizens of Fresno no longer have to fear being drafted for posse duty, and teachers are no longer hired on the basis of their marital status and church attendance, the traditions of public involvement in the service professions remains strong. School boards, citizen panels, advisory boards, parent-teacher organizations, hospital guilds and a host of informal organizations fuel and direct the growth of medical and educational institutions. Neighborhood Watch groups and the opportunity to take one's turn on jury duty keep citizens close to law enforcement.

Interest and involvement are reciprocal, for educators, physicians, attorneys and allied professionals make up a small army of involved citizens and civic leaders. The judicial, medical, educational and health establishments of the area are major employers, prime purchasers and important landholders, and are an integral part of Fresno's economic development. The service professions comprise a tremendous support system for business and industry. They represent a major purchasing base for goods and services, property and products. As such, they are vital to the area's economic well-being, as well as to its quality of life.

EDUCATION

When the first superintendent of schools was appointed in 1860, education in Fresno was intended to serve three purposes: 1) to train students in the subject matter of the core instructional curriculum, 2) to promote moral development, and 3) to foster enculturation and integration of children of diverse cultural backgrounds into the American way of life. More than 100 years later, the principles underlying the educational process remain remarkably similar.

The idea of educating for enculturation has been supplanted with an emphasis on educating for mutual understanding and enhancing pride in one's heritage. As the influx of immigrants from foreign lands continues, Fresno teachers are on the front lines easing culture shock and guiding their students to a common understanding of their new nation.

The quality of teachers is still a matter of pride, as it was in 1900 when Superintendent George Ramsay publicly

(Continued on page 98)

STATE CENTER COMMUNITY COLLEGE DISTRICT

FRESNO CITY COLLEGE & KINGS RIVER COMMUNITY COLLEGE

The fountain area of Fresno City College is a focal point for student relaxation.

State Center Community College District was established in 1964 to administer Fresno City College and Kings River Community College in Reedley and is governed by a seven-member board of trustees. The district serves approximately 650,000 people and covers an area of 5,580 square miles in four counties. The colleges drew almost 20,000 full and part-time students during the 1985-86 school year and summer sessions.

Fresno City and Kings River are as diverse in nature as the populations they serve. FCC, founded in 1910 as the state's first community college, is the larger of the two in terms of the enrollment. It is located in the middle of Fresno and has the hustle-bustle feel of an active urban college.

Since 1970, over 11 new buildings have been added to the 103-acre campus, including a science building, a college theater and a business education complex. Today Fresno City College is a thriving, vibrant facility with almost 16,000 students and a faculty of 450.

A wide variety of people attend Fresno City College. Recent high school graduates, non-high school graduates over 18, high school honor students, and people of all ages are coming back to school. More than half of the students at Fresno City College both work and attend school. Students work part-time, and some even full-time, often arranging their classes around work schedules.

Fresno City College offers over 110 high quality programs leading to an Associate Degree in Arts or Science. Vocational programs are also plentiful, where students can earn a vocational training certificate which can open up opourtunities in many job fields. What's more, educational costs at Fresno City College are minimal and the college has services available to make the transition to college life easier.

Kings River Community College is located approximately 35 miles southeast of Fresno in Reedley. The campus is near lakes, mountains, national parks and the Kings River.

The rural community of Reedley has a population of 13,000. It is a small town with a keen eye towards development. The college also draws from the surrounding areas of Dinuba, Selma, Kingsburg, Sanger, Orange Cove and Parlier. Populations in these towns range from 6,000 to 12,000. Kings River also attracts students from the metropolitan area of Fresno.

SOMPM

The Social Sciences Building on the FCC campus is one of the many focal points of academic life.

Kings River Community College is the sister institution to FCC, and its serene campus is located in Reedley.

Kings River's total student population is approximately 4,500. Three thousand attend class in Reedley, while another 1,500 attend college classes at one of the following seven community campus sites: Clovis, Fresno Arts Center and Museum, Kerman, Madera, Oakhurst, Sanger and Selma.

The Kings River campus is 487 acres making it the fourth largest community college in California. A 300-acre farm and an 8-major agricultural department make Kings River a trendsetter among agricultural programs.

The college takes full advantage of its location and maintains a 600-acre forest at Sequoia Lake — an invaluable teaching "laboratory" for forestry majors. The California Conservation Corps, United States Forest Service and National Park Service all use the college as a home base for emergency training.

Kings River has one of only 16 certified aeronautics programs in California, and the geographical diversity of its students attests to the programs far-reaching reputation. Students work on "live projects" in a 19,000-square foot facility.

State Center Community College District is proud to be part of a thriving community by offering valley residents quality education at both Fresno City College and Kings River Community College.

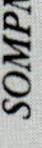

Visitors are impressed with the spaciousness of the FCC campus.

praised the excellence of teachers in the county's 122 school districts. Although unification has reduced the number of districts dramatically, teacher training and continuing in-service education give modern day superintendents much to extol. Even in the early grades, specialists have replaced generalists. Students have access to enrichment experiences provided by exceptionally well-qualified staff. Whereas the first Fresno teachers were examined for competence in 21 subjects, depth of knowledge is a more important consideration today. From pre-school to PhD, Fresno students are fortunate to have a wealth of high quality educational opportunities at their fingertips.

ELEMENTARY AND SECONDARY SCHOOLS

From the earliest age, Fresno children can experience the challenge and excitement of education. A wide variety of preschools, some accepting students as young as age two, offer informal training in social skills as well as helping children to unravel the mystery of shapes, colors, sounds and sizes. By age four or five, most Fresno children can sing, dance, recite the alphabet, sit somewhat still for short presentations, and count many far beyond 100! While their parents busy themselves with the mundane matters of the world, these eager explorers may go off on a trip to the zoo, picking their own jack-o-lanterns at a pumpkin patch, or visiting with a firefighter, nurse or even Mickey Mouse! Some parents select schools with an emphasis on music while others may prefer a church-related preschool experience. Whatever their preference, Fresno families have a variety of options available for their youngsters' introduction to the joys of learning.

Fresno Zoo Director Dr. Paul Chaffee shows a reptile to curious school children.

(Continued on page 102)

CALIFORNIA STATE UNIVERSITY FRESNO

EXCELLENCE IS A TRADITION

The Henry Madden Library is one of the best in the entire university system.

The Henry Madden Library collection includes over 700,000 volumes, over 4,500 different periodicals, an extensive music library and a number of special collections.

Established in 1911, California State University, Fresno has become a major regional university in Central California. It is one of the oldest and most prestigious of the campuses of the California State University system.

The university is fully accredited by the Western Association of Schools and Colleges, and ranks third highest among the 19 CSU campuses in the number of nationally accredited professional programs available to students.

CSU Fresno offers programs leading to the bachelor's degree in 55 different fields of study and the master's degree in 42 fields of study.

CSU, Fresno's 1,410-acre campus includes a 220-acre main campus and an extensive University Farm. The main campus features 40 major buildings linked by tree-lined sidewalks. Because of the beauty of its 4,000 trees of 85 different species, the campus has been officially designated an arboretum.

The Henry Madden Library is one of the best in the CSU system. The collection includes over 700,000 volumes, over 4,500 different periodicals, an extensive music library and a number of special collections. The library is also a selective depository of U.S. government and state publications.

CSU, Fresno's sports complex includes 30,000-seat Bulldog Stadium for football and soccer games, a 3,500-seat baseball stadium, an all-weather track, tennis courts, a swimming pool and facilities for intramural sports activities.

The 1,190-acre University Farm is one of the most modern and best-equipped university agricultural facilities in the West. Visitors especially enjoy the dairy, the horse unit, the livestock pens and nearby O'Neill Park.

CSU, Fresno's campus community bustles with activity. With over 200 student organizations, honor societies, fraternities and sororities, social change groups, cultural clubs and professional, vocational and recreational organizations, students have many opportunities for involvement.

In addition, the campus boasts an active student government organization, a full calendar of social and cultural events, daily and weekly student-edited newspapers and Division 1A intercollegiate athletic competition in 11 men's and seven women's sports.

CSU believes in the importance of current, specialized training that will sharpen students' knowledge.

Extracurricular activities enhance student life at CSUF.

The 75-year history of CSU, Fresno is a history of quality education. The university is committed to the comprehensive preparation of its graduates. The school believes in the importance of current, specialized training that will sharpen students' knowledge of the most recent developments in their chosen fields. CSU, Fresno also believes in the value of lifelong learning experiences, so the General Education Program offers a rich, traditional background in the arts and sciences. In short, an education at CSU, Fresno will enhance your growth in both your personal and professional pursuits.

The late Leon S. Peters, one of Fresno's foremost civic leaders, is memorialized by the new CSUF Business School Building funded in part by local business and individual donations.

An artist's rendering of the Valley Business Center Wing of the Leon S. Peters Business Building, the newest addition to the CSUF campus.

FRESNO PACIFIC COLLEGE

BUILDING FOR FRESNO'S FUTURE

Several of the students that make up the thousand-plus student enrollment at Fresno Pacific College.

Fresno Pacific College is a small, private Christian College located on 39 acres in the Southeastern section of Fresno. In the fine tradition of liberal arts education, it provides a distinctive form of value-oriented, quality higher education.

Fresno Pacific College is associated with the Mennonite Brethren Churches, offering undergraduate degrees, graduate degrees in teacher education and a variety of in-service courses for working schoolteachers.

Full-time enrollment exceeds 1,000 students with another 10,000 working schoolteachers taking in-service courses.

At Fresno Pacific College, every professor actively seeks to integrate biblical truth with his or her academic field. Many sides of a theory, idea or issue are presented and thoroughly examined, but the final authority is always God's Word.

Faculty and students alike view all truth as God's truth and apply that truth to the problems of our modern world.

Although students are ultimately responsible for discovering God's direction for their lives, Fresno Pacific faculty are uniquely qualified to assist them in that effort.

As dedicated Christians, they are living examples of lives made whole through a vibrant faith in Jesus Christ. As dedicated teachers, they are talented and highly prepared.

The superior quality of instruction is one of the reasons Fresno Pacific College is accredited by the Western Association of Schools and Colleges through the master's degree level.

Sixty percent have earned doctorates. The superior quality of their instruction is one of the reasons Fresno Pacific College is accredited by the Western Association of Schools and Colleges through the master's degree level.

Fresno Pacific faculty also act as Mentors, personal guides and counselors to help students through the sometimes complex world of college education. Each mentor advises

The arts are a vital part of student life.

Fresno Pacific faculty also act as mentors, personal guides and counselors to help students through the sometimes complex world of a college education.

about 20 students on an individual basis. There is always someone to talk to on campus. The Mentor's students also meet as a group, or collegium, forging strong bonds of friendship as they perform service projects and fellowship together. Later, when students choose their majors, they have the option of joining another collegium dedicated to the particular field of study. Friendships between students and professors are lasting ones.

Because of the college's commitment to growth and improvement of the campus, Fresno Pacific has embarked upon an ambitious $10 million building plan that includes a new cafeteria and student center, library expansion, a theater, athletic facilities, dormitories and a swimming pool.

Students have already helped to kick off the swimming pool construction project by raising $100,000. Fresno Pacific hopes to move forward soon with the new student center and dining hall that will cost an estimated $2 million.

The definition of success in our society usually means a good job that pays well. At Fresno Pacific College it means a great deal more.

Alumni believe that the education they received is among the best in the nation. At Fresno Pacific College students have everything they need to build a rewarding career and a full life that will compliment them and honor God.

However, students' academic experience is only part of their education. This is why Fresno Pacific's holistic approach to education focuses on the development of students' social, spiritual and academic needs. Fresno Pacific College believes that this is the best possible way to prepare their students to face a rapidly changing society.

Edison High School's specialized Computech program has received statewide acclaim and has proven to be immensely successful.

With over 60,000 students and gaining — at a rate of 2,000 per year — the Fresno Unified School District is the fourth largest school district in the state. District schools offer comprehensive special education, career education, adult education, community education, a complete spectrum of sports, and highly-regarded programs of computer education, fine and performing arts, and education for the gifted and talented. All this in addition to "regular" school classes that are anything but routine!

The school district serves its diverse constituency through a variety of magnet schools, alternative schools, year-round schools and special programs. It has developed comprehensive enrichment programs for students with exceptional potential and ability. Identification strategies enable these students, who rank in the top three to five percent of their age group, to be located as early as the first grade. At the time of identification, parents and guardians are encouraged to assist their students in selecting the most

NATIONAL UNIVERSITY

MEETING THE NEEDS OF MODERN ADULTS

Fresno's National University campus is designed to meet the educational needs of modern adults.

Fresno's National University campus, one of 12 in the United States and Costa Rica, is designed, like its sister institutions, to meet the educational needs of modern adults. System-wide, over 14,000 students attend National's one-month long courses in pursuit of over 100 degree programs. Fresno's students have access, at the 5140 E. Dakota Ave. site and at satellite locations, to MBA, BBA, Bachelor of Arts in Behavioral Science, M.S. in Administration, M.S. in Instructional Technology and Teacher Credentialing programs. With classes meeting in two four-hour sessions each week, plus an additional Saturday or two, students may enroll at any time for the month-long courses. Continued enrollment in the intensive classes for a period as short as 12 to 15 months may be sufficient for completion of a Master's Degree. This unusual delivery system for college and graduate programs is fully accredited by the Western Association of Schools and Colleges, signifying that the

appropriate of the Gifted and Talented Education (GATE) programs. Options range from participation in satellite part-time and multiple-grade GATE enrichment programs at several elementary schools to attending Manchester GATE School, where the entire program is geared to students in grades two through six with outstanding ability.

The SPARC program has been designed to serve young people with promise in economically disadvantaged or culturally diverse areas.

The Students with Promising Academic and Reasoning Capabilities (SPARC) program has been designed to identify and serve young people with promise in economically disadvantaged or culturally diverse areas. An outgrowth of the innovative model Migrant And Gifted Impact Center (MAGIC) program which located and provided academic enrichment to exceptionally able migrant children, SPARC promises to have substantial impact on lowering the disturbingly high drop-out rate among the poor and minorities. It is also intended to build community leadership skills so important to people of all economic and cultural backgrounds.

The Bullard Project TALENT school provides a strong and stimulating humanities-based curriculum for elementary students from throughout the district with exceptional talent and interest in the performing arts.

instructional program meets or exceeds all the standard quality requirements for university level academic instruction.

The story of National University's development is a classic marketing example of responsiveness to client need. University President David Chigos in 1969 interviewed some 2,600 business, government, industry and education leaders. These executives were asked what they hadn't liked about their own university educations, and what they disliked about the organization of their current businesses. From these survey results, the need for faculty with successful work experience, flexibility of scheduling and an academic support system emerged with great clarity. These components have become the hallmarks of National University's program, and the keys to its strength. Students can meet with counselors to plan an entire course of study at one sitting, and can enroll on any business day of the year, beginning their classes the very next month after enrollment. Schedules fit the needs of working adults, and faculty are chosen for their experience with and sensitivity to the demands of the world of work. Classrooms look like executive conference rooms, encouraging intensive student interaction around sprawling tables in seminar-style settings. Counselors and administrators are approachable — in fact, barriers, whether walls or secretaries, are consciously avoided.

Not surprisingly, this unorthodox, ultramodern university excels in high-tech educational applications as well. Two IBM mainframes allow 250,000 daily transactions by staff and students in this, the most sophisticated computerization of any educational institution anywhere. Paperwork redundancy simply doesn't exist at National University. Instead of memos and forms, enrollments, grades, veteran status for students, and the like are entered electronically. Students in the software engineering degree programs can tie into the massive NU computer with ordinary home computers and modems, bringing the power of real-world application and modern equipment to every assignment. Former Navy Commander Robert C. "Bob" White, an important part of the NU team, says "We teach tomorrow's technology today."

State-of-the-art equipment and a sense of the future help draw superior faculty to National — people who are at the top of their fields, and who enjoy an occasional chance to teach. National's unique class schedule allows such people the opportunity to teach for as short a period as one month, permitting them to schedule teaching during less demanding periods at the office. Many sign up to teach month after month, however, because they find that the stimulation keeps them sharp in their everyday world of work. In addition to these professional adjunct faculty, National has a core staff of full-time, mostly PhD-qualified faculty who develop the curriculum and select the adjunct teachers.

National University's students place great demands on the institution—expectations the school is proud to meet.

National University's students place great demands on the institution — expectations the school is proud to meet. Ninety-five percent of them have tried other educational institutions before coming to National. Unlike students in the past, they are unwilling to go to school in the daytime and settle for a deadend, part-time job in the evening. Deep in their careers, and committed to advancement in those careers, they require a university that recognizes their scheduling limitations as well as their willingness to work. National University, Fresno's innovative alternative, is meeting this need for increasing numbers of tomorrow's leaders today.

At the secondary level, ten middle schools and all high schools provide GATE academic classes. Both GATE electives and Advanced Placement (college credit) classes are available for students of exceptional ability. Some students elect participation in the Fresno City College enrichment program, which offers subjects not taught in the high schools to GATE ninth and tenth graders. The area's two magnet schools draw students of outstanding ability and interest to their specialized programs: Computech at Edison High School attracts those who are interested in mathematics and computers to its highly technological environment, while Roosevelt Performing Arts draws those interested in visual and performing arts. A third specialized high school, Duncan Polytechnic, offers an education with a vocational emphasis for students interested in career training and preparation.

The Fresno Unified School District administration is justifiably proud of the splendid array of educational options it offers the city's children. The students give their parents and the district reason for pride because of their excellent performance on the California Achievement Test (CAT), an annual evaluation of basic skills. Even with the growing

Roosevelt Performing Arts program draws students interested in the visual and performing arts.

CALIFORNIA SCHOOL OF PROFESSIONAL PSYCHOLOGY

A SOUND THEORETICAL FOUNDATION COMBINED WITH PRACTICAL TRAINING

The California School of Professional Psychology, the nation's first autonomous graduate school of professional psychology.

The California School of Professional Psychology was founded by the California State Psychological Association in 1969 as the nation's first autonomous graduate school of professional psychology. Cited in the American Psychological Association's publication the APA Monitor as "the most respected professional school in the country....the model to which all others are held" and by Robert Perloff, President of APA as a national pacesetter in professional education, CSPP leads the professional school movement.

Today it s four campuses (Berkeley, Fresno, Los Angeles and San Diego) offer an integrated program combining psychological theory, professional growth and research coursework to provide the board training that enables graduates to function effectively as practitioners and as scholars. The school currently awards nearly 12 percent of the accredited doctoral clinical psychology degrees granted annually in the United States.

CSPP Fresno was founded in 1973. The Fresno campus is

number of non-English speaking students, district scores continue to rise — particularly in mathematics. These test results are a positive indicator of the effectiveness of administration and staff in encouraging excellence in all the district's classrooms, in spite of formidable obstacles.

Outstanding performances by a number of student organizations as well as individual students also bear witness to the dedication and competence of the district's teachers and the eager involvement of its students. A Fresno High School student took first place in the 1986-87 National Forensics Voice of America — best in a field of 300,000 competitors! Another Fresno High student took second place at the National Future Business Leaders of America competition, and an Edison Computech student scored 99 percent on a national examination in German. State, regional and area

Duncan Polytechnic offers education with a vocational emphasis for students interested in career training and preparation.

The campus is dedicated to offering state of the art support to the student throughout the degree program.

housed in three buildings adjacent to downtown Fresno.

The Psychological Services Center, located across from Fresno Community Hospital, opened in September 1985 and provides needed services to the community as well as being an excellent training facility.

The youngest and smallest of the four campuses, CSPP Fresno was recognized with an American Psychological Assocation Presidential Citation of Excellence in 1979. The Journal of Rural Community Psychology, the national scholarly journal in the field, is published biannually by the campus.

CSPP Fresno's doctoral program in clinical psychology received regional accreditation by the Western Association of Schools and Colleges in 1977 and was fully approved by the American Psychological Association in 1984. In addition to training in Clinical Psychology, CSPP Fresno offers students an opportunity to gain experience in proficiency areas such as Behavioral Medicine, Child/Family Psychology and Clinical Neuropsychology.

The 212 students (185 full-time and 27 part-time) currently studying at CSPP Fresno represent 37 states and three foreign countries. The campus is enriched by the student's diverse backgrounds.

The faculty of CSPP Fresno, recruited nationally, reflect the dedication of the campus to the Ph.D. training program in professional psychology. The emphasis on excellence in both research and practical training is mirrored in the faculty. While there are a number of faculty who are engaged in private practice or employed in clinical settings, most are engaged fulltime in academic pursuits and consultation.

From its inception, CSPP has combined a solid foundation in theoretical and research coursework with an emphasis on development of professional skills. Students at CSPP build these skills through field experiences, which are an integral part of the curriculum, and through association with practicing psychologists in the fields of clinical, organizational, industrial, health and community psychology.

CSPP Fresno is committed to the philosophy that the completion of the doctoral program is a joint responsibility. Accordingly, the campus is dedicated to offering support to the student throughout the degree program. This process strengthens the learning environment on campus and prepares students for ongoing self-evaluation and personal development throughout their professional careers.

contests yield far longer lists of winners, but to the city of Fresno, its students — the hope of the future, are all winners!

Voters resoundingly voiced their approval and support of the schools and their students at the polls in 1987. At that time they voted by a margin of four to one to pass Measure A, which assures funding for urgently needed additional classrooms by releasing income derived from existing taxes for the purchase of new classrooms and for other educational uses. As many as four elementary schools will be built with these funds, and additions will be made to middle and high schools. Portable buildings will be purchased and a food processing center and maintenance years will be constructed.

Fresno's superb public schools are supplemented by a broad selection of fine private schools, such as the Fresno Christian School.

Fresno's excellent public schools are complemented by a broad selection of private schools. Most of these schools are affiliated with religious organizations, but a second group is designed to preserve the languages and traditions of particular ethnic groups. Still other schools are based upon a unique philosophy of education, while some have specific vocational emphases. From preschool through college, Fresno students have a wealth of educational opportunities available for the asking.

HEALD 4C'S BUSINESS COLLEGE

PRACTICAL TRAINING FOR THE FUTURE

The mission of Heald College is to prepare students to qualify for entry level jobs in business and industry in the shortest possible time.

Getting a good education today is just as important as it was 96 years ago when Heald 4C's Business College first opened its doors in Fresno.

The mission of Heald College is to prepare students with the knowledge and skills that enable them to qualify for entry level jobs in business and industry in the shortest possible time. Emphasis is placed on practical job-oriented instruction. Heald 4C's training is designed to develop analytical problem-solving abilities, professional conduct and the attitudes, values and habits required for success in business careers.

Heald 4C's is one of 15 schools which comprise the statewide system of Heald Business Colleges of California. Founded by Edward Payson Heald in San Francisco in August 1863, Heald Colleges have recognized the need for business

EDUCATIONAL OPTIONS

Additional educational opportunities are available to Fresno students through branch offices of other institutions. The University of San Francisco offers academic programs through the regional office of its College of Professional Studies, which offers degree programs to mid-career professionals. The evening and weekend courses lead to the BS in Organizational Behavior or Public Administration. There are also master's programs in Human Resources and Organizational Development, Administration, and Public Administration with a Health Care specialization.

The Central Valley Regional Office of the University of California offers selected continuing education, undergraduate and certificate-preparation course work. Programs include agriculture, transportation studies and business administration. In 1987, University of California at Davis Continuing Education courses became available in Fresno through the coordinating efforts of the U.C. Regional Office.

FRESNO: THE ATHENS OF CENTRAL CALIFORNIA

Fresnans have long recognized the importance of advanced education and training to sustain their position as the hub of a wealthy and economically diverse area. As Central California mushroomed at the turn of the century, higher education assumed a place of importance in the expenditure of public funds. Teachers were needed, and locals were loath to import them from the midwest. Doctors, lawyers and other professionals were in demand, and a vigorous business climate called for ever higher skill and training levels in management. In 1908, negotiations began which led to the establishment of the Fresno State Normal School in 1911. The school was so popular that its growth exceeded projections by 400 percent in the first 25 years! In the beginning, agriculture classes were required of all students, in recognition of the importance of research and training in the field which forms the economic foundation of the county.

Today, the farmer trading opinions on the stock market

Faculty and staff at 4C's take a personal interest in the individual student.

and technical employees. From the beginning, Heald emphasized quality education through practical programs designed to get its graduates the jobs they want!

Heald Colleges are accredited by the Accrediting Commission for Community and Junior Colleges of the Western Association of Schools and Colleges.

Students at Heald 4C's represent a wide range of ages. While the majority are 18-23 years old, others are between the ages of 23-60, have some college or work experience and are preparing to enter or reenter the job market.

Whatever the age or educational background of the student, the faculty and staff take a personal interest in the individual. Before and after school, faculty members offer personal guidance and assistance with classroom work and assignments on an individual basis. Classes have between 15 and 25 students, with the maximum class size limited to 36. This student-teacher ratio allows for individual attention while providing efficient classroom management and an atmosphere conducive to the exchange of ideas among teachers and students.

Instruction at 4C's reflects the realities of today's modern business environment. Programs are designed to provide each graduate with a solid background of practical applications and to produce graduates who can think on their feet and solve problems.

Individual student counseling is a hallmark of Heald Colleges. Counseling is done by the Dean and is designed to help students with their college planning, academic programming and personal problems.

Before each quarter the Dean meets with each student individually to review that student's program and projected graduation date. At this time a class schedule based on program requirements and personal needs is determined by the Dean.

The Dean and Director maintain an open-door policy for all students who at any time feel the need for help or guidance in academic or personal affairs.

Heald 4C's Business College is recognized by business, government and nonprofit organizations as an excellent resource for qualified clerical, secretarial, accounting and data processing employees. The Placement Director stays in contact with area employers and arranges job interviews for Heald graduates.

It is this environment of personal attention, practical training and dedicated job placement that has enabled Heald 4C's to consistently place over 90 percent of its graduates in business careers during the school's history in Fresno.

Classes have between 15 and 25 students, with the maximum class size limited to 36.

with his dentist at a meeting of one of the local Rotary clubs is likely to be a college graduate who relies on his advanced education in managing a vast and complex enterprise. Along with business and industry leaders, professionals and civil servants, the farmer of today understands the vital role of higher education both to the individual and as an investment in the economic health of the entire region.

Public support of higher education runs deep in Fresno. The people believe, with California State University Chancellor Ann Reynolds, that college graduates are an important community resource — a pool of economic and civic leaders who participate in community affairs, support the arts, live wholesomely and contribute significantly to an area's economic growth. So strong is this belief in Fresno that, in addition to the multifaceted university, the area is home to a variety of colleges, graduate schools, medical schools, professional schools, junior colleges, technical training centers and other post-secondary institutions. So impressive are these institutions that Fresno has been dubbed "The Athens of Central California."

(Continued on page 112)

SAN JOAQUIN COLLEGE OF LAW

ACADEMIC AND INSTRUCTIONAL EXCELLENCE

The San Joaquin College of Law combines the high caliber instruction of the major law schools with the personal atmosphere of a smaller institution.

San Joaquin College of Law offers the prestige and academic caliber of major law schools with the personable atmosphere of a smaller institution.

Outstanding local faculty, coupled with a stiff, objective grading standard, ensure competent graduates. Their success is reflected in SJCL's overall California Bar passage rate of 85 percent, and in the significant roles graduates have assumed in the legal community throughout the valley.

SJCL has been recognized as a candidate for accreditation by the accrediting commission for senior colleges and universities of the Western Association of Schools and Colleges (WASC). WASC officials indicate San Joaquin is the only California law school of its kind and size to achieve this distinction in the past decade.

WASC is an independent agency that sets and monitors standards of educational "integrity and excellence." Candidacy is granted to those schools meeting the commission's criteria for institutional quality in higher education.

San Joaquin has also been recognized by the U.S. Department of Education's Division of Eligibility and Agency Evaluation. As a result, students qualify to participate in state and federal financial aid programs.

Although SJCL has been fully accredited by the California State Bar since 1976, WASC candidacy is the first regional recognition of the school.

The school was founded in 1969 by the late Judge Dan B. Eymann and attorneys Oliver Wanger and John Loomis. It is a nonprofit, private and independent educational institution offering a law program, a paralegal training program and a graduate program in taxation. Faculty includes 41 practicing judges and attorneys who serve as part-time adjunct professors.

The founders believed legal education should combine theoretical knowledge with practical skills. From the beginning of instruction in the Fall of 1970, the school adopted the uncompromising standards essential to the achievement of this goal.

The law section is a four year evening program. Students who successfully meet academic requirements are awarded the Juris Doctor (J.D.) degree. Alumni now comprise approximately 18 percent of the Fresno County Bar.

The paralegal program is an intensive one year course of study meeting two nights weekly. Graduates receive a certificate in paralegalism. The taxation program makes continuing education courses available in addition to offering degrees of Master of Laws (LL.M.) and Master of Science (M.S.)

In 1985, San Joaquin was named Small Claims Court Advisor for Fresno County. According to the California Judicial Council, it is one of only two schools in the state to provide this community service through a clinical program.

San Joaquin has fulfilled its founders' vision of serving the community by providing highly motivated individuals the opportunity to study law.

UNIV. OF CALIFORNIA, SAN FRANCISCO

FRESNO-CENTRAL SAN JOAQUIN VALLEY MEDICAL ED. PROGRAM

The UCSF Fresno — Central San Joaquin Valley Medical Education Program was established in 1974 and provides internship and residency training, clinical clerkships for medical students and continuing education for physicians.

A LEADING UNIVERSITY MEDICAL PROGRAM

All major clinical disciplines are represented in the Fresno UCSF medical program.

Approximately 200 graduate and undergraduate medical students are studying in Fresno through the UCSF Fresno-Central San Joaquin Valley Medical Education Program.

This major clinical branch of the UCSF School of Medicine, established in 1974, provides internship and residency training, clinical clerkships for medical students and continuing education for physicians.

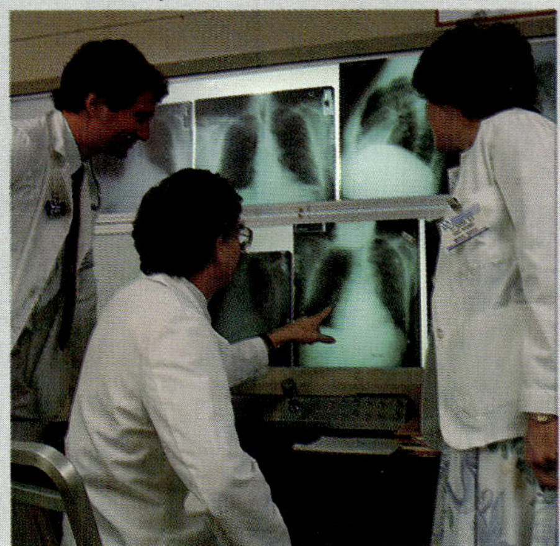

The program is regional in scope and provides unique opportunities for young physicians to prepare for careers as practitioners in rural localities.

All major clinical disciplines are represented in the Fresno program, with emphasis on primary care fields. They include: emergency medicine, family practice, internal medicine, obstetrics-gynecology, ophthalmology, pediatrics, psychiatry, radiology and surgery.

The program is regional in scope and provides unique opportunities for young physicians to prepare for careers as practitioners in rural localities, a feature commensurate with the rural characteristics of the Central Valley. Physician training is based principally in three Fresno teaching hospitals: Valley Medical Center, Veterans Administration Medical Center and Valley Children's Hospital; although some teaching takes place in health care facilities and practitioners' offices throughout the area. The Milo E. Rowell Education Building adjacent to VA Medical Center houses the program administrative offices, a regional biomedical library, research laboratories and support services.

Half of the graduating physicians in the program remain in the Central Valley to practice medicine. The program also attracts scholarly physician-scientists to the area and its continuing education programs assist practicing physicians to keep up to date.

UCSF's School of Medicine is one of the leading university medical programs in the United States.

INTERNATIONAL ENGLISH INSTITUTE

CONTRIBUTING TO WORLD UNDERSTANDING

I.E.I. was founded in 1980 to serve international students who need further language training to meet college and university entrance requirements.

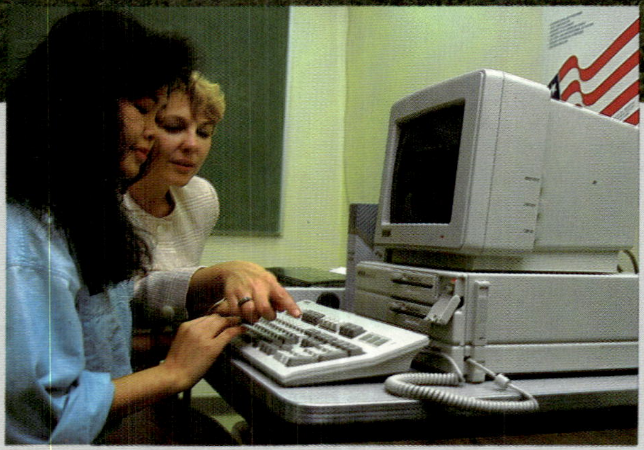

In addition to instruction in the English language, I.E.I. provides students assistance in university placement.

Cosmopolitan and friendly, Fresno is the perfect setting for the International English Institute (I.E.I.). President Anne Speake founded I.E.I. in 1980 to serve international students who need further language training to meet college and university entrance requirements. I.E.I. now serves annually hundreds of students from over 40 nations on six continents.

Seminar-size classes, with an average of 12 to 15 students, allow ample individual attention. Instructors are selected, not only for academic credentials and skill, but also for prior experience abroad or in intensive English training with international students in this country. Many hold advanced degrees and all take a personal interest in each student's progress. Students may be placed in any of ten steps of instruction for four week sessions which continue throughout the year. The College, or highest, Level is designed to refine the language skills necessary for academic success. Special courses are offered to assist students in preparing for the Test of English as a Foreign Language (TOEFL).

In addition to teaching all English language skills, I.E.I. provides assistance in university placement. Among the top-rated academic institutions which accept qualified I.E.I. graduates are the UC and CSU systems, Colorado School of Mines, Texas A&M, University of Michigan, Notre Dame, Columbia, and MIT. This is only one of many services provided by a dedicated staff of counselors and the student services director. Airport greeting, doctor's appointments, medical emergencies, DMV appointments, help with purchasing a car or bicycle, opening bank accounts, outfitting apartments for students with families, travel reservations, and an almost

Seminar class sizes at I.E.I. average about 12 to 15 students.

I.E.I is located on Shaw Avenue in close proximity to transportation and university resources.

endless list of other student needs, are dealt with daily.

To complement the year round academic program, and to serve the language interests of a wider variety of international students, I.E.I. has introduced two vacation programs. The Holiday Homestay English Program is designed for groups of ten or more. It includes three hours of intensive English instruction each day, combined with total immersion in the U.S. culture through a homestay experience with a Fresno family. Daily extra-curricular activities are planned on a seasonal basis and range from swimming and picnics to ice skating and bowling. Optional weekend trips introduce students to the recreational diversity of California. Disneyland, Yosemite National Park, and San Francisco are among the most popular choices.

The California Cultural English Program is designed for individuals who wish to combine an American vacation experience with intensive English language training. Five hours of daily instruction provide thorough training in reading, grammar, listening comprehension, writing, and conversation. This program is available in either four or eight week sessions, with graduation certificates awarded upon completion of the course.

English for the Professional and individually tailored ESP (English for Special Purposes) programs, are available to individuals, businesses, and other organizations. Short or long term courses of study in business English, English for technicians or technical professions, for agriculture, medicine, graduate study, or other uses will be prepared upon request. Among the organizations that have used the programs and services of I.E.I. are ARAMCO, Mazda, AFGRAD, Kubota Tractor, the Malaysian Ministry of Education, Dow Chemical, USA-Schulen, Saudi Arabian Airlines, Mobil Oil Indonesia, Sysorex International, BPPT Indonesia, and Japan Travel Bureau.

Enhancing the classroom experience is the Homestay Program. These "second families" open their homes and their hearts to I.E.I.'s young students, sharing meals, weekend outings, hobbies, and family activities to enrich the academic experience and build bridges of understanding. Often, lifetime friendships develop from these sharing encounters. Many of the host families, some of whom have been with I.E.I. since its beginning, express their deep satisfaction in terms that are both intensely personal and universal, for they view the arrangement as a personal contribution to world peace. For their part, the students find the Homestay Program to be a significant help to them in learning about American culture, and in feeling at home in a very short time.

The hub of all this inspirational international activity is I.E.I.'s impressive and attractive facility located at 2743 East Shaw Avenue, a short walk from the university. Proximity to bus lines provides convenient transportation for the students, and the university's library and its varied student population and activities provide an additional, readily accessible learning resource. Well placed within Fresno, and capitalizing on Fresno's central location among California's many attractions, I.E.I. has, in a few short years, attracted numerous students who have, or will have, substantial leadership roles in their home nations. The Institute's potential for and promise of contributing to world understanding is welcomed by the diverse and internationally-minded people of Fresno.

Students whose career interests require business or vocational training have their choice of more than 50 educational institutions in the Fresno area. They offer courses ranging from auto mechanics through dental assistance and electronics to hotel management and security officer training. Whether interest and aptitude lead to court reporting, travel agency operation or management training, there are schools in Fresno equipped to provide the courses necessary to prepare area residents for productive careers.

Some of Fresno's higher education institutions bring students into the community from other areas, enlivening the academic atmosphere. One such program is the Clinical Branch of the University of California at San Francisco School of Medicine, which serves medical students through overseeing their clerkships and residencies in the Fresno area. Fresno's central location made it a promising candidate

Students seeking vocational education have quality opportunities as pictured in this autobody repair class at Fresno City College.

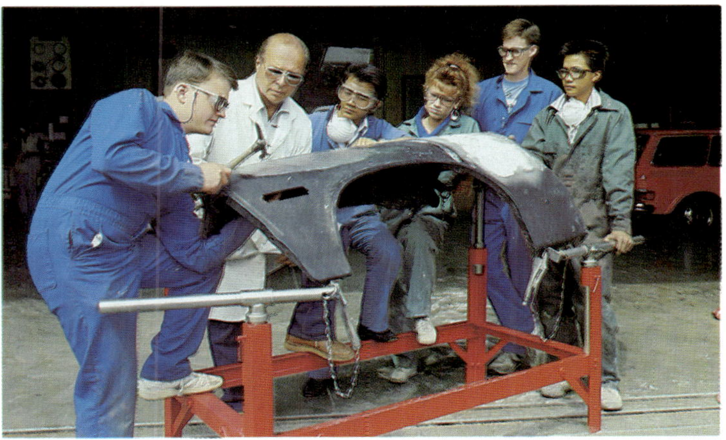

(Continued on page 115)

VALLEY CHILDREN'S HOSPITAL

ONE OF A KIND CARE FOR KIDS

Little red wagons dot the hallways and are used to cart pint-sized patients around Valley Children's.

"My two year old son has had a temperature of 104 to 105 for the past six days. He's totally lethargic and hasn't talked to us or walked in three days." That was Joy Soares' statement to the emergency room at Valley Children's Hospital one Monday evening two years ago.

"Little did I know the concerned and caring voice on the telephone was only the beginning of how Valley Children's Hospital helped me and my family cope with the nightmare we were going to experience with A.J."

"When the most precious thing in the world to you is in a life or death situation, an intense and specialized treatment is exactly what you need," said Soares.

For most people, the very thought of a child struggling to overcome an illness or handicap is emotionally wrenching at best. At Valley Children's Hospital the staff helps not only children, but also families, just like A.J.'s.

It takes a special person to work in health care and it takes some very special qualities to dedicate oneself day in and day out to the special needs of children. The challenges offered at Valley Children's Hospital have enabled the hospital to attract an extremely talented team of professionals who have committed themselves specifically to care for children.

The doctors, nurses, therapists and hospital staff at Valley Children's Hospital never forget that they are not only treating an illness, they are treating a child. Little red wagons dot the hallways and are used to transport the kids around, popsicles are used to soothe scratchy throats following surgery, specially designed playground equipment is available for both able-bodied and disabled patients, plus a playroom and a special wing for teen-age patients.

Long gone are the days when a critically ill or severely injured child had to be rushed to San Francisco or Los Angeles. Today valley children are transported from as far north as Modesto and as far south as Bakersfield. To the east the Bishop, Mammoth Lakes area and to the west Santa Maria and San Luis Obispo, are served.

Valley Children's critical care transport vans help bring children to their future. With the mobile transport vans and

Educational needs of the young patients are also met at Valley Children's.

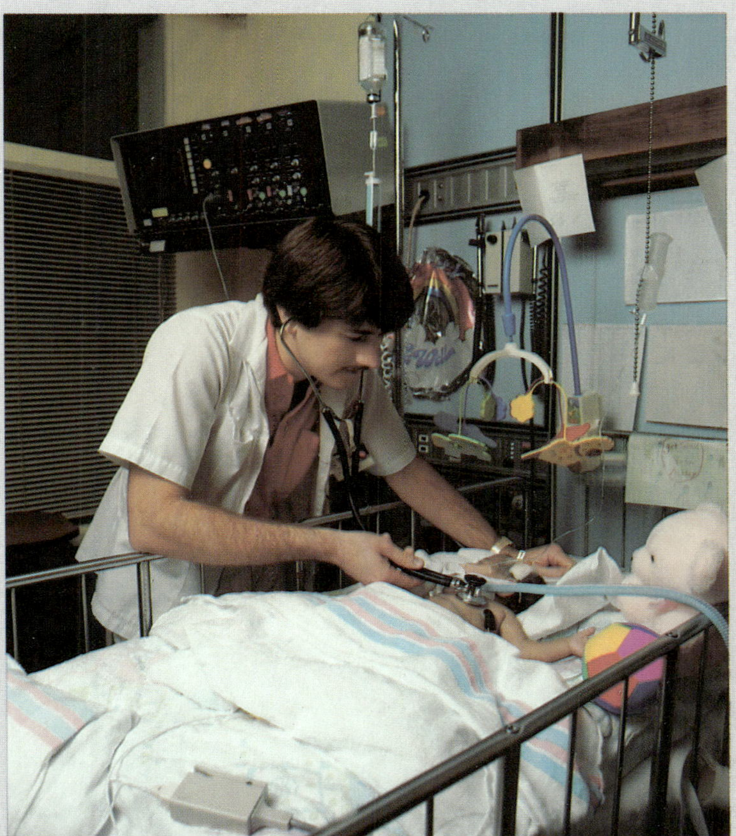

The challenges offered at Valley Children's have enabled the hospital to attract an extremely talented team of professionals who have committed themselves specifically to the care of children.

highly trained transport teams that staff them, location isn't a big factor for a premature or critically injured child. Children in the outlying communities now have the same chance as a child who may just be across the street from the hospital.

It has taken over 30 years of love and dedication to bring this type of hospital to the children of the San Joaquin Valley. Women throughout the valley got together and formed the guilds of Valley Children's Hospital, which are now 18 strong with over 1,500 members. From small towns to big towns they formed an underlying network of support in the Central Valley. Like the roots that nourish the crops of the valley, the guilds helped nurture the dream of building a children's hospital.

It's kids like A.J. who benefit from the fruits of that labor, love and commitment. A.J. was diagnosed as having Kawasaki Syndrome, a rare disease that affects the arteries of the heart. He is now doing just fine. "Only four months later and our little boy is back to normal," said Soares.

Without the care, understanding and love given to not only our child, but to us, the family, it would be hard to cope with the reality of the situation."

As Soares said, "Valley Children's provides the 'extra' needed element to make it through the difficult times. It's not just a hospital, it's a very special family-oriented health care facility."

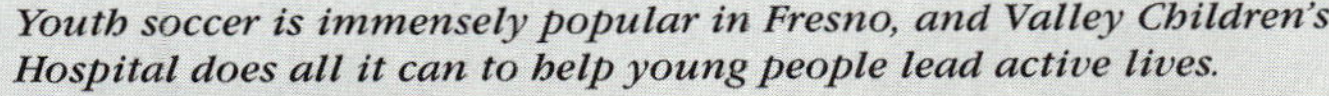

Youth soccer is immensely popular in Fresno, and Valley Children's Hospital does all it can to help young people lead active lives.

"Sunny" the California Bowl mascot, entertains youngsters. Proceeds from the California Bowl go to Valley Children's Hospital.

DE MERA DE MERA CAMERON

A PROFESSIONAL ACCOUNTANCY CORPORATION

DeMera, DeMera, Cameron Professional Accountancy services clients in many diverse fields.

for establishment of the additional medical school envisioned by the state legislature ten years ago. This new facility would be open to students not served by the existing campuses at Davis, San Francisco and Los Angeles. Although these expansion plans were abandoned, the need to work with medical patients remained. Thus the Clinical Branch was developed as a compromise solution.

Some 120 to 190 undergraduates a year serve their clerkships of four to eight weeks in Fresno County, where many gain valuable rural experience. In addition, 150 residents serve three to five years working at Valley Medical Center and the Veterans Administration Hospital in Fresno, using their newly developed skills and postgraduate training to benefit patients at those facilities.

HEALTH CARE

Fresno's citizens lead vigorous lives, taking full advantage of the athletic and recreational opportunities which abound in the area. These active lifestyles are supported and extended by the sophisticated network of accessible health care

The Veterans Administration Hospital in Fresno has a 275 bed capacity.

The firm stands ready to assist clients with business planning, personnel evaluation, financing, computer system selection and implementation, and many other forms of management advisory services.

The growth of the public accounting practice of De Mera De Mera Cameron has paralleled the growth of the Fresno business community. Just as Fresno's businesses have grown in numbers, size and complexity, so too has the certified public accounting firm of De Mera De Mera Cameron.

In 1949, the late James V. De Mera Sr. founded the firm with the opening of his office in the "Brix" building in downtown Fresno. In so doing, he demonstrated his confidence in the vitality and growth of the Fresno area and its businesses. That confidence has been more than justified over the past 38 years.

Today, De Mera De Mera Cameron is one of the largest public accounting firms in the Fresno area.

The firm's well educated and motivated staff of certified public accountants and support personnel are true business advisors. The firm's clients and numerous community and church organizations benefit from the staffs' professionalism and dedication. The owners and many employees of De Mera De Mera Cameron serve in positions of leadership in a wide variety of civic, philanthropic and arts organizations in Fresno.

The company's current shareholders, Howard J. De Mera, Mark D. Cameron, John B. Houlihan, John A. Renna, R.M. "Tripp" Pound III, James Hering II and Craig M. Horn are members of the American Institute of Certified Public Accountants and the California Society of CPA's. All of them are recognized as professional and community leaders.

In addition to providing tax, auditing and accounting services, the firm assists clients with business planning, personnel evaluation, financing, computer system selection and implementation and many other forms of management advisory services.

De Mera De Mera Cameron services clients in many diverse industries. These fields include medical and dental practices, construction, agriculture, finance, real estate, automobile agencies, manufacturing companies, convalescent homes, nonprofit organizations, retail outlets, restaurants, fast food franchises, trucking firms and a number of service industries.

As has been the case since its inception, the firm is committed to providing outstanding client service, and is equally committed to improving the city in which its people live and work.

This physical therapist at Saint Agnes is typical of the many health care professionals in Fresno.

facilities. Of the 69,208 licensed physicians in California in 1985, 1,159 practiced their trade in Fresno County. The Fresno-Madera Dental Society estimates that nearly 400 dentists serve the region. In addition to licensed physicians and dentists, there are hundreds of other health care professionals in the valley, including chiropractors, optometrists, pharmacists, physical therapists, psychologists, nurses and the many veterinarians who serve the health care needs of pets and livestock. Allied health care professionals include lab and x-ray technicians, convalescent and nursing home attendants, health maintenance organizations and other third party health care insurer employees, all of whom make substantial contributions to the area's economy and vitality.

The range of medical facilities is equally broad, encompassing several full service hospitals as well as specialized sports injury treatment facilities, psychiatric hospitals, women's health centers, eye clinics and walk-in treatment facilities. In many of these facilities, as in nearly all the medical clinics in outlying county areas, care givers

CENTRAL CALIFORNIA FACULTY MEDICAL GROUP

QUALITY MEDICAL EDUCATION AND PATIENT CARE PROGRAMS

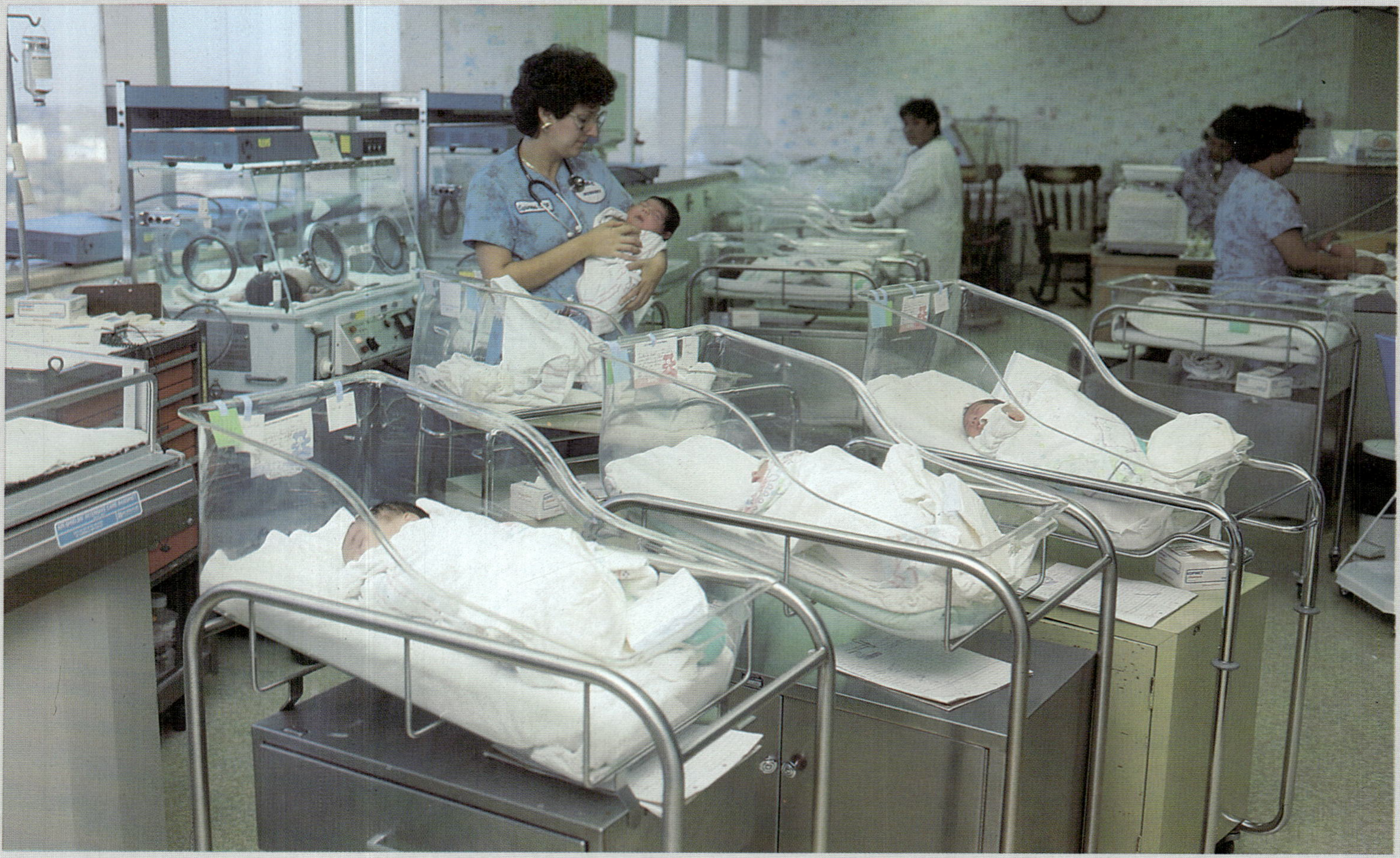

Pediatrics is just one of several health care services available through the Central California Faculty Medical Group.

The Central California Faculty Medical Group is the only organization of its kind in the central San Joaquin Valley. It is a professional corporation founded in 1979 with two purposes: to provide quality health care at an affordable cost to people in the Fresno/Clovis community, and to advance the state of medical knowledge and technology.

CCFMG is made up of more than 100 dedicated physicians, many of whom provide patient care at the Family Practice Health Centers and the Multi-Specialty Center. The centers are designed to offer a complete range of health care services at single locations, in the comfortable setting of private doctors' offices.

communicate their concern in Spanish as well as in English, and the use of Asian dialects is becoming increasingly common.

When Dr. Lewis Leach built the first county hospital of poles, thatch and willow matting, his compassionate care included both soldiers and Indians who sustained injuries in the Indian Wars. That tradition of compassion, acceptance and service continues unabated. The only difference is that its delivery system is now a multi-million dollar industry with a technological sophistication Dr. Leach and his patients could not have imagined in 1870.

VALLEY MEDICAL CENTER

Fresno County's inpatient and outpatient medical care facility is the 417-bed Valley Medical Center. The principal teaching hospital in the Central Valley since 1921, VMC serves as the base hospital for the University of California's San Francisco School of Medicine. Residents serve in emergency medicine, family practice, internal medicine,

VMC residents serve in emergency medicine, family practice, internal medicine, obstetrics and gynecology, ophthalmology, pediatrics, general dentistry and oral surgery.

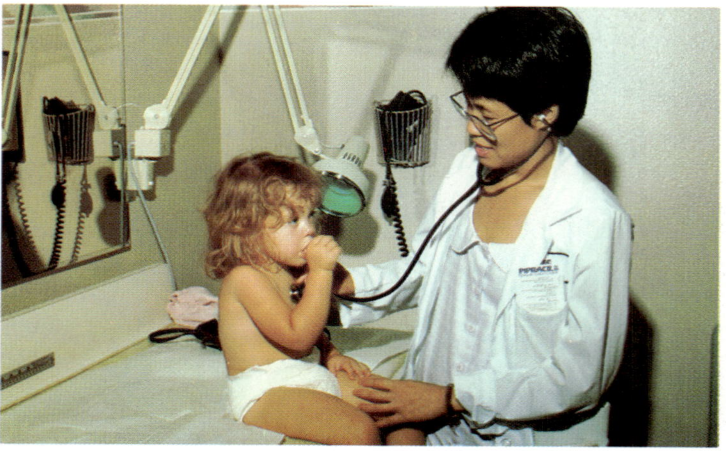

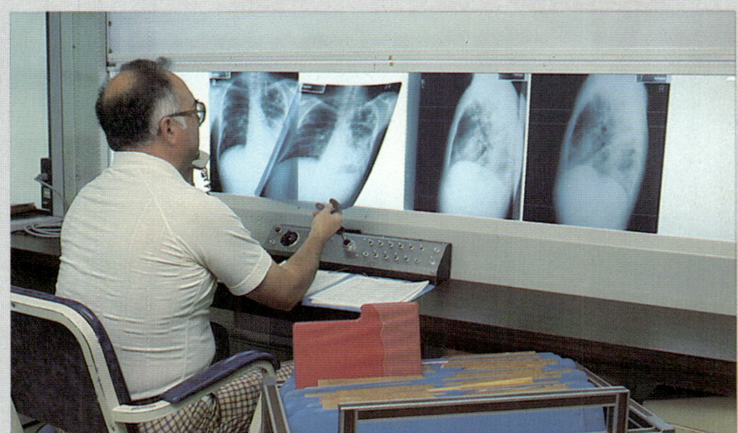

The 8,300 square foot CCFMG Multi-Specialty Center has private exam rooms, full x-ray and lab facilities, and is equipped to handle many outpatient and surgical procedures.

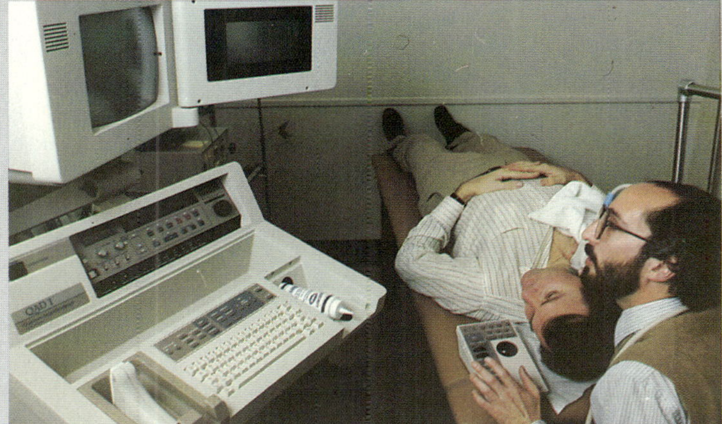

The Multi-Specialty Center is staffed by physicians representing all of the major medical specialties.

Other physicians of CCFMG practice full-time at Valley Medical Center and comprise the faculty group that provides instruction to medical students and post graduate trainees affiliated with the University of California, San Francisco. CCFMG conducts residencies in nine departments at VMC. CCFMG faculty physicians are unique in that they are involved both in research and in patient care. Because of this involvement, people in this community benefit from skills and technology that are not available even in many of the country's largest cities. For example, CCFMG and VMC recently introduced the Duplex Scanner; a state of the art diagnostic tool, and one of only eight such instruments in the world.

In order to make specialty care available to more people in the community, CCFMG developed the Multi-Specialty Center, located in the heart of Fresno. The center is a unique, single-location facility staffed by physicians representing all of the major medical specialties. The 8,300 square foot center has private exam rooms, full x-ray and lab facilities, and is equipped to handle many outpatient surgical procedures. Like the Family Practice Health Centers, the Multi-Specialty Center is warm, friendly and comfortable.

The CCFMG Multi-Specialty Center offers the most complete range of specialty services, absolutely unmatched by any similar single-location facility in the community.

There are two CCFMG Family Practice Health Centers located in Fresno and Clovis. Both are staffed by experienced family practice physicians and are well-equipped to handle a multitude of illnesses and injuries. All kinds of people are helped; from newborn babies to senior citizens, and all of the doctors encourage a strong physician-patient relationship. Patient-families have their "own" doctors, and visits take place in the doctors' private offices.

Patients can be seen at all CCFMG facilities and admitted to any area hospital. CCFMG physicians maintain privileges at all area hospitals so that should the need arise, patients can be cared for at the best equipped facility nearest the patient's home.

In addition to being unique to the central San Joaquin Valley, CCFMG is assuming a leadership role in the way you receive and pay for your health care. CCFMG is creating alternatives that conveniently meet your medical needs and allow you more control over your health care costs.

CCFMG has a commitment to health care and the community.

No one can predict what the future holds. CCFMG knows that the preservation of quality in medical care will not happen by accident. Caring for people is what CCFMG is all about. Every patient care program and every research project is centered on your needs. CCFMG, the doctors who practice what they teach.

VMC's Primary Care Center provides specialized medical assistance in internal medicine, obstetrics, gynecology and pediatrics.

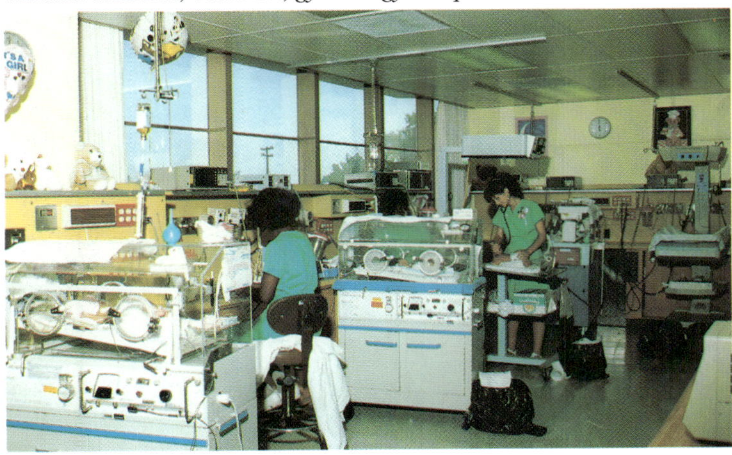

obstetrics and gynecology, ophthalmology, pediatrics, general dentistry and oral surgery. Additional training programs expand available staff in psychiatry, radiology and other therapeutic programs.

Valley Medical Center's Emergency Department is among the state's ten busiest, and its specialized Intensive Care Units meet the needs of patients of all ages. Specialized services are available for patients from throughout the San Joaquin Valley through the regional Level I Trauma Center, Burn Center, Sexual Assault Center and Dialysis Center. The Woman's Choices program provides education and medical guidance for area women, and the Heart Care Center provides consultation as well as inpatient and ambulatory services. The Primary Care Center, located on the northeast corner of the 80-acre VMC campus, provides gateway services and specialized medical assistance in internal medicine, obstetrics, gynecology and pediatrics.

(Continued on page 126)

COMMUNITY HOSPITALS OF CENTRAL CALIF.

A HERITAGE OF CARING, COMMITMENT TO THE FUTURE

Pictured is the modern Fresno Community Hospital.

In the late 1890's, a strong, caring woman, Mrs. Celia Burnett, began a boarding house located in the southeast corner of what is now Fulton and Calaveras in Fresno. Her house was occupied by single men who had left their families to travel west in search of their fortunes. Whenever these boarders would become ill, Mrs. Burnett would take the role of nurse and, with her skill and caring, return the men to health.

Mrs. Burnett's small enterprise evolved into Fresno Community Hospital and Medical Center which affiliated in 1982 with Sierra Hospital Foundation to create Community Hospitals of Central California (CHCC), the San Joaquin Valley's largest health care provider. CHCC employs more than 3,600 people and maintains over 900 beds. Eight hundred volunteers give their time and effort to aid in providing quality health care.

Throughout the years central San Joaquin Valley residents have come to expect the best from CHCC. When a service is needed, CHCC was the first to develop and deliver it. For example, Sierra Hospital Foundation recognized area residents' need for convalescent care and in 1967 pioneered the concept of acute-care-hospital affiliated convalescent care.

Other outstanding examples of such service are ARC (A Recovery Center for people with chemical dependencies), Renaissance Adolescent Center (for young people with chemical dependencies), In Vitro Fertilization (for couples who are unable to have children on their own), the Neurological Retraining Center (for the ongoing treatment of people with head injuries), Insight: Employee Assistance Program (intervention and short term counseling to help people resolve problems), Eating Disorders (inpatient and outpatient services for people suffering from anorexia, bulimia and compulsive eating) and CareFinder (a physician and health care telephone referral number).

An architectural model depicts the future Clovis Community Hospital.

Sierra Community Hospital has made a name for itself by providing unsurpassed excellence in orthopedic surgical procedures.

Each Community Hospitals of Central California acute care facility has developed a special health care expertise. At Fresno Community Hospital and Medical Center, the Leon S. Peters Rehabilitation Center offers the most comprehensive spectrum of rehabilitation services in the central valley. Sierra Community Hospital has created a name for itself because of its unsurpassed excellence in orthopedic surgical procedures.

Soon Clovis will be able to boast that, in the new Clovis Community Hospital, it has one of the most modern and attractive facilities in the state. Plus, CHCC hospitals help bring more new Fresno County life into the world than any other area health care provider with over 5,500 babies delivered annually.

In addition to programs, CHCC has introduced the community to the latest in medical technology. Mobile Magnetic Resonance Imaging was brought to town by a joint venture with another local hospital. Also, the open heart program has been enhanced by the new cardiac catheterization laboratories at Fresno Community Hospital and Medical Center which allow patients to undergo complex procedures with minimum discomfort.

Maintaining the personal touch for which Clovis Community Hospital, Fresno Community Hospital and Medical Center and Sierra Communtiy Hospital have become well-known is a CHCC priority. At the same time, an eye is kept on the future. Determined to honor its long-standing commitment to provide the finest, most caring and up-to-date health care in affordable ways, CHCC will continue to seek ways to contain costs without sacrificing quality.

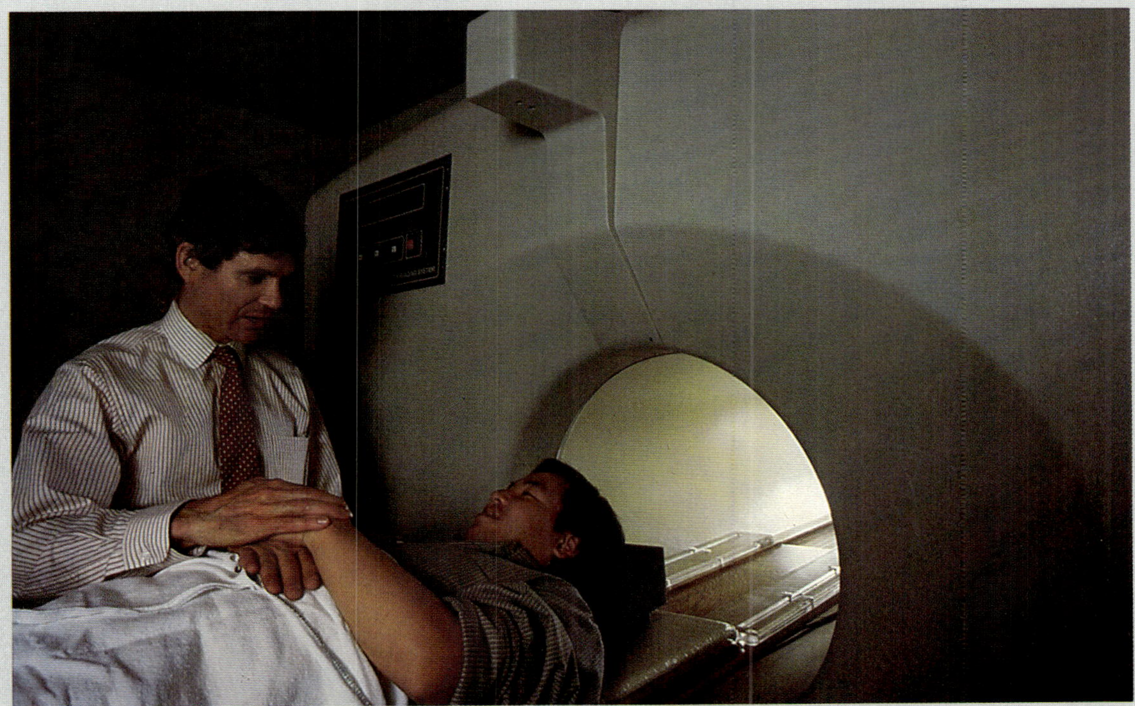

Pictured above is a superb example of major hospitals in partnership as Community Hospitals of Central California and Saint Agnes Medical Center join in providing state of the art diagnostic technology. Through shared usage of this magnetic resonance imager, which is housed in a mobile unit and shuttles between Fresno Community Hospital and Saint Agnes Medical Center, Central Valley residents have access to the very finest medical diagnostic equipment.

KAISER PERMANENTE

"GOOD PEOPLE – GOOD MEDICINE"

The Fresno offices of Kaiser Permanente are part of the nation's largest private medical care program.

The Kaiser Permanente Medical Care Program evolved from the vision of two men. Dr. Sidney Garfield and industrialist Henry J. Kaiser created the first prepaid health care program for construction, shipyard and steel workers in the late 1930s and early 1940s. In 1945, the medical program was opened to the general public on a voluntary basis. Mr. Kaiser prophetically claimed he would be remembered chiefly for his health care program.

Today, Kaiser Permanente is the nation's largest private medical care program. Over five million people nationwide are members of the Kaiser Foundation Health Plan. Over 5500 physicians work for The Permanente Medical Group, the largest group practice in the world.

Several things make Kaiser's approach to medicine unique. First, the plan operates on a prepaid basis, so it's in Kaiser's best interest to help its Health Plan members stay healthy. Kaiser does this by emphasizing health promotion and preventive care.

Second, Kaiser Permanente believes an individual has the right to choose among several health plans to determine which one suits his needs. When the size of the group permits, Kaiser is offered only if employees have a selection of at least one other plan.

Kaiser's program has always been nonprofit. Ninety-seven cents of every premium dollar is spent directly on patient care.

Kaiser's approach to medical care attracts highly qualified physicians. As members of this unique group practice, Permanente physicians can devote all their professional time to caring for patients. Some also teach residents and medical students, and conduct medical research.

Each Permanente physician in Fresno must become board certified within three years, which means the physician must complete strict requirements for training and knowledge established by medical boards. People who join the Kaiser plan are encouraged to select one of these doctors to be their personal physician and oversee all their medical care.

Walt Puhn

Quality health care allows Fresno residents to take advantage of outdoor recreation as shown here at Shaver Lake.

Dr. Eugene Gilpin, one of Kaiser's fine cadre of physicians.

Kaiser physicians can opt to devote all their time to the care of patients, or they can elect to teach residents and conduct research.

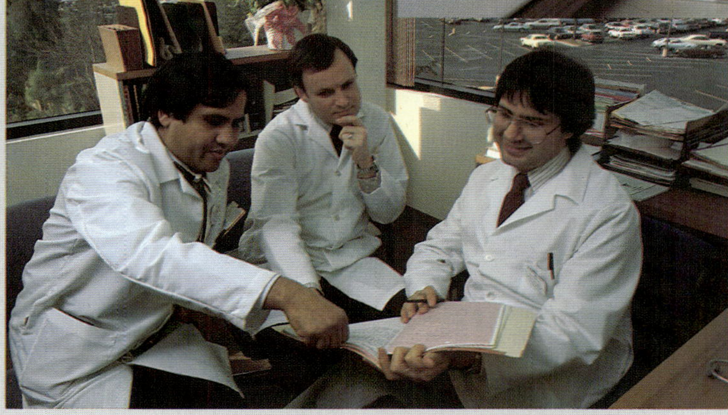

As a major employer in California, Kaiser Permanente believes it has a responsibility to play an active role in communities. Kaiser physicians and employees are encouraged to join professional organizations, and to serve in their choice of civic groups and local agencies.

One community program made possible by Kaiser Permanente is Professor Bodywise's Traveling Menagerie. This award-winning theatrical performance of costumed characters entertains and educates school children about the importance of healthy lifestyles.

Kaiser Permanente believes good health habits and quality medical care enhance life for everyone in the community. Kaiser sponsors health education classes for both its members and the general public.

Kaiser Permanente is excited to bring to Fresno its 40-plus tradition of reasonably priced, quality medical care.

Walt Puhn

The benefits of good community health care can be seen at an early age as Fresno's PeeWee Baseballers exhibit their skills.

GARY TIMAN VIGEN, AIA AND ASSOC., INC.

DIFFERENT BY DESIGN

An award-winning firm, Gary Timan Vigen, AIA and Associates, performs quality architectural planning and design services throughout the central valley.

Established in 1980, the firm is one of the fastest growing in the area. Its commitment to the community is reflected in visually-pleasing, landmark-quality buildings that complement the environment, the firm's participation in Preview Fresno, and Mr. Vigen's chairmanship of Fresno's Urban Design Task Force sub-committee addressing hi-rise issues.

McDonald's on Shaw Avenue.

Innovative detailing is exhibited in the architecture of Motion Designs.

Vigen and Associates combines in-depth experience with a client-focused approach that results in innovative, fully-integrated and purposeful designs for industrial, commercial, retail, office, civic, educational, and religious facilities.

A hallmark of the firm's expertise is Vigen and Associates' sensitivity to space, structure, and economies that fully satisfy the client's needs, as evidenced by numerous diverse projects that include: the corporate headquarters of Motion Designs, the new facilities for Blackstone Bowl, expansion of Grundfos Pumps regional offices in Clovis, the award-winning McDonald's 30th Anniversary restaurant, the United States Postal facility at Woodward Park, and the Wine Press Shopping Center.

Vigen and Associates' performance is characterized by attention to detail, through the use of high-level CAD/D systems (computer-aided drafting and design), time-and-cost control systems, budget management, and personal monitoring of all work in progress.

Vigen and Associates' many projects throughout the community exemplify excellence in architectural planning and design whether for new facilities, current or future expansions, efficiencies in work or traffic flow, or expression of a corporate identity. Committed to architectural expressions that exceed expectations, Gary Timan Vigen, AIA and Associates is.....#1.

HCA CEDAR VISTA HOSPITAL

COMPASSION AND QUALITY CARE

Activity therapy is just one of the services offered to patients of HCA Cedar Vista Hospital.

Located in one of Fresno's fastest growing areas and centers for total health care is Cedar Vista Hospital, a Hospital Corporation of America (HCA) affiliate. The new 60-bed facility on Cedar Avenue, just north of Herndon, provides easy access and convenience for patients and their families as well as the professional community.

Cedar Vista Hospital is divided into specialty treatment units tailored to meet the individual needs of children, adolescents and adults experiencing a broad range of psychiatric disorders and emotional problems. Among the services available to patients are individual therapy, daily structured programs which provide therapeutic community, interaction, group and family therapy, activity therapy and after-care planning.

Because the quality of care delivered can be no better than the people charged with providing it, Cedar Vista, through the HCA Network, maintains a strong commitment to the recruiting, training and development of management and clinical professionals. When staffing, HCA seeks the most highly skilled personnel available and devotes tremendous energy to fostering the professional growth of each individual.

The hospital is accredited by the Joint Commission on Accreditation of Hospitals, JCAH, and recognized as a health care provider by Federal Medicare and Champus programs. The hospital is affiliated with the National Association of Private Psychiatric Hospitals, the American and California Hospital Associations and the Hospital Council of Central California.

The demonstrated excellence that has fostered the HCA psychiatric facilities' impressive record provides the foundation for facing the health care challenges of tomorrow. Looking ahead to meet the needs of the residents of Fresno and its surrounding communities will continue to be the highest priority for Cedar Vista Hospital.

A healthy mind and body come together as this youngster studies during his Sierra camping opportunity with Northwest Church.

SAINT AGNES MEDICAL CENTER

LEADING THE WAY

Saint Agnes Medical Center serves the health care needs of the valley with a medical staff of over 800 physicians, 1,800 employees, and more than 500 active volunteers.

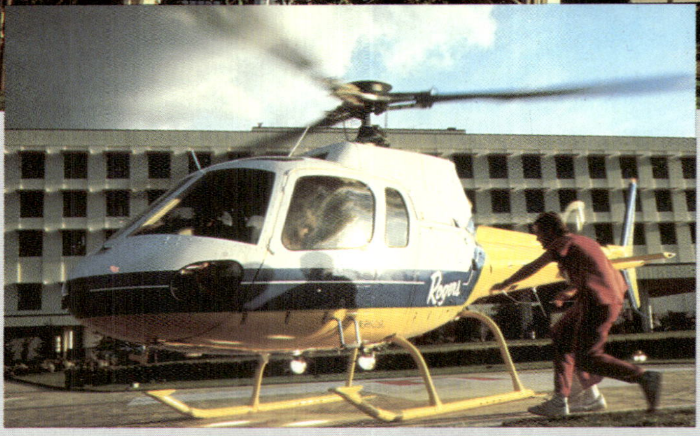

The medical center's 24-hour emergency department provides expert care in life threatening situations as well as for minor cuts and sprains.

The Sisters of the Holy Cross made a commitment to serve Fresno when they founded Saint Agnes Hospital in 1929. The hospital quickly built a reputation for modern treatment, and attracted a staff whose attitude was especially caring and sensitive.

That reputation has grown over the years, just as the commitment to the valley community shows in everything Saint Agnes does. Today Saint Agnes Medical Center serves the health care needs of the valley with a medical staff of 800 physicians, 1,800 employees and more than 500 active volunteers.

From the most advanced microsurgery to the most tender care for newborns, Saint Agnes provides the care you need. Both outpatient and inpatient surgical care are provided. Surgery is performed in modern facilities fully equipped with the most sophisticated medical technology available.

The Medical Center's maternity facilities provide optimum comfort and support for mother, baby and loved ones. Complete medical backup is available for high risk and caesarian deliveries, and neonatal intensive care is provided by Valley Children's Hospital, right in Saint Agnes Medical Center.

The Medical Center's 24-hour emergency department provides expert care in life threatening situations as well as for cuts and sprains. Physicians, nurses and technicians are trained and experienced in emergency procedures, and are supported by the latest medical technology.

In addition, Saint Agnes provides special health services, wellness programs and outreach activities.

The medical center's maternity facilities provide optimum comfort and support for mother, baby, and loved ones.

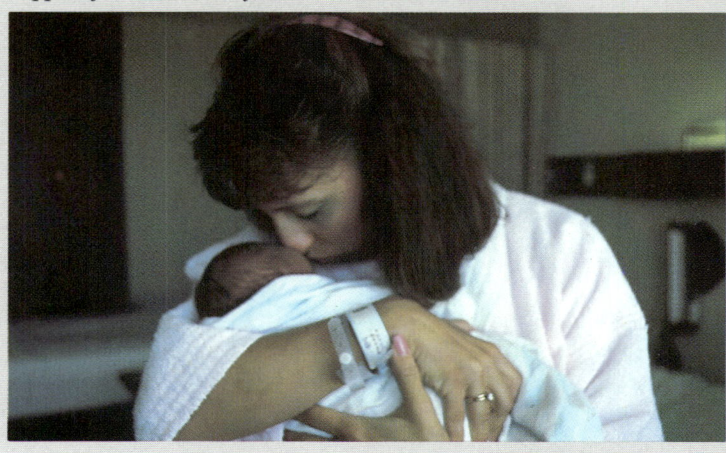

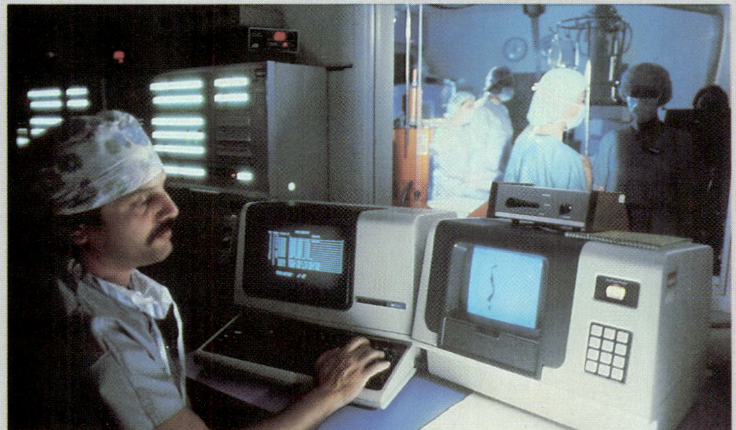

Staff at Saint Agnes is supported by the latest medical technology.

The Sports Medicine Center at Saint Agnes offers expert diagnosis and treatment of sports-related injuries, plus physical therapy and counseling in nutrition, fitness and weight management.

The Breast Imaging Center is the only facility in the valley to offer both low-dose x-ray and ultrasound mammography in one location. The center makes possible the early detection of breast cancer.

The California Eye Institute at Saint Agnes is nationally recognized as not only a center for routine eye care but also a center for sophisticated vision care and education including cataract treatment, lens implants, radial keratotomy, microsurgery and laser surgery.

Saint Agnes is also dedicated to community involvement. Three programs illustrate this commitment. The Hospice of Fresno at Saint Agnes serves the needs of terminally ill patients, their families and friends. The Holy Cross Center for Women serves as a shelter for women and their children and a health clinic at the Poverello House is operated by Saint Agnes.

Every year more than 100,000 people are served by Saint Agnes. That's 20 percent of the population of Fresno. Saint Agnes Medical Center is leading the way to a healthier tomorrow.

THE BUSINESS OF LAW

The imposing towers of the Fresno County Courthouse call attention to the hub of legal activity for the city and county. As Central California's regional service center, Fresno is home to one of six appellate district courts. A small army of attorneys, clerks, peace officers and support staff are engaged in carrying out all aspects of the legal activities of the Fifth Appellate District Court of Appeals, located in the State Office Building, as well as the rigorous schedules of the Municipal, Superior and Federal District Courts. Justice Courts located at eight rural sites provide access to the judicial system for county residents from the foothills to the Coalinga oil country.

Municipal Courts serve the greater metropolitan area, including Clovis. The 12 judicial positions in these courts are filled by ten elected judges, whose unexpired terms may be filled by gubernatorial appointment, and one referee and one commissioner who assist with the mounting case loads. The traffic referee may hear matters pertaining to traffic infractions or small claims, and the court commissioner may hear all cases heard by district judges, with the exception of felonies.

SOMPH photo

The Fresno County Sheriff's building, an integral part of the area's criminal justice system.

(Continued on page 129)

WILD, CARTER, TIPTON & OLIVER

FRESNO'S OLDEST LAW FIRM

Wild, Carter, Tipton and Oliver was founded over 90 years ago and remains Fresno's oldest law firm

Founded in 1893, the law firm of Wild, Carter, Tipton & Oliver has provided legal services to a wide range of clients throughout Central, Northern and Southern California. Even as it prepares to address legal issues which will affect clients in the 21st century, the firm is proud that it maintains a number of client relationships begun by the firm's founders over 90 years ago.

Wild, Carter, Tipton & Oliver has grown to become a full service professional law corporation with a highly specialized staff of attorneys. In addition to general business law and litigation, the firm offers its clients expertise in tax, estate planning and administration, probate and probate litigation, real estate law, agricultural law and financing arrangements.

The firm prides itself on a careful and thoughtfully controlled growth pattern that ensures a close professional relationship with each of its clients. They approach client problems with the belief that by working closely with the clients, effective solutions to legal problems, compatible with the client's goals, can be achieved.

Wild, Carter, Tipton & Oliver believes that the best way for the client to win in court is often to avoid being there. As potential litigation matters are explored, alternative approaches are thoroughly reviewed. If litigation is required, the litigation staff acts in a coordinated manner to aggressively pursue the client's interest.

Real property law constitutes a significant area of practice and expertise at Wild, Carter, Tipton & Oliver. They have developed a solid reputation with bankers, agricultural interests, commercial and industrial developers, property owners and managers for dealing effectively with a wide range of real property matters.

Left to right — G. Dana French, William H. Leifer, Bruce M. Brown.

A commitment to effective "preventative law" is an important facet of the firm's work. They have developed comprehensive programs and seminars which have been presented throughout California to help owners and managers of commercial and residential property anticipate and prevent potential legal problems. The firm also works with clients' marketing and sales departments to create a sensitivity to pricing and fair trade issues, and with personnel departments to minimize unnecessary conflicts with employees.

Wild, Carter, Tipton & Oliver provides significant counsel to financial institutions, property owners and creditors regarding the structuring of acquisitions and sales, exchanges, leases, debt work, work-outs, zoning, planned unit developments and syndications.

The firm has made a commitment to the community. The attorneys who comprise the firm enjoy a well earned reputation as civic leaders. They are involved in many volunteer and charitable activities, including the Metropolitan Museum of Fresno, Fresno Arts Center, Fresno Zoo Society, Saint Agnes Hospital & Medical Center, Rotary Clubs, KMPH-Public Television, and various churches and synagogues. By giving back a portion of the many good things which have come to the firm, Wild, Carter, Tipton & Oliver believes it is contributing to the continued viability and quality of life of the community.

The business of law continues to change dramatically. At Wild, Carter, Tipton & Oliver the firm's commitment is to adapt to changes in the law and society and to create progressive and unique solutions to the clients legal and business needs regardless of the sophistication or technical nature of the issue. With this philosophy, the firm looks forward to the same success in the next hundred years that it has enjoyed to date.

Left to right — Robert H. Oliver, Robert G. Carter, Jack M. Tipton, M. Bruce Wild.

Fresno-based public television station Channel 18 pictured here has been well supported by the firm of Wild, Carter, Tipton and Oliver as well as thousands of other valley businesses and individuals.

KMTF Channel 18 is the public broadcasting station serving the Central San Joaquin Valley. KMTF is operated by a non-profit corporation, KMTF Channel 18, Inc. Channel 18 provides 100% of the public broadcasting programming to the residents of the Central Valley and each year, in May, airs the "Great TV Auction" where thousands of merchants provide goods and services to be auctioned off to support the Station. At the same time, some 1,200 Valley residents volunteer their energies for the seven-day event. This, along with the pledge drives and many other activities, keeps Channel 18 on the air.

The four departments of the Municipal Court decide civil and criminal matters ranging from small claims and traffic infractions to major crimes or felonies.

From 15 to 20 percent of the cases heard in Municipal Court are appealed to Superior Court. The 16 Superior Court judges are the court of first hearing for all felonies, civil claims in excess of $25,000, divorces, probates and child custody matters. The Fifth District Appellate Court and the U.S. District Court provide yet other levels of judicial expertise and leadership.

There were 1,136 licensed attorneys in Fresno County in 1986. The California State Bar monitors the activities of all attorneys and reviews their preparation for professional practice. The Committee of Bar Examiners, a component of the State Bar, administers the licensure examination. The Bar monitors all ethics and discipline issues, acting as a review committee of peers when questions of propriety arise. The Bar also has the responsibility of accrediting law schools within the state to ensure that training meets its high standards.

Several linking agencies assist citizens in gaining access to qualified legal assistance in time of need. Legal aid services are available through several sources in the county, and the Bar Association provides referrals from among its members.

Each of these fields — education, health and the law — represents a growing sector of the national economy, as well as a vital factor in the development of Fresno County. The monetary value of health care, for example, is expected to more than double by 1990, reaching a national total of $760 billion a year. The strength of the health care sector is important not only in providing citizen access to ever more amazing treatment capabilities, but also to the economic well-being of the entire region. Physicians, like educators and attorneys, tend to be productive, informed and committed community leaders. The Fresno area is fortunate to include a solid base of these service sectors, and can look forward to continuing high levels of productivity in these crucial arenas.

A light fog settles over a panoramic stretch of rural Fresno County.

STOUGHTON DAVIDSON

ACCOUNTING FOR OUR GROWTH

Since Stoughton Davidson was founded in 1924, Fresno has grown from a relatively quiet farming region into a populated, metropolitan hub of commerce that is capable of attracting and servicing international and regional business.

Reflecting the growth of the city and county of Fresno, the accountancy corporation of Stoughton Davidson has moved to keep pace — and remain in step — with the times. As a local leader in the accounting profession, the firm has evolved to service more completely the needs of the region and has developed a broad range of up-to-date accounting, auditing, tax, consulting and management services.

What has not changed since the early days is Stoughton Davidson's commitment to providing services that extend beyond the traditional accounting firm. At the same time, the scope of expertise has grown to help clients meet the challenges of financing operations, managing information, tax planning, computerization and coping with a variety of other specialized industry and systems demands. Through diversified capabilities, extensive experience, on-going education and involvement in community service and professional organizations, the company's professionals can continue to better serve clients' immediate and long-range needs.

For six decades, Stoughton Davidson has anticipated and met many exciting challenges and opportunities by serving businesses of all sizes in a wide variety of industries; from agriculture and real estate to manufacturing, distribution, sales and service. From government to the private sector, the firm's client experience represents a varied array of Central California's most vital and growing commerce.

The growth of Stoughton Davidson has mirrored the growth of Fresno commerce. The firm seeks to develop its professionals as broad-based business advisors to its clients and believes that business participation in political and government affairs is essential to maintaining a healthy climate for economic growth and community well-being.

Today, as in 1924, Stoughton Davidson operates on the belief that the key to providing tax, accounting and consulting services is a close, professional relationship with clients. It is the execution of this philosophy that has established the firm as one of Central California's largest and most progressive accounting firms.

The Stoughton Davidson team continues to address the clients' immediate and long-range needs with innovation.

CPC SIERRA GATEWAY HOSPITAL

HELP FOR EMOTIONAL AND CHEMICAL DEPENDENCY PROBLEMS

Sierra Gateway Hospital is a state of the art facility that makes the well-being of a patient a top priority.

It may be difficult to know when to seek professional help for emotional or chemical dependency problems, especially when the help is for a family member or close friend. There is always hope that in time such a problem will resolve itself, and sometimes that happens. But other times the problem may persist. Even worse, it could become more complex.

People don't have to be alone when they struggle with disordered thoughts, anxiety or feelings of depression. CPC Sierra Gateway Hospital is designed to help during those times. Whatever the nature of the situation, we can help.

As a leading international health care corporation, Community Psychiatric Centers (CPC) has created a state-of-the-art facility in Clovis - a hospital that places the well being of the patient as its top priority. A 91-bed facility, capable of serving adults and teens, each with a variety of challenges to overcome. It's been a CPC tradition, spanning more than two decades, to help return patients to healthy, normal and productive life-styles.

Under the direction of a psychiatrist, each patient is thoroughly assessed both medically and psychologically. A treatment plan tailored specifically to the needs of each patient is developed by the staff, which includes psychiatrists, social workers, psychologists, nurses, therapists, teachers and dietary professionals. Each staff member has been hand selected from the area to provide the best care available in the San Joaquin Valley for the services provided.

The range of programs available at CPC Sierra Gateway Hospital covers a large number of emotional health needs, with programs structured in either intensive care or open unit settings, providing the appropriate environment for each patient.

ADULT CARE offers a supportive milieu, including intensive individual and group psychotherapy coordinated through occupational, recreational and other therapeutic modalities.

ADOLESCENT CARE is tailored to meet the special needs of teens during this sometimes difficult transition period. The

(Continued bottom of page 132)

LUNDBERG & ASSOCIATES

MEETING VALLEY RESIDENT'S INSURANCE NEEDS

The prospects looked bright to Walker Lundberg when he first opened his doors in Sanger, becoming one of the pioneer independent insurance agents in the San Joaquin Valley. Today, after more than 50 years of service, Lundberg & Associates has earned a reputation as one the valley's most respected insurance agencies. The reputation has enabled the company to grow to more than 45 employees with headquarters in the Fresno Airport Complex, and branch offices in Dinuba and Sanger.

Lundberg & Associates offers a complete array of commercial and personal insurance coverages, including workers compensation, group health, bonding and crop insurance. In each area of specialization, there is a Lundberg representative able to help with knowledge and experience in that field.

A deep commitment exists throughout the company to provide the best client service possible. This feeling is inherent in every staff member, and to achieve this goal, management has adopted specific objectives:

1. To attract the best qualified candidates to represent the firm based on attitude, experience and product knowledge.
2. To provide employees with as many tools possible, such as a state-of-the-art computer system capable of networking product ideas and information.
3. And finally, to seek out the best match between product and client based on need.

In fact, a key stated management objective is: "To make Lundberg & Associates an enjoyable place to work, and a place to make a great career." Even the casual visitor can't help but sense a unique esprit de corps.

In addition to their commitment to clients and employees, Lundberg & Associates maintains a strong alliance with the community-at-large, through support of community organizations such as the Chamber of Commerce, the Fresno Arts Center, The Metropolitan Museum, Rotary International, Storyland in Roeding Park and others.

Believing that the entire region holds immense promise with its strong agricultural base, growing industrial base and superb quality of life, Lundberg & Associates is proud to be part of Fresno and the San Joaquin Valley. All in all, looking to the 1990s and beyond, Lundberg & Associates considers Fresno an ideal place to be.

After more than 50 years of service, Lundberg and Associates has earned the reputation as one of the valley's most respected independent insurance agencies.

program is designed for those between 13 and 18 years of age.

CHEMICAL DEPENDENCY TREATMENT utilizes accepted medical methods to stimulate recovery from alcohol and drugs, and is offered through CounterPoint. This service is available for both adults and adolescents.

**DUAL DIAGNOSIS CARE meets the needs of patients who suffer from psychological problems in addition to chemical dependency, rendering them inappropriate for regular drug or alcohol abuse programs.

Our care and commitment extends beyond the patient. The hospital offers family therapy, pastoral care and a vast array of educational programs. There is also an accredited school program coordinated through the prestigious Clovis Unified School District, allowing students to continue their education.

Sierra Gateway Hospital offers programs structured either in intensive care or open unit settings, providing the appropriate environment for each patient.

HOPE MANOR

A REPUTATION FOR EXCELLENT SENIOR HEALTH CARE

Hope Manor provides skilled health care and a safe, comfortable environment to "Yesterday's Youth."

In a historic section of downtown Fresno, surrounded by fine homes of restored Victorian beauty, Hope Manor provides skilled health care and a safe, comfortable environment to "Yesterday's Youth." The pleasantly decorated health care facility provides appropriate medical attention, nutritious meals and a wide variety of interesting activities to the 225 senior citizens who call Hope Manor home.

Residents bring a favorite sofa, a treasured desk or several lamps and pictures to maintain a homelike atmosphere and express their personal tastes. The brightly lit, carpeted hallways are lined with paintings and jigsaw puzzles completed by a patient resident, and flowering plants frame many a window in the private and semiprivate rooms. Posters of puppies and kittens advertise pet therapy, and the social hall and lounges buzz with laughter, music and the soft voices of residents engaged in card games and hobbies. The director greets each guest by name, for each is a respected individual with a history of accomplishment.

The private facility was originally purchased in 1960 as a 24-bed home. In 1966, Mr. and Mrs. John F. Einhart expanded the home to 54 beds, and their partnership increased the facility to its present size in 1977. Continuing the administration of the home after her husband's death, Genie Einhart has strengthened its staffing, improved the appearance and comfort level of the residents' rooms and common areas and maintained a standard of service which has brought accolades to Hope Manor, earning it a reputation as one of the Cadillacs of the health care industry. Mrs. Einhart maintains a good mix of patients and residents, in the belief that the variety gives more of a homelike feeling.

Some residents have been at Hope Manor as long as ten years, and a few remain only several months. For those who are ambulatory, Residential Care provides a 24-hour a day attendant, meals, housekeeping and an emergency call button for added peace of mind. Intermediate Care provides licensed nursing services 12 hours each day, and a number of certified nursing assistants to respond to residents' needs. Skilled Nursing Care provides 24 hour a day service for those who need it, with a licensed nurse on duty at all times, supplemented with a number of certified nursing assistants. These three levels of care meet the needs of patients and residents with a broad range of requirements, catering to the individual with sensitivity and skill.

The center of this care and activity is a five story, modern health care complex located in downtown Fresno. Patient and resident rooms are approximately 15 x 20 feet, and each has a large bay window overlooking the mature trees which beautify the grounds. Rooms can be single, double or triple, with occupancy arrangements suited to the level of care needed and the resident's desires. The main floor includes

Fresno is blessed with great cultural and religious diversity and customs. Friendships and social opportunities are evident today as in years past.

administrative offices; a main dining area; a large activity room, complete with two well-tuned pianos; a beauty shop and a physical therapy room. The kitchen area is also on the main floor, along with a dental care area and a TV room newly refurbished with skylights and ceiling beams.

Attention to tasteful, cheerful decorating, as well as to scrupulous standards of cleanliness, mark Hope Manor as an exceptional home away from home. Serene, odorless and staffed with attentive, caring personnel, the facilities' program is guided by 14 well-trained department heads. Innovative measures, such as staffing the nursing director position with not one, but two, skilled people in a job-sharing situation, guarantee that Hope Manor will retain its well-deserved reputation for excellence in senior health care.

Residents at Hope Manor enjoy the afternoon sun on the immaculately kept grounds.

McCORMICK, BARSTOW, SHEPPARD, WAYTE & CARRUTH

GROWING WITH CENTRAL CALIFORNIA

The rapid urbanization of Central California has created an ever-increasing demand for legal services. McCormick, Barstow, Sheppard, Wayte & Carruth is aggressively responding to that demand with a growing and diverse practice.

From a handful of seasoned trial attorneys practicing in tort litigation exclusively, the firm now boasts more than 50 attorneys and is recognized as one of California's premier trial firms. McCormick, Barstow's statewide reputation is reflected in its clientele, and demonstrated by the frequent appearances of its attorneys as lecturers and panelists on programs sponsored by national, state and local bar associations.

While the firm has retained its original emphasis on trial work, its practice has expanded to include corporate and tax law, estate planning, appellate practice, banking, securities, commercial litigation and insurance coverage among its specialties.

To assure continuing excellence in representation, MBSW&C has instituted a farsighted recruiting program attracting talented individuals from all over the country eager to relocate to the Fresno area.

Integral to the firm's tradition is its long history of community involvement and philanthropic pursuits. Members serve on the boards of directors and promote numerous civic, cultural and charitable organizations, including the Fresno Philharmonic, Fresno Metropolitan Museum, Fresno Arts Center, Valley Business Center, YMCA, YWCA, Boy Scouts, Rotary and the California State University Bulldog Foundation.

McCormick, Barstow has maintained downtown offices since the firm's inception almost 40 years ago. The firm recently built its own three story 36,000 square foot building on the downtown Fulton Mall, which houses a staff of 140, the largest private law library in the valley, and a computerized legal research system.

McCormick, Barstow is proud of growing harmoniously with Fresno and Central California. This area provides a relaxed atmosphere free of the congestion, traffic problems and pollution associated with larger urban centers, while allowing an opportunity to pursue a sophisticated law practice.

Larry Wayte (L) and Jim Barstow of McCormick, Barstow, Sheppard, Wayte & Carruth.

The firm now boasts more than 50 attorneys and is recognized as one of the state's premier trial firms.

McCormick, Barstow, Sheppard, Wayte and Carruth has maintained downtown offices since it first began in Fresno 40 years ago. It recently built its own three-story office building on the Fulton Mall.

SUMMA HEALTH PLAN

QUALITY OF LIFE ROOTED IN THE VALLEY

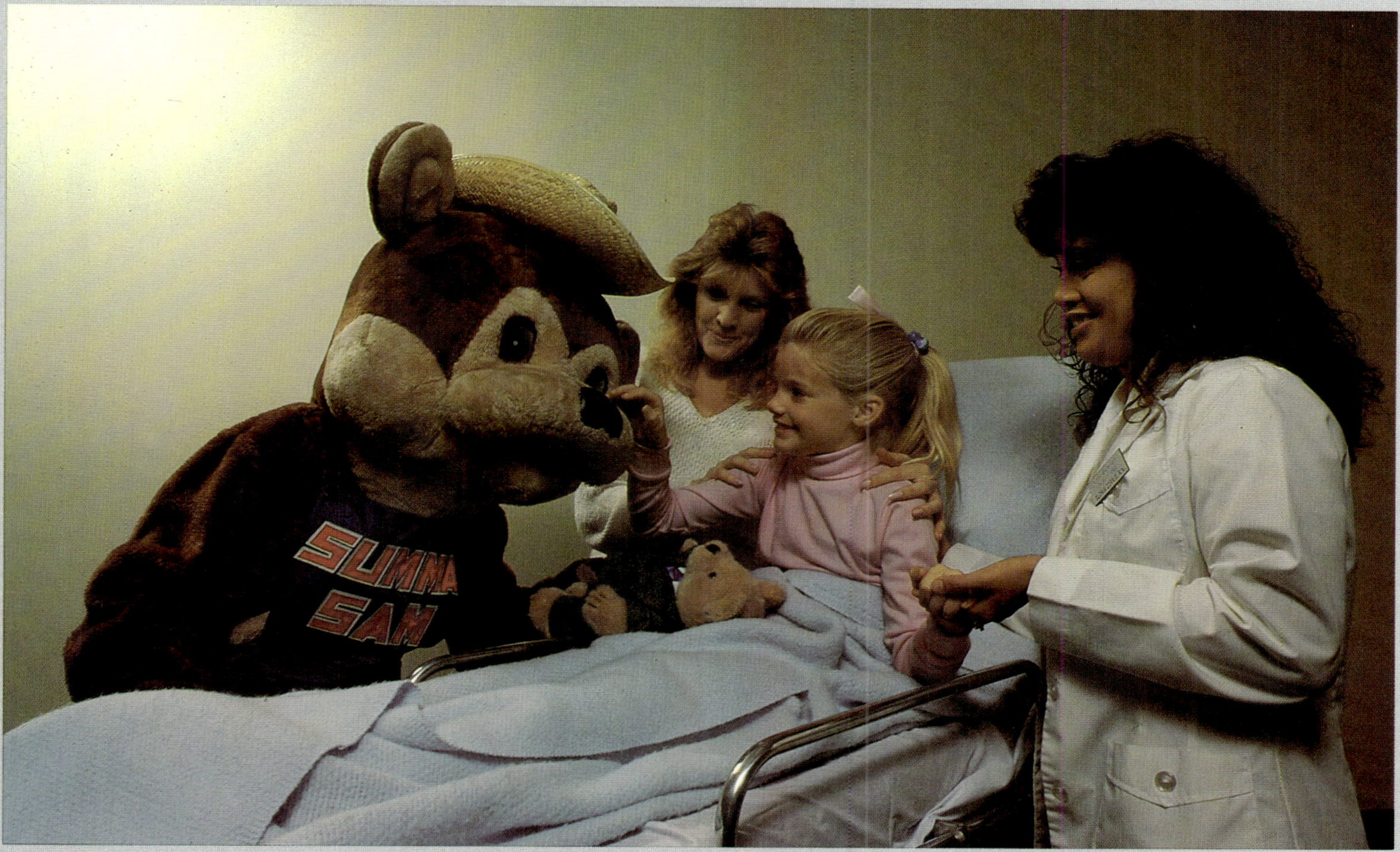

Summa Bear makes this little one's hospital stay happier.

After nearly ten years of planning, Summa Health Plan, Inc., emerged on the marketplace as an alternative health care delivery system for the businesses and residents of the San Joaquin Valley.

Soon after its arrival in the health care field, Summa proved to be a legitimate contender among health maintenance organizations (HMOs). Summa Health Plan, Inc. is now the largest HMO in the area. Its operations extend throughout Fresno, Madera, Kings and Kern counties.

Summa offers a comprehensive health care plan by and for the people of the valley. It took local people, local physicians and local health care providers to design a health plan as uniquely right as Summa is for the people of this valley.

Summa is a locally-owned company with a management team that is known and respected throughout the San Joaquin Valley. The experienced management team has given Summa a breadth and depth of knowledge needed regarding managed health care delivery service. Summa members benefit from local roots in two ways. First, well-regarded physicians have and continue to support Summa, providing it with the largest physician panel available. And second, Summa is the only plan uniquely responsive to service situations that occur in the valley.

Summa has evolved into the new generation of health maintenance organizations — managed care. Summa offers quality health care services in exchange for a predictable monthly fee, maximum freedom of choice in an HMO setting and reliable, usable data.

When compared to traditional insurance plans there are advantages with Summa. There are smaller co-payments and deductibles and no claim forms. In addition, Summa promotes preventive and alternate-site care. In short, Summa offers a generous benefit package at competitive prices. Summa provides these benefits to over 400 local firms and it is also proud to service many statewide and national companies doing business in the San Joaquin Valley.

Summa enjoys the distinct advantage of being the largest HMO in the valley in terms of enrollment. Summa has also been well-received, accepted and respected throughout the four-county area it presently serves, especially in the smaller, rural areas. Future plans include expansion into the remaining six counties of Central California by the 1990s.

With the leadership of a strong management team, Summa anticipates continued growth in Fresno and the Central Valley. Summa's local roots are a source of pride for the company and provide loyalty among employers concerned about providing quality health care for their people.

Summa is hometown people who put a high value on valley health care. Summa Health Plan is ideally suited to valley living.

Summa enjoys the distinct advantage of being the largest HMO in the valley in terms of enrollment.

Anna Woodward

Fresno's Courthouse Park

Networks in Action

CHAPTER 6

A helpful Fresno policeman adjusts a child's bicycle.

Human civilization. In far too many of the nation's great metropolitan centers, the words "human" and "civilization" seem almost contradictory. City dwellers often yearn for an earlier era, before the advent of traffic gridlocks, smog alerts and take-a-number service counters, when people seem to have lived more graciously and met their daily needs more readily. In these often noisy, chaotic, polluted concrete canyons, humankind may be failing its final exam.

In all communities, rural or urban, essential services must be provided and human problems must be resolved. In cities that have grown topsy-turvy, the sheer number of people people requiring these essential services boggles the mind and challenges the creativity of city officials. Where foresight and planning have been lacking, the resulting confusion, inefficiency and bureaucratic excess mean gaps in the provision of necessary services. The resultant economic and psychological costs have been well documented in the tragic chronicles of human waste.

But in Fresno, visionary leadership and abundant natural and human resources have combined to preserve the human qualities which make civilization something more than a dreary exercise in technology. Essential services are provided efficiently, and crises have been dealt with promptly and effectively. There is in Fresno the same sense of personal belonging, communication and understanding which made life more satisfying in an earlier era. The enviable quality of life Fresnans enjoy stems in large part from the fact that their needs for safety, security and growth are being met in an atmosphere of acceptance, individual recognition and challenge.

In Fresno, as in other cities where the quality of life is important, linkages are the key to success. A remarkable array of services is provided through the city and county governments. Vast communication and transportation networks weave patterns of interaction throughout the metropolitan area, connecting it with the larger world. What makes these networks special, and their services particularly appropriate and productive, is an active commitment to quality and efficiency. To a great extent, this goal is met through the establishment and provision of innovative programs, resources, linkage structures and forums.

THE COUNTY SEAT

Fresno County's five-member elected Board of Supervisors develops policies which direct the activities of more than 6,000 employees and the expenditure of its $400 million annual budget. The county's nearly 600,000 people are dispersed throughout an area larger than that of many states and nations — 6,000 square miles. In recent years, the board has faced a difficult challenge: to provide administrative, financial, health, justice, library, public works and development services, as well as public assistance and capital improvements, to a steadily growing population.

Under board direction, the County Administrative Officer has developed a lean, streamlined operation which relies upon innovative, effective delivery of services and coherent management, contract and personnel policies, together with strategies of consolidation and vacancy elimination, to meet the mandate of providing comprehensive services at the lowest possible cost.

Consolidation of four departments into a single Public Works and Development Services Department has improved efficiency, as has the merger of the Weights and Measures Department with the Department of Agriculture. Innovative depopulation strategies have reduced jail funding costs while emphasizing work furlough and substance abuse rehabilitation programs. With these and similar administrative measures, the county strives to deliver top-quality services to a diverse, and expanding population. With its open door policy and commitment to serving its citizens from infancy through retirement, Fresno County's leadership is a model for high-quality, cost-effective service delivery.

The GAIN program enabled this man to re-enter the work force.

PUBLIC-PRIVATE PARTNERSHIP FOR GAIN

On June 30, 1986, California Governor George Deukmejian inaugurated Fresno County's GAIN, or Greater Avenues for Independence Now, program. On that date, Fresno County became the first of California's 58 counties to implement the program, which significantly restructures public assistance.

The GAIN program was created to assist individuals in reaching their employment goals through the provision of education, training, employment and support services such as child care and transportation. GAIN's operation in Fresno County is exemplary in its utilization of effective linkages. The Private Industry Council, the County Department of Education, the State Center Community College District, community-based organizations, non-profit agencies and government offices are linked in a network coordinated by the Department of Social Services.

The goal of each of these participating agencies is to assist individuals and families to achieve and maintain improved living standards by encouraging the maximum possible degree of self-sufficiency in each person. This frequently means the removal of barriers which have prevented people from entering the economic and social mainstream. These barriers include inadequate child care and transportation, lack of job skills or lack of self-confidence. The employees of the County Department of Social Services work vigorously to overcome these barriers through many programs, but none has been more dramatically effective than GAIN.

Every qualified GAIN program participant benefits from the innovations developed at the Department of Social Services to link individuals to the economic marketplace. Each participant is tested for English and math skills and referred, if necessary, for remedial education. Each is taught basic job-seeking and job-keeping skills such as punctuality, cooperation and persistence. Job specialists schedule interviews for those who are ready to "graduate" into the work force.

Employers who have hired these pre-qualified and pre-screened candidates not only enjoy the benefit of increased stability and productivity in their work force, but also realize a number of significant tax credits. GAIN is a winning partnership all around.

To date many county residents have obtained employment as a result of the GAIN public-private partnership. As the business community continues to expand, the GAIN network will provide a readily available pool of trained and motivated employees.

ADDITIONAL TRAINING PROGRAMS

The comprehensive GAIN program is but one of a number of training programs available to offset start-up labor costs for new and expanding industry in Fresno County. Programs designed to prepare new employees, as well as to upgrade job skills of existing human resources, range from pre-employment and on-the-job training to industry-specific training sessions coordinated through the excellent facilities of Fresno City College; Kings River Community College; West Hills Community College, California State University, Fresno, and other public and private skill-specific training schools located throughout the county.

A network of Employment Development Department field offices provides applicant screening and job placement assistance for industry. Under the provisions of the Job Training Partnership Act, the Fresno Private Industry Council offers a wide variety of employment training programs to private business and industry. Federal funds are available to custom design training programs to enable qualified applicants to fill a company's specific labor needs. Each of these programs is designed to match employer needs and employee resources in a way that maximizes benefits for both.

PRESCRIPTION FOR PROGRESS: HEALTHY PEOPLE, HEALTHY ENVIRONMENT

Fresno County's Department of Health provides comprehensive health care and environmental health services. Health education services and protection are key ingredients of Fresno's vigorous, competitive business environment. The young (average age-27.5 years) work force, refreshing Mediterranean climate and outstanding recreational opportunities combine to create a lifestyle where health truly is wealth.

Six accessible, affordable county-staffed community health centers are strategically located throughout the county,

(Continued on page 141)

PACIFIC BELL

FOREMOST PROVIDER OF TELECOMMUNICATIONS

From the early telegraph and telephone wires which served Fresno residents in 1882, to today's high-tech fiber optic cable, Pacific Bell continues to be the foremost provider of telecommunications in the San Joaquin Valley as well as the state of California.

The 17 telephone subscribers linked by phone wires on fence posts a century ago in the City of Fresno pale in comparison to the 180,000 business and residential telecommunications customers served by Pacific Bell in 1987-1988.

Pacific Bell's story involves far more than the familiar telephone. Since the breakup of the Bell System in 1984, Pacific Bell's mission has broadened dramatically to include all manner of digital and electronic transmission.

Pacific Bell is more than a provider of dial tone. It's a fast-track marketer of Information Age technology. It supplies the all-important network lines that link customers – locally as well as to a variety of long distance carriers – in an increasingly complex system capable of responding to a wide range of personal and business needs.

"Fresno was the first community in the state to be served 100% by computerized electronic switching equipment," said W.E. "Bill" Beavers, Division Manager over Pacific Bell's San Joaquin Valley operations.

"Thanks to Pacific Bell's state-of-the-art digital and electronic network here, the City and County of Fresno can attract the types of industries that utilize our sophisticated telecommunications network," said Beavers.

Although Pacific Bell faces a new era in telephone network applications, it continues a history of providing quality service in Fresno. Because the business necessitates close involvement with its customers, the company has always encouraged and supported the contributions made by its employees in Fresno.

In addition to supporting the Fresno County United Way, Pacific Bell's 1,200 active employees are joined by 500 Fresno retirees who carry out a variety of community service projects. The Sierra Pacific Chapter of the Telephone Pioneers of America is part of a nationwide organization – of retired and active telephone employees – that serves the volunteer interests of the community. In Fresno, Pioneer volunteers help feed the needy at the Poverello House, help families of critically-ill children with transportation needs to and from Valley Children's Hospital, help solve communications problems with the disabled and more.

As a major entity in the Fresno community, Pacific Bell recognizes that it is in everyone's best interest to stimulate the community's vitality. Corporate contributions are a part of that process. Together with Pacific Telesis Foundation, the company looks for ways to improve the quality of life in four principal areas: community and civic, health and welfare, education and culture. The contributions, which are made at shareholder expense, take the form of resources and people and support the company business plan.

Community involvement in Fresno reflects Pacific Bell's commitment to good corporate citizenship. The volunteer activities of Pacific Bell employees – active and retired – are an example of this commitment. It is the belief that such community involvement benefits Pacific Bell's business as well as that of Fresno.

Pacific Bell is a subsidiary of Pacific Telesis Group, a telecommunications and diversified holding company based in San Francisco.

bringing a full range of preventive and primary treatment services within reach of both rural and urban communities. In addition, a wide spectrum of specialty clinics for infants and children are held in churches and community centers throughout the area. Public health nurses offer specialized screening, data collection and follow-up services for communicable disease. Significantly, the department focuses on health promotion and disease prevention activities with an emphasis on education.

County Health Department environmental technicians work with consumers, business, industry and growers to reduce environmental health hazards. These efforts, combined with high quality natural resources, mean that most county residents enjoy pure water running from the ground to the tap. Increasing awareness of the joint responsibility of all sectors for maintaining a healthy community environment bodes well for meeting the environmental challenges of the future.

Mental health care planning and service delivery is the responsibility of county health employees, too, as the local area responds to national de-institutionalization policy trends. The continuing care system of services developed by the County Mental Health Authority encompasses a comprehensive range of programs designed to ensure a meaningful, productive lifestyle for all county residents.

SAFETY AND SECURITY

With an enviable record of decreases in many property crime categories, the decentralized Sheriff's Department of Fresno County can feel justifiable pride in its prevention efforts. The staff of approximately 400 works in the areas of criminal apprehension, evidence collection, prison management, crime prevention and the service of legal documents. Department patrol officers drove more than three million miles performing their duties in 1986. With a county-wide response time of 10.4 minutes, the department has maintained a reputation for promptness and reliability, especially in the metropolitan area where response time averages two to three minutes.

The department's headquarters in downtown Fresno is supplemented with seven substations and 17 community service centers. Centralized dispatch, homicide, arson, vice and intelligence investigation services ensure cost-effective, professional operations. Contract law enforcement services cover several unincorporated cities as well as the National Parks Services and the U.S. Army Corps of Engineers at Pine Flat.

Innovative programs identify and target career criminals, decentralize patrol operations and keep deputies in personal contact with the neighborhoods they serve. Together with enhanced crime prevention and community involvement efforts, these programs have held the crime increase to a modest .3 percent (using the FBI crime Index), and have actually contributed to a decrease in reported crimes within the county.

The Fresno County Sheriff's Department is widely recognized as an innovative, aggressive leader in crime prevention. Its solid reputation also includes recognition for its search and rescue operations. Lost or injured outdoors enthusiasts were retrieved from within the county's thousands of square miles of recreational areas by department personnel. The dive team responded to boating or vehicle accidents on the county's waterways, and 1,926 contacts with boaters improved recreational safety for all residents. Reserve units donated 5,955 hours of volunteer time, and community service officers conducted thousands of business and home security inspections, neighborhood watch meetings, and educational crime prevention programs, thereby freeing deputies for urgent safety and security missions on behalf of county residents.

THE RICHES OF THE WRITTEN WORD — FREE TO ALL

With health and safety under the watchful eye of county staff, Fresno's citizens are actively pursuing individual growth and development through the many public and private opportunities available throughout the area. Chief among these high-quality services is the extensive public library system. County residents respond enthusiastically to a wide variety of library services. More than two million books, records, tapes, documents and films circulate in the county each year. From traditional books to modern on-line database searching, the professionally staffed county library system meets the public's information needs through an up-to-date, effective, interactive service network. Thirty-one library branches and two bookmobiles effectively cover the county's 5,066 square mile service area.

Special populations deserve special attention. The library has thousands of "talking books" available without charge for the blind. Correctional institution residents receive library services for productive educational and recreational uses. Each year, more than 18,000 children receive special attention through the library's creative programming, which includes preschool story times and summer reading and activity programs.

Newly developed services reach a special population most people were unaware of until about a decade ago — the adult illiterate. The Fresno County Library's Adult Literacy Program, originally designed to reach incoming Southeast Asian refugees, has become a model program. Illiterates from many backgrounds are reached through its effective, personalized training program. Volunteers provide a substantial proportion of the library's services to the adult illiterate, as well as to the blind and physically handicapped.

With a collection of almost a million books and numerous microfilms, documents, recordings and pamphlets, the library serves as a primary source of information for area residents. Its staff responds to more than 475,000 questions annually; they tap inter-library loan and on-line database resources to provide the most accurate and current information available. From introducing preschoolers to the joys of reading to responding promptly to a complex business information request, the county library plays a critical role in ensuring the high quality of life Fresno County residents have come to expect and enjoy.

(Continued on page 143)

H. MARKUS & CO.

FINE PRINTING AND BUSINESS FORMS

H. Markus & Co., Fine Printing and Business Forms, is a reflection of its founder's philosophies and goals. Harry Markus believes that printing is a demanding craft yet for him it is also a labor of love. "I enjoy seeing the client's look of excitement when he or she first sees a finished piece that we've printed." Harry Markus is committed to high quality. "Although we cannot achieve perfection every time, we strive to reach that goal in service and quality. With our resources, an experienced, caring staff and the latest in print technology, we offer the valley the best in putting ink on paper."

Harry Markus has made printing his career for the past 24 years. "My first love is quality commercial printing. Quite frankly, our goal is to be the best print production plant in our area. Our company is prepared to grow with the future of Fresno."

"Market studies indicate enormous growth for the Fresno area in the next 10 years. We believe we must position ourselves in the marketplace with the capacity and capabilities to meet the present and future demands of the printing needs of commercial business."

Harry Markus, President

"Our success is not something we take for granted. We express our appreciation by investing in Fresno. H. Markus & Co. supports California State University at Fresno, The Bulldog Foundation and the American Lung Association to name a few organizations."

H. Markus & Co. is located at 1003 N. Abby, Fresno.

THE CITY OF FRESNO

Fresno's mayor and six-member city council preside over a modern, thriving, industrious metropolis of nearly 100 square miles and close to 300,000 persons. The annual budget, which approaches $100,000,000, funds important services as diverse as police and fire protection and pothole repair. General government revenue sources and expenditures are graphically depicted below.

CITY OF FRESNO ANNUAL BUDGET

THE GENERAL USE BUDGET DOLLAR

WHERE IT GOES

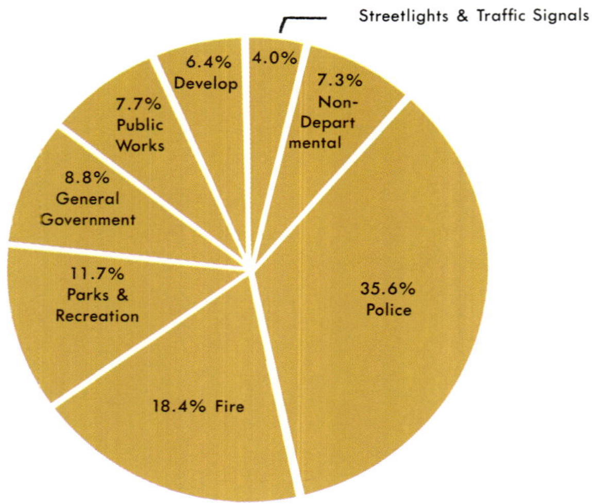

WHERE IT COMES FROM

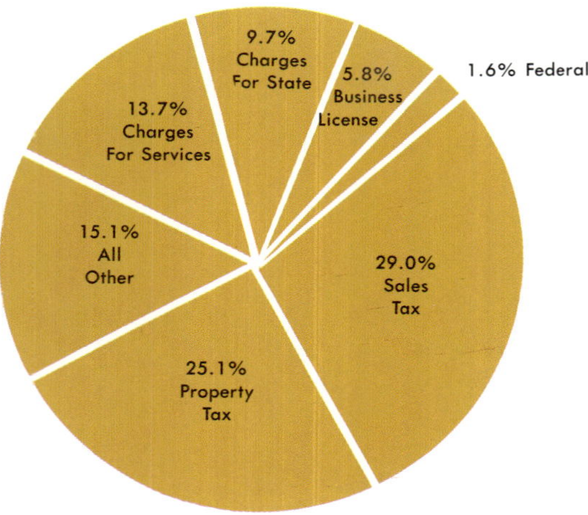

To deliver the services mandated by its city charter, city government is organized into 14 departments, each with a set of clearly delineated responsibilities. The Public Informa tion Office provides an information and referral service to connect citizens with appropriate departments. Public involvement with city government is extensive in Fresno. Each council meeting provides citizens an opportunity to voice concerns, and numerous citizen boards, commissions, and advisory committees draw upon the expertise and interest of the public in resolving present concerns and planning for Fresno's future.

THE FRESNO BEE

INFORMING THE VALLEY SINCE 1922

For more than six decades, The Fresno Bee has grown through aggressive pursuit of the news, and it claims the six county Central California region as its beat. The Bee provides a broad mix of news, sports, features, entertainment and analysis, giving major weight to stories from San Joaquin Valley communities in Fresno, Tulare, Kings, Madera, Merced and Mariposa Counties.

The Bee is one of the valley's major employers, with nearly 800 people on its payroll. It has a daily circulation of more than 140,000 and a Sunday circulation of nearly 170,000. It is the only newspaper of more than 100,000 circulation within 150 miles.

Fresno was a bustling city of some 70,000 when the first edition of The Bee was published on October 17, 1922. There were two other dailies in Fresno then; the Evening Herald, which The Bee purchased in 1924, and the Morning Republican, acquired by The Bee in 1932.

Originally an afternoon newspaper, The Bee in 1976 switched to morning publication. The move strengthened the newspaper and provided its more than 400,000 readers with more current information.

The Bee is recognized for editorial excellence, particularly in its coverage of news pertaining to Fresno and the surrounding region. It regularly wins state, national and

international awards. The Bee was nominated to receive the Pulitzer Prize for general reporting in 1984, a decision overturned by the Pulitzer board of directors.

The Bee is printed in a 17 year old, 166,000 square foot plant on nearly 15 acres in downtown Fresno in an area that has been revitalized by public and private investment in a city redevelopment project. The Bee donated its former offices to a Fresno foundation and helped established the Fresno Metropolitan Museum there.

Since its first issue in 1922, The Bee has been a strong, consistent advocate of natural resource conservation, a supporter of public ownership of utilities and a defender of the "little man" who has no one to look out for his interests when he confronts the powerful.

The health of agriculture, the area's major economic base, has long been of great concern to The Bee. The newspaper supports water development and land reclamation projects, and is concerned with environmental issues and the quality of life of valley residents.

This emphasis on issues affecting the quality of life, plus its role in insuring honest, efficient government has brought The Bee acclaim as a newspaper which reports all the news without fear or favor.

The city manager is responsible for implementation of city council policies and supervision of all city departments except those of the city attorney and the city clerk. In addition, the city manager prepares the city's annual financial plan and maintains the daily operations of city government. With a total city staff of approximately 2,500 and an annual expenditure of $292.22 per capita for services, the demands on the city manager and staff are substantial. Dedicated and capable staff bring order to the process of managing growth while equitably providing necessary services.

Fresno's overall growth is guided by its General Plan. This is closely monitored by the Development Department, which oversees the city ordinance standards for construction and administers building, health and safety standards. Fresno's Finance Department serves as the city's banker, accountant, auditor, insurance agent, investor and purchasing manager. Most citizens encounter this department in paying their water and sewer bills, or in the pursuit of a business permit or a license for the family pet. In addition to its role as the city's financial watchdog, the Finance Department compiles statistical portraits of the fiscal impact of policy decisions at the local and state levels, and provides a database for monitoring the city's financial health.

The General Services Department is the city's property management system, with responsibility for repair, maintenance and any necessary remodeling of city property. The department is responsible for all fleet vehicle purchases, inspections, maintenance and repairs. Additional responsibilities include printing, storage, telecommunications facilities, and provision and upkeep of all traffic lights and some street lights. The Public Works Department analyzes traffic flow and provides signs and markings for traffic safety. Its responsibilities include the design, construction, inspection and improvements to all city-owned facilities. It also serves as the repository for all survey records, engineering records and maps. The enormity of this department's responsibility is indicated by the sheer size of the territory governed. The city holds more than 8,000 acres of city streets and alleys, 2,000 acres of airport properties and another 2,000 acres in waste disposal property.

Fresno City Manager James Aldredge pictured in front of City Hall.

COMMERCIAL TRANSFER, INC.

A TRADITION OF QUALITY FOR OVER 75 YEARS

The Fortier family has been in the local trucking industry for four generations.

The Fortier family ownership of Commercial Transfer, Inc. is a continuance of the Fortier's association with hauling and trucking for over 75 years.

Terry D. Fortier, President and C.E.O. of Commercial Transfer, followed the tradition established by his grandfather and father by creating this firm in 1963. Terry Fortier's

Staff for these and other city departments is recruited, tested, trained and employed under the supervision of the city's Personnel Department. Its strengths in affirmative action and in employee safety training have contributed much to the professionalism, reliability and performance record of Fresno's city employees. The tasks of recruitment, retention training and monitoring career development are indeed demanding.

In the eyes of many, the most visible city services are fire and safety functions. Fire companies are located strategically throughout the Fresno urban area, ready to respond immediately to threats to life and property. The department carries out complete investigations of fires of suspicious origins, implements a comprehensive fire safety inspection plan, and administers a wide-ranging public safety education program. Fresno's Fire Department operates a widely respected paramedic service, which provides emergency life support to citizens in need. The area's Emergency Medical Service System, developed in 1974 with federal funding, was designed to effectively provide critical care to citizens while freeing the aerial truck companies for their primary fire fighting responsibilities. In addition to paramedic services, this highly respected service is characterized by prompt fire response times, fire prevention investigations, public education programs and vigorous prosecution of fire violations.

One of the hook and ladder trucks of the Fresno Fire Department, ready to respond to threats to life and property.

Terry D. Fortier, President and C.E.O. of Commercial Transfer, Inc.

"trucking heritage" and formal education prepared him to run his own business. He earned a degree in business in 1964 from the University of San Francisco, and then persevered through night school to obtain his law degree, being admitted to the California Bar in 1976.

Known for state of the art equipment and exceptional quality standards, C.T.I. has recently expanded its headuarters site from five to twelve acres, including a $600,000 addition housing its corporate offices, warehouses and equipment storage areas.

Serving California with its 27 million people is no small task, and C.T.I. hauls a variety of products including building materials, glass containers, machinery, as well as a host of general commodities.

The Fresno headquarters employs sixty people with twenty more working at terminals in Los Angeles and Lathrop.

The Fortier philosophy stresses corporate excellence both in appearance and performance, and this is reflected in the state of the art equipment and the high standards expected of Commercial Transfer employees.

While meeting the trucking needs for the central valley for most of America's mechanized lifetime, C.T.I. has put a lot of their success back into the Fresno community.

The scope of civic involvement includes supporting telethons, public television (channel 18), the Fresno Convention and Visitors Bureau, the Fresno County and City Chamber of Commerce, as well as a host of other community-oriented causes.

It's been 75 years since Conrad L. Fortier launched his two-horse team and a drop "A" Frame wagon for his hauling business and throughout all those years, the Fortiers have sought to lead the pack in ideas and performance.

With his brother Timothy as vice president and son Russel as equipment manager, Terry Fortier and C.T.I. have positioned themselves to keep the Fortier name associated with premier trucking, quality and service throughout the central valley and all of California.

One of the Commercial Transfer fleet.

The largest share of public expenditures, about 35 percent, funds police services, ensuring that Fresno maintains itself as a safe place to live, work and visit. In providing its mandated educational, protection and justice administration services, the Fresno Police Department has developed a number of outstanding programs that have gained national recognition. The department provided emergency services, maintained civic order, educated the public regarding crime prevention, fought the incursion of narcotics traffickers, and responded to traffic accidents and personal safety needs.

In addition to activities focusing on crime control, Fresno's police make significant strides in crime prevention. Five community-wide police/public partnership conferences were held in 1987 to clarify community concerns, and the model Southeast Asian Neighborhood Service Representative program was implemented.

Innovative programs effectively reach out to widely diverse segments of the community, bringing police protection and safety services to meet their needs. With programs especially targeted to young people, members of the youth education component of the Community Services Bureau make presentations to over 16,000 students during the year. In addition, children tour "safety town," and crime prevention presentations are made in the schools.

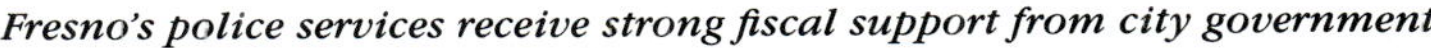

Fresno's police services receive strong fiscal support from city government.

In response to the cultural and ethnic diversity that characterizes Fresno, the Police Department's Community Affairs Officer negotiates sensitive community issues. The city's Human Relations Commission provides expert direction in these matters, and the Crime Prevention Unit produced a brief film in four Southeast Asian languages to help new resident populations understand the American judicial system and its impact on their daily lives. Neighborhood Services Representatives provide translation services, give community talks, assist in police report preparation and help educate refugees about crime prevention and police services. The department's multicultural staff, integrated into all service units, now has the capability of bringing police services to the community in ten different languages, an important aspect of effective service delivery.

Other special populations are the focus of special police outreach programs as well. A Senior Awareness Program seeks to educate and prepare senior citizens to reduce their vulnerability to crime. Similarly, "Women Awareness" and "Business Brown Bag" forum series have been developed to help women and business owners learn how to make themselves less vulnerable to crime.

The Fresno Police Department's exceptionally effective Neighborhood Watch program has sought to address residential crime through a variety of meetings, activities, newsletters, demonstrations and educational programs. New Neighborhood Watch groups are continually being formed as citizens unite to protect the peace and security of their homes.

Through strong youth education programs, active community outreach, and the support of home and business owners alike, the Fresno Police Department will continue to lead in its effective mission of crime prevention and control.

Fresno Transit provides efficient and economical daily transportation throughout the metropolitan area.

TRANSIT — THE NETWORK ON THE MOVE

The contemporary city is a city on the move, and nowhere is this more true than in Fresno today. The city boasted an automobile in the year of its invention and has never lost its affection for this most personal mode of transportation. Its most recent declaration of this sentiment, the passage of the highway support taxation Measure C, surprises no one who knows the city well. Its people are citizens with vision and the projected integrated highway network is a primary form of this linkage.

Freeway 41 will one day speed vacationers northward to the mountains.

With Measure C monies, Highway 41 will be extended northward a new freeway will speed vacationers to the mountains, crosstown access will be vastly improved, and a number of additional connections, upgradings and expansions of the excellent highway system will be made possible.

Measure C commits 75 percent of funds each year to the state highway programs, and the remaining 25 percent is apportioned directly to each city for local transportation purposes.

For many of Fresno's workers, economical, efficient daily transportation is provided throughout the metropolitan area by Fresno Transit, the city's bus system. To improve service to its 8 million riders a year, Fresno Transit embarked on a five-year, 20 million dollar capital improvement program replacing and moderizing the large bus fleet as well as upgrading shelters, bus stops and providing more convenient fare boxes. Older citizens receive rate reductions, and the disabled may avail themselves of the comfortable, accessible demand response transportation via Fresno Transit's Handyride operations. The new Manchester Transit Center at Manchester Mall is indicative of the Transit System's commitment to providing up-to-the minute convenience and service to the riding public.

Fresno Transit's employees exemplify the community spirit and pride of many of the city's professional staff. A recent news story reported the initiative of one driver who briefly delayed his scheduled route in order to rescue a lost toddler from nearby railroad tracks and return the child to his worried mother. Bus employees traditionally raise funds and decorate one "Christmas Bus" which distributes holiday remembrances to school children, to hospitalized children and to senior citizens who might otherwise be left out of the festivities.

Passenger train service to and from Fresno is provided by Amtrak, with Caltrans operating the San Joaquin Valley line. Two trains run daily in each direction from Fresno. A northern route takes travelers to the Bay Area, and the southern route runs to Bakersfield with connections to Los Angeles by bus. Amtrak proudly dubs these trains the "fogcutters" because they have never missed a day's service even in the Valley's heaviest winter fog. The equipment is all two-story Superliners, which provide the ultimate in comfort and in spectacular views of the snow-covered Sierra, on the scenic Valley route. Each train has a snack bar and

The Southern Pacific Railway is one of two railroad companies that help fill Fresno's commercial and industrial transportation needs.

dining service is available with some departures. Many Fresnans make an outing of the one-half hour ride to Hanford, visiting that city's Chinatown and enjoying historic tours of the area before the comfortable ride back to Fresno.

For commercial and industrial transportation needs, Fresno has convenient scheduled service from both the Santa Fe and Southern Pacific Railway Companies. The Atchison, Topeka, and Santa Fe's mainline operation through Fresno provides several transcontinental trains daily. Consistent fourth morning Chicago arrivals are matched by similar schedules to the Texas Gulf ports. Rapid loading and unloading of the trailer-flatcar combinations enables the Calwa Yard on the south side of Fresno to handle 35,000 trailers on flatcars per year. This efficiency has resulted in a 70 percent usage rate for this intermodal traffic movement system, as compared to traditional carloading methods. Santa Fe's business development and valley division headquarters offices in Fresno assure top-notch, responsive, and effective attention to all those who patronize the system.

The Southern Pacific railroad has literally shaped the city of Fresno, so closely have their histories been intertwined. The original settlement, now downtown, parallels the Southern Pacific tracks. Outlying areas are aligned in neat geometric squares, with north-south and east-west streets. Out in the county as well, the location of most cities and towns was determined by optimum placement of railroad shipping points to ensure speedy delivery of Fresno County's agricultural bounty to the rest of the nation.

The Southern Pacific continues to play a vital part in area commerce and industry, with as many as 16 trains a day through Fresno. Local service is available to nearly all San Joaquin Valley communities. The Southern Pacific serves all major west coast ports except Seattle-Tacoma, and provides consistent second morning delivery to Portland. Connections to eastern carriers can be made at New Orleans, Memphis, Kansas City and St. Louis; all major ports of entry to Mexico, with the exception of Laredo, are served. The Southern Pacific has emphasized innovation in service improvement, and has been a pioneer and leader in double-stack intermodal operations. Its new intermodal container transfer facility (ICTF)) is the largest rail transfer terminal in the world, with an annual capacity of 360,000 container loads. Although the Southern Pacific is a massive system, comprising a network 13,400 miles in length, its Fresno-based San Joaquin Valley sales office offers transport tailored to meet the needs of local business and industry.

(Continued on page 150)

PSA/USAir

A LEADER IN THE AIR TRANSPORTATION INDUSTRY

Pictured above is PSA/USAir's 737-300 airplane.

Pacific Southwest Airlines (PSA) began operations on May 6, 1949, flying a leased DC-3 aircraft with a seating capacity of 31 once a week between San Diego and Oakland via Hollywood/Burbank.

From those humble beginnings, PSA grew into a major airline. The PSA smile is a common sight to valley travelers.

And soon, PSA will be making a move that will in one fell swoop significantly strengthen the company's place in the air transportation industry. PSA will be merging with USAir. When USAir, PSA and Piedmont Aviation join forces, they will together serve 75% of the United States population.

USAir began in 1938 as All American Aviation. It was the first airline to be certified by the former Civil Aeronautics Agency.

Today USAir operates a fleet of approximately 148 jet aircraft: 727-200s, 737-200s, 737-300s, DC-9s and BAC 1-11s. Joining the fleet in 1988 will be the first of at least 20 new Fokker 100s.

Stretching from Canada to Florida and westward to California, USAir's route network spans the heartland of America and includes nearly all the major getaway cities in the U.S. As one of the largest and most profitable airlines in the United States, USAir has grown to carry over 14 million passengers a year. The 120 plus jet fleet operates some 900 daily flights linking more than 80 cities in nearly 30 states, the District of Columbia, and two Canadian provinces.

Key to the USAir route system is the Pittsburgh connecting complex. Through Pittsburgh, the hub of the system, USAir offers nonstop or direct services to more than 60 airports. A combination of on-the-ground efficiency and well-timed departures and arrivals at Greater Pittsburgh International Airport enables USAir to offer over 400 connections between cities on the USAir network at several peak times throughout the day.

All of this supports USAir's primary product — time savings. The millions of people who fly USAir each year do so to get to their destination — quickly, comfortably and conveniently. USAir designs its schedule, whenever possible, to fit the business travelers' needs by providing same day, out and back services between many cities. Business travelers account for approximately 70 percent of USAir's customers.

An added convenience for the many business travelers is USAir's unique relationship with the Allegheny Commuters, independent airlines working in association with USAir. Allegheny Commuters provide frequent and well-timed service from smaller and medium sized cities to Pittsburgh and other large cities served by USAir, as well as frequent service between major short-haul markets, e.g. New York and Baltimore, and New York and Philadelphia.

For leisure travelers, USAir has something for everyone. The airline serves a host of vacation destinations, including Arizona, California, Canada, Colorado, Florida, Louisiana, New England, and, of course, many historic Eastern locations. Numerous value-priced tour packages are available as well as USAir's full range of money-saving fares.

A bird's eye view of the Fresno Air Terminal.

FRESNO'S AIRPORTS

Fresno's rapid growth and its major city outlook are reflected in the modern Fresno Air Terminal. While the supersonic Concorde has never landed in Fresno, it could — the main runway is long enough, wide enough, and strong enough to support any plane currently in use, from the Concorde to the fastest super-secret spy plane.

Fresno is headquarters for the California Air National Guard's 144th Fighter Interceptor Wing, flying F-4 Phantoms, and F-16s scheduled for the 1990s. The California Army National Guard has a major aircraft repair depot at the airport, and there's a Marine Corps Air Reserve unit located there as well. These military aviation bases share facilities with Fresno's 200 daily scheduled passenger flights, private aircraft, air freight services and support services. The 800,000 passengers who enjoy the attractive, convenient terminal each year have their choice of major airlines and several commuter lines, which offer a mix of Boeing 727s, 737s, the new, quiet McDonald Douglas MD-80s and British BAe-146s. Commuter lines use jet turboprops, for the most part, and all are linked with major airlines for convenient connections in hub cities.

Fresno Air Terminal is the largest airport in the central San Joaquin Valley. Its personalized service, excellent seat availability, convenient parking, updated baggage claim facilities and ample support services provide VIP service for every passenger. With its convenient location, just 7.5 miles northeast of downtown, its good support services for general aviation and its readily available rentals, sales and

The tower at FAT coordinates local air traffic.

The California Air National Guard is a major contributor to the Fresno economy.

Fresno is proud to be the corporate home of United Express.

lease of aircraft of all types, the airport meets every business aviation need with dispatch. Five full-service fixed base operations provide fuel, repairs, and hangar services for private and corporate aircraft of all types. On the north side of the airfield, new office facilities and land for custom development offer convenient runway access and two golf courses within walking distance for the executive's relaxation. Around the corner, rapidly growing airport business parks offer attractive, convenient office space to an ever-expanding list of progressive companies.

Fresno's second airport, Chandler, is located just one mile west of downtown. Equipped to handle smaller aircraft, it provides convenient access to downtown offices for the corporate traveler. Its two paved runways and several fixed base operations provide convenience and service for those to whom center city location is critical.

The ultimate in luxury for the general aviation enthusiast is the hangar-plus-home combination pioneered at Fresno's north side Sierra Sky Park. After a leisurely patio breakfast, take off for a day's business or fishing over on the coast, and taxi back into your own garage before dinner.

The Fresno Air Terminal, Chandler Field, and Sierra Sky Park, combined with the variety of private and municipal airstrips scattered throughout the valley, graciously and conveniently meet every need for the traveler on the move. From the airfreight importer who relies on Fresno's Port of Entry Customs Inspector to the family that decides on a spur-of-the-moment dinner outing — flying over to Harris Ranch, Fresno's aviation needs, large and small, are well met by its modern air transit facilities. With approximately $26 million earmarked for improvements to be made by 1991 at the Fresno Air Terminal alone, this standard of readiness and responsiveness will be maintained for years to come.

COMMUNICATIONS CONNECTIONS

The contemporary Fresno resident, listening to an insightful news program between calls on the transportable cellular car phone, takes excellence in communications capabilities as a necessary, even natural part of everyday life. Not long ago, however, things were quite different. News of the 1906 San Francisco earthquake was received at the Fresno train depot in Morse Code. The 1917 championship series between the Chicago White Sox and the New York Giants was played out on an elaborate lighted board.

Now, telex and fax machines, transportable phones, cable TV and the finest in electronic and print news services are available at the touch of a button. Some traditions remain — the educational and religious programs of early radio and the public-spirited campaigning of *The Fresno Bee*'s early years all have their contemporary echoes, but convenience, quality and instantaneous connection mark today's communications world.

From the earliest Fresno area radio station, broadcasting two hours nightly in 1925, service has grown to include 34 stations, all broadcast networks, several languages and two public radio stations — the local KVPR and the KFCF signal, which rebroadcasts Berkeley's KPFA public affairs and music programming. KPFA, with its flourishing drama and literature department, offers a wide range of poetry, readings, dramatic performances and interviews along with news and musical programming. On both KPFA and KVPR, Fresno residents can enjoy classical music programming, a tradition in Fresno since the Fresno Symphony Orchestra broadcast over the California Radio System in 1937. Public Radio, with strong local support since its 1975 founding, broadcasts classical music, jazz, news and information, night service and entertainment 24 hours a day. As the Central Valley's exclusive non-commercial professional, fine arts radio station, KVPR reaches a wide spectrum of listeners with a substantial proportion in the highly educated demographic segments.

Fresno's television offerings span as wide a range as its radio stations, reflecting a tradition of competitive marketing and service orientation. Fitting its capability of bringing the world into the living room, the first show broadcast over Fresno TV was the coronation of Queen Elizabeth. By 1979, a Spanish language channel was in operation. Two years earlier, public sponsored television was being broadcast over Channel 18. That same year saw the introduction of cable TV. All networks are represented and programming is available in several languages in addition to English and Spanish. Transistors, microchips, satellite dishes, big screens with rear projection and the ubiquitous home VCRs have continued to revolutionize the industry, keeping information quality, entertainment value and convenience a state of the art for the Fresno audience.

(Continued on page 155)

UNITED EXPRESS AIRLINES

IN PARTNERSHIP WITH THE COMMUNITY

When WestAir Airlines, known as United Express, began its search for a new city in which to locate its headquarters, Fresno was immediately one of the leading choices. Boasting a prime location in the center of the state, reasonable costs, friendly people and a business-minded local government, the city known as the "Raisin Capital of the World" soon convinced the airline's management that it need look no further.

Located in a large building complex adjacent to the busy runways at Fresno Air Terminal, United Express officially opened its new corporate facility in April of 1986. Nearly 200 people settled into their new offices – and for many, new homes, as well – while continuing to do their part to keep the busy airline flying.

United Express has grown to become California's largest regional air carrier, employing more than 750 people. In Fresno, its daily workforce has nearly doubled, and now exceeds 400.

As its name implies, United Express is a travel partner with United Airlines. Coordinated schedules give United Express passengers excellent connections to hundreds of United flights at San Francisco and Los Angeles. In addition to these two cities, the airline also provides Fresno with frequent daily nonstop flights to such destinations as Burbank, Ontario, Orange County and San Diego in Southern California; and San Jose, Oakland, Sacramento and other valley cities to the north. All told, Fresnans can now choose from at least 50 United Express departures every business day.

This impressive flight schedule has been optimized by the airline's fleet of more than 36 aircraft, each chosen for its ability to provide reliability, efficiency and passenger comfort. Composed of 15-seat Embraer Bandeirantes, 30-seat pressurized Embraer Basilias and 36-seat Shorts 360s, the United Express fleet is one of the most modern now in operation, reflecting the state of art in regional aircraft design and innovation.

With more than 400 associates on the job in Fresno, United Express can certainly be considered one of the area's larger employers. Yet it has never lost the unique family-feeling that exists throughout the company. Indeed, this feeling extends to the community itself through the airline's participation in and sponsorship of numerous local events. It's a further indication of the United Express commitment to serving the needs of its hometown.

Also unique to such a large company is the airline's reliance on the merit system for evaluating the work of the associates. If an associate excels in a position, it's standard procedure for the associate to be promoted to a position with even more challenging responsibilities. At United Express, personal development opens doors – and open doors are the hallmark of the airline's management style.

As it continues to grow, the airline's economic contributions to the community, in the form of payroll, property and sales taxes, become ever more significant. But United Express has come to mean more than jobs and local revenues. With the exceptionally high level of air service it has brought to the city, and its ongoing support of local activities, United Express has become a partner in Fresno's future.

KMJ and KNAX RADIO

THE FIRST 65 YEARS

In one respect, KMJ hasn't changed much in the last 65 years, and that's a point of real pride!

When it first signed on the air in 1922, KMJ was the most listened to station in the area. It had to be. It was the only one.

Now, after six and a half decades, News/Talk 58 is still, more often than not, the most listened to station in the area. And today there are dozens of AM and FM stations around.

When KMJ-FM signed on at 97.9 mhz back in 1949, hardly anyone noticed. Now as KNAX, everyone seems to be noticing it.

The reasons lie in what could be called "The History of the Heavyweights."

By the mid-1920's, KMJ had already shown its feelings for the community. There were regularly scheduled newscasts, agribusiness reports, weather forecasts and an idea exchange among listeners. Local concern kept listeners trust and confidence in KMJ right through the decades of big name network radio stations and into the present.

The "Man on the Street" and the studio discussion programs of the 20's and 30's evolved into three-way conversations involving talk show hosts such as Craig Mollison, the listeners, and the newsmakers, policy shapers and innovators.

The valley's largest radio news team is joined by Captain Scotty's Traffic Helicopter, reporting on traffic conditions. Meterologist Harry Stockman, reports the weather outlook for city people and the grower alike, and Roy Isom reports on Valley agribusiness.

When listening habits began to dramatically change in the 50's and 60's, and radio broadcasters searched for a "sound," KMJ didn't need to change. It just expanded upon what it had consistently done best: providing information broadcasts by people the listener could identify with and look to as friend.

But friendship doesn't indicate a lack of meaningful controversy. Lively debate is an important part of the news-talk format. And it's nothing new for KMJ.

Captain Scotty Sample aboard the KMJ-Bird monitors the local traffic conditions weekdays.

There were a number of raised eyebrows back in 1937 when KMJ decided to broadcast a weekly discussion program involving Catholic Monsignor James Dowling, Dean James Mallock of the Episcopal Church and Rabbi David Greenberg. It was an ecumenical ideal considered risky in those times, but in its 17 years, "The Forum of Better Understanding" facilitated major accomplishments. A statue in Fresno's Courthouse Park honors those three clergymen. "The Forum" was so unique, it was often picked up by the NBC radio network and the Voice of America.

One KMJ tradition that's gotten stronger over the years is a dedication to Bulldog athletics. It began with Fresno State College as far back as 1934, when not many people away from the campus cared about the sports program. Whatever the "FSU" Bulldog fans want, (women's sports, too), they can find on KMJ with Bill Woodward, the trusted voice of Fresno State sports since 1969.

Changing times have meant changes in programming over the years. Long gone are relics of an earlier era, such as the studio band, the daily broadcasts of live accordion music and the poetry reading.

The regular KMJ broadcasts of country music that dated back to 1931 disappeared too, only to be rediscovered on KMJ's FM station. KMJ-FM had given its classical music tapes and equipment to support Fresno's struggling public radio station. It was a good move for both stations. With its new name and contemporary country sound, KNAX has become the most listened to country music station in Fresno. What was once the "kid brother" is now a dynamic force and service in its own right.

With roots in the city's past, KMJ and KNAX look to the future with new and fresh ideas, as they constantly work for an always higher quality of life for Fresno and its neighbors.

This historic photograph depicts an early business site of KMJ Radio.

MARKETING PLUS

OFFERING A FULL RANGE OF SERVICES

Robert Hance, Marketing Plus, planning a new product introduction.

Paul Zylka, Zylka Design, developing a new brochure for Marketing Plus.

Marketing Plus has established itself as a true marketing driven advertising and promotion agency, dedicated to producing specific results for its clients. Established in 1983 by Robert W. Hance, the agency has grown from a small base of national food oriented accounts, to a medium size agency representing a broad base of diversified national, regional and local companies.

The name of the agency is indicative of the range of services provided to its clients. In many cases, the agency actually serves as the marketing department for the company, thus providing a truly integrated form of advertising. Operating in this manner is ideal because all forms of communication can be tied together in a consistent and coordinated effort. Additionally, the client benefits by the efficiency under which the programs are executed.

The background of the agency head, Robert W. Hance, is somewhat unique among other advertising firms in the valley, due to his strong advertising and sales experience with several international businesses known for their outstanding marketing expertise. These include General Foods, American Can, Beech-Nut, LEGO Toys and Seabrook Foods. This experience, says Hance, has provided the foundation upon which sound advertising objectives and strategies are developed to meet specific client goals.

The diversity of services range from product development, packaging, promotion and public relations to the more traditional support in media, copy and graphic design. Almost all forms of communication are employed, such as television, radio, print and direct mail. Perhaps one of the most underrated marketing tools available to almost all clients, at virtually no cost, involves the use of consumer premium programs.

While the agency has grown over the last several years, the underlying commitment to provide professional results-oriented programs on a cost effective basis has never changed. This comes from servicing a limited number of clients, selecting highly talented professionals and using proper budgeting to control costs.

The agency is closely involved with the Fresno community, having actively participated in many local fund raising activities such as The Association for Retarded Citizens Tennis Tournament, The Greater Valley Concours D' Elegence Car Show and Storyland at Roeding Park.

While electronic media rate rave reviews for immediacy and vitality, print has always played a significant role in Fresno, as in all the nation's cities and towns. From time to time, as various immigrant groups settled in the Valley, Armenian, Russian, German, Japanese and Spanish language newspapers have been published, and neighborhood and special-interest papers still appear from time to time.

But for most Fresnans, the newspaper means *The Fresno Bee*. Founded in 1922 and rapidly acquiring the competing *Fresno Morning Republican* and *Fresno Evening Herald*, the *Bee* has enjoyed an unbroken record of independent reporting. When the *Bee* was merely three years old it introduced a technological marvel, wirephoto transmitted pictures of President Coolidge's inauguration, published on Inauguration Day! Within its first decade, the *Bee* introduced another tradition, as characteristic of its reputation as its technological currency: the mounting of public information campaigns in matters of local significance.

The *Bee* has been an editorial advocate of projects which its management feels are in the best interests of Fresno and the San Joaquin Valley. Since its first issue, it has been a consistently strong supporter of natural resource conservation and public ownership of utilities. It has supported water development and land reclamation projects, expressing concern for the health of Fresno's agricultural base. The *Bee* has explored the environmental issues of pesticides and of soil and ground water contamination which impact the lives of the thousands of Valley residents who work in the fields and vineyards. Most recently, the paper has been at the forefront of the movement to protect land along a 21-mile stretch of the San Joaquin River from Freeway 99 to Friant Dam for development as a parkway.

The *Bee*'s role as a good corporate citizen reaches beyond advocacy in print. When the newspaper outgrew its original plant, *Bee* owners contributed the elegant building to house the Fresno Metropolitan Museum of Art, History and Science. Charitable support of the arts did not end with donation of its outgrown physical plant; over the years, the *Bee* has been a consistent supporter and reliable friend of cultural, educational, health, civic and athletic causes.

For six decades, the *Fresno Bee* has been a dedicated corporate citizen of Fresno. Part of the Sacramento-based McClatchy Newspapers, the *Bee* is a major employer, a community supporter and a concerned advocate for maintaining Fresno as a fine place to live. With its Disney-designed logo, its computerized, modern plant, and its commitment to preserving and enhancing Fresno's quality of life, the *Bee* plays a most important role in the community's life and growth.

The California Advocate is a Fresno-based weekly newspaper with an area circualtion of 22,500. The paper has been in business since 1967, and although the paper's readership is quite diversified, it attempts to focus on the black and minority community, acting as an advocate for the enhancement of the minority communities throughout the San Joaquin Valley.

Owned and operated by the Les Kimber family, the paper has championed a number of community causes, especially meaningful to West Fresno, including economic development, district representation, and anti-drug efforts.

Channel 24 was Fresno's first T.V. station to have complete satellite linkage.

LINKAGE RESOURCES — MAKING THE NETWORK WORK

The impressive resources of Fresno's city and county governments, and of its communication and transportation networks, would be of no use were it not for the agents of access. These resourceful and catalytic organizations serve the crucial function of linking need and solution, question and answer.

Prominent among these organizations is the Fresno Economic Development Corporation. Funded in part by city governments, and in part by the Chamber of Commerce, the EDC exists to market the Fresno community. It seeks to attract new businesses and encourage expansion of existing operations, serving as a facilitator by opening doors to commercial development. Its high visibility makes it a place for newcomers to find one-stop answers to their business questions.

At the vigorous, productive Chamber of Commerce, the Small Business Resource Center serves as an information clearing-house. A public service arm of the chamber, the center operates a referral network comprised of 30 local agencies providing services exclusively to small businesses. A wealth of resources is available from the center, including brochures on starting businesses — and identifying the resources to finance them, directories of firms, organizations and associations, and a full range of demographic and statistical information on area markets.
Its services include in-house consulting, workshops for new business owners, and seminars for owners of existing businesses. The Business Hotline telephone answer service meets an important need.

The Small Business Resource Center, true to its network-in-action nature, maintains a vital relationship with the Fresno Private Industry Council (PIC). It places an impressive number of employees each year through its contract with the PIC. The Private Industry Council works through a network of contractors, like the Small Business Resource Center, to place laid-off workers and low income citizens in appropriate vocational training and employment settings. Its staff develops, implements and monitors job

(Continued on page 158)

KSEE, TV-24

FRESNO'S FIRST TELEVISION STATION

KSEE, TV-24, brought television to Fresno.

KMJ-TV, as it was called prior to 1983, took to the air on June 1, 1953, broadcasting programs, as it still does today, that inform, and entertain viewers in Fresno and the heart of Central California.

One of the first programs carried by KSEE was the Inauguration of Queen Elizabeth II. Since then hundreds of thousands of San Joaquin Valley families have grown up watching KSEE news, sports, comedy and drama programs, just as television itself has grown up from its early beginnings.

In the over three decades that have followed the premiere telecast, a steady and diverse influx of people and businesses have rocketed Fresno into one of California's fastest growing large cities and made it the 63rd largest broadcast market in the country.

In 1983 Meredith Corporation bought the station. Meredith is a diversified media company with interests in publishing, broadcasting, printing and real estate. Meredith publishes and prints Better Homes And Garden magazine as well as other related Better Homes And Garden products for the family.

KSEE, TV-24's programming reflects its commitment to be responsive to local needs. KSEE's Newscenter 24, consistently an industry leader, covers Fresno and San Joaquin valley news all seven days a week.

KSEE's news firsts include:

* First to use news film
* First to use color
* First to use sound on film
* First to use electronic news gathering
* First Live Remote Unit

KSEE is especially proud of its commitment to community involvement which is reflected in both award winning public affairs programming and personal involvement at all levels of community activities by many members of the KSEE staff.

Recently, KSEE moved to brand new facilities, becoming Fresno's premiere, state of the art broadcast and production center.

In addition to being able to broadcast the highest quality television picture and sound, KSEE's two 40x60 foot news and production studios, three Phillips color cameras, Chyron IV character generators, Ampex production switchers, digital effects and video tape recorders make it the best equipped production center between Los Angeles and San Francisco.

KSEE also became Fresno's first network affiliated station to broadcast its programs in stereo and one of the few in the nation to be able to originate local programs in stereo.

KFSN-TV 30 FRESNO

FRESNO'S LEADING TELEVISION SERVICE

From left to right: ACTION NEWS personalities Dan Taylor, Rudy Trevino, Nancy Osborne, Don Postles, Liz Harrison and Angelo Stalis.

On May 10, 1956, the ancestor of what was to become KFSN-TV, Channel 30, began its television service to Fresno and the six county area of Central California. In 1971, the station was purchased by Capital Cities Communications, Inc. and, since then, Channel 30 has become the most popular station in town according to the Arbitron Ratings reports.

Channel 30 programming reflects its staff's commitment to be responsive to the local community. The station's Action News broadcasts have long attracted the largest audiences of any other local news competitors. Action News programs are seen daily at 7:25 and 8:25 a.m.; 12 Noon, 5, 6 and 11 p.m. Four newscasts over the weekends are also available. Viewers in Fresno and the Central Valley have come to rely on Channel 30 Action News for extensive, reliable and credible local news coverage. State-of-the-art technical equipment in the hands of experienced producers, reporters, photographers and research staff guarantee the best results. Channel 30 Action News provides Fresno and the Central Valley with exclusive Accu-Weather forecasts.

In addition to the programs of the ABC Television Network, Channel 30 televises many of the most popular nationally syndicated programs. The Oprah Winfrey Show and the Phil Donahue Show provide viewers with stimulating talk/information each afternoon from 3 to 5 p.m. From 6:30 to 8:00 p.m., the most popular game shows, including Wheel of Fortune and Jeopardy, provide fun-filled entertainment. Saturday evenings, Channel 30 is the exclusive Fresno area television station broadcasting the California Lottery's Big Spin and Lotto programs.

KFSN-TV, Channel 30, is the area's acknowledged television leader in community affairs broadcasting. Each spring, the station televises the Miracle Network Telethon on behalf of Valley Children's Hospital, an effort which raises more than half-a-million dollars annually. Each January, the station televises the United Cerebral Palsy Telethon. NEA, the National Education Association, cited Channel 30 for one of the first Stay in School campaigns aimed at curtailing student dropouts. The nationally successful Moments for MS (Multiple Sclerosis) campaign had its origins at Fresno's Channel 30. The station provided the impetus for the Fresno Unified School District's Here's Looking at You anti-drug campaign now in place at every grade level in the district's classrooms.

In the more than 30 years that Channel 30 has served Fresno and the valley, the area's population has grown rapidly. Recent studies show the growth continues at a rate two-and-a-half times faster than that of the rest of California. The television industry has grown, too, with eight local stations available and large numbers of homes equipped for cable reception, the program choice is even greater. However, through the years, Channel 30's firm commitment to news, quality programming and community affairs has kept KFSN-TV the number one television station in the area.

All of which is summed up by the station's motto: Channel 30 Action News . . . Leadership that Works for You!

training and employment programs under the expert guidance of a volunteer board of directors. Careful pre-screening and on-the-job monitoring helps to provide cooperating client companies with appropriate employees. The PIC also works closely with the Fresno Economic Development Corporation, thereby enabling new and expanding businesses to take advantage of this effective, economical employee recruitment system. Older citizens, the disabled and refugee groups have been identified by the Fresno Private Industry Council as sources of capable and willing workers.

For specific business needs, the Small Business Administration (SBA) and the co-located Service Corps of Retired Executives can provide pertinent information and individualized assistance. In addition, the SBA sponsors — often in conjunction with California State University's Valley Business Center — a number of informative workshops each year.

Under a cooperative agreement with the U.S. Department of Commerce, the Fresno-based NEDA office offers full service business consulting services, with a special focus on minority business development. Among the NEDA services are management support, marketing development, procurement assistance, construction and contracting development, financial development and assistance in selling to the private sector. NEDA also presents a weekly small business information program on cable television, and assists business owners and managers in identifying potential sources of both business and employees, relying on the PIC linkages.

The Convention and Visitors Bureau offers a broad array of support services to the company or organization contemplating Fresno as a meeting center. Whether the meeting is an industry-wide trade show or a regional professional association retreat, the bureau assists meeting planners in securing the right facilities, programs and support services for a first-class event.

Fresno's active network of problem solvers responds not only to the myriad business needs for information and service, but also provides a parallel network of effective resources for individual needs. The Fresno County Library, in collaboration with the Fresno County Department of Social Services, has each year for nearly a decade published the Fresno County Resources Directory. This monumental volume catalogs, describes and cross-references every social service agency and human service office in the county. Potential clients can find out what documentation is required to initiate assistance, the kind and cost of services available, and even the waiting time to expect in obtaining desired services. From child care to mental health, convalescent homes to legal services, this is the standard reference — comprehensive, current and exceedingly useful. While other referral agencies serve areas of specific need, such as dental care or mental health, this single volume efficiently steers the newcomer or long-time resident to qualified area service providers.

To avoid problems of duplication of services, inefficiency, inconsistency and gaps in service provision, the Fresno Interagency Committee sponsors studies, written reports, and implemented effective programs in various kinds of youth services. In 1987, an adult Interagency Committee was formed, building on its predecessor's success, to better serve the needs of Fresno's adult population. With initiatives like these, Fresno's solid reputation as a community of caring, committed and effective networks in action is certain to grow.

Channel 30 sports covers one of America's premier swimming competitions at the Clovis School's Olympic Swim Complex located on the Clovis West High School campus.

Steve Dzerigian

Recreation and Cultural Arts

CHAPTER 7

Clair E. Nelsen

Steve Dzerigian

Yosemite Valley reflected in crystal waters.

"So much; so close!" proclaims the Convention and Visitors Bureau, and with good reason. There's a multitude of wonders, adventures and attractions minutes away from every Fresno doorstep. Have a free hour at lunchtime, or perhaps a few hours on Saturday morning? Take in the latest show at the Arts Center, wander through the shops in Farmers' Market, scan the newspaper's entertainment section to plan a fun-filled evening on the town, or pack a picnic dinner for enjoyment at a mountain lake shore after work. All possible for the Fresnan. But there's more.

An unexpected day off? If you can resist the golf courses, tennis clubs, zoo, and Japanese Garden in town, pack a lunch and head for the giant Sequoias in Kings Canyon National Park. Or drive to Monterey for an afternoon at the beach and a tour of the wonderful new aquarium.

But for most Fresnans, and for millions of less fortunate people who must travel great distances to find the ultimate in rest and recuperation for fragile psyches or frayed nerves — or just for sheer wonderment — Yosemite National Park, the Range of Light, is the temptation extraordinary, the loveliest spot on earth.

These attractions and many more are at the fingertips of the average Fresnan. Pleasures as diverse and as satisfying as a fresh, juicy plum on a summer evening, a world-class show at the Metropolitan Museum, chamber music at a garden wine-tasting, or champion bronco-busting at the rodeo are here for the taking. Whatever one's work-weary heart might desire can be found in or around Fresno.

THE GATEWAY

Minutes from downtown Fresno, in the gateway to the greater splendor of California's alpine majesty, lie oak- and granite- covered rolling foothills, dotted with lakes and brimming with history and excitement. Modern-day visitors can pan for gold, pick luscious apples, marvel at artifacts in the Mono Indian Museum, ride on an authentic steam-driven logging train or scoop up bargains at the Peddler's Fair. Stern-wheeled boat rides compete with melodrama for attention, and boating, camping and horseback riding take the visitor miles and years from the cares of the day. Pleasant, comfortable small towns offer every amenity, including four-star French cuisine which has been extolled in *The New York Times*! There's enough variety to satisfy the most jaded appetite. Spring wildflower gathering, summer waterskiing, fall hiking in the Ansel Adams Wilderness Area, and winter cross-country skiing beckon city-dwellers to the rustic, clean, quiet beauty of the Gateway area.

SEQUOIA AND KINGS CANYON NATIONAL PARKS

An easy half-hour drive from Fresno takes one to the "convenient wilderness" of Kings Canyon and, just beyond, Sequoia National Park. Sequoia, the first to be established, was set aside by Congress in 1890 to prevent logging interests from destroying the great natural wonders of the giant redwood trees. Sequoia's 604 square miles and the adjoining 719 square miles of Kings Canyon offer refreshingly clean mountain air, the grandeur of the Great Western Divide, and the amazing and inspiring pillars of the Giant Sequoias to more than a million visitors each year.

Largest of all living things, the Giant Sequoias rise as high as 274 feet into the crisp pine-scented air, supported by cinnamon-red trunks as much as 30 feet in diameter. When the largest, the General Sherman, sprouted about 3,000 years ago, Egyptian armies were in the process of conquering the known world. A thousand years old when the star shone over Bethlehem, this tree and its neighbors have silently witnessed the sorrows and joys of much of human history. The General Sherman was at one time named in honor of Karl Marx by a Utopian community nearby. The second largest of the big trees, the General Grant, stands in neighboring Kings Canyon as the nation's Christmas Tree, and serves annually as the focal point for a non-denominational commemoration of the nation's war dead.

Horses graze in the pastoral beauty of Wonder Valley.

Clair E. Nelsen

The crystal blue waters of Hume Lake, located in the Sequoia National Park.

Judy Baker

In all their towering beauty, the Sequoias are somewhat fragile. With no tap root, they are vulnerable to high winds and to the compaction of the soil about their shallow root system. Diligent park system management has helped to ensure they will remain an inspiration for generations to come. Born in the Mesozoic era and spread at one time across the vast continent, these few remaining Giant Sequoias are national treasures.

Although the groves of Giant Sequoias are the best known feature of these national parks, a multitude of other high-country delights tempt the visitor to tarry. The southern terminus of the 188-mile John Muir Trail is in Kings Canyon, linking it to Tuolumne Meadows in Yosemite at the northern end. Altogether there are 900 miles of backpacking trails in the two parks, as well as fishing, horseback riding, camping, bus tours, and such attractions as Moro Rock, Crystal Cave, Crescent Meadow, Tokopah Falls and Wolverton Ski Bowl. Seventy-five miles of cross-country ski trails weave among the giant trees, offering the adventurer an unforgettable experience. The beautiful Kings Canyon invites the wilderness lover to pitch a summer camp far from the frantic hustle of the city below.

From hundreds of sites in Kings Canyon, one can find unsurpassed views of the Great Western Divide. No better vantage points exist to marvel at the majestic Sierra Nevada, the longest unbroken mountain range in the United States. Lying between the arid eastern desert and the fruited plain of the San Joaquin Valley, the range is capped by awe-inspiring Mt. Whitney, which at 14,494 feet is the highest mountain in the continental United States. In contrast to the gentle roll of the Appalachians or other geologically old ranges, the Sierra Nevada is relatively new, raised up by shifts in the earth's crust during the Pleistocene Epoch. California's wondrous Sierra supports hawks, deer, bears and many other species of wildlife in addition to the noble Sequoias of Kings Canyon and Sequoia National Parks.

An elk pauses in a field in the Sierras.

Galen Rowell

YOSEMITE, STUNNING BEAUTY

Approximately 60 million years ago, an earth fault of almost incomprehensible magnitude angled a 440 mile long, 80 mile wide mass of rock upward to form the jagged peaks of the Great Western Divide. Rapidly tumbling streams etched deep V-shaped gorges in the rock, leaving behind, high on the side walls, the waterfalls of a hundred smaller, slower tributaries. As the snows of the ice age piled up deeper and deeper, sheer weight compacted them into rivers of ice. These glaciers etched, gouged and polished the granite over which they moved, leaving behind broad U-shaped valleys and towering walls of polished rock. Exfoliation — the expansion and cracking off of onion-like layers of rock — rounded and shaped great bald domes of granite high above the valley floor. The warming ages brought pine, fir and abundant wildlife to these lovely lands. Giant Sequoias stood guard over sparkling streams, and sentinels of stone waited silently for the poet, the laborer and the lover to discover the wild grace of what Teddy Roosevelt called "the most beautiful place in the world."

Galen Rowell

Galen Rowell

A storm clears to reveal the grandeur of Yosemite's El Capitan.

Each summer weekend, more than 40,000 visitors stream into Yosemite National Park to marvel at the handiwork of the ages, painstakingly preserved for the nation to enjoy. They come to breathe the clean, pine-scented air, to stroll beside the sun-dappled river, to relax in the soul-satisfying beauty that is Yosemite. The story of how this unusual harmony of civilization and nature came about is one of idealism, commitment, love and luck.

Yosemite was officially discovered in 1851 by the Mariposa Battalion as it chased an Indian raiding party back into the mountains. However, the site was recorded in a gold miner's journal in 1849, and it was well known to the mountain tribes which summered in its meadows. It is from one of these tribes, the Grizzlies, or Uzumati, that Yosemite gets its name.

By the latter half of the 19th century, the American frontier had all but disappeared, and with it, cheap farming land. A national network of railroads was in place, and the nation was rapidly becoming urbanized. There was a growing awareness of the devastation wreaked in the nation's wilderness areas by unregulated logging and mining. Concerned citizens banded together in conservation associations to put an end to the pillaging of mountains and forests.

The American Association for the Advancement of Science was founded in 1874 to protect natural resources of high economic value from exploitation by any single corporation. In 1875, the American Forestry Association moved to encourage government management of public lands. A variety of mountain clubs sprang up in the east, and the Audubon Society was founded in 1886. Teddy Roosevelt's vigorous Boone and Crockett Club was formed in 1887 to promote sport hunting and to preserve existing herds of large game in the American wilderness.

Spurred by a growing interest in Yosemite and the impassioned defense of the mountain area by John Muir, a group of 27 San Francisco intellectual and political leaders organized the Sierra Club in 1892. Its purpose: to protect Yosemite from commercial exploitation and destruction. As early as 1855, a tour group from the Bay area visited Yosemite Valley. Sketches of Yosemite by tour member and artist Thomas A. Ayres were widely published. In 1859, the influential *California Magazine* published photos of Yosemite's scenic wonders, and in the summer of 1864, a total of 653 hardy souls endured the grueling pack trip into Yosemite Valley.

The Gold Rush spurred hopes of mineral wealth throughout the Sierra. In 1860, the state legislature authorized California State Geologist Josiah Whitney and his assistant, botanist William H. Brewer, to map the high terrain. For the next four years, their party diligently documented every peak and valley, named the meadows, and correctly surmised the role of glaciation in the formation of

Picture at right courtesy of Galen Rowell.

A daring climber scales the face of Yosemite Falls.

Bob Barnes

Mt. Whitney is the highest mountain in the contiguous 48 states.

the spectacular valley. They bestowed the names of eminent geologists — an American, Dana, and an Englishman, Lyell — on the highest peaks. The highest peak of all was named for Whitney, even though the party's journals indicate he did less actual climbing than other party members.

Hetch Hetchy, Yosemite's sister valley, was the subject of prolonged debate. As lovely as Yosemite, but more compact in arrangement, the wonders of Hetch Hetchy could be grasped with one sweeping view. However, San Francisco water interests — with a powerful lobby in the state legislature — wanted to flood Hetch Hetchy Valley to meet the city's water and power needs. Disunity within the Sierra Club crippled its impact and led to a tragic but instructive loss; the city won the right to flood the valley. In the 12-year battle over Hetch Hetchy the nation faced, perhaps for the first time in so conscious and public a fashion, a choice between preserving the beauty of the wilderness or destroying it for commercial purposes.

The mark of the early pioneers and park zealots is still evident in Yosemite. The John Muir Trail stretches along the Sierra crest from Yosemite Valley to Mount Whitney. Tioga Road, frequently called the Tioga Pass, was purchased by Steve Mather in 1914; it provides an eastern access to the park — at least during the summer. Rangers take visitors on nature walks and interpret the eloquent insights of geologist Francois Matthes, who speculated on the geologic origins of Yosemite years ago. Matthes' Yosemite Field School still attracts both scholars and amateur scientists. A naturalist's paradise, Yosemite — with 1,187 square miles of unsurpassed beauty — stands as a monument to the glory of nature. Visitors year after year testify to the truth of John Muir's prediction: "You will want to stay forever."

But desire isn't enough, and most visitors have to face the inevitable departure sooner than they'd like — vowing, no doubt, to return at the earliest opportunity. The southeastern entry, an hour and a half from Fresno, takes one through the Giant Sequoias of Mariposa Grove. These living giants are a fitting introduction and departure point to this land where the human perspective on things suddenly seems insignificant. Overlooking the valley is the breathtaking vista of Glacier Point. Its panoramic views orient the visitor to the marvels to be seen from a closer range on the valley floor.

Once through Wawona Tunnel, the visitor must stop to absorb the compelling view of the valley. From this vantage point, the sheer massiveness of El Capitan, 3,500 feet in elevation, the rugged, glacier cut of Half Dome, and Bridal Veil Falls, a 620- foot high floating mist of prismic splendor, are planted in the memory in one sweeping view. The looping road through the seven-square mile valley brings visitors in touch with wonders too magnificent for words: the splashing extravagance of Yosemite Falls — 2,425 feet of purest beauty, the mystery of Sentinel Rock, the camps, the hotels and shops, and the chill beauty of the crisply churning Merced River, pausing from time to time in pools that tempt one to dip in a finger, but ever moving in its undercurrent of momentum toward the San Joaquin Valley below.

Beauty abounds in every direction. A leisurely drive on through the valley leads to the Alpine splendor of Tuolumne Meadows. Hiking trails tempt the hardy to sample still more wonders of the high Sierra showplace. Lumbering bears — never, never feed them — can be seen in many areas of the park, and deer may be sighted morning and evening. The trill of bird calls, the lush profusion of wildflowers and the crisp fragrance of pine combine to cleanse and stir one to

The sun illuminates one of the beautiful waterfalls in Yosemite.

Bob Miksch, Jr.

the soul's very depths. Mountain climbing, painting, skiing, photography, Nordic touring and horseback riding are there for the taking. At times, just breathing deeply of the pure mountain air seems to be enough.

The visitor leaves Yosemite with a glance over the shoulder, a farewell until next time, a silent promise to return, to wonder again and live more fully for having been embraced by the wondrous beauty we call Yosemite.

Clair E. Nelsen

Enthusiasts enjoy the thrill of white water rafting on the Kings River.

MOUNTAIN LAKES AND RIVERS

Just minutes from the city, families and friends can gather for an evening or a weekend of sailing, fishing, waterskiing or just lazing on a "party boat" on the foothill lakes of Millerton and Pine Flat. Formed by dams, these easily accessible lakes feature well-marked, paved, boat launch areas, picnic tables and rest rooms. Windsurfing classes take advantage of morning and evening breezes, and swimmers and surfers dot the shoreline. Oak-dotted rolling hills surround the lakes, and vistas of distant, snow-capped mountains grace the scene.

Another hour of driving brings the recreation enthusiast to the high country lakes: Bass, Shaver and Huntington. Tall pines, clear, cool water and rustic cabins are the attractions here; the lakes seem to be worlds away from the dry summer heat of the valley below. Swim, fish, ride the "Bass Lake Queen," jet ski or rent a paddle boat — there's always something exciting to do at these refreshing mountain lakes. Midsummer finds the region's best sailors competing in the renowned Huntington Regata. On a summer Sunday, entire congregations from Fresno churches journey to Bass Lake for an inspirational "church in the mountains" service followed by picnics, swimming and a softball game. Scout camps, church camps and vacation resorts lie hidden in the pines, offering weeks of enjoyment in the invigorating mountains. The lakes are popular honeymoon locations as well. It's not uncommon to see couples who are returning years later with their families to this pleasant summer paradise.

In the winter, skis and snowmobiles are the order of the day. A stream of cars, complete with chains against a sudden storm, bring snow enthusiasts to this winter wonderland. Snowshoe to a lodge for a cup of hot cocoa, or just snuggle up to the hearth in a cozy cabin. Winter or summer, the beautiful mountain lakes so close to Fresno offer a world of wholesome outdoor recreation for the entire family.

Galen Rowell

Wildflowers grace the Sierra foothills.

In contrast to the placid lakes, the rivers of Central California offer the sporting enthusiast a sometimes more vigorous outing. For incomparable fishing, or for the ride of your life, try the mightiest of California's famous whitewater rivers — the glorious Kings River! Rushing down from its high Sierra birthplace, the roaring river divides Sequoia and Sierra National Forests and flows westerly through beautiful Kings Canyon National Park. At Twin Pines Camp on the banks of the upper Kings, about 60 miles east of Fresno, excitement is intense during the Spring high water season — from late April through mid-June. Adventurers from all over the world gather to challenge the river in the experience of a lifetime. Under the expert guidance of expedition staff, the rafters work their way through "side winder," "fang tooth," and many other rapids, each more formidable than the last. Deli lunches, barbecue dinners and camp volleyball games add the comforts of civilization to the great outdoor adventure. While only the fittest adults take on the river in high water days, after the river warms in mid-June even children as young as nine enjoy the thrill of rafting through the beautiful valley of the Kings River. *(Continued on page 170)*

WONDER VALLEY RANCH RESORT

CONFERENCE, PICNIC AND BANQUET HAVEN

Clair E. Nelsen

Horseback riding is one of many pleasures guests enjoy at Wonder Valley Ranch.

Clair E. Nelsen

A profusion of wildflowers grow in Wonder Valley.

Rolling oak covered hills, groves of giant sycamores, a sparkling creek, a quiet lake – this is Wonder Valley. Nestled in the foothills of the Sierras, 35 minutes east of Fresno, the grandeur of Wonder Valley remains unspoiled and little changed.

The ranch grounds cover fifty-two acres of the valley floor, and the trail rights include the surrounding 1600 acres. The 600 foot elevation assures visitors of sun filled days and starry nights.

Wonder Valley was California's first guest ranch. In 1911, George Pierson, a horse and cattle rancher, purchased the land. His visitors were so impressed with the beauty of his property that they soon became paying guests.

Paul and Becky Webb purchased the ranch in 1948 and continued the tradition of warm hospitality.

In 1973, Stan Oken, President of Western Camps, Inc., fell in love with the ranch as a guest. Wonder Valley offered the perfect setting for tour groups, conferences, picnics and children's summer camp. The ranch was purchased and the Oken family still operates it together. Stan and his three children help create the family atmosphere that has become a tradition at Wonder Valley. Roy Oken and his wife Liz manage and operate the resort. Nancy Oken Nighbert and her husband, Jeff Nighbert are directors of the River Way Ranch children's camp. Larry Oken oversees the business operations.

Wonder Valley is the ideal place for conferences and seminars. It offers a secluded and peaceful country environment, complimentary meeting rooms, package plans at reasonable group rates and a Group Services Coordinator to assist in planning the event and activities for spouses while delegates meet.

Wonder Valley's professional picnic planners can guarantee groups of 100 to 5,000 people fun, excitement, great food and an experience that won't soon be forgotten. You can choose a poolside, lakeside or patio picnic.

And there won't be an idle moment. Picnic activities can include any combination of activities, such as: sailing, swimming, horseback riding, hayrides, dancing, horseshoes, goat milking, fishing, softball, volleyball, dunk tanks and cowchip throwing. In addition, there can be strolling musicians, bands, barbershop quartets, sing-a-longs, clowns, staged gunfights and casino activities.

Experience old California. The western decor of the ranch facilities and accommodations have all the charm of the past with all the conveniences of today. Ranch fresh produce and dairy products, carefully selected meats and freshly-baked breads and pastries are delicious traditions in the kitchen. Relaxation, fun, excitement – Wonder Valley has them all. The staff, who offers warm western hospitality, await your arrival.

Clair E. Nelsen

The spectacular beauty of Pine Flat Lake is captured.

HISTORIC FOOTHILL DUDE RANCH

A scenic 40-minute drive from Fresno, but a world apart, lies the lovely secluded Wonder Valley. Yokut Indians were the first inhabitants of this area. Later, the infamous Dalton Gang terrorized passing trains from its Wonder Valley hideout. Today's guests at the Wonder Valley Dude Ranch are likely to meet up with a modern-day version of the gang, gone "crazy with guilt," who pass out tokens for the contests and games of chance at the resort.

When California's first guest ranch was established on this site, celebrities filled the guest books. Tour groups, corporate retreats and family vacationers now find the same warm hospitality and old-fashioned fun that once drew so many of the famous. Forty different activities entice the vacationer, from canoeing on the private lake to horsedrawn hayrides and goat milking contests. Tennis and golf are available, and guided nature walks criss-cross the 1600 shaded acres of this beautiful foothill valley. The program staff has established 12 "wanders" or tours of the area's attractions. The Turn-of-the-Century Tour, the Fresno Tour and the Historic Homes Tour all include a sampling of Fresno's points of historical significance. The National Parks Tour, the Rodeo Tour and the County Fair Tour capitalize on festive seasonal offerings. Informed guides help each visitor gain the most from every trip before returning to the comfortable guest rooms and exceptional meals that have been a resort tradition since 1911.

Guests accosted by 20th century desperadoes at Wonder Valley Ranch Resort.

Wonder Valley Ranch guests discover the joys of goat milking.

SIERRA SUMMIT SKI AREA

HOT SPOT IN THE HIGH SIERRA

Three skiers get a lift.

Sierra Summit, Central California's winter hot spot in the high Sierra, is just 65 miles northeast of Fresno on Highway 168. It's an easy drive for a day of skiing from either the Central Valley or Central Coast cities. Sierra Summit offers some of the best ski terrain in the Central Sierra and has become well known for both its fine skiing and friendly atmosphere. The Sierra Summit Inn, located at the base of the slopes, offers comfortable lodging, fine dining and a cozy lounge for after-ski enjoyment.

The mountain rises up 1600 vertical feet to the top of Chinese Peak, elevation 8,709, and has annual snowfall over 200 inches. Sierra Summit offers 230 acres of cleared ski runs (over 12 total miles), with an abundance of terrain to suit beginners through seasoned experts. To provide more consistent snow coverage and to enhance the skiing experience, Sierra Summit has installed a supplemental snow making system in its first phase, covering most of the lower one half of the mountain and in several areas of the upper slopes.

SKIING IN THE SIERRA

Fresno area skiers have an incredible variety of choices for their winter enjoyment. Cross-country enthusiasts can choose from ten Sierra resorts providing miles of groomed track, or they can simply glide through the mountains on informal trails and tracks found near every high country resort. A simple, inexpensive and wholesome family entertainment, cross-country skiing is attracting many Alpine skiers as a second ski experience. It serves for many as an introduction to the world of winter sports. Family members of all ages can enjoy cross-country skiing, and can make new friends at the strategically-located warming huts. Closest to Fresno are the 16 trails of Montecito Sequoia with their 65 kilometers of groomed trail. Located in Sequoia National Park, this resort offers lodging, meals, rentals, day care and warming hut facilities.

At Yosemite's Badger Pass, 35 trails provide 32 kilometers of groomed ski track across the spectacular wilderness area. The day lodge includes a cafe, ski school, rentals and day care; there are two warming huts. Nearly 500 beds are available within a ten-mile radius for overnight guests. Farther north, east of Stockton, lie the 90 kilometers of groomed trail at Bear Valley Nordic, one of the largest trail systems in the west. Tahoe's trails, as well as those at Mammoth, await the traveler who ventures farther afield. Throughout the Sierra, beginners and experienced skiers alike can be assured of delightful days of skiing in the grandest scenic areas imaginable!

Downhill ski enthusiasts have their choice of two excellent, readily accessible ski areas: Sierra Summit and Yosemite's Badger Pass. Sierra Summit offers beginner-friendly runs as well as those calculated to challenge intermediate and advanced skiers. The ski school staff holds daily classes, giving encouragement for graded progress through the Firebowl to the chair lifts. Steep and bumpy

The expert grooming crew works hard nightly in their state-of-the-art grooming vehicles to prepare the best possible skiing surface each day.

The first-time skier will find Sierra Summit's Introduction-To-Skiing program a tremendous bargain. The resort has an excellent bunny slope to get started, an easy-to-ride handle tow, and a full-time, highly trained staff of ski teaching professionals. Novice and low intermediate skiers can spend all day on Academy Run, a two-and-one-half mile trail that winds down the mountain from the top of Chair #1 to the base lodge. Intermediate skiers can enjoy a wide variety of terrain suited perfectly to their abilities, and experts will also find plenty of skiing to their liking. The wide open areas of the "The Face," "China Bowl" off of Chair #5 and the steep slots of "Waterfall," "Dynamite" and "Buckhorn" all attract a wide following of top level skiers.

Sierra Summit offers all the amenities necessary for a complete ski trip, beginning with a full service rental shop with over 800 pairs of skis and boots, and a large inventory of junior equipment. The resort's Ski School and Race Department have lessons and clinics for the never-ever skier through the expert racer; classes are available daily, and Standard Races run Wednesday through Sunday. The Sierra Summit Sport Shop carries a large selection of the latest ski fashions and accessories, gift items and a deli with beer and wine.

Food services are plentiful, including the Inn, which serves a cafeteria-style breakfast daily, lunches on weekends and holidays, and a full service dinner in the evenings; the Daylodge serves hot and cold lunch items, and has barbecues daily (weather permitting); the Midway House at the bottom of Chair #2 has cold snacks, sandwiches, beverages and barbecues; and the Snack Bar at the base of Chair #3 features sandwiches, snacks, drinks, and a barbecue. For kids six and under, the Daycare Center is open daily and provides adult supervision and a snow-play area.

China Bowl, smooth and wide open runs on chair lift 2, and the easy beginner slopes offer something for everyone. Sierra Summit Inn offers good food and service at reasonable prices; the convenient accommodations are excellent. Friendly, enthusiastic instructors and well-groomed slopes conspire to tempt even the most dedicated snow bunny away from the lodge. Advantageous group arrangements and the delightful view of Huntington Lake combine to make skiing at Sierra Summit a memorable experience.

Yosemite's Badger Pass, in operation since 1935, offers delightful skiing for all ability levels. The nine runs provide 50 percent availability for intermediate skiers, 35 percent for beginners, and 15 percent for those with advanced skills. Clinics, races and special events enliven the skiing season. Special children's and seniors' ski programs make the slopes accessible to all, and a carefully planned range of after-ski buffets, dances and other activities keeps the fun going long after dark. Capable instructors led by veteran Ski School Director Nic Fiore offer one-day "learn to ski" packages which boast an impressive 99 percent success rate!

These nearby resorts offer everything a skier needs for winter fun, but for Fresno skiers with wanderlust, Squaw Valley, Sugar Bowl, Mammoth, Bear Valley and the many fine areas of Lake Tahoe are within easy range. Good highways, Amtrak and frequent airline flights offer the adventurous skier ready access to the joys of the entire Sierra every winter.

The brightly-dressed clowns are a regular feature of the Clovis Rodeo.

OTHER RECREATION NEAR FRESNO

Closer to home, convenient leisure activities abound. The annual Clovis Rodeo draws large crowds, as the best cowboys and cowgirls in the country compete for top prizes. Clovis Lakes offers family fun just seven miles east of town. It's a popular summer spot for family and company picnics, with such cool and wet attractions as a wave pool, super fast speed slide, raft ride, four water slides, kiddie complex and olympic-size pool. In addition to these water sport facilities, Clovis Lakes includes two softball diamonds, seven volleyball courts, horseshoe pits, picnic groves and fishing. There are catered meals available as well as snack bar treats. Another attraction in the Clovis area is Blackbeard's, a family-style recreation center for the young and young at heart. Its three 18-hole miniature golf courses, batting ranges, water slides, slic-trac races, baby bumper boats and picnic area offer hours of fun for the family at play.

(Continued on page 176)

A child has some summer fun on the water slide at Clovis Lakes.

CLOVIS LAKES

THE BLUE WAVE IN CLOVIS

The Blue Wave is a popular attraction at Clovis Lakes.

Clovis Lakes is one of California's largest water amusement parks. The 52 acre park boasts the wettest, wildest waterways anywhere and fun for the whole family.

Park attractions include White Water rafting, the spine tingling innertube ride on the Rapids and the hair raising ride down the Black Hole speed slide. If that's not enough to take your breath away, try riding the Rampage water coaster ride.

One of the newest attractions at Clovis Lakes is the Blue Wave. Sure to be one of the favorites at the recreational park, the 27,000 square foot pool is one of the largest in the nation. The million dollar attraction incorporates a unique wave machine which can produce ocean-type waves ranging from two to four feet high every two and a half seconds.

Other parks with similar wave pools report that everyone from five years old and up is anxious to ride the waves in some fashion.

You do not have to be "a surfer" to enjoy the thrill of riding the machine-made waves. Men, women, young and old, will find the thrill of catching a big one just as exciting.

The Blue Wave features crystal clear ocean-type waves for body surfing, bodyboarding, inner tubes and other safe flotation devices provided by the park. Surfers will have nearly 100 yards to test their skills or just enjoy a cool ride in the 180 by 300 foot pool. Surfing fans will be challenged by wave patterns that include the Diamond, Double Diamond, Pyramid waves and Roller waves.

Besides these thrilling water rides you will also find four water slides; an olympic swimming pool; a kiddie slide complex; picnic groves; game facilities for softball, volleyball and horseshoes and fishing lakes, which are stocked with bass, bluegill, catfish and trout (in May). A gift shop and arcade complement the recreational facilities.

A delicious Tri-Tip Bar-B-Q is served each evening after five p.m. and there are also three concession stands with food and ice cold refreshments available.

And when your group comes to visit Clovis Lakes, you won't need to worry about feeding them. The chef at Clovis Lakes has 20 years experience catering to groups and can easily feed from 30 to 1000 or more guests.

Summertime parties are Clovis Lakes' specialty. Whether you choose a traditional backyard cookout or an authentic Hawaiian luau complete with grass skirts and hula dancers on the shores of the Blue Wave, Clovis Lakes can take care of all the details.

Clovis Lakes invites you to take a short drive east of Fresno, to enjoy a refreshingly fun day.

FRESNO METROPOLITAN MUSEUM

A COMMITMENT TO ART, HISTORY AND SCIENCE

The Fresno Metropolitan Museum features exhibitions and programs in art, history and science.

The Fresno Metropolitan Museum opened in 1984 to serve the people of the San Joaquin Valley with exhibitions and programs in art, history and science. The museum is recognized as a valley treasure. More than a quarter million people have visited the Met including 60,000 school children who have enjoyed special tours.

The Met's collections are extraordinary, unmatched anywhere else in the valley. Some significant pieces include an outstanding array of over 200 ancient Chinese snuff bottles and Asian objects, original photographs by Ansel Adams and a rare gold coin from California's mining days. The museum has also acquired a major collection of still life and trompe l'oeil paintings from Southern California collector Oscar Salzer, who served as the Met's Curator of Painting until his death in 1987. Through the years the museum's collection has grown and its present value exceeds $3 million.

Visitors discover works of art reaching back through the centuries and representing many lands, cultures and artistic styles with attention focused on the valley's rich cultural heritage. Special exhibits are frequently curated with the help of local collectors and organizations. Various cultural groups, California State University, Fresno and the Fresno City and County Historical Society regularly participate in the Museum's programs.

Science exhibits take visitors from the art and history of the past to man's adventures into the future. The natural wonders of the valley and the mysteries of outer space are showcased.

One striking measure of the museum's achievement has been the number of "firsts" in its schedule of major exhibitions: first U.S. museum to show the 3,000-piece jade exhibit from the Taiwan government; first California museum to mount a display of San Joaquin Valley dinosaurs; only museum West of the Rockies to show "Weavers, Merchants and Kings: The Inscribed Rugs of Armenia" in 1986; and, first in the valley to exhibit NASA's "25 Years of Space Photography."

Featured in this interior view of the Met is the Goddess of Justice statue (right) formerly part of the old Fresno County courthouse and restored for display.

A primary feature of the Fresno Metropolitan Museum is the building itself. Constructed in 1922 to house The Fresno Bee, it is a five-story brick structure with arched windows, terra-

approved the idea and offered to donate the building. City engineers and private architects examined the 100,000 square foot building and judged it structurally sound. The building was granted City Historical status in 1978, and accepted for the National Register of Historic Places in 1983. The Fresno Metropolitan Museum continues to maintain the integrity of the exterior of the 1922 building.

Sponsorship for the Fresno Metropolitan Museum is provided by the Pacific Telesis Foundation.

cotta ornaments, and a recessed porch and balcony. Architects followed the style of the Italian Renaissance in the design. With its bright blue decorative accents, the building is a departure from the conservative architectural style of Fresno.

By the 1970's, the building could no longer be adapted to the needs of a modern newspaper, and The Bee planned to have it demolished. Lewis S. Eaton, a local banker, read about the demolition plans and thought the building might be suitable as a major museum. Officials at the Fresno Bee

One of the elegantly adorned living Christmas trees decorated for the Met's annual Illusions of Christmas exhibit.

RECREATION AND CULTURE IN FRESNO

High quality leisure and cultural activities have long enriched life in Fresno. The city boasts three historical museums, a fully-accredited contemporary Arts Center and Museum, a Discovery Center science museum and the new Metropolitan Museum of Art, History and Science. It supports the professional Fresno Philharmonic Orchestra, numerous dance and performing companies, dinner theaters, and a wide range of musical and artistic organizations served by the umbrella Alliance for the Arts, the arts council for Fresno City and County.

Art education in a variety of disciplines and media is available to persons of all ages through private groups, the California Arts Council, and the recreation department's Creative Activities for You (CAFY) program. Through the Alliance for the Arts, professional artists are contracted to provide city and county school children performances and instruction in the arts. Public outdoor sculpture is showcased in several areas of the city, and excellent galleries offer art exhibits of many media and styles. Private and public interests have joined in beautification efforts in several areas of the city, and an annual festival celebrating the area's ethnic diversity is underwritten by individuals, corporations and public agencies. Historic preservationists have succeeded in restoring and preserving many area architectural treasures.

The Meux Home is a fine example of Fresno's heritage.

So rich is the artistic array and so tempting are the choices that a lifetime of leisure in Fresno would permit only a small sampling. Fresno is a region blessed with abundance, and nowhere is it more evident than in these mind- and spirit-enriching activities.

(Continued on page 178)

FRESNO ARTS CENTER AND MUSEUM

EXPLORE THE MODERN VITAL CULTURAL SHOWCASE

Many fine collectibles can be found in the Fresno Arts Center and Museum Gallery Shop.

The Fresno Arts Center and Museum, established in 1960 in Fresno's Radio Park, today occupies an elegant state-of-the-art 25,000 square foot facility of spartan contemporary lines. The only accredited museum in Central California, the Arts Center provides a forum for 19th and 20th century art widely recognized for its quality, scope and innovative programming. More than twenty exhibits are presented each year. With an extensive interpretative program featuring lectures, tours, concerts, performances and published catalogs, the Arts Center attracts 100,000 visitors annually. Recently reaccredited by the American Museum Association, the center is administered by an elected board of trustees and an expert staff, assisted by many dedicated volunteers.

Each year, the Center's wide-ranging schedule features works from the growing permanent collection as well as from international traveling exhibitions. The Center staff has gained a reputation for creative presentations of significant and distinctive exhibits presented in Fresno for the first time anywhere. Among the finest in recent years was the multi-faceted "Passages: A Survey of California Women Artists 1945 to Present." Extending over a period of a year, the 13 exhibits comprising this series traced the evolution of women's art in California. Gallery displays, lectures, performances, a symposium and a publication provided the most extensive review of this topic ever undertaken by a community institution. Significant components of this unusual and informative project included an exhibition of watercolors with regional themes, a historical exhibit

focusing on prominent women artists whose eminence predated the women's movement, and the exquisite, detailed collaborative textile work, The Birth Project, produced over a five-year period under the artistic direction of Judy Chicago. The overall impact of the project has been to sensitize, enlighten, inform and enrich the artistic experience of area residents.

Subsequent exhibit calendars include a retrospective entitled Director's Choice, representing 40 years of museum acquisitions; an exhibit of pre-Columbian clay sculpture; a Rodin exhibit; watercolors; doll houses and miniatures;

The Childspace Gallery features a constantly changing, high-quality exhibit of particular interest to children.

Inspired pieces are displayed in the Fletcher Benton exhibit.

Ansel Adams' photography; Morris Broderson's still life and portrait work; the Rockefeller collection of Mexican folk art; recent marble sculptures of Professor Bill Minschew; school children's art; drawings and ceramics by Suzanne Sloan Lewis; June Wayne's paintings, prints and tapestries; oils by Fresno artist Merry Scott; and a newly-acquired, extensive collection of prints by Johnny Friedlander.

From its inception, the Center has sought to enlarge the audience for contemporary art. A key element of its programming is service to the youngsters of the community. The Childspace Gallery features a constantly changing, high quality exhibit of particular interest to children, and the Center's educational program reaches many children through classes, workshops and demonstrations. From folk concerts to paper folding, these activities help to ensure an ever-growing number of enthusiasts for the contemporary arts so well showcased at the Fresno Arts Center and Museum.

THE VISUAL ARTS

Enjoyment of the visual arts in Fresno is enhanced by the presence of fine museums and educational institutions. At the Metropolitan Museum of Art, History and Science, as well as at the Fresno Arts Center and Museum, the world-class exhibits are of such variety as to make membership nearly mandatory! Supplementing the offerings of these private agencies are the activities of the many fine studios and galleries and the educational programs and gallery showings of the area's university, colleges and private schools.

THE MET

One of the newest and brightest stars in Fresno's cultural crown is the Metropolitan Museum of Art, History and Science, fondly known locally as "the Met." Elegantly housed in the five-story, 1922 Italian Renaissance-style building that formerly housed *The Fresno Bee*, the museum began to acquire significant collections before its grand opening in 1984. In contrast to centuries-old European institutions whose collections came nearly intact from kings, churches and the plunder of war, the Met is a typically American institution. Gifted and dedicated professionals and business leaders have sought to share their insight and love of the arts through loans and donations from their private collections. The museum's collection is valued at more than $3 million. The first significant acquisition of the museum, the "Portraits and Objects" collection of Oscar and Marie Salzer, exemplifies the spirit of public support surrounding the Metropolitan Museum. This collection of 60 extraordinary still life and trompe l'oeil works brings to the region the finest of a 300-year tradition.

The quality and range of the museum's artistic displays can be gleaned from its list of impressive "firsts:" first U.S. museum to show the 3,000 piece jade exhibit from the government of Taiwan; first California museum to mount a display of San Joaquin Valley dinosaurs (1985); only museum west of the Rockies to show "Weavers, Merchants and Kings: The Inscribed Rugs of Armenia" (1986); and first museum in the valley to exhibit NASA's "25 Years of Space Photography" (1986).

The Met's role in education, entertainment and enrichment for all ages is being fulfilled with relish. Each Christmas, the "Illusions of Christmas" exhibit features a magnificent array of designer-decorated trees, ethnic holiday breads and cookies, music, dance and bell concerts in a month-long celebration. When the Youth Gallery opens, children's projects, arts and crafts will be on year-round display. Family classes and school tours will help make the museum a festival for all seasons and ages.

In addition to the fine collections and exhibitions of its museums, the people of Fresno can claim an exceptional collection of publicly-owned art. Outstanding pieces of sculpture, mosaic, painting and bronze architectural detail add immensely to the ambience of the city. A walk through Fulton Mall or Courthouse Park will bring one into contact with the work of some of the world's most gifted artists. The Convention Center and Fresno Air Terminal proudly display other fine examples of public art. The discerning eye will note an abundance of privately-owned sculpture gracing corporate offices and courtyards throughout the city, attesting to the artistic sensitivity of Fresno's business and civic leaders.

Outstanding theatrical productions are performed at the area's university and colleges, like this one at Fresno Pacific College.

THE LIVELY ARTS

Several outstanding theatrical performances are offered each season by the area's university and colleges. In addition, stage enthusiasts can enjoy the presentations of a variety of professional theater groups. Storyland at Roeding Park is the site for summer performances geared to the younger set; many of these are original, and all are performed by youngsters enrolled in the summer Young Actors' Workshop program started in the late 1970s by Fresno performer Jeri Nagle.

Roger Rocka's Music Hall and the nearby Second Space Theater host the outstanding theatrical productions of Fresno's Good Company Players. The intimate dinner theater atmosphere of Roger Rocka's is an exceptional setting for the performance of comedies and Broadway musicals. A special feature is the outstanding work of the Junior Company, a group of young people who add to the fun of each performance with a mini-show of their own. Second Space offers a theater-in-the-round setting for the performance of a wide variety of masterpieces of the American stage. The reservation of the entire theater for special group fund-raisers has become an enjoyable tradition at both sites.

DANCE

The lively art of dance is well represented in the Fresno area. Several of the city's ethnic groups boast their own troupes, which are available to perform at special events. In addition to these outstanding performers, several fine local dance schools hold recitals and professional dancers delight the public through several excellent Dance Repertory offerings each year.

Anyone who tingles to the tango or swoons to Swan Lake will want to be present at one of the next performances of the Fresno Dance Repertory Association. For more than 20 years, this dedicated group of volunteers and its excellent staff have brought the magic of dance to the people of Fresno. The organization strives to promote dance as a major art form, enrich the cultural dance experiences of area residents, provide local dancers with professional performance opportunities, and to provide a forum for both local and nationally-known choreographers. The Fresno Dance Repertory Association's companies include the Fresno Ballet, the Jazz Company, and the Aloha Polynesian Dancers — a troupe which performs ethnic dance. The group offers ballet, jazz and Polynesian dances each year in a variety of settings for the enjoyment and enrichment of the community.

Fresno citizens support the endeavors of the Dance Repertory in a number of important ways. The Fall Fandango fashion show and dance is a significant fund-raiser. Many community organizations request the Hawaiian, Tahitian and Maori authentic dances of the Aloha Polynesian Dancers for their social and cultural events. Because a primary goal of the non-profit Dance Repertory is to expand the audience for dance, senior citizens and students receive discounted rates at performances. Professionally designed sets as well as costumes are acquired in a program designed to build the groups' repertoire and ensure high quality dance performances for years to come.

THE SOUND OF MUSIC

Throughout the year and around the clock, Fresno music lovers of every persuasion have an outstanding selection of live and recorded performances from which to choose.

Fresnans support the performing arts.

Major concerts of top rock, country and gospel musicians are scheduled regularly at area stadiums, theaters, concert halls and the fairgrounds. Jazz and Dixieland enthusiasts enjoy a number of concerts each year. Concerts and programs of exceptional quality are available at a touch of the dial from Valley Public Radio, KVPR-FM, the valley's National Public Radio affiliate, and KFCF, which broadcasts

the signal of Pacifica station KPFA in Berkeley.

Live performances featuring talented local musicians and guest artists from around the world are offered by area organizations dedicated to the support of fine music. For 15 years, the Fresno Free College Foundation has sponsored an annual series of keyboard concerts which offer established masterworks of the past and a wide variety of contemporary compositions performed by distinguished artists from around the world.

Chamber music devotees enjoy the work of Orpheus, an outstanding ensemble directed by Professor Jack Fortner. The Central Valley's finest chamber music artists provide a series of performances each year featuring a unique repertoire; thorough program notes add to the educational value of each concert.

THE FRESNO PHILHARMONIC

Since its premiere concert in the spring of 1954, the Fresno Philharmonic Orchestra has grown from a small ensemble to a fully professional organization of nearly 80 talented musicians dedicated to the performance of fine music. Support from the National Endowment for the Arts, the California Arts Council and local government enables the orchestra to provide an outstanding program for valley residents each year.

The repertoire for the subscription concerts in a typical year ranges from "The Nutcracker" — performed in conjunction with the Fresno Dance Repertory Company — to works by such diverse composers as Bach, Stravinsky and Mahler. Choral works add another dimension to the program, as does the enthusiastically-received evening of popular music. In addition to its regular schedule, the Philharmonic performs eight special youth concerts, engages in a variety of educational activities, and tours throughout the Valley. Youth orchestras, young artist competitions and demonstrations in public schools help to ensure a continuing appreciation for the classics in years to come. The annual Young Artist Awards Competition, supported by local Rotary clubs, draws gifted young musicians from the entire western United States.

A popular Sunday concert series features informative commentaries by the conductors, adding a feeling of intimacy and superlative educational value to these enjoyable events. With the arrival of conductor Andrew Massey in the fall of 1987, the Fresno Philharmonic entered a new and highly productive phase of musical development.

In addition to the Philharmonic, outstanding vocal and instrumental performances are presented in the area under the auspices of educational, religious and civic groups. These concerts range from spectacular seasonal religious works to the unusually fine presentations of local high school choral and instrumental groups.

(Continued on page 182)

FRESNO ZOO

OPEN THE DOORS TO THE ANIMAL KINGDOM

The Fresno Zoo is one of the premier zoological facilities in the state.

Established in the early 1920's, the Fresno Zoo has expanded to 15 acres with over 400 specimens of mammals, birds and reptiles. Located within Roeding Park's 160 acres, the zoo's winding pathways and dense vegetation provide beautiful surroundings for visitors' enjoyment.

Over the years the zoo has developed natural exhibit areas, created attractive landscaping projects and designed innovative animal care facilities conducive to species survival and conservation.

The Fresno Zoo is home to the world's first and only computerized Reptile House. Environmental chambers inside the exhibit area control temperature, humidity and light cycles to create an environment that is as close to each species natural habitat as possible. Since the building opened in 1979, the Fresno Zoo has had considerable success in both maintaining and breeding reptiles and amphibians in captivity.

Reproductive research is being conducted on several endangered species of reptiles in an effort to enhance captive propagation. The zoo has won two national awards for the first captive reproduction of two species of rare snakes.

A two-acre elephant exhibit is one of the few Asian elephant breeding centers in North America. It features a naturalistic waterfall which plunges from a lushly planted cliff into a deep pool for the zoo's family of three females and one male elephant to swim and play.

The Fresno Zoo is also one of five zoos to maintain a breeding colony of American flamingos. During the spring and summer months, visitors are delighted by the sights of hatching eggs and fluffy baby flamingos.

Recently completed is a $2.1 million Tropical Rainforest Exhibit. Visitors feel like they are in a real tropical forest with dense foliage, a variety of free-flying birds and small monkeys surrounding them. A waterfall and river provide a habitat for wading birds, ducks and brilliantly colored amphibians, and a special building re-creates the habitat of the hummingbirds and tanagers.

Zoo visitors can open the doors to the animal kingdom through a wide variety of classes and activities offered by the zoo's Education Department. Training of docents, volunteer tour guides, is one of the functions of the education department. The docents help zoo visitors experience the magnificent animal collection with year-round personalized tours which are available with advance arrangements to any community group.

Both children and family wildlife workshops are offered during the summer. The recent completion of the Karl and Doris Falk Wildlife Education Building permits classes on a year round basis.

The "Zoomobile" outreach program is highly successful. Docents take the Zoomobile to schools and retirement homes to share the world of animals with the entire community.

The Fresno Zoo Society is a nonprofit organization which works to support the Fresno Zoo. Society volunteers give their time and financial support to serve as a force, working to expand community awareness of the facility and its role in the conservation of our national wildlife.

PARKS AND ATTRACTIONS

The Discovery Center

The cultural scene is considerably enlivened by the presence of several outstanding attractions. The Discovery Center, Fresno's hands-on science center, features science exhibits and an Indian room. It includes a six-acre park with a cactus garden, tortoise pen, rabbits, a worm farm and picnic areas. Summer evenings provide an opportunity to view the stars through the center's telescope. This year-round operation hosts school tours and provides a unique informal learning environment for kids of all ages.

The Fresno Zoo

The Fresno Zoo, fully accredited by the American Association of Zoological Parks and Aquariums, is dedicated to wildlife conservation and public education. In a 15-acre park-like setting, more than 400 mammals, birds and reptiles live in surroundings as close to their natural habitats as possible.

The Reptile House, one of the zoo's most popular features, is the only facility of its kind in the world with computerized climate control to ensure an optimum environment for each of its reptile guests. As a part of its commitment to the preservation of endangered species, the zoo conducts research on the reproduction of its captive species.

The new two-acre Asian Elephant exhibit is another example of the zoo's successful growth. With its naturalistic waterfall and deep pool, the exhibit provides a pleasant playland for the zoo's elephants and an attractive site for visitors. Fluffy baby flamingos attest to the success of another zoo breeding program; the sizeable colony of flamingos delights photographers and school children alike.

Located inside Fresno's 160-acre Roeding Park, the zoo provides a wide variety of exhibit areas connected by graceful paths which wind through dense vegetation. Bison, tigers, giant tortoises, zebras, giraffes and several varieties of monkeys provide an enchanting and educational focus for curious and delighted visitors. Classes and other educational activities are provided by the zoo's education department. The recently-completed Karl and Doris Falk Wildlife Education Building provides an ideal setting for the popular summer zoo school as well as classes held during the school year. A mobile zoo travels throughout area school districts with its informational presentations.

The Rainforest, newest of the zoo's exhibit areas, provides a naturalistic home for a variety of birds and animals. Part of the zoo's continuing renovation and expansion program, the Rainforest bears witness to the dedication, imagination and commitment of the expert staff and supportive community volunteers who have developed and maintained this fine facility. With its adjacent Playland and Storyland, the Fresno Zoo is an irresistible attraction for young and old alike!

OTHER PARKS

Fresno's beautiful Woodward Park, with its lovely lake, picnic areas, playgrounds, bird sanctuary and exceptional Japanese Garden, is one of the loveliest attractions in the area. Plantings in the Japanese Garden are designed for enjoyment in all seasons; the garden has become one of the area's most popular locations for weddings and other special events.

The City of Fresno's Parks, Recreation, and Community Services Department provides a wide variety of recreational activities for area residents. Classes, organized sports, after school recreation, swimming instruction, bicycle events, therapeutic services and a lively seniors program ensure that people of all ages have an opportunity to respond to the department's challenge, so appropriate for Fresno's active populace:
"Life — be in it!"

Community Spirit

Fresno's people are a mosaic on the move — a lively, warm, gregarious and hospitable collection of cultures and interests blended in the progressive harmony of the American spirit. Scores of early morning joggers, hundreds of construction workers putting in a new subdivision, thousands of family members of all ages singing together at Saint Agnes' Fourth of July "America Sings" — all these are the pulse, the heartbeat, the pride of the community, a vigorous, robust, life-loving people.

Fresno is a "think tank" of community leaders, volunteering arduous hours to plan for the city's future, concerned citizens who support and monitor their elected officials, teens who spend an evening playing cards and singing along with nursing home residents, executives who hammer nails at a Habitat for Humanity home, volunteer docents who introduce awe struck children to the world of art at the Met. All these are snapshots of life in Fresno. Together they form a character sketch of a city with an enormous heart.

The energy and enthusiasm with which Fresnans meet life shows in many ways: the Red Wave of Bulldog fans, the hundreds of clubs and organizations that serve so many useful purposes, the passionate commitment to health and the good life, the hundreds of churches representing every denomination, the libraries, museums, galleries, and the selfless sharing of resources at home and abroad. These are the marks of a community with maturity, vigor and dynamism. Whether on the athletic field or at a charity auction, Fresno's people have a vitality that's contagious, that

Bulldog Stadium represents the tremendous spirit and support of the greater Fresno area. Stimulated by the 1977 championship year of the Fresno State football team, a massive fundraising effort was launched to raise 7½ million dollars to construct a 30,000-seat stadium. The dream became a reality three years later as FSU played its first game in its new home to conclude the 1980 season.

The spirit which built the stadium soon became physically evident as red-clad football

CHAPTER 8

ıns became consistent overflow crowds cheering on their Bulldogs to two conference ıampionships and two California Bowl victories.

ıe California Bowl, played annually in Fresno, was one of the major benefits sulting from the construction of Bulldog Stadium. Receiving NCAA Bowl sanctioning 1980, the first California Bowl game was played in 1981 and immediately became e premier sporting event in all of Central California.

prompts even the shyest to step forward and participate.

Voluntary organizations have played a significant role in our history as a nation, and they have figured importantly in the development of Fresno County as well. Individuals over the years have derived immense joy and satisfaction from the service they give as members of charitable organizations; their generosity has had a significant impact on the health and in some cases even the lives of the recipients of this generosity.

When hardship, persecution and natural disaster drove waves of immigrants from southern dust bowls or foreign shores to the fertile San Joaquin Valley, charitable associations provided food, shelter and the opportunity for productive work. In more prosperous times, musical clubs, literary associations, athletic teams and social clubs do much to enliven and enrich the life of the community. Hundreds of network and service organizations are listed in *The Fresno Bee* each Sunday, making it easy for the newcomer or long-time resident with a new interest, or a little free time, to find a congenial group. The organizations are divided into categories such as "professional," "political," "hobbies" and "retirees," making it a simple matter for the reader to find the meeting time, place and contact person for a group which suits his or her fancy. An informative box at the top of this Agenda page each Sunday notes new organizations, joint membership drives, special events or other newsworthy items.

New organizations appear regularly, and some are remarkable in their appeal and impact. One such organization, the Fresno Women's

(Continued on page 187)

FRESNO COMMUNITY AND CONVENTION CENTER

A HUB OF ACTIVITY

Fresno's community and convention center complex viewed from "M" Street showcases the William Saroyan Theatre followed by the Exhibition Hall and newly expanded multipurpose arena.

"May the uses of these facilities bring joy, entertainment, enlightenment and increased knowledge; may they promote goodwill and better understanding among us; may they broaden our horizons; and may they increase the economic stability of this community."

With those words, United States Circuit Court Judge Gilbert H. Jertberg announced the opening of the Fresno Community and Convention Center to the public in September of 1966.

It was one of the first major convention centers constructed in the western United States and was made possible by a "joint powers agreement" between the City and County of Fresno. The Convention Center, consisting of an arena, theater and exhibit hall was constructed at a cost of less than 10 million dollars including land acquisition.

The Convention Center has been a tremendous success from the day it opened. Sporting fans have enjoyed the spacious 11,300 seat Selland Arena taking in such athletic events as professional boxing, wrestling, basketball, ice hockey, rodeos, motorcycle races, tennis and ever-popular Fresno State University basketball. The arena plays host annually to many family oriented shows such as the Ice Capades, the Ringling Brothers Barnum and Bailey Circus and the Harlem Globetrotters. In addition, popular entertainers and groups have performed in the arena such as Journey, Huey Lewis and the News, Whitney Houston, Kenny Rogers and Dolly Parton.

The William Saroyan Theatre with its plush 2,359 seat interior, elegant lobby and superb acoustics, provides an ideal environment for stage plays, ballets, concerts and convention meetings. Some of the renowned performers who have appeared here are Van Cliburn, Isaac Stern, James Whitmore, Hal Holbrook, Ginger Rogers, Mary Martin, David Copperfield and Mikhail Baryshnikov. The theater is also home to the Fresno Philharmonic, the Fresno Musical Club and the San Joaquin Valley Town Hall Lecture Series.

The 32,000 square foot Exhibit Hall with its eleven separate meeting rooms has been popular for local luncheons, banquets, charity events, receptions and exhibit shows. The hall can comfortably accommodate 2,400 people for a meal function and is the site for many convention meetings and trade shows.

In recent years the Convention Center has added a plush 13,120 square foot conference center ballroom (divisible into 7 separate rooms), increased the seating capacity to 11,300 in Selland Arena and increased its parking capabilities to accommodate 1,500 automobiles.

The Convention Center was built in part to enhance the economy of the area by attracting large conventions to Fresno. In this regard, the convention center has been a resounding success. During the fiscal year 1986-87, 75 conventions and conferences convened at the center attracting 89,258 people who spent in excess of $20,975,630 while in the area. In 1986, Fresno helped host over 325 conventions and 157,000 delegates. These conventioneers contributed an estimated $36,000,000 to the local economy.

The Ice Capades is a consistently popular attraction in the Arena.

The Fresno Falcons bring exciting hockey to the Fresno-area sports fans.

Ringling Brothers Circus appears annually in Fresno.

The William Saroyan Theatre regularly hosts a wide variety of the performing arts to appreciative Fresno audiences.

One of the many trade shows in the 32,000 square foot Exhibit Hall.

Fresno State Basketball plays to consistent sellout crowds and has led all California Universities in home basketball attendance.

The Fresno City and County Convention and Visitors Bureau is the designated marketing arm for the City and County of Fresno. The agency works to attract convention groups, tour operators and individual travelers to the Fresno area. The agency also provides support services for travel writers, film producers and convention delegates.

Considering Fresno's outstanding Convention Center, convenient central California location and numerous visitor attractions, it is easy to see why Fresno is consistently a favorable site for state and regional conventions.

Network, was established in 1986 with 500 eager members at its very first meeting! While such an enthusiastic response is unusual, the fact that it occurred is a source of encouragement to people considering forming new groups.

In addition to providing opportunities for socializing, these groups perform a variety of welcome services. Hundreds of thousands of volunteer hours are donated to a myriad of worthy causes in Fresno each year. Each group responds to need in its own way — some with funding, some with in-kind donations, some with services, and still others by providing education or training opportunities for their beneficiaries. As is often the case, the donors find they have gained and grown through the experience of giving, and the entire community is strengthened by the efforts of these individuals. In some cases the charitable efforts of Fresnans have reached beyond the city limits, as children have been brought from Northern Ireland for a summer vacation or from Africa for surgery, and ambulances have been donated and driven to villages in Mexico. The world seems a bit smaller and more unified as a result of this kind of sharing.

PHILANTHROPY

The charitable work of Fresno's clubs and organizations is but one avenue of response to human need. In Fresno as in the rest of the nation, there is a tradition of government support for the truly needy. Churches and other private agencies have established programs to alleviate hunger, homelessness and the pain of psychological and social trauma.

The Easter Seals Annual Balloon Festival brings great color and visual delight to multitudes of Fresno-area residents.

People give through many channels. For many, the United Way simplifies the choice: one gift, conveniently deducted from the paycheck, supports numerous worthy projects — such as the Chicano Youth Center and the Marjaree Mason Center for abused women and their children. United Way's annual budget, steadily increasing each year, is distributed through a unique allocation process.

Other donors choose to give through a new consolidated health care charitable organization (CHAD), or directly to the non-profit agency or charity of their choice. From the Fresno Philharmonic to the Rosecrest women's alcoholism recovery home operated by the Salvation Army, Fresno offers abundant opportunity for its citizens to express their philanthropy through volunteer service or monetary donations — all to the betterment of the community in which they live.

A few years ago, several area leaders established the Fresno Regional Foundation to accept gifts and bequests and to manage their disbursement.

The Estate Planning Council, a group of attorneys, CPAs and investment professionals, works to maintain expertise in the field of charitable giving with the goal of better assisting clients in this kind of financial planning. Another group, the Charitable Giving Council, was formed in 1984 to unite representatives of area non-profit organizations with legal and financial advisors for mutual information exchange.

With the implementation of these organizations, philanthropy has reached a new level of sophistication in Fresno.

At the present time, of the $64 to $73 million donated in the county in 1984, approximately 47 percent was given to religious institutions (calculation based on national averages). It is possible that in Fresno County, with its rural values and strong religious traditions, that proportion is even greater. The remainder of the charitable gifts is distributed among athletics, the arts, health care, poverty relief, education and the many other avenues for individual and community improvement arrayed before the civic-minded citizens of Fresno.

ATHLETICS: FRESNO GAINS NATIONAL ACCLAIM

Competition for donor dollars is extensive. In Fresno, athletics have been consistently successful in the generation of donor dollars. As individuals and as part of the Red Wave, Fresno's fans are intensely supportive, loyal and vocal in their love of sport.

Organized sports have had a strong following in the city since the debut of baseball in the 1880s. In the 1920s and 1930s, Fresno was home to professional league teams, including some strong Japanese-American clubs. Frank L. Chance, elected to the Baseball Hall of Fame, left Fresno for the Chicago Cubs. Former Cy Young Award winning pitcher Tom Seaver hails from Fresno as well. Spring training for several pro clubs and exhibition games featuring Ty Cobb, Lou Gehrig and the inimitable Babe Ruth kept Fresno sports fans loyal to the great American pastime. Softball has a glorious history in Fresno too, with well-known men's teams and the outstanding women's Rockets, which counts several Hall of Famers among its members.

Prior to World War II, boxing had a strong following in Fresno, and many a neighborhood scuffle was settled properly in the ring. Young Corbett, 1934 World Welterweight Champion, got his start in Fresno; the city proudly commemorates his accomplishments with a likeness at Selland Arena.

A number of county towns fielded impressive football teams even prior to 1900, with Selma's the most outstanding. Football had gained in strength at the college level by the 1930s, when Fresno State began to show consistently good performance. Tom Flores, who played at Fresno City College in 1954, went to the Oakland Raiders. Darryle Lamonica, a Clovis High player, won the American Football League's Most

(Continued on page 189)

DONAGHY SALES, INC.

THE LEADING BEER DISTRIBUTOR IN THE SAN JOAQUIN VALLEY

A stunning interior shot of Donaghy's beautiful new facility.

Donaghy Sales, Inc., is the largest beer distributorship in the San Joaquin Valley. The company is headquartered on a 20-acre site at 2363 South Cedar Avenue in Fresno, California. The warehousing, loading and office facilities comprise more than 200,000 square feet. The company also has extensive shop facilities for maintaining its fleet of local delivery trucks and long-haul vehicles.

Donaghy Sales has achieved one of the largest market shares of any beer distributorship in the United States. Anheuser-Busch has recently awarded Donaghy Sales the Dimensions of Excellence "Ambassador/Gold Eagle Award" which is given to only eight distributors out of approximately 1,000 Anheuser-Busch wholesalers nationwide. This award is based on six performance categories which include: sales and marketing, delivery procedures, warehousing, personnel management, administration and community involvement.

As a major distributor of Anheuser-Busch products, Donaghy Sales distributes Budweiser, Bud Light, Michelob, Michelob Light, Michelob Classic Dark, Natural Light, LA and King Cobra brands as well as the Anheuser-Busch European beers Carlsberg and Elephant Malt. They also distribute Master Cellars wines, Zeltzer Seltzer soft drinks and 'a Santé' mineral waters.

In conjunction with the distributorship, Donaghy Sales also operates a recycling facility for glass and cans. The recycling plant is open seven days a week, and is the largest volume beer distributor recycling plant in the United States.

Donaghy Sales appreciates the support they have received over the years from the more than 1,600 retailers in Fresno and Madera Counties.

Donaghy exterior signage displays their diversity of products.

Valuable Player designation not once but twice. Fresno football got an important boost in 1980 with the completion of the 30,000 seat Bulldog Stadium, built through the generosity of local fans. Under the tutelage of coach Jim Sweeney, Bulldog Football is played before overflow crowds and season ticket sales have reached 28,000!

The construction of Selland Arena brought basketball into the limelight, as Bulldog Stadium had done for football. Nationally ranked teams added Fresno State to the slate, and Coach Boyd Grant's FSU team played to sellout crowds in the arena year after year. The team's 194 win-74 loss record for the years from 1976 to 1984 gave the name "Grant's Tomb" to the arena, a dispiriting sign to competitors!

Auto racing was an important sport in Fresno in the 1920s, when the Fairgrounds boasted a one-mile board speedway and crowds of 50,000 at its championship races. Midget racer Billy Vukovich, two-time Indianapolis 500 winner, was a product of Fresno racing. Thoroughbred Horse racing has dominated the Fairgrounds since the auto track burned down in 1924. Harness racing prevailed into the 1950s, when quarter horses became more popular.

Ice skaters Bill and Julie Barrett trained a number of national champions at Fresno's ice rinks. The Falcons, the Fresno ice hockey team organized in 1946, plays to enthusiastic crowds at Selland Arena.

The West Coast Relays have brought track and field fans to Fresno's Ratcliff Stadium starting in 1927. Several records have been established here. Recent major improvements to the track at Ratcliffe Stadium have made it one of the premier track facilities on the west coast. Soccer is becoming increasingly popular, especially as a youth sport, because of its team emphasis and relative safety. The Fresno Pacific and Fresno State teams have helped gain recognition for the sport, and adults of both genders are joining the growing number of teams all over town. Fresno State Soccer set the NCAA Soccer attendance record and also holds the honor of being the first FSU team to attain preseason No. 1 ranking. Competitive cycling has brought Olympic teams to Fresno's foothill resorts for training. The number of serious recreational cyclists is increasing dramatically each year.

Swimming has come into its own as an important sport with strong representation in Fresno. The world class swim complex at Clovis West High School, recently treated to a $50,000 refurbishment, hosted the 1987 national long course swimming championships. Olympic class swimmers broke record after record at the meet, bringing national media attention to the facility and its host town. *Sports Illustrated* alone devoted four pages to the meet, which the school first hosted in 1983.

Tennis clubs, racquet clubs and fitness centers operate in all areas of the city, attesting to Fresnans' passion for fitness. Competitive wheelchair tennis games at the national championship level have been held in Fresno frequently in recent years, gaining more publicity for the sport and for Fresno's excellent facilities.

Golf is a popular sport and recreational pastime in Fresno and Fresno is blessed with numerous beautiful and challenging courses. The city's two publicly owned courses, Riverside on the San Joaquin River and Airways near the Fresno Air Terminal, are complemented by a number of private clubs. Sunnyside in southeast Fresno was opened in 1911, and Fort Washington opened in 1922. More recently, the Belmont, Fig Garden and San Joaquin Country clubs have added variety to the golfer's selection. Competitive bowling leagues and miniature golf competitions round out the organized sports scene.

Fresno City College's Ratcliffe Stadium showcases their superb new track which became the original host site for the famous West Coast Relays in 1927.

THE RED WAVE

Back in 1981, when the Fresno State team played at San Jose, a wave of loyal, red-clothed fans followed them across Pacheco Pass to cheer on their team. A local reporter coined the term "Red Wave" to describe the crowds, and the tradition of filling the stadiums and arenas with red for every game, home or away, began. With fans in each section rising in sequence to cheer, the stands truly resemble a massive wave of red, flowing back and forth, to terrorize — or at least mesmerize — the opposition.

California State University, Fresno, hasn't always been the beneficiary of such strong and loyal fan support. Up until the mid-1970s, Fresno State — as it is fondly known athletically and by the National Press — was recognized in athletics primarily for its baseball successes. In 1977, the university began to lay the groundwork for its remarkable recent record. In 1977, Coach Jim Sweeney guided the football team through an overall 9-2 season and a Pacific Coast Athletic Association (PCAA) championship. In that same year, basketball coach Boyd Grant, who had inherited a team that finished 7-20 the previous season, engineered a remarkable turnaround, guiding the university's team to a 21-6 record and a PCAA championship. With that double-barreled performance, the university began to pick up steam — and demonstrative supporters — in a momentum that, ten years later, is still building!

Athletic director Gary Cunningham, a former UCLA basketball coach, points out that Fresno State's athletic program has made great strides in recent years, gaining recognition as one of the West Coast leaders in both men's and women's intercollegiate athletics. The former teacher's college now has a number of programs which are nationally ranked, and dozens of its athletes have earned All-American honors. These include Doug Fraley, a pole vaulter who swept both the indoor and outdoor National Collegiate Athletic Association (NCAA) titles in 1987. The FSU soccer team

(Continued on page 191)

THE CALIFORNIA BOWL

BATTLE OF CHAMPIONS, FIGHT FOR LIFE

The California Bowl, one of the NCAA's elite sanctioned college football bowl games, takes place each December in Fresno's Bulldog Stadium.

The Bowl annually matches two Division I conference champions representing the Pacific Coast Athletic Association (PCAA) and the Mid-American Conference (MAC).

With the building of Fresno State's beautiful new 30,000 seat stadium assured in 1979, the idea of the California Bowl event evolved from concept to reality when a strong contingent of Fresno Bowl enthusiasts, headed by the eminent retired Congressman Bernie Sisk, obtained Bowl sanctioning from the NCAA. Since gaining the NCAA's blessing, the new stadium and the new Bowl game have grown together in providing an annual classic matching two conference champions seeking ever increasing national acclaim.

The Bowl game even through its first six years has already established itself as the premier sporting event in central California. In the first three years, the winner was not determined until the final seconds as both conferences displayed some storybook endings in achieving their victories.

For all of the pomp, excitement and pageantry of the Bowl game, the heart and soul of the entire effort rests with the charitable recipient which is Valley Children's Hospital in Fresno. The highlight of the week for the teams is their visit to Valley Children's Hospital. Prior to kickoff, one of the most meaningful sights to witness is the players with their little buddies from Valley Children's Hospital all meeting at mid-field in an emotional coming together that would have made Norman Rockwell proud.

The California Bowl usually kicks off the college football post-season play as the opening Bowl game in December and is carried nationally by ESPN sports.

With several sellout games under its belt, the California Bowl has proven Fresno's reputation as a great sports town and demonstrated the tremendous community spirit which exists in the central valley.

From grand marshals of national acclaim to the lovely Bowl queens, marching bands and championship teams, the California Bowl represents all that is good and positive about collegiate football.

To see the healthiest and strongest of America's collegiate youth striving for victory on the field of athletic competition on behalf of youngsters, many of whom are battling for their lives, is living testimony to the California Bowl's motto, "Battle of Champions, Fight for Life."

THE BIG FRESNO FAIR

ONE OF A KIND ENTERTAINMENT

Every year the Big Fresno Fair delights hundreds of thousands of people bringing them diverse attractions. In 1986 during the Fair's 14-day run, 637,900 people attended.

Fair grounds cover 165 acres, including 15 major buildings which cover 230,000 square feet.

Each year Fair management books top-name entertainers to perform in the 5,200-seat Paul Paul Theater. These shows are held twice daily-the first at 5 p.m., the second at 8 p.m. Because of the Fresno fair tradition, established during the tight money days of the Great Depression, there is no extra

advanced all the way to the NCAA final four, and the softball team made its third appearance in the last six years in 1987 at the Omaha, Nebraska College Softball World Series. The university has hosted the NCAA soccer playoffs and the NCAA women's softball regionals, a tribute to its standing as a regional leader.

The 1977-78 PCAA wins in football and basketball fueled so much enthusiasm in the university, community and region that Fresno State has one of the most successful, fastest growing athletic departments in the country. For each of the past three seasons, nine of the university's 18 varsity sports have been ranked at one time or another in their respective national polls. The men's golf (number 3), women's softball (number 6) and water polo (number 10) teams were all ranked among the top ten in the 1986-87 final polls. This kind of impact on the intercollegiate athletic scene is in large part attributable to the excellence of the university's well-rounded and highly respected coaching staff. Well-deserved recognition has come not only to Fresno State athletes, but also to those who have guided the school's athletic successes. In the past three years, both soccer's Jose Elgorriaga and volleyball's Leilani Overstreet have earned national coach of the year honors.

Honors have been extended to university athletes in impressive numbers as well. In just the last four years, 63 of Fresno State's athletes have achieved All-America status. In the 1985-86 season alone, the university had a total of 19 athletes named to various All America teams. They include football star Henry Ellard, now with the Los Angeles Rams, basketball players Rod Higgins, Bernard Thompson and Ron Anderson, all now in the National Basketball Association, baseball Olympian John Hoover, a former first round pick of the Baltimore Orioles, and volleyball player Ruth Lawanson, a former member of the U.S. national team.

Five members of the Fresno State 1986 football team were drafted into the National Football League; this was a record number for the school and one of the highest numbers for any West Coast school. The university appeared on both the Associated Press and United Press International top 20 polls, and went on to post a season log of 9-2. The 1985-86 season was just as impressive; the Bulldogs finished as the only unbeaten NCAA Division 1-A team in the country, and completed the season with a UPI final ranking of 16th and a near-perfect 11-0-1 overall record, winning a second

charge for these star-studded performances once the nominal gate admission has been paid.

Since the first Fresno Fair in 1884, horse racing has played a major role in the Fair's activities. Races are run on a dirt-surface, one-mile oval track. The racing mounts—appaloosas, quarter horses, thoroughbreds and Arabians—are housed in 700 stables maintained at Butler and Maple Avenues.

After the day's horse racing activities are cleared away in the 6,000 seat grandstand, evening performances begin there at 8:30 p.m. The 1987 schedule included four days of a Professional Rodeo Cowboys Association sanctioned Sierra Circuit rodeo, a Mexican rodeo, a Hispanic show (all sponsored by Coors), the Budweiser amateur boxing championships, a tractor pull and demolition derby.

But first and foremost, the Big Fresno Fair is an agricultural show, the largest in the nation and some even say it is the largest in the world. Foreign visitors are among the fairgoers who come annually to marvel at the quality and variety of produce grown in Fresno County, the largest agricultural producing county in the world in terms of gross national product. Eleven San Joaquin Valley communities have, since 1934, competed in a Community Agricultural Booth contest at the Fair. Premium money, amounting to thousands of dollars, is used by each community for service projects in its home area.

Ten competitive departments of exhibits are on the grounds, two of these—Junior exhibits and Industrial Education—are devoted exclusively to projects made by youth.

In 1987 premiums of $426,722 were offered for all exhibits. For five consecutive years, Butler Amusements has served the Fair as carnival concessionaire, offering 20 kiddie and 30 major and spectacular rides. On the seven-acre midway visitors can enjoy approximately 85 games and food concessions each year.

On grounds performers, including mimes, clowns, strolling musicians, fancy rope twirlers, jugglers, singers, comedians, harmonica artists, mariachis and brass ensembles contribute their talents to provide a continuous flow of entertainment. Some of these specialists entertain as they move through the crowds; others perform on stages throughout the grounds.

A long-time Fair favorite is the children's Petting Zoo. Bleachers are provided for parents and grandparents to watch their little ones enter pens where gentle small animals are temporarily housed for petting.

Every year the Fair brings the finest in entertainment. It's no wonder opening day is met with such anticipation.

This young fair-goer is pictured thoroughly enjoying her roasted ear of corn.

The Big Fresno Fair has a variety of exciting rides.

California Bowl championship. Quarterback Kevin Sweeney surpassed Doug Flutie and established a new NCAA 1-A career passing record of 10,623 yards and finished second and ninth, respectively, in the voting for the Davey O'Brien National Quarterback Award and the Heisman Trophy in his final, 1986-87, season.

These two terrific seasons, back to back, provided enormous momentum for the enthusiastic Red Wave. Sellout crowds are the norm at home, and on the road the Red Wave has gained a reputation for flooding the arenas and stadiums of its opponents with hundreds, and even thousands, of Bulldog fans clad in red. In 1983, more than 2,000 fans followed the Bulldogs to New York's Madison Square Garden to see the team defeat DePaul for the National Invitational Tournament basketball championship. In 1985, 7,000 Red Wavers thronged into Pauley Pavilion to watch Fresno State meet UCLA in the NIT quarterfinal game.

The Red Wave has built a regional reputation for its overflowing support of home games. In basketball, Fresno State was the highest drawing school on the West Coast in 1986, averaging over 10,000 fans per game. Selland Arena has been a season ticket sellout for eight straight years! In football, too, Fresno State leads the PCAA in attendance and annually outdraws a number of Pacific -10 schools and half the schools in the Western Athletic Conference. The 1986 game average was more than 33,000 fans in the 30,000 seat Bulldog stadium. For three straight years, baseball fans have

(Continued on page 195)

THE BULLDOG FOUNDATION, FRESNO STATE UNIVERSITY

#1 IN ATHLETIC VOLUNTEER FUND RAISING

As the sun sets on another special Fresno evening, over 1,200 Bulldog Foundation members gather in Bieden Field to kick off another Fresno State University athletic year.

Highlighted by current annual donations of $2-million, the ledger shows The Bulldog Foundation, the athletic fund raising arm for Fresno State University, can rightfully claim a number #1 ranking among all universities and colleges in America using volunteers to raise donations. In less than two decades, Bulldog Foundation members have contributed $14-million to scholarships, recruiting and special Athletic Department requests. Bulldog Foundation members have also purchased an additional $8-million in season tickets, and they have since 1980 been the core group in providing $14-million for football, basketball and baseball stadium improvements. Few if any collegiate athletic programs can claim these marks as achieved by 350 volunteers during a one month annual drive. There are only three paid staff members and the operation costs have averaged under 15 percent of monies collected.

But, it's not just dollars donated that make The Bulldog Foundation unique. Research shows that over 60 percent of the 4,000 plus Bulldog Foundation members support other University programs as well. All eight academic schools benefit from Bulldog Foundation scholarship monies. Monies raised have helped initiate nationally recognized student support services in academics, in counseling and treatment in all areas of alcohol and drug abuse, and in fifth year and summer school scholarship programs. Bulldog Foundation members help take the lead for other University fund raising causes outside athletics. FSU can boast of being among the very few in the nation that is sold out in both football and basketball. Soccer attendance led the nation. Bulldog baseball is played before some of the largest crowds in "the best" collegiate park in the United States. Bulldog Foundation volunteers don't just live in Fresno County, but rather represent this regional University with fund raising efforts in Kern, Kings, Tulare and Madera Counties. The way the "Red Wave" supports its Bulldog student-athletes on the road is amazing when many times more FSU rooters are on hand than the home teams have in support. Even Madison Square Garden sophisticates were stunned when 5,000 Red Wavers traveled coast to coast to witness the Bulldogs' National Invitational Basketball Tournament Championship in 1983. But at FSU it's not just the football and basketball programs that the Bulldog Foundation supports, but rather the total program of 18 intercollegiate sports which has had in one year as many as 10 mens' and womens' programs in the Top Twenty nationally.

Fresno State Athletics play an important role in the economic life of Fresno and the San Joaquin Valley. The donations and ticket sales plus facilities provided by Bulldog Foundation members have helped make FSU's enrollment grow at nearly twice the rate of the other 19 campuses in the state university and college system, generating an additional $11-million impact per year on the valley economy. Sixty percent of Fresno State graduates, including student-athletes, go to work each year in the central valley, generating new salaries of more than $1-million.

Bulldog Foundation members are proud of their accomplishments and want to maintain their national leadership position.

CENTRE PLAZA HOLIDAY INN

A COMMITMENT TO EXCELLENCE

The Centre Plaza Holiday Inn is located in the heart of Fresno, across from the city's Convention Complex. The hotel is easily accessible from both Highway 41 and 99, and it's close to shopping, parks, California State University of Fresno, golf courses and much more. Yosemite National Park is only one and one-half hours away, and it's a short 15 minutes from the Fresno Air Terminal.

The Centre Plaza Holiday Inn is beautifully designed. It features an eight story atrium with gentle indirect sunlight filtering down from above. 322 guest rooms surround the atrium lobby displaying a 14-foot waterfall in the center with lush plants and richly colored carpeting.

The hotel offers the finest in accommodations and entertainment, for both the individual traveler and the conventioneer. Exquisitely decorated rooms include eight interconnecting Poolside Suites, two Deluxe Suites, 16 rooms specially designed for the handicapped and a Presidential Suite.

Guests will enjoy the indoor/outdoor swimming pool, saunas, whirlpool, exercise room, electronic game room, boutique and beauty/barbershop.

The Centre Plaza Holiday Inn is a full service convention and corporate hotel with 13,000 square feet of functional space ideal for meetings, banquets or exhibits, which can accommodate 1,200 persons. The Conference Center divides into seven sections to seat 50-200 persons, in addition to five small meeting rooms to accommodate 10-40 persons. Directly across the street from the hotel is the Fresno Convention Center which has the Saroyan Theatre (seating capacity 2,359), the Selland Arena (seating capacity 11,300) and the Exhibit Hall (32,000 square feet, 10 small meeting rooms to accommodate 10-200 persons).

The hotel offers guests their choice of two excellent restaurants. John Q's is a fine restaurant noted for elegance and exceptional cuisine. Recipes Atrium Cafe is perfect for a relaxed meal of breakfast, lunch or dinner. And the hotel features two popular lounges, Beethoven's and the Atrium Tavern, where guests can have their music and conversation, too.

When visitors walk through the doors of the Centre Plaza Holiday Inn, they instantly recognize that the hotel's commitment to excellence is much more than a slogan.

FRESNO HILTON

AN ELEGANT DELUXE HOTEL

Located in the heart of downtown Fresno, the Fresno Hilton has been a landmark of excellence and elegance to Central Valley visitors and residents since its opening in 1972. The Hilton is a full-service deluxe hotel with 195 oversized rooms and suites.

Ideally located between beautiful Courthouse Park and the Fulton Mall and only four blocks from city, county, state and federal buildings, the Hilton's guest list includes businessmen, celebrities, government officials, conventioneers and tourists.

The Hilton offers its guests three restaurants; two lounges; and outdoor, Grecian-style pool and a spa. The "Sky Room" is Fresno's only rooftop restaurant. It sits on the ninth floor of the building and gives diners an unparalleled panoramic view of the city. "Baker Street" is one of the area's newest and most popular spots for dinner and dancing and the "Muffin Shop" provides guests with a quick, delicious meal.

With a complete convention and conference level located on the second floor, the Hilton can accommodate groups of up to 800 people. This level includes its own lobby, five garden-terraced meeting/banquet rooms, hospitality rooms and suites, bar and a separate banquet kitchen to assure quick and efficient service.

The Hilton was developed, designed and built by Steve Pilibos of Stephens Investments in the same distinctive architectural style as his other buildings on the city block. And it has been filled with fixtures, antiques and rich woods that create an air of elegance. The lobby stands a tall one and one half stories high and boasts three impressive Austrian crystal chandeliers custom designed and imported especially for the Hilton. Diners in English Tudor-style "Baker Street" enjoy large, floral cushioned antique chairs and brass chandeliers, and mirror domed dance floor. The magnificent mirrored Grand Ballroom boasts 17 crystal chandeliers making it Fresno's most elegant ballroom. And there will soon be a fully equipped gym and exercise room for guests to enjoy.

The Fresno Hilton's complete and luxurious facilities, outstanding service and convenient location set it apart. It represents the finest Fresno can offer.

kept Fresno State among the top ten schools in paid attendance. Beiden Field which is considered one of the premier facilities in all of college baseball has served as an NCAA regional site four times since 1979. Since 1980, Fresno State has drawn more than 140,000 soccer fans to its games. The 8,529 fans on hand to witness the 1986 NCAA semifinal Fresno State-Akron match helped make that event the highest attended collegiate soccer match in the country that year.

Fans have shown their support not only through record-breaking attendance but also in hard cash, contributing to the most successful capital fund raising project ever undertaken in the San Joaquin Valley: the building of the 30,000 seat Bulldog Stadium. The on-campus football-soccer facility was followed by a $2.2 million baseball stadium, a $1.3 million office-locker room facility and the $11.5 million expansion of the city-owned basketball arena; $2 million of the funds used to expand Selland Arena were raised by Bulldog supporters. The Bulldog Foundation, the primary support group of the athletic department, has become the number one athletic fund raising organization in the nation utilizing volunteer fund raisers. For the past several years, the Bulldog Foundation has raised an average of $2 million in donations during its five-week May drive. With support like this, the Red Wave is certain to gain the attention of universities throughout the nation.

Although it is a relative newcomer to power in collegiate athletics, Fresno State has accumulated an impressive record. The breadth of its athletic program, the quality of its coaching and athletic administration, and its record-breaking fan support all attest to a new power in the Golden State, a power to be reckoned with. As the most visible focal point for Fresno's community spirit, the Red Wave is an engaging tradition which has only begun to show its stuff!

In Woodward Park stands Fresno's tribute to America's astronauts lost in the 1986 space shuttle tragedy.

THE PARKS OF FRESNO

Fresno's residents and visitors can choose from a wide variety of publicly owned and operated parks for their leisure enjoyment and team sport activities all year long. In 1985, the county operated 14 parks, five fishing access areas and one boat launch area on a budget of $2.4 million. In addition, the city Parks, Recreation and Community Services Department administers parks, playgrounds, the zoo and extensive youth and adult sports programs. Within the county system, Shaver Lake — 50 miles northeast of Fresno, has a boat launch. Lost Lake, below Friant Dam, is a 305-acre river park. Pine Flat Recreation Area offers camping, fishing and boating in a 120-acre park below Pine Flat Dam. Choihumini Park on the Kings River near Piedra has fishing and camping. Avocado Lake Park, 23 miles northeast of Fresno, has an 83-acre fishing lake, and the Kings River access park provides boating and fishing.

Entrance to Storyland, a favorite Children's attraction located in Roeding Park.

The Kings River Green Belt Park is as yet undeveloped, but Winton Park near Trimmer Springs offers fishing as well as overflow camping. Laton Kingston Park, 25 miles southeast of Fresno, has playgrounds, a soccer field and fishing in the Kings River. Millerton Lake, closest to the city, offers boating and picnicking. The State Recreational Area at Millerton offers a number of amenities, and Millerton's upper lake is considered a sportsman's paradise. Publicly owned Camp Fresno, on Dinkey Creek in the Sierra National Forest, provides 60 acres of wilderness fun just 62 miles northeast of the city.

On the west side, the county operates the Delta-Mendota Pool Launch Ramp, the Fairfax fishing access, Skaggs Bridge Park, Three Rock fishing access, Los Gatos Creek Park — including a baseball field and camping areas — and the Huron fishing access. The Coalinga Mineral Springs Recreation Area is on the 35-acre site of the mineral springs which were popular earlier in the century; it includes both day use and camping facilities. In addition, the Coalinga School District leases Camp Yeager, in the Cambria area near the coast.

City playground planning began as early as 1908, and took a major step forward with the hiring of recreation director Howard Holmes in 1950. Holmes worked with park land donors to plan comprehensive social and cultural programs and to plan for the development of Woodward Park on Fresno's north side. Cooperation with schools in planning for recreational facilities was an important part of Holmes' leadership.

The recreation division now administers an adult sports program which fields 400 teams each year. In addition, it oversees a comprehensive youth sports program and cooperates with area schools in providing swimming instruction to children throughout the area. The therapeutic services division offers an comprehensive program of adaptive sports and recreation for the disabled of all ages. Community centers provide hot meals for seniors in addition to recreational activities and a school restart program to encourage dropouts to complete high school.

The city's popular CAFY (Creative Arts for You) program provides a wide array of classes, tours and festivals, with special emphasis on ethnic foods, arts and crafts.

CHAPTER 9

The year-round green citrus trees of "Navelencia" country.

Throughout the Central Valley, sprinkled like a constellation of sparkling stars, lie the 14 other incorporated cities of Fresno county. To the east, nestled against the foothills, lie Reedley, Parlier, Orange Cove, Fowler, Kingsburg and Selma. Rich with the citrus groves and vineyards that form their economic base, these cities share a wholesome lifestyle. They have developed from small farming settlements to modern cities, each with a distinctive character. Metropolitan Clovis and the smaller Sanger, with their lumber center histories, share life with a western flavor.

To the west of Fresno, Firebaugh, Mendota, Huron, San Joaquin, Coalinga and Kerman dot the open plains. Cotton, melons, grapes and almonds form their agricultural base. With easy access to the lovely central California coast, these cities have grown from dusty prairie towns to lush urbanized centers of commerce. The discovery of oil in the far western regions stimulated railroad development, which supplemented the access provided by the San Joaquin River.

Each of these cities has its unique blend of people, business and recreational opportunities, and they retain the friendly openness that once typified the entire west. The county is enriched by their special history and culture. Linked by a love of the land and the know-how to make it outperform any other agricultural area in the world, the people of Fresno County bring the resources of diverse cultures, a zest for life and a positive spirit to the task of meeting the challenges of the future.

REEDLEY: FRUIT BASKET OF THE WORLD

Twelve miles east of Freeway 99, midway between the metropolitan centers of Fresno and Visalia, lies the charming, bustling south county commercial hub of Reedley. Its well-educated, ethnically diverse population is growing at a steady 3.5 percent a year, which will bring the community size to approximately 15,000 by 1990. With a warm climate moderated by breezes from the beautiful Kings River, Reedley offers an enviable lifestyle.

Civil War hero Thomas Law Reed settled here in the mid-1800s to provide wheat for Gold Rush miners. His donation of land for a railroad station site established the town as the center of the Valley's booming wheat business. Railroad officials commemorated his vision by naming the fledgling city in his honor.

When mining fever began to fade, wheat demand slackened. Kings River water was diverted for crop irrigation, and the region began to enjoy the bountiful field, tree and vine fruit harvests which have characterized it for the past 100 years. European immigrant farm families were attracted by the abundance of water and the presence of the railroad, and the settlement was incorporated in 1913. Among these immigrants was a colony of German Mennonites whose values and traditions shape Reedley to this day.

Reedley is a multi-cultural city; about 45 percent of its population is Hispanic. Each of the town's major ethnic groups exhibits strong civic leadership, a desire to maintain cultural and religious traditions, and the ability to work

Reedley's Main Street Clock graces its busy downtown.

together successfully for the betterment of the community. The city is home to 27 churches and 55 charitable, cultural and civic organizations which include a Filipino Community, a Finnish Brotherhood and a Syrian-American Women's Club. In 1988 the city will celebrate its one hundred years of multi-cultural heritage and the 75th anniversary of its incorporation.

Reedley's attractive homes reflect the pride and industry of its residents. With an average household income in 1980 of $22,880, approximately 41 percent of the population had owner-occupied property values in the $50,000 to $80,000 range. The median property value in that year was $54,092. Reedley, with a fourfold increase in retail sales over the period from 1970 to 1983, has kept pace with overall county growth. Sales tax revenue indicates a quickening pace. Revenues were up 14 percent in 1986 from 1985, with the last quarter up by 35 percent. First quarter 1987 sales tax revenue exceeded projections by 40 percent. Gift boutiques in Reedley's historic downtown, new shopping centers and a wide variety of restaurants add to the town's atmosphere of prosperity.

Education is vital to Reedley community life. Including public and private institutions, there are seven elementary schools, two junior high schools and two high schools. Nearly 4,000 students are served by these excellent facilities, which are part of the Kings Canyon Unified School District. For more than 60 years, Kings River Community College has capped the local educational structure, providing area residents with a lively assortment of classes, programs, activities and community events. Part of the 106-campus California Community College system, it has an on-campus enrollment of 3,000; another 1,000 students are served by seven off-campus locations. Small classes, on-campus housing, an excellent library, strong career guidance resources and a spirited athletic program add to the college's appeal. Two of its most popular majors are aviation maintenance and agriculture, but students can select certificate or associate degree programs in a wide variety of majors.

Within a 30-mile radius of the city are California State University, Fresno; West Coast Christian College; Fresno City College; two law schools and a graduate professional psychology school. A local cable television station and two local radio stations complement the television and radio stations received from outside the community. A local newspaper, *The Reedley Exponent*, keeps residents abreast of community news and adds a local perspective to the newspapers from Fresno, Los Angeles and San Francisco which circulate in the city. An active historical society and an impressive local museum round out Reedley's educational profile.

Reedley contributes a wide variety of agricultural products to the county's economy. The area's rich, fertile soil produces fruit, nut, vegetable, grain and cotton varieties of the highest quality. Reedley leads the nation as a supplier of fresh fruit, a distinction which earned it the title "Fruit Basket of the World" in 1946. Twenty-four fruit and vegetable packing and cold storage facilities join area wineries in supplying the nation with tree and vine fruit products of consistently high quality. Agriculture-related industries include logging and lumber products; boxes, packing machinery and automatic packaging equipment are also manufactured.

Although agriculture is king, Reedley has a wide variety of other employers. Many residents find work in government, education and health services. Others are employed by the forklift and glass product industries which form part of the city's economy while still others work in retail businesses and communications. A 60-acre industrial park houses a number of light industries; phased development to 640 acres is planned. Firms are being recruited from the midwest as well as from rural Fresno County to join Reedley's development surge. An ample, qualified labor force is included in the population of 90,000 who live in the market

A plum packing operation in Reedley.

(Continued on page 201)

SALWASSER MANUFACTURING

A FAMILY SUCCESS STORY

The Salwasser family management team. Pictured left to right are Les, Mel, and Dennis Salwasser.

From humble beginnings in 1949, Salwasser Manufacturing has grown to become a world leader in the manufacturing of high performance automatic casing machinery. The company's success is the result of its ability to grow not only in size but also in its wealth of knowledge. The company's employees are constantly building on their experience in engineering and production. This commitment to progress has helped keep Salwasser in the forefront of the industry.

The company was established by Fred Salwasser and his sons, Mel and Les, to manufacture an automatic carton checkweigher and to provide service and repair of machinery for many local industries. Fred Salwasser's experience in raisin processing, led to his realization that there was a great need for a flexible and adaptable case packing machine. With this information in hand, Mel and Les Salwasser designed their first semi-automatic case packer which was sold to West Coast Growers and packers for casing cartons of raisins.

The increasing demand for high speed casing was recognized by the young Salwasser company which set out in the late 1950s to develop Salwasser fully automatic case packers. The first one was delivered to Uncle Ben's Rice in Houston, Texas. By the early 1960s precision, high performance Salwasser automatic case packing equipment was being used by the leading companies throughout the country.

Salwasser automatic case packing machinery meets a vast variety of production line needs. Cases can be set up to handle cartons or cans, and sealed with either hot melt or cold glue systems. Fast, medium or slow speed units are designed and built to specifications. In many "cases" Salwasser standard machines "plug in" to the needs. The flexibility of Salwasser is the key to its effectiveness in satisfying customer requirements.

For many years Salwasser Sure-Way case packing equipment was sold nationally and internationally by a representative company. Constantly growing, evolving and adapting to meet customer needs and expectations, Salwasser now sustains its own marketing network with exclusive sales offices and representatives located throughout the nation. International sales are directed from the central headquarters in Reedley, California.

The Reedley, California location has proven to be important to the company for reasons other than it being the home city of its founders. Reedley's central location in the "World's Center of Agribusiness" keeps Salwasser in the mainstream of industry's dynamic demands. California's central location also provides uncongested, convenient accessability.

In every respect, Salwasser Manufacturing embodies American free enterprise. With the passing of Fred Salwasser in 1956, Mel Salwasser and Les Salwasser have continued to guide company operations. Dennis Salwasser directs marketing and sales for the company established by his grandfather, father and uncle.

The success of Salwasser Manufacturing was built upon Mel Salwasser's conviction that "it takes 'U' and 'I' to make QUALITY," a statement displayed on a large sign posted on an interior wall of the main plant. The Salwasser success story is a direct result of this philosophy.

NATIONAL RAISIN COMPANY

Twenty years ago, Ernest, Krikor and Kenneth Bedrosian were San Joaquin Valley farmers, making their living from the fertile valley soil. Today, the Bedrosian brothers are the driving force behind one of the most respected names in the California raisin industry — National Raisin Company.

Virtually 100% of the raisins distributed throughout the United States — and 30% of the worldwide export supply —

Inset picture shows Governor George Deukmejian flanked by Kenneth Bedrosian (left) and Ernest and Krikor Bedrosian touring National Raisin facilities.

area surrounding the city center. More than 20 new businesses opened in Reedley in 1986, and that pace is expected to accelerate.

A four-lane divided highway connects the city with Interstate 99, 12 miles to the west. State Highway 180, which leads to Sequoia and Kings Canyon National Parks, is eight miles north. Both highways are used heavily by local, regional and national motor carriers. Reedley is served by bus lines and by the Santa Fe and Southern Pacific railroads. Fresno Air Terminal's passenger and freight facilities are 25 miles to the north.

Reedley's council-manager government administers a full service municipal generalized budget of over $3 million; the city's total budget is in excess of $6 million. The city has had a planning commission since the 1940s, and it provides a full range of services to its residents. Police staffing includes 20 full time and 16 reserve officers; both contract and volunteer fire services are available. A modern acute-care hospital, with a comfortable new maternity wing, provides comprehensive medical care. One of the finest inpatient psychiatric treatment facilities in the west is located nearby. The active Chamber of Commerce and Reedley Downtown Association are responsible for significant revitalization and beautification of the city. It is an exceptionally attractive location for business as well as for family life.

The key to Reedley's charm, however, lies in its recreational amenities. The sandy beaches and clear water of the Kings River lure swimming, fishing, boating and waterskiing enthusiasts. Parks alongside the river attract families and civic groups for picnics and games. The area is second only to California's Sacramento River in popularity for river sports.

The city boasts public parks, swimming pools, three golf courses and a comprehensive recreation program. Outdoor lovers can enjoy nearby Pine Flat Reservoir as well as the redwoods, lakes, streams and hiking trails which are only minutes away in the surrounding mountains. Reedley's come from California. And most of those sweet, sun dried, all-natural California raisins are grown right here in the San Joaquin Valley, within a 20 mile radius of Fresno. National Raisin Company — selling primarily under the Champion brand name — is responsible for growing, packaging and distributing upwards of 25,000 tons of raisins annually. Champion is among the top-selling raisin brands in the United States, and the number-one seller in many large retail chains.

Located on a 25 acre site just southeast of Fresno in Fowler, amid a sea of Thompson seedless (the ideal raisin grape) vineyards, National Raisin is a modern study in high-tech efficiency. Years of hands-on research have gone into the design, placement and operation of each piece of specialized equipment within the 80,000 square foot facility, making National one of the finest state-of-the-art raisin packing plants in California. Innovative methods for stem removal and moisture control are exclusive to National, and among the reasons their product is rated so highly in every type of market in which they compete.

In the minds of the wholesale and retail customer, the Champion brand name is synonomous with superior quality raisins. Stringent quality control measures are incorporated into every phase of processing, from one end of the line to the other. The result is a consistent high quality product that far exceeds industry standards.

Champion Raisins are attractively packaged in a large variety of boxes and bags, and new resealable cannisters, to meet the needs of every type of consumer. From single-serving snack boxes to two-pound family-size bags, the distinctive red, yellow & blue packages are highly visible on grocery and convenience store shelves in every part of the country, and around the world. An on going high-profile marketing campaign — including radio, television, newspaper and magazine advertising, as well as sponsorship of special events — is responsible for Champion brand's high level of top-of-mind awareness among consumers. Rounding out their product line, National also produces and packages Champion brand Golden Raisins, Raisin & Nut Snacks, and Pitted Prunes.

Champion raisin products are marketed throughout the world.

The Company is also heavily involved in the industrial market, their success being largely due to quality control and aggressive marketing. Some of the regular industrial customers who use Champion raisins in their products include Kelloggs, General Foods, Quaker Oats, General Mills, Ralston Purina and Nabisco.

As a major employer in the Fresno area, National Raisin provides jobs for approximately 75 full-time staff members. During harvest, employee rolls swell to over 500, making National one of the largest employers in the county.

Ernest, Krikor and Kenneth Bedrosian were born and raised in the valley, and have always been dedicated to supporting the community that supports them. They made that commitment two decades ago, when National Raisin Company was a small business with a big vision. Today, both the business and the vision have grown. But the commitment remains the same — to show the country, and the world, that some very good things come from Fresno, California.

spectacular setting is enhanced by annual pageants and festivals, and by easy accessibility to entertainment and shopping in larger metropolitan centers. The city continues to build on the strengths of its close-knit community of involved citizens.

PARLIER: A FINE COMMUNITY

"Parlier — A Fine Community" says the highway sign greeting travelers on four-lane Manning Avenue a few miles east of central California's Highway 99. And a nice place it must be, for centrally-located Parlier was the fastest growing city in the San Joaquin Valley in 1986, and the fastest growing city in the entire state for the years 1982-1985. Distinctions like these warrant closer review, and this friendly, hospitable city of 6,600 (up to 12,000 in peak season) bears up well under scrutiny.

Since its incorporation in 1921, Parlier has managed to grow on its own terms. Its city council is the only council in Fresno County that also sits as the planning commission and redevelopment agency.

Four separate sources of development financing are available to support the city's development, and a period of community revitalization is well underway. Eighty-two acres of industrial park parcels are available, with rail service provided by the Southern Pacific and Santa Fe through a reciprocal switching agreement. Rural transit bus lines serve Parlier, as do all major motor carriers. Fresno Air Terminal and Amtrak are just minutes away on Highway 99, nine miles west. Highway 41 is 15 miles west of town, and Interstate 5 is 62 miles west. Parlier's children attend local schools through high school, and have easy access to nearby colleges and universities in Fresno and Reedley. Local medical and dental care is excellent, and the hospital ably meets the general medical needs of the community. Two city parks, a public library and three civic clubs provide leisure activities.

The city's economy is widely diversified. Major manufacturing employers include several fruit packing companies and a new box manufacturer. Diversity is characteristic of the non-manufacturing sector as well; education, health care, fuel oil and an agricultural consulting firm are important employers.

Parlier has been honored by being selected as the site of the University of California's Kearney Agriculture Center. This will be the largest agricultural research facility in the state, with 20 separate laboratories, including one devoted to teaching.

The University's decision to locate the research center in Parlier is an indicator of the city's progressive spirit and capable leadership.

One of many citrus groves near Orange Cove

ORANGE COVE: CENTER OF FRUIT SHIPPING

Snuggled against the Sierra Nevada foothills, fragrant with the perfume of millions of orange, peach and plum blossoms, the tiny community of Orange Cove straddles the decades as surely as it straddles the rails of the Santa Fe spur. With traditions tied to the measured pace of an agrarian economy, the government of Orange Cove faced potentially devastating demands when the city's population doubled in a single decade. The spirit of Orange Cove's community leaders, and their commitment to preserving their charming city, promise success in overcoming the problems of rapid development.

The even temperatures and gentle winds of a "thermal corridor" create optimum fruit growing conditions all along the base of the foothills in central California. In the early 1900s, growers discovered the area was ideally suited to the production of high quality citrus. By 1916, the economy of Orange Cove was sufficiently developed to support formation of the Orange Cove Citrus Growers Association. Its characteristically colorful orange crate labels projected the glamour of California, the healthful qualities of citrus fruits and the proximity of the giant Sequoia groves. Among these labels, now collectors items, are "Grant Park," "Live Wire," "Assurance," "Orange Gold," "Souvenir" and "Orange Cove."

In the heyday of the growers associations, a local newspaper, *The Orange Cove News*, printed its first issue in 1928. Although the town was not incorporated until 1948, a strong sense of community developed much earlier, as evidenced by the newspaper, the establishment of numerous churches and the initiation of local celebrations by active civic associations.

With a year-round population of 5,000 and seasonal influxes that double the population, Orange Cove's new leadership faces a challenge: to maintain the community's pride in its quality of life while making the changes necessitated by rapid population growth. A zero vacancy rate, for example, has created pressure for construction of housing for low and moderate income persons. The Redevelopment Agency, one of the first to be established in the county, is working to make land and services available to developers, light manufacturing and industry. The large available work force — up to 17,000 in the service area — is an incentive to employers seeking to relocate.

The city has qualified for federal funds to upgrade and renovate its sewer system and purification plant. Water is provided by the Friant-Kern Canal and four city wells. Fire protection is delivered by full-time and volunteer staff, and police protection is provided through the County Sheriff's Department.

Orange Cove is a center of fruit shipping. More than a hundred motor carriers travel through the town daily. This is in addition to extensive railroad shipping services. Local bus service is available, and air terminals in Fresno, Visalia and Reedley are nearby.

The community's 1,000 students attend two elementary schools and one junior high school. High school students are bused to Reedley, although the city's General Plan shows both a need and a desire for a local high school. Health services are available in local clinics, with both public and private hospitals accessible in surrounding communities.

Orange Cove is a gateway to the splendors of the Sierra Nevada. The city's main thoroughfare converges with Highway 63 to the east, offering ready access to the scenic and recreational attractions of Kings Canyon and Sequoia National Parks. Residents and visitors also enjoy the boating and camping facilities — and excellent fishing — of Pine Flat Lake, 25 minutes away.

In town, the annual Cinco de Mayo celebration draws the community together for two days of folk dancing, ethnic foods, music, a fashion show, a parade and a queen pageant. Speakers use the opportunity to remind enthusiastic audiences of the special pleasures and privileges offered by life in this southeastern corner of the county.

Orange Cove City Hall

FOWLER: A CITY POISED FOR GROWTH

The city of Fowler, incorporated in 1908, took its name from a strong-willed and vastly popular Irishman, "Honest Tom" Fowler. He was a cattle rancher whose popularity boosted his election to the state senate in the 1860s. Pioneers settled in this cattle and sheep prairie south of Fresno following the opening of the Central Pacific Railroad line in 1872.

The pioneers began growing wheat, and with the arrival of irrigation water in 1881, raisin grapes became the town's primary crop. For more than three decades, Fowler was the nation's second-largest shipper of raisins and other dried

Fowler pride exhibited in its beautiful high school campus.

fruits. The decline in raisin prices in recent years has made available choice parcels of Fowler's prime agricultural land for industrial and business development.

Some of the aura of earlier days lingers in Fowler, despite fluctuations in the town's economic base. Tree-lined streets celebrate the planting efforts of the first women's club. Lovely churches, many of them reflecting the culture of their members' native lands, stand as monuments to community spirit. The cleanliness for which the town was noted in its first decades is still a point of local pride.

With a population of just over 3,000, Fowler is growing. Its proximity to Freeway 99, seven miles south of the Fresno-Clovis metropolitan area, ensures ready access to the resources and markets of a substantial city.

Housing is plentiful in Fowler; there are both low and moderate income single family homes and apartment complexes in the area. A development of low income homes is underway near the high school, and 92 apartments are being constructed nearby. In the same vicinity a 15-acre site will be developed in moderate income single family homes.

Officials in the new unified school district offices administer the city's four schools, which serve more than 1,000 students from kindergarten through adult levels. Residents have ready access to area technical, business and junior colleges, and to California State University, Fresno. In addition, a number of education and training institutions offer evening and weekend classes in the area.

The city operates a municipal hospital, one of only three in the state. Area general and special purpose medical facilities ensure a broad range of high quality health services. The city's police department includes both full-time and part-time staff. Fowler's volunteer fire department, known for its prompt and capable response to emergency medical calls, is supplemented in the industrial core by a contracted fire service.

An efficient water system utilizes five large capacity wells and interconnected supply lines to bring the area's abundant water to city residents. Ample energy is available to support industrial development. The area sanitation district can treat eight million gallons of waste water each day.

More than 1,000 acres is available for industrial development in parcels ranging from one to 75 acres. A well-trained, highly-motivated labor force resides in Fowler and its environs, and the area boasts excellent truck, rail, air and bus transportation. Three area airports, the Southern Pacific Railroad and Freeway 99 are readily accessible.

The City Recreation Commission directs a broad range of sports and recreation programs. Both the Fowler Fall Festival and the area-wide April Band Review draw crowds from throughout the region. In addition to local recreation and entertainment opportunities, residents are within minutes of the cultural offerings of the Fresno-Clovis metropolitan area. The mountain parks and lakes for which central California is famous are but a short drive away.

KINGSBURG: VALKOMMEN TO KINGSBURG

Just about halfway between San Francisco and Los Angeles on Freeway 99, the traveler's eye is caught by the large

Kingsburg Swedish Festival street dancing.

windmill of a popular Kingsburg smorgasbord restaurant. Welcomed into the neat little town by a water tower painted to look like a coffee pot, visitors are apt to think they've made a trans-Atlantic crossing to Sweden. In the downtown area, steeply peaked shingled roofs, side paneling with cross boards and used brick, gable and dormer windows proclaim a proud Scandinavian heritage. Gaily painted Dala horses add a touch of old world charm to each street light standard; souvenir replicas are available in the many gift shops. The hand carved, richly decorated Dala horses were used for barter in medieval Sweden; today they serve as cheerful reminders of an important craft tradition.

Kingsburg owes its origins to 50 Swedish families who came to the area from Ishpeming, Michigan in 1886. In a short time, the area boasted five churches that held services in Swedish. By 1921, 94 percent of the population within a three-mile radius of Kingsburg was of Swedish descent. Although the proportion of its population claiming Swedish roots has dropped to about one-third, Kingsburg still celebrates the influence of its early settlers. Wide, clean streets, neatly manicured parks and festive celebrations throughout the year remind townspeople of their heritage. In December, Santa Lucia presides over a lively holiday festival and lighted Christmas trees decorate each light post on the city's main street.

Visitors by the thousands flock to Kingsburg each May for the Swedish Festival. A representative of the Swedish Consulate joins local dignitaries in welcoming folks to the pancake breakfast, parade, band competition, concerts, art show and smorgasbord — and to the traditional Pea Soup

(Continued on page 206)

RICHLAND SALES COMPANY

QUALITY FRESH FRUIT AND VEGETABLES

Peach blossoms exploding with color.

Founded in 1969 by Alvin Peters and Mel Lewis, Richland Sales Company produced 120,000 boxes of soft fruit for market in its first harvest year. The varietal selection was small and the season was short, but the foundation was laid for the company to become one of the valley's largest fresh fruit and vegetable operations. Today, Richland packs, sells and ships over 3 million boxes of fresh fruit and vegetables and employs over 600 workers during the peak season. Its domestic and international harvest provides over seventy-five varieties of fresh fruits and vegetables throughout the year, and includes such volume items as peaches, plums, nectarines, grapes, apples, apricots and Asian pears.

In 1987 the company completed another major expansion, moving into a modern 120,000 square foot packing and administrative complex. The new packing facility utilizes the latest state-of-the-art technology and equipment. Computer generated compressors can be activated at a four stage level to ensure proper temperature maintenance, which is vitally important to all perishables. A 10,000 cubic foot ammonia refrigerated hydracooler has a capacity to run 17,000 gallons of water per minute. Processing products in this fashion reduces the field temperature of incoming fresh fruit from 100° to 34° in approximately 30 minutes. Because of these achievements, fresh fruit is routinely picked, packed and shipped all in the same day.

The executive office center is the hub for the network of nationwide and overseas sales distribution. Here, Mark Lewis and other members of the marketing department are in constant communication with supermarket retailers and merchants across the country and around the world. Making sales, handling orders and answering inquiries, they work to make sure the products meet individual specifications and delivery schedules. The high standards Richland places on the quality of service to its customers is matched by its detailed attention to product standards. Special attention starts in the fields long before the fruit appears. As a grower, Richland is a totally integrated company, and knows from experience what it takes to deliver the finest quality fruits and vegetables. Shape, size, color and flavor are continually evaluated to improve consumer satisfaction.

Pictured above is the Richland management team from left to right: Frank Duerksen, Alvin Peters, Mel Lewis, Mark Lewis, Helmut Schnitzler, and Frank White.

Richland Sales has made a commitment to be the best. Working with trade associations and taking part in activities locally, nationally and internationally, personnel listen and learn from others. Through a spirit of shared values, the company not only meets the challenges of today, but builds a sound foundation for a better tomorrow.

and Pancake Supper. Flower-decked Maypoles and Dala horses add a festive touch, and blue and yellow Swedish flags flutter alongside the stars and stripes.

Recreational activities are important year 'round in Kingsburg. The nearby Kings River supports an abundance of water sports. Two museums, three city parks, a country club, a gun club, a library, eleven restaurants and 23 civic clubs provide a variety of activities for Kingsburg's 6,000 citizens. Two thousand Kinsgburg children attend its three elementary schools, high school and continuation school. The population is well served by the local hospital.

Kingsburg's location on Interstate 99, near Highway 44, provides access to reliable and frequent bus and motor carrier transit. Passenger and freight railroad service is available, and the Fresno Air Terminal is just 25 miles away. The city is operated by a council-administrator government which manages a municipal budget of just over $1 million.

Early in its history, Kingsburg was the busiest wheat shipping point in the nation, located as it was at the site of a Central Pacific railway switch. Its economic base is still agriculture, but fruit has replaced wheat in importance. Sun Maid Growers and the Del Monte Corporation, the two largest employers, each provide jobs for five times as many workers as any other local industry. The Sun Maid Growers plant is the largest dried fruit processing plant in the world! In addition to raisin grapes, major crops in the area are tree fruits, watermelon, cotton and truck farmed vegetables.

Several Kingsburg citizens enjoy reputations which extend beyond the quiet family- and church-oriented community. John Forney, developer of the white leghorn chicken, grew up in Kingsburg, as did actor Slim Pickens. Professional football player Jim Johnson and coach Monte Clark share a Kingsburg background. The city's most famous son is Rafer Johnson, renowned for his 1960 Olympic Decathlon championship. He had the honor of lighting the Olympic torch at the 1984 summer games in Los Angeles.

Kingsburg was recently honored by the Swedish Counsel General with the designation of "Jubilee City" in recognition of its participation in "New Sweden '88." Citizens will be joining in activities designed to promote friendship between Sweden and the United States during 1988, proclaimed as "The Year of the New Sweden" by the 99th Congress.

Frontier Village showcases historic preservation in Selma.

SELMA: RAISIN CAPITAL OF THE WORLD

Tradition is important in Selma, the only city in Fresno County other than Fresno that was incorporated prior to 1900. Even before the town's incorporation in 1893, the *Selma Weekly Free Lance* had begun publication (1882), and the *Selma Enterprise* — the newspaper with the longest continuous publishing record in the county — rolled off the presses for the first time in 1888. As early as the 1890s, the town's high school boasted the best football team in the region, a tradition that continued until the Depression hit in the 1930s.

By 1900, Selma was much more than a frontier town. It had schools, churches and a diversified business district. Following a decline in wheat prices, fresh fruit increased in agricultural importance. In 1904, after a long and lively debate, Selma became the first in the Valley to go "dry." A thriving illegal liquor business sprang up in Selma's Chinatown, and systematic raids and consequent fines enriched the city coffers. More refined entertainment was available as well; the Chautauqua visited Selma regularly from 1915 through the mid-1920s, bringing lectures, plays and music. The women of Selma commanded a great deal of respect because of their role in the cultural arts as well as their leadership in the Prohibition movement. In 1911, the city went on record in support of women's suffrage.

Three years after Selma's incorporation, a boy named Art Gonzales was born in the barren desert area known as Selma Briggs Tract. As he grew up, he developed a great respect for the sacrifices made by the city's early settlers. In 1935,

SUN-MAID GROWERS OF CALIFORNIA

SINCE 1912, THE WORLD'S FAVORITE RAISIN

For more than 75 years, the smiling girl in the red sunbonnet has brought an important part of Fresno County to millions of people throughout the world. Sun-Maid raisins are synonymous with natural goodness and the highest in quality and are a shining example of the excellence of California agriculture.

Sun-Maid Growers of California is a farmer-owned cooperative. Its 1,600 grower-members produce nearly 25 percent of the United States raisin crop on 55,000 acres of prime San Joaquin Valley vineyards. Most of these vineyards are located within a 50-mile radius of Fresno.

During late August and early September, mature grapes are picked and naturally dried in the sun until they become raisins. The raisins are then delivered to Sun-Maid's massive 650,000 square foot processing and packaging plant. Each year this facility handles nearly 100,000 tons of raisins.

following the death of his wife, Gonzales began collecting articles of historic interest and value, ranging from his own childhood bicycle to a large assortment of wagons and buggies. His collection became a small country museum. Later, with the help of the city and the Selma Museum-Historical Society, and the donation of a 15-acre tract of land for a museum site by Carl Ruegg, the Pioneer Village of Selma was created. It was a dream come true for Art Gonzales.

Nine years of work and over $230,000 in grants and donations turned a strip of land alongside Freeway 99 into an authentic 1880-1920 period village, complete with church, Victorian house, barn, farm store, opera house, north and south exhibit buildings, and the 1887 Southern Pacific Railroad depot — the first building to be moved to the site in 1974. The village includes a dentist's office, a barbershop and a doctor's office as well as historic farm vehicles and implements. Antique furniture is on display along with the thousands of items from the Gonzales collection. Hundreds of letters from area school children express delight in visiting the village, a wonderful reminder of early days in the San Joaquin Valley.

A song written in 1915 by Louis W. Everson extolled "Selma, the Home of the Peach." A Libby, McNeil and Libby cannery opened in Selma in 1911, and the peach business peaked in the 1920s. But the town's continuing good fortune lay in its stunning success in the raisin grape industry. The Selma Raisin Festival was held as early as 1910, complete with tray-turning competition, raisin-baking contest, food booths, and the popular parade and queen contest. The raisin grape industry began when an enterprising farmer hit upon the idea of marketing his shriveled grapes as a delicacy.

Raisins have been enjoyed as a nutritious, portable food in the middle east's nomadic cultures since 1490 B.C., but they were unknown in this country until the early 1900s. In 1904, Thomas H. Elliott invented the raisin seeding machine; this was followed by other innovations designed to speed

After delivery to the plant, Sun-Maid raisins are meticulously cleaned, processed and inspected to assure that only the finest quality raisins are packaged. U.S.D.A. and Sun-Maid inspectors regularly pull samples from the processing lines to insure only quality raisins are packed.

From its beginning in 1912, Sun-Maid has been a pioneer in the California raisin industry. In the early days, the cooperative's aggressive national advertising programs encouraged consumers to try the dried fruit. Sales grew tremendously as the public enjoyed the delicious sweet flavor and dependable quality of Sun-Maid raisins.

Today, Sun-Maid processes and sells half of all consumer-packaged raisins in the United States with annual net sales averaging $165 million. Depending on the time of year, the Sun-Maid plant employs between 500 and 900 employees.

Sun-Maid packs four types of raisins to suit consumers' needs. Natural seedless are the familiar dark raisins, naturally sun-dried from Thompson Seedless grapes. They are equally popular for snacks and as an ingredient in cooking.

Golden Seedless come from the same Thompson grape but are mechanically dehydrated and processed under special conditions to become golden in color. Goldens are slightly more tangy in flavor than sun-dried Thompson Seedless and are a favorite for light fruitcake recipes and other baked specialties.

Muscat raisins are large, dark and extra sweet. Naturally sun-dried from the Muscat grape, seeds are removed by an ingenious mechanical process. Muscat raisins are exceptionally fruity in flavor and highly prized for special recipes.

Zante Currants are tiny, seedless raisins (no relation to the berries of the same name) which are naturally sun-dried from Black Corinth grapes. Their unique sweet taste makes them an ideal addition to salads, sauces, desserts and many baked goods.

Sun-Maid's modern packaging equipment provides the grocery trade with a variety of consumer packages and offers great flexibility in satisfying the demands of cereal manufacturers, bakeries and other industrial users.

Although the greatest volume of raisins go into the 15 ounce cartons, the speediest packing lines in the Sun-Maid plant are the six lines which together turn out miniature 1/2-ounce cartons at the rate of 70 per second. Sun-Maid estimates that during its 75-year history it has packed more than 13 trillion raisins.

The famous Sun-Maid brand is synonymous with the utmost in quality, an achievement proudly shared by all involved in packing the product during the past seven decades.

Sun-Maid is proud to have played such a key role in the California raisin industry, an industry which is a significant part of the history and economy of Fresno and Fresno County. The Cooperative's grower-members and employees remain committed to producing a product which exemplifies the excellence of California agriculture. After all, that's one important reason that, since 1912, Sun-Maid has been the world's favorite raisin.

processing and protect quality. With mechanization, the industry thrived. Now, more than 95 percent of U.S. raisins are grown in Selma, 55 percent are packed here, and nearly half the world's supply of raisins is produced here. Selma's nickname, "Raisin Capital of the World," is completely accurate. The Raisin Festival, held in May each year, now includes entertainment at Pioneer Village in addition to the traditional parades, contests and dances celebrating the source of Selma's economic well-being.

Selma has started an ambitious renovation and expansion program to turn the city into south Fresno County's regional commercial, retail and industrial service center. A $3 million facelift is turning the city center into a vintage Main Street. Lights which once graced Hollywood Boulevard are in place along Second Street in Selma. The city's program for restoring downtown building facades to their original beauty has received enthusiastic response from building owners. City-owned buildings will be the first to be restored; ten privately-owned properties will be transformed soon afterwards.

The three-phase downtown restoration is only one of the redevelopment agency's projects as Selma moves into position as the south county trade center. With a planning commission in place since 1963, the city has done its background work. A new commercial area is being tied to the downtown area with landscaping, and a 4-1/2 acre shopping center has been approved. A major automobile marketing center is partially in place, and a new industrial district is in the planning stages. Plans are being made for a large housing development surrounding a golf course at the north end of the city. This will be an excellent spot for the many Selma residents who commute to metropolitan Fresno for work but enjoy Selma's small city atmosphere for family living. Two additional single family subdivisions are under construction, as are condominiums, townhouses and apartment developments. A new motel is available for tourists and travellers.

New promotional brochures highlight the advantages of this lively, forward-looking community of 13,500. City population is expected to reach 16,000 by 1990, and the trade area is already serving 37,000. The city's sphere of influence embraces more than ten square miles, and is served by a council-city administrator government managing a budget of $4,429,031 for 1897-88.

The full-service city offers police, fire, paramedic-ambulance, public works, public transportation and park and recreation services. Its location on Highway 99 gives Selma good access to commercial transportation. Nearby mountain and coastal recreation areas add to the charm of life in Selma.

Education and medical services are first rate. Nearly 4,000 students are enrolled in the seven elementary schools, one junior high school, one high school and one private school. Selma District Hospital, with its newly expanded emergency care facilities, is the south county's largest medical institution. Its services are supplemented by a health center, an industrial medical center and two nursing homes. With its broad range of up-to-date services, its vigorous economic climate and its desirable quality of life, Selma provides an ideal atmosphere for family living and an attractive site for business and industrial development.

Steer roping at the popular Clovis Rodeo.

CLOVIS: IT'S A WAY OF LIFE!

"Clovis — it's a way of life!" So proclaim the bumper stickers, many of them on pick-up trucks with a couple of friendly dogs in the back. The driver wears a ten gallon hat, and if you hail him at a corner he'll be glad to direct you to the rodeo grounds, or to one of the many antique shops or colorful saloons lining the downtown streets.

Tucked into the northeast corner of the Fresno metropolitan area, Clovis is one of central California's most attractive and appealing small cities. Its history is typical of communities born during the early settlement of the west. Only an occasional trapper or missionary disturbed the Indian villages until the Gold Rush brought miners in force in the 1860s. Sheep and cattle replaced the prospectors as the mines played out. Homesteaders' fences, in turn, crowded out the grazing livestock. Farms were established, and before long thousands of acres were devoted to grain cultivation. Clovis Cole, for whom the city is named, was dubbed "Wheat King of the Nation" in the 1880s; his operation included 40,000 acres of wheat. Cole and other wealthy landowners contributed land for a railroad right-of-way planned by Marcus Pollasky to provide an economical means of transporting lumber from the Sierra.

Although the railroad project was short-lived, the lumber industry thrived nevertheless. Huge boards were transported down the mountain from Shaver Lake to the mill in Clovis — a distance of 45 miles — via a V-shaped flume, truly a marvel of engineering. The 40-acre mill and finishing plant provided work for many early settlers. When the mill burned to the ground in 1898, residents rallied to rebuild what had become the economic and social focal point of their town.

A constable kept the peace, relying on the local jail to remove troublemakers from circulation. The city incorporated in 1912 in response to the pressures for governmental services which accompanied rapid expansion. Fire, water and sewer services were soon in place; this led to still more rapid growth. Public-spirited associations and service clubs sprang up. Only two years after incorporation, Clovis held its first Spring Festival — forerunner of today's annual Rodeo.

While retaining its friendly, small-town flavor, Clovis has grown to 12 square miles and is home to over 42,000 residents. The current development boom is expected to double the population of this "Gateway to the Sierras" within 20 years. Originally settled as a convenient center for the grain and cattle industries, and for its location halfway between the mountains and the county seat of Fresno, Clovis is now attracting newcomers because of its attention to "quality of life" components such as education, medical care and a vital downtown area.

The Clovis Unified School District provides top-notch, comprehensive, individualized education for over 20,000 students in 13 elementary schools, two intermediate schools, two high schools, one adult school and one continuation school. The 177-square mile district is known for its emphasis on excellence and competition. Challenging academic and co-curricular programs have resulted in the achievement of student standardized test scores which rank well above state and national averages year after year.

A $32 million Clovis Community Hospital is under construction on a 143-acre site in the northeast sector of the city. A general acute care facility with 120 beds, the new hospital will incorporate such features as the Birthing Center, which has proved so popular in the presently existing facility. The hospital, designed to allow easy expansion as the population grows, will feature innovative, energy-saving heating and cooling systems.

Civic pride is also evident in the Community Development Agency's ambitious projects for the revitalization, restoration and beautification of the city center. Storefront refurbishment and street beautification work combine to call attention to the city's turn-of-the-century heritage. Early frontier style storefronts entice shoppers. Nearby, a 500,000-square foot regional shopping center is under construction; it will provide a controlled-climate retail alternative for area shoppers and merchants.

No description of the Clovis life would be complete without mentioning its star attraction, the Clovis Rodeo. More than 40,000 rodeo enthusiasts flock to the city each April to enjoy the parade, horse show, western arts festival, banquet, dance, queen contest and — of course — the rodeo. The world's finest cowboys and cowgirls compete for

(Continued on page 211)

GRUNDFOS PUMPS

COMPANY PUTS CLOVIS ON THE WORLD MAP

Product line of Grundfos Pumps.

One of the nation's largest manufacturers of circulating pumps for plumbing and heating has a home right here in the valley.

Grundfos Pumps Corporation in Clovis manufactures a variety of water pumps for use in homes, on farms and in commercial and industrial applications. Locally, many Grundfos pumps are found in water wells for domestic and agricultural use as well as in solar heating systems. By using stainless steel as the primary construction material, Grundfos has a unique position in the marketplace and a reputation for superior quality and innovative engineering in its products.

From this manufacturing plant in Clovis, hundreds of thousands of pumps are distributed throughout the United States, Canada and Latin America. Grundfos Pumps is one of twenty Grundfos companies found worldwide, with the parent company, Grundfos International, headquartered in Denmark. The company was founded in 1945 and worldwide now produces 20,000 pumps each day.

Grundfos Pumps began marketing its products to the U.S. market only a decade ago. In ten short years, the company has expanded its facility four times and tripled the square footage and employs nearly 200 people. Company-owned distribution centers have been established in Allentown, Pennsylvania; Toronto, Canada; and Atlanta, Georgia.

Visitors can stay right at the plant in one of four master suites and a full-time hostess is on staff to provide meals for guests in the company's dining room. Customers from across the country attend product training seminars in the 3,500 square foot training center.

In the air-conditioned manufacturing plant, computer-controlled and state-of-the-art machinery is used for production. Because of the high tensile strength of stainless steel, huge presses exert 300 tons of pressure per square inch to flatten sheets of stainless steel to fabricate components. Automated lines use robots to assemble the submersible pumps and send them through a maze of conveyors for final assembly and testing. Every pump Grundfos produces is tested before it is shipped from the factory.

This attention to quality and efficient manufacturing processes is paramount to Grundfos' growth and development. Grundfos is committed to being the leader in superior quality, unique design and high volume/low cost products in the pump industry. The company has adopted "Just-In-Time" manufacturing techniques to produce pumps when the customer places the order to be more responsive to the customer and provide faster service. Each year new products are being added to the product line and aggressive marketing is keeping sales at record breaking levels.

Because of the success Grundfos has found in the San Joaquin Valley, the company established a 100 acre industrial park in Fresno and is promoting the central location, excellent work force and local pride to bring other companies to the area.

prizes in one of the largest professional rodeos in the country.

An Oktoberfest which draws 7,000 is a lively attraction also, as are the numerous events and activities sponsored by the city's 44 service clubs and organizations. The city's proximity to the mountains provides easy access to Shaver Lake, Huntington Lake, Sierra Summit Ski Area and the many other attractions of the Sierra Nevada. In the foothills just a few miles out of town, Millerton Lake offers year-round recreational opportunities within minutes of downtown Clovis.

Small town values are an important part of Clovis' appeal. Twenty-nine churches offer spiritual nourishment to its people. A modern senior citizens facility provides a variety of activities to serve this important segment of the population. Clovis is truly, in the words of its new motto, "a nice place to be" — for people of all ages.

Respect for tradition does not prevent Clovis from moving swiftly into the future. Local leaders are pushing for rapid development of Freeway 168, which will connect Clovis with the growing foothill communities to the east and the metropolitan freeway system to the west. Plans are being drafted to ensure quality control in all such development. Clovis appears to be well equipped to preserve and enhance its cherished way of life.

SANGER: RAPIDLY GROWING

Sanger, just 15 miles east of Fresno, is the third largest city in Fresno County and the third fastest growing city in California. The Chamber of Commerce projects a population of 20,000 by 1992, up substantially from the 1982 population of 13,129. Forty-eight percent of the city is now under redevelopment as the city heads into the 21st century at full speed.

Named in 1887 for the Secretary of the National (railroad) Yardmaster's Association, Sanger gained fame early as a center of wheat shipping. Lumber soon displaced wheat as the city's primary product; the 65-acre Kings River (later Sanger) Lumber Company was the largest in the state. Its 54-mile long flume reached high into the Sierra timber country; narrow gauge railroad and hoist connections further extended its reach. The high volume logging activities supported a booming industry by the turn of the century. However, prosperity waned following a series of fires and a recession, and the company sold its holdings to the Forest Service; they are now part of Sequoia National Park. Ironically, the largest Sequoia in the depleted forests of Converse Basin bears the name of lumber company manager Frank Boole.

Fruit displaced lumber as Sanger's economic base in the 1920s; many colorful orange crate labels of the time originated with the growers' cooperative established in Sanger in 1920. "Target" used a logo reminiscent of a section of log, while the "Orange Gold" label evoked memories of Gold Rush days in the surrounding mountains.

Sanger had developed a solid reputation of prosperity at the time of its incorporation in 1911. *The Sanger Herald*, established in 1889, was the first newspaper in the county. Its early issues illuminate the county's development. In its pages we learn that Oscar Brehler, a Sanger resident, traded with the foothill Yokuts to obtain a large collection of baskets and artifacts. His vision led to the establishment of the Sanger Historical Society, which acquired the old Southern Pacific Depot and converted it to a museum of history. In addition to the Yokut artifacts, the museum houses replicas of an early town home and city block. The lumber industry is chronicled here, and there is an exhibit of pioneer life, which is rotated periodically.

The city is proud of its school system: ten elementary schools, a junior high school, and a high school. The high school's exemplary ROTC program graduated the greatest number of military academy appointees from a single school in the nation. Sanger parents are enthusiastic supporters of extracurricular activities; their volunteer labor built an extensive sports complex on the high school campus, and their enthusiasm brings them out to fill the 6,000 seat stadium every Friday night during football season. This kind of parental and community support and encouragement keeps Sanger's students in school; 65 percent of its graduates go on to college.

Sanger's council-manager government administered a $4.3 million budget in 1983-84. Its well-staffed police and fire departments provide excellent protection. Sanger's active redevelopment agency has enjoyed success in recent recruitment efforts; a manufacturing plant for fruit product containers, a biomass plant and a food product boxing equipment plant are among new businesses in the area.

The city center is being beautified with extensive street work, and planners envision construction of a four-square-block "Mercado" of shops and plazas soon after the 1988 centennial. A $3 million sewer development project is underway, and the major highway that runs through the city is being widened to four lanes.

Vigor and diversity characterize Sanger's economic base. Fruit packing outstrips all other industries in labor demand, especially in the peak summer season. Employment opportunities also exist in the medical, clothing, electrical, wood product, food, refrigeration, government and retail trade areas. Excellent motor, rail and air transportation is available. Branches of several major banks provide financial support services for development and are readily available to meet the needs of the burgeoning business population.

The City Parks and Recreation Department provides many opportunities for citizens to relax in their own home town. The town boasts a country club and five city parks. The nearby mountains offer many opportunities for sport and recreation. The fishing and camping facilities of Pine Flat are less than a half-hour away, and there is abundant hunting, fishing and hiking in Kings Canyon, Sequoia and Yosemite National Parks. Theater and spectator sports are readily available in nearby Fresno.

Sanger's numerous civic clubs have year-round activities of wide appeal. Best known, however, is the Trek to the Nation's Christmas Tree, an annual motorcade to the General Grant Tree in Sequoia National Park. The trek has been a tradition since the 1920s, when Sanger's Chamber of Commerce secured the "Nation's Christmas Tree" designation for the 4,000 year-old, 267-foot Sequoia.

The Sanger Rotary Club hosts the annual Grape Bowl Festival, featuring agricultural exhibits, food booths, a queen pageant, barbecues and the selection of "Mr. and Mrs. Farmer" each fall. On September 16, the town celebrates Mexican Independence Day with an all-day festival in the park. Mexican music, folk dancing, food and a queen contest highlight the event. These celebrations reflect Sanger's pride in its growing, vigorous multiethnic community.

Rice fields near Firebaugh.

FIREBAUGH: HUB OF WEST SIDE AGRICULTURE

Major Andrew J. Firebaugh was with the U.S. Cavalry troops who discovered Yosemite Valley in the mid-1800s while chasing some Indians into the mountains. He settled on the open land on the county's west side, establishing the Firebaugh Ferry and Trading Post on the San Joaquin River in 1854. The ferry served the Butterfield Overland Stages on the San Francisco to St. Louis route, and provided passenger, freight and livestock transport for travelers as well as area residents. Shepherds used the ferry to take their flocks to the cooler foothills for summer pasture. Rates seem quite reasonable from today's perspective: two cents per head for sheep and 50 cents for a one-horse buggy.

By 1900, the settlement of Firebaugh, an important sheep shearing station, had become a company town — headquarters for the vast Miller and Lux ranches. Henry Miller recruited his workers from specific ethnic groups to capitalize on their special knowledge and experience. Significant numbers of Italian, Irish, Basque and Portuguese descendants of those early sheepherders and dairy farmers reflect Miller's recruitment. Old timers tell of sheepherders brought to the area for a salary of $90 a month who went on to prosper and retire as millionaires.

When Miller died, his vast holdings were sold off in small parcels. Many people bought 40 to 80 acre tracts, expecting to develop profitable small farms. Firebaugh was incorporated in 1914 to meet the needs of these new settlers and those who had established homesites near the Delta Standard Oil pumping station a few miles south.

Firebaugh is the hub of west side agriculture; it is best known as a growing and shipping center for cotton, tomatoes and cantaloupe. In 1939, the U.S. government established a sizeable migrant camp for housing seasonal workers. Tenants were allowed to exchange labor for their housing. The city's annual Cantaloupe Roundup, celebrating the beginning of the August harvest, was first held in 1941. Nowadays the festival lasts several days and includes a parade, a queen's pageant and a community barbecue.

Civic pride is evident in Firebaugh. Its council-manager government provides municipal services with a $2.8 million annual budget. The population of more than 4,000 enjoys the protection provided by a city police force of eight full-time and nine reserve officers, and a volunteer fire department of 26 with one part-time paid staff member. Health care is provided at clinics as well as by individual dentists and physicians. The public and private elementary and secondary schools serve nearly 1,400 students; the student-teacher ratio is a desirable 25:1. Evening vocational classes are offered in Firebaugh by West Hills Community College.

Transportation and shipping services are readily available. Highway 33 follows the Southern Pacific Railroad through town, and Interstate 5 is 18 miles west. All major motor carriers provide service to Firebaugh, and both local and Greyhound buses are available. The Firebaugh Municipal Airport provides general aviation facilities and Fresno Air Terminal is 45 miles southwest.

The city's redevelopment agency, vested in the city council, has projected growth in agriculture related enterprises. A 32,000 square foot, $3 million cold storage facility is under construction to assist in making crops such as broccoli, asparagus, cantaloupe and lettuce more stable, year-round commodities. Inexpensive land and abundant labor resources contribute to Firebaugh's agricultural success. In addition to farming, farm equipment companies are a major source of employment. Education, government and support services provide work for a substantial number of Firebaugh residents.

Firebaugh's climate is comfortable, even in the mid-summer heat which is so vital to the area's high quality crops. Low daytime humidity and the cool evening ocean breezes which blow over Pacheco Pass moderate the temperature of even the warmest July day. Citizens enjoy a comfortable, unhurried way of life. The carefully maintained 13-acre city park with its expanse of lawn, specimen trees, playgrounds, ball diamond and picnic areas is well used throughout the year. A public pool adds to in-town summer fun, and residents make good use of the fine hunting and fishing opportunities available along the Delta-Mendota Canal. Water attractions are abundant: the San Joaquin River, the California Aqueduct, the San Luis Dam and numerous lakes and streams in the mountains. The city's organized soccer, baseball and football programs and movie theatre complete the recreation picture. Rain-free summers with cool, breezy evenings combine with a traditional lifestyle and civic pride to create an appealing quality of life for the city of Firebaugh.

MENDOTA: CANTALOUPE CENTER OF THE WORLD

The town of Mendota was not incorporated until 1942, but its history began with the establishment of a Southern Pacific Railroad storage and switching facility in 1891. This service point was unusually large and well equipped, including a roundhouse and repair facilities. By 1900, a good-sized business district had grown up around the station, but development came to an abrupt halt when the railroad stopped using the roundhouse in 1910. For a time a diatomite mine operated in the area, and substantial numbers of farm workers settled there. Pressure for municipal services led to incorporation in 1942.

Nearby waters attracted sports enthusiasts; the sturgeon, salmon and bass fishing were legendary. In 1868, government pressure forced construction of Mendota Pool to facilitate ship passage on the river. Regulations were changed, however, and the turntable gate was never used. The county established Mendota Pool Park at the site in 1964. Its 85 acres include a launch ramp, playgrounds and picnic areas, and excellent fishing.

At the turn of the century, the alkali sink east of Mendota was home to thousands of antelope. As late as the 1950s, deer were still found in the area. The state of California, in an effort to maintain the area's attractiveness to migratory birds, established the 12,000-acre Mendota Wildlife Refuge for waterfowl management. While elk and deer are no longer seen here, snow geese and pintail, some from Siberian breeding grounds, winter in this natural prairie. Although concern has been expressed over dwindling wetlands and toxic buildup in some basins, the nesting grounds and waterfowl wintering areas are among the loveliest reminders of the Valley's history and beauty.

The teeming wildlife refuge to the east of town is complemented by abundant croplands. Throughout its history, Mendota has depended upon agriculture for its economic well-being; it has a reputation as the Cantaloupe Center of the World. Three of the largest cantaloupe packing houses in the state are located here. The community's leadership has mapped out a development strategy that builds upon Mendota's agricultural base. The Planning Commission, established in 1968, laid the groundwork for the careful research and planning which preceded the current development surge.

The city plans to move from dependence on seasonal crops — lettuce, tomatoes, corn, onions, broccoli and cantaloupe — to a steady year-round economy. A key factor in this strategy is the projected Biomass Power, Ltd., plant. The plant, to be built on a 25 to 50 acre site in the Mendota Industrial Park, will produce electricity by burning agricultural waste products. The electricity will be sold to Pacific Gas and Electric Company. In addition, the plant will produce low grade steam capable of efficiently running hothouse operations. Interestingly, shrimp farming is an additional possibility. The steam could be used to maintain optimum temperatures for producing this lucrative food source. The plant is due to be completed by November of 1989, and is expected to be a strong stimulus to the local economy.

City leadership is working to find ways to motivate children to stay in school and to create new employment opportunities for youthful citizens. An $8 million high school has been approved by the state. Citizens are eager to keep the youth in their home town for the entire educational cycle to maintain community identity and racial balance. Community leaders expect the new high school will bring increased opportunities for after-school activities, athletics and work experience.

Mendota is growing rapidly; 350 homes and a shopping center are under construction. A 60-acre parcel has been set aside for the high school and for an agriculture-related facility. A shopping center and rental units are being built on a 120-acre parcel north of town. The city is eager to provide the infrastructure for developments geared to meeting the needs of its young and growing population.

The population of Mendota, up by 83 percent in the decade from 1970 to 1980, now stands at 7,000. The city has a school age population of 1,200. Its labor force of 2,000 increases significantly during harvest season. The council-city manager government administered a budget of $1.7 million in 1984-85. It provides water, sewer, police and contracted fire and paramedic services. Medical and dental services are available, as are all retail trades.

Sugar beet processing is the major source of employment and produce packing is the largest non-manufacturing employer. Government, education, banks and retail shops complete the employment picture. Routes 33 and 180 intersect in the city, and Interstate 5 is just 15 miles west, making transportation convenient. The Southern Pacific Railroad, a multitude of motor carriers, and bus lines serve Mendota.

Mendota has three city parks in addition to county and state park lands. The city sponsors a sports and activity program, and eight service clubs provide additional community events. The August Harvest Festival, a four-day carnival sponsored by the Chamber of Commerce and the Westside Youth Center, is the biggest community event of the year. Dancing, amateur boxing, food booths and mariachi music add to this annual celebration of the melon harvest. Hunting and fishing are excellent, and the attractions of the Pacific Ocean, the San Francisco Bay and the Sierra Nevada are only a few hours away.

HURON: AGGRESSIVELY PURSUING DEVELOPMENT

By the time of its incorporation in 1951, Huron — the last city to be incorporated in Fresno County — had a substantial history. It was described in the 1891 county atlas as an "important wool and sheep shipping center." Huron had rail service as early as 1877, and by 1915 it led the nation in sheep shipping. Huron's station house included an unusual, human-powered roundhouse.

Its location on the road to the Coalinga oil fields made Huron an important distribution station for oil pipeline construction. Pipeline construction, a labor-intensive process, at one time employed as many as 1,000 horse and mule teams hauling the pipe to Kettleman Valley for installation.

Although Huron experienced a decline in its early prosperity at the turn of the century because of water supply problems and changes in the oil industry, it managed to keep pace with the times. Electrical and telephone services were in place by 1909, and automobiles came to Huron in 1910. Fresh drinking water was brought in by truck or rail to ease the water shortage; deep wells were drilled to provide a more permanent supply. But Huron suffered another devastating blow in 1919 when fire destroyed most of the town. Population figures shortly after that show only 25 residents, the all-time low.

Buoyed by the 1927 Kettleman Hills oil boom, Huron became an important supply point and prosperity returned. Several businesses settled in near the railroad. Churches were established, and the population stabilized. During the war years, transient labor came to step up food production to meet increased war-time demands.

In the years following World War II, a new packing shed and ice plant stimulated growth. However, even though productivity improved, mechanization lowered the demand for labor. With the declining population, retail business suffered, and Huron entered a period of decline. City and county leaders are making vigorous efforts to pull the town out of its slump.

Huron's council-manager government is pursuing an aggressive redevelopment and revitalization program. The work of a planning commission, established in 1952, has led to the development of a 200-home residential area, plans for a local high school, development of a 10-acre community center and park, and numerous other civic improvements. Two anchor stores have already committed to locating in the planned 80-acre shopping mall. Three hundred sixty acres are available for industrial park development. Huron has much to offer relocating business and industry. It has a general aviation airport and is served by all major motor carriers and by a line and spur of the Southern Pacific Railroad. Interstate 5 is only five miles away.

A new city hall serves as a visible indicator of Huron's commitment to provide all the municipal services necessary to sustain a comfortable way of life for its citizens. Contracted fire protection and municipal police service ensure the community's safety; local medical and dental services are available to safeguard the health of the populace.

Huron's new City Hall.

Water from the California Aqueduct, purified locally, is readily available. The Huron Community Park and Recreation Center provides swimming, picnic areas and sports facilities for relaxation and family fun. The Fresno County Parks Department maintains the Huron Fishing Access on the Aqueduct. City sports programs, a library, a theater, restaurants and the activities of local civic clubs keep residents busy. Each Fourth of July the community joins the Boy Scouts for a parade, games, food booths and a raffle. A new community celebration, the Festival of Hope, expresses a commitment to the future, as the people of Huron continue to work hard to bring their dreams to fruition.

City Hall at San Joaquin.

SAN JOAQUIN: A TRADITIONAL LIFESTYLE

San Joaquin, incorporated in 1920, was originally part of a ranch established in the 1850s by Jefferson G. James. When James moved to San Francisco in the 1890s, he leased out his land in 38 parcels totalling 72,000 acres. Landholders faced legal disputes over water rights with the other giant west side ranch, owned by Miller and Lux, during the area's tempestuous early development. In 1912, the James Company sold the land around San Joaquin to a Chicago man, Benjamin F. Graham, who envisioned a Fresno of the west side, a "city beautiful" on the site which he named Graham. Graham's dream was short lived, however. He lost control of the property to Los Angeles investors; the town of Graham lasted only two days. The investors, seeking a marketing tool to spur land sales, chose the name San

Joaquin to take advantage of promotional material featuring the beautiful San Joaquin River.

The Los Angeles syndicate established an irrigation district, and for a number of years the fertile land and ample water combined to give San Joaquin an air of prosperity. The Southern Pacific Railroad helped business development. A creamery was established, and a large nitrogen plant went into operation. The average size of farms increased with improvements in mechanization, and a cohesive community developed. San Joaquin celebrated its prosperity each May with San Joaquin Days.

The establishment of a planning commission in 1963 reflected the desire of community leaders to monitor growth in the interest of preserving San Joaquin's traditional style of life. The community numbers just over 2,000. The largely agricultural labor force is composed of permanent, not seasonal, residents. The council-manager government had a 1984-85 municipal budget of $642,700. Fire services are provided by the Mid-Valley Fire District, and the County Sheriff's Office provides police protection.

Major manufacturing employers include piping, garlic processing and seed companies. A variety of retail, government and educational institutions provide non-manufacturing employment. A physician is established in town, and the fine hospitals of major Valley cities are minutes away. Six hundred students are enrolled in the local elementary and high schools, as well as in the vocational and college-level institutions nearby.

Civic clubs, parks, restaurants, a library and a city sports program provide leisure activities. Fresno County's mountain rivers, lakes and streams are minutes away. Interstate 5 is only 21 miles to the west; Highway 99 is 28 miles east of town, and Highway 145 is eight miles east. Major motor carriers provide service to the city, and the Southern Pacific runs through town. Bus, Amtrak and airline services are available in Fresno.

The city is experiencing a modest boom. A $2.5 million melon packing and processing plant is being expanded to include vegetable processing. Housing is going up rapidly, with a constant demand for more. City leaders have started to develop an industrial park and have made additional acreage available for commercial and residential use. Premium lots are available for development in the city center, and local government is eager to work with new business and industry that is compatible with the city's treasured way of life.

San Joaquin's charm can be summed up by listing what it doesn't have: smog, stress, urban sprawl and strangers. People here call each other by name and stroll down the quiet streets to take care of daily business. Some folks don't bother to use their cars at all, except for church on Sunday. Occasionally they may visit the "big city" for some special purchase, but they are happy to return to the peaceful, productive small town that is San Joaquin.

Harris Ranch is I-5's most elegant travelers' oasis.

COALINGA: HORNED TOADS AND BLACK GOLD

Horned toads and an iron zoo? Coalinga is definitely, delightfully different! Each May, "coaches" root for their favorites in the Horned Toad Derby, a 50-year Coalinga tradition. At the clang of the fire bell, the horned toads scamper from the center to the edge of a 25-foot circle. Well, to be absolutely honest, sometimes the scampering looks more like a slow strut, and the stopwatches are replaced with an hourglass. When the main event is over, and the spectators know whether "Flash," "Petunia" or "Ole Jerry" is the winner, there is more fun in store.

Visitors enjoy the tricycle race, a ten kilometer run, the parade, a barbecue and lots of other good, homespun fun. Class reunions are held in conjunction with Derby Days, and the townspeople honor significant civilian and military leaders in special ceremonies. Once, when Derby Days was rained out, the owner of a Coalinga liquor store set out decoys and used the shrubbery in front of his establishment as a duck blind. His duck call could be heard for blocks, a spirited response to the dismal weather conditions.

(Continued on page 217)

HARRIS RANCH

A TRAVELER'S OASIS

Enter the world of Harris Ranch. A brilliant display of fresh flowers, red tile roofs, lofty palms, stone columns and stately archways await you. The ranch was built in the tradition of an early California hacienda. Truly an oasis in the desert, Harris Ranch Restaurant and Inn Resort has become a San Joaquin Valley landmark.

Guests have come to expect only the finest food and hospitality from Harris Ranch, whether for casual dining in the Ranch Kitchen, or for formal dining in the elegant Fountain Court Dining Room. Both restaurants serve only premium cuts of famous Harris Ranch U.S.D.A. choice beef in addition to homemade pies, breads, desserts and other specialties.

And for those who haven't visited the Harris Ranch in a while, they're in for a big surprise: the Inn at Harris Ranch. The new resort facility has just been completed by the Harris family. The Inn is the newest addition to the first-class restaurants, shops and conference facilities that make up the legendary Harris Ranch. As a corporate meeting place, or an overnight getaway, the Inn at Harris Ranch is a destination of distinction. Private conference rooms and guest rooms are beautifully decorated in light scrubbed-pine and fresh country floral prints. Many guest rooms are comfortably appointed with French doors leading to private patios that overlook the terraced courtyard, 25-meter lap pool and jacuzzi spa. Other amenities include wireless remote control cable television; superior mattresses; silent, efficient climate control; extra-high ceilings and deep pile carpets.

Inside and out, Harris Ranch is a showcase of tasteful western architecture and furnishings.

And the nicest surprise is the great value, with guest rooms moderately priced.

Located midway between San Francisco and Los Angeles, on the west side of the valley just 55 minutes from Fresno, the Harris Ranch also features a paved, lighted 2,800 foot airstrip easily accessible to private planes. With the addition of the Inn, Harris Ranch has become the ideal, central location for business meetings as well as leisure activities.

Guests describe the Inn as the perfect accompaniment to the familiar Harris Ranch hospitality. "Harris Ranch has provided the ideal overnight accommodations to complement the conference and restaurant facilities, with the same charm and comfort the Harris name is known for," said one visitor.

Discriminating guests are discovering the Harris Ranch.

Many of the oil wells around Coalinga are decorated as animals, giving rise to the name "The Iron Zoo."

Coalinga's civic pride and resilience is evident in today's attractive downtown, painstakingly rebuilt after the devastating 1983 earthquake which brought national attention to this small west side city. City and county officials worked with local merchants to plan and implement an efficient rebuilding program, and Coalinga stands today as a monument to the hardy spirit of its people.

The first inhabitants of Fresno County, the Yokut Indians, had a trading center near present day Coalinga. Coastal Indians came through the mountain passes to trade shells and dried fish for the oil the Yokuts obtained from seepage in the foothills. Early white settlers later discovered that oil dug by hand in this region was of such high quality that it could be used unrefined.

Ranching, not oil, was the main interest of the area's first non-Indian settlers — Spanish-Mexicans who raised livestock in the middle of the 19th century. During this period the west side gained its first notoriety; its low brown hills provided convenient shelter for bandits and desperadoes, one of whom was the legendary Joaquin Murrieta.

Near the end of the century, other settlers were attracted by stories of "live" oil seepage and by coal mining activity. A narrow gauge spur line called Coalinga Station A drew miners and merchants to the small community built to serve the Southern Pacific.

When the oil boom hit in the 1890s, speculators poured into Coalinga, a wild frontier town with 13 saloons and flowing oil. The first big well, drilled in 1896, yielded 300 barrels a day. By 1908, 100 wells were being drilled in fields to the east and west of the town. The coal mines have been shut down, unable to meet competition from Utah, but oil production in the Coalinga field has been steady and reliable. Gravel is quarried in the region as well. A list of major employers reads like the roster of an oilers' convention.

To keep pace with the town's rapid growth, Coalinga's leaders have been diligent in providing community services. The city boasts a hospital, a complete range of professional health care services, four parks, a museum, a library, 16 churches and five schools that serve nearly 2,000 students. West Hills Community College, with over 350 employees, provides Associate degrees and vocational education to 2,500 students.

Recreational opportunities abound in the area, including Camp Yeager, a state championship rifle range, off-road motorcycle racing, and hunting and fishing areas. The mayor-council government manages a $5 million annual budget. A complete range of services is provided to businesses and residents by retail, service, financial and manufacturing operations. Interstate Highway 5, connecting Los Angeles and San Francisco, is nearby, and the area enjoys bus and general aviation services as well.

The whimsical iron zoo which greets people entering Coalinga from the north is another example of local energy. Artist Jean Dakessian secured funds from the Shell and Standard oil companies to fund a design contest in 1973. There were 178 entries; 53 of those creatures inhabit the oil fields outside Coalinga, bobbing up and down in full character dress to the delight of passers-by. A turtle, rhino, grasshopper and pink rabbit join Uncle Sam, an Indian chief and a cowboy in promoting the special charm of this western corner of the county.

This hand-held horned toad, along with many others, has been the impetus for Coalinga's Annual Horned Toad Derby.

The famous Thompson Seedless Grapes.

KERMAN: HOME OF THE THOMPSON SEEDLESS RAISIN

At the turn of the century, a post office was established in the small townsite of Collis, located by the railroad tracks in central Fresno County. After a temporary move to Rolinda, the post office was reopened in 1904 at the Collis site. By 1906 the name had been changed to Kerman. A composite of the names of several of the town's founders, the name also identified the area's newspaper, the *Kerman Times*, which was succeeded in 1905 by the town's current paper, the *Kerman News*. Skagg's Bridge was built across the San Joaquin at Kerman in 1907, and by 1910 the town boasted a telephone company, a branch library, a volunteer fire department and the Kerman Creamery Company. The high school opened in 1912, allowing graduates of the town's three elementary schools to continue their education in their home community.

In 1902, Kerman had 200 residents in town, and a population of 4,000 lived in the surrounding area. Fresno Farms Company extolled the virtues of small town prosperity in its 1925 pamphlet, "Kerman the Wonderful," promoting the town as "The Home of the Thompson Seedless Raisin." The town prospered during the 1920s. The Fresno Irrigated Farms Company sold 26,000 acres of land, and wildcatters found oil in areas previously considered worthless. During this period, Kerman school students rode to school in modern buses. The elegant Kerman Inn was built to host prospective land buyers.

Incorporation occurred in 1946, and growth accelerated. The 200 telephone subscribers listed in the 1946 directory had grown to 5,000 by 1986. Farming continued to attract new settlers as alkaline land was successfully reclaimed by using new technology.

Community spirit led to the first September Harvest Festival in the 1940s. Sponsored by the Chamber of Commerce, this festival continues to draw crowds to its queen pageant, parade, band music and food booths. New businesses opened: a tallow works, a winery and a chemical plant. The first major residential subdivision went up in 1950, and the city's Planning Commission was formed in 1955.

To serve the anticipated population growth in the 1990's, Kerman has developed a new 120-acre industrial park next to the Southern Pacific Railroad line. The park is anchored by an institutional food packaging company which relocated from Southern California. The plant uses a spur line put in by the city. That spirit of cooperation helped advance the city's goal: to attract clean new industry which is compatible with its agricultural base. Within the city's planning area are an additional 430 acres set aside for industrial development, available in 1/2-acre to 40-acre parcels. The city's abundant clean water and large capacity sewage plant are added enticements.

Kerman is classified as a general law city. Its council-city administrator government administered a budget of $2.7 million in 1984-85. Transportation is convenient: Interstate 5 is 40 miles west, Highway 99 is 15 miles east, and Highways 145 and 180 run through town. Motor carriers, railroads and bus transit systems serve Kerman, and the Fresno Air Terminal and Port of Stockton are within easy reach.

Agricultural products and concrete are the major manufacturing industries. Education, government and banking are the primary non-manufacturing employers. Physicians and dentists serve the Kerman area, and Fresno's hospitals are easily accessible. A local radio station and newspaper supplement the television channels, radio stations and newspapers received from major cities.

Community recreation facilities include a golf course and three city parks. The city sponsors a sports program, and 13 civic clubs are active. Kerman's ethnic groups provide additional activities for residents. The Portuguese community, for example, sponsors a festival six weeks after Easter, with a parade and free community dinner of Sopas — a hearty beef and cabbage dish which is served with French bread. The custom commemorates Queen Isabella's tradition of feeding the poor in Portugal on religious holidays.

The community also boasts concentrations of Russians, Germans, Italians, Armenians, Scandinavians, Asian Indians and Hispanics, as well as an active relationship with its Japanese sister city, Kannami. Its music club, school plays and Harvest Festival add to the homespun charm of Kerman.

Cattle graze on the lush grass in the outlying foothills of Fresno.

Vistas of Tomorrow

CHAPTER 10

Hiker surveys Whitebark Vista in Yosemite.

MANAGING GROWTH FOR QUALITY OF LIFE

Central Californians have long been conscious of the importance of maintaining a balance between growth and the preservation of the enviable quality of life their region affords. More than a hundred years ago, when gold fever lured thousands of immigrants to the Sierra foothills, environmental activists persuaded Congress to set aside vast areas of wilderness land for Yosemite National Park. The need to preserve valuable natural resources was apparent to only a few visionaries at that time, but it is now a common concern of Californians from the halls of government to the backyard barbecue.

News of oil spills, toxic waste dumps and inversions of polluted air has made Californians aware of the fragility of their Golden State. Families and corporations are increasingly making decisions about lifestyle and industry in the light of environmental concerns.

Population in Fresno County and surrounding areas is growing as a result of a nationally-documented change in population settlement patterns. Beginning in the 1970s, the trend to urbanization has been offset and even reversed by increasing immigration to smaller cities and towns as well as open country areas. Companies are relocating to smaller cities where their presence makes a difference and where willing workers are readily available. More and more individuals are settling in smaller towns and rural areas to raise their families.

The result of such corporate and individual decisions for Fresno County is an expected population growth rate of between 16 and 25 percent for the period from 1984 to 1990.

Fresno was the fastest growing of California's ten largest cities in 1986. Parlier has been tops in overall growth in the state since 1980, although much of that growth is attributable to annexation. This population explosion is likely to continue into the 1990s, placing severe stress on the environment as well as municipal services. Governments throughout the county are grappling with issues of land management and environmental protection.

The factors which have influenced the national trend to urbanization of rural areas are strongly present in Fresno County. The relationship between the farming industry and the environment, as well as to other sectors of the economy, has been altered as a result of the fact that agriculture is now capital intensive rather than labor intensive. The migration of manufacturing and, more recently, service industries to the countryside has placed steep demands on existing transportation and communication networks. Government itself has become a growth industry, with intensive employment, often in rural military or service installations.

These factors have combined to create a rural renaissance, a network of countrified cities (low density urban conditions in a rural setting) that has permanently altered

(Continued on page 222)

FRESNO COUNTY ECONOMIC DEVELOPMENT CORP.

CREATING JOBS FOR COUNTY RESIDENTS

AVK is a Danish-based firm manufacturing water valve products. Fresno is AVK's first U.S. plant site and serves the West Coast market.

The Fresno County Economic Development Corporation (EDC) was established in 1981 as a subsidiary of the Fresno County and City Chamber of Commerce, but with a separate board of directors and independent funding. It grew out of a recommendation in the 1980 "Market Fresno" study which called for a concerted effort by business and local government to promote Fresno as a place to do business, visit and hold conventions. This effort was led by Fresno County, the cities of Fresno and Clovis, the Chamber of Commerce and the Convention Bureau, and it resulted in the formation of the Economic Development Corporation.

The EDC operates with a permanent staff of five people and an annual budget of approximately $360,000. The funds are contributed by the County of Fresno; the cities of Fresno, Clovis, Sanger and Selma; the Fresno Private Industry Council and private businesses. With these resources, the EDC:

* Responds to an average of over 800 enquiries annually from local and out-of-the-area businesses. These queries include requests for general information as well as requests for more specific research and referrals to business services.
* Sponsors a national and international advertising and marketing campaign that increases the outside community's awareness of the attributes and benefits of Fresno County.
* Assists expanding businesses by providing referrals to financing sources, training funds and guidance with the development process.
* Assists local communities in developing strategies to attract local investment and new jobs.
* Serves as the host to visiting businesses that want to do an on-site assessment of the Fresno County area as a location for their new facilities.

The rapid growth of Motion Designs was aided by the EDC staff and resources.

The recent years have been successful ones for the EDC. In the last fiscal year, EDC was responsible for the direct creation of over 700 jobs and indirectly assisted in the creation of almost 600 more. These jobs represent a new payroll contribution of well over $10 million and an increase of thousands of dollars in new tax resources. The re-employment of these workers also provides relief to the already overburdened public services.

The success of the last year is encouraging and will create a momentum that will lead to even better things in the future. However, in order to achieve full employment in Fresno County, EDC believes the community needs to do a great deal more.

The Economic Development Corporation is committed to continuing its good work and to encouraging others to support this important effort.

Hartt Porteous

Fresno is fast becoming a regional headquarters site for many businesses necessitating state of the art computer capability.

the landscape and our relationship to it. As these trends persist and accelerate, the ability of local governments to plan for and respond to changing conditions will be critical to the maintenance of the safe, attractive and productive lifestyle of this bountiful region.

Informed citizen participation is a key element in effective management of growth. In contrast to an earlier era, when citizen activism often meant disruptive actions, citizens are now participating through established civic, professional, development, industrial and public interest groups in making decisions regarding the use of the county's land. Developers in particular are coming to the realization that environmental sensitivity can contribute to profitability.

Among the key issues involved in balancing growth with maintenance of the quality of life in Fresno County are air and water quality, protection of prime farmlands and ensuring a supply of labor.

Planners recognize that air pollution is potentially the most serious environmental threat to the Central Valley. Not only does air pollution pose a serious threat to health, but it is also extremely detrimental to vegetation, animals and property. Area farms, for example, are experiencing a ten to 20 percent decline in crop yield due to pollution. Farmers are being forced to change their cropping patterns, selecting crop varieties resistant to damage from airborne pollutants. In response to this threat to their economy and way of life, all local jurisdictions in Fresno County jointly produced the 1982 Clean Air Plan.

Neither the county's tremendous agricultural productivity nor its recreational lifestyle would be possible without its abundant and precious water resources. The history of California is marked by continuing controversy over the equitable distribution of water. Agriculture alone accounts for 85 percent of the state's total water usage. Federal, state and local entities play important and sometimes conflicting roles in the water saga.

Water quality is another high priority issue on the California state agenda, as toxicity and drainage problems pose tremendous threats to agriculture, wildlife and health. Fresno County's west side, which produces over $600 million in direct farm output annually, is dealing with salt buildup and the impact of shallow water tables. It has become something of a proving ground for cooperative solutions to water issues which are of state and national significance. Drainage and salt removal technologies being tested and proven on the west side will be exportable applications, hard evidence of the resilience, durability and commitment of the people of Fresno County, for whom agriculture is primary.

The long term viability of Fresno County depends upon agriculture. Acre for acre, the soils of Fresno County are some of the most productive in the world; they have made agriculture the number one industry in the county. Land is a finite resource which must be protected from uncontrolled growth. For every 1,000 new residents of the county, 142 acres of land are converted from agricultural to other uses. Area planners are moving to preserve prime agricultural land and to share development in ways compatible with this strategy.

Labor is another resource critical to the area's economy. While statewide figures for agricultural employment hover around three percent of the market, 25 percent of the labor force in Fresno County is employed in agriculture. The labor needs of agriculture fluctuate with strong seasonal demands. Large numbers of undocumented workers who have long contributed to the area's agricultural productivity may, under the 1986 Immigration Reform and Control Act, receive legal status. This would enable them to look for work in other industries, thereby diminishing the supply of readily available farm labor. Area business and farming communities are taking an active role in assisting in the legalization process while working with area planners to recruit new agribusiness industries and expand existing ones. These coordinated efforts should minimize the impact of federal legislation and help to maintain optimum stability in the area's agricultural work force.

In each of these key areas — air and water quality, agricultural land preservation, and labor force stabilization — impressive strides are being taken toward resolution of shared problems. Preventive measures are being implemented to ensure maintenance of the area's human and natural resources. Public and private sector interests are working together to protect Fresno County's abundance for future generations. As part of this, residents are playing an active role in planning for recreational opportunities, an appropriate stance for residents of an area so rich in natural scenic resources.

THE SAN JOAQUIN RIVER PARKWAY: A DREAM WITHIN REACH

After years of neglect and abuse, it appears that the San Joaquin riverway north of Fresno may become an integrated 22-mile-long series of parks and river front recreational areas. The San Joaquin River Committee has launched an intensive educational and lobbying effort to alert citizens to the potential of the area. Using the beautiful and immensely popular American River Parkway in Sacramento as a model, the committee is publicizing the many benefits to be gained from developing the area as a parkway. These include river reclamation, wildlife preservation and the establishment of roadside reststops along busy highways.

The National Audubon Society has encouraged the effort to develop the parkway, for the area holds great promise in the effort to preserve California's fragile waterfowl. Voters are circulating petitions to qualify the California Wildlife, Coastal and Parkland initiative for the 1988 ballot, in hopes of passing a bond measure that would include $5 million for the proposed San Joaquin River Parkway. The City of Fresno has already gone on record in support of the parkway, and the matter is before the County Board of Supervisors.

The focus of all this attention is a 22-mile stretch of river that meanders westward from Friant Dam across the flat valley floor to Highway 99. The first leg of the parkway, at the eastern end, is already established as the Lost Lake Recreation Area. This easternmost segment includes a 42-site campground, more than 200 picnic areas and a large primitive nature area and wildlife preserve. The committee's proposal calls for additional long stretches of the parkway to be wildlife refuge areas much like that at Lost Lake.

Eighteen miles downstream, the City of Fresno is considering the development of a regional park on the south bank of the river, near Sierra Sky Park. Two ponding basins would become fishing and boating lakes, and a full range of park facilities would be developed on 440 acres of reclaimed sand and gravel lands.

The plan calls for these two parks to be linked by a 22-mile hiking and riding trail that would at times touch either the Fresno or Madera side of the river. Although motorized vehicles would be restricted, the trail would be open to hikers, joggers, bicyclists and horseback riders.

In addition, work is already underway on another hiking and equestrian trail which would connect the river parkway at Friant with the San Joaquin River Trail, a 73-mile trans-Sierra path. This trail would run from the valley floor to the crest of the Sierra, where it would intersect the famed Pacific Crest Trail near Mammoth Mountain. When both trails are complete, riders and hikers could make the 95-mile trek from Highway 99 to the Sierra crest through some of California's most colorful landscapes, climbing from the hot arid semi-desert valley floor to the cool alpine peaks thousands of feet above.

With the Sierra Sky Park area and the Lost Lake Recreation Area as anchors, the parkway would provide a series of small river front parks, interspersed with wildlife areas and linked by a continuous hiking and riding trail. Roadside rests have been proposed to serve motorists along busy Highways 99 and 41. Camping and picnic areas at the roadside rests would enable families on their way to Yosemite to enjoy a

Clair Nelsen

The beautiful San Joaquin River beginning its southward journey is the subject of discussion for a 22-mile river parkway project.

PARAGON GROUP/COOMBS, INC.

A QUALITY DEVELOPMENT COMPANY

A Paragon Property similar in quality to the proposed complex to be built in Fresno by Paragon/Coombs, Inc.

Paragon Group, founded in Dallas in 1978, is one of the largest privately owned development companies in the country. The company's major business objectives are development and long-term ownership of prime properties. By retaining management of its properties, Paragon believes it is best able to assure their proper maintenance and to increase their value as income producers and assets.

The company's real estate portfolio is valued at approximately $2 billion. It owns, operates or has under construction 180 income properties comprised of more than 12 million square feet of commercial projects and 27,000 rental housing units in 45 cities within 15 states. Paragon Group is involved in virtually all facets of real estate development—office buildings, shopping centers, office/showrooms and apartments.

Approximately 600 of the Fortune 1000 companies are Paragon tenants. Quality details and a prestigious image are offered to the discriminating tenant. For example, Paragon's attention to detail is reflected in Redwood City's Paragon Point, an exceptional corporate office complex.

The two four-story office buildings front a magnificent 200-acre lagoon, which is the focal point of Redwood Shores. The campus-like setting at the water's edge allows employees to enjoy the adjacent parks and lagoon for jogging, leisurely strolls and water-related activities. Landscaped plazas are available to tenants for outdoor eating, meetings or relaxing. Shower and locker room facilities are provided for tenants' exclusive use.

In a joint venture with Fresnan Dennes Coombs of Coombs, Inc., Paragon is planning an impressive project in Fresno at the intersection of Shaw Avenue and Highway 41. Construction of the 450,000 square foot office compex will begin in the spring of 1988.

The project will be marked by the unparalleled excellence Paragon tenants have come to expect. Owned and managed by those who are highly attuned and responsive to tenants' needs, Paragon is looking to the future with confidence.

head start on their vacation. An access corridor from Fresno's Woodward Park is planned. Other access ways along the parkway would allow recreation enthusiasts to canoe or float down the river on rafts.

The San Joaquin River Parkway holds much promise for visitors as well as area residents. Park planners, landscape architects and other parkway enthusiasts are eager to implement their ambitious plans, and the public support needed to make this dream a reality is gaining momentum. It may well be that the parkway will become an important enhancement to the quality of life for Fresnans within this generation.

Effective coalitions such as the San Joaquin River Committee are made up of informed, committed individuals, people who invest their time, talent and energies in preserving and enhancing the distinctive characteristics of their communities. Although Fresno has always been gifted with enlightened and devoted leaders, a program was established in the city in 1984 to build and sustain that talent pool.

GESCO CORPORATION

LEADER IN THE DATA PROCESSING INDUSTRY

The GESCO Corporation is a leading provider of specialized financial data processing services for savings and loans.

GESCO Corporation is a leading provider of specialized financial data processing services for savings and loans. A leader in a highly competitive and volatile industry, GESCO has enjoyed steady growth and burgeoning success since the company was founded more than 20 years ago. In 1987, GESCO became the nation's third largest data processing servicer to the savings industry.

GESCO has successfully maintained this leadership position through its commitment to developing new products and services that give GESCO clients the leading edge they need in today's competitive financial environment. GESCO's company-wide dedication to customer satisfaction has also been a key factor behind the Fresno-based corporation's expanding client roster and continued, long-term success.

LEADERSHIP FRESNO–DYNAMIC TRAINING GROUND

In the fall of 1984, the Fresno County and City Chamber of Commerce and *The Fresno Bee*, with the support of corporate sponsors, began a joint venture in leadership development. Each year, a community-wide recruitment effort yields a Leadership Fresno class of 30 members selected from numerous applicants. These individuals represent agriculture, business, the professions, government, education and the media, and are chosen on the basis of their track records in community action.

Each month, the class spends a full day learning about the problems, needs, opportunities and political realities of the community. Together they select a class project as a vehicle through which to demonstrate their commitment. Year after year, this program has added to the pool of qualified leaders equipped with the information and motivation to tackle the tough problems of community life. Alumni can be expected to play a significant role in both public and private sectors, planning and working with other community leaders for a bright future.

PLANNING TOGETHER

The people of Fresno have an impressive track record of establishing and relying on community groups for preventing or resolving problems. The Fresno Interagency Committee, for example, has so successfully discharged its mission in the area of consolidating, integrating and improving youth services that an adult interagency committee has been modeled upon it. Advisory boards composed of informed community leaders serve to guide the development of area nonprofit organizations and community service agencies and their combined wisdom has brought a wealth of resources to the area.

In the area of human services, the innovative United Way allocation process relies on hundreds of volunteers to work out an equitable distribution of resources among the many projects serving the needs of the community. In the arts, the umbrella Alliance for the Arts has stimulated a number of outstanding programs and brought inspirational artists into the schools as artists in residence. In government, citizen boards and commissions guide the work of many departments, ensuring their responsiveness to community

Incorporated in 1969 as a wholly owned subsidiary of Guarantee Savings and Loan — also headquartered in Fresno — GESCO now serves 36 saving institutions throughout the Western U.S. with combined assets of more than $110 billion. GESCO's clients include some of the largest savings institutions in the country, including American Savings and Loan of Stockton, Great Western Savings Bank of Beverly Hills and World Savings and Loan of Oakland.

GESCO provides real-time access and immediate transaction processing capabilities for more than six million client accounts. To handle the transaction processing needs of such a large account volume, GESCO maintains a complete telecommunications network of more than 10,000 client terminals residing at over 1,000 branch locations. GESCO also supports more than 250 automated teller machines (ATMs) and offers processing on two regional ATM networks.

GESCO's data center is the largest single data center serving the savings industry today. This means that while other servicers may use multiple data centers for processing, GESCO's one data center is equipped to handle all of the processing needs of its clients.

However, GESCO believes the key to its success does not rest with its data center. At GESCO, people are what count most: both customers and employees. The company takes great pride in responding to the needs of its clients, a commitment that requires a dedicated and highly qualified staff, strongly motivated to provide customer service.

Long ago, GESCO moved toward establishing the high standards in employee recruitment it maintains today. GESCO's national recruiting program attracts highly skilled technical and administrative employees from all over the country — employees who bring to GESCO invaluable experience and innovative ideas.

GESCO is dedicated to attracting motivated and talented individuals who will do a better job for its customers because customer satisfaction continues to be the company's number one goal. And as a result of this philosophy, GESCO boasts one of the highest client satisfaction levels across the country in its industry. Many of GESCO's satisfied clients have been on the GESCO system for five, ten and even fifteen years.

GESCO recognizes that it is the talents and efforts of its staff of more than 400 people that have created and maintained such a high level of customer satisfaction. This high satisfaction level has, in turn, allowed GESCO Corporation to emerge at the forefront of the data processing industry.

GESCO's data center is the largest single data center serving the savings industry today.

priorities. At the grassroots level, the Fresno Organizing Project unites area churches, unions and community organizations in working for the alleviation of poverty. In these and many other ways, Fresnans work together to safeguard the unique social, cultural, environmental and economic characteristics of their community, and to plan intelligently for its future.

This historic sign embodies the spirit of Fresno. No longer a small city, the pride of Fresno, however, is still vibrant and the Frank Caglia family has done much to keep this landmark symbol properly preserved.

VISION 90—PLANNING FOR THE FUTURE

In August of 1987, the Fresno Chamber of Commerce, in cooperation with Fresno City College and the State Center Community College District, released the Vision 90 report. The report summarizes six months of intensive assessment and planning on the part of hundreds of community leaders, who volunteered for this unusual, taxing and highly productive assignment.

The history of economic development in Fresno County has been one of moving from an embryonic state to a skilled professional unit. There has been a lack of coordination among the multitude of chambers, cities, state and county offices, corporations, bureaus, financial institutions and programs, and other key players in the economic arena. Yet the time is surely at hand for cooperation. The urbanization of farmlands impacts taxation bases. Pure air and water concern everybody. Developments in one community have repercussions in other communities. Concerns such as these motivated the chamber and the college to take the initiative in starting the joint planning process which resulted in the Vision 90 report.

JOHNNY QUIK FOOD STORES, INC.

A LICENSING CONCEPT ON THE LEADING EDGE

Johnny Quik Food Stores is a state of the art licensing concept which has positioned itself to be at the leading edge in convenience store development. The success of Johnny Quik Food Stores, Inc. began 20 years ago when two teenage brothers, George and Ernie Beal, began working for a convenience store chain.

It wasn't long before the two brothers began their own store in Reedley, California, in 1973, which grew to a chain of 25 stores located between Tulare and Modesto. Their success culminated with the sale of their company owned stores to a large national chain in 1985. Shortly thereafter, the birth of the new Johnny Quik Food Store licensing program came about.

These new stores were developed on the leading edge of convenience stores concepts achieving a happy balance between the traditional convenience store and a quality fast food provider. Since July of 1985, 12 Johnny Quik Food Stores have been built with 12 more scheduled in 1988. These new stores contain sit-down seating areas, interior restrooms, a quality fast food bar and state of the art gasoline pumping equipment.

The initial growth area targeted for Johnny Quik Food Stores ranges from Bakersfield to the Oregon border. The Beal brothers have always been regarded as superb operators of quality stores and their philosophy is that they genuinely desire to see their stores exist as a "good neighbor" to the surrounding homes and businesses in their area. Serving on the average of 1600 customers a day, the Johnny Quik Food Stores reflect the Beal's goals of building stores in convenient locations, attractive both inside and outside with quality products and services as the foundation for their growth and success.

In addition to innovative appearance, products and services of their stores, the Beal brothers have also introduced a very attractive aspect to the normal licensing concept with their "equity ownership program." Unlike the normal convenience store franchise, the Johnny Quik approach allows the licensee to gain ownership of all equipment at his location, in addition to gaining ownership of all the inventory for a significant equity advantage.

If the present rate of growth and success continues, the Johnny Quik Food Store concept could well move eastward across America in continuing the California tradition of giving birth to national franchises.

George and Ernie Beal are proud of their good neighbor business philosophy and coupled with their new state of the art stores are poised for significant expansion throughout all of northern California.

In the process, subcommittees met for several months to wrestle with the issues, including the general plan, quality of life, agriculture, financing economic development, coordination of the general plan with economic development of the county and city, and Fresno's image. Each subcommittee gathered data and developed recommendations in its particular area of study. These recommendations were compiled into a preliminary report which was distributed for review, analysis and refinement at the Vision 90 charrette.

The charrette process gets its name from the medieval practice of architectural students traveling by cart, or charrette, to important examinations. Along the way, the students would put their heads together to analyze and improve their preliminary plans and designs. In a similar way, the Vision 90 charrette brought together more than 100 community leaders for a Saturday of intensive re-examination of the work of the subcommittees. Preliminary solutions were modified and strengthened by the combined wisdom of the group.

Out of this effort a general strategy for economic development and a number of carefully considered recommendations to implement that strategy have been gathered in the Vision 90 report. The participants issued a clear call for regional coordination, for the Fresno Economic Development Corporation to take a leadership role, for economic development which will enhance agriculture, and for the preservation of Fresno's desirable quality of life.

Included in the report are thoughtful analyses of the air quality, water quality, employment and land use issues which will determine the quality of life for Fresno County residents of the future. Some of the Vision 90 recommendations, such as the call for a local planning and procedures ordinance in the City of Fresno, have already been implemented. Many of the water and agricultural land preservation recommendations are currently under consideration by the appropriate boards and agencies.

Vision 90 participants are heartened by this prompt response to their recommendations. They realize, however, that continuing diligence is required to ensure the success of these first tentative steps in the direction of coordinated planning for the future. Vision 90 has given Fresno a head start down the road toward its goal of maintaining economic health while preserving the quality of life. It has also shed light on the pathway ahead.

INFORMATION AND TECHNOLOGY

Fresno has been an active participant in the much-touted information revolution. This was well illustrated in the Vision 90 process, where subcommittee members — ordinary citizens with an extraordinary interest in community betterment — had at their fingertips an impressive array of facts and figures upon which to base their recommendations. Among the many tools available in Fresno for data gathering, tools which were scarcely dreamed of a decade ago, are database search capabilities and electronic directories which bring to the research information that runs the gamut from funding sources to the names of top experts in any given field. Inexpensive searches can put the latest information in nearly any field, including the titles of all catalogued pieces of printed material on the subject, into the researcher's hands in a matter of seconds.

Computerization, the technology for database searches, is making its presence known in Fresno. The Fresno office of IBM ranks among the top ten in the nation. It boasts that a single customer today utilizes more computer "horsepower" than did the entire region just a decade ago. In financial services, one large mainframe user services a network of 10,000 terminals. County governments up and down the valley are intensive computer users, particularly in the areas of criminal justice and social services, where computerization streamlines services and helps hold down personnel costs.

In retail computer installations, Fresno's users employ state-of-the-art technology for point-of-sale terminals. Agriculture is among the area's most intensive users of mid-range processors. All the large farming operations have been computerized for many years. They employ sophisticated applications for vehicle and equipment maintenance, crop costing, payroll monitoring and record keeping.

Fresno is one of the eight best test markets in the country and is used by market researchers to test new products and advertising campaigns. Metropolitan Fresno, with its many ethnic groups and clustered population segments, can be easily stratified for research sampling. Because the population tends to be conservative, market research conducted in Fresno yields predictive, rather than faddish, results.

Fresno's colleges, universities and vocational schools have produced a pool of capable workers for computerized business and industrial applications. The population of Asian immigrants is proving to be a source of reliable, efficient and quality-conscious workers in the information and technology industries, thereby giving Fresno some of the advantages traditionally associated with overseas labor markets.

The colleges and universities contribute to the information base in fields other than computer science. The University of California's research station at Parlier and the California State University, Fresno, graduate programs add to the pool of knowledge, particularly in agriculture. Articles written by students and published in national scholarly journals point to the area's advancements in air quality monitoring, integrated pest management and a host of other fields.

(Continued on page 230)

The technology of CSUF is exemplified in its nationally acclaimed enology program. Shown here are students involved in evaluating various wines, always seeking improvements.

ATWOOD GROVE CONSTRUCTION

A TOTAL CONCEPT IN BUILDING

The law office building of Wild, Carter, Tipton and Oliver is a recent example of the quality work done by Atwood Grove Construction.

Atwood Grove Construction was founded and incorporated in 1962 by Atwood Grove. The company's business is commercial, industrial and agricultural construction and development.

The spectrum of services, capabilities and crafts combine to offer what Atwood Grove calls the AGC Total Concept in building.

Atwood Grove Construction offers a wide range of services including design and engineering through the actual construction phase. Financing, site selection, site development and landscaping are all integral parts of every construction project and AGC stands ready to assist in these important aspects.

AGC emphasizes a client relationship that combines ideas on systems, esthetics and economics to develop a coordinated plan. This cooperative pre-construction planning results in a building that represents the best dollar investment and optimum plant performance.

Particular emphasis is placed on the way a new plant looks, inside and outside. AGC offers the design talents of some of the best people in their fields. Interior and exterior design, color coordination and landscaping are all essential components in the total design expression. The skills and talents of AGC's artists and craftsmen mold these components into the best esthetic impression for the best dollar value.

Among AGC's Total Concept services is site selection. AGC's interests in a wide range of outstanding commercial and industrial sites, along with access through lease and purchase to numerous Central California locations, make site selection a matter of intelligent choice.

AGC believes in proper planning and strives to give prudent cost estimates. AGC has a well-deserved reputation for pinpoint estimating and the company is proud of it.

AGC's goal is to have its clients move in and start "living with" their new plant as soon as conveniently possible. The company can help secure a broad spectrum of financing through banks, insurance companies and various private funds.

AGC hand picks its crews for performance and reliability. From AGC's older and more experienced personnel to the company's young foremen and leadmen, there is a certain personal pride in workmanship and an unequaled, coordinated team effort. Personal on-site inspection is always invited during every phase of construction.

AGC's guarantee is that construction will be completed as scheduled and every attention will be given to finishing details. AGC guarantees timely completion in addition to pledging continued service following occupancy. AGC's pride in workmanship has made that guarantee possible and that guarantee has established Atwood Grove Construction as a quality builder for 25 years.

The Fresno campus of the California School of Professional Psychology provides an ideal research environment for studies of human behavior. Each year, between 25 and 30 doctoral dissertations produced at the school advance our knowledge in such fields as substance abuse treatment, gerontology, child development and cross-cultural understanding. At each of Fresno's institutions of higher learning, faculty and graduate assistants engage in research aimed at broadening human knowledge. The reputation of the community is enhanced in the bargain.

A century ago, before the advent of railroads and radios, the West was left out of the flow of information. Now, with timenet and telenet networks, compact disc information processing capabilities, ISDN, fiber optics and 800 system telephone networks, location is irrelevant for information access. Factors such as labor availability, climate and lifestyle impact corporate location decisions to a greater extent than ever before. With its abundant labor supply, low costs and highly desirable quality of life, Fresno is launching much of its new growth from technology's cottage industry springboard.

In leisure and entertainment as well, Fresno is reaping the rewards of advances in information and technology. The "Fresno" mini-series in the fall of 1986 provided an unusual opportunity for an all-city, multi-media, giant screen party. High tech may very soon become a routine leisure activity, even outside homes with the ubiquitous VCR.

The Metropolis, an entertainment district enterprise currently on the drawing board, features production studios, 25,000 square feet lit for filming, an electronic cafe installation like those at the Summer Olympics in Los Angeles, a stage and two large screens for performance, teleconference capability, interactive video for performance and social events, as well as live and recorded television production. In addition, the building would house flower and newspaper kiosks, a full-service restaurant and lounge named Joaquin's after the valley's romanticized outlaw, a cafe, an ice cream specialty shop, a bakery, a deli and office and service features.

With satellite transmission linking patrons to their counterparts in Paris, Moscow, Hong Kong or Nairobi, the Metropolis has the potential of connecting multi-cultural, middle-America Fresno with the larger world in a most exciting and effective fashion.

This lovely girl, Alyssa, is a living example of how technology has touched people's lives. She is the first baby conceived and born as a result of the San Joaquin Valley's in vitro fertilization program.

WORLD AGRITRADE CENTER–UNDER STUDY

Fresno is exploring a unique opportunity to position itself as the world leader in international agricultural trade. The results of its World AgriTrade Center Feasibility Study, based on a survey of other world trade centers and released in 1987, indicate that no other world trade center exists or is being planned with a focus on agriculture.

This photo showcases but a fraction of the astounding crop production of Central California available to a world market.

As a one-stop center combining state of the art services and facilities, conceptually the center would benefit government and the educational system as well as the agribusiness community. Serving a wide range of domestic and international interests, the AgriTrade Center could combine retail, office, restaurant and hotel accommodations.

As the evaluation process continues the tasks to be accomplished under the direction of a steering committee include development of an interim facility to test the market, investigation of financing, solidifying leadership support, identifying prospective tenants, integrating ancillary services, and promoting and marketing the project throughout the United States and abroad, with special attention to Pacific Rim countries.

As part of the feasibility study process, the city sponsored a World AgriTrade Center Conference to educate the community and build support for the project. The 16 speakers and panelists included representatives of two California ports and six world trade centers. Twenty-two exhibitors provided informative displays. Topics included timing, marketing, benefits and implementation. As a test of the AgriTrade Center idea, the conference was a cautious first step.

Community response to a market survey indicated a high level of interest, demonstrating that the time may be right for this indepth exploration in planning for the future growth of California agriculture.

AIS MARKET RESEARCH

A GIANT IN THE MARKETING SERVICES INDUSTRY

AIS Market Research was started in 1959 by President Patricia Alviso.

AIS Market Research was started by Patricia Alviso in 1959 and is the oldest marketing, social and political research firm in California's Central Valley. With its primary telemarketing and research facilities located in Fresno, AIS has field research offices in both Bakersfield and Modesto and employs a staff of over 50 people.

AIS is considered a full-service research firm because the staff includes professionals who can design studies and then analyze collected data, making appropriate conclusions and recommendations. AIS also employs a field staff of data collectors and interviewers. Many research firms subcontract out the field work or hire temporary employees but AIS feels its own staff insures better quality control and improved study turnaround time.

Fresno (and to a lesser extent, the entire Central Valley) has earned a reputation for being an excellent national test market city. This has given AIS the opportunity to work with a wide variety of clients from all over the country. AIS numbers among its clients multinational corporations, hospitals, governments, banks, advertising agencies and newspapers.

AIS also offers marketing consulting services. This division was originally formed to help clients implement the information that was provided to them from research. AIS has the consulting experience in all areas of the marketing mix - from new product evaluation to organizing a complete marketing division. Most commonly, AIS works with clients preparing marketing plans and strategies. As a result of her success in research, Alviso has identified a new area of business that offers and extremely promising opportunity — professional telemarketing.

PASSPORT FRESNO: AN IDEA THAT IS GROWING

When the Chamber of Commerce created the Downtown Association in 1955, it had no idea that one of the association's inspirations would turn out to be Passport Fresno. Originally a special event designed to draw people to the downtown area, Passport Fresno has grown to become a strategy for revitalizing a 60-block area of the city. This plan capitalizes on Fresno's natural advantages, including international trade and ethnic diversity.

The Downtown Association searched for a way to communicate the positive elements of Fresno to all segments of the city. Their solution? Passport Fresno!

The festival began as an annual celebration which drew thousands to enjoy the parade, food booths, ethnic arts and crafts displays and music. The celebration has grown in size and scope each year. It is now a three-day carnival enjoyed by 80,000 Fresnans. They come to the Fulton Mall Complex and Courthouse Square — transformed into a 750,000 square foot outdoor exhibition mall — to see handicrafts from 33 nations, and to relish the cuisine and folk music. Ever expanding, the festival in 1987 added 14 countries to the 19 represented in 1986 and an international theater program to this downtown extravaganza.

These Polynesian dancers embody the spirit of Passport Fresno where thousands annually enjoy the parade, food booths, ethnic arts, crafts and music.

The Passport Fresno Trade Conference is a second phase of Passport Fresno and is planned for 1988. Complementing the exuberance of the multi-cultural festival, this three-day regional trade conference is designed to promote economic development and domestic and foreign trade through educational workshops and seminars.

AIS has consulting experience in all areas of the marketing mix from new product evaluation to organizing a complete marketing division.

Right now, the AIS Telemarketing facility is the premier operation in Central California, with nationwide capabilities, state of the art telecommunications equipment and again, the finest staff that Alviso could assemble. In fact, the AIS Telemarketing goal is to become the pioneer firm in telemarketing through innovation and application of research based telemarketing programs.

It is this integration of research based marketing endeavors that sets Patricia Alviso and AIS apart from any other marketing services firm in California and the nation. In that vein, Alviso's long range plans encompass the development of a broader based business consulting firm specializing in marketing research, planning, professional telemarketing and "other services as determined by an ongoing research program."

While the firm primarily conducts its business through the Fresno headquarters—with field service offices in Modesto and Bakersfield—the ultimate goal is to service the entire West Coast and the Pacific Rim Countries.

This AIS Telemarketing facility is the premier operation in Central California.

With more than 200 businesses already active in international trade, and with its status as a Port of Entry, the City of Fresno is well positioned for increasing the volume of its international trade. A Trade Exhibition, part of the Passport Fresno Conference, is designed to inform conference participants about available business and government services. With representation from businesses as well as government trade agencies, the exhibition is sure to spur interest and promote expertise in international trade.

Most comprehensive by far is the third component of Passport Fresno: a master plan for redevelopment and revitalization of a 60-block area of the central city with an international festival marketplace as its cornerstone. Modeled on Boston's Faneuil Market and other large-scale festival marketplaces, the installation would provide permanent housing for trade missions, ethnic restaurants, shops and museums, and home offices for international businesses. This development is intended to create an identity for central city Fresno which could enhance the positioning of the city in the local, regional, national and international markets.

A comprehensive plan has been set in motion, a plan which combines strategies for improving public access to downtown, responding to public safety concerns, attending to visual improvements and marketing the downtown area. Passport Fresno is one of the most exciting manifestations of the spirit that keeps Fresno vital and growing.

Pictured below is the Fulton Mall area of downtown noted for its variety of artistic sculpture, fountains and aesthetically attractive landscaping.

Author's Acknowledgements

A book of this scope is clearly the creation of a number of people. Throughout the interview and research phase, while I was gathering data, it quickly became apparent that the sense of community celebrated in this book is a vibrant truth. The pride and ownership of all that is special about Fresno are palpable throughout the County, from the halls of government to the corner grocer in the most remote hamlet.

Chamber Board President Gene Clayton's confident leadership smoothed the way for the entire publication effort. Of course, Executive Director Russ Sloan is primarily responsible for any success of these efforts, for it was his vision that gave birth to the project, and his genius for sharing that vision which secured its funding. Ernie Hergenroeder's experienced eye and technical skill created the visual appeal which could so easily have been lost, given the large number of photographic contributors and the diversity of graphics necessary to tell the Fresno story. Editor Sharon Stochler's competence, patience, reliability, and skill have been truly remarkable.

Finally, I want to acknowledge my parents, Walter and Evelyn Conger, who spent much of their California vacation touring Fresno County on assignment with me, and my husband, John, and children, Eileen, Heather, Michael, and Brian for lending me so wholeheartedly to this project. Their patience is a tribute to their shared belief that the Fresno story is well worth the telling. While each of these named, and many others as well, have contributed to the success, accuracy, and inspiration in this work, its limitations are entirely my own.

My grateful appreciation should also be extended to the following people who contributed in many different ways to the development of this book.

Jeanne F. Adams
C.W. "Bill" Allison
Shirley Armbruster
Byron Astida
Jane D. Avedikian
Robert Barrett
James D. Barri
Leland Bergstrom
Ken Billings
James Bort
Fred Brusuelas
Thomas Butch
Carla Byers
Al Camin
Marcos Casarez
Yvonne Cashion
Jackie Church
Charles W. Clough
Edwina Collins
Ronald H. Corliss
Terri Cowling
Robert Cox
Sid Cox
Mitzi Esteva-Jones
Rose Fisher
Tony Focarelli
Phil Forhan
Edith Forsstrom
Richard Francois
Dennis Gaab
Linda J. Gilmore
Connie Gomez
Janet Gray
Duff Green
James D. Grigsby
Vi Grinsteiner
Reid Groomis
Shellie P. Grude
Don Hall
Sharon Hiigel
Betty Hinton
Nick Housepian
Cosmo C. Insalaco
Bill Jirsa
David Jones
Donald D. Laub
Gayle P. Ledford
Michale Lehman
Annette Leifer
Michael Lipson
LaFonda Lobmeyer
John Luthy
Richard Markarian
Douglas Martin
David McClelland
Ross McGuire
Walter A. McKinney
Barbara Mecca
Blanche Milhahn
Philip R. Minnehan
Joe Mixer
L.P. Molina
Dee Moody
Richard Nagle
Dick Nichols
Bruce Obbink
Pat Ogle
Liz Olson
Larry Pesch
Marcy Phillips
Don Pierce
Jan Pierce
John D. Popp
Perry Powers
Judith Preuss
Sue Quigley
John E. Quiring
Craig W. Reid
R.R. Rhodes
J.M. Rodriques
Gene Rose
Louise Schneider
Nancy Shepherd
Wesley Slade
Theresa E. Smith
Al Solis
Tina S. Sonnier
Bruce Spaulding
Gayle Surabian
Robin Swanson
Bill Thompson
Charles Topjian
Tom Van Nortwick
Robert D. Vandergon
Alex Vavoulis
Lieutenant Art Venegas, Jr.
Perry A. Walker
Jerre Weber
Frances White
Berton K. Wills
Harvey Zimmerman

Approaching a Century of Chamber of Commerce Leadership

William M. Lyles
President
1986

Gene R. Clayton
President
1987

Paul O'Rourke
President
1988

Octavia Diener
President Elect
1988

Board of Directors Presidents

Name	Year(s)
ALEX GOLDSTEIN	1895
ARTHUR R. BRIGGS	1896
LOUIS GUNDELFINGER	1897
JOHN REICHMAN	1898
JOHN C. NOURSE	1898
T.C. WHITE	1899
S.F. BOOTH	1900
W.T. MATTINGLY	1901
JOHN A. NEU	1902-03-07-16
LEWIS H. SMITH	1904
F.A. JONES	1905
A.L. HOBBS	1906-09-10
M.F. TARPEY	1908
WYLIE M. GIFFEN	1911
W.W. PHILLIPS	1912-13-14-15
W.G. COCHRANE	1917
W.F. CHANDLER	1918
WILLIAM GLASS	1919-20
CHARLES OSBURN	1921
C.T. CEARLEY	1922
W.A. SUTHERLAND	1923-24
L.A. NARES	1925
FRANK BRADFORD	1925-26
E.M. PRESCOTT	1927-28
CHESTER WARLOW	1929
HENRY AVILA	1930
EDWIN M. EATON	1931-32
STANLEY PRATT	1933
JESSE E. RODMAN	1934
FRANK G. EVERTS	1935
DAVID E. PECKINPAH	1936
E.C. SMITH	1937
GILBERT H. JERTBERG	1938
KENNETH T. CRAWFORD	1939
CHARLES G. CONNORS	1940
B.M. HOBLICK	1941
PAUL STANIFORD	1942
WALTER STAMMER	1943
HARRY S. BAKER	1944-45

Name	Year(s)
J.C. KIMBLE	1946-47
AL. J. BROWN	1948
PAUL V. LORTON	1949
J.K. HERBERT	1950-51
MELVILLE E. WILLSON	1952
DENNIS B. WHEELER	1953-54
MAYNARD MUNGER	1955-56
LEON S. PETERS	1957
EDWARD H. MARSELLA	1958
C.W. RICHARD ATKINS	1959
OLIVE M. JAMISON	1960
B. FRANKLIN KNAPP	1961
JAMES B. MAYER	1962
HERBERT N. FERGUSON	1963
RICHARD M. WORREL	1964
HAROLD M. SCHUPPERT	1965
GENE FORD	1966
LEWIS S. EATON	1967
JACK E. OLIVER	1968
GILBERT T. CASWELL	1969
PHILLIP C. WEIGAND	1970
TED F. BAUN	1971
GERALD B. BREWER	1972
JAMES K. BARNUM	1973
RICHARD J. RUDY	1974
NORMAL LIDDELL	1975
FRANK J. SANDERS	1976
JOSEPH W. LEVY	1977
MARTIN C. NELSEN	1978
J. MARTIN TEMPLE	1979
DONALD J. SCHAFER	1980
VANCE L. CLARK	1981
GRANT N. RADFORD	1982
SHELDON P. LEWIS	1983
GERALD L. TAHAJIAN	1984
HELEN SMADES	1985
WILLIAM M. LYLES	1986
GENE R. CLAYTON	1987
PAUL O'ROURKE	1988

Distinguished Patrons

The following individuals, companies, institutions, and organizations have made a valuable contribution to the quality of this publication. The Fresno County and City Chamber of Commerce gratefully acknowledges their participation and support of FRESNO: VALLEY OF ABUNDANCE.

AIS Market Research
Atwood Grove Construction
Automated Office Systems
Bank of America
Builders Concrete and River Rock Products
California School of Professional Psychology
California State University-Fresno
Capri Sun
Central California Faculty Medical Group
Centre Plaza Holiday Inn
Chihuahua, Inc.
City of Fresno
Clovis Lakes
Commercial Transfer, Inc.
Community Hospitals of Central California
CPC Sierra Gateway Hospital
DeMera, DeMera and Cameron
Donaghy Sales, Inc.
Electric Motor Shop, Inc.
Fashion Fair Mall
Fig Garden Village
First American Title Insurance Company
First Interstate Bank
Fleming Foods
Fresno Arts Center and Museum
Fresno Community and Convention Center
Fresno Convention and Visitors Bureau
Fresno County Economic Development Corporation
Fresno Hilton
Fresno Metropolitan Museum
Fresno Pacific College
Gary Timan Vigen, AIA and Associates
GESCO Corporation
Gottschalks
Grubb and Ellis
Grundfos Pumps
Grupe Development Company
Guarantee Savings
Guardian Industries
H. Markus and Company
H.P. Metzler and Sons
Harris Ranch
HCA Cedar Vista Hospital
Heald's 4-C's Business College
Hope Manor
International Business Machines
International English Institute
Johnny Quik Food Stores, Inc.
Kaiser Permanente
KFSN-TV 30 Fresno
Kirkwood's Design Gallery
KMJ and KNAX Radio
KSEE, TV 24
Leo Wilson Construction
Lundberg and Associates
Lyles Diversified, Inc.
Manchester Center
Marketing Plus
McCormick, Barstow, Sheppard, Wayte and Carruth
Motion Designs
National Raisin Company
National University
New York Life
Northwest Church
Pacific Agricultural Services, Inc.
Pacific Bell
Pacific Gas and Electric
Paragon Group/Coombs, Inc.
Peabody Floway
Pepsi Cola San Joaquin Bottling Company
Producers Dairy
PSA/USAir
Reedley Chamber of Commerce
Richland Sales Company
Riverbend International Corporation
Saint Agnes Medical Center
St. Anthony of Padua
Salwasser Manufacturing
San Joaquin Business Services Group, Inc.
San Joaquin College of Law
Sandalwood Development Corp.
Schoenwald - Oba - Mogensen - Pohll- Miller, Inc.
Shearson Lehman Brothers
Sierra Summit Ski Area
Stars To Go, Inc.
State Center Community College District
Stoughton Davidson
Summa Health Plan
Sun-Maid Growers of California
The Big Fresno Fair
The Bulldog Foundation, Fresno State University
The Farmers Market
The Fresno Bee
The Peoples Church
University of California, S.F. Medical Program
United Express Airlines
Valley Children's Hospital
Valley Community Church
Wells Fargo
Wild, Carter, Tipton and Oliver
Wonder Valley Ranch Resort

Bibliography

Bean, Walton and James J. Rawls. *California: an interpretive history.* New York, McGraw-Gill, 1983.

Butcher, Devereux. *Exploring our National Parks and Monuments.* 8th ed. Harvard, Mass., The Harvard Common Press, 1985.

California State Job Training Coordinating Council, The. *Tomorrow's Workers at Risk.* n.p., n.d.

California Table Grape Commission. *Grapes are Always in Good Taste.* Fresno, 1984.

Carter, Louis, Superintendent of Banks. State of California. *Seventy-Seventh Annual Report.* San Francisco, 1986.

City of Fresno. State of California. *Comprehensive Annual Financial Report for the Fiscal Year Ended June 30, 1985.* Fresno, 1985.

Clough, Charles W. and Twenty-two Co-authors. *Fresno County in the 20th Century: from 1900 to the 1980s.* Bobbye Sisk Temple, ed. Published in cooperation with the Fresno City and County Historical Society. Fresno, Panorama West Books, 1986.

Clough, Charles W. and William B. Secrest, Jr. *Fresno County — The Pioneer Years: From the Beginnings to 1900.* Fresno, Panorama West Books, 1984.

County of Fresno. *County Administrative Officer's 1986-1987 Recommended Budget* as submitted to the Fresno County Board of Supervisors, July 17, 1986.

County of Fresno. *County Administrative Officer's 1987-1988 Recommended Budget* as submitted to the Fresno County Board of Supervisors, July 27, 1987.

County of Fresno. Department of Agriculture. *1986 Agricultural Crop and Livestock Report.* Fresno, 1987.

Educational Extension Systems. *Ethnic Cultures of America Calendar 1987.* Washington D.C., 1987.

Fresno, City of. Development Department. *Fresno Statistical Abstract: a data resource book on Fresno.* Fresno, 1986 (updated).

Fresno City and County Historical Society. *Imperial Fresno.* Facsimile Reproduction 1979.

Fresno City and County Historical Society. *M. Theo Kearney's Fresno County California and the Evolution of the Fruit Vale Estate.* Facsimile Reproduction 1980.

Fresno County and City Chamber of Commerce. *Fresno County Wage and Salary Survey.* prepared by M. Newell, M. Esteva-Jones, and A. Camin. Fresno, 1987.

Fresno County and City Chamber of Commerce. *Industrial Directory 1986-1987.* Fresno, 1986.

Fresno County and City Chamber of Commerce. *1987 Membership Directory and Buyers' Guide.* Kathleen Nave, Ed. Fresno, 1987.

Fresno Interagency Committee. *Report of the Fresno Interagency Task Force on Youth Substance Abuse.* Fresno, 1984.

Fresno World Agritrade Center Feasibility Study: findings, conclusions, and recommendations. Prepared for the City of Fresno by The Mentor Group, May, 1987.

Great Mountains of North America. by the editors of Country Beautiful. Waukesha, Wis., 1976.

Jones, Holway R. *John Muir and the Sierra Club: the battle for Yosemite.* San Francisco, Sierra Club, 1965.

McFarland, Jon R. (Randy) *Village on the Prairie: the story of Fowler's first 100 years.* Fowler Mothers' Club, 1972.

National Cottonseed Products Association, Inc. *Cottonseed and its Products.* 8th ed. Memphis, 1978.

National Geographic Society. Washington D.C. *The New America's Wonderlands.* 1980.

O'Neill, Elizabeth Stone. *Meadow in the Sky: a history of Yosemite's Tuolumne Meadows region.* Fresno, Panorama West Books, 1983, c1984.

A Portrait of Fresno: 1885 to 1985. Centennial Celebration Edition A publication of the Centennial History Committee, City of Fresno 1985.

Sargent, Shirley. *Yosemite & its Innkeepers; the story of a great park and its concessionnaires.* Yosemite, Flying Spur Press, 1975.

Sargent, Shirley. *Yosemite's Rustic Outpost Foresta, Big Meadow.* Yosemite, Ca., Flying Spur Press, 1983.

*State of California. Health and Welfare Agency. Employment Development Department. Employment Data and Research Southern Area Labor Market Information Group. *Annual Planning Information. Fresno Metropolitan Statistical Area (MSA) 1986-1987.* Los Angeles, 1986.

Turner, John. *White Gold Comes to California.* Bakersfield, Ca., California Planting Cotton Seed Distributors, 1981.

Index

Bold Italicized numbers indicate pictures.
*Asterisks indicate corporate and institutional profiles.

A
Abbott, Linda M.C., 233, ***239***
Adult Literacy Program, 141
Air National Guard, ***151***
*AIS Market Research, ***231, 232,*** 235
Aldredge, Jim, ***144***
Alexander, George E., ***40***
Almonds, 72
Alviso, Patricia, ***231***
April Band Review, 204
Arakelian, Stuart, ***40***
Armenians, 28, 50
Arestanos Mexicanos Childspace Gallery, ***178***
Astronaut Memorial, ***196***
*Atwood Grove Construction, ***229,*** 235
August Harvest Festival, 213
*Automated Office Systems, ***79, 80,*** 235
AVK Co., ***221***

B
Ballet, ***159***
*Bank of America, ***10, 83,*** 235
Barstow, Jim, ***135***
Barton Opera House, ***35***
Baseball, Pee Wee, ***122***
Bass Lake, 168
Bedrosian, Krikor, ***201***
Bedrosian, Ernest, ***201***
Bedrosian, Kenneth, ***201***
Beiden Field, ***193***
Bennett, Allen, ***76***
Biomass Power Ltd., 213
Bishop, Norman, ***92***
Board of Supervisors, 138, 139
Board of Trade, 27
Bonneville, Captain Benjamin, 21
Brehler, Oscar, 211
Brown, Bruce M., ***127***
Brush House, ***23***
Buckner, Inc., ***79***
Bufe Karraker, ***14***
*Builders Concrete and River Rock Products, ***93,*** 235
Bullard High School, 38
Bullard Project Talent, 103
Bulldog Stadium, ***183, 184***
Butler, A.B., 27

C
Caglia, Frank, ***34, 226***
Caglia, Franklin J., ***34***
Caglia, Richard M., ***34***
California Air National Guard, 36
California Fruit Growers Exchange, 31
*California School of Professional Psychology, ***105, 106,*** 235
*California State University, Fresno, 38, 46, ***99, 100, 228,*** 235

Production Team

LINDA M.C. ABBOTT
AUTHOR

The author, Linda M.C. Abbott, is president of the management and consulting firm, Abbott & Associates. She holds a PhD from Iowa State University, an MS from the University of Wisconsin-Lacrosse, and a BA from the University of Colorado. Her books include *An Evaluation of International Educational Services Offices* and *The No-Nonsense Resume.* She is listed in *Who's Who in the West, The World Who's Who of Women* and a number of other biographical listings of national and international scope. She is married and the mother of four children.

ERNIE HERGENROEDER
DESIGNER

The design and layout of this book was done by Ernie Hergenroeder of Advertising Design. Ernie, a Fresno native, is a cartoonist, layout artist, and author of the book *The Communicator.* He has illustrated 24 children's books and 48 parent-teacher education books.

Ernie Hergenroeder has also created a presentation system that has been instrumental in raising over $75 million in venture capital for start-up, high tech companies in the Silicon Valley. His firm, Advertising Designs, creates presentations, direct marketing pieces, and market strategies for clients.

RUSS SLOAN
PUBLICATION COORDINATOR

Much of the success of this book is credited to project coordinator and chamber executive director Russ Sloan. Sloan performed much of the hands on work of the book and secured the substantial financial sponsorship for this endeavor.

Sloan was named executive director of the chamber in May of 1985, and is best known to Fresnans for his productive career in intercollegiate athletics.

During his leadership tenure with Fresno State athletics, the annual fundraising grew from $468,000 to $2.4 million. Sloan is also a former executive director of the California Bowl.

Index

*The Fresno Bee, 39, 44, ***143, 144,*** 155, 235
The Fresno Canal Company, 28
The Fresno Historical Society, 27, 34
The Fresno Traction Company, 30
The Fresno Zoo, 30, 38, 182
The Hume-Bennett Lumber Company, 32
The Orange Cove News, 203
*The People's Church, ***6,*** 235
The Sanger Herald, 211
The Sanger Lumber Company, 32
The Sugar Pine Lumber Company, 32
The Tower District, 18
The West Coast Relays, 35
Thompson Seedless Grapes, ***217***
"Timeout" — Fresno State's Mascot, ***193***
Tipton, Jack M., ***128***
Torrano, Ron, ***17***

U

Ulbrich Stainless Steel, 54
*United Express, 54, ***151, 152,*** 235
University of California, Kearney Agricultural Center, 201, 203
*University of California, San Francisco Medical Program, ***110,*** 235
Ura McCray's Oak Hotel, 47

V

*Valley Children's Hospital, ***113, 114,*** 235
*Valley Community Church, ***17,*** 235
Valley Medical Center, 117, ***117, 118,*** 118
Van Ness Extension, ***14***
Veterans Administration Hospital, ***115***
Victor Gruen and Associates, 36
Villegas, Fidencio, ***43***
Villegas, Frank, ***43***
Vineyard, ***27***
Volga Germans, 51, ***51***

W

Wayte, Larry, ***135***
*Wells Fargo, ***85,*** 235
West Coast Relays, ***189***
Western Kraft, Inc., 54
Western Mono Indians, ***47***
Westlands Water District, 39
Whitebark Vista, ***220***
Wild, Bruce M., ***128***
*Wild, Carter, Tipton & Oliver, ***127, 128, 229,*** 235
Williams, Joe, ***45***
Wine, ***228***
*Wonder Valley Ranch Resort, ***169, 170,*** 235
Wonder Valley, ***161,*** 169, 170
Woodward Lake, ***1, 2, 18***
Woodward Lakes, 18
Woodward Park, 182, ***196***
Woodward Park, Japanese Gardens, ***11***

Y

Yosemite Falls, ***166***
Yosemite National Park, ***163, 164***
Yosemite, 21, 163, 164, 165, 166, 167, 168
Yosemite Water Fall, ***167***

Z

Zapps Park, 21
Zoological Society, 38

Hardy

Heather *Species*

and some related plants

D Metheny

with contributions by
Arthur P. Dome
Alice and Robert M. Knight
Donald A. M. Mackay

ISBN (Soft Cover): 0-939116-29-4 Price: $24.95 U.S.
ISBN (Hard Cover): 0-939116-31-6 Price: $39.95 U.S.

Published by
Frontier Publishing
P.O. Box 441
Seaside, OR 97138

Cover by Tracy Noot

Printed in U.S.A.

Acknowledgments

At their September 1982 annual meeting, the members of the North American Heather Society (then the Pacific Northwest Heather Society) expressed consensus that the Society support, to the extent economically feasible for them, publication of what has become this book. Since that time they have been solidly supportive of the project through what must sometimes have seemed endless years. At last year's annual meeting the Society voted authorization for the printing and distribution costs. —A number of members have contributed more funds in support of the publication. To the Society and to these individuals goes the credit for the book having been accomplished, and my profound thanks.

I am particularly indebted to the kind friends who, without having their arms twisted, contributed their expertise to the writing of this book: Art Dome has spent many hours growing and observing his Cassiope plants, and researching and writing the section on Cassiope species.

Alice and Bob Knight, who surely without question have grown more heather plants than anyone else in North America, and have supplied so many of the heather plants growing in our gardens, worked together to provide for all the rest of us the knowledge of propagation, cultivation, and pests and diseases gained from their long experience. They have also added an explanation of color names applied to heather flowers.

Donald A. M. Mackay, President, Applied Microbiology, Inc., New York City, New York 11205, and currently President of the North American Heather Society, has provided the extraordinarily interesting and up-to-date information on the role of mycorrhizae in the growth of heathers, on their native heaths and in our gardens.

Judy Young, co-translator of the learned volume by a Chinese Professor of Botany, *RHODODENDRONS OF CHINA*, Editor of the former Rhododendron Species Foundation yearbook, *NOTES AND RECORDS* and an avid student of the Chinese language, most kindly translated two more recently published Chinese cassiope species.

I am signally indebted to Maj. Gen. P. G. Turpin, Surrey, England, Chairman of the Heather Society, who having been defeated by the postal system in sending me fresh flowers of *Erica sicula*, prepared and sent me the dried specimens from which the drawings of that species were done.

Though not directly apparent as the author of a particular article, the name of David McClintock, Kent, England, author of *A GUIDE TO THE NAMING OF PLANTS* published by the Heather Society in 1980 and many learned articles on heathers and other plants and now President of the Heather Society, will be encountered many times by anyone reading this book. He has for years most generously supplied the latest available information to the grateful author of this book.

My late husband, Davie, was unfailingly encouraging and photographed literally hundreds of heathers for me.

Countless other kind friends and avid gardeners have contributed over many years to whatever familiarity with heathers I may have gained. But whatever errors may have crept into this text are entirely my responsibility.

D Metheny, May 1991

Dedication

To my loving children
and grandchildren

Hardy Heather Habitats

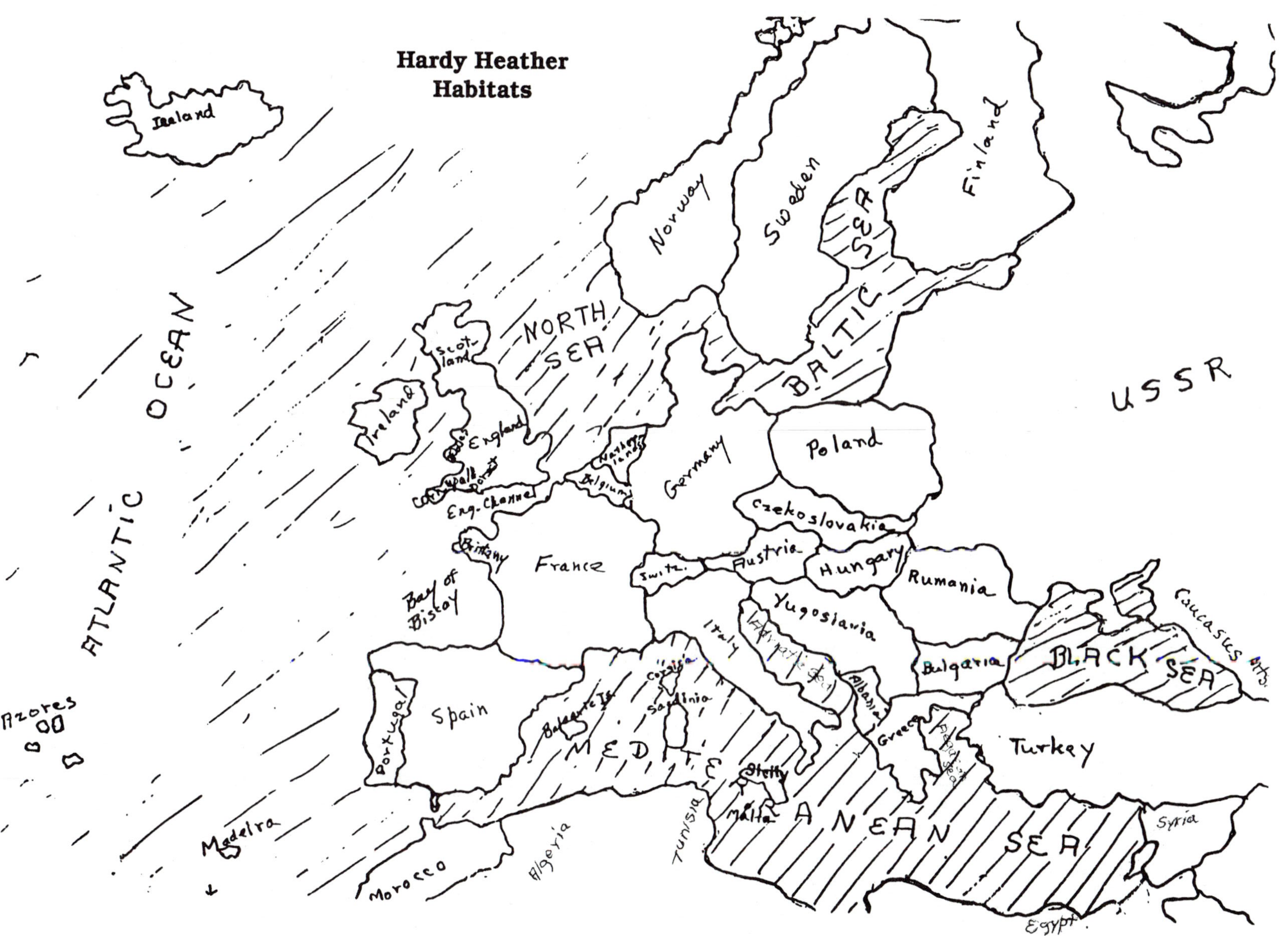

USDA Plant Hardiness Zone Map

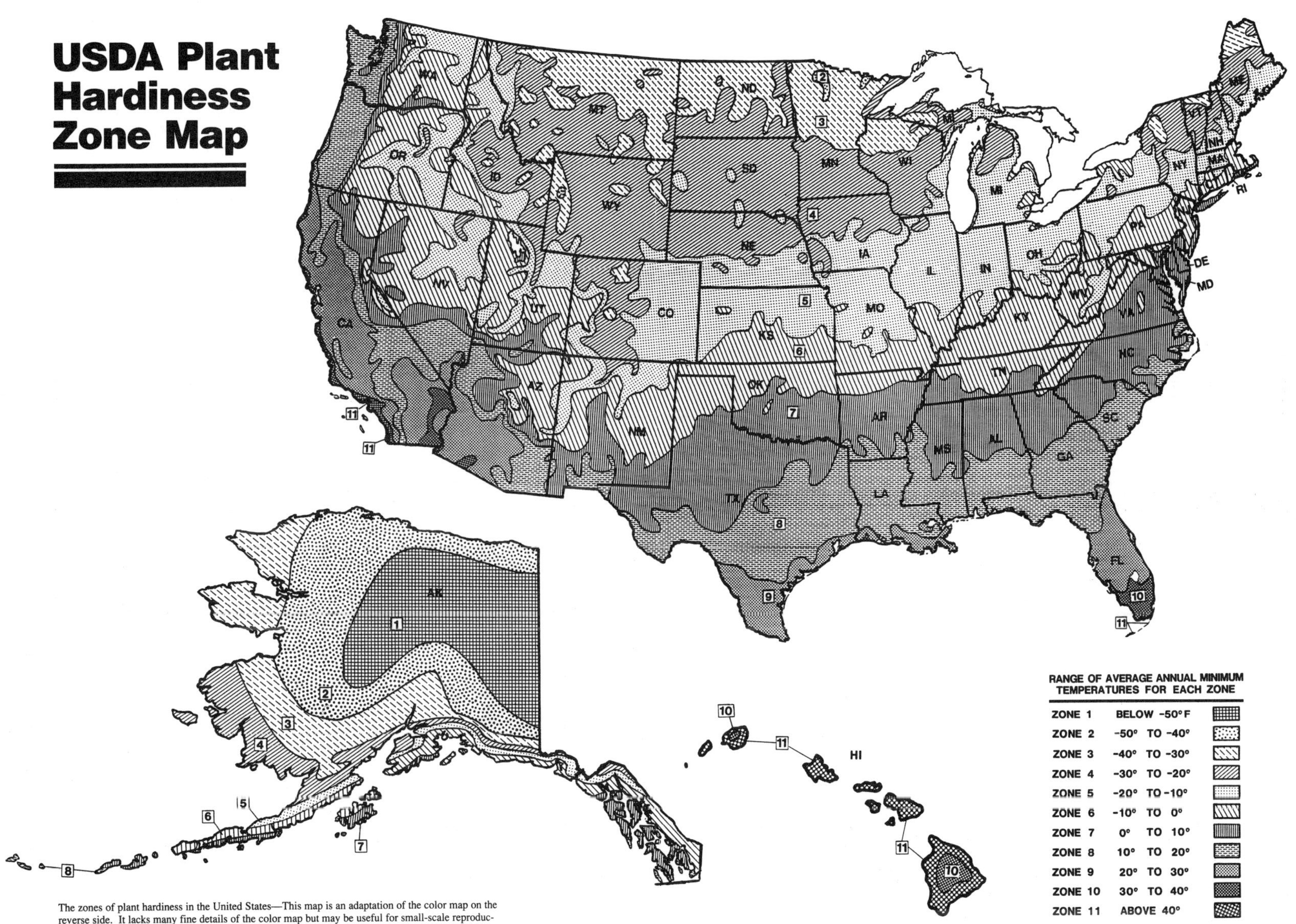

The zones of plant hardiness in the United States—This map is an adaptation of the color map on the reverse side. It lacks many fine details of the color map but may be useful for small-scale reproduction in books, magazines, and nursery catalogs.

Contents

Page
Acknowledgments III
Map—HARDY HEATHER HABITATS IV
Map—USDA PLANT HARDINESS ZONE MAP V
Preface, Hardy Heather Species 1
What is a Heath, a Heather? 2
Moor, Down, Bog 4
Maquis 5

HEATHER SPECIES

Andromeda 6
Bruckenthalia 8
Calluna 11
Daboecia 15
D. azorica 17
D. cantabrica 20
D. x scotica 24
Erica 27
Tree Heaths 28
E. andevalensis 29
E. arborea 32
E. australis 38
E. carnea (E. herbacea) 42
E. ciliaris 46
E. cinerea 50
E. x darleyensis 55
E. erigena 60
E. Lusitanica 65
E. mackaiana 68
What can I Do With My Heathers? 73
E. maderensis 74
E. manipuliflora 76
Heather Wreath 81
E. multiflora 82
E. scoparia 84
E. sicula, E. bocquetii 87
E. x stuartii 92
E. terminalis 96
E. tetralix 99
E. umbellata 103
E. vagans 106
E. x veitchii 110
E. x watsonii 114
E. x williamsii 117

RELATED PLANTS

Cassiope, Arthur P. Dome 120
Phyllodoce 134
X Phylliopsis hillieri 144
X Phyllothamnus erectus 148

Propagation, Alice and Bob Knight 152
Cultivation, Alice and Bob Knight 156
Pests & Diseases, Alice and Bob Knight 159
Heather Colors, Alice and Bob Knight 160
Hybridizing Heathers 161
Mycorrhizal Associations of Heathers, D. A. M. Mackay 164
North American Cultivar List 170
The Why of Plant Names 174
Heather Cousins 176
Bibliography 178
Glossary 182

HARDY HEATHER SPECIES

This book is presented for the purpose of enabling those who like to grow heathers to identify their heather species and thus be able to inform themselves about how to grow them.

By HARDY HEATHER SPECIES we mean those which are native to a Temperate Zone and, providing other conditions are suitable, can be grown in one or another part of a Temperate Zone.

The word *heather* has long been an uncertain entity meaning a more limited group of species to one person and a more extended group of species to others. However, the International Horticultural Congress, in 1969, designated The Heather Society (Gr. Br.) as the International Registration Authority for Heather Cultivar Names, including cultivars of the genera *Andromeda, Bruckenthalia, Calluna, Daboecia* and the hardy *Erica* species, thus defining for our purposes what a "heather" is. For the practical gardening purposes of this book and to help dispel the general confusion, we are adding to species of the above five genera very limited description of some of the species known in North America as "Mountain Heath" and "Mountain Heather," *Phyllodoce* and *Cassiope* and some of their attractive and useful hybrids.

Gardeners particularly interested in heathers have formed societies for the study of heathers and for fellowship among those with like interests.

THE HEATHER SOCIETY was initiated in London in 1963 and publishes an annual *Yearbook* and three quarterly bulletins.

In Holland, Nederlandse Heidevereniging (1971) publishes the quarterly *Ericultura.*

In Germany, Gesellschaft der Heidefreunde (1977) publishes *Der Heidegarten.*

In North America (Canada and the United States), nurseries have been offering and gardeners have been growing heathers for much of the Twentieth Century if not earlier. However, it was not until October 1977 that the Pacific Northwest Heather Society, later widened to become the North American Heather Society, got its start. It publishes its quarterly journal, *Heather News* and welcomes members from all across the United States and Canada as well as others who may be interested. Anyone interested in information on membership, may write to:

Ellen Norris, 1205 Copley Pl., RR 1, Shawnigan Lake, B.C. VOR 2WO, Canada

Walter Wornick, P.O. Box 101, Alstead, NH 03602

WHAT IS A HEATH, A HEATHER?

When presenting a HEATHER program I have frequently been asked at the start to explain What is a *Heath* and What is a *Heather*. I have answered with drastically truncated definitions because the whole story goes back a long way. But for readers of this book:

The voluminous Oxford English Dictionary (1933, 1970) explains *heath* and *heather* and their numerous hyphenated uses thus:

Heath, in one spelling or another and referring both to a particular kind of countryside and to the individual plants that grow on it, goes back over a thousand years to Old English (Anglo-Saxon), Middle Low German, Middle Dutch, Old High German and Old Norse. In modern Dutch and German it has become *Heide*, which serves for both *heath* and *heather*. A couple of centuries after the Romans left Britain (410 A.D.), the earliest English Christian poet, an inspired herdsman called Caedmon, was reported to have sung of the *haeth* (*th* as in *then*). Chaucer, in the *Prologue* to the *Canterbury Tales* (1386), wrote charmingly

> "Whan Zephirus eek with his swete breeth
> "Inspired hath in every holt and **heeth**
> "The tendre croppes, and the yonge sonne
> "Hath in the Ram his halfe cours y-ronne
> ". . . Then longen folk to goon on pilgrimages,"

Shakespeare's (1605) horrid mischief conniving witches arranged to meet,

". . . Where the place? Upon the **heath**, There to meet with Macbeth . . ."

In the course of the centuries *heath* has not only changed its spelling, but has also gathered to itself a number of meanings and uses:

A **heath**, as indicating the kind of terrain where the witches met MacBeth, is open, infertile, uncultivated, waste land, "now chiefly applied to a . . . tract of land naturally clothed with low herbage and dwarf shrubs, especially with the shrubby plants known as heath, heather or ling." This name was originally used for such places in the south or middle of England. In Scotland, they were more likely to be moors, though these are usually thought of as with peat or Sphagnum moss overlying the sand, and more or less marshy.

Heath is the ordinary name for shrubs of the genus *Erica*, whose hardy members are part of this book's concern. When heather gardeners speak of their **"Heaths and Heathers,"** they are likely to be referring to their *Erica* and *Calluna* plants.

"Heath" is sometimes extended to cover other members of the *Ericaceae,* the Heath Family—*Rhododendron, Pieris, Kalmia, Gaultheria, Oxydendrum, Arbu-*

tus, etc.—about 70 genera and in the neighborhood of 1,900 species.

The word ***Heather*** (variously spelled hathir, hadyr, haddir, hadder, hather, hether) is of much more recent origin. It first appeared in the 18th C. and might have been a compromise between the Scottish *hadder* and the English *heath*. (In northern England, the word for *Calluna* was ***ling***, inherited from the early Norse invaders.)

Heather was the Scottish common name for the plants so generously clothing their Highlands. Linnaeus called them *Erica vulgaris*, but in the early 19th C., for botanical reasons, that was changed to *Calluna vulgaris*. *E. cinerea* is the "Scottish Heath," in England commonly called "Bell Heather."

Less legitimately, nowadays, retail merchants, loving the phrase **"Scotch Heather,"** apply it indiscriminately to various plants, especially tender South African species of the genus *Erica* which appear in the supermarkets under this alias, especially around Christmas time. Let the buyer beware!

Enjoying your heathers will not necessarily make you a ***heathen***, but folk so described were originally dwellers on the heath.

There are plants commonly called "heath" or "heather" that are **NOT "true heaths"** or **"true heathers."** They are probably so-called because they are small shrubs with small evergreen leaves and thus somewhat resemble heaths or heathers:

Cassiope and *Phyllodoce,* are two circumpolar small shrubby genera of mountain habitats at or above tree line. In North America, they occur on mountains of both east and west coasts. They are often commonly known as "Mountain Heath", *P. empetriformis* and "Mountain Heather," *C. mertensiana*. They are members of the family of *Ericaceae*, and thus are *Heaths* in that sense, but they are quite unlike our heather garden heaths and heathers in the growing conditions in which they are most happy.

"Australian Heath" (*Epacris impressa* and other species of *Epacris*) are members of the *Epacridaceae* Family, also in the Order of Ericales and thus cousins of the *Ericaceae*, and they are similar to our hardy heaths in being tubular-flowered, fine-textured evergreen shrubs of heath-like land; but they have differently arranged stamens and one-celled anthers, and they are not very hardy. (Some more or less hardy members of the *Epacridaceae* are grown in the northwest, but they are not so heath-like. *Cyathodes fraseri*, for example, is a hardy, very small, evergreen, rock garden plant with erect stems and tubular white flowers and it spreads by its roots underground. Its cousin, *C. colensoi,* is a small, greyish-leaved shrub also with small white bell flowers but is less hardy. Unlike true heaths, both develop fruits in the form of berries.)

"Beach Heather," *Hudsonia,* with three species native to eastern North America are members of the *Cistaceae,* the Rock Rose Family. They are small evergreen shrubs with very tiny leaves and rather fleeting, yellow, 5-petalled open flowers, solitary at the ends of branchlets in May and June. All are reported to thrive best in sandy soil, but to be difficult to grow in the garden and short-lived. The three species are: *H. ericoides,* "Golden Heather," which occurs from Newfoundland and New Brunswick south to North Carolina; *H. tomentosa,* "Wooly Heather," New Brunswick to North Carolina and around the shores of the Great Lakes to Minnesota; *H. montana,* in the high mountains of North Carolina.

In California we have sometimes heard "New Zealand Heather" applied to the small-leaved shrubs, *Leptospermum scoparium,* extremely floriferous garden ornaments. They are members of the *Myrtaceae,* the Myrtle Family, which also claims *Eucalyptus,* the Bottle Brushes, guava, and other genera commercially important for their fruit, oils, etc. When you see a plant labelled "Heather," you can't always believe it!

HEATHER HABITATS

down—A treeless chalk upland along the coast of southeast England.

heath—A tract of waste (infertile) land; an open level area clothed with low shrubs, many of the *Ericaceae* Family

moor—An extensive area of waste sandy ground overlaid with peat and usually more or less marshy. In Europe heathers are often the prevailing plants.

peat bog—Peat, formed by the partial decomposition in water of such plants as sphagnum moss, lying in a soft, wet, miry situation.

AND THEN THERE IS MAQUIS

Around the shores of the Mediterranean, where the climate differs markedly in its rainfall pattern from that of Britain and the European Continent, a number of lower-growing species of heath plants and of tree heaths that are less tender than those of South Africa grow in a kind of plant community known as ***maquis* (*ma-kee'*)**—sometimes spelled **macchie**. (My venerable Cassell's French-English Dictionary prefers ***makis*** but admits ***maquis***, and defines it as a thicket.) This is in an area of long dry summers and winter rainfall, the so-called "Mediterranean Climate" similar to the climate that prevails on the North American west coast. Thus, the *maquis* bears the Mediterranean species of *heath-plants*.

The Mediterranian *maquis* is a special kind of community. To quote the alluring description of Polunin and Huxley, "It forms very dense and sometimes impenetrable thickets of tall shrubs, two meters or more high, with stiff densely twiggy branches and small dark green leathery leaves. In springtime it brightens the hillsides with splashes of colour, with the pink and white of the Cistuses, the yellows of the brooms and the snowlike dusting of the myriads of flowers of the Tree Heather *(Erica arborea)*. During the remainder of the year it forms a dark green mantle over the hillsides, thickening in the valleys and thinning on the drier ribs of the hills. . . . ."*

The low altitude maquis is composed of lower-growing shrubs 1.5 to 2 m. (5-6.6 ft.) high, in some places including *Calluna* and *Erica* species. High *maquis* 500-700 m. (1,650-2,300ft), includes *Erica arborea* among the larger shrubs, and a number of tree species, the ericaceous *Arbutus unedo* and *A. andrachne*, and some oaks, pines, *Cercis*, Juniper, Olive, etc. There are other specialized types of *maquis* such as *Calluna maquis* in Italy.

As there are many useful products to be derived from the *maquis* it is continually being altered by the activities of its human inhabitants, and this results in leaving a great number of variations on what might have been its primeval components.

* Polunin, Oleg & Anthony Huxley, *Flowers of the Mediterranean*, 1966, p. 9

ANDROMEDA L.

As far as we know, *Andromeda* has never been considered a heather; but it is a member of the *Ericaceae* Family and because the nomenclature of its cultivars has been given into the care of the Heather Society (UK), we are including it here. In 1767 Linnaeus called *Daboecia* (one of our heathers) an *Andromeda*, but this quirk was corrected by D. Don in 1834. In the past the genus *Andromeda* has also housed species now known as *Cassiope, Chamaedaphne, Leucothoe, Lyonia, Oxydendrum* and *Pieris* the last of these still sometimes referred to as "Andromeda."

Andromeda, like *Daboecia* (and also *Cassiope* and *Phyllodoce*, our so-called "Mountain Heather" and "Mountain Heath") has deciduous rather than persistent corollas, i.e. when spent, its flowers drop off instead of remaining on the flower stem and turning brown, as do those of *Bruckenthalia*, *Calluna* and *Erica*. *Andromeda* flowers are 5-parted, with 10 stamens and usually pink. Its two species occur in the colder parts of the northern hemisphere. Both species are rated USDA Zone 2 (1) and both are in flower from April or May to July.

A. polifolia is a native plant of high acid bogs in northwest North America (Alaska south to Washington and Idaho) and also of northern and central Europe and Asia. We have seen it growing happily in a very wet bog at 4,000-5,000 ft. (1,200-1,550 m) in the northern Cascade Mountains (vicinity of Mt. Baker) in Washington. A white-flowered form occurs in Japan.

A. glaucophylla, is a native of northeast North America (Newfoundland and Labrador to Manitoba and south to New Jersey, Indiana and Minnesota). It differs from *A. polifolia* in having whitish pubescent leaves. It has been reported, by Arthur Gilman(2), from Groton State Forest, Vermont, in a very acid bog where there are stunted specimens of Spruce and Larch but the *Andromeda* seems to derive adequate nourishment from the cold sphagnum and does not show any stunting.

Andromeda is accordingly recommended to be grown in cool, moist, peaty shade, on acid soil. If so situated its rhizomatous roots can slowly spread.

For ***A. polifolia*** L.D. Hills(3) suggests taking cuttings of non-flowering wood between February and June and inserting them in a peat and shade frame. Arthur Gilman mentions that *A. glaucophylla* is among the easiest ericaceous plants to propagate. September cuttings of current year's wood are stuck in a mixture of 50% peat (well decomposed) and 50% sand with 70°F (22°C) bottom heat in a polythene tent. No fertilizer at all to be applied until they have rooted. Keep fairly warm over the first winter.

There are a number of *A. polifolia* cultivars. The one depicted here is *A. p.* 'Minima,' a delightful dwarf shrub, 10-12 cm (4-5 in) high with pink bells in April-May in a sea level garden. It is considered a choice plant for the alpine

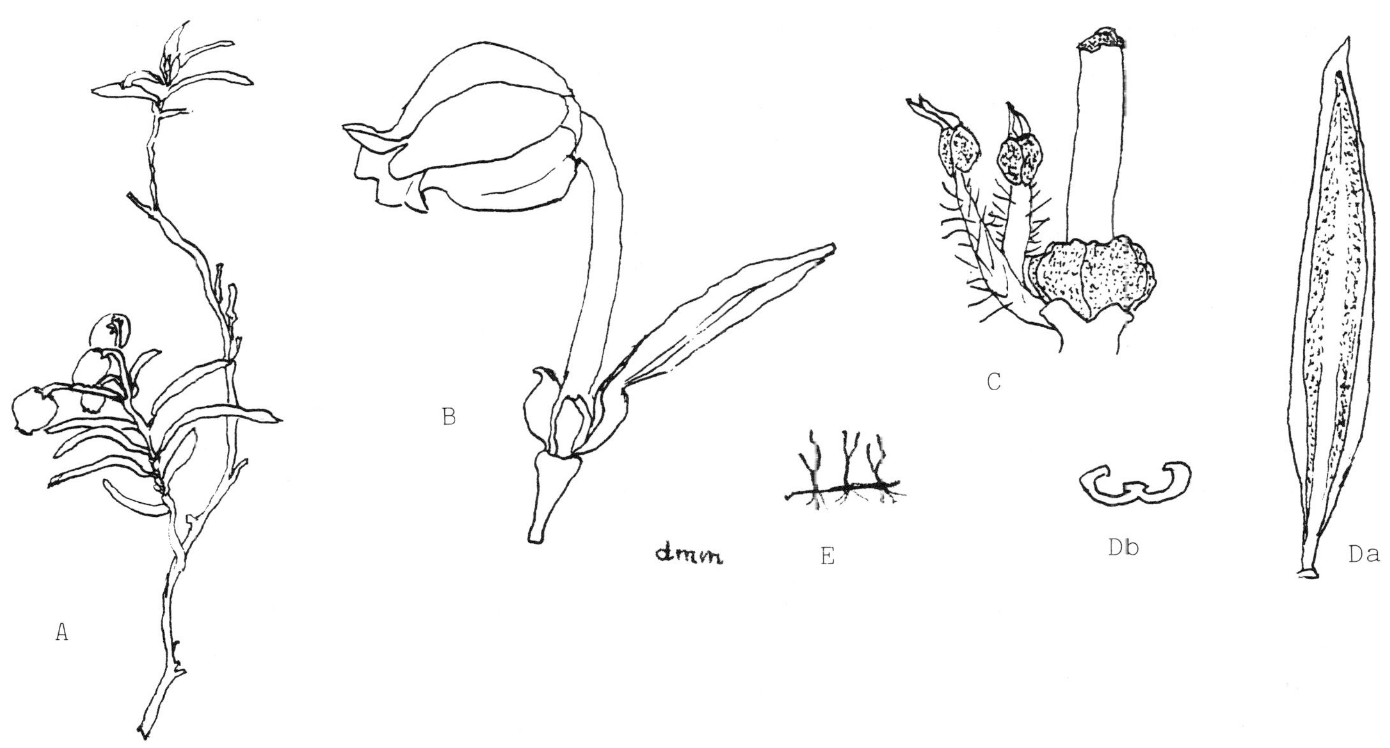

***Andromeda polifolia* L. var. 'Minima':** A, flowering stem 1X; B, flower 5X; C, pistil and 2 of the 10 stamens 10X; Da, leaf beneath 5X; Db, leaf cross section 5X (under side of leaf shown at top); E, plant habit.

---

garden.

***A. p.* 'Compacta,'** a compact form of the species, was given an A.M. (Award of Merit) by the Royal Horticultural Society in 1964.

***A. p.* 'Macrophylla,'** having been awarded an A.M.in 1971, received an F.C.C. (First Class Certificate) in 1982.

References:

1) Rehder, Alfred: *MANUAL OF CULTIVATED TREES & SHRUBS,* 1956.

2) Gilman, Arthur: *Native Plants of Vermont. BULL. AMER. ROCK GDN. SOC.*, Vol. 43, No. 4, Fall 1985, pp. 189-194.

3) Hills, L.D.: *THE PROPAGATION OF ALPINES,* 1959.

BRUCKENTHALIA SPICULIFOLIA Reichenb.

The so-called Spike Heath, or Balkan Heath, formerly not included in heather garden books, is an attractive little shrub very suitable for the heather garden. It has been welcomed there since the International Botanical Congress, at its 1969 meeting, approved The Heather Society (UK) as the naming authority for garden cultivars of *Bruckenthalia*, along with *Andromeda, Calluna, Daboecia, and Erica.* (1)

Bruckenthalia occurs in acid subalpine pastures in the mountains of Romania and the Balkan peninsula, south to northern Greece. There is also a disjunct population in the mountains of northern Anatolian Turkey, for example on the summit of Mount Olympus (2,600 m, 8,343 ft), across the Sea of Marmara to the south from Istanbul. P. H. Davis(2) describes these plants as having densely puberulent stems and red corollas. Plant explorers and Alpine Garden Society hikers in the Balkans reported having seen *Bruckenthalia* at elevations of from about 1,400 to 2,800 m (4,000-9,000 ft).(3) The explorers mention that the plants occur more densely as they ascend to higher elevations.

Dr. R. H. Munson(4) found Bruckenthalia very little affected by temperature down to -5°F (-23°C) with occasional brief drops to -20°F (-28°C) in Ithaca, N.Y., when grown in gravelly clay-loam amended with sphagnum peat or perlite in the planting hole and not fertilized. Snow cover was not mentioned but would surely have helped. In very severe climates it can perhaps be protected by a mulch of salt hay or dry leaves.(5) Rehder rates it Zone V, equivalent to USDA zone 6a.(6) It seems to me to flourish most abundantly where its roots can get under a moisture conserving rock.

At a glance *Bruckenthalia* much resembles a small *Erica*. In fact it was given the name *Erica spiculifolia* by Salisbury in the early 19th Century, then because of differences in its floral parts, was changed by Reichenbach to *B. spiculifolia*. (Now its name stability may perhaps again be threatened as we are told that Dr. E. G. H. Oliver, co-author of *ERICAS IN SOUTHERN AFRICA*, thinks it may be after all not sufficiently different from *Erica* to warrant its being in a separate genus.(7)) The specific epithet refers to the tiny spikes (spicules) at the tips of its little leaves. As the stem which bears the dense raceme of flowers at its tip, the pedicels which hold the florets to it, the calyx, the corolla and the exserted style are all (usually) clear pink, it could be said to get a lot of mileage out of its tiny size.

Botanically, it is very closely related to both *Calluna* and *Erica*, having persistent corollas (flowers remaining attached to their stems when spent), and small seemingly needle-like leaves sharply reflexed at their margins, usually in whorls of four. It differs from *Calluna* in having a calyx smaller than the corolla, from *Erica* in having its sepals united to form a campanulate calyx, and from both of them in its pedicels without bracteoles.(8) Its flowering height is

Bruckenthalia spiculifolia Reichenb.: A, top half of flowering stem 1X; B, flowers 5X; Ca, pistil and 2 of the 8 stamens 10X; Cb, anther enlarged; Da, leaf beneath 10X; Db, leaf cross section 10X (lower surface shown at top); E, plant habit.

about 20-23 cm (8-9 in). A small clump put at the top of a brick wall in 1951 gradually spread, over 30 years, to cover a square meter (10 sq ft); then all of the self-layered but not very well rooted part of the unprotected plant was killed by a December freeze. In moister, peatier soil it might have done better. It needs acid soil. Its flowering commences in June, before the mass of the summer-flowering heathers, and continues for two months.

It reportedly can be grown from seed, but in my Seattle garden there have been no self-sown seedlings. It is most satisfactorily propagated by cuttings of soft side shoots in Aug.-Sep. The low-growing branches are fairly easily layered, in fact occasionally layer themselves, but plants from this method are less reliably sturdy than those from cuttings.(9)

Bruckenthalia has three named forms: *B. s. f. albiflora*, white-flowered, published in 1986 by David McClintock; *B. s.* 'Balkan Rose,' dark pink; *B. s.* 'Scotica,' darker pink, growing at Harlow Car, England, source unknown.(10)

References:

1) McClintock, David: *GUIDE TO THE NAMING OF PLANTS*, 1980.

2) Davis, P.H.: *FLORA OF TURKEY*, Vol. VI, Edinburgh, 1978.

3) *BULL. ALPINE GARDEN SOC.*, Vol. 40, No. 3, Sept. 1972, pp. 232-3.

4) Munson, R.H.: *HEATHER NEWS*, No. 11, p.5, Sept. 1980.

5) Wilder, Louise Beebe: *THE GARDEN IN COLOR*, MacMillan, N.Y., 1937.

6) Rehder, Alfred: *MANUAL OF CULTIVATED TREES & SHRUBS*,1956.

7) McClintock, David: personal communication, 10 Apr. 1987.

8) *FLORA EUROPAEA*, 1972.

9) Hills, L. D.: *THE PROPAGATION OF ALPINES*, 1959.

10) McClintock, David: personal communication, 15 Oct. 1986.

CALLUNA VULGARIS L. Hull

Calluna vulgaris, the Scotch Heather(1), has been in cultivation for centuries. Its name is derived from the Greek word *kalluno*, meaning to beautify or to sweep clean, giving one a choice between its aesthetic use for garden decoration and its practical farm and household uses. The latter have included making brooms, stuffing mattresses, brewing heather wine, feeding bees for honey, providing pasture for sheep or grouse, etc., running the gamut of uses of the vegetable kingdom, all of these uses from a plant which grows naturally on infertile soil good for very little else.

In 1753, Linnaeus called it *Erica vulgaris* (Common Heath), a name still occasionally met with in plant lists; but R. A. Salisbury in 1802 and John Hull in 1808 thought its flowers, with calyx larger than and often concealing the corolla, and its leaves opposite and often imbricate instead of whorled and spreading, provided sufficient botanical difference to warrant making it a separate genus, and so gave it the name *Calluna*. Most botanists, and modern investigations of chromosome count bear them out. It is a monotypic genus (one species only), but with infinite variety of form.

Calluna is a summer-autumn flowering, small-leaved, evergreen shrub for well-drained acid soil, in a range of climates typified by its natural occurrence over much of Europe west of the USSR, Albania and Greece. It has been collected from Iceland and northernmost Norway south to the Azores and northern Morocco. There is a disjunct population in northeast Anatolia in northwestern Turkey. In this southeast corner of its distribution, however, it never dominates its areas as do the *Calluna* masses of the Scottish Highlands.(2) There are introduced stands on the Atlantic coast of North America, and reportedly on the west coast of Vancouver Island, in British Columbia, Canada. But not all *Calluna* cultivars will tolerate all these diverse climates. Those originating from very mild climates may prove not hardy in the colder areas. It grows on open heaths, moors and sand dunes, where it relishes the wind and sun, but is also found in open woods,—in any case never where there is any liminess to the soil.(3)

The plant habits can be cushion/hummock, creeping/trailing, spreading, horizontal-branching, compact, with ascending or erect stems, all of these of varying sizes. The height is 5-80 (-120) cm (2-30(-48) in). The greatest number of cultivars fall in the 30 cm (12 in) height group; very few can be expected to achieve over 70 cm (28 in). Recently introduced cultivars include a number not exceeding 5 cm (2 in), many of them creepers from the windswept St. Kilda Islands, 115 miles west of the Scottish mainland. Most *Calluna* cultivars have been found in the wild, or in gardens; they have not come from deliberate hybridizing.

Leaves are tiny, 2.5-3.5 mm (1/10-1/8 in) or even smaller. The smallest foliage often occurs on cushion and low-growing varieties, but occasionally on larger cultivars, giving them a distinctive fine-textured appearance. New growth tip leaves are appressed to the stems, later may spread to about 45°. Introductions since about 1950 have resulted in the available list's including over one-third foliage color forms which provide varying garden color throughout the year. Even the shades of green vary from the nearly white felted 'Hirsuta Typica' to glabrous medium to dark green. There are numerous cultivars with year-round yellow foliage, and some changing to various shades of orange, red, or bronze in the winter. The latter should be situated where they get plenty of sun; a touch of frost seems to intensify the reds. Place your plants if possible so that they will be viewed from the sunny side where the color will be most vivid.

Erica, Bruckenthalia, and *Calluna* form the small ericaceous group whose corollas are persistent, remaining on their stems and turning varying shades of brown after their season of summer flower color is over. The flowers may be borne in long, plumy panicles to 30 cm (12 in), to straight racemes of a few inches, or medium between these. On some small cushion plants attractive for their form, there may be few or no flowers at all. The flower color season, according to cultivar, stretches from June to December, with the greatest number showing in August-September, when the Scottish Highlands are so warmly colored. Likewise, the duration of flower color in the garden can be 1-2-3-4 months. Double flowers are among the longer lasting and will keep their color if cut when fresh and dried for winter display. (Note illstration Bd. Double flowers usually have no reproductive parts and so set no seed.) Some so-called bud-bloomers never expand their sepals from the bud stage, e.g. 'David Eason,' 'Underwoodii,' and, having not been fertilized by pollinators, they too keep fresh color in the garden for 3, 4 or 5 months. The florets are usually single, but there is an increasing list of doubles, by 1986 about thirty. Flower colors range through white, mauve, lavender, lilac-pink, purple, crimson, shell-pink, rose-pink, amethyst, salmon, heliotrope, and bicolor. Mauve flowers are, to many, the least attractive, but they often seem to appear on plants that have particular appeal of habit or foliage color and so are tolerated.

Calluna vulgaris (L.) Hull: A, 'Durfordii' inflorescence 1X; Ba, 'Hammondii' flowers 5X; Bb, 'Hammondii' flower 5X; Bc, seed plant flower 5X, showing bracteoles on pedicel; Bd, cross section of double flower, 'Tib' 10X; C, pistil and 2 stamens of seed plant 10X; Da, twig 1X; Db, short shoot ca. 10X; Dc, short shoot leaf 15X; Dd, short shoot leaf cross section 15X (the groove is on the side away from the stem); E, plant habits: Ea, common wild form; Eb, 'Californian Midge'; Ec, 'Mrs. Ronald Grey'; Ed, 'Kuphaldtii,' Ee, 'Foxii Nana'; Ef, 'Humpty Dumpty'; Eg, 'Bess Jr.'; Eh, 'White Lawn.'

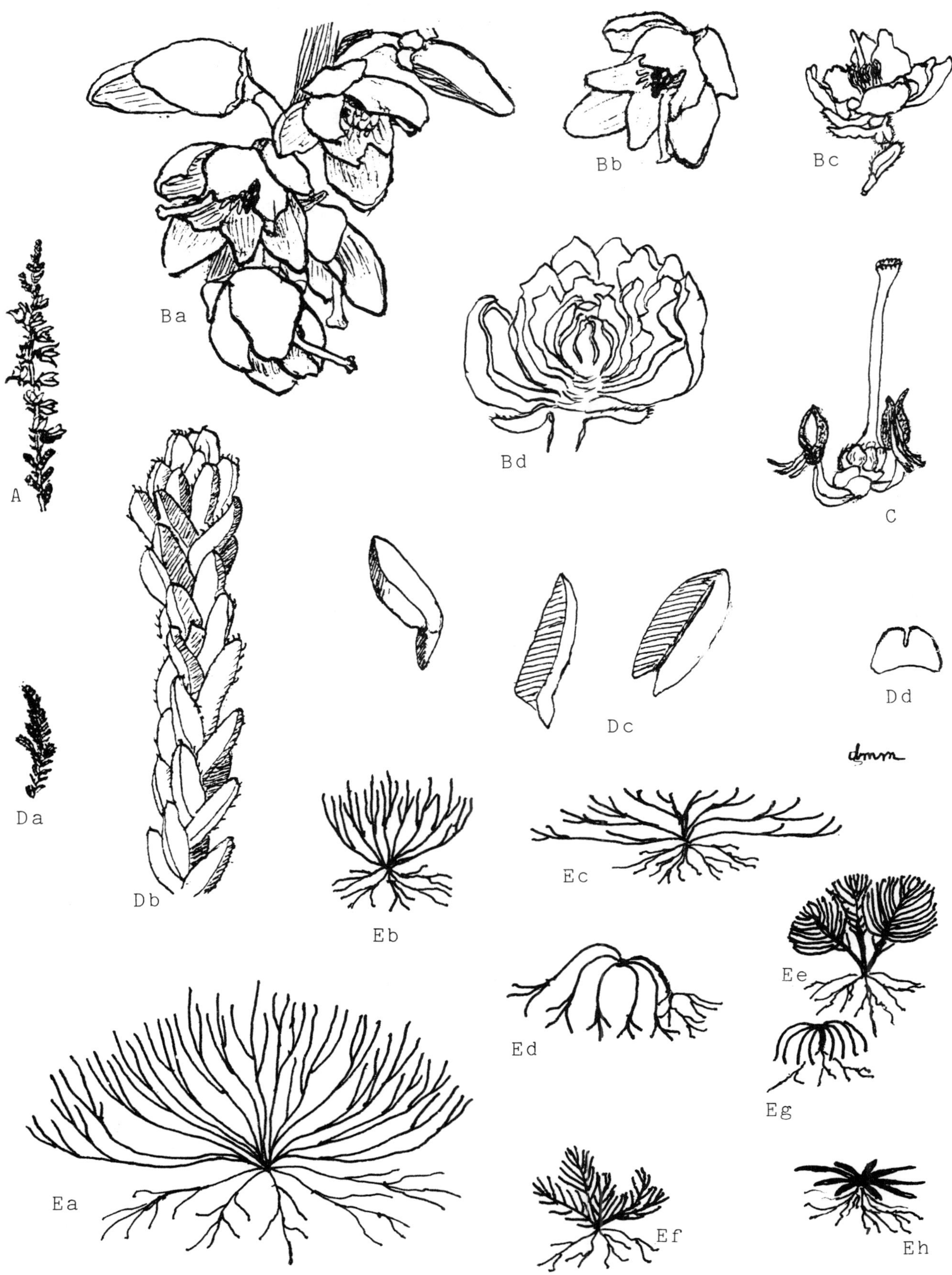
Bb
Bc
Ba
A
Bd
C
Dc
Dd
Da
Db
Eb
Ec
Ee
Ed
Eg
Ea
Ef
Eh

Rehder(4) gives the species a Zone IV (USDA 5) hardiness rating, but some of its cultivars, those of Mediterranean origin, are not that cold-tolerant. It should be remembered that those *Calluna* plants native to the far north are accustomed to being protected by a snow blanket in bitter weather.

Considering the mathematical implications of combinations of all of these possible variations, it is apparent that the resulting cultivar list could be all but endless. Geoffrey Yates's "Pocket Guide to Heather Gardening," 1978 describes 320 cultivars that were available somewhere at that time, and many more have since been introduced. Another some 450 cultivar names have been used for plants that are currently not available, are old, no longer used names, etc. etc. A grower needs to be very hesitant about conferring a new name on a plant without first making certain it **is** something new and worthy of introduction. We already have a very wide choice of these "found" plants, chance seedlings or from sports,—gifts from heath or garden.

As the cultivars often do not come true from seed, they must be propagated by vegetative means - cuttings, layering or deep planting and division. Cuttings are best.

Some gardeners have an urge to prune off the spent flowers in the autumn but the best time of year for pruning is probably early spring, before the flush of new growth is well under way.

References:

1) Beijerinck, W.: *CALLUNA, A Monograph on the Scotch Heather*, Amsterdam, 1940. Outdated but still the classic work of reference relating to this genus.

2) Davis, P. H.: *FLOWERS OF TURKEY AND THE EAST AEGEAN ISLANDS*, Edinburgh, 1978.

3) *FLORA EUROPAEA*, 1972 ed.

4) Rehder, Alfred: *MANUAL OF CULTIVATED TREES & SHRUBS*, New York, 1956.

DABOECIA D. Don

The *Daboecia* species are delightful low evergreen shrubs, broader than they are high. Their lanceolate to elliptical leaves are arranged alternately on the stems, to which they are attached by short petioles, and they are broader than the leaves of other heathers. Their flowers are relatively larger, variously lantern-shape and fresh colored and are individually more conspicuous than are those of other low-growing hardy heathers. The plants are thus a bit larger-textured than are *Bruckenthalia*, *Calluna* and the hardy *Erica* species. But they grow on similar acid, peaty soil, are harmonious in design values, and offer flower color and charm, some at early and some to late summer and thus are desirable for any gardener who can grow them.

In the past there was a division of opinion among horticulturists over whether *Daboecia* should be considered a "true heather". Purists said no. The rest of us clung to it for our heather gardens where it is a charming addition giving extended color and interest. Since The Heather Society was given responsibility for its cultivar nomenclature(1), the debate has subsided and *Daboecia* has become a more frequent subject in the heather literature.

In at least one respect the genus *Daboecia* does differ markedly from *Bruckenthalia*, *Calluna* and *Erica*. The corollas of its 4-merous flowers normally drop from their stems while still plump and fresh-colored, when their season of fertility is over, leaving only the stem with the small brown developing seed capsules at intervals along it. (Note drawings of *D. cantabrica* and *D. x scotica..*) We are now blessed with two species, *D. azorica*, from the islands of the Azores, and *D. cantabrica*, from western Ireland, northern Portugal and Spain, and southwestern France (around the Bay of Biscay) and the hybrid between them, *D. x scotica*.

In 1700 a Welsh naturalist collected *D. cantabrica* in western Ireland and reported that the local name for it was "Frych Dabeog," St. Dabeoc's Heath *(Erica Dabeoci)*. John Ray, having seen the dried specimens, described the species in 1704 and called it *Erica S. Dabeoci Hibernis* (St. Dabeoc Heath of Ireland). In 1719 the French botanist de Tournefort described it from its location in the Cordillera Cantabrica of northern Spain and called it *Erica cantabrica flore maximo* (the large-flowered *E. cantabrica*). In 1762 Wm. Hudson, in his *FLORA ANGLICA*, described the same plant as *Vaccinium cantabricum*. In the 1762 edition of his *SPECIES PLANTARUM*, Linnaeus listed it as *Erica daboecii* (note reversal of *eo*). He had also elsewhere spelled it *Dabeci* and *Dabeoci*. In 1765 Peter Collinson called a plant grown from Spanish seed *Erica Cantabrica &c*. In 1769 it was being culltivated at Kew Gardens as *Andromeda Daboecia*. In 1834 David Don concluded persuasively that it should be separated from *Erica* and become a genus in its own right. He retained Linnaeus' misspelling and named it *Daboecia*. For good measure it had also been listed as *D.*

polifolia D. Don and *Menziesia polifolia* Juss.(1)(2) To be added to this bewildering array is the late 18th century French Noel Joseph de Necker who called his plant *Boretta*.(3)

References:

1) McClintock, David: *A GUIDE TO THE NAMING OF PLANTS*. The Heather Society, 1980.

2) Nelson, E. C.: *Dabeoc—A saint and his Heather. YEAR BOOK OF THE HEATHER SOCIETY*, 1984.

3) Rehder, Alfred: *MANUAL OF CULTIVATED TREES AND SHRUBS*, 1956.

DABOECIA AZORICA Tutin & E. F. Warburg

The home of *Daboecia azorica* is on five of the Islands of the Azores where it is an endemic found above 490 m (1,600 ft) and reaching almost to the summit of Pico mountain, elev. 2,200 m (7,611 ft). After a 1974 visit there David McClintock wrote, "The higher you go on Pico the more is the ground cover solidly *D. azorica.*"(1) *Erica scoparia ssp. azorica* occurs at lower elevations (2). The Azores are somewhat humid volcanic islands almost mid Atlantic, the nearest landfalls being Portugal (830 miles east) and Cape Race, Newfoundland (1,000 miles west); but because of their climate and flora they are considered to be European. Their latitude is roughly equivalent to northern California, from Monterey Bay north to above Fort Bragg, but the higher heathland where *D. azorica* flourishes is reported to be blanketed with snow for much of each winter.(3) Existence of the Azores *Daboecia* plants has been known since at least 1838, but they were not separated from *D. cantabrica* and given their own specific epithet till after the 1929 Azores visit of the British botanists, Tutin and Warburg, who published it in 1932.(4) The species has been in cultivation in Britain since 1929.

D. azorica differs from *D. cantabrica* most noticeably in habit, which is low and spreading, with branches parallel to and less than one inch above the ground, in the dense top growth, in size, scarcely achieving a height of more than 15 cm (6 in) when flowering, in much smaller foliage size, the little leaves fresh green in summer and becoming bronzed in winter; and in flowers, which are smaller, much more red on average (ruby, cerise or purple on the Heather Soc. colour chart), and have an earlier season of a few weeks (May-June in Seattle, June-July in the Azores). On close inspection the corollas can also be seen to lack the glandular hairs found to some extent on those of *D. cantabrica.*

These Azores natives are also less frost hardy than their Biscayan cousins, but reports from growers in the Puget Sound area indicate that a snow cover will protect them here as it does in the Azores. In locations periodically visited with sharp drops of temperature with no snow protection, some good gardeners at elevations of a few hundred feet have lost their plants. My original plant was given to me in 1963 by an expert gardener friend living at a considerably higher location, who had sadly concluded that her climate was too harsh for it. It was cut back from 75 cm (30 in) diameter to almost nothing in December 1968 (9°F, -13°C), slowly reached that diameter again, lost all its foliage in December 1978 (11°F), achieved 37 cm (15 in) and flowered vigorously by 1980. Its top foliage was again badly scorched by the 9°F (-13°C) of December 1983. This plant is on a slight west slope but otherwise completely unprotected. If you are thinking to yourself that it wouldn't be worth the trauma, I can only urge that a good sized planting of *D. azorica* in full rosy-crimson flower is such a joyous sight as to be worth some effort and periodic waiting. A number of the self-sown seedlings

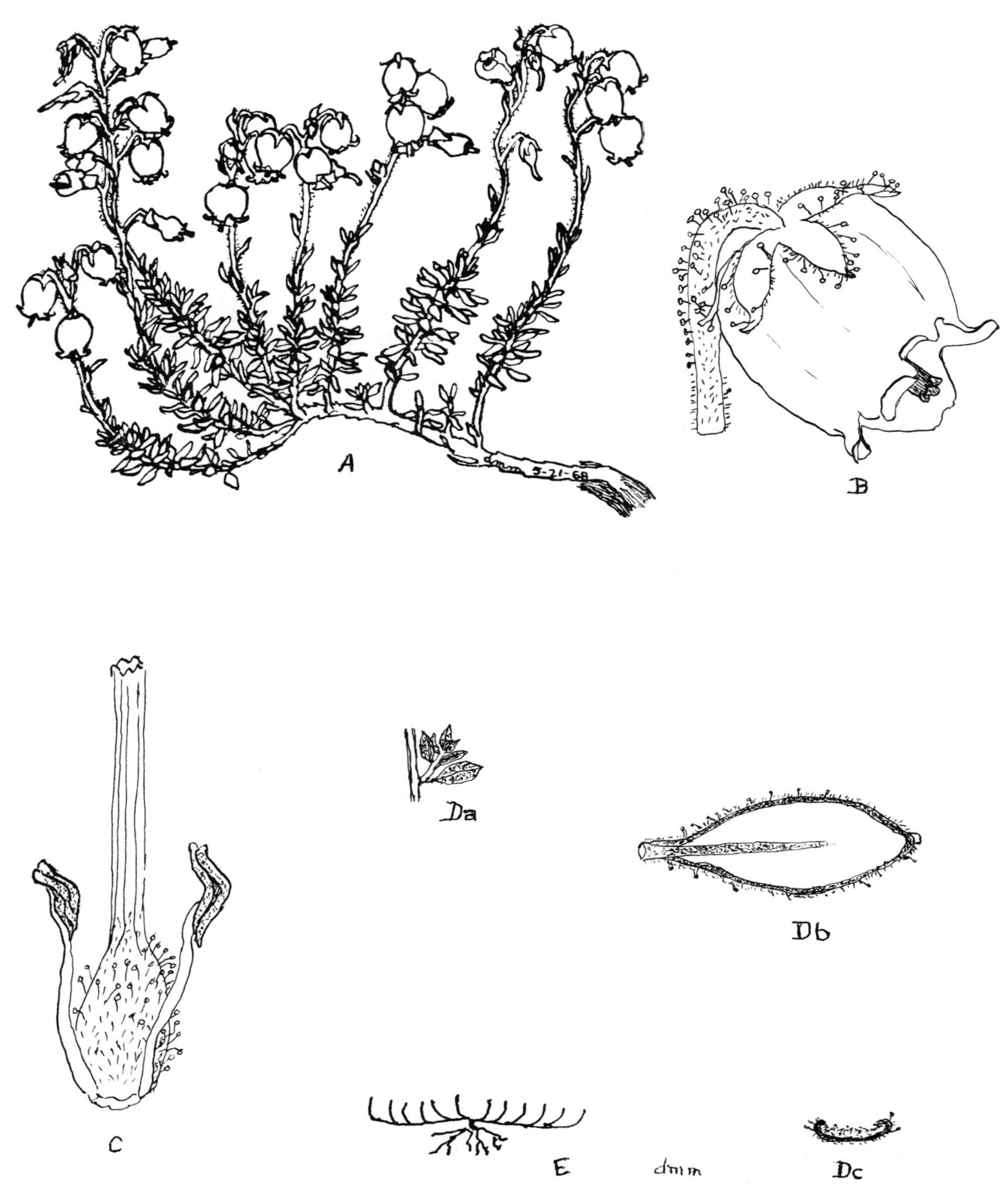

Daboecia azorica Tutin & E. F. Warburg: A, flowering branch .8X; B, flower 5X; C, pistil and 2 stamens 10X; Da, side shoot 1 X; Db, leaf 5X; Dc, leaf cross section 5X; E, plant habit.

around my original plant appeared still lively despite the weather.

The seedlings appear in the peat-sand soil around the perimeter of the parent. As until the last year or so it has always ended its flowering sometime in May or early June (depending on seasonal weather variations), before the *D. cantabrica* season commences, and there has thus been no opportunity for cross pollination, these seedlings have very closely resembled the parent plant. In North America, in any case, there were up to February 1984 no named color forms of *D. azorica*.. But Mr. Richards, of Eskdale, Cumbria, England, reported in the *HEATHER SOCIETY YEAR BOOK* having seen flowers from white through pale pink to "many different shades of flower colour" in the Azores.(2) As Mr. McClintock(3) mentioned, "some of these forms have recently been collected," so cultivars are now available. Incidentally, it should be noted that Mr. Richards described *D. azorica* in England as forming "dense bushes some 8 in (20 cm) across. In May and June there is a blaze of red-purple blooms and then an odd bell or two during the summer. In the Azores they form stunted, straggling, carpeting plants . . . ." Dimensions indicate that the low, spreading plant in my garden may have come from different stock, perhaps a different elevation on Pico. Or perhaps it is just that I do not ordinarily prune it hard back.

Propagation by cuttings may be difficult. L. D. Hills(5) recommends soft cuttings one-half inch long in May-June. Mr. Richards, though an experienced propagator, succeeded with only "one in a thousand". With bottom heat, I did succeed in getting roots on 2 of 10 cuttings late in June, 1970; none at all in August.

References:

1) McClintock, David: personal communication.

2) Richards, D. A.: *Mostly Erica maderensis and Daboecia azorica, YEAR BOOK OF THE HEATHER SOCIETY*, 1976.

3) McClintock, D.: *THE GARDEN*, Royal Horticultural Society, March 1978.

4) McClintock, D.: *A GUIDE TO THE NAMING OF PLANTS*, The Heather Society, 1980.

5) Hills, L. D.: *THE PROPAGATION OF ALPINES*, 1959.

DABOECIA CANTABRICA (Hudson) K. Koch

This beautiful little evergreen shrub takes its specific epithet from its home in the Cordillera Cantabrica, the mountains which stretch along northern Spain parallel to the coast on the Bay of Biscay. It also occurs in France, Portugal and the west coast of Ireland.

Mr. D. A. Richards(1) visited *D. cantabrica* at its home in the Cantabrian Mountains and reported that there it grew to normal size [presumably 10-15 in, 25-40 cm] up to tree line. Above that height and to over 3,000 feet [900 m], "it grows in a curious stunted form, usually about three inches [7.5 cm] tall, flowering freely with bells of the normal colour [purple] and size." Of the species in its boggy Irish stands, Dr. Webb wrote(2) that it is "widely distributed . . . from the extreme west to the edge of the limestone"; he added that it is found to 1,800 and 1,900 feet [550 m], respectively, on two mountains. "Commences flowering in May, and blooms throughout the summer and autumn. A rather straggling plant, growing best when trailing through other shrubby species . . ." At the Liverpool University Garden, Ness, we photographed a plant of what appeared to be *D. cantabrica* 'Praegerae' flowering at a height of three or four feet (1m) over the top of cotoneaster bushes.

In the garden *D. cantabrica* is usually an upright shrub to 25-40 cm (10-15 in) high and somewhat broader, depending on cultivar, with decumbent to ascending stems. Its leaves are of variable length, from 9 to 14 mm (3/8 to 1/2 in) long, narrowly lanceolate to ovate-elliptical, darker or lighter green or variegated above, white tomentose beneath and narrowly revolute at the margins. Its flowers are variously ovoid-globular, white to lighter (the usual color) or darker purple, 9-14 mm (3/8-1/2in) long, spaced out and usually pendent in racemes of 9 to 12 flowers above the body of the plant. The flowering season is variously long - June to November, with the bells beginning to expand at the base of the raceme and progressing higher on the raceme as the season goes on, so that the newest flowers are always nearer the tips.

Rehder(3) rates *D. cantabrica* hardy <u>with protection</u> in the equivalent of USDA zone 6a. Ken Wilson(4) reported from British Columbia that *D. c.* 'Praegerae' withstood the hard winter of 1972 better than an unnamed form and *D. c.* 'Alba', showing there is variation among cultivars.

D. cantabrica, generally is lime tolerant, some forms reportedly to pH 7.8 or 8.0 (but not *D. azorica* or *x scotica* which demand acid soil.) In the garden *D. cantabrica* does well in peaty soil with enough moisture supplied during droughty seasons. Lacking water in such drought as we have just endured (1988) the *Daboecia* flowered poorly through the summer then when the rain finally came in October some of the plants in sun bore masses of flowers. Its native habitats are in acid soil, but, as mentioned above, recently reported experience of several growers indicates that it will also stand a good deal of

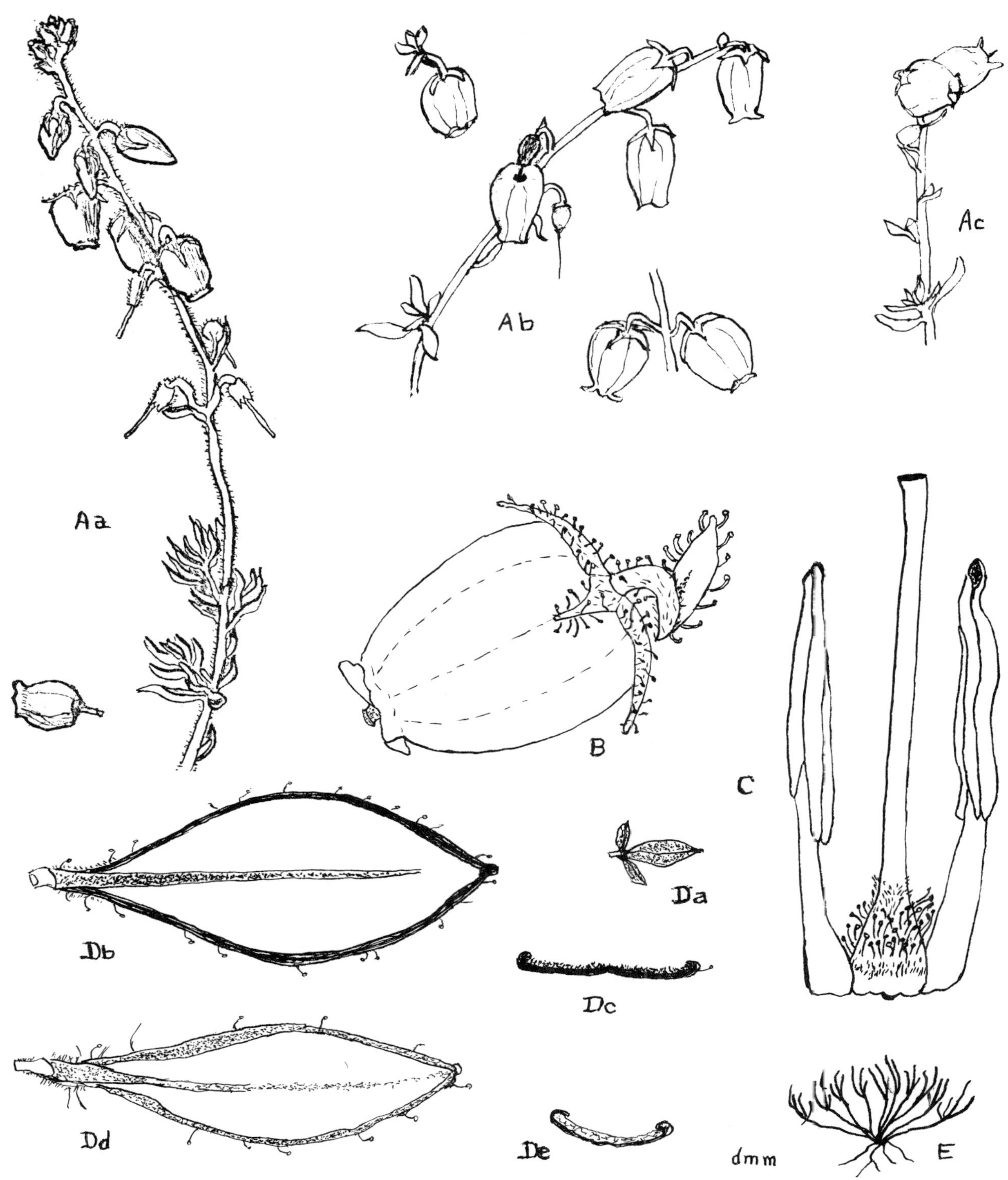

Daboecia cantabrica (Hudson) K. Koch: Aa, inflorescence *D. c.* 'Alba' 1X; Ab, corolla sizes & shapes 1X; Ac, 'Praegerae' 1X; B, flower 'Alba' 5X; C, pistil and 2 stamens 'Alba' 10X; Da, vegetative side shoot 'Praegerae' 1X; Db, 'Alba' leaf beneath 5X; Dc, 'Alba' leaf cross section 5X; Dd, 'Praegerae' leaf beneath 5X; De, 'Praegerae' leaf cross section 5X; E, plant habit.

liminess, even in cutting flats. It certainly tolerates full sun, but in my garden also flowers well in the shade of deciduous trees.

Some authors advocate promptly cutting off spent flowered stems, to keep the plant neat; but if this is done the fun and beauty of self-sown seed plants will be forgone. The seedlings will be unlikely to resemble the parent, but of all those in my garden there is not one without some charm. My plants are trimmed back in March along with the other summer flowering heathers. Hard pruning at that time will much benefit any *Daboecia* plants that are looking less than in vigorous condition; and *D. c.* 'Praegerae' in particular, if looking peaked, will make a wonderful comeback from a fairly murderous pruning.

In the 1978 *POCKET GUIDE TO HEATHER GARDENING*, Yates(5) listed 22 cultivars of *D. cantabrica*. New cultivars continue to be noted in the *YEAR BOOK OF THE HEATHER SOCIETY*, not to mention the 60 plus absentees in Yates's "Other Heather Names". 'Hookstone Purple' and 'Porter's Variety' are said to commence flowering in May, most cultivars are listed for June-October, and 'Alba' (at least in my garden) is reliable June-November. A recent notable variation is 'Charles Nelson,' a double-flowered form with the stamens converted to petaloid filaments and no pollen-bearing anthers. David McClintock(6) describes this variety as having flowers that look distinctly globular, are "the same color as the usual wild plant" but the browned corollas remain on their stems instead of dropping off as those of the single flowers do. This is, so far as we know, the first double-flowered *Daboecia* on record. Another recent note by the same author(7) is of *D. c. f. blumii*, with erect instead of nodding flowers. The North American Cultivar list (cf. p. 171) holds six cultivars of *D. cantabrica*, namely 'Alba', 'Atropurpurea', 'Cinderella' (white), 'Mrs. W. V. Manning', 'Praegerae' and 'Rubra'. 'Bicolor', a particularly charming plant for cutting, was formerly available hereabouts but seems to have disappeared. I think special mention should be made of 'Praegerae', which is a wide-spreading plant to about 34 cm (13 in) high. It differs so noticeably from other *D. c.* cultivars that for a number of years the specific epithet (*cantabrica*) was omitted from its name. It is now listed as a *cantabrica*, but its habit is more spreading, its foliage is smaller and turns bronze in winter, and its flowers have a different stance on their stems and are a brilliant "shocking pink," characters that suggest it might be half way to *D. azorica*. If it has normal reproductive organs I have never had a seedling plant I suspected of having come from it; and Mr. Jones(9) mentions not having been able to grow it, possibly because of his limy soil.

References:

1) Richards, D. A.: *Daboecia cantabrica* at home, *YEAR BOOK OF THE HEATHER SOC.*, 1970.
2) Webb, D. A., Sc. D.: *AN IRISH FLORA*, 1953.

3) Rehder, Alfred: *MANUAL OF CULTIVATED TREES & SHRUBS*, 1956.

4) Wilson, Ken: *The Botanical Garden, The University of British Columbia, YEAR BOOK OF THE HEATHER SOC.*, 1975.

5) Yates, Geoffrey: *POCKET GUIDE TO HEATHER GARDENING*, 1978.

6) McClintock, David: *A double form of Daboecia cantabrica, YEAR BOOK OF THE HEATHER SOC.,* 1982.

7) McClintock, D: *Daboecias with erect flowers, YEAR BOOK OF THE HEATHER SOC.,* 1984.

8) *North American Heather List, HEATHER NEWS,* Mar. 1983.

9) Jones, A. W.: personal communication, 1982.

DABOECIA X SCOTICA D. McClintock

Hybrids of D. *azorica* and *D. cantabrica* which appeared in a Glasgow garden in the 1950s, were given the name of *Daboecia x scotica* by David McClintock in 1978.(1) They had appeared as seedling plants in the garden of William Buchanan, who gave three differing plants to the Scottish nurseryman, Jack Drake. After propagating them Jack Drake named the strongest growing one in honor of Mr. Buchanan. On trial at the R.H.S. garden at Wisley it was awarded an A.M. in 1968. One of the three seedlings, designated "seedling No. 2," which was considered similar to 'William Buchanan' but inferior to it, was discarded by Mr. Drake. The third plant was eventually named 'Jack Drake' for the propagator and distributor. Yates (2), in 1978 listed 'Bearsden' (which had been reported by A. T. Johnson in 1942), 'Cora' (from Holland), 'Jack Drake', 'Silverwells' (white), 'Tabramhill', 'William Buchanan' and 'William Buchanan Gold.' His 1985 book(3) added 'Robin.' Since then 'Red Imp' has come from Holland, and the Heather Farm, Sebastopol, CA found 'Mrs. W. V. Manning'. If you are so fortunate as to be able to grow the two parent species, *DD. azorica* and *cantabrica*, close to each other, and they should happen to flower together, keep an eye out for possible hybrid seedlings, which may be valuable garden assets.

As would be expected, the hybrids vary over a range approaching the two parent species. Their ascending stem habit more resembles *D. cantabrica*. Height is smaller than *cantabrica*, reportedly ranging from 15-40 cm (6-16 in), though if left unpruned they may ascend through overhanging shrubs to a meter. Their leaves vary in size but are mostly intermediate and proportionately broader than those of *cantabrica*. The corollas are larger than those of *azorica*, smaller than *cantabrica* and the flowering season here seems generally to be divided—early, then rest, then flower again. The flower colors I have seen of course vary with the cultivar—some more purple, less red than those of *azorica* and ranging to white. Yates(2) mentions that, unlike other hybrid heathers they set fertile seed. In my garden I do not recollect any freeze loss of *cantabrica*, but David McClintock reports the hybrids are "much hardier than either parent," and Mr. Julian(4) reported the *x scotica* plants to be "regenerating themselves" at Harlow Car after the severe freeze of Jan. 1 to Apr. 1, 1979. My plants were not affected by our 7°F (-14°C) of February 1989.

They are **not** lime tolerant. The plants look reasonably tidy if not pruned back, but pruning will not hurt them.

Propagation from seed would be worth trying, but of course the offspring cannot be expected to be identical to the parent.

A plant of 'Jack Drake' acquired in 1975 was killed by December 1978 freeze. Its replacement, after five summers, was still a little, small-textured plant with flower stems to 25cm high and a spread of 25-30cm (10 X 10-12 in). The illustration in the Proudleys' book(5) indicates the plant should eventually

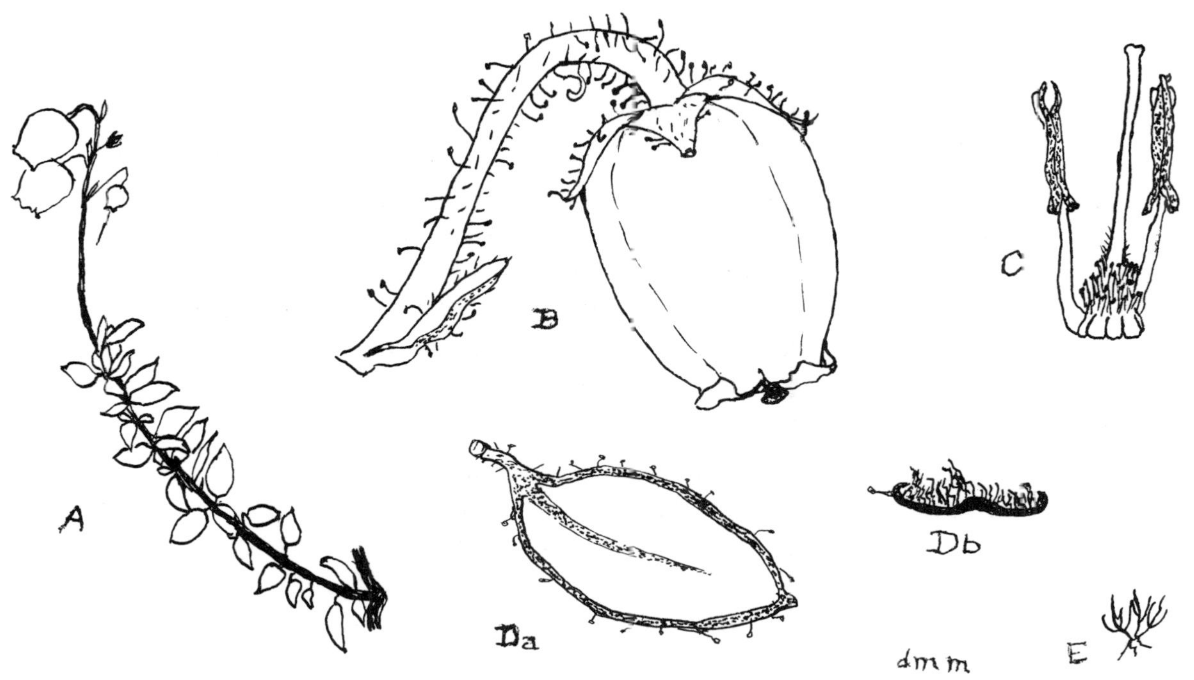

D. x scotica **"Jack Drake":** A, flowering stem 1X; B, flower 5X; C, pistil and 2 stamens 5X; Da, leaf beneath 5X; Db, leaf cross section 5X; E, plant habit.

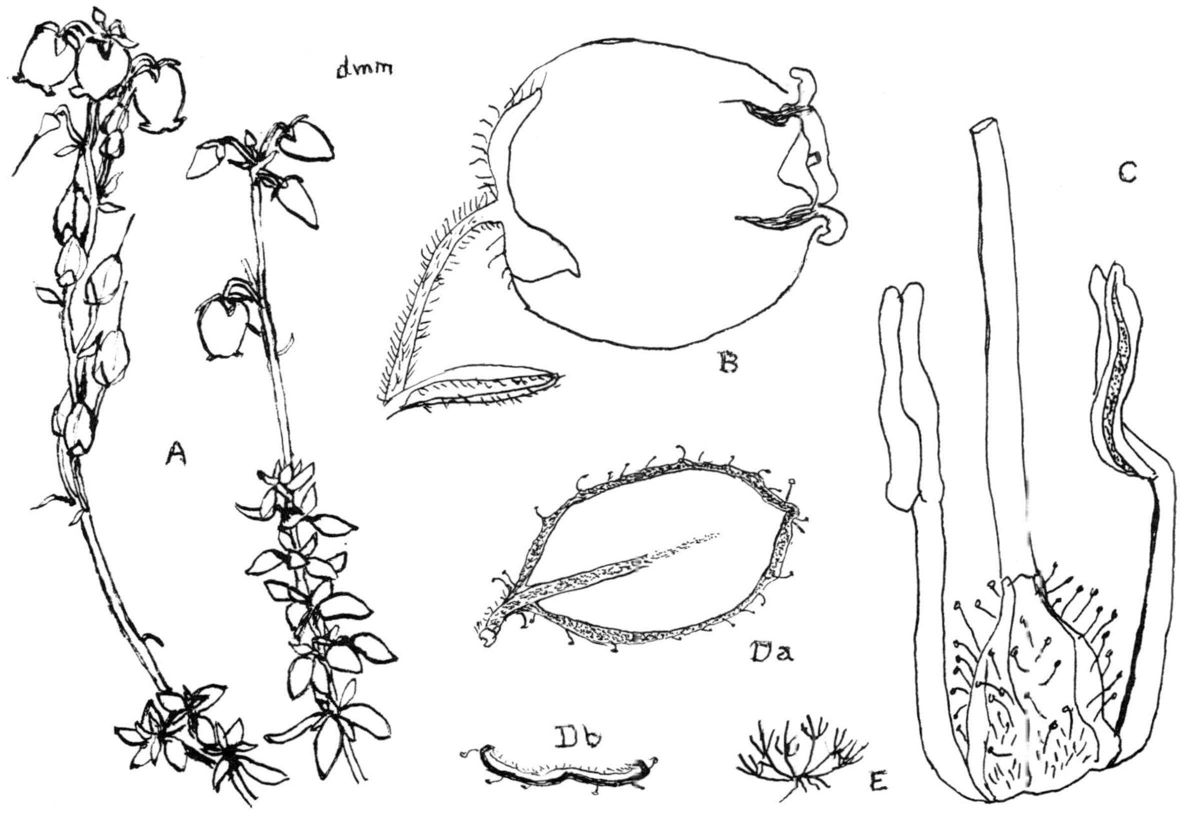

Daboecia x scotica **"William Buchanan":** A, flowering stems 1X; b, flower 5X; C, pistil and 2 stamens 10X; Da, leaf beneath 5X; Db, leaf cross section 5X; E, plant habit.

increase to a more substantial size. Its flowers are slightly smaller and a glowing vivid red with not much purple mixed in. Flowering June-Aug.

I have not succeeded in obtaining a start of 'Mrs. W. V. Manning', but its leaves much resemble those of *D. azorica*. Both 'Jack Drake' and 'William Buchanan' resemble their *azorica* parent in having their leaves change from fresh green to bronze with the advent of winter. 'William Buchanan,' a vigorous growing plant, is cut back each spring but has its stems ascending to 40 cm (16 in) and produces plenty of glowing reddish-purple bells over the 70 cm diameter (28 in) of its spread from June to October.

'William Buchanan Gold', a lovely plant, is a sport from the above and similar to it except that it is a bit smaller, has yellow flecks on its leaves and very dark purple flowers, which appear in satisfactory profusion even in part shade.

References

(1) McClintock, David: *St. Dabeoc's heaths and their hybrids*, Royal Horticultural Soc., *THE GARDEN*, Mar. 1978.

(2) Yates, Geoffrey: *POCKET GUIDE TO HEATHER GARDENING,* 1978.

(3) Yates, Geoffrey: *THE GARDENER'S BOOK OF HEATHERS*, 1985.

(4) Julian, T. A.: *Winter Damage at Harlow Car, YEAR BOOK OF THE HEATHER SOCIETY*, 1980.

(5) Proudley, Brian & Valerie: *HEATHERS IN COLOUR*, 1974.

THE GENUS ERICA L.

The genus *Erica* is one of the 70 or so genera in the very widely distributed Ericaceae (Heath) Family. Most members of this family are shrubs, some are somewhat woody perennial herbs, a few trees or trailing vines. Among its members are many familiar ornamental shrubs: *Rhododendron, Gaultheria, vaccinium* (including the blueberries and cranberries). *Arctostaphylos* (manzanita, bear berry, etc.), *Gaylussacia* (the huckleberry), *Leucothoe, Epigaea* (trailing arbutus), *Pernettya, Pieris, Cassiope, Phyllodoce, Ledum* (Labrador tea), *Kalmia*, our heather group, the trees *Arbutus* (madrona) and *Oxydendrum* and many others. Various ones of them are native to the northern, southern, eastern or western hemispheres. Of the 1,900 or so species in the family most occur on acid soil and are more or less highly calcifuge. Some of the genera in the family are composed of one species only, e.g., *Calluna vulgaris, Bruckenthalia spiculifolia.*

Erica, a genus of evergreen shrubs or rarely small trees, derives its name from *Ereike*, the ancient Greek name of the Heath. It is represented by perhaps 650 species, over 600 of which occur only in Southern Africa and are not temperate zone hardy. (Capetown, near the southern tip of Africa, is at about 34° S and has a temperature range which corresponds to that of the French and Italian Riviera, or California.) Only those species, the hardy heathers, which occur naturally in temperate Europe and the British Isles are our concern. These hardy *Erica* species vary considerably in their degree of hardiness.

The various species have short petioled evergreen leaves which are whorled and linear, or so revolute as to appear linear. The flowers have a single pistil and (usually) eight stamens. The corollas are variously campanulate, most have four short lobes and remain on the stems when spent. The fruit is a capsule which splits open when ripe, and the numerous seeds are minute.

DIFFERENTIATING TREE HEATHS—ERICA species

(sh=shrub, i.e. with several stems from the base;
T=tree, with a trunk or trunks)

If there is a need to differentiate tree heaths when they are not flowering, the following, with the use of a 10x lens, may be helpful:

	arborea	*australis*	*erigena*	*lusitanica*	*scoparia*	*terminalis*	*x veitchii*
Habit	erect shrub or tree, 1-4m	shrub with 1-several main stems 1-2.5 (-3m) high	erect shrub 50-150cm	erect shrub 1-2(-3.5)m	erect shrub 1-3(-4.5)m	bushy erect shrub 1-2.5m	erect shrub to 2.5m, with erect branches; very similar to *E. arborea* but more compact and with lighter, brighter green new foliage than on many but not all, *E. arborea*—certainly distinquished by pollen grains
Branches	ascending-erect	ungainly, ascending-spreading	± erect; ridges decurrent from leaf bases	erect	erect-spreading -bent down-ward, lax	suberect; in very young plants, in whorls of 4	
New growth stem hairs (illustrations are much enlarged)	densely pubescent, with partly longer, branched, partly short, smooth hairs	puberulent	finely puberulent	pubescent, with simple hairs	glabrous or puberulent	puberulent	
Leaves (note apex)	whorls of 3; spreading giving feathery effect; very narrow, 3-6mm long, glabrous	whorls of 4 at 45° angle; 4-6mm long, wider than *arborea;* glabrous	whorls of 4;spreading; 5-8mm long; glabrous	whorls of 3-4 irregular; 3-4mm long	whorls of 3-4; spreading; 4-7mm long; glabrous	whorls,4(-6);3-5.5mm long;	
Leaf Margins	revolute, contiguous	revolute, contiguous	revolute, not quite contiguous	revolute, contiguous	revolute, not contiguous	revolute; contiguous at apex only	

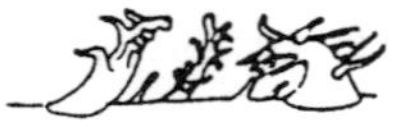

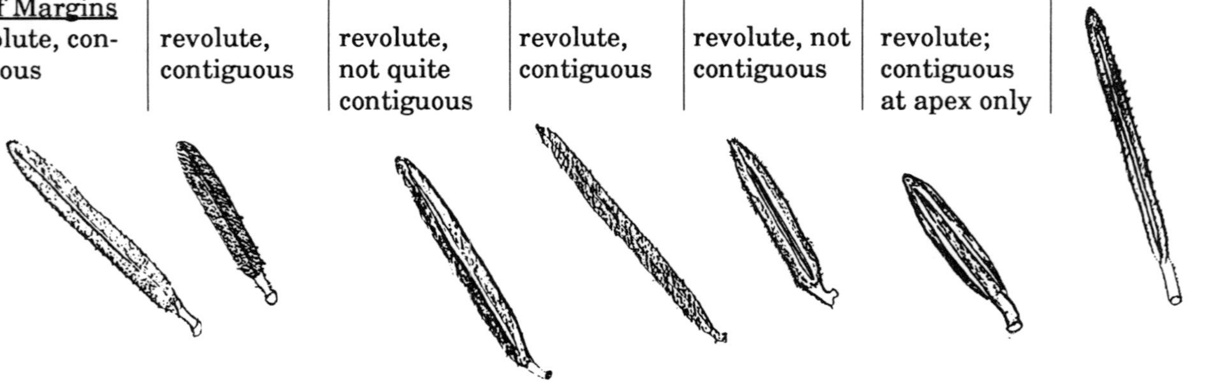

ERICA ANDEVALENSIS Cabezudo & Rivera

In 1980 two Sevillian botanists, B. Cabezudo and J. Rivera, published in the Spanish journal, *LAGASCALIA*, their report and description of what they had decided must be a new *Erica* species.(1) The plants were growing in what seemed a strange habitat for heather—the spoil heaps around pyrites mines (pyrites: metallic-looking sulphides of copper, iron, tin, etc.), in the southwestern Spain area of Huelva, an Atlantic seacoast city somewhat over 100 miles northwest of Gibraltar, at the mouth of the Rivers Odiel and Tinto.

The low evergreen plants, height 20-180 cm (8-72 in), with pink umbellate inflorescences, appendages on the anthers, and leaves in whorls of four, appeared to belong to the heather group of *Erica tetralix* and *E. mackaiana*; but they differed from the former in having entirely glabrous ovaries, and from the latter in the number, character and location of the hairs on the margins and undersurfaces of their leaves.

In addition to these structural differences, the distribution of the new species is markedly different. Such *E. mackaiana* as is found in the Spain-Portugal peninsula is confined to a relatively small area in the extreme northwest corner of Spain, in the part of the Province of Galicia that juts up to the Bay of Biscay(2). *E. tetralix* has wider distribution in the northwest and east-center of the Iberian Peninsula, but has not been found in that extreme southwest corner where *E. andevalensis* is situated. For these reasons, Cabezudo and Rivera published and described *E. andevalensis*, a name derived from the district of Andeval in which it was found, as a new species.

Following a July 1982 visit to Spain with Charles Nelson and David Small, David McClintock reported in the Heather Society *YEAR BOOK*, 1983(3) the findings resulting from their trip, which involved driving 3,500 miles in Spain. They found the plants in the location described by the Spanish botanists, then explored further and found more of them in more normal heather habitats, on the banks and stony beaches about 40 miles up the River Odiel from Huelva. Some even grew where, during the rainy season, they would undoubtedly be submerged by the river water, which was polluted by copper and tasted salty.

McClintock describes the bushes as stout, stiff and erect, many smaller but some reaching to a height and width of three or four feet (90-120 cm). All had thick stems. They seemed to differ in no important way from either Spanish or Irish *E. mackaiana*. The usual flower color was pinkish-purple (Amethyst H1 on the Heather Society color chart), but a group of five white-flowered plants was found in the River Odiel population. In 1983 the white-flowered form was published as *E. andevalensis f. albiflora*.(4) As noted above the observation of the Spanish plants was made in July, but in a cooler climate their flowering season seems to be late summer—autumn.

David Small, of Suffolk, England air-mailed cuttings of plants grown from the

Spanish collections to D Metheny in mid-July, 1984. The cuttings were inserted in peat/perlite with bottom heat. Two pink-flowered and two of the whites rooted, but the whites did not survive. One of the pinks was given in 1985 to Art Dome, who fertilized it and succeeded in having a 16-inch (40 cm) high plant flowering in September, 1987, at which time the accompanying drawing was made from it. (The other rooted pink has kept alive but not grown much in three years.)

So far the two plants have not been tested by exposure to severe freeze in their Seattle gardens.

Pruned annually, Art Dome's plant seems to not exceed 16 inches (40 cm) in height. Its leaves are dark green above and whitish beneath. Its flowers are of a dark pink color. He considers it to be interesting but not particularly decorative. It does have the advantage of a late flowering season when not many heathers are still showing much color.

After seeing a copy of this drawing, David McClintock wrote in mid-November, 1987, "I looked at the plants now in good flower in my garden [in Kent, England] . . . and I found that there was variation in how thickly the leaves grew and in how upright the flowers held themselves—always nodding here, mostly upright in Spain, and larger. . . . In mine. . .the leaves are much closer and tidier—some have rather larger leaves. It could be that the smaller leaves and flowers here are environmental. . . ."(5)

References:

1) Cabezudo, B. and J. Rivera: *Erica andevalensis, LAGASCALIA*, No. 2, pp. 223-6, 1980.

2) Fraga, M. I: *Notes on the Morphology and Distribution of* Erica *and* Calluna *in Galicia, Northwestern Spain, GLASRA*, No. 7, pp. 11-23, 1983.

3) McClintock, David: *Iter Hispanicum Ericaceum, YEAR BOOK OF THE HEATHER SOCIETY*, 1983, p. 33.

4) Nelson, E. Charles and D. C. McClintock: *Two New Wild White-flowered Heathers (Erica andevalensis and E. mackaiana) from Spain, GLASRA*, No. 7, 1983, pp. 35-40.

5) McClintock, David: personal communication, 13 Nov. 1987.

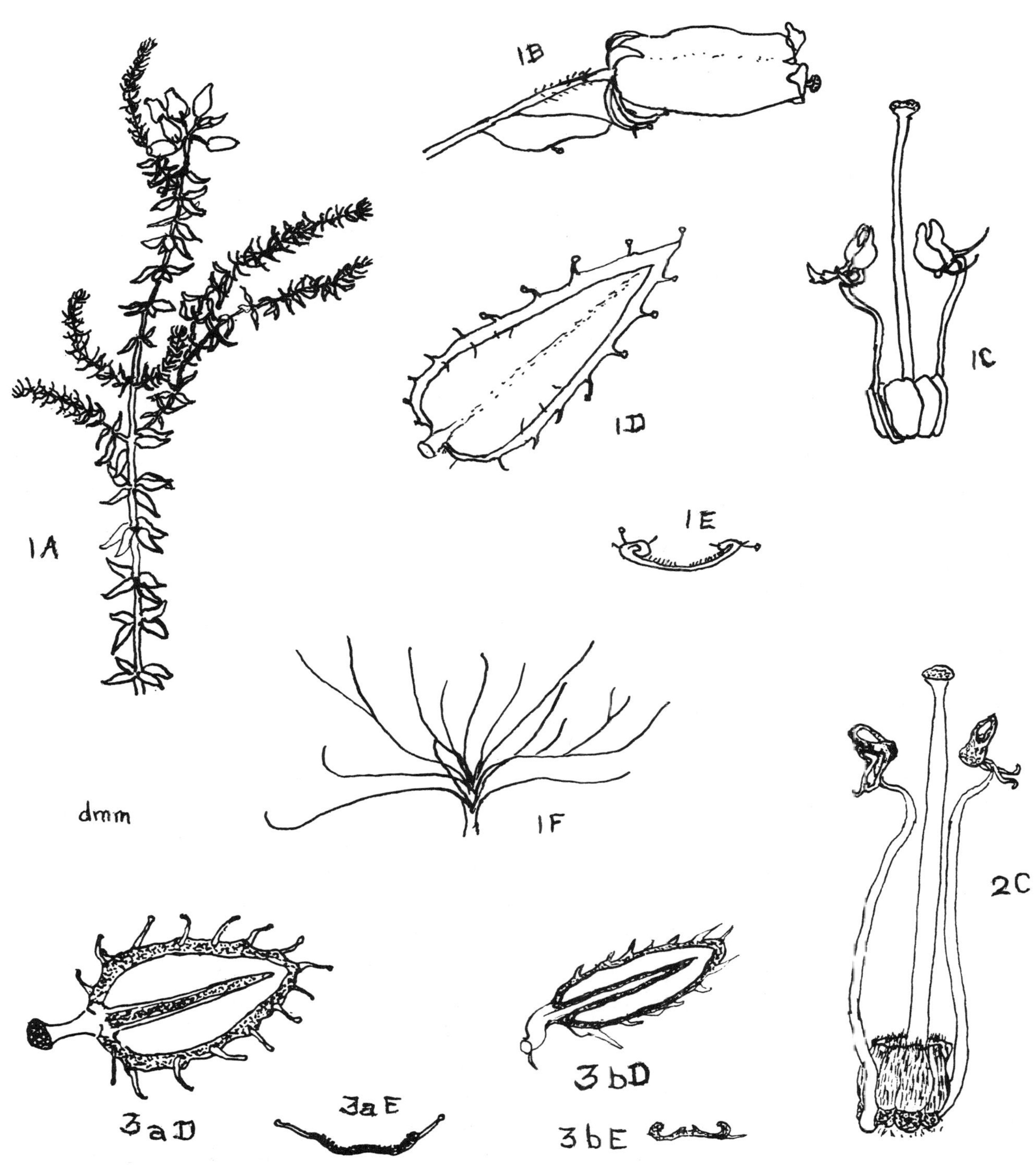

1, *Erica andevalensis* Cabezudo & Rivera; **2, *E. tetralix* 'Alba Mollis; 3a, *E. mackaiana* 'Plena'; 3b, *E. mackaiana* 1'Dr. Ronald Grey':** 1A, flowering stem 1X; 1B, flower 5X; 1C, pistil and 2 stamens 10X; 1D, 3aD, 3bD, mature leaf beneath 10X; 1E, 3aE, 3bE, leaf cross section 10X; 1F, plant habit.

ERICA ARBOREA L.

"In springtime it [the maquis] brightens the hillsides with splashes of colour, with the pink and white of the cistuses, the yellows of the brooms and the snow-like dusting of the myriads of flowers of the Tree Heather." Thus Polunin and Huxley(11) describe the maquis around the shores of the Mediterranean.

Of the natural distribution of *E. arborea*, Ronald Good(7) says, "this, the only wide species in the whole *[Erica]* genus, connects the tropical African [Cape Heaths] with the remaining group of European and Mediterranean *[Erica]* species." It has been found in widely separated locations: in the East African Highlands on Mt. Kilimanjaro, Tanzania, about 200 miles south of the Equator; on Mt. Ruwenzori, just north of the Equator in Uganda; about 1,700 miles northwest on summits of the generally dry and rocky Tibesti Mountains of northern Chad; another 800 or so miles north to the shores of the Mediterranean, where there are concentrated occurrences; in the Mediterranean Islands where there is acid or neutral soil; to southernmost France and the Iberian Atlantic shores - some 4,000 mi (6,400 km).

East and west, it occurs from the Atlantic islands of Madeira and the Canaries, off the northwest coast of Africa, to as far east as the foothills of the western Caucasus, in the Asia Minor segment of Turkey - a span of nearly 5,000 miles (8,000 km).(2,7)

It should be noted that the African montane colonies of the species are at elevations which catch considerably more moisture than falls on the surrounding lowlands. Of the colony on Mt. Ruwenzori, Patrick Synge(15) wrote, "Gradually the bamboos diminished in size . . . until suddenly we emerged into a zone of tree heathers [10,000-12,000 ft (3,000-3,700 m)], [above which *Senecio* and *Lobelia*(8)] . . . there were trees fifty feet high . . . twisted into weird shapes and gnarled . . . and bearded with streamers of lichens and mosses . . . these shapes stand out dimly from a background of swirling mists."

Depending on the climate from which *E. arborea* is reported, it achieves varying heights: in the mountains of equatorial Africa, trees of 15 m (50 ft); on the summit of Mt. Emi Koussi (11,204 ft (3,500 m)) in the Tibesti Mountains (ca. 20°N, sometimes thought of as the backbone of the Sahara Desert) of northern Chad(3), old plants are said to have attained 5-6 m height (17-20 ft) and trunk diameter of 33-40 cm (13-16 in); on the sandy soils of the Canary Islands, to 7 m (23 ft) with stout trunks—abuzz with bees, it is an important honey producing plant; in gardens around Puget Sound in northwest Washington, 4.5 m (15 ft). The rule seems to be: the harsher the climate, the less the height.

Botanically, "Flora Europaea"(5) places *E. arborea* close to *E. lusitanica*, from which it differs in having many new-growth stem hairs which are branched, along with some simple ones, the corolla generally

shorter, rounder and greyish-white, without *lusitanica*'s red flower buds, the base of the calyx saccate, the stigma capitate and the anther appendages shorter and flatter (fig. Ab). But, as shown in the accompanying drawings, the corollas and other reproductive parts of the numerous seedlings which appear can vary considerably in shape and size.

The branches of *E. arborea* are generally ascending. The great masses of flowers are arranged in pyramidal or cylindrical panicles to 45 cm (18 in) long, and are delightfully fragrant. Its leaves, though narrow, are relatively wider than those of *lusitanica*, are densely packed in whorls of three and, in some forms, very dark green. Seedling foliage can be assortedly more yellowish and there is the glorious form, 'Estrella Gold' whose leaves gleam in the winter sun. *E. arborea* wood provides the "briar" (from the French "bruyere", heath) from which smoking pipes are manufactured. Mr. Richards(14) mentions that on the Island of Madeira, which is in many places precipitous, security fencing is made of Tree Heath stems, whose hard wood needs no preservative. *E. arborea* hedges are used as windbreaks in some English gardens.

E. arborea bells are expanded in March-April and remain into May.

As described by botanists, *E. arborea* seems to be a fairly certain entity which, if unprotected, cannot tolerate much sharper freeze than 18°F (-8°C) without extensive damage. It is a plant for the Mediterranean climate, a long hot summer which is rainless or nearly so, and a short, mild, rainy winter, during which severe frosts seldom occur.(6) In the Pacific Northwest, this climate description is most nearly met in coastal northern California. In a relatively mild (not far from salt water and with good air drainage) Seattle garden it was barely possible to keep a plant of the tender form of *E. arborea* from spring 1967, when four plants from University of Coimbra, Portugal seed were put out in a close group in a somewhat protected (by overhead trees) situation. Three of these were killed by the 9°F (-13°C) of December 1968. The survivor (fig. A), though cut back, regrew from the base. All but its lowest, snow-covered branch was killed by freeze (16°F, -9°C) in January 1972, made a fine recovery and flowered beautifully before again having all but one low branch frozen in December 1978 (11°F, -12°C). Recovery from this third attack was been much less vigorous, though it commenced flowering reasonably well at 60cm (2 ft) height, two years later, with the typical mass of fragrant, greyish-white flowers, and continued till killed by 9°F (-13°C) in December 1983. Rehder(12) rates *E. arborea* for Zone VII (+5 - +10°F, USDA zone 7b)), but experience indicates this may be an optimistic assessment for at least the tender forms of the species.

It is hard to know just where to place the Washington Park Arboretum's *E. arborea* plants (figs. Ba, Bb, Bc). Grown from seed labelled *E. arborea*, imported from the University of Lisbon, Portugal, they were apparently planted out in 1952. If so, they survived the devastating November 1955 freeze, six days with lows of 16°, 15°, 10°, 11°, 13°, 17°F (-12°- -8.5°C) with no snow cover and unprepared by autumn "hardening" weather. Thirty years later they were large plants about 3 m, 4.5 m, and 3.5 m high (10, 15 and 11.5 ft) and nearly as wide. It seems possible only to conclude that the species is considerably more variable than the botanists' descriptions indicate, with a fairly wide range including some more tender and some more hardy forms. This variation is probably to be expected in a species with so wide a geographical distribution.

Fortunately for those of us who garden in less reliably mild areas, the *E. arborea* plants available in our nurseries are the more hardy forms of this species, which, except for known clones of *E. arborea* 'Alpina', can be referred to as *E. arborea alpina* (without the single quotes and capital A.)(10) The parent of *E. arborea* 'Alpina' was collected by the German nurseryman, Dieck at tree line in mountains of southeast Spain, in 1892. Clones of it were acquired by the Royal Botanic Garden, Kew, in 1899.(2). Plants vegetatively propagated from this original import (or its German forebear) are now properly called *E. a.* 'Alpina'. (Probably figs. C). Krussman(9) describes this cultivar as usually no higher than 1m (3.3 ft), rigidly erect, with brighter green foliage and cleaner white flowers than the type. Bean's 1973(2) report was that the Kew plant "is now 8 to 10 ft high and 24 ft across." None of the plants we have observed have stopped at Krussman's 1 m.

In congenial garden situations *E. arborea*/*E. a. alpina* self-sow fairly generously, providing a range of hardier forms. These plants vary widely in leaf color

---

Erica arborea L., ***E. a.* 'Alpina'** Dieck, ***E. a. var. alpina;*** Aa, *E. arborea* (Coimbra), flower and pedicel (all flowers 5X); Ab, pistil and 2 stamens (all pistils and stamens 10X); Ba, Bb, Bc, *E. arborea* (Lisbon), Washington Park Arboretum 989-50; Ca-Ce, plants acquired as *E. a.* 'Alpina'; D, dmm *E. arborea* 325.2; Ea-Ed, plants from self-sown seed; Fa, leaf arrangement 1X; Fb, leaf beneath 10X; Fc, leaf cross section 20X; Ga, Gb, plant habits.

A
Ba
Bb
Bc
Ca
Cb
Cc
Cd
Ce
D
Ea
Eb
Ec
Ed
Fa
Fb
Fc
dmm
G

(yellowish to dark green), flower shape (rounded to longer and narrower), flower color (greyish- to cream-white), shape of stigma (capitate to subobconical), and length of style; and in shape of inflorescence (cylindrical to pyramidal). The ovaries are all similarly squat-rounded, and the anther appendages all have the distinctive more-or-less short, flat appearance, with ciliate margins. All the pollen grains I have observed, using low-power microscope, while somewhat various in size, have the same shape as those of the presumably true, frost-tender *E. arborea*.

In their analytical key, Polunin and Smythies(12) give as one character of *E. arborea* that the anther appendages are one-fourth the length of the anther. This limitation in length is met by some of the plants illustrated here (notably fig. A) but not all of them. As mentioned in the *FLORA EUROPAEA*(5) description, the bracteoles are below the middle of the pedicels and can number two or three. All have new-growth stems clothed with a mixture of branched and simple hairs. All have delightfully fragrant flowers. Some of these seed plants very closely resemble in appearance the tender *E. arborea* but are a few weeks later to expand their bells, probably will achieve less than the reported maximum height, and are surely more frost-hardy (e.g. fig. Ed). No established specimens have suffered noticeably from the 7°F (-14°C) to which they were subjected in February 1989.

In any case, the species is of easy garden constitution as long as it is in poor, well drained sandy-peaty soil. Floras mention its native habitats as dry, sandy(3), on banks, cliffs(4), in woods, evergreen scrub and by streams(5). Experience shows that it does equally well in full sun and in the light shade of deciduous trees, but will probably grow larger and take longer before starting to flower in shade. If old branches have a tendency to die out, cut them back and fresh new growth will spring from the base.

As indicated above, the species can be propagated by seed, with interestingly variable results, or by summer cuttings in peat with sand, perlite or vermiculite.

Of the more recently reported cultivars only 'Estrella Gold' is known to be currently available in North America, not 'Albert's Gold.' Two cultivars originally supposed to be of *E. arborea* parentage, have since been determined to be probably forms of *E.x veitchii*. They are 'Gold Tips' and 'Pink Joy'(16)

References:

1) Baker, H. A. & G. H. Oliver: *ERICAS IN SOUTHERN AFRICA*, c. 1968.

2) Bean, W. J.: *TREES & SHRUBS HARDY IN THE BRITISH ISLES*, 1973 ed.

3) Chopinet, R.: *Les Bruyeres rustiques, PLANTES DE MONTAGNE,* No. 63, 1967.

4) Davis, P. H.: *FLORA OF TURKEY,* 1978.

5) *FLORA EUROPAEA*, 1972 ed.

6) Gleason, Henry A. & Arthur Cronquist: *THE NATURAL GEOGRAPHY OF PLANTS*, 1964.

7) Good, Ronald: *THE GEOGRAPHY OF THE FLOWERING PLANTS*, 1964 ed.

8) Heawood, Edw.: *Ruwenzori, ENCYCLOPAEDIA BRITANNICA*, 11th ed., 1911.

9) Krussman, Gerd: *HANDBUCH DER LAUBGEHOLZE*, 1960-1980.

10) McClintock, David: *A GUIDE TO THE NAMING OF PLANTS*, 1980.

11) Polunin, Oleg & Anthony Huxley: *FLOWERS OF THE MEDITERRANEAN*, 1966.

12) Polunin, Oleg & P. E. Smythies: *FLOWERS OF SOUTHWEST EUROPE*, 1973.

13) Rehder, Alfred: *MANUAL OF CULTIVATED TREES AND SHRUBS*,1956.

14) Richards, D. A.: *Mostly* Erica Maderensis *and* Daboecia azorica, *YEAR BOOK OF THE HEATHER SOCIETY*, 1976.

15) Singe, Patrick: *IN SEARCH OF FLOWERS*, ?1985.

16) Turpin, P. G.: *The Tree Heaths* 'Gold Tips' and 'Pink Joy', *YEAR BOOK OF THE HEATHER SOCIETY*, 1979.

ERICA AUSTRALIS L.

E. australis is a native of Spain and Portugal and Linnaeus (1770) derived its name from the Latin for southern. The only presently recorded synonym, *E. aragonensis* (from Aragon), was published by the 19th Century German botanist, H. M. Willkomm, whose plant is now classed as a variety of *E. australis.*(1) Aragon, the old name for a section of northeastern Spain just south of the French border, is the area of the city of Zaragoza and the Ebro River. This region has been described thus, "... parched, chalky soil .... As the mountains of Valencia and Catalonia effectually bar out the fertilizing moisture of the sea-winds, much of the province is a sheer wilderness, stony, ash-coloured, scarred with dry watercourses, and destitute of any vegetation except thin grass and heaths."(2) If, as Willkomm's name suggests, *E. australis* is the heath which adorns this discouraging sounding plain, Aragon must, in their flowering season at least, be blessed with shrubs of great beauty.

E. australis is grouped botanically with those ericas having anthers appendaged at the base, leaves in whorls of 4 with contiguous, revolute margins completely concealing their under surfaces, and 3 bracteoles near to the flowers and partly overlapping the sepals. The foliage is fairly dark green, varying slightly among plants of seed origin; and such plants, after 16 growing seasons in a Seattle garden, ranged in size from .8 m high and 1.2 m wide (32 X 48 in) to 2.5 m high and almost as wide (8 ft).

"Flora Europaea"(3) locates *E. australis* in acid soil, in Portugal and north, central and west Spain, in heaths, scrub and open woods. The white-flowered *E. a.* 'Mr. Robert' was reportedly(4) found in 1912 by Lt. Robert Williams (who died in action in WWI) in the mountains near Algeciras, a coastal city near the extreme southern tip of Spain, across a small bay from Gibraltar. Of the species, the Proudleys(5) say, ". . . perched high up on a crag in Andalucia [extreme southwest Spain] we found two other" [color forms].

As is also true of the other tree heaths, young plants, whether from seed or cuttings, exhibit early-on the tendency for a main stem to stretch up before side branches develop. Many *E. australis* plants from seed will then develop a few fairly sturdy, more or less erect trunks (some to 2 m (6.6 ft)) with only short laterals, before developing additional sprawling, spreading stems - though some of my seed plants sprawl at only a few years and never do grow very tall. Some

---

E. australis L.: Aa, flowering branch, 1X; Ab, flowering branch, 'Mr. Robert' 1X; Ac, flowering stem tip, seed plant 8 1X; Ba, flower, 5X; Bb, flower, 'Mr. Robert' 5X; Bc, flower, seed plant 8 5X; Ca, flower cross section 5X; Cb, pistil and 2 stamens, 8X; Da, leaf beneath, 10X; Db, leaf cross section, type 10X; E, plant habits. (Flowering branches Aa and Ab drawn by Jean McConnell. All other drawings, dmm.)

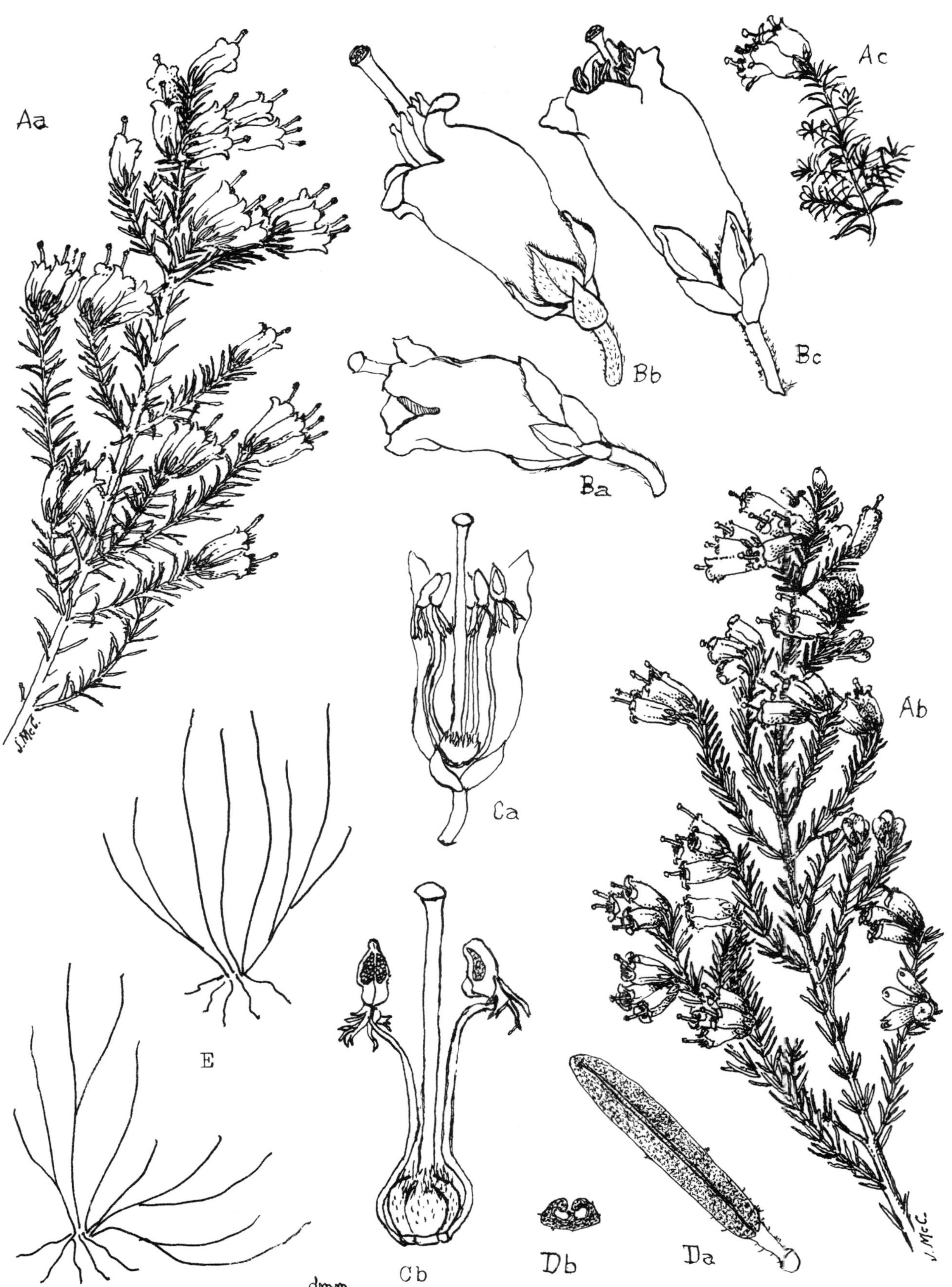
Aa
Ac
Bb
Bc
Ba
Ab
Ca
E
Cb
Db
Da

authors describe the species habit as "ungainly" and the French Chopinet(6) recommends cutting the branches hard back to give the plant a more regular form. They will stand the pruning, which may be done in spring immediately after flowering. Some gardeners delight in their irregularity. - The wood is fine-grained, hard and somewhat brittle.

The Proudleys' description of the common *E. australis* corolla color as pale mauve-pink seems to me more realistic than others', who use such terms as rose pink, bright pink, bright purplish-red, etc. However, the description of the flowers, the largest of the hardy heaths, as born in clusters of 4-8, terminating short shoots of the previous year's growth, while accurate, gives hardly a hint of the spectacular effect of a large solidly flowering plant. A very close look at the flowers reveals small areas of intense bright red on sepals, bracts and style, adding warmth to the over-all effect,—except with the white 'Mr. Robert' where bright green is substituted. The flower colors of my seed plants, so far, range from pale pinkish-purple to the light warm rose of seed plant 30, which may resemble 'Riverslea' (but seems more cold resistant) and some have more intense color at the base of the corolla. There have been no white seedlings here.

Seed plant 8 had larger than usual flowers very early (January or sooner) but was all but killed in December 1983, when it was in full flower; and it appears to be finally gone following February 1989 drop to 7°F (-14°C). Several of the seed plants have proven more resistant to cold.

Except for Mr. H. M. Scantlin, Surrey, England, the Hampshire nursery from which came 'Riverslea,' and Brian and Margaret Mulligan, Kirkland, WA, gardeners are not on record as having self-sown seed plants of *E. australis.* My original plant of the type was planted out in 1958. 'Mr. Robert' followed in 1961. The first seedlings appeared in 1966 and, all told, in over 20 years I numbered 47 seedlings. Over half of these expired at an early age, most from temperatures below 18°F (-8°C), some from distress at having been moved, even when young. Some of these appear to be seedlings from seedlings, having appeared close to seed plants and nowhere near the original clones.

Thinking of that arid plain in Aragon, my own sandy hillside, and the rock crevices from which some of my seed plants have sprung, I suspect that a very well-drained situation that encourages the plant roots to head for the nether region not only keeps the roots from being water-logged but also ensures that they will be far enough from the surface to survive vagaries of weather. It has usually been some of the young plants whose roots are not yet deep that have succumbed. Freezes of 16° to 18°F (-9° to -8°C) will leave some of the top of *australis* (type) scorched, but no drastic harm. When there has been a very rainy season just preceding hard freeze, there is a tendency of older and thicker or even younger stems to literally explode from the ice formation where too much water remains in the xylem, the woody part of the stem. Hard freeze is also noticeably devastating when the preceding season's high average temperatures have encouraged many of the tree heaths into precocious flowering before the drop occurred.

My original *E. australis*, planted in 1958, has had its entire top frozen to the ground three times, with temperatures of 8°, 9°, or 12°F (-13°, -13°, -11°C). From these three attacks it has grown again from the roots.

The best time to move a flowering size plant, at least in this more or less mediterranean climate, seems to be autumn after the rainy season is under way.

Yates(7) lists as cultivars only:

'Mr. Robert,' a spendid plant with white flowers, is more erect-growing than the type, to 3m (10 ft) here. Its dark green leaves are straighter and more regularly set at a 45° angle to the stems, whereas those of the type are more spreading. It has a tendency to be showing a sprinkling of its white flowers off and on throughout the year, with a great mass in the usual flowering season. It is notably more able to withstand hard freeze.

'Riverslea' has brighter-colored flowers than the usual pink-flowered form, but has twice succumbed to freeze here when still young.

Some writers list *E. a.* 'Aragonensis,' some declare it to be no different from the type. Chopinet says its flowers are smaller. My slide of it at the Royal Botanic Garden, Edinburgh shows flowers of a more intense pink.

Other formerly listed cultivars are now said to be extinct, or not to justify a separate cultivar name.

References:

1) McClintock, David: *GUIDE TO THE NAMING OF PLANTS*, 1980.
2) *ENCYCLOPAEDIA BRITANNICA*, 11th ed., 1911.
3) *FLORA EUROPAEA*, 1972 ed.
4) Maxwell, D.F. & P.S.Patrick: *THE ENGLISH HEATHER GARDEN*, 1966.
5) Proudley, Brian & Valerie: *HEATHERS IN COLOUR*, 1974.
6) Chopinet, R.: *Les Bruyeres Rustiques*, *PLANTES DE MONTAGNE*, Bull. de la Soc. des Amateurs de Jardins Alpins, No. 63, 1967.
7) Yates, Geoffrey: *POCKET GUIDE TO HEATHER GARDENING*, 1978.

ERICA CARNEA L.(syn. **E. HERBACEA** L.)

"*Erica carnea* . . . has the breath of moorland, and yet it is neat and elegant. It is, in a sense, a solitary, flaming away long before the crocuses have shown the smallest flicker of gold, and yet it is companionable, blending happily with all its neighbors. . . . What other flower will produce this blaze through the snow, so that after a storm you can have the sheer enchantment of seeing what seems to be an embroidery of brilliant pink on a coverlet of white satin? . . . What other flower has so sure and masterly a manner with weeds?" This paean of praise from Beverly Nichols.(1)

At the start, perhaps, should be mentioned the recent division of opinion over whether the species is properly called *E. carnea* L. or *E. herbacea* L. This debate has somewhat more interest than most nomenclature disputes because the confusion was brought about by an error of the great Linnaeus (1707-1778) himself. Because he did not understand the seasonal variation of the plant and the old (pre-Linnaean) literature about it, at various times he gave the plant five different specific *Erica* epithets: *carnea, herbacea, pallido-purpurea, purpurascens* and *mediterranea.* Recently some botanists have been opting for *herbacea*; much of the horticultural world, including The Heather Society, for *carnea*, each side citing arguable botanical reasons in its favor. Early on, Linnaeus had named the species in its flowering stage *E. carnea*, and the summer-autumn green-bud stage *E. herbacea*, which he described as having exserted anthers (which it does), the anthers with basal appendages (there are none), and leaves in whorls of three (they are in whorls of four). Finally, he combined his *carnea* and *herbacea* under the latter name but most botanists continued using *carnea*, and since that has been the generally accepted name for over 200 years, and the old *herbacea* description does not fit the species we have, we use *carnea*.(2) Recently (1990), *carnea* has become again the official name. But gardeners need to remember that *herbacea* is the same plant.

The natural habitat of this species is coniferous woods and stony slopes, usually limy, mainly in mountains; in the Central European Alps, west to Switzerland, north to east central Germany, south to central Italy, and east to Jugoslavia. It is found as high as 2,650 m (8,700 ft), where it flowers as the snow melts.(3)

The flowering stems of *E. carnea* are generally ascending; cultivar heights range from 10 cm to 30 cm (4-12 in), the majority falling in the 15-20 cm (6-8 in) range. A plant of the usual wild form of the species will spread to cover about 60 cm (2 ft). Such cultivars as the white-flowered 'Cecilia M. Beale' and 'Snow Queen' keep to an even more modest foot or so and need to be protected from their pushier siblings; the majority of cultivars will cover an about one-meter (3 ft) diameter circle in about ten years; but a number of others such as the 'Springwood' varieties are very determined spreaders, a fact which needs to be

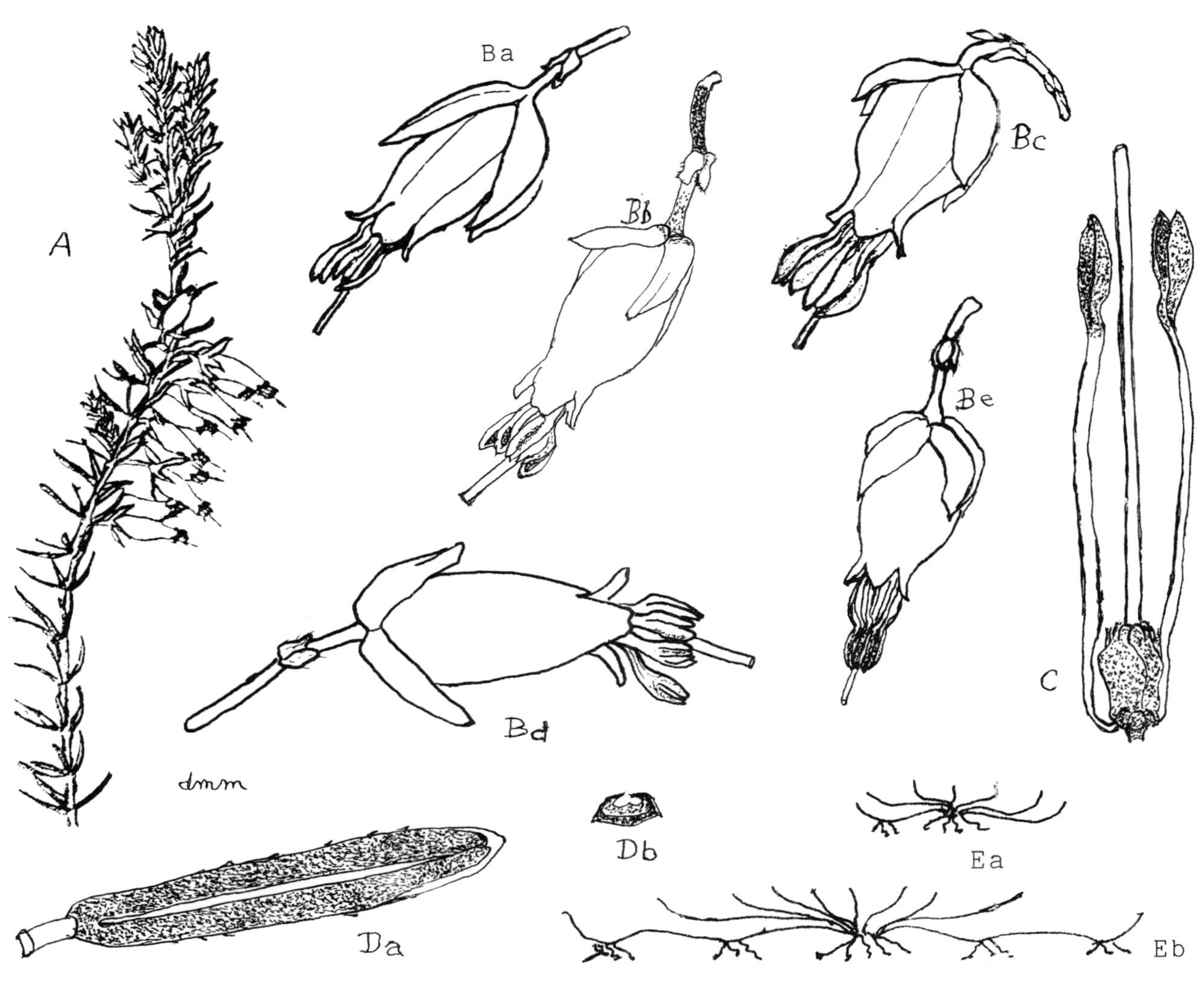

Erica carnea L. (syn. ***E. herbacea*** L.): A, flowering stem 'Springwood White' 1X; B, flowers 5X: Ba, wild form; Bb, 'Cecilia M. Beale'; Bc, 'Ruby Glow'; Bd, 'Springwood White'; Be, 'Vivellii'; C, pistil and 2 stamens, 'Cecilia M. Beale' 10X; Da, stem leaf beneath 10X; Db, leaf cross section 10X; Ea, habit 'Cecilia M. Beale'; Eb, habit 'Springwood White.'

---

taken into consideration when locating them in the garden.

E. carnea is distinguished from other hardy erica species by its exserted anthers, its pedicel about as long as the sepals, and its procumbent and more or less hairless stems with ridges running down more or less evenly from the leaf bases. Its leaves are 5-8 mm long (3/16-5/16 in), in whorls of four, taper to an acute angle or even have a small sharp point at the tip, and have their margins rolled back to nearly cover the lower surface. It is particularly distinguished by its flowering season: winter, where the winters are mild; spring, where winters are more harsh.

As the multitude of *E. vagans* seedlings appearing in my garden and the very few seedlings of *E. carnea* resemble each other at a glance, I need some way of distinguishing them before flowering age. As seen through a 10X lens, the under sides of *E. carnea* leaves show only a single furry white stripe visible between the rolled-back margins. The under sides of the leaves of *E. vagans* show a pattern of two white stripes with the green midrib between them.

The flowering racemes are terminal on the stems; the corollas, 5-7mm long (3/16-1/4 in), according to the cultivar, and the flowers do not quite surround the stem. Those of the common wild type (available as *E. carnea*), 'Springwood Pink' and others open a pallid pink and intensify to brighter color as their long season progresses. Some cultivars are bright-colored throughout their season, 'King George' and 'Porter's Red', for example. What gives particular sparkle to such cultivars as 'King George' (deep pink), 'Sherwood's Early Red'(deep pink), 'Eileen Porter' (deep pink to red) and 'Pink Spangles' (bright pink) is the contrast of the white, or in any case much paler, sepals against the more intense-colored corollas. And such as 'Vivellii' (deep pink, with bronze new foliage tips) are intensified in color by the darker pink, or even reddish sepals supporting their show, while 'Alan Coates' corollas (bright pink) are brighter colored at the lip. The firiest red *carnea* in my garden are the flowers of 'Porter's Red', slightly outdoing 'Myretoun Ruby' which was given a First Class Certificate by the Royal Horticultural Soc. in 1988.

In the garden, *E. carnea* is very tolerant of a variety of growing conditions, but not to a direct blast of automobile exhaust. As leafy new growth tends to quite quickly conceal spent flowers in late spring, necessity for trimming is mostly reduced to keeping the plant in bounds. If trimming is indicated it should be done at the end of the flowering season, because the next winter's flower buds are set in summer (by July in a Seattle garden), and later trimming will remove next winter's flowers. I have cut a hopelessly over-grown 15-year-old bed of 'Springwood White' and its seedlings back to the ground; and after six months 3-inch shoots (8 cm) were dotting the site; a year later the bed was back to flourishing again, resurrected from its roots. But success of so drastic a procedure is not guaranteed with all cultivars of all ages. Occasionally a plant will become barren of foliage and flowers at its center. Whatever the cause, the treatment suggested is to trim the plant's long-growing stems back somewhat and give the bare spot a cover of mixed sand and damp peat, which will encourage new growth to sprout from the center.

My experience indicates that *carnea* situated in part shade, though a little later to open its flowers, will keep fresh flower color considerably later in the spring than those exposed to full sun.

In selecting cultivars for the garden, a prime consideration must be the plant's growing habit, which can range all the way from the modestly compact and very slow-growing 'Cecilia M. Beale' and 'Snow Queen' to such ground-covering cultivars as 'Springwood White', which sometimes seems to have ambition to cover the earth. If you are looking for ground covers, the more or less rampant varieties are:

'Accent'	'Pink Spangles' (NA) +
'C.J.Backhouse' (NA)	'Pirbright Rose' (NA)
'December Red' (NA)	'Sherwood Creeping'
'Foxhollow' (NA)	'Smart's Heath'
'Foxhollow Fairy' (NA)	'Springwood Pink' (NA) +
'James Backhouse' (NA)	'Springwood White' (NA) +
'Loughrigg' (NA)	'Sunshine Rambler'

(NA), on the North American cultivar list, March 1983.(4)

+, especially wide spreading.

Foliage color of the cultivars ranges through lighter and darker shades of green with other color variations:

'Adrienne Duncan', dark bronze
'Ann Sparkes', yellow turning bronze-red in winter
'Aurea', golden
'Foxhollow', light yellow
'Jack Stitt', red in spring (sometimes listed incorrectly as an *E. x darleyensis* cultivar)
'Lesley Sparkes', new growth creamy, tipped salmon
'Sherwoodii', yellow-green
'Smart's Heath', bronze-tipped
'Sunshine Rambler', yellow
'Vivellii', bronze

E. carnea cultivars used fortunately in the landscape can be heart-warming jewels in very dreary winter weather when such embellishments are not common, between October and April. Add to these recommendations its ability to withstand the eastern North America winter cold, and a degree of alkalinity in the soil and it must be at the top of any list of most useful heaths.

References:

1) Nichols, Beverly: *MERRY HALL*, 1953.

2) McClintock, David: *A GUIDE TO THE NAMING OF PLANTS*, 1980.

3) *FLORA EUROPAEA*, 1972.

4) Eighme, Lloyd: *Heathers in North American Gardens*, *HEATHER NEWS*, No. 21, Mar. 1983.

ERICA CILIARIS L.

E. ciliaris L., the Dorset Heath or Fringed Heath, is a resident of Dorset, Cornwall and Devon in southern England, and of Portugal, Spain, the western half of France and a small spot in Connemara, Ireland. In the latter location, however, as reported by Dr. E. C. Nelson(1), there are just six plants, a biotype and possibly a single clone, which flower very late (autumn) and have not been found to set seed. If it is a relict population, as Dr. Nelson points out, comfort can be taken from the fact that "this colony has survived intact for over 130 years since the species was first seen in Connemara . . . . At least the Dorset Heath is tenacious!"

Its tiny ovate to oblong-lanceolate leaves, 2-4 mm long (3/32-3/16 in), are usually arranged in whorls of three. All of its vegetative top, when seen at close hand, is sparklingly decorated with gland-tipped hairs (cilia, whence its name), those on the apparent margins of the leaves at neatly spaced intervals. The leaf margins are revolute but only to cover up to 1/3 of the under surface. When its flowers appear for their long July-October season, they are uniquely bottle-shaped, with a well-defined neck topped by the small reflexed lobes of the corolla. Flowers of some cultivars, e. g. 'Wych,' have narrower, more pronounced necks than others. The corollas, which are 8-12mm long (5/16-1/2 in), appear in terminal racemes with the flower often standing out at right angles to the stems, very regularly, in 2, 3, or 4 directions. As the spent bells are left behind down the stem while fresh blossoms and swelling buds supersede them toward the top, the inflorescence keeps its comely appearance for the duration of the season. Maxwell-Patrick(2), who lived and worked in Dorset, say the inhabitants where *E. ciliaris* is native refer to it as "the pink heather." Many of its flowers are bright, clear pink, except where they are red, white or bicolored. In the wild it is a straggly plant, the wood softer and limper than that of other hardy heathers, and *ciliaris*, regrettably, is the least freeze tolerant of the British natives.

On Hartland Moor, in Dorset, where the botanist accompanying our Heather Society group declared the soil of that gently rolling ground to be "the most infertile in Britain," *E. ciliaris* set itself up in the lower areas where the surface layer of peat was closer to the water table. *E.cinerea* preferred the sandier hillock tops, and *Calluna* the peaty slopes. We did not see *E. tetralix* in that particular area, though it is reported to join *E. ciliaris* in other stands where it seeks out still wetter boggy places. The whole area had suffered from Britain's 1976 drought but, 3 years later, was making a good comeback. Maxwell-Patrick say *ciliaris* plants, being easily crushed by grazing animals, "are often replaced for this reason by members of the three common and more purposeful species."

In the garden, *ciliaris* succeeds very well in ordinary acid soil where it gets periodic watering in dry spells so that its roots do not dry out. Unpruned in the garden *ciliaris* plants will become thick pillows of tangled stems, and the inside

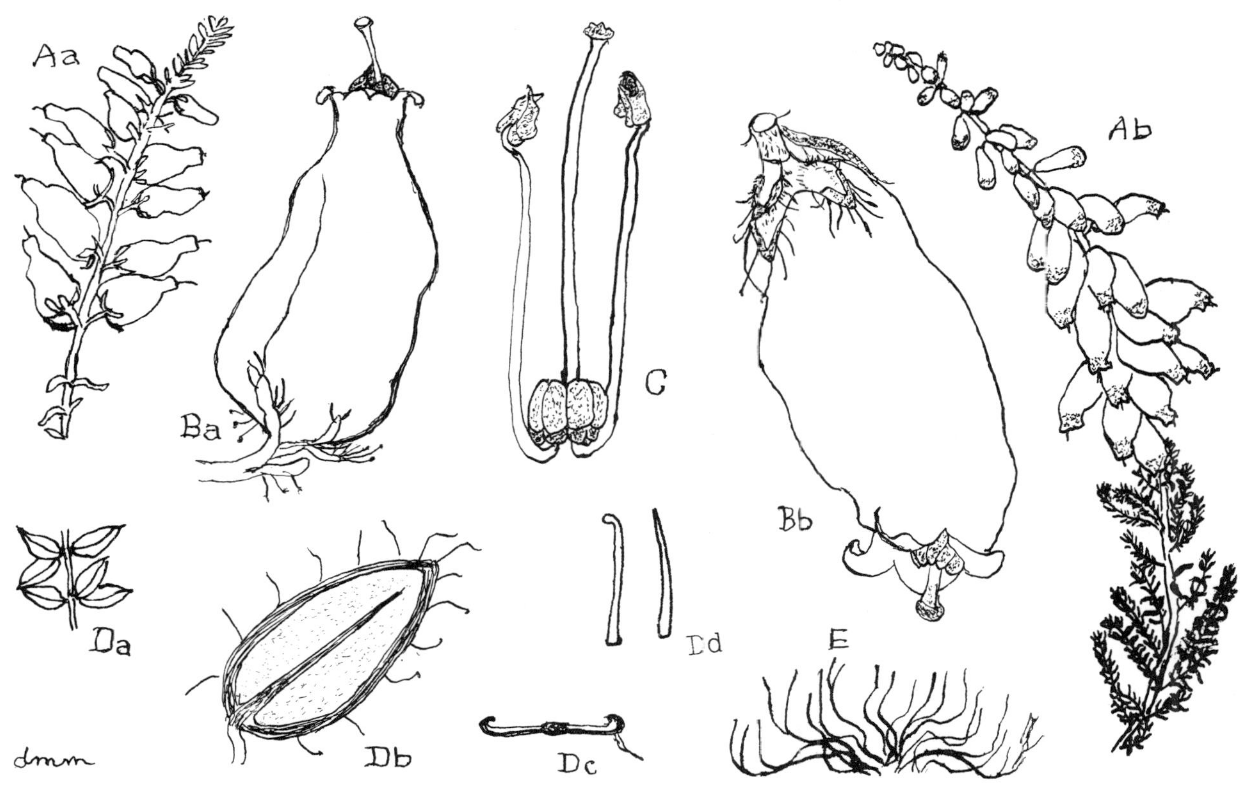

Erica ciliaris L.: Aa, inflorescence 'Wych' 1X; Ab, 'David McClintock' 1X; Ba, flower 'Wych' 5X; Bb, flower 'David McClintock' 5X; C, pistil and 2 stamens 5X; Da, leaf whorls 2X; Db, leaf beneath 10X; Dc, leaf cross section 10X; Dd, glandular and eglandular leaf cilia ca. 40X; E, plant habit.

---

stems will suffocate. Annual pruning and thinning out will keep them in more attractive condition.

The horrendous freeze around Puget Sound of November 1955 (-15°C, 5°F) with no snow cover, meant sudden death to *E. ciliaris*; it will be damaged by but may survive similar low temperatures later in the winter,but successive attacks of such cold may finally be too much for some cultivars. On the other hand, other cultivars, though sometimes cut back, may survive through one, two, three or more not too severe freezes. They may emerge with dead tops but then come back from the roots. The older, thicker stems seem to suffer more bark damage (and therefore dieback) than the younger, narrower ones.

On Hartland Moor there seemed a considerable range of flower and foliage color, but the published cultivar list is relatively short. Yates(3) lists a baker's dozen, but as I am familiar with only the cultivars in my garden and they are very good plants, I shall mention only those. All of these plants are broader than they are high. (No self-sown *ciliaris* seedling has ever appeared here.) The following will be back after a winter freeze of 7°F (-14°C):

'Aurea' This is the only yellow-leaved *ciliaris* so far in trade. It is a good plant with some, if not many mauve flowers, still evident into October. It is 40 cm high, 60 cm wide (16 x 24 in).

'Corfe Castle' Another cultivar unmistakable with its bright cerise flowers. Like its namesake, ancient Corfe Castle which spreads picturesquely over a hilltop between Hartland Moor and the English Channel, it is a lovely addition to the landscape. It is 30 cm high, 40 cm wide (12 x 16 in).

'David McClintock' Unique bicolor bells, the mauve at the corolla tips tending to suffuse the whole flower as the season progresses. A strong grower, it is 55 cm high, 70 cm wide (22 x 28 in). Only a few flowers are left in October.

'Maweana' Flower buds are an impressive ruby color and expand to gradually become more mauve, giving an over-all pink effect. An unpruned plant has grown to 30 cm high (12 in). Yates thinks this one less hardy than the others, and experience here indicates he may be right.

'Mrs. C. H. Gill' Plants acquired in 1961, expired from 16°F (-9°C) in 1972. Another group acquired in 1967 were hard hit by 9°F (-14°C), Jan. 1968, but recovered and remained in reasonably good shape since. Now its tops look dead again, but there are hopeful small bits of green around the bases of the plants. It is 50 cm high, 60 cm wide (20 x 24 in). Flowers a rather intense mauve and still good in October.

"Forma Rosea" Not recognized as a cultivar, but listed in Yates's "Other Names", and the plant in my garden has survived several freezes, with at least half its top green. Its flowers are pinker than mauve, the foliage dark green. It is a moderate grower, 35 cm high, 50 cm wide (14 x 20 in), and has good flowers in October. No real freeze trouble after 13 winters in the garden. It seems it should be given official status.

'Stoborough' Undoubtedly handsome, with white flowers and medium green foliage, but three plants acquired in 1961 and two in 1967 gradually succumbed to freezes in the 1970s. It is attractive enough to be worth trying again.

'Wych' A not very vigorous grower, 30 cm high, 40 cm wide (12 x 16 in), but with large delicate shell-pink flowers still looking fresh in October. Of three plants acquired in 1969, one survived for four years and then succumbed.

References:

1) Nelson, E. C.:*Erica ciliaris in Connemara*, November 1981, *YEAR BOOK OF THE HEATHER SOCIETY*, 1982.

2) Maxwell, D. F. and P. S. Patrick: *THE ENGLISH HEATHER GARDEN,* 1966.

3) Yates, Geoffrey: *POCKET GUIDE TO HEATHER GARDENING*, 1978.

ERICA CINEREA L.

"It is perhaps the most beautiful of the dwarf summer- and autumn-flowering heaths and produces an enormous profusion of blossom"(1), and "This is the commonest of British Heaths, as opposed to the Heather (*Calluna vulgaris*) and the most spectacular in flower of all those hardy enough to grow in our climate . . . ."(2) All those who object to greyed flower color can without question turn to *E. cinerea*, whose clear colors, in a recklessly mixed bed, are joyfully vivid, many with a glowing luminous quality.

To the English, it is The Bell Heather; to the Scots, Scottish Heath; and it has also been referred to by numerous other common names, none of which appears to have followed it to North America. However, its Latin name, *Erica cinerea* has been undisputed since Linnaeus published it in 1753.(3) The specific epithet is from the Latin word for ashes, (cf. cinders) referring to the somewhat greyed pubescent new growth stem color.

Its natural habitat is on rocky ground, in woods, and over dry moorland in well-drained acid soil(4). I have seen it growing out of rock crevices, but that was in western Scotland where prolonged summer drought is not expected. It extends from about the southern quarter of Norway and the Faeroe Islands south into northern Portugal, Spain and Italy; and from the British Isles in the west to western Germany, but in Holland occurs only in the southeast corner where there is high ground (to 1,000 ft, 300 m). It has been reported to be rarely naturalized in Massachusetts and on Nantucket Island(5). Of its occurrence in Britain, Bean says, "In cultivated ground in the Thames Valley it is apt to be short-lived, growing too fast in the early summer and often scorched by excessive heat in July and August." It is highly calcifuge.

E. cinerea is a dwarf, generally rather lax-growing shrub, though there are some more upright cultivars. Its height can range from 10 cm and 12 cm (4-5 in) to 75 cm (30 in) in the wild.(4) A baker's dozen cultivars are described(6) as 15 cm (6 in) plants, a dozen cultivars as reaching 35 cm (14 in), and some can reach 40-45 cm (16-18 in). The great majority fall in the 20-25-30 cm (8-10-12 in) range.

The leaves have a distinctive arrangement in complicated bundles on short side shoots from the stems below the terminal flowering racemes. The foliage color is usually dark, medium or bright green; but there are a number of cultivars with shades of pale or golden yellow, or even bronze leaves, which in winter deepen to from bright red to mahogany.

The terminal racemes or umbels are of urn-shaped flowers, which vary conspicuously in size as well as in color, have 4 slender sepals with scarious margins, to 3 of which the small bracteoles are appressed. The corolla lobes can be erect or spreading; the anthers are included and the exserted stigma is capitate. If you have a sufficient range of cultivars, one or another of them will

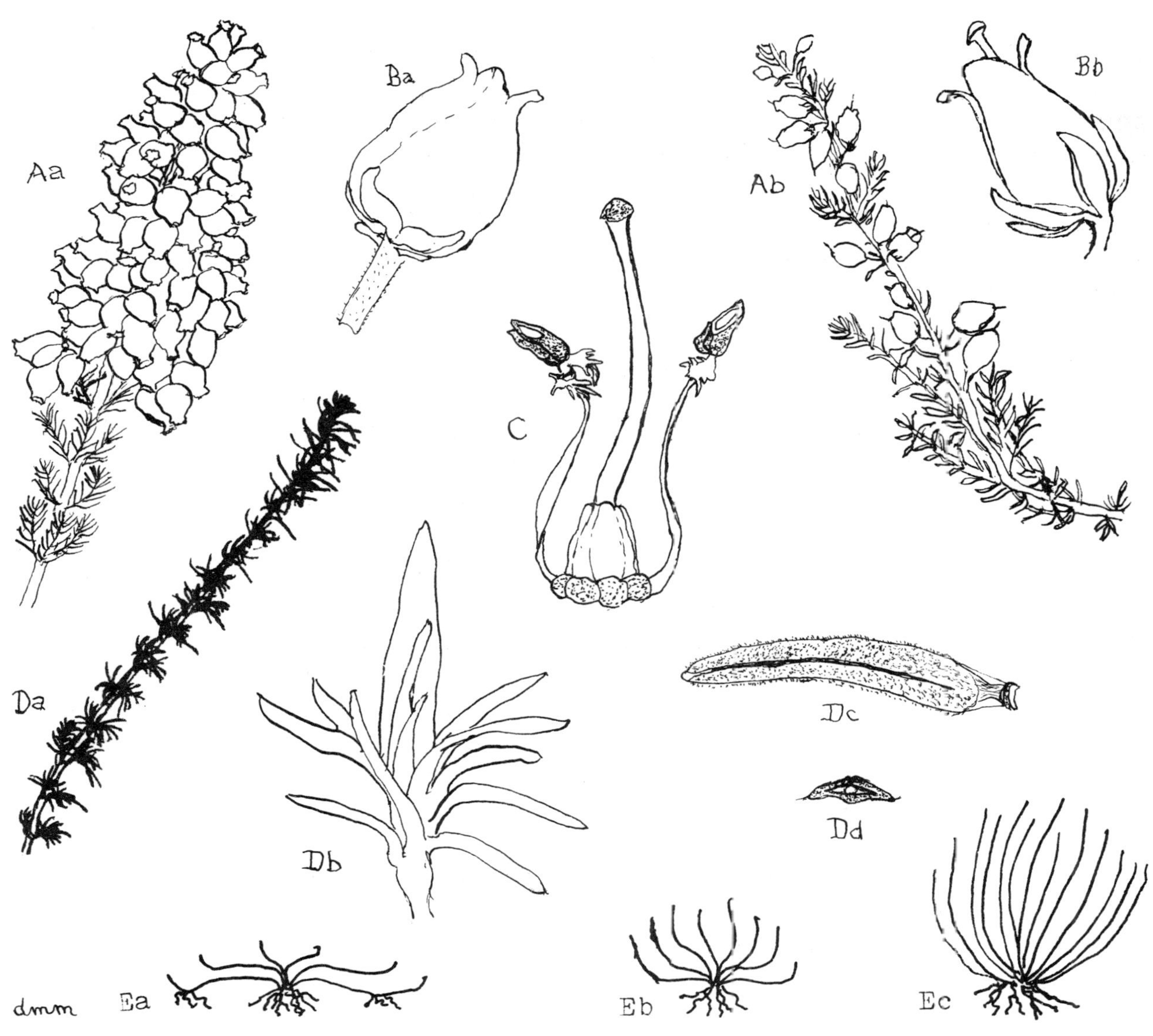

Erica cinerea L.: Aa, inflorescence 'Colligan Bridge' 1X; Ab, inflorescence 'P.S.Patrick' 1X; Ba, flower 'Colligan Bridge' 5X; Bb, flower 'P.S.Patrick' 5X; C, pistil and 2 stamens 10X; Da, leaf arrangement on stem 1X; Db, lateral shoot 10X; Dc, leaf beneath 10X; Dd, leaf cross section 20X; E, plant habits: Ea, 'Golden Drop'; Eb, 'Alba Minor;' Ec, 'Golden Hue,' 'Rose Queen.'

---

be flowering from May or June to November.

It should be mentioned here that as long ago as ca. 1575 a Belgian plant lover was reported to be growing an *E. cinerea* (though not by that name), a curiosity with its corollas more or less split into 4 petals. Similar variations began being reported in Britain in the 19th Century, and in 1912 a botanist surmised that these plants must be hybrids between *E. cinerea* and *Calluna vulgaris*. In 1960, Dr. Gerd Krussmann published, in *DEUTSCHE BAUMSCHULE*, a new hybrid, *X Ericalluna bealeana* with the cultivar 'W.G.Notley' as the type of the species. Other botanists could not agree, and finally, a few years later, Dr. Krussmann himself had become convinced that these plants were just abnormal forms of *E. cinerea* rather than hybrids.(7). There are other named forms of this oddity (*f. schizopetala*(6), 'Winifred Whitley'), but they are more interesting botanically than as garden embellishments. There are other variations of form with assorted characteristics, all botanical curiosities rather than of garden value. For example, among the many *E. cinerea* seed plants that have appeared in my garden is one with attractive yellow and green foliage, seeming to have no flowers but dark red color at the stem tips, which turns out on lens inspection to be tiny flowers with no corollas. It has been diagnosed by Mr. McClintock as *E. cinerea var. kreussmaniana subvar. depauperata.* All this for a plant not worth naming! But I'm rather fond of it.

A species with so northerly a range might be expected to endure severe cold with no damage, but this is not always the case. Plants of *cinerea* in the Pacific Northwest showed varying degrees of damage following the December 1983 cold, (to 9°F, -13°C), and Mr. Julian's comments in his assessment of winter damage at Harlow Car following Britain's hard winter of 1978-79 are to the point: "37 of a total planting of 75 were damaged in some degree; however most of the plants have recovered substantially. Unlike the *Calluna* plants, stems of the *cinereas*, in the areas where the foliage had died, have thrown up new shoots; also new growth has appeared at the bases of some of the dead stems. Many of the damaged plants have flowered freely and should regain their normal shape."(9) Some cultivars are more resistent to cold than others.

About growing *E. cinerea*, Maxwell and Patrick wrote, "The roots of *E. cinerea* are generally longer, looser and less fibrous than those of any other species of dwarf heather . . . the most difficult . . . is 'Golden Drop' . . . it is quite a problem to move young plants with a ball of soil still round the roots, and the number of casualties is abnormally high . . . it is safer to give the young plants plenty of space in the nursery beds and not attempt to move them until early middle age." **Pot plants are the safest buy.**(8) Their soil needs to be acid and well-drained, but moisture-retentive. Yates(6) says, "It enjoys a hot, dry position if planted with generous quantities of peat or other humus."

An annual pruning back will keep the beds in handsomer condition.

As indicated above, they can be grown from seed; but if plants of a particular cultivar are wanted they must be propagated by soft cuttings in early summer.

Yates(6) listed 125 cultivars in 1978, others have been introduced since then. It can be said that every one of these is a good plant, though there is considerable variation in the amount, size and season of flower among them. They flower early in the summer and there is not a muddy color in the lot. Every seedling can be confidently expected to have enjoyable color. This being said, the choices remain of foliage color, height of plant and flower colors, ranging from white, and bicolor white-pink or white-lavender, through amethyst, mauve, lavender, lilac, ruby, cerise, rose pink, lighter to darker shades of pink, shell pink, paler or deeper salmon, magenta, crimson, heliotrope, purple, to beetroot and the darkest of all, 'Velvet Night', an extraordinary dark red-purple with blackish areas on the corollas, which to be seen needs to be against some kind of lighter background, yellow foliage or a grey rock.

In my garden, one of the taller and most enduring cultivars has been 'Rose Queen,' with plentiful deep rose pink flowers, it is also the lone survivor of a good deal of neglect in the Washington Park Arboretum, Seattle. Equally in the among-those-present list is the little 'Alba Minor'. After 20 years, it is still just 15 cm high and of 40 cm diameter (6 X 16 in), its foliage bright green and its white flowers shining through a long season. 'Golden Drop', eventually a low-growing mat with tangled stems, produces only a sprinkling of dark mauve flowers, but is admired for its foliage, golden in summer and turning to almost mahogany red in winter, depending on the amount of cold. 'Golden Hue', on the other hand, is a 60 cm (24 in) upright-stemmed variety, with lemon yellow foliage in summer, becoming bright red in winter. It completely gave up producing its vivid purple flowers after just 5 years in the garden, but its foliage is so attractive that the perhaps too contrasting flowers are not missed. I prefer it not cut back. It seems unfair not to mention each one of all the cultivars we have grown. Try whatever you can find available.

". . . in the central Highlands in Scotland, I came across a southeast facing hillside covered with large irregular patches of rich purple Bell Heath (this was July so none of the *Calluna* had flowered yet). It was unusual, in that such large colonies of the Bell Heath are rare, though the rather dry, stony hillside would account for its healthy proliferation. Purple is the common color of the wild plant . . . ."—Stuart Fraser.(10)

References:

1) Bean, W. J.: *TREES & SHRUBS HARDY IN THE BRITISH ISLES*, 1973 ed.

2) Haworth-Booth, Michael: *THE FLOWERING SHRUB GARDEN TODAY*, 1961.

3) McClintock, David: A GUIDE TO THE NAMING OF PLANTS, 1980.

4) *FLORA EUROPAEA*, 1972 ed.

5) Seymour, F. C.: *THE FLORA OF NEW ENGLAND*, 1969.

6) Yates, Geoffrey: *POCKET GUIDE TO HEATHER GARDENING*, 1978.

7) McClintock, David: *Bell Heathers With Split Corollas, THE PLANTSMAN*, Vol. 2, No. 3, 1981.

8) Maxwell, D. F. & P. S. Patrick: *THE ENGLISH HEATHER GARDEN*, 1966.

9) Julian, T. A.: *Winter Damage at Harlow Car, YEAR BOOK OF THE HEATHER SOCIETY*, 1980.

10) Fraser, Stuart: *Erica cinerea cultivars, HEATHER NEWS*, No. 14, June 1981, p. 3.

ERICA X DARLEYENSIS Bean

Erica x darleyensis Bean, synonym *E. mediterranea hybrida* Hort., is commonly offered at nurseries in a cultivar form as "Med. Pink" or "Med. White." It is a hybrid between *E. carnea* L. and *E. erigena* R. Ross. It is natural for all of us to look with interest on new forms, in the gardener's case forms of plants, and to give them an enthusiastic welcome if they appear to have some new and desirable qualities. And so it was when a new and different plant appeared by chance, early in the 1890s, in the nursery of James Smith & Son, Darley Dale, Derbyshire. The nursery proprietors, assuming the plant to be a cross between *E. carnea* and *E. erigena* (then called *E. mediterranea*), marketed it as *E. mediterranea hybrida*. W. J. Bean, noted British horticulturist, in 1900 reported it as *E. hybrida*, a name already assigned to a South African *Erica* and so not available for the new plant. Other epithets were suggested, but in 1914 Bean, having realized his earlier error, published, in the first edition of his famous *TREES AND SHRUBS HARDY IN THE BRITISH ISLES*, *Erica x darleyensis* (honoring Darley Dale), which accords with the presently accepted International Code of Botanical Nomenclature, and so has been the correct name ever since.(1)

The assumption that this plant was the result of cross fertilization between *EE. carnea* and *erigena* was made because of its character midway between those two species, which are themselves very closely related. So far as is known, the available cultivars listed under *E. x darleyensis* have mostly resulted from chance cross fertilizations of cultivated plants. The species do not occur in proximity to one another in the wild. Until relatively recently, assignment of the plants as of hybrid origin has been based on surmise. Beginning in 1972, Mrs. Anne Parris, then in southeast Wales, undertook to make controlled crosses using *E. erigena* as the female and *E. carnea* as the male parent, and raised seven plants resembling the *E. x darleyensis* taxon(2), thus helping to confirm the assumption.

In the 1970s, microscope and scanning electron microscope examinations revealed a difference in the shapes of the pollen grains of the parent species, those of *E. carnea* being spherical, and of *E. erigena* being roughly pyramidal. Those of *E. x darleyensis* cultivars so far examined had a collapsed appearance and contained no cytoplasm from which growth could start, a character which can be indicative of hybridity.(3)

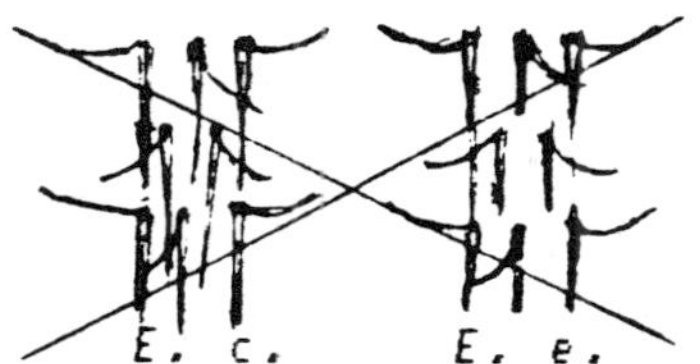

For centuries botanists have been disagreeing on classification of the two parent species. Suggested criteria for differentiating them have included **habit:** *E. carnea* procumbent with ascending branches, *E. erigena* erect; **infrafoliar stem ridges**: *E. carnea* constant width and running from leaf base down through an internode, *E. erigena*, ridges petering out before arriving at next internode, but this has not proven valid; **leaf apexes: E. carnea** acute to apiculate, *E. erigena* obtuse to subacute; **anthers:** *E. carnea* usually exserted, *E. erigena* usually only part exserted. But the botanists' "usually" renders some of these criteria often unhelpful. No one seems to have mentioned that, often, **sepals** of *E. carnea* are somewhat divergent from the corollas, and those of *E. erigena* clasp the corollas.

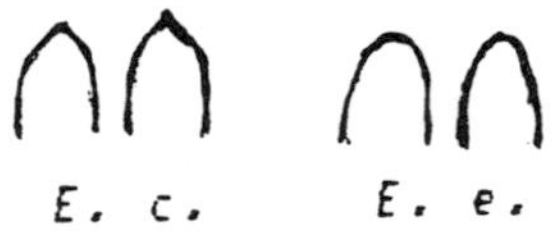

In any case, the cultivars considered to be of *E. x darleyensis* show degrees of colored foliage at the leaf apex, especially in the spring when the new-growth foliage can be cream to bright copper-gold. On this subject A. W. Jones(3) says one can safely assume that if a hardy winter-flowering heath plant does not have colored foliage it is not a hybrid, but if it does there is still a slight chance that it is not. With some *E. x darleyensis* cultivars, one must wait for the spring new growth to see this color; e.g., *E. x d.* 'Silberschmelze' leaves are entirely green in December.

No botanist's description of this taxon is available, but observation of the limited selection of cultivars in my garden seems to suggest the following characteristics as compared with those of *E. carnea* and *E. erigena*:

habit: the cultivars of *E. x darleyensis* are very vigorous- growing plants with ascending branches and no main stems.

height: 50-100 cm (1.5 to 3 ft).

width: one and one-half to two or more times the height.

infrafoliar stem ridges: varying.

foliage: whorls of 4 or 5, leaves sometimes larger than in parent species, more or less variegated by yellow at the apex, margins revolute, mostly tightly contiguous and apparent margins entire.

apexes: obtuse, subacute or acute, but none apiculate.

inflorescences: racemes of varying lengths on well-branched stems.

pedicels: ca. 4 mm (5/32 in) long, perhaps generally longer than those of either parent, with bracteoles at or above the middle.

corollas: 4.5-6 mm (3/16-1/4 in) long, crowded around or secund on stems.

sepals: (3.5-)4 mm long.

anthers: partly exserted.

stigmas: no wider than style.

In the Pacific Northwest they flower for several months between October and May, varying with the cultivar and climate where growing.—They are more resistant to freeze than *E. erigena*, less than *E. carnea*. My first 'Darley Dale' came in 1937 and has survived all freezes, however harsh, since. None of the

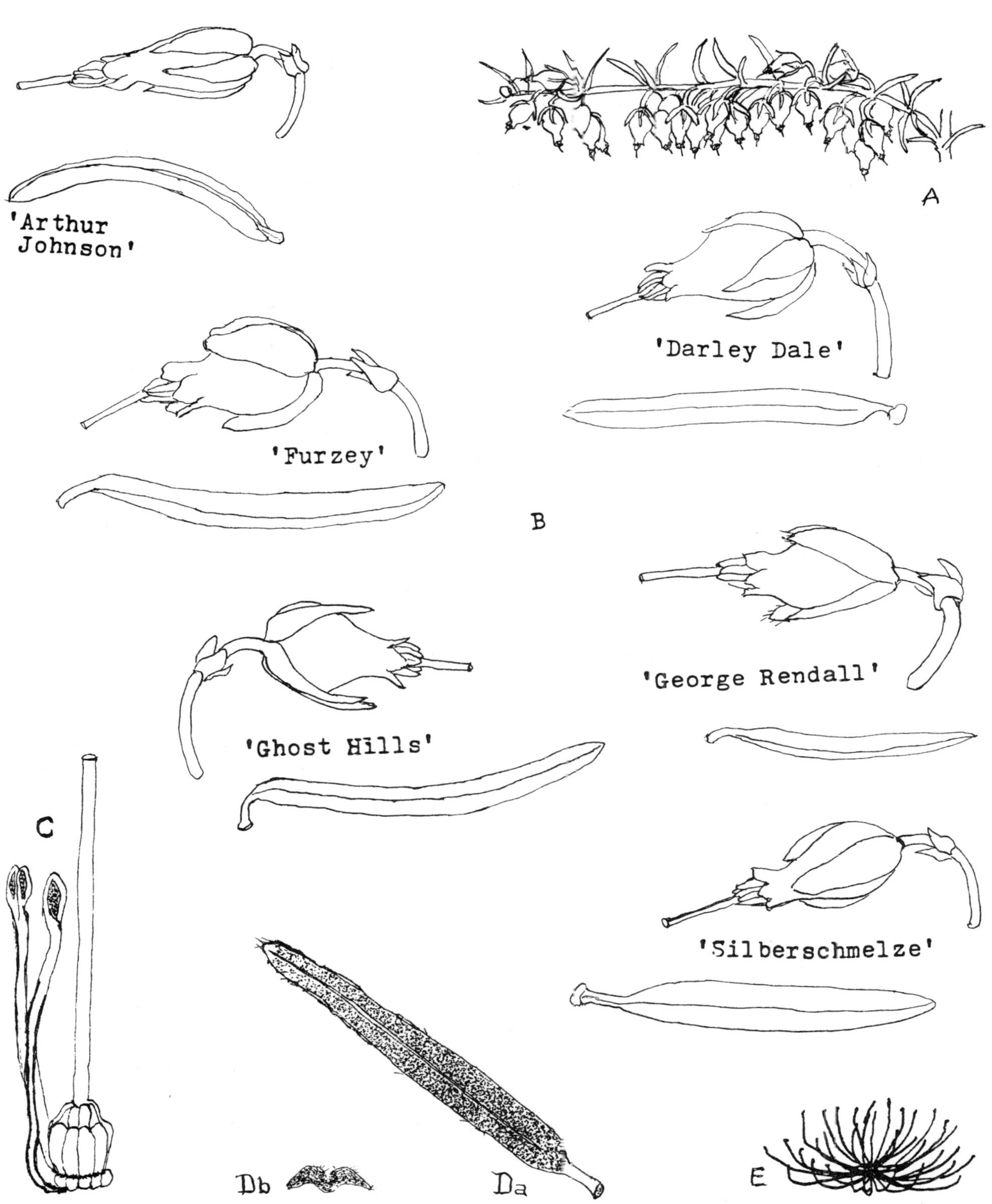

Erica x darleyensis Bean: A, inflorescence *E. x d.* 'Darley Dale' 1X; B, flowers 5X; C, pistil and 2 stamens 'Darley Dale' 10X; Da, stem leaf 'Silberschmelze' 5X; Db, leaf cross section 10X; E, plant habit.

cultivars acquired since 1960 has been frost-killed, but 'Arthur Johnson' has been noticeably cut back. (The Daystar Nursery, of Litchfield, Maine, lists those we grow except 'Arthur Johnson.') *E. x darleyensis* are said to be tolerant of a wide variety of soils and conditions, including some lime but not stiff clay. They cannot be expected to flower well in solid shade. They may be pruned back in May, or soon after flowering is over, to keep them more compact, but this does not very much affect the size of mature plants. Pruning later in the season will remove the buds for next winter's flowers.

The cultivars we grow differ from each other in height, foliage color and flower color and season; but considering they presumably mostly originated from seed there is remarkably little difference in the shape and size of their florets. Before their flowers have been exposed to much sunlight, their color is a pale harbinger of what it will become; but when corollas are expanded, scrutiny with a 10X lens of the already colored styles will give a reliable clue to what is in store.

Geoffrey Yates(4) listed 16 *x darleyensis* cultivars. (He included 'Jack Stitt', which has since been determined to be *E. carnea*, not *x darleyensis*.) Of these, 10 were on the 1983 North American heather list. The six (cf. illustration) of which we have mature plants are:

'Arthur Johnson' The tallest grower, medium dark green foliage; lilac-pink flowers (heliotrope-lilac on Heather Soc. color card), Nov.-May. Somewhat damaged by December freeze to 9°F (-13°C).

'Darley Dale' Dark green foliage; rather muddy pale lilac-lavender flowers, but lots of them, commencing to open in October, just as the *vagans*, *cinerea* and *ciliaris* are on their way out and only the late *Calluna* and *Daboecia* are still really flowering; to May.

'Furzey' Very dark yellow-green foliage; flowers becoming deep pink (heliotrope on color card), Jan.-May.

'George Rendall' Medium green foliage, old leaves tending to yellow; flowers mauve-purple (amethyst on color card), Dec.- May.

'Ghost Hills' A beautiful, very floriferous shrub; foliage medium dark green; flowers warm bright pink (heliotrope on color card), Dec.-May.

'Silberschmelze' ('Molten Silver,' 'Alba', "Med. White") Relatively large dark green leaves, many in whorls of 5; flowers appear white until seen against fresh snow, when the "silver" in its name is seen to be justified, very floriferous, Dec.-May.

Four further cultivars available in N. America are:

'Jack H. Brummage' A low-growing cultivar with heliotrope pink flowers; our August photograph of it at Royal Botanic Garden, Edinburgh shows glistening gold foliage tips; Yates(5) says it has orange and deeper gold tints in winter.

'Jenny Porter' Flowers so pale they can be described as white with a flush of pale lilac.

'J.W.Porter' Red tips to very dark foliage in spring; sparse pink flowers.

'Margaret Porter' 20 cm (8 in) high, spreading but not tall; deep lilac flowers.

Other desirable cultivars, concerning which Mr. A. W. Jones has written(6) are:

'Ada S. Collings' White flowered. "Highly regarded by some people. . . "

'White Perfection' "David McClintock and I both consider it to be outstanding . . . Here [Somerset, England] it flowers from mid-September until I trim it in late April . . . the flowers are rather creamy-white, and totally different to the other whites . . . "

References:

1) McClintock, David: *A GUIDE TO THE NAMING OF PLANTS*, 1980.

2) Parris, Anne A.: *Notes on a cross between Erica erigena and E. carnea. YEAR BOOK OF THE HEATHER SOC.*, 1976-77-78-80.

3) Jones, A. W.: *The Classification of Hardy Winter-flowering Heaths with Notes on Erica x darleyensis. YEAR BOOK OF THE HEATHER SOC.*, 1979.

4) Yates, Geoffrey: *POCKET GUIDE TO HEATHER GARDENING*, 1978.

5) Yates, Geoffrey: *THE GARDENER'S BOOK OF HEATHERS*, 1985.

6) Jones, A. W.: personal communication, January, 1982.

ERICA ERIGENA R. Ross (E. MEDITERRANEA, E. HIBERNICA)

In the 400 years since botanists first referred to the Bay of Biscay populations of *E. erigena* and, since the western Ireland ones were discovered in 1830, the species has been given specific epithets: *mediterranea, lugubris, carnea var. occidentalis, mediterranea var. hibernica, hibernica, purpurascens, carnea ssp. occidentalis,* and in 1969 *erigena*. As this name accords with the now generally accepted Rules of Nomenclature of the International Botanical Congress, it can be hoped that these heaths are permanently released from the Purgatory of changing names.

Part of the difficulty stems from the fact that taxonomists, since and before the time of Linnaeus, have relied heavily on the characters of the reproductive parts of vascular plants to serve as significant criteria in their classification.(1) The flowers and fruiting structures of *E. erigena* are very similar to those of *E. carnea* except that the anthers of fully expanded flowers of *erigena* are usually (but not always) somewhat less exserted than those of fully expanded *carnea;* and the corolla lobes of *erigena* are usually (but not always) flared while those of *carnea* are usually pursed at the lip.

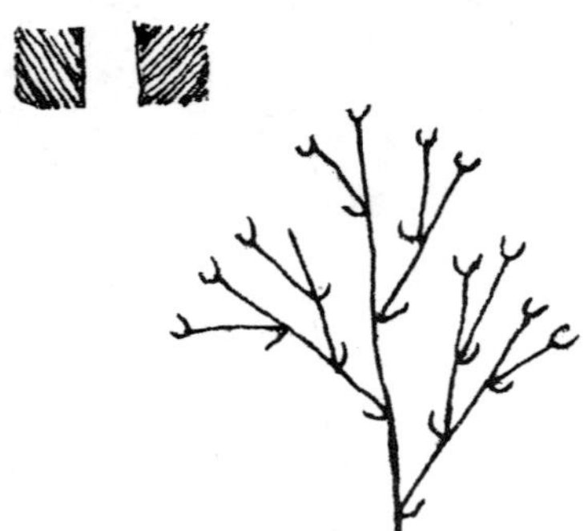

Also, *erigena* has linear leaves which are less acute at the apex, and are less completely revolute, so that there is a relatively wider white stripe beneath. In other respects, the vegetative differences are obvious: *E. erigena* is an erect-stemmed shrub, (30-)60-200cm (1-) 2-6.5 ft) tall; and the flowers, though smaller than those of many *carnea* cultivars, are often grouped into extensive panicles, which in most cases give an elegantly floriferous show over a period of months in winter-spring.

E. carnea is a low species of high in the Alps while *E. erigena* is a tall species of lowland areas in northern Portugal and Spain, southwest France (Gironde), and the west coast of Ireland (Mayo and Galway). Its Continental habitats are on siliceous soil; the Irish communities inhabit seaside bogs. Both locations are relatively mild and more or less humid. Also, it tolerates chalky or limy soils.

In the hardiness sweepstakes, the *carneas* win hands down. Rehder's(2) rating of Zone VI? (USDA 6b-7a) for *erigena* is certainly too optimistic. Hardiness varies rather widely with the cultivars. About 25 years' observation of 25 plants of 10 varieties of *erigena*, of which half survive, has shown that though most of their tops are killed by lower temperatures, they come back from their bases and are flowering again in two years. Our experience is that most *erigena* cultivars do pretty well down to about 15°F (-12°C), but below that there will be degrees of trouble. They have sometimes seemed to suffer more in exposed situations than where somewhat protected by groups of shrubs or walls, just

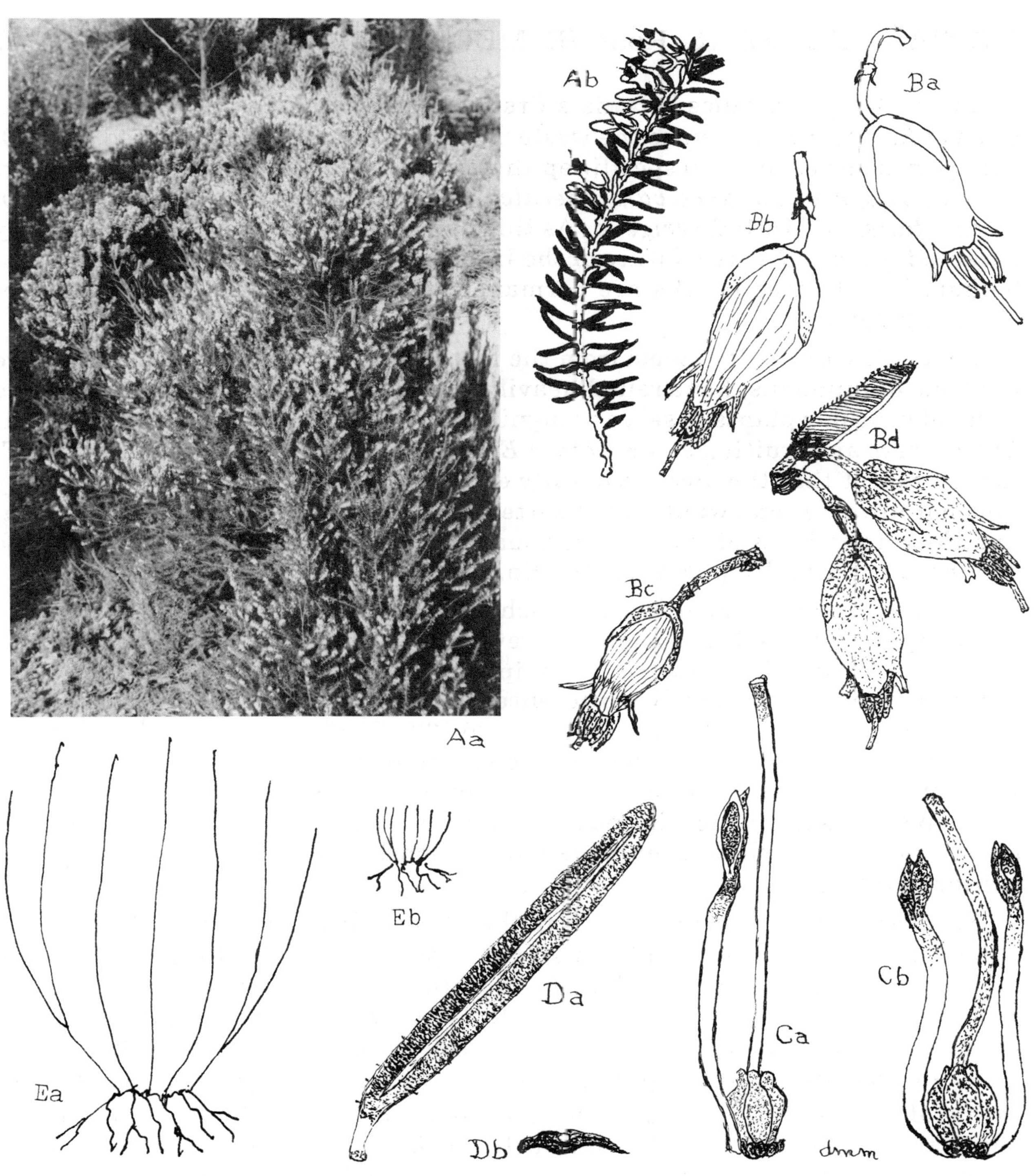

Erica erigena R. Ross Aa, 'Maxima,' plant; Ab, flowering stem tip, 'W.T.Rackliff' 1X; Ba, flower, 'W.T.Rackliff' 5X; Bb, flower, 'Superba' 5X; Bc, flower, 'Occidental Dwarf' 5X; Bd, flowers, 'Irish Dusk' 5X; Ca, pistil and 1 stamen, 'Superba' 10X; Cb, pistil and 2 stamens, 'Irish Dusk' 10X; Da, leaf, 'Maxima' 10X; Db, leaf cross section 20X; Ea, plant habit, 'Superba'; Eb, plant habit 'Occidental Dwarf.'

making sure that they are not unduly shaded out by receiving little or no sun. In the Puget Sound climate they are chancy, but rewarding for those with the patience to wait for the survivors to regrow from the base every few years.

The other winter hazard, if you are gardening where there is the likelihood of heavy snow, is that it can bend the somewhat brittle stems to breaking. To prevent this, where heavy snowfall may be expected, Maxwell-Patrick(3) suggest encircling the bush, half way up, with stout twine, looping it round the stronger outside branches, to give the plant support.

This is a species which we can't refrain from trying at the northern end of its range, but it should be ideal for such climates as northern California where its tolerance of a great range of soil conditions and summer heat may stand it (and the gardener) in good stead.

The cultivar heights mentioned below are those of my own mature plants. (The cultivar heights given by Yates (4) seem to bear not much relation to my plants at maturity, possibly because of climate difference.) As with many of the *carnea* cultivars, some *erigena* flower colors start pallid and then intensify as the spring progresses. The colors given here for my plants are as of mid-March in the Pacific Northwest.

Yates(4) listed 17 cultivars in 1978, and twice that many in 1985(5). I have had experience with, or at least seen, most of the following:

'Alba' Bright green foliage. Young plants I have had with this label were flowering generously in early March and at a very early age. Given height is 60 cm (2 ft). Unhappily, my plants did not survive long enough to even guess at their ultimate height here, freezing weather permitting.

'Brightness' A compactly erect shrub to 135 cm high and 70 cm wide (52 x 27 in). The flower buds are bright red and expand in February to small corollas, which by mid-March are are a light pink, with dark brown exserted anthers. Flower colors are sparklingly effective against the background of very dark bronze-green foliage. I had one plant 22 years before it succumbed to freeze. Its replacement was here only 5 years.

'Golden Lady' Said to have originated as a sport on 'W.T.Rackliff', it has year-round golden foliage and a sprinkling of white flowers beginning in February, and at an early age. Expected to achieve 60 cm (2 ft), but if so it must be slowly. One of my 2 plants has now succumbed to 7°F (-14°C), the other just managed to survive.

'Hibernica' This cultivar I have not grown, but our slide of it in the Washington Park Arboretum Rock Garden, in April 1967, showed it to be a 60 cm (2 ft) tall plant with light pink flowers against dark grey-green leaves. Two plants of this cultivar survived there for at least 15 years.

'Irish Dusk' This variety has flowers of a delicious deep peach-pink color against dark greyed foliage, from December to May. Probably grows to only 40 cm (16 in). Entire top killed by freeze, but is bravely coming back from the base.

'Irish Salmon' Said to have flowers of similar color, but a shorter Feb.-May season, lighter green leaves, and a taller, looser habit. These two were confused on introduction and Yates says thousands of 'Dusk' were mistakenly distributed under the 'Salmon' label.

'Maxima' Plants placed in front of a west-facing 4 ft high wall have grown to 6.6 ft high and 3 ft wide (2 m x 90 cm). Their flowers come a little later than some, expanding in March, at first a pale pink, but by the end of April have intensified to a very bright deep pink (heliotrope on the Heather Society Colour Chart.) Very floriferous and have made rapid comeback whenever mostly frozen to the ground.

'Nana Alba' Plants started from cuttings in spring 1961 were about 1 ft (30 cm) spherical bushes after six years, and 1.5 ft (45 cm) two growing seasons later. They somehow survived 1968-69, but gave up in 1978. Very copious white flowers in season while they lasted.

'Occidental Dwarf' This one, was given to me in 1975 by the Mathesons' Heather Farm, near Sebastopol, CA and is a unique dwarf with erect stems. Acquired in a 4 in pot, six years later it had grown no taller than 11 in (28 cm) with diameter of 11.5 in (29 cm), apparently its ultimate size. Its very dark foliage looks all but black in the garden. The leaves in compact whorls of 4, are up to 5 mm long, with apparent width of .75mm (3/16 x 1/32 in). The flowers are in short, 2 cm racemes (3/4 in) at the stem tips; from ruby buds, they expand, toward the end of March to bright little bells 4 mm long and 2 mm wide (1/8 x 3/32 in), mauve in center but keeping the ruby color on the sepals and at the corolla lips, with blackish anthers and very dark maroon style. It will not survive a really hard freeze, so taking cuttings is probably advisable as it is a rock garden natural.

'Superba' With 'Maxima', the strongest growing of the *erigenas* when young, this cultivar can increase by 10 in (25 cm) a year, and has reached 6 ft (195 cm) here with width of 5 ft (155 cm). It has endured in the garden for 25 years, sometimes drastically cut back by freeze, but regrowing strongly. The foliage is a good deep green and the heliotrope flowers, early out and long lasting, are noticeably plumper than those of the other cultivars we have.

'W.T.Rackliff' In its four-month flowering season, this cultivar is a mass of snow-white bells against foliage which is lighter on the new tip growth and then becomes a fine medium-deep green. In its first few years forming a rounded shrub, plants here have reached height of 4 ft (120 cm) and diameter of 3 ft (90 cm). Regrown several times from hard freeze damage, it now appears to have finally succumbed to the recent 7°F (-14°C). Plants less than five years old from cuttings have given up more easily. Considered in Britain to be among the hardier of the tall heaths.

References:

1) Lawrence, G. H. M.: *TAXONOMY OF VASCULAR PLANTS,* 1966 ed.

2) Rehder, Alfred: *MANUAL OF CULTIVATED TREES & SHRUBS,* 2nd ed., 1956.

3) Maxwell, D. F. & P. S. Patrick: *THE ENGLISH HEATHER GARDEN,* 1966.

4) Yates, Geoffrey: *POCKET GUIDE TO HEATHER GARDENING,* 1978.

5) Yates, Geoffrey: *THE GARDENER'S BOOK OF HEATHERS,* 1985.

ERICA LUSITANICA Rudolphi

The Portuguese Tree Heath has a fairly recently used synonym, *Erica codonodes* Lindley, but its publication did not occur until 36 years after the German, Rudolphi, in 1799, proposed *lusitanica*, priority of which makes it the valid one.(1)

It occurs naturally in damp heaths and along wood margins from southern Portugal up across Spain and into southwestern France(2). It is naturalized on railway embankments in Cornwall and on heath near the Poole Estuary in southwestern Britain.(3) The Proudleys(4) report having seen it growing naturally on dry barren hillsides. In France(5), it is said to be a plant of wasteland, moors and talus slopes. Obviously it does not require rich soil, but it must be lime-free or neutral.

In the wild *E. lusitanica* grows erect to 1-3.5 m (3-12 ft). In my Puget Sound garden the erect stems of a 16-year-old plant rose to 2.5 m (8 ft) and half as wide before being killed by freeze. Botanists relate it closely to *E. arborea*, and young plants of the two species are sometimes confused. Existence of *E x veitchii*, the hybrid more or less midway between them, further complicates the identification. Differences between the species are:

E. lusitanica		***E. arborea***
	new-growth hairs	
all short, simple		longer, some bristly-branched
	flower color	
cerise buds opening white		greenish white buds, white fls.
	corolla	
4-5 mm long, tubular		2.5-4 mm long, campanulate, with erect lobes
	stigma	
obconical, small, red		more or less broadly capitate
	ovary	
Greek vase-shaped		somewhat flattened spherical
	base of calyx	
non-saccate 		saccate, pouch-like 

These differences are easily observed with a 10X or higher lens. Further difference is in the leaf arrangement, those of *E. lusitanica* being partly in close-packed jumbles, while those of *E. arborea* are neatly spaced out on the stems.

Once the plant has achieved flowering there is no mistaking it. The buds at the tops of the massive panicles are bright deep pink where touched by the sun, approximately H6, cerise, on the Heather Society Colour Chart. (The only other tree heath with red flower buds, up to now, is *E. x veitchii* 'Pink Joy'.) As they

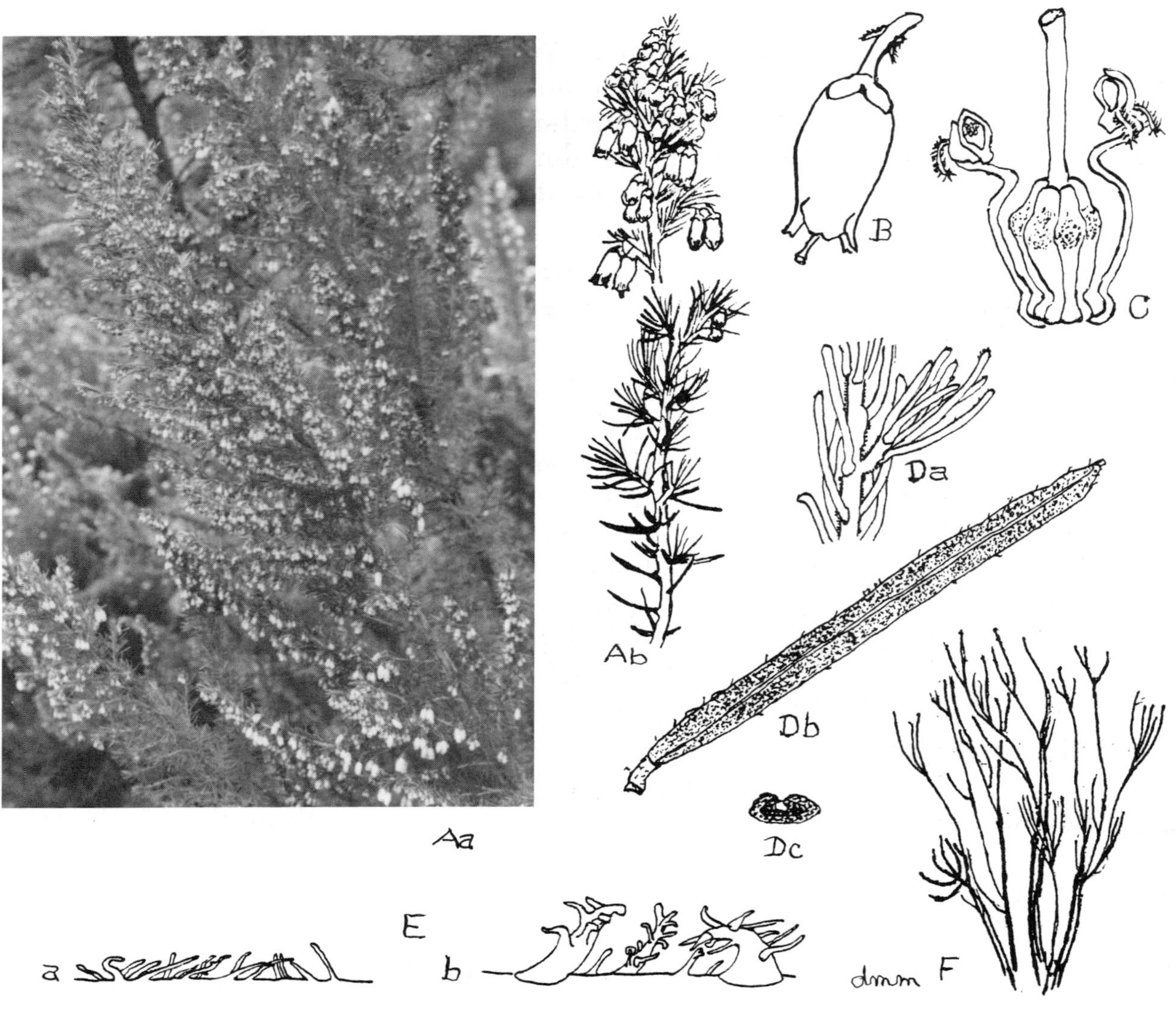

Erica lusitanica Rudolphi: Aa, flowering branches; Ab, flowering twig 1X; B, flower 5X; C, pistil and 2 stamens 10X; Da, leaf arrangement 3X; Db, leaf beneath 10X; Dc, leaf cross section 10X; E, new-growth stem hairs ca. 30X, a, *lusitanica*, b *arborea*; F, *E. lusitanica* plant habit.

---

expand from below upwards, the corollas gradually become white so that for several weeks there is a beautiful pink and white perfection of inflorescence. The flowers are slightly fragrant, but less so than those of *E. arborea*.

The flowering season depends to a certain extent on the weather. Provided the weather cooperates, its flower buds may be bright pink by early November and flowering can be expected to continue till April or May. The Heather Society(6) notes that it flowers better when untrimmed.

Unhappily *E. lusitanica* is much less hardy than is *E. arborea*. Bean(7) says it will tolerate 20° of frost, i.e. down to 12°F (-11°C), which approximately accords with my experience, though my last survivor of 10 plants lived through 8°F and 11°F (-13 °, -11.5°C) before succumbing to 9°F (-13°C) when in full flower in December. Perhaps, it was better hardened for the earlier freezes. The most possible sunlight probably helps to harden its wood, and having just the right genes may help, too. Age is another possible factor.

E. lusitanica can be propagated by seed in finely sifted peat, or by July cuttings 1 1/2-2 in long (4.5-5 cm), inserted in 3 parts of sand to 1 of peat.(8)

As mentioned above, there is the varietal form E. l. 'George Hunt', with yellow foliage. This plant is or was patented, with proceeds to benefit the National Cancer Research Campaign, of Britain.

We have had none from self-sown seed but the Mathesons, Sebastopol, CA had a *lusitanica* seed plant which they assumed to be a hybrid. It was reported to be 26-28 in high and 36 in wide (70 x 95 cm), more broad than tall, unlike *E. lusitanica* itself. The new-growth stem hairs of this plant appear to be all simple; in any case, I have observed none that are branched on my small plant. New-growth leaves are light medium green, rather than the yellow-green of the parent. The profuse flowers from pink buds are white and 6 mm long by 5 mm wide (1/4 x 3/16 in), noticeably larger than those of the species, which are usually 5 mm long and 2.5 mm wide. Experience here indicates it is even less hardy than the species. In any case, it differs from the known *lusitanica* hybrid, *E. x veitchii*, which lacks the color in the flower buds except in its form 'Pink Joy', and is proportionately very much larger-growing than the Mathesons' plant.

References:

1) McClintock, David: *A GUIDE TO THE NAMING OF PLANTS*, The Heather Society, 1980.
2) *FLORA EUROPAEA*, 1972.
3) Underhill, Terry L.: *HEATHS AND HEATHERS*, 1971.
4) Proudley, Brian & Valerie: *HEATHERS IN COLOUR*, 1974.
5) Chopinet, R: *Les Bruyeres Rustiques, PLANTES DE MONTAGNE*, La Societe des Amateurs de Jardins Alpins, Vol. IV, No. 64, 1967.
6) The Heather Society: *HEATHER TRIALS*, 1971-75.
7) Bean, W. J.: *TREES & SHRUBS HARDY IN THE BRITISH ISLES*, 8th ed., 1973.
8) Sheat, Wilfrid G.: *PROPAGATION OF TREES, SHRUBS AND CONIFERS*, 1953.

ERICA MACKAIANA Bab.

E. mackaiana had apparently been mistaken for *E. tetralix* until noticed and collected, in September 1835, by William McCalla, a schoolmaster of Scottish descent, residing at Roundstone, Connemara, due west from Dublin on the west coast of Eire.(1) Remarkably, it had also been discovered and collected in June of that same year, in Asturias Province, northern Spain, by a French army officer out plant hunting in the mountains there.(2) McCalla, sounding very much like a late 20th Century nature lover, had previously published a note lamenting the fact that the native plants were left "heedlessly to decay without the knowledge of a botanist", and he set forth to remedy the situation. When the distinguished Cambridge University botanist, Charles Babington, came to visit his district McCalla took him to see the *Erica* and other plants of interest in the district. Other botanists agreed that the *Erica* was a new species. It was Babington who published the report of it.

Besides a number of locations in Connemara, there is a quite separate and somewhat different-looking (taller and with showy umbel-like inflorescences) population of the species in Donegal, the extreme northwest county of Eire, as well as the even more widely separated stations of the "stout, stiff and erect" form and others in northern Spain.

To quote Maj. Magor (3), "*E. mackaiana* was . . . collected [in Donegal] in 1909, but not recognized as such until much later." Except for the easily distinguished *E. m.* 'Plena', the species is still not too readily distinguished from *E. tetralix.* The main easily recognizable differences are:

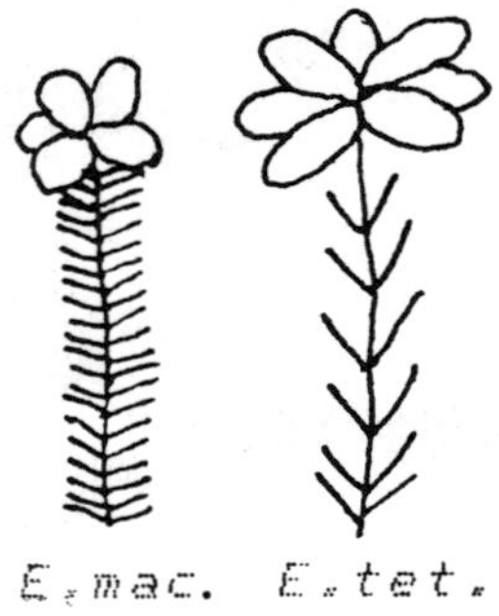

E. mac. E. tet.

E. mackaiana		*E. tetralix*
compact, bushy	HABIT	straggling
2-4.5 mm long, all patent	LEAVES	3-6 mm, appressed below inflorescence
internodes all about equal		internodes longer below inflorescence
shorter and broader	COROLLA	longer, cylindrical
glabrous or comparatively glabrous	OVARY	pubescent

E. mackaiana Bab. **'Dr. Ronald Gray'**: A, flowering twig 1X; B, inflorescence 10X; C, pistil and 2 stamens 10X; Da, leaf beneath 10X; Db, leaf cross section 10X.

E. mackaiana Bab. **'Plena'**: A, flowering stems 1X; B, flower 5X; C, flower cross section 10X; Da, leaf beneath 10X; Db, leaf cross section 10X; E, plant habit.

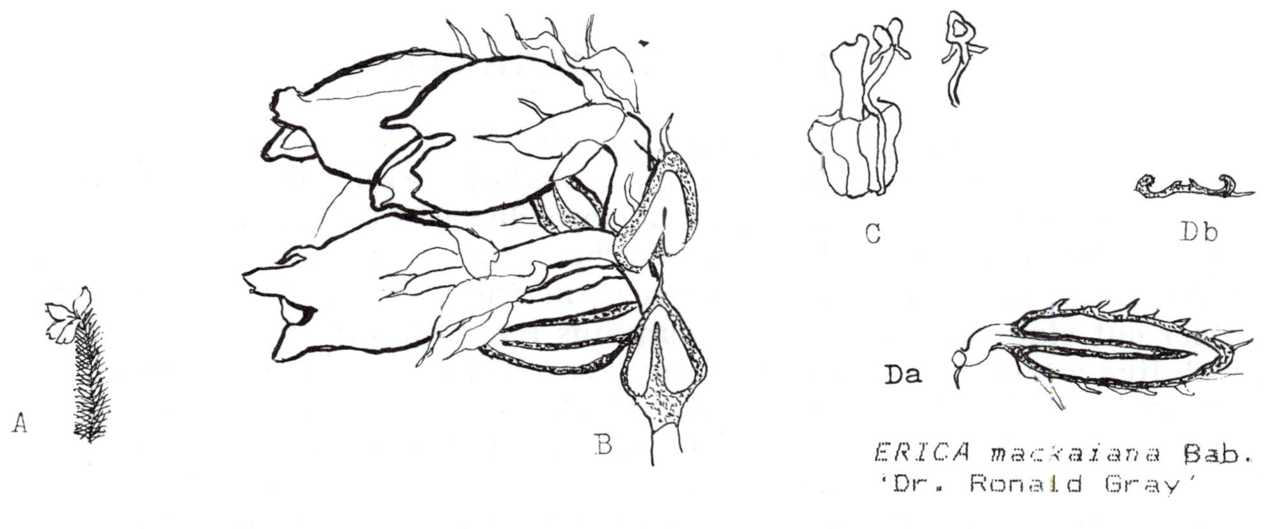

ERICA mackaiana Bab.
'Dr. Ronald Gray'

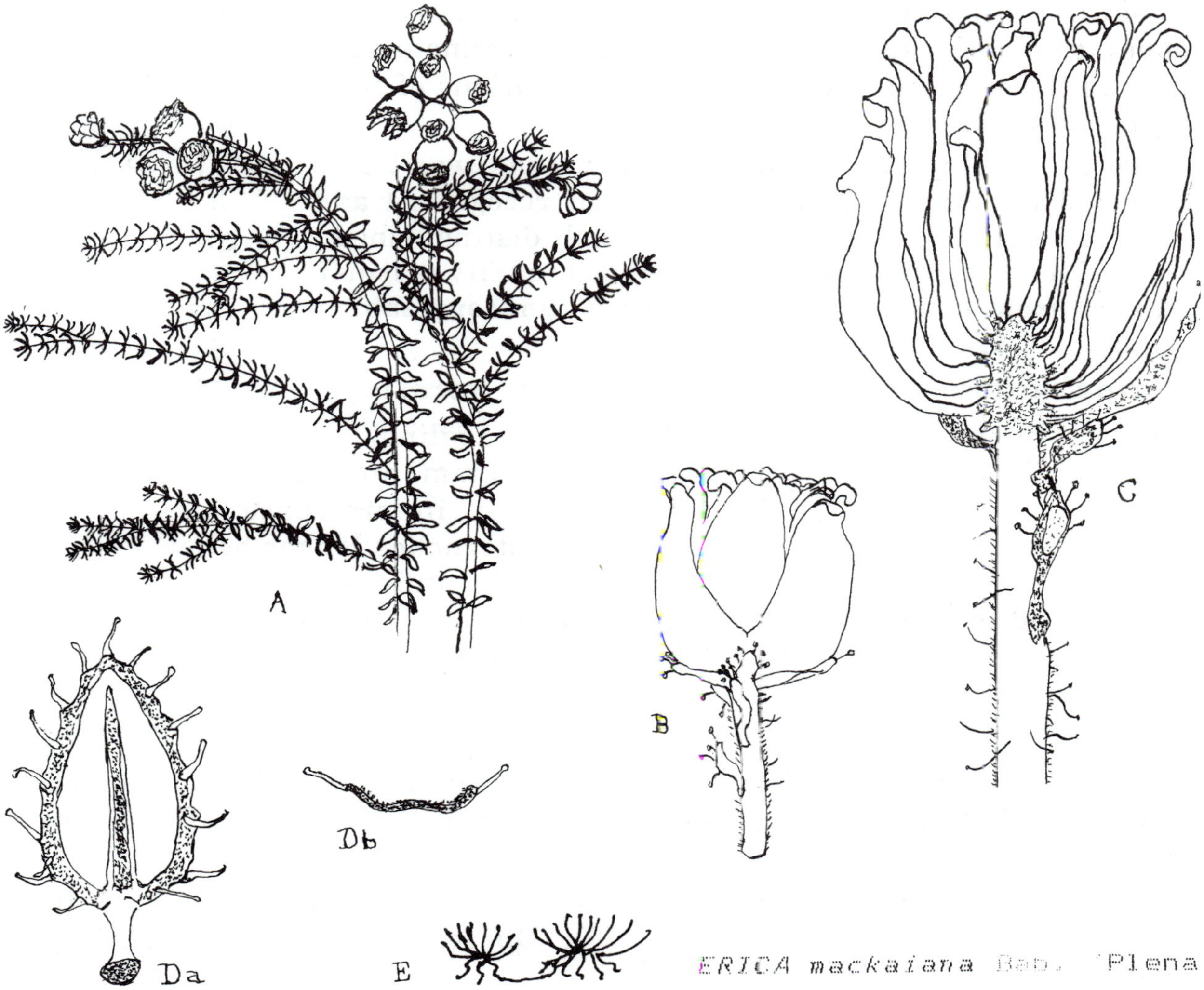

dmm

A
B
C
Da
Db
E

ERICA mackaiana Bab. 'Plena'

In the Pacific Northwest, *E. mackaiana* 'Plena' has sometimes seemed less hardy than *E. tetralix*. Following the December 1983 cold snap, with temperature down to 9°F (-13°C), plants of *E. mackaiana* 'Plena' were only too easily distinguished by their freeze-scorched tops; but they did recover. Harry van de Laar(4) reported some forms to survive in the Netherlands.

To further confuse the issue, the several forms of *E. x stuartii* have been determined to be hybrids of *mackaiana* and *tetralix*, occur intermingled where the parents naturally grow together, and are intermediate between the parents in their characters.

The Irish populations are reported(5) to have little fertile seed, though there is a higher percent in Spain. Much of their spread in the wet, boggy valleys of Connemara is attributed to some layering and especially, as Maj. Magor says, to spreading at length and in all directions by its shallow rhizomes.

Now that we know it is *E. mackaiana* we are looking at, *FLORA EUROPAEA*(6) describes it as a compact, bushy dwarf shrub 15-60 cm (6-24 in) high; its stems are decumbent to erect, with suberect branches; the young twigs are hairy. Leaves are 2-4.5 mm (1/16-3/16 in) long, in whorls of 4, patent in all parts of the plant, oblong, glabrous except for long, stout, gland-tipped cilia on true and apparent margins; margins are slightly revolute, leaving most of the white lower surface exposed. Internodes on the flowering stems are all about equal in length. The flowers are in terminal umbels; the pedicels have 1 or 2 bracteoles on the upper half. The sepals are 2-3 mm (ca. 1/16-1/8 in) long, glabrous except for long cilia; the corolla is 5-7 mm (3/16-1/4 in) long, urn-shaped, with spreading or revolute lobes; the anthers are included, with long, narrow basal appendages. The ovary is glabrous and the stigma capitate.

The species is distinguished by including the only known double-flowered hardy *Ericas* in which as the illustration shows all reproductive parts may be replaced by a multiplicity of petals or, sometimes, petaloid filaments. David Small(7) mentions such a form, "we travelled to Carna to see the colony of *Erica mackaiana* plants which have petaloid stamens much like the cultivar 'Maura' which came from this site." (Major Magor(3) described 'Maura' as with fused petaloid stamens and split style. David McClintock, in "The Garden," May 1980(8), mentioned that Maj. Gen. Turpin had found that all 12 florets in one umbel of 'Maura' differed in the extent to which they had stigmas or anthers, up to five, or how they were attached to the wall of the corolla. Interestingly, Mr. Leslie B. Patrick, Argyll, Scotland(9) reported having found both double and single flowers on the same shoot of an *E. m.* 'Plena.' These forms are obviously not very stable.)

The forms of the species are best propagated by summer cuttings, though well-rooted layers can be carefully separated.

The North American List, 1983(10) included only the forms 'Dr. Ronald Gray', 'Lawsoniana', and 'Plena.' Others have been introduced and some imported since.

Geoffrey Yates (11 and 12) mentions:

'Ann D. Frearson' A double form flowering much more freely than 'Plena.'

'Donegal' June-Sept; 24 cm (9.5 in); large magenta flowers, spreading, rather open growth.

'Dr. Ronald Gray' July-Oct; 15 cm (6 in); attractive white form raised from a sport on 'Lawsoniana'.

'Lawsoniana' July-Sept; 15 cm (6 in); pale lilac flowers, with lighter than usual green leaves.

'Maura' Beautiful clear pink flowers without any trace of blue in the colouring.

'Plena' July-Oct; 15 cm (6 in); double magenta flowers with a white center; foliage dark green, turning bronze in winter.

'Wm. M'Alla' (A variation on the formal spelling) July-Sept; 15 cm (6 in); lilac-pink flowers in clusters on a dark green spreading plant. Formerly listed as just *E. mackaiana*.

Mr. J. Platt described two recent acquisitions:

'Ann D. Frearson'(13) The flowers each have a ring of petaloid stamens within their H11 (lilac pink) corollas, rather more like 'Maura' than 'Plena.' It is also said to be hardier than 'Plena.'

'Errigal Dusk'(14) A 60 cm (24 in) plant flowering in Aug.- Sept. A strong growing plant with an upright habit. The flowers are darker magenta than those of 'Donegal' and barrel shaped.

Several other forms collected from Ireland and Spain in 1982 and sent to me from England by David Small under collection numbers, are being propagated. These include:

DHN 11-82. Not seen in flower.

DHN 15-82. White, from Spain. A very choice compact plant, 13 cm (5 in) high spreading to 30 cm (12 in) diameter at five years from cutting; leaves medium green; it has a very generous offering of good-sized white flowers over a long season. Not damaged by our 7°F (-14°C) with an 8-inch snow cover, of February 1989.

DHN 41-82 Pink, from Spain. A somewhat less compact plant 15 cm (6 in) high spreading to 30 X 45 cm (12 X 18 in) in five years; leaves medium green; its relatively large flowers, 7 mm (1/4 in) long and 4 mm wide, are in tight umbels of 15 or 20. The color effect is deep pink but it most closely matches H1, amethyst on the Heather Society Colour Chart. Flowering well in mid-June. Also not damaged by the freeze.

References:

1) Nelson, E. C.: *William McCalla, Discoverer of Erica mackaiana, YEAR BOOK OF THE HEATHER SOCIETY*, 1983.

2) McClintock, David: *Iter Hispanicum Ericaceum, YEAR BOOK OF THE HEATHER SOCIETY*, 1983.

3) Magor, Maj. E. W. M.: *Riddles of the Irish Heaths, YEAR BOOK OF THE HEATHER SOCIETY*, 1981.

4) Van de Laar, Harry: *THE HEATHER GARDEN*, 1978.

5) McClintock, David: *Species of Heather in Britain, YEAR BOOK OF THE HEATHER SOCIETY*, 1964.

6) *FLORA EUROPAEA*, 1972.

7) Small, David: *Champagne in Connemara, THE HEATHER SOCIETY BULLETIN*, Autumn 1983.

8) McClintock, David: *A Day in my Heather Garden, THE GARDEN, Jour. of the R.H.S.*, May, 1980.

9) Patrick, Leslie B.: *Making a Garden in Argyll, YEAR BOOK OF THE HEATHER SOCIETY*, 1974.

10) Eighme, Lloyd: *Heathers in North American Gardens, HEATHER NEWS*, No. 21, Mar. 1983.

11) Yates, Geoffrey: *POCKET GUIDE TO HEATHER GARDENING*, 1978.

12) Yates, Geoffrey: *THE GARDENER'S BOOK OF HEATHERS*, 1985.

13) Platt, J.: *New Acquisitions, YEAR BOOK OF THE HEATHER SOCIETY*, 1985.

14) Platt, J.: *New Acquisitions*, *YEAR BOOK OF THE HEATHER SOCIETY*, 1988.

WHAT CAN I DO WITH MY HEATHERS?

One of the best known and most interesting of the (Ericease) family is the common heath, heather or ling, *Calluna vulgaris* . . . In all moorland countries the ling is applied to many rural purposes; the larger stems are made into brooms, the shorter tied up into bundles that serve as brushes, while the long trailing shoots are woven into baskets. Pared up with the peat about its roots it forms a good fuel, often the only one obtainable on the drier moors. The shieldings (e.g., shepherd's huts) of the Scottish Highlanders were formerly constructed of heath stems, cemented together with peat-mud, worked into a kind of mortar with dry grass or straw; hovels and sheds for temporary purposes are still sometimes built in a similar way, and roofed in with ling. Laid on the ground, with the flowers above, it forms a soft springy bed, the luxurious couch of the ancient Gael, still gladly resorted to at times by the hill shepherd or hardy deerstalker. The young shoots were in former days employed as a substitute for hops in brewing, while their astringency rendered them valuable as a tanning material in Ireland and the Western Isles. They are said also to have been used by the Highlanders for dyeing woolen yarn yellow, and other colours are asserted to have been obtained from them . . . The young juicy shoots and the seeds, which remain long in the capsules, furnish the red grouse of Scotland with the larger portion of its sustenance; the ripe seeds are eaten by many birds. The tops of the ling afford a considerable part of the winter fodder of the hill flocks, and are popularly supposed to communicate the fine flavour to Welsh and Highland mutton, but sheep seldom crop heather while the mountain grasses and rushes are sweet and accessible. Ling has been hardly sufficiently fibrous for that purpose. The purple or fine-leaved heath, *E. cinerea*, one of the most beautiful of the (*Erica*) genus, abounds on the lower moors and commons of Great Britain and western Europe, in such situations being sometimes more prevalent than the ling. The flowers of both these species yield much honey, furnishing a plentiful supply to the bees in moorland districts; from this heath honey the Picts probably brewed the mead said by Boetius to have been made from the flowers themselves.

—*ENCYCLOPAEDIA BRITANNICA*, 11th edition, 1910

ERICA MADERENSIS (Benth.) Bornmueller

E. maderensis (signifying from the Island of Madeira) was first mentioned in the literature, in 1839, by George Bentham, who assumed it to be a varietal form of *E. cinerea*. Sixty-five years later, in 1904, the German botanist, J. F. N. Bornmueller wrote that it was closely related to *E. cinerea* but sufficiently different to warrant raising it to specific rank. Bornmueller's opinion did not draw much attention and the plant has continued to be referred to as *E. c. var. maderensis*. At this time the only available (to us) published articles on *E. maderensis* are those in recent *YEAR BOOKS* of The Heather Society.

In a 1981 article, David McClintock(1) listed the characters of the two species and also of *E. terminalis*, which has also been mentioned as a possible close relative of *E. maderensis*. As can be noted in the illustrations of the species, *E. maderensis* leaves are in 3s, like those of *E. cinerea* but not in the fascicled bundles, and the leaf cross sections are noticeably different; its inflorescence is paniculate, rather than racemose; its corolla is a noticeably longer, narrower bell; and, it would seem significantly, its anther appendages are a long narrow shape quite unlike the broad fringed ones found on *E. cinerea*. Further variations are found in its habitat (montane, rather than moorland), habit (where not exposed to high-altitude gales it is an erect-bushy plant to two feet tall and across, where exposed it becomes lower and more spreading), and in the nature of its aging stems. In *cinerea* they remain thin and don't live long; in *maderensis* they become thick and are long-lived. Whatever similarities to *E. terminalis* there may be, the pollen grains of the two species are quite different, a definitive character.

It is interesting to consider the situation of *E. maderensis*, isolated for an unknown period of time on the Madeira Islands, about 400 miles west of the coast of Morocco, where it grows at elevations between 3,000 feet and the mountain top 6,000 feet (850-1,700 m). Mr. Richards(2) gives a lively account of precipitous Madeira Island and the plant-hunting visit he and Mr. McClintock made there in 1974. He writes, "On the bleak top of Pico do Ariero it is quite common as tight cushions or mats draping the rocks. Some of these plants are ancient with a main stem thicker than one's thumb and close pressed to the rock up to 6 ft across (1.8 m). . . . We never found *E. maderensis* growing in competition with any other plant, but it survived on the bleak, rocky mountain tops where practically nothing else could find a living." Lower down, uncultivated ground is populated by a scrub of *E. arborea* and *E. scoparia*; but they found no *E. cinerea*.

David McClintock writes, "This species has been growing in my garden at Platt [Kent, southeast England] for some years now. Here it does not really thrive or make the floriferous display to be seen in the climate of Madeira. In D[on] Richards' garden in Cumbria [northwest England] however, seedlings

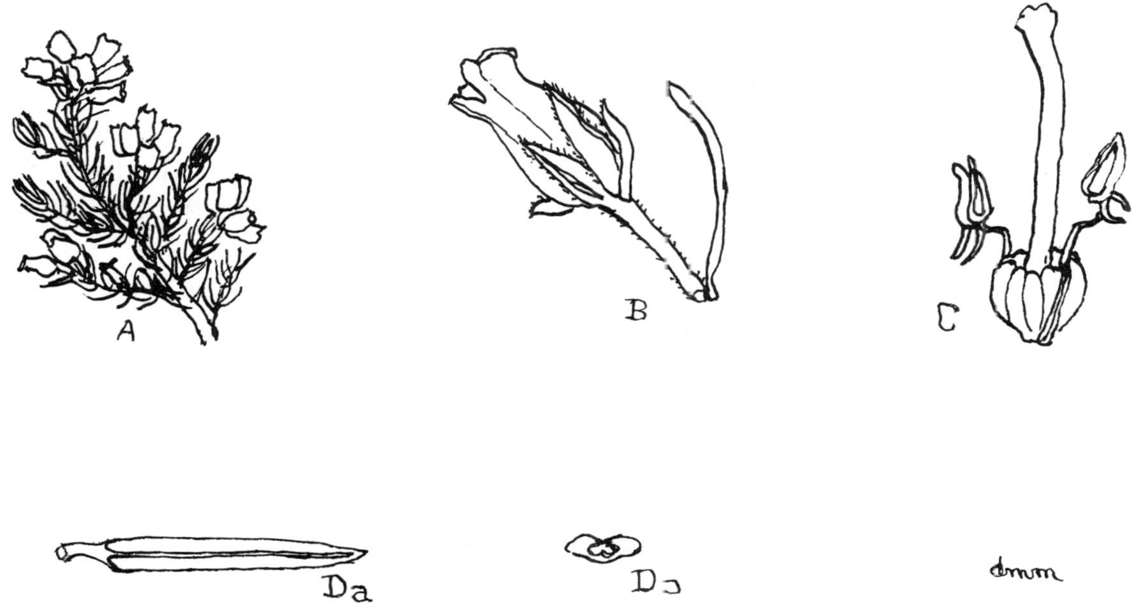

E. maderensis: A, inflorescence 1X; B, flower 5X; C, pistil and 2 stamens 10X; Da, leaf beneath 5X; Db, leaf cross section 10X.

'keep popping up all over the place.' Until they flower he cannot tell them from seedlings of *E. arborea*, *E. lusitanica* or *E. australis*. . . ." The flower color is said to be mauve, identical with that of *E. terminalis*, and its season, in England, is May to October.

It can be propagated by seed or cuttings.

References:

1) McClintock, David: *The Bell Heather in Madeira, YEAR BOOK OF THE HEATHER SOCIETY*, 1981, pp. 48-51.

2) Richards, D. A.: *Mostly Erica maderensis and Daboecia azorica, YEAR BOOK OF THE HEATHER SOCIETY*, 1976, pp. 15-20.

ERICA MANIPULIFLORA Salisb.

Erica manipuliflora was reportedly introduced to Great Britain over 200 years ago but is nevertheless a late comer to most heather gardens there. It has also been neglected by many authors of fairly comprehensive works treating other heather species; but it was included by Polunin and Huxley, 1965(1), by Terry Underhill, 1971(2), and by Harry van de Laar, 1974(3). It was not indexed in the *YEAR BOOK OF THE HEATHER SOCIETY* until 1980 when Mr. P. L. Joyner, of Southampton, reported the undamaged survival of his very young plants in the open during the hard British winter of 1978-79, and also mentioned that Mr. A. W. Jones's plants, in Somerset, not only survive but grow well on his high pH soil.(4)

There has been confusion over its name. It was long known as *E. verticillata* (flowers arranged in a whorl), the name given it by P. Forskal in 1775. However, that name, having already been used for a South African Cape Heath in 1767, was not available according to the accepted rules of nomenclature. Next choice was Salisbury's *E. manipuliflora* (flowers in small handfuls) published in 1802.(5) In the 18th C. Sibthorp called plants from the vicinity of Istanbul *E. purpurascens*; then Lamarck classed it as *E. vagans*, but more recently, botanists decided that it is a separate species.(6)

E. manipuliflora is classed in a group with *EE. vagans* and *multiflora*, botanically similar species, each of the three occupying its own geographical area, with some overlaps: *vagans* to the north and west in Britain, Spain and France; *multiflora*, to the south and west from the Atlantic coast of Morocco up to Spain, southern France, the Mediterranean islands, Italy and the eastern shores of the Adriatic; *manipuliflora* from the shores of the Adriatic eastward to Turkey. These three taxa form the Erica Section Gypsocallis (lime-loving, a clue to their soil tolerance).(7)

There are distinctions between the species. *FLORA EUROPAEA*(7) describes the habit of *E. manipuliflora* as with stems 50(-70cm), (less than *vagans* (60(-80 cm)) and with decumbent to ascending stems, straight or somewhat flexuous, the plant rarely erect; the leaves smaller (to 8 mm long) in whorls of 3-4, mostly erect or erecto-patent (at a 45' angle); the corollas somewhat resembling those of *vagans*, but in more lax inflorescences, which are smaller than those of the usual *vagans*, not more than 6 cm (2.5 in) long. It occurs in evergreen scrub and dry, rocky places.

P. H. Davis, *FLORA OF TURKEY AND THE EAST AEGEAN ISLANDS*(8), gives an interestingly different picture of *E. manipuliflora* as it occurs in these furthest eastern stands. Here it is described as an erect shrub to 4 m (13 ft) tall, the stems white, sparsely pubescent; the leaves usually in whorls of 4, adpressed or spreading, with all intermediate angles occurring. Davis' description of the

E. manipuliflora Salisb.: A, inflorescence 1X; B, flower 5X; C, pistil and 2 stamens 10X; Da, vegetative leaf beneath 10X; Db, leaf cross section 20X; Ea, habit of plant in my garden; Eb, habit, of Athens plant.

inflorescences does not differ much from that given in *FLORA EUROPAEA* but adds that the flowers are rose-pink in bud and when newly opened, but they become paler, almost white, later. He traces the occurence of *manipuliflora* from western (European) Turkey down along the Aegean coast and on eastward to the extreme northeast corner of the Mediterranean, and from sea level to 1,500 m (5,200 ft), in open places, maquis, under *Pinus brutia*, and on limestone, serpentine and schistose rocks.

The plants we saw and photographed on November 1st, 1965 in the Ancient Agora, Athens, and later along roadsides to the south in the Peloponnesus, were erect (height ca. 1 1/3 X width) and about 80 cm (30 in) tall. We had also seen similar plants of it growing in a roadside ditch at an elevation of 500 ft (150 m) on the Island of Rhodes, in flower on Oct. 24th. The flower colors of all these plants ranged from nearly white through mauve, to light pink, to deep pink. The inflorescences were very numerous over the whole plants.

Recent studies of its reproductive parts have shown that the ovary of *E. manipuliflora* is of a height 1 1/3 times its diameter, while the ovary of *E. vagans* is of squatter proportions and that of *E. multiflora* is taller. The drawings accompanying these articles may help to make those distinctions clear. It has also been observed that the stems of *E. manipuliflora* are often stiff and grey and its flowers are scented.

Whatever the form of *E. manipuliflora* I have, its flowering season lasts five months, from July to November.

Since Mr. Joyner's report in 1980, other British gardeners have found plants of *E. manipuliflora* to be surprisingly hardy and there has been a surge of interest in it. This has been accompanied by reports in the *YEAR BOOK OF THE HEATHER SOCIETY*. Dr. John Griffiths, has worked in his garden in Yorkshire, hybridising his more eastern, more upright form of *manipuliflora*. Fortunately for the hybridizer his plant had shown itself to be of remarkably low self-fertility, but gives good seed set with suitably compatible pollen from other plants. He embarked in 1981 on experiments in crossing it with a number of other *Erica* species. In 1985(9), he reported that crossing *E. manipuliflora* with various forms of *E. vagans* resulted in a high set of fertile seed which gave a good crop of 1st generation hybrid plants. In 1987(10), he was able to provide a description of the hybrids as upright, with stiff grey stems, leaves very short and of a dark green color, with inflorescences interrupted. He had also found that the hybrid plants were vigorous, floriferous, long-flowering, scented and "extremely hardy", but they did not bear viable pollen, indicating that the parents, *EE. manipuliflora* and *vagans* are indeed two separate species.

[Dr. G. H. M. Lawrence(11) says that the degree of fertility of a hybrid may give some indication of the degree of genetic relationship between its parents. Thus, in general, hybrids between less closely related parents tend to be sterile or of low fertility [they do not produce fertile seed], whereas hybrids between more closely related parents tend to be more fertile.]

In October, 1988, A. W. Jones(12) and David McClintock visited southern Yugoslavia to observe the species in the wild there. They hired a car at Dubrovnik (on the Adriatic coast) and, more or less paralleling the coast on a sometimes hair-raising road, drove northwest as far as a little north of Makarska, having side-tripped to the island of Korcula. Returning to Dubrovnik, they drove inland to an altitude of about 1,000 ft (300 m) where *E. manipuliflora* plants were still present; but they petered out after about 35 km (21 mi) from the sea shore.

They saw and collected herbarium specimens and cuttings of numerous forms of *E. manipuliflora* from prostrate, not over 2 in (5 cm) tall, one of these with yellow foliage, or growing from clefts and hanging down over rocks, to ascending and 2 ft (60 cm) tall (like vagans), to erect and 1.8m (6 ft) and 2.25 m (7 ft) tall; with leaves set at a variety of angles; with flower colors ranging from white to lilac pink. Clearly a considerable range of forms of this valuable species is to be anticipated for gardens able to accommodate it.

Following this trip David McClintock addressed the Linnean Society and his paper was published in their Botanical Journal(13). Having studied the plants and the literature, he had come to the conclusion that these species "were well muddled by authors in the last [19th] century . . . " and should have been stated to be four species: *E. dydima* Stokes, *E. vagans* L., *E. anthura* Link and *E. manipuliflora* Salisb. in the order of their occurrence from west to east.

Mr. Jones has suggested(14) that some cross pollenation experiments are needed to sort the problem out.

In 1982 we heard that there were four clones of this species being grown in Britain, namely one possibly from Kew Gardens (the most widely available in Britain), one collected from the island of Korcula, Yugoslavia, one of unknown origin, and one from the Greek Island of Corfu. They differ in pollen fertility. These clones have apparently all withstood the recent hard winters in Britain. A. W. Jones reported that his plant (the one possibly from Kew) survived -18°C (-2°F) in the open.

Because Mr. Jones very kindly sent us flowering branches in September 1982, we are so fortunate as to have a start of one of them in the Pacific Northwest. Seven days after they were cut in England, Lavonia Leo, Seattle and I inserted every possible cutting of the clones "A", "B" and "C" on hand. Lavonia's medium was sand/peat, mine vermiculite/peat. Our results were remarkably similar: clone "A" gave us some little rooted plants; clone "B" lingered for a while before giving up; clone "C" was more quickly discouraged. These results accord with the experience of British growers. We have not heard details on the rooting of clone "D". Whichever is the one I have, it was quite unaffected by our 7°F (-15°C) in February 1989. Its flowers are small but a nice pink and flaunt gracefully about on long pink pedicels for that long five month season.

References:

1) Polunin, Oleg and Anthony Huxley: *FLOWERS OF THE MEDITERRANEAN*, 1965, first American edition, Boston, 1966.

2) Underhill, Terry: *HEATHS AND HEATHERS*, Newton Abbot, Devon, 1971.

3) van de Laar, Harry: *THE HEATHER GARDEN*, 1974, English ed., London, 1978.

4) Joyner, P. L.: *Erica manipuliflora, YEAR BOOK OF THE HEATHER SOC.*, 1980.

5) McClintock, D.: *A GUIDE TO THE NAMING OF PLANTS*, The Heather Soc., 1980.

6) Jones, A. W.: *Notes on Erica manipuliflora, E. vagans and their hybrids, YEAR BOOK OF THE HEATHER SOC.*, 1987.

7) *FLORA EUROPAEA*, (Webb and Rix), 1972.

8) Davis, P. H.: *FLORA OF TURKEY AND THE EAST AEGEAN ISLANDS*, Edinburgh, 1978.

9) Griffiths, John: Hybridisation of the Hardy Ericas, *YEAR BOOK OF THE HEATHER SOC.*, 1985.

10) Griffiths, J.: *Hybridisation of the Hardy Ericas, Part 2, YEAR BOOK OF THE HEATHER SOC.*, 1987.

11) Lawrence, G. H. M.: *TAXONOMY OF VASCULAR PLANTS*, 1951.

12) Jones, A. W.: *Erica manipuliflora Salisb. in Southern Yugoslavia, October 1988, YEAR BOOK OF THE HEATHER SOC.*, 1989.

13) McClintock, D.: *The heathers of Europe and adjacent areas, BOTANICAL JOURNAL OF THE LINNEAN SOC.*, 101, 1989.

14) Jones, A. W.: personal communication, 30 Jan. 1990.

HEATHER WREATH

Heather Wreath, clockwise from top center:

1. *Daboecia cantabrica*
2. *D. azorica*
3. *Erica arborea*
4. *E. australis*
5. *E. carnea*
6. *E. ciliaris*
7. *E. cinerea*
8. *Calluna vulgaris*
9. *E. erigena*
10. *E. terminalis*
11. *E. tetralix*
12. *E. vagans*
13. *E. umbellata*
14. *Bruckenthalia spiculifolia*

ERICA MULTIFLORA L.

E. multiflora is a species concerning which there is no argument with the Linnaean name of 1753. Such confusion as there has been has related to identifying the plant, because of its similarity to *E. vagans* and *E. manipuliflora*. *E. multiflora* appears often to have been mistaken for *vagans*, from which it differs, however, in having an upright habit, potentially tree heath-like; inflorescences always at the branch tips never with a flush of leafy new growth out beyond them; corcllas which are more or less ovate and twice as long as they are wide, rather than rounded bells; calyx half as long as the corolla rather than the shorter stubbier sepals of *vagans*; and anther lobes which are parallel and contiguous for most of their length rather than widely divergent. It usually achieves a height of 30-80 cm (12-32 in) though *FLORA EUROPAEA*(1) suggests 250 cm (8 ft 4 in) is possible in the wild, and the late Dr. Violet Gray(2) reported the plants in her garden at Hindhead, Surrey to be 4.5 and nearly 6 ft (1.35-1.8 m) tall. Chopinet(3) describes its branches as ascending and glabrous, the new growth pulverulent. Its leaves are to 11 mm (7/16 in) or more long and in whorls of 4, 5, or 6. The Proudleys(4) found plants in the wild with flowers in varying shades from almost white to mauve-pink, but the cultivated plants are generally clear pink. The flowering season in the wild is variously reported between July and February. The specimens for drawing which Mr. David Small sent to me (from Dr. Gray's garden) were mailed from England on September 12th, indicating an autumn flowering season in Surrey.

This is another species of dry, rocky hillsides and woods near the sea, and tolerant of calcareous soil. It occurs from the Atlantic coast of Morocco across to the northern shores and islands of the Mediterranean and as far east as Dalmatia, in Jugoslavia.

E. multiflora was introduced to England in 1731 but has been scarce to non-existent in gardens there since. The scarcity could be accounted for by two reasons: first, it is not very hardy. Mr. Small, whose nursery is in Suffolk on the colder east side of England, sent flowering specimens from Dr. Gray's Surrey garden because his own plants had not recovered to flowering condition from the hard winter two years earlier. Dr. Gray mentioned in her article that her late husband's original plant survived for 25 years at Hindhead, 750 ft (230 m) above sea level, but was protected by an overhanging beech tree.

Second, *E. multiflora* is difficult to propagate by cuttings. Dr. Ronald Gray "had great difficulty in getting successful cuttings from that original plant, but fortunately he got some going before the parent plant petered out owing to overgrowth of its competitors. The young plants progressed slowly, . . ." Mr. Small(5) has written that "it is very difficult [to propagate]. In fact we rooted it for Kew." We did not succeed in rooting any of the material sent to us. We have

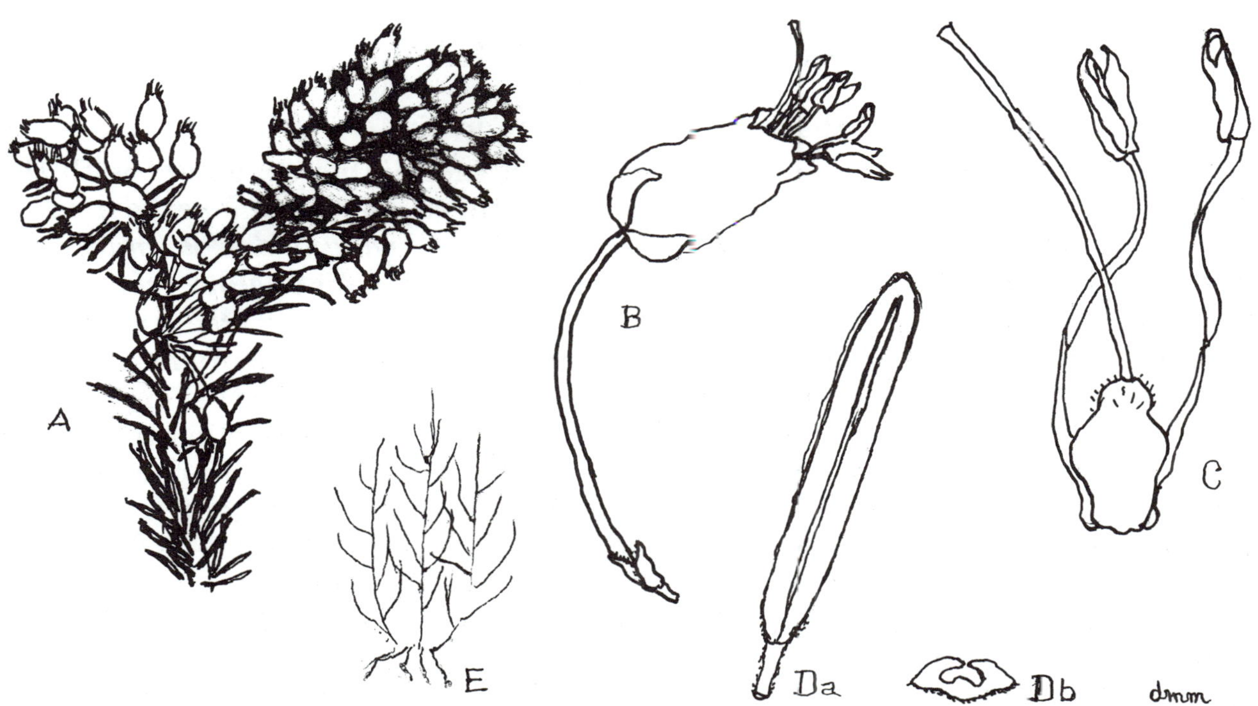

Erica multiflora L.: A, inflorescence 1X; B, flower 5X; C, pistil and 2 stamens 10X; Da, leaf beneath 5X; Db, leaf cross section 10X; E, plant habit.

---

not seen much mention of seed except Dr. V. Gray's comment that "even the seedling plants have a strong central vertical spike."

It is to be hoped that it will be possible to establish *E. multiflora* in USDA zone 7b-8a or milder gardens. There are certain to be areas of our long coastlines where the climate will suit it; and surely there are some dedicated propagators among us who will finally succeed in producing at least a few rooted plants from their cuttings. If it insists on lime, that can be provided, but other species occurring naturally on limey places appear contented in our mildly acid soil. Further variety in our selection of heathers is always welcome; *E. multiflora*, with its upright habit, will give welcome variety to our garden designs, and its autumn flowering will help to round out our flowering year.

References:

1) *FLORA EUROPAEA*, 1972 ed.

2) Gray, Dr. Violet: *YEAR BOOK OF THE HEATHER SOCIETY*, 1970.

3) Chopinet, R.: *Les Bruyeres Rustiques, PLANTES DES MONTAGNES*, Bul. de la Soc. des amateurs de Jardins Alpins, 1967-1968.

4) Proudley, Brian & Valerie: *HEATHERS IN COLOUR*, 1974.

5) Small, David: personal communication, 1983.

ERICA SCOPARIA L.

E. scoparia L. still has the uncontested name originated by Linnaeus in 1753. The specific epithet *scoparia* is derived from the Latin *scopa*, meaning broom. The British common name for the plant is Besom Heath - a besom being a brush of twigs for sweeping; and the French common name is *Bruyere a balais* -Broom heath. (The Scottish definition of the word *besom*, can also be *sloven*, *drab*, - or worse.) The type form, an erect-growing shrub of height variously stated to be from 50 cm to 2.5 m (20 in to 8+ ft), is native in the islands of the western Mediterranean, is in northern Africa (Tunisia), is associated with other tree heaths in Spain, occurs as far north in France as the base of the Brittany peninsula and extends as far east as Italy and possibly the eastern Adriatic. Forms of the species also occur in the Atlantic islands: the Canaries, Madeira, and the Azores where, as David McClintock says(1), long isolation has given rise to variations of form that justify giving subspecies names to the colonies on each group of islands; i.e., *ssp azorica* (the Azores), *ssp platycodon* (the Canaries), and possibly a special designation for the Madeira group when they have been further studied by the botanists concerned. The type form on the continent is *ssp scoparia*.

Outstandingly, over the years, this species has been the ugly duckling of all the hardy heather brood. Except for an occasional kind word for the conifer-like dwarf form, sometimes used as low hedge in Britain, our authors have used up their entire vocabularies of disparaging remarks on it, the exception being the big-hearted W. J. Bean(2). The mature plant's gracefully erect main stems justify his comment, " . . . though loose and irregular in habit, it is decidedly elegant . . . it is only for its beauty of habit that it is desirable." But the rather hopeless sprawl of its "besom" side branches might cause others to call its habit ungainly. Perhaps it is a cranky plant for cranky gardeners.

Its leaves are usually lustrous dark green, to about 7 mm long (1/4 in), with the margins so revolute that the leaves appear less than 1 mm wide (1/32 in); but they are very numerous, occur in whorls of 3 or 4, and stand out from the stems at about a 45 degree angle, so that they give the plant a very well-furnished appearance.

One cause of the species' low place on the popularity scale has been its flowers. Although very numerous (May-June), they occur in the axils of the leaves, are so small (2.5-3 mm (1/8 in) long) as to be barely perceptible, and besides are generally green, more or less tinged with brownish-red. In *ssp azorica*, which is said to grow to as much as 6 m high (20 ft), the flowers are reportedly even smaller with conspicuously exserted reddish-purple stigmas.

The small, conifer-like form with light green foliage has been distributed as 'Minima', 'Pumila', 'Nana', 'Compacta', all the same plant. Now David McClintock(1) urges the use of only 'Minima' for this form, on grounds of the word's

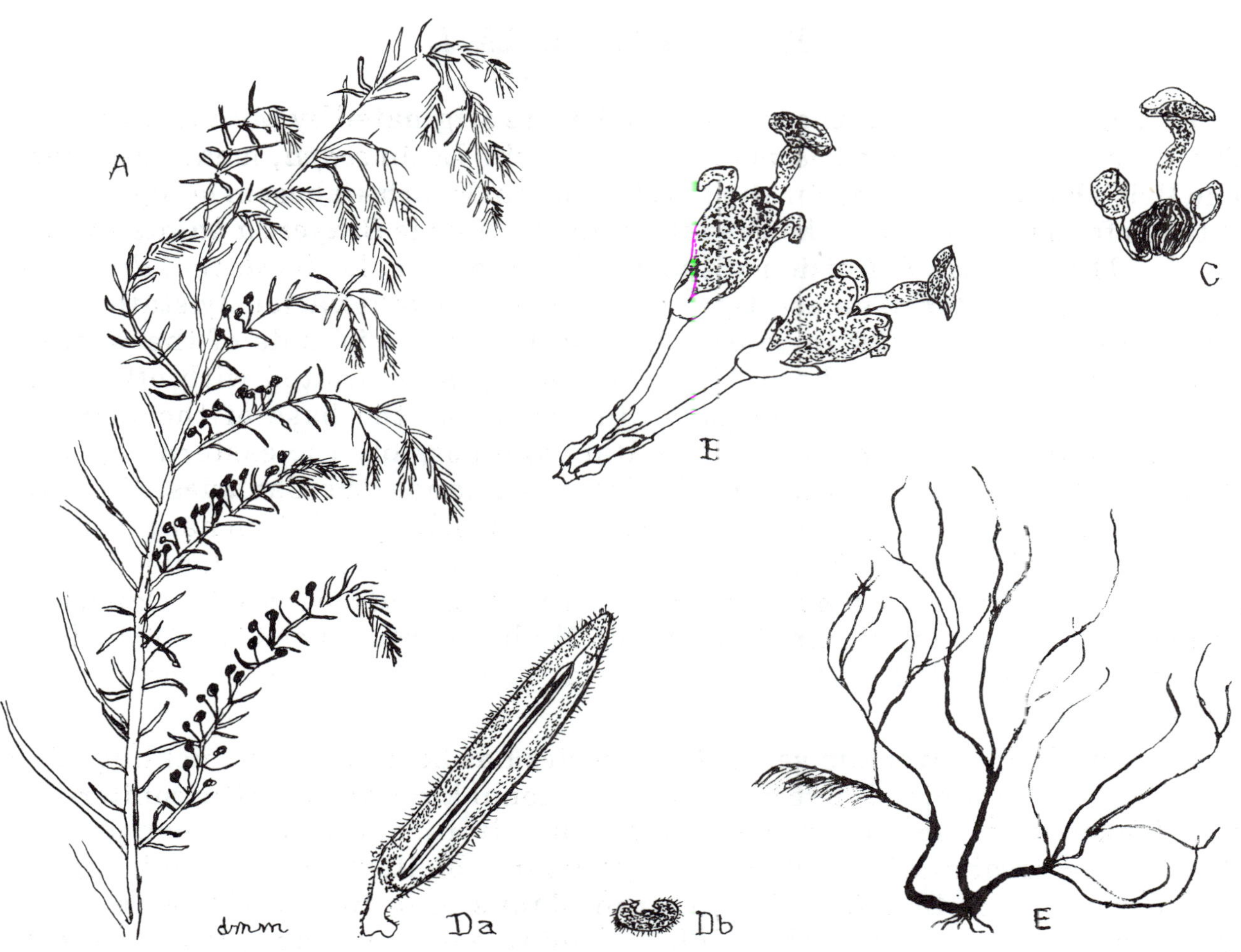

***Erica scoparia ssp platycodon* 'Lionel Woolner':** A, flowering twig 1X; B, flowers 10X (NB: twice the usual enlargement); C, pistil and 2 stamens 10X; Da, leaf beneath 10X; Db, leaf cross section 10X; E, plant habit.

---

priority (1808).

In 1965, we saw and photographed at The Royal Horticultural Society's garden, Wisley, plantings of what were presumably *E. scoparia* type form, and also of *E. s. 'Minima'*. In 1969, at the Royal Botanic Garden, Edinburgh, we saw *E. s. ssp azorica* (then labelled *E. azorica*), which turned out to have been given to the garden by Prof. Warburg, author of *FLORA OF THE AZORES*. But not many others were willing to give space in their heather beds to a plant chiefly noted as an implement for sweeping.

Then, in 1969, Mr. and Mrs. Woolner (Lionel and Thelma), of Gloucestershire, were on holiday at Tenerife, Canary Islands and enterprisingly went exploring in the Mercedes Mountains. As Mr. Woolner tells it(4), "at a height of 4,000 ft [1,200 m], we found *E. scoparia* more or less taking over from *E.*

arborea . . . the *scoparia* was not in flower but, at one point, I noticed a few small golden-leaved seedlings which I brought home, although suspecting that they would soon revert to green. ... in 1973 I was intrigued to see that the shoots of one of the reverted [to green] plants were packed with buds. As these developed there was no suggestion of green about them and when fully opened at the end of May the by no means insignificant clusters of flower were coloured a rich cedarwood-red, ultimately dying to a warm rust. ..." This is the cultivar which has been named *E. scoparia ssp. platycodon* [broad-belled] 'Lionel Woolner'. It is reported to have larger leaves and corollas than the mainland plants.

Despite its circum-mediterranean origin, *E. scoparia* somehow manages to survive some freezes in not-so-warm gardens - for which I am thankful. Rehder(3) rates it Zone VII? (USDA zone 7b). In my garden, though unaffected by previous exposure to 9° to 13°F (-13° to -11°C), it was mortally damaged by 7°F (-14°C).

It prospers in the ordinary acid soil of the Pacific Northwest.

The *E. scoparia* seedling which retained its golden colored foliage was introduced in 1972 as **'Mercedes Gold'**, but I have not seen it and no description of it is at hand.

E. scoparia ssp platycodon **'Lionel Woolner'** came to me as a rooted cutting from Pamela Harper in 1973. Eleven growing seasons later it was 135 cm high and 1 m in diameter (54 X 40 in), having increased its height in two seasons by 57 cm (23 in). It was flowering in 1980 (8 years from cutting) and, except when freeze damaged, it has flowered ever since extraordinarily profusely with a pair of bells at every leaf node over the entire top of the plant. The foliage is a soft, medium green in effect. The corollas are minutely puberulent (with very short hairs), and are intense dark brownish-red with orange-red overtones. The well-exserted broadly capitate stigmas are deep maroon.

References:

1) McClintock, David: *A GUIDE TO THE NAMING OF PLANTS*, 1980.

2) Bean, W. J.: *TREES AND SHRUBS HARDY IN THE BRITISH ISLES*, 1973.

3) Rehder, Alfred: *MANUAL OF CULTIVATED TREES AND SHRUBS,* 1956.

4) Woolner, Lionel R.: *Erica scoparia*, *YEAR BOOK OF THE HEATHER SOCIETY,* 1974, pp. 13-15.

5) Proudley, Brian & Valerie: *HEATHERS IN COLOUR*, 1974.

6) Jones, A. W.: *Observations on Lime Tolerance*, *YEAR BOOK OF THE HEATHER SOCIETY,* 1977, p. 39.

ERICA SICULA Guss.; **ERICA BOCQUETII** (Pesmen) P.F.Stevens

(*Pentapera sicula* Klotzsch; *P. bocquetii* Pesmen)

Erica sicula

In 1821, Italian botanist, Giovanni Gussone reported a new species of *Erica*, which he named *sicula* from its habitat on the Island of Sicily. It was growing, remarkably for an *Erica*, on calcareous cliffs by the sea. Then, in 1838, the German botanist, Johann Friedrich Klotzsch, presented in the botanical journal, *LINNAEA*, his view that this plant, having five- instead of four-part flowers, as do most *Erica* species, should therefore be considered not as *Erica*, but as a new genus, which, because of its five-part ovary, he named *Pentapera*; so it became known as *Pentapera sicula*, and, although several authors disagreed, it was grown (by a few expert gardeners) mostly under this name for well over a century.

In his article on *E. sicula* in the *YEAR BOOK OF THE HEATHER SOC.*, 1980 David McClintock, cites twelve references from the 19th C. and sixteen more from the 20th. Others have written about the plant throughout this period and since. More recent writers, since the late 1960's, have chosen to return the species to the genus *Erica*. Dr. P. F. Stevens, author of *Ericaceae* articles in P. H. Davis's *FLORA OF TURKEY AND THE EAST AEGAEAN ISLANDS*, 1978, has expressed his opinion that Gussone's original classification was the right one after all. He says, "The only difference between *Pentapera* and *Erica* is that flowers of the former are habitually 5-merous whilst those of the latter are 4-merous. Individual 5-merous flowers are found in several species of *Erica*, and the difference in the meristicity of the flowers [i.e., variation in the number of flower parts] is clearly insufficient for generic status." So it seems we may have another more or less hardy *Erica* on our list.

Ripley, 1937 described the Sicilian plant as "a tight, symmetrical bush of fat leaves crowded along the stem, from which there issued an umbel of three or four large pale-pink cups, as delicately tinted as a sea shell, emerging from the narrow divisions of a pink calyx." In similar form plants occur in Cyrenaica, which is along the coast of Libya, over toward Egypt and across the Mediterranean from Greece. The latter form has been designated as *ssp. cyrenaica*.

E. sicula is also found on the Island of Cyprus, in Lebanon and rarely in the Province of Antalya (in southwest Anatolian Turkey). It is reported here also to grow on limestone cliffs. In 1949, P. H. Davis, having visited southwest Anatolia, wrote, "It was very satisfactory to find that wonderful Heath, *Pentapera sicula* (var. *libanotica*?) hanging down the shadier parts of the limestone cliffs in 3-foot bushes of Yew green. . . . The large pentamerous bells are pink in the Oriental variety - at least in Cyprus—but in the Sicilian form (which flowers more readily in cultivation) they are white."

In 1980 and again in 1989, after extensive study and also consultation with knowledgeable members of the Alpine Garden Soc., David McClintock expressed doubt, lacking further investigation, of the validity of the distinction of the three suggested subspecies: *sicula*, *cyrenaica* and *libanotica*.

Comparison of the descriptions of the species in *FLORA EUROPAEA*, 1972 and *FLORA OF TURKEY*, 1978 indicates the main differences between the Sicilian and Turkish plants are in the flower colors; and, more importantly, that Webb & Rix, *FLORA EUROPAEA* authors, give anthers without appendages, while Stevens, in *FLORA OF TURKEY*, says there are very small appendages at the apex of the filaments [not anthers].

An Alpine Garden Soc. *BULLETIN*, 1951 photograph of a plant exhibited in June and identified (after some initial confusion) as *E. sicula ssp. libanotica*, shows a rather sprawling plant 5 inches (13 cm) high and 18 inches (45 cm) across with soft-pink flowers, described as Amaranth Rose [equivalent to somewhere between Heather Soc. Colour Chart H11, lilac pink and H12, heliotrope], and said to eventually reach about 30 cm (12 in) high. A 1952 A.G.S. *BULLETIN* photograph finally identified as of *E. sicula ssp. sicula* shows an erect bushy shrub with ascending branches and said to be 46 cm high (18+ in), exhibited in May. It has flowers described as "white with a tinge of pink." Both forms were given Awards of Merit.—Krussman adds that it is "very long lived when left untouched."

In 1958 Roy Elliott wrote that his plant was quite distinct from either of the above, "stiff and upright in habit, yet has leaves and colouring of [the low sprawling plant]. The flowers are a drab white . . ." P. F. Stevens, in *FLORA OF TURKEY* etc. describes the Turkish form as not low and straggling but an erect bushy shrub to 60 cm (24 in) and with pink flowers. It would seem that the habits vary, but perhaps the pink color is found only in the more eastern plants. Maj. Gen. Turpin has written that his erect plant has flowers of H.S. Colour Chart H16, shell pink. This was as of May 11, 1984.

Two little plants were most kindly sent to me in 1984 from the Cambridge University Botanic Garden. The one labelled "white-flowered, from Sicily" failed to survive; the one labelled "pink flowered from Lycia" [southwest Turkey] has healthy appearing light green foliage, but has been extremely slow growing, with one erect stem growing about 2.5 cm (1 in) a year and an even slower erect side branch. (This plant, so far, is erect, but J. G. Elliott wrote, in 1958, that some plants "remain upright for a year to two, until each stem has grown about six inches long when it becomes procumbent.) Worried by the report of the calcareous situation said to be its natural habitat, I potted it in sandy loam with perlite and a teaspoonful of Dolomite lime. Perhaps repotting it in more nourishing soil will encourage it to grow!

All locations for forms of the species have lain between 30° and 40° North Latitude, often at only 60-100 m (200-330 ft) above sea level, but also reported

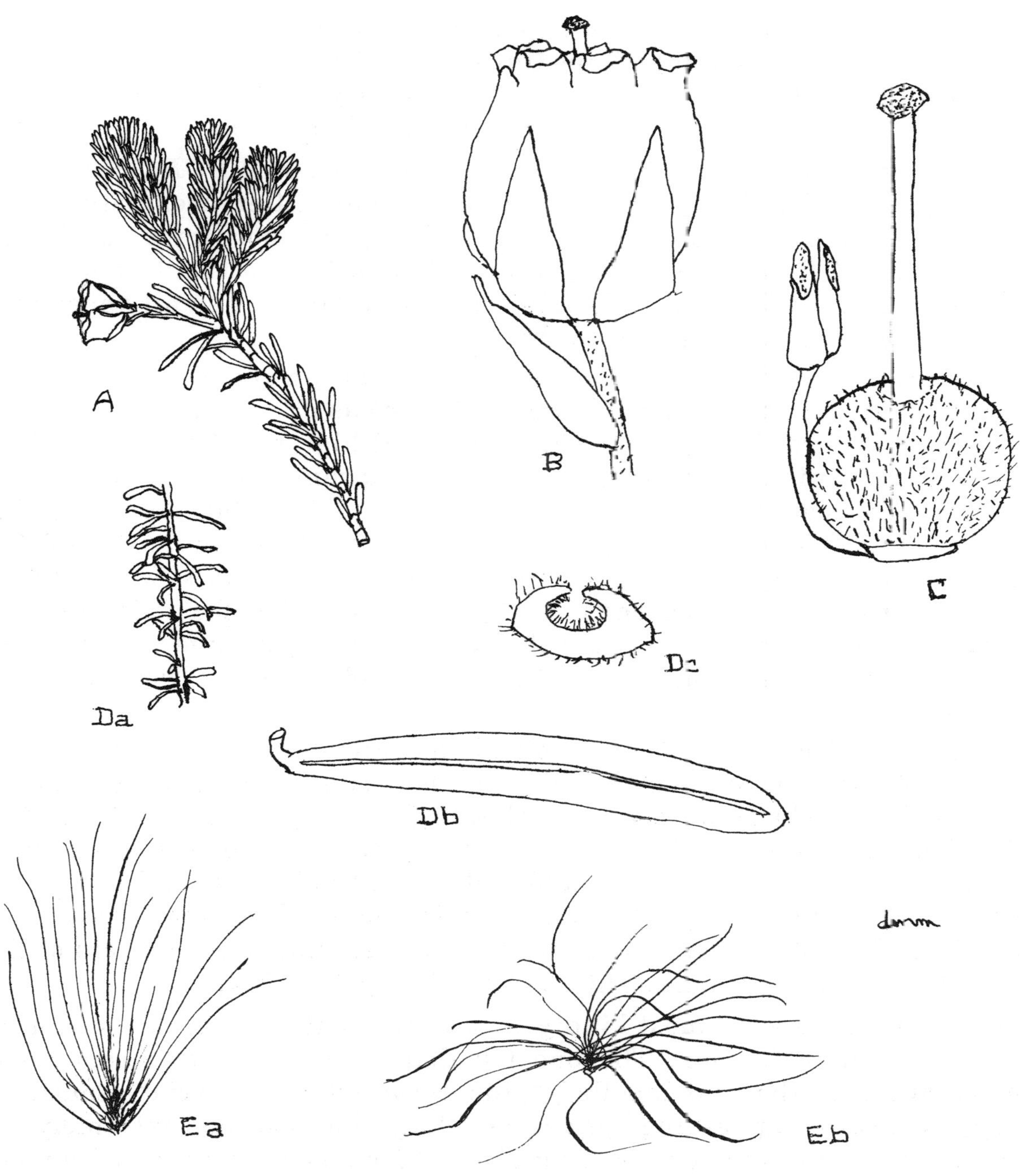

E. sicula Guss.: A, flowering stem 1X; B, flower 5X; C, pistil and stamen 10X; Da, vegetative stem 1X; Db, leaf beneath 10X; Dc, leaf cross section 20X; Ea, plant habit erect; Eb, plant habit decumbent. — A, B and C were drawn from dried, pressed specimens kindly sent me by Maj. Gen. P. G. Turpin, Surrey, England; all leaf drawings were done from a small plant in my garden; plant habits from photographs in the Alpine Garden Society *BULLETINS*, Vol. 19, 1951 and Vol. 20, 1952.

from Lebanon at 1,100 m (3,500 ft). At first *E. sicula* was assumed to be too tender for growing in the open in England except in very favorable localities. But by 1958 J. G. Elliott was reporting that they "seem to survive with simple cold frame treatment"; and in 1980 David McClintock mentioned that *E. sicula* "spent the [severe] winter of 1978-1979 in the open at Kew and was unscathed, and other growers here had theirs survive outside, yet it is better for protection in our climate." From elsewhere in the *YEAR BOOK* we are informed that in that cold winter temperatures in various parts of England had fallen to -10° to -13°C (9°-14°F). My own small potted plant in just cold frame protection came unscathed through over a week of temperatures to 7°F (-14°C) in February 1989 when elsewhere the garden suffered much damage.

Royton Heath, in *SHRUBS FOR THE ROCK GARDEN AND ALPINE HOUSE*, 1954, suggested that *E. sicula* (*Pentapera s.*) be treated as recommended for pot culture of the rarer sun-loving shrubs and more difficult plants. He suggests one part of heavy loam and leaf mould, rubbed through a 1/6 in sieve, to two parts of coarse sand, over good drainage, a good supply of water during the growing season, dryish but not arid condition in winter. Repot as necessary in early spring once growth has commenced.—Maj. Gen. Turpin, Chairman of The Heather Soc., has written me, "I have never bothered much about the soil in which I have grown my *E. sicula*, but have just used the same peaty mixture which I use for other heathers. Perhaps I should give it a little taste of limestone."

Propagation is by seed sown in March or by green cuttings taken in July and rooted in the propagating frame. Stoker, in the R. H. S. *DICTIONARY OF GARDENING*, 1952 and 1984, mentions also the possibility of layers. Seed is said to have been sometimes available to members, in the R. H. S. annual seed list, but it is not listed in autumn 1989 or 1990. I hope that seed will somehow become available as it seems our best hope for trying the species in North America.

Erica bocquetii

In 1968, another, similar plant was found at a much higher elevation (1,750 m, 5,800 ft), also on calcareous rock, also in mountains, in the vicinity of Antalya but in forest clearings instead of on shady cliffs by the sea. It flowers in July, instead of April—May. This plant also has 5-part flowers but differs from *E. sicula* in being generally smaller in all its parts and having pale purple corollas instead of pink or white ones. Its leaves are usually in whorls of 3 (instead of 4). These differences would be insufficient to justify making it a new species; but Dr. Stevens reports that while *E. sicula* has a very small and difficult to see spur at the apex of the filament, this new smaller, pale purple flowered plant does not. It was therefore given, by Pesmen, its finder, the status of a new species with a new name, *Erica bocquetii*.

I have so far not seen any reports of cultivation of *E. bocquetii.*

References:

1937, Ripley, D.: Some plants of southern Europe, *QUAR. BULL.OF THE ALPINE GARDEN SOC.*, Vol. 5, p. 69.

1949, Davis, P. H.: *A journey in southwest Anatolia, JR. OF THE R.H.S.*, Vol. 74, pp. 155-164.

1951, Anon.: *Pentapera sicula, JR. of the R.H.S.*, Vol. 76, p. 332.

1951, Anon.: *Pentapera sicula, QUAR. BULL. OF THE A.G.S.*, Vol. 19, p. 377.

1952, Anon.: *Pentapera sicula, QUAR. BULL. OF THE A.G.S.*, Vol. 20, p. 344.

1952, Anon.: *Pentapera sicula, JR. OF THE R.H.S.*, Vol. 77, p. 423.

1952, Stoker, F.: *Pentapera sicula, R.H.S. DICT. OF GARDENING,* (Repeated in the 1984 edition).

1954, Heath, Royton: *Pentapera sicula, SHRUBS FOR THE ROCK GARDEN AND ALPINE HOUSE*, pp. 135-136.

1955, Anon.: *Pentapera sicula, List of Plant Awards, QUAR. BULL. OF THE A.G.S.*, Vol. 23, p. 89.

1958, Elliott, Roy: *from Alpine House to Scree Frame, QUAR. BULL. OF THE A.G.S.*, Vol. 26, p. 5.

1958, Elliott, J. G.: *Pot Luck, QUAR. BULL. OF THE A.G.S.*, Vol. 26, p. 170, pp. 276-277.

1972, Webb, D. A. & E. M. Rix: *Ericaceae, FLORA EUROPAEA.*

1978, Stevens, P. F.: Ericaceae, *FLORA OF TURKEY AND THE EAST AEGAEAN ISLANDS*, P. H. Davis.

1980, McClintock, David: *Erica sicula, YR. BK. OF THE HEATHER SOC.*, pp. 45-54.

1981, Everett, T. H.: Pentapera, *NEW YORK BOTANICAL GARDEN ENCYCLOPEDIA OF HORTICULTURE.*

1984, 1986, Turpin, P. G.: personal communications.

1985, Krussman, Gerd: *Pentapera, MANUAL OF BROAD-LEAVED TREES AND SHRUBS.*

1989, McClintock, David: *The heathers of Europe and adjacent areas, BOTANICAL JOUR. OF THE LINNEAN SOC.*, 1989, 101, p. 287.

ERICA X STUARTII E.F. Linton (E. X PRAEGERI Ostenf.) (*E. mackaiana x E. tetralix*)

The name of *E. x stuartii*, first published in 1902, applied to clones of a single plant found once only, in 1890, in west Galway, Ireland by Dr. Charles Stuart. Dr. Stuart died in 1902 and in that year the Rev. E. F. Linton published the name honoring the finder. For the next 75 years the plant, which is sterile, was the subject of periodic debate over what were its status and, if hybrid, its parents. Various writers hazarded various guesses including *erigena, mackaiana* and *tetralix*, among the latter two of which it had been found. The debate was brought to a definite close so recently as August 1977 when the observant Dutch nurseryman, Rinus Zwijnenburg, noticed a plant of *E. x stuartii* with a branch which was a reversion to undoubted *E. x praegeri*. Recognizing this as a significant find, Zwijnenburg started the specimen on its way and it eventually came to the attention of Prof. D. A. Webb, Trinity College, Dublin, Ericaceae Editor for *FLORA EUROPAEA*. Prof. Webb finally determined that the mutant branch passed every test for *E. x praegeri*, the already established hybrid between *E. tetralix* and *E. mackaiana*. Prof. Webb's photograph showing part of the plant with the small bicolored bells of *x stuartii*, but one branch with a terminal cluster of the much larger typical flowers of *x praegeri*, is strikingly convincing.(1) It was thus settled that *x stuartii* and *x praegeri* are both cultivars of a single taxon.(2) However, since the name *x stuartii* had been published ten years earlier than the name *x praegeri*, the rules of botanical nomenclature in effect since 1975 require that this group of plants, including all their varieties, be designated as *E. x stuartii* E. F. Linton. All members of the group of plants, including all their varieties, be designated as *E. x stuartii* E. F. Linton. All members of the group have been found in western Ireland, Galway, Donegal and Connemara, where their *mackaiana* and *tetralix* parents are cohabitants.

EE. mackaiana and *tetralix* have a number of characters in common: both have pubescent young twigs; leaves in whorls of 4 and with revolute, ciliate margins; flowers in terminal umbels and urn-shaped corollas; anthers included in the corolla and with long, narrow basal appendages; and stigma capitate (somewhat mushrooming). They differ in the size, shape and vestiture (with or without hairy surface) of their leaves; the length of the spaces between leaves on the flowering stems; the vestiture of their sepals; and the vestiture of their ovaries (in *mackaiana* glabrous, in *tetralix* pubescent.)

The progeny of this union (at least, all we have so far observed) have glabrous green leaves that are white beneath, are proportionately less broad than those of *mackaiana* and have revolute margins; included anthers with long, narrow basal appendages; and ovaries clothed with pubescence. In various respects the varieties differ from each other, most obviously flower color.

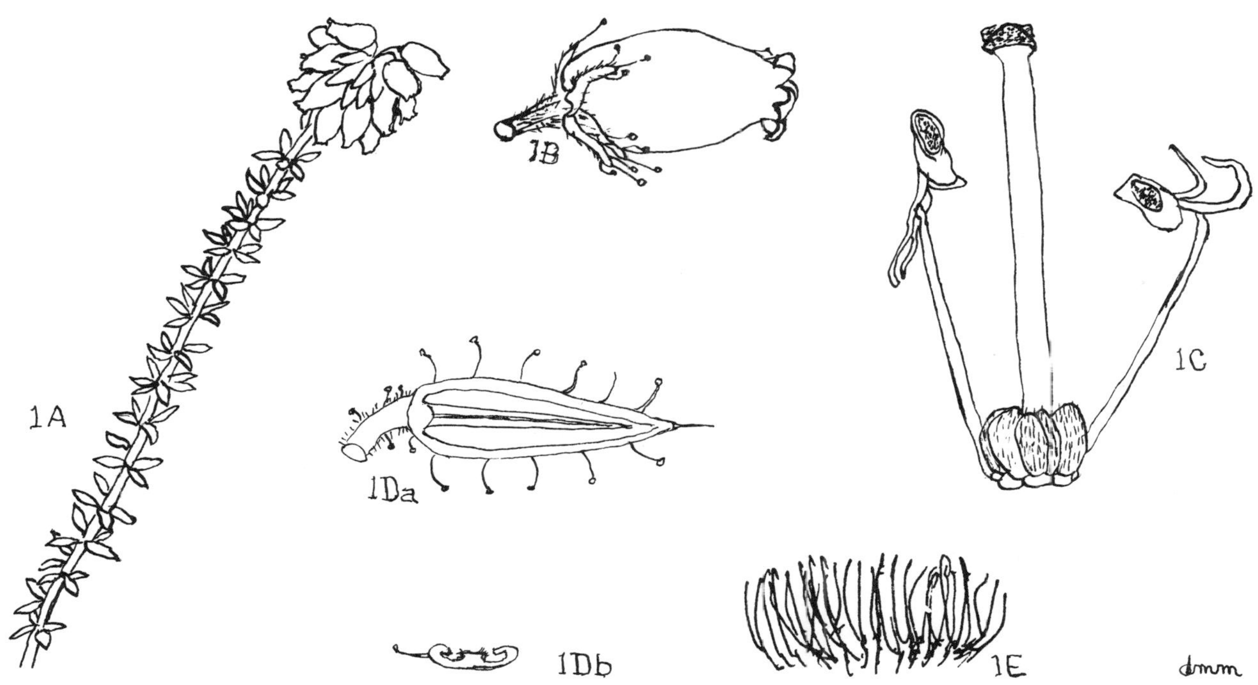

Erica x stuartii E. F. Linton, 1) **'Connemara'**: 1A, flowering stem 1X; 1B, flower 5X; 1C, pistil and 2 stamens 10X; 1Da, leaf beneath 10X; 1Db, leaf cross section 10X; 1E, plant habit.

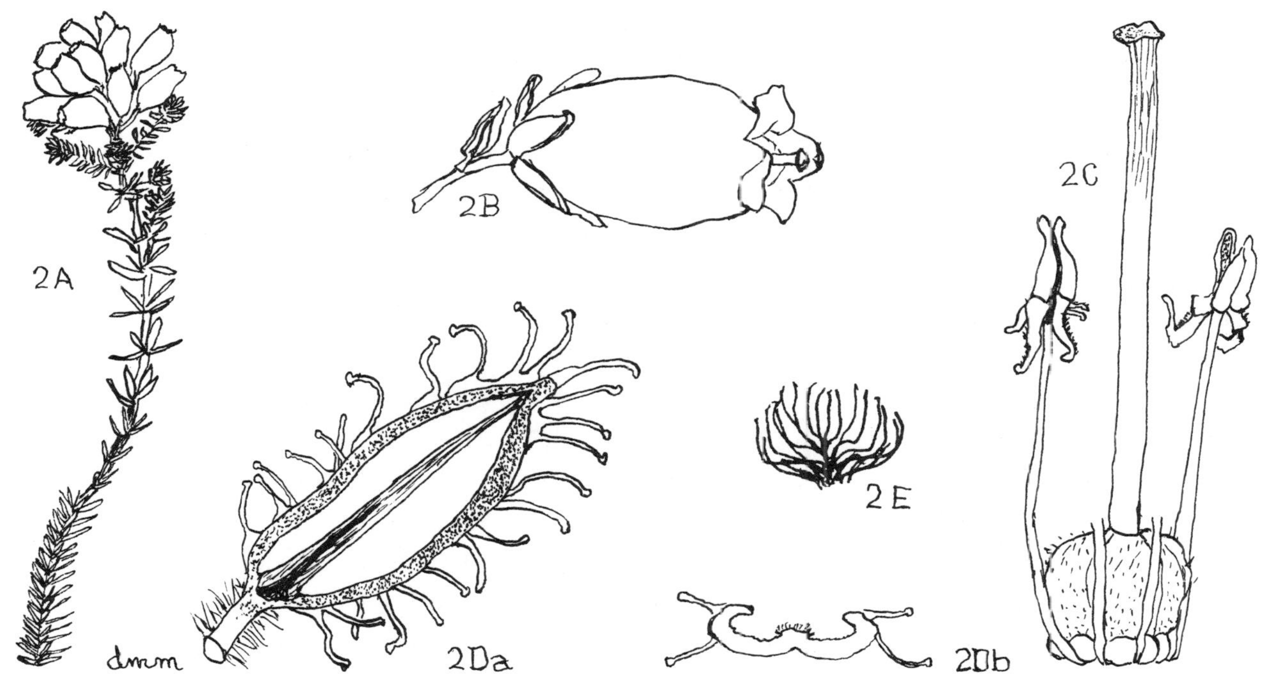

2) ***E. x s.* 'Irish Lemon':** 2A, flowering stem 1X; 2B, flower 5X; 2C, pistil and 2 stamens 10X; 2Da, leaf beneath 10X; 2Db, leaf cross section 10X; 2E, plant habit.

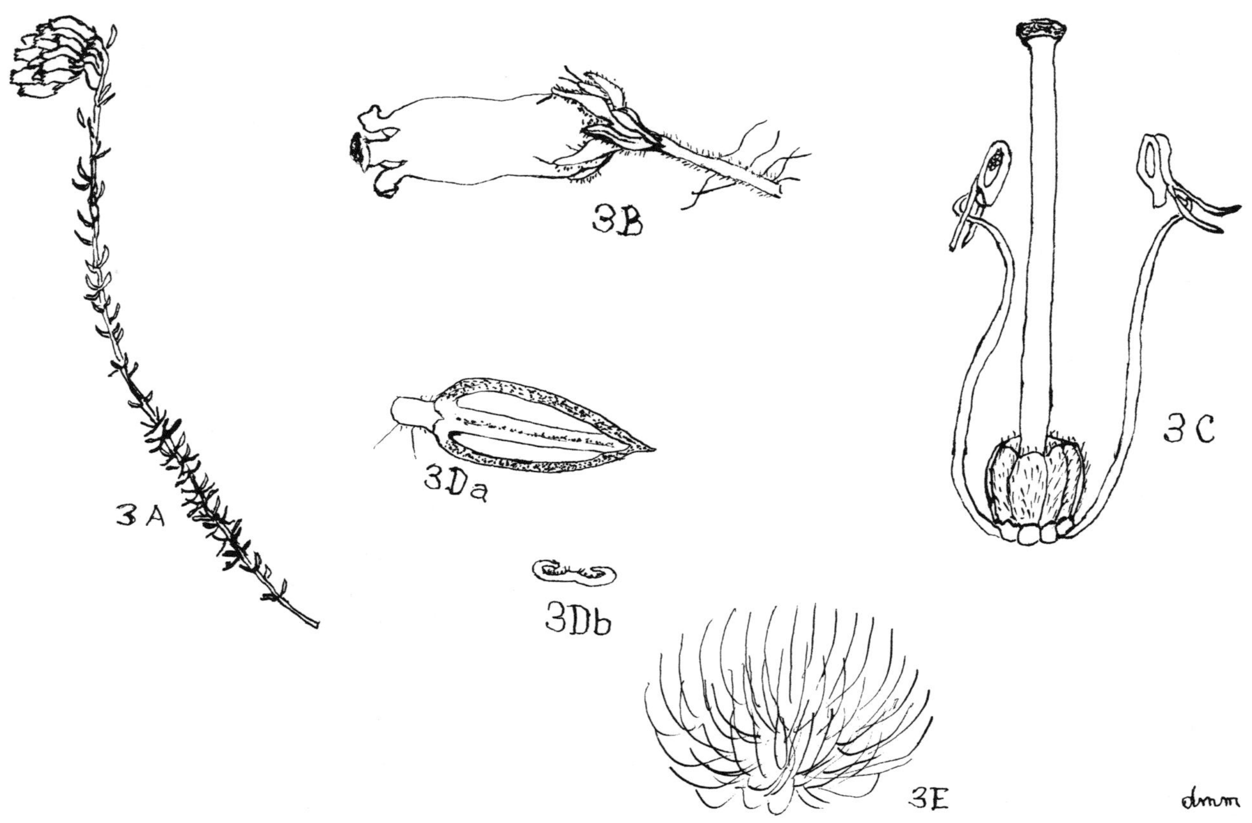

3) ***E. x s. 'Stuartii':*** 3A, flowering stem 1X; 3B, flower 5X; 3C, pistil and 2 stamens 10X; 3Da, leaf beneath 5X; 3Db, leaf cross section 5X; 3E, plant habit.

'Connemara' (formerly *E. x praegeri*)—In the garden 23 years, 30 x 90 cm (12 x 36 in); new-growth stems with very short, fine hairs; leaves small, narrow. Darker flower buds open to light (not pale) pink flowers, August-September.

'Irish Lemon'—After 3 years, 20 cm high x 40 cm wide (8 x 16 in); longer hairs on new-growth stems; leaves larger, broader, lemon yellow in spring. Flowers deep lavender-pink, June-September.

'Stuartii'—At 12 years, 45 x 90 cm (18 x 36 in); fewer hairs on new-growth stems; leaves small, with no cilia on margins but short hairs on petioles and a few very small hairs at base of leaf surface above. Flowers narrow tubes, bicolor, red-purple on distal half, whitish at base. some apparent freeze damage.

Yates (3 and 4) also listed: 'Irish Orange'—June-Sept. 25 cm (10 in). Lilac-pink flowers. spring foliage yellow with an orange flush.

'Nacung'—June-Sept. 30 cm (12 in) Lilac-pink flowers much larger than on 'Connemara'.

A plant acquired by me in 1960 as "*E. tetralix Mollis*", ultimate source unknown, seems likely on closer inspection to be probably a *x stuartii* form. Its size is 40 x 75 cm (16 x 30 in); it has new-growth stems with very short fine hairs; its leaves are similar in size to 'Connemara' but darker green, more crowded on the stems and in whorls of 5 (instead of 4). Its flowers are slightly larger, and darker than 'Connemara', and slightly more lavender-pink.

References:

1) Jones, A. W.: *YEAR BOOK OF THE HEATHER SOC.*, 1979, p. 33 and pl. 2.

2) McClintock, David: *The status of and correct name for Erica x stuartii, WATSONIA,* Feb. 1979.

3)Yates, Geoffrey: *THE POCKET GUIDE TO HEATHER GARDENING*, 1978.

4) Yates, Geoffrey: *THE GARDENER'S BOOK OF HEATHERS*, 1985.

ERICA TERMINALIS Salisbury

The Corsican Heath has been in cultivation in Britain since about 1765. Before the priority of Salisbury's epithet, *terminalis* (flowering at the branch tips), was determined it was also referred to variously as *E. corsica, E. stricta* (erect) and by Salisbury himself as *E. multicaulis* (many-stemmed). *Stricta* was the name in common use for a long time, till *terminalis* took over in about 1950.(1)

The only summer-flowering Tree Heath, it is usually somewhat taller than it is wide, said in native stands to achieve 100-250 cm (40-100 in)(2). Mature plants in a Seattle garden range from 125-180 cm (50-72 in). In Holland it is said to achieve only 60 to 70 cm (24 to 28 in)(3), so perhaps we can infer that it is less high in colder climate. It is definitely erect in habit. Young plants from seed or cuttings shoot up single first stems which soon exhibit the erect-parallel growth of side branches. As the seasons pass more stems rise from ground level and the total height of the plant increases a few inches a year till maturity. Thus the plant gradually broadens, but the width seldom becomes equal to the height. Old stems tend to become bare where shaded beneath as more fresh growth initiates from ground level. The small neat foliage, at about 45° from the stems and a fresh yellow-green when young, will eventually become more patent (spreading) and a dull darker olive-green. The flowers, as indicated by the accepted epithet, are terminal on the erect twigs, are pink, and may be seen over a long July-October season. They usually occur in umbels of 3, 4 or 5 to 8 or 12; but we have one plant (from self-sown seed) which has rounded flowering heads 4 cm (1.5 in) in diameter on some of its twigs, 50 or more florets in each, and gives a quite distinctive effect, but for a less extended season. Seed plants also vary in depth of color.

As with other Tree Heaths, the stem wood is hard and somewhat brittle, and British writers say it is easily damaged by snow, a problem not encountered here. The stems are too erect to hold a great deal of even wet snow. W. J. Bean's well-justified summation is, "Although one of the tallest of the heaths, it is perfectly hardy at Kew . . . strikes freely from cuttings and flowers well when 12 in (30 cm) high . . . a most desirable shrub. Yet it is almost neglected in gardens."

Considering its relative hardiness, (H. M. J. Blum(3) writes that its winter hardiness is better in the Netherlands than other tree heaths except *E. arborea alpina*) virtually complete indifference to soils, limy, chalky or acid, and the semi-frequency with which self-sown seed plants appear, one only wonders why its natural distribution is limited to southern Spain, Italy, Corsica, Sardinia and northwest Morocco. David McClintock(4) mentioned, that a colony of naturalized *E. terminalis* has been established since the 1920s on the Magilligan Dunes, in Londonderry, North Ireland.

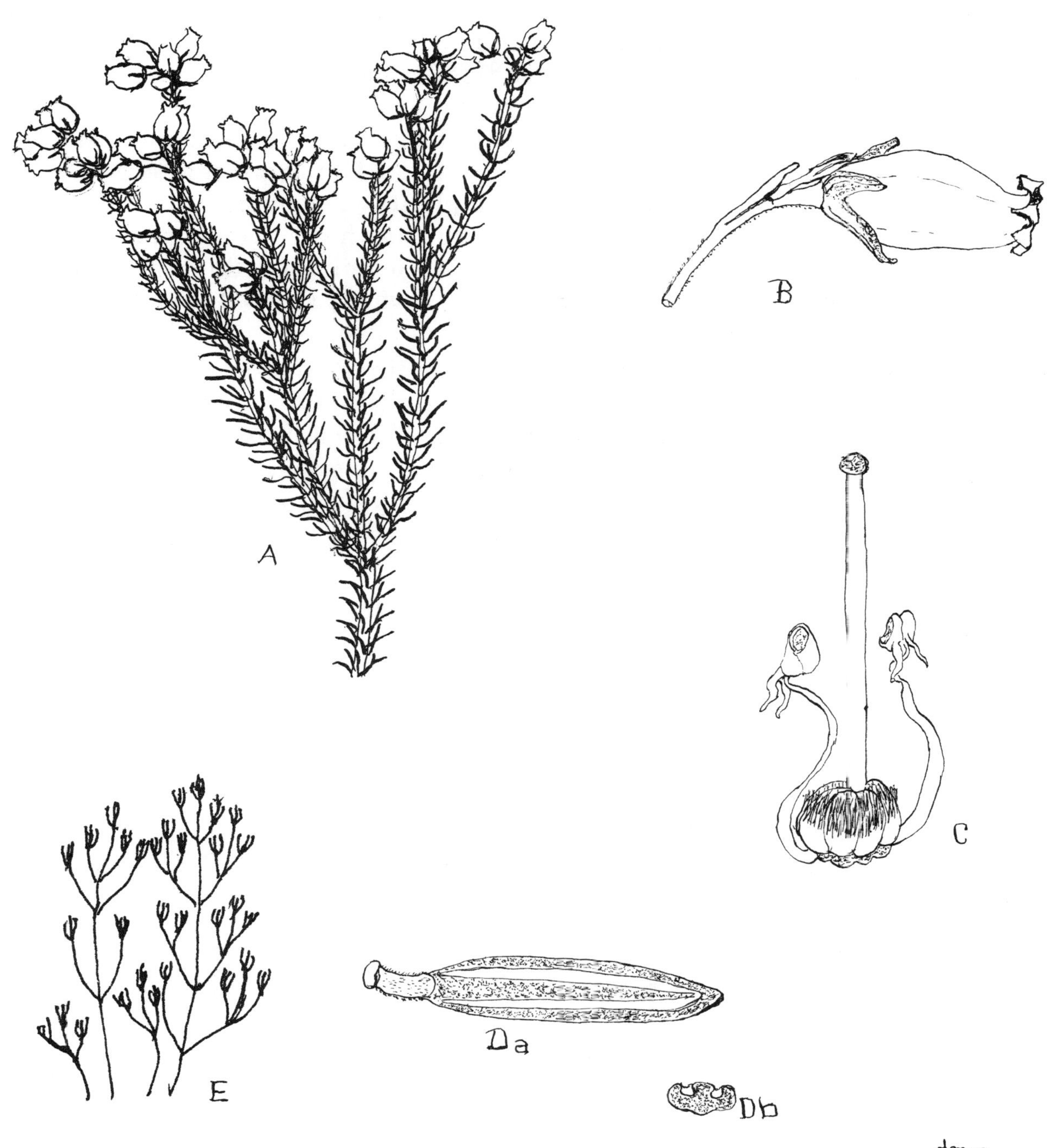

Erica terminalis Salisbury: A, flowering stem 1X; B, flower 5X; C, pistil and two stamens 10X; Da, leaf beneath 10X; Db, leaf cross section 10X; E, plant habit.

Mention of the species has been sparse in the 25 years of the Heather Society *YEAR BOOK* and most mention has been of the "among those present" variety, though Maj. Gen. Turpin, Society Chairman, has called it "a heather garden work horse." Perhaps lack of much enthusiasm for the species is accounted for by D. F. Maxwell's(5) comment, "These flowers do not expand consecutively up the stem, as is the case with most Heathers, but burst into bloom here and there about the bush, just as the spirit moves them. General effectiveness is thus sacrificed to a lengthened flowering period . . . ." But there can be a solid flush of flowering on young or carefully pruned plants - removing all of the previous year's spent flower heads. Also, some uses that have been made of it in the Pacific Northwest have not been such as to enhance its reputation; e.g., landscape designers have planted it in rows to make clipped evergreen hedges, a treatment heaths should not be asked to endure.

Free-grown mature plants are probably improved by cutting well back some of the oldest stems in spring, removing unsightly bare lower branchlets and encouraging the fresh young growths which will rise from the base.

The only cultivar listed by Yates(6) is 'Thelma Woolner' which he says has lilac-pink flowers, an improvement over the ordinary form. The progenitor of this variety was found in Sardinia, in 1967, by Mr. Woolner, of Devon, England, who named it for his wife.

In 1966 a plant called *E. t.* 'Nana' was available from at least one nursery, in Maple Valley, Washington. Its origin is unknown to us. Now 147 cm (58 in) tall, it is not particularly "nana" but its current width of 175 cm (70 in) makes it the only one of ten plants here which has always maintained wider-than-high proportions.

References:

1) Bean, W. J.: *TREES AND SHRUBS HARDY IN THE BRITISH ISLES*, 1973.

2) *FLORA EUROPAEA*, 1972.

3) Blum, H. M. J.: for *ERICULTURA*, translation by Pauline Croxton, Feb.1988.

4) McClintock, David: *Notes on British Heaths, YEAR BOOK OF THE HEATHER SOCIETY,* 1964.

5) Maxwell, D. F.: *THE LOW ROAD*, 1927.

6) Yates, Geoffrey: *POCKET GUIDE TO HEATHER GARDENING*, 1978.

ERICA TETRALIX L.

Erica tetralix was formerly commonly referred to as "The Tetralix," a reference to its leaves in whorls of four and an old classical plant name of Theophrastus and Pliny, adopted in 1753 by Linnaeus for the Cross-Leaved Heath.(1) As a parent, with *E. mackaiana*, it bequeaths its hardiness to *E. x stuartii*, and with the somewhat tender *E. ciliaris*, to *E. x watsonii*.

In the wild, *E. tetralix* is reported to grow in acid soil in bogs, wet heaths and pine woods(2). It is distributed over much of northern Europe, from possibly Iceland and certainly Scandinavia to Spain and Portugal, and onward east to central Finland and Latvia in the north, and Poland in the south. It is found all over Britain but is less prevalent than *Calluna*. There are naturalized stands in Switzerland and Czechoslovakia, and also introduced North American representatives in coastal Maine and Massachusetts.(3) Rehder(4) gives it a hardiness rating of Zone III (USDA ca. 4). Its extensive distribution suggests it is tolerant of a variety of climates, but it does not take kindly to lime. In mixed heaths, it takes the lower, wetter areas, leaving the higher, better-drained places to other heathers which are intolerant of water-logged conditions; and it is found in flat, wet moors where other heathers are not accommodated. Stuart Fraser(5), gardening on a western Oregon hillside, said it does best on a cool north slope.

It is distinguished from other summer-flowering, low-growing heaths by its flowers, ovoid campanulate with small revolute lobes, nodding in umbels of 4 to 12, or more, at its stem tips. The anthers are included and the stigma capitate and slightly exserted from the corolla. As noted above, its leaves are in whorls of 4. The leaf margins are somewhat revolute but not sufficiently to prevent the lower surfaces from being at least partly visible. It forms straggling dwarf shrubs 15-70 cm (6-28 in) high, with weak ascending stems and rather few suberect branches; young twigs are clothed with shorter or longer soft hairs, varying with the cultivar. Leaves on mature stems are divergent, with long, stout often gland-tipped cilia on both the true and apparent margins. Flowering period is June to October.

Seen in the garden, its pubescent leaves and stems give it varying degrees of silver-gray appearance, which often combines with its flower colors to make a charming picture. Many of its cultivars seem to have a problem with public approval, perhaps accounted for by Maxwell-Patrick(6), who write, "The flowers expand from June until October. Since the season's crop of flowers have to straggle out through this long period it is a rather less effective plant than most of the other species." We would add that, as with other species, the problem of browned-off umbels mixed with those of fresh color turn off many viewers, - except Mr. Chapple, who found the faded corollas "picturesque" and the plants "ultra-reliable."(7) It probably remains somewhat more compact in well-drained

Erica tetralix L. **'Alba Mollis':** Aa, flowering stem 1X; Ab, inflorescence 1X; B, flower 5X; C, pistil and 2 stamens 10 X; Da, leaf beneath 10X; Db, leaf cross section 20X; E, plant branching pattern.

garden soil, but should have an annual spring pruning to remove old spent bells and keep it tidy. The compilers of the Harlow Car Heather Trials 1971-75 reports noted(8), "... We have found, after the drought of 1974, that a dry season curtails the flowering and lightens the colours. They much prefer a dull wet season." [This garden was not supplied with a watering system.] But it still needs sun.

Since there is so confusing a multitude of heather cultivars listed, attempts are occasionally made to determine which varieties are the most peoples' favorites. Because of differences in taste and objectives, the results often tend to be less than helpful. Some gardeners don't like strong colors, some don't like pale colors. *E. tetralix* does not produce any muddy colors. Of the cultivars that have been with us for some time (a limited selection) we would speak particularly kindly of the following:

'Alba Mollis' Rather erect growing, to 25 cm (10 in). Among the most popular heathers for its year-round silver-gray foliage (in sun) and its Jun.-Oct. gleaming white flowers, which keep the attention away from the spent corollas. Among the indispensables.

'Con Underwood' At 30 cm (12 in), it is one of the taller *tetralix*. Its corollas are so deep a crimson color that the spent ones are absorbed in the color of the fresh throughout its July-Nov. season. Several experienced growers are on record as considering it among the best.

'Daphne Underwood' 25 cm (10 in). Deep bright pink flowers against grey-green foliage. June-Sept.

'Darleyensis' 15 cm (6 in). Of lower stature than some of the others, this cultivar is enjoyed by everyone for its salmon-pink flowers and its silvery foliage. A good edging plant.

'Hookstone Pink' 30 cm (12 in). Another taller plant with reddish flower buds opening to deep pink. June-Oct.

'Ken Underwood' 20 cm (8 in). One of the few colored heathers with no trace of purple in its deep salmon flowers, handsome against its dark grey-green foliage. June-Oct.

'L. E. Underwood' 22 cm (9 in). A particularly luscious combination of terra cotta buds opening to deep apricot flowers, against silver foliage. June-Oct.

'Pink Glow' 20 cm (8 in). Its deep crimson flowers and silver foliage share the virtue of 'Con Underwood' color, but it is lower growing and earlier flowering, June-Sept.

'Pink Star' 15 cm (6 in). Mr. Yates(9) calls this one his favorite *tetralix*. It has light lilac pink flowers against furry grey foliage. July-Oct. It is nearly horizontal-growing.

Besides these favorites are some not yet on the North American list that, according to Geoffrey Yates, we should be on the lookout for: **'Bartinney,'** with masses of white flowers starting in May; **'Foxhome,'** with the "reddest-colored" flowers of all; **'Hailstones,'** the only cultivar rated excellent for amount of flower by the Heather Trials committee; **'Melbury White,'** which "displays its large white flowers to perfection"; **'Ruby's Variety,'** with off-white, salmon-flushed corollas, light purple at the tips(9). Formerly listed 'Morning Glow' and 'Sunrise' have been determined to be actually the same as *E. x watsonii* 'F. White.'

References:

1) McClintock, David: *A GUIDE TO THE NAMING OF PLANTS*, 1980.
2) *FLORA EUROPAEA*, 1972.
3) Seymour, F. C.: *THE FLORA OF NEW ENGLAND*, 1969.
4) Rehder, Alfred: *MANUAL OF CULTIVATED TREES AND SHRUBS*, 1956.
5) Fraser, Stuart: Heathers in the Pacific Northwest, *YEAR BOOK OF THE HEATHER SOCIETY*, 1983.
6) Maxwell, D. F. & P. S. Patrick: *THE ENGLISH HEATHER GARDEN*, 1966.
7) Chapple, Fred J.: *THE HEATHER GARDEN*, 1964.
8) The Heather Society: *HEATHER TRIALS*, 1971-75.
9) Yates, Geoffrey: *POCKET GUIDE TO HEATHER GARDENING*, 1978.

ERICA UMBELLATA L.

It is generally agreed that this is a particularly beautiful heath. A native of the western half of the Iberian Peninsula (Spain and Portugal) and of northern Morocco, it was included by Linnaeus in his 1753 edition of *SPECIES PLANTARUM* and so has been known to the world of botany for a long time. Somehow it failed to be introduced to gardens (in Britain, in any case) until the 1920s, when it was brought in by the noted alpine plant nurseryman, W. E. Th. Ingwersen, and another form by another noted alpine gardener, Dr. Giuseppi.

FLORA EUROPAEA(1) describes it as 20-80 cm high (8-32 in). W. J. Bean(2) mentions that it can be erect or semi-prostrate. Its small leaves are in whorls of 3 and, like many other dry area plants, have revolute margins to reduce moisture loss. Somewhat greyed by pubescence when young, at maturity they become a glabrous rather dark green. The species' most striking feature, its masses of intense rosy purple flowers at the branch tips, are particularly welcome in the May-June period when not many other heathers are showing color. The corollas, occurring in terminal umbels of 2 to 8, are squat little bowls somewhat broader than long, pinched in at the mouth and with erect lobes, and the eight chocolate-colored exserted stamens contribute appreciably to the effectiveness of the inflorescence. This description applies to the plants I have had.

However, there are references in the literature to variations of flower form and color. *FLORA EUROPAEA* adds that, occurring here and there throughout the species' range, are plants, possibly hybrids, generally similar to this description but with longer pedicels, larger corollas, and anthers abortive and included in the corollas. If they are hybrids the identity of the other parent is unknown. Terry Underhill(3) says that at least four varieties can be found in the wild: *alba*, with white flowers; *anandra*, with anthers sterile and not exserted; *major*, with leaves longer and thicker, corollas larger and anthers longer and exserted; and *subcampanulata*, with the upper part of the throat more open and the anthers less exserted. An article entitled Living with Lime by Mr. Harold Street(4), who gardens in Gloucestershire on "heavy, alkaline clay" (pH not specified) says, "but more intriguing are the umbellatas raised from seed collected in the mountains of Spain by Dr. H. A. McAllister. These did not bloom until August and are still blooming in November . . . ." So it seems variations are certainly a possibility, but perhaps we already have the most attractive of the lot.

Expressions of opinion on what kind of soil the species requires run the gamut from calcifuge to reports of good tolerance of alkaline soil. It does occur naturally on acid soil. Perhaps it's indifferent.

So, with all these virtues, why is it so scarce in our gardens? The answer, of course, lies in its questionable hardiness. Here again opinions have varied

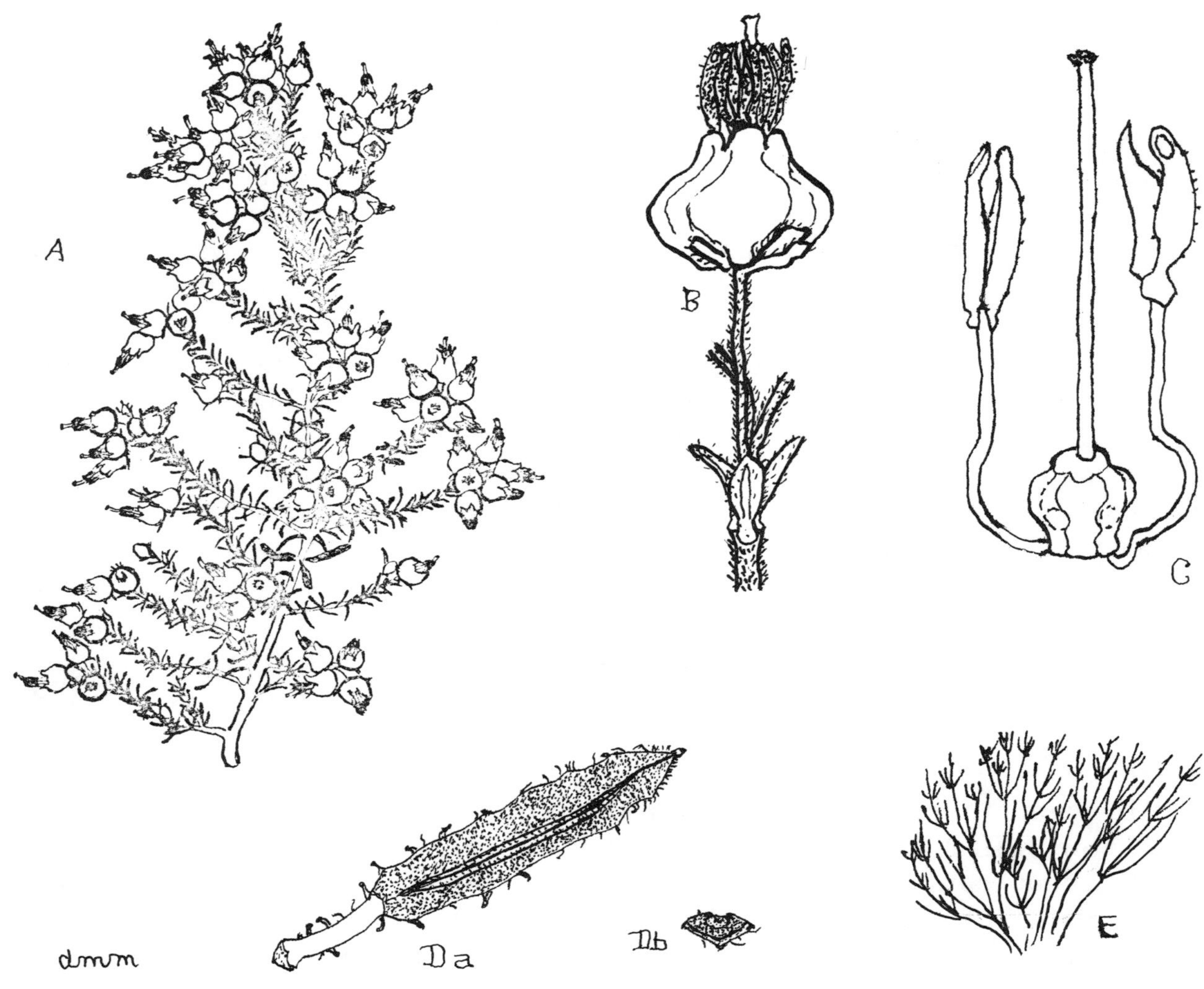

Erica umbellata L.: A, flowering branch 1X; B, flower 5X;C, pistil and 2 stamens 10X; Da, leaf beneath 15X; Db, leaf cross section 15X; E, plant habit.

---

to extremes. Harry van de Laar(5) says, "quite hardy." The Harlow Car trials reports of 1976(6) rated E. umbellata "outstanding." In the 1983 *YEAR BOOK*, Mr. Julian(7) reports that all plants of the species at Harlow Car were killed by the very hard winter of 1981-82. Worth quoting, I think, is the Proudleys' statement in *HEATHERS IN COLOUR*, 1974(8), "One cannot consider it to be entirely hardy over the whole of Britain, although in the south-west of England we have yet to lose a plant due to hard weather. . . . A position that gets full sun, is sharply drained, [situated] where the wood will get fully ripe before winter sets in, will result in more flower and of a better colour." That was before recent severe freezes.—In my Puget Sound garden in the past 25 years I have lost nine plants, mostly to one freeze or another. An *E. umbellata* plant acquired in October 1974 survived to mature size through four relatively mild winters, two with a day each down to 23°F (-5°C) and one with a day down to 21°F (-6°C), before succumbing in December 1978 to 13°F (-11°C) and 11°F (-12°C). If you can guarantee it no drops below about 20°F (-12°C) it may do very well for you.

References:

1) *FLORA EUROPAEA*, 1972.
2) Bean, W. J.: *TREES & SHRUBS HARDY IN THE BRITISH ISLES,* 1972.
3) Underhill, Terry: *HEATHS & HEATHERS* 1971.
4) Street, Harold: Living with Lime, *YEAR BOOK OF THE HEATHER SOCIETY*, 1979.
5) Van de Laar, Harry: *THE HEATHER GARDEN*, 1974-78.
6) The Heather Society: *HEATHER TRIALS REPORTS*, 1971-75.
7) Julian, T. A.: Damage at Harlow Car During the Winter of 1981-82, *YEAR BOOK OF THE HEATHER SOCIETY*, 1983.
8) Proudley, Brian & Valerie: *HEATHERS IN COLOUR*, 1974.

ERICA VAGANS L.

The Cornish Heath has been properly *Erica vagans* since it was published by Linnaeus in 1770. The only confusion in connection with its nomenclature came in 1762 and again in 1839 when it was mistaken for the more eastern Mediterranean species, *E. multiflora* and *E. manipuliflora* or they for *vagans*.(1)

The common name, Cornish Heath, masks the extent of its distribution. *E. vagans* is a native of not only Cornwall, but also elsewhere around the Bay of Biscay. It is reported in Spain as far south as the center.(2) Chopinet(3) says it is common in France (where it is called "bruyere vagabonde"—the vagabond heath) in the southwest and appears here and there in the central west and isolated spots in Haute Savoie and Isere in the extreme southeast where France borders Switzerland and Italy. A small entirely white-flowering stand has long since been reported in a remote area of County Fermanagh, in northwest Ireland. Members of the Heather Society visited it there in 1980.(4) In Cornwall it is probably confined to the Lizard Peninsula, which juts out to the south at the west entrance to the English Channel.

A peculiarity of *E. vagans* is that its natural occurrences are above serpentine rock, which causes a slightly high pH, 5.5-7.5, in the soil; but the alkalinity is magnesium-rather than calcium-based. The *vagans'* constitution permits it to succeed in heavy soils, with added peat, where other heather species would not survive.(5) Observing it in Spain, David McClintock commented, "*E. vagans* showed itself constantly the most lime tolerant of all the heathers we saw, frequently growing where no others did, and accompanied by many plants typical of chalk or lime soils(6)." But it also does very well in moderately acid soils.

Vagans, the Latin for wandering, is a suitable descriptive epithet for a shrub whose low-growing branches may develop roots where they are in contact with the ground, thus forming new plants which spread to cover ever larger areas. Where happily situated it also seeds itself copiously.

The decumbent to ascending stems of the cultivars range from 15 cm to 45 cm (6 to 18 in) in height, and the width of the plants can be several times as much. *E. vagans* is a leafy species, and its foliage varies from rather dull to fresh green, or golden-leaved. The small bell-flowers are borne in leafy clusters, intercalary in some cultivars, terminal in others, in late summer and autumn. A common color of wild stands is a light mauve-lavendar, and some such plants of not very exciting color do have the virtues of being very floriferous and keeping their color till late November. The cultivars on nursery lists range from various shades of white through very pale to deeper shades of pink, rose pink and lilac to near-red. Seedlings will produce flower colors more or less resembling those of the parents. Except for some of the mauves, flower colors are

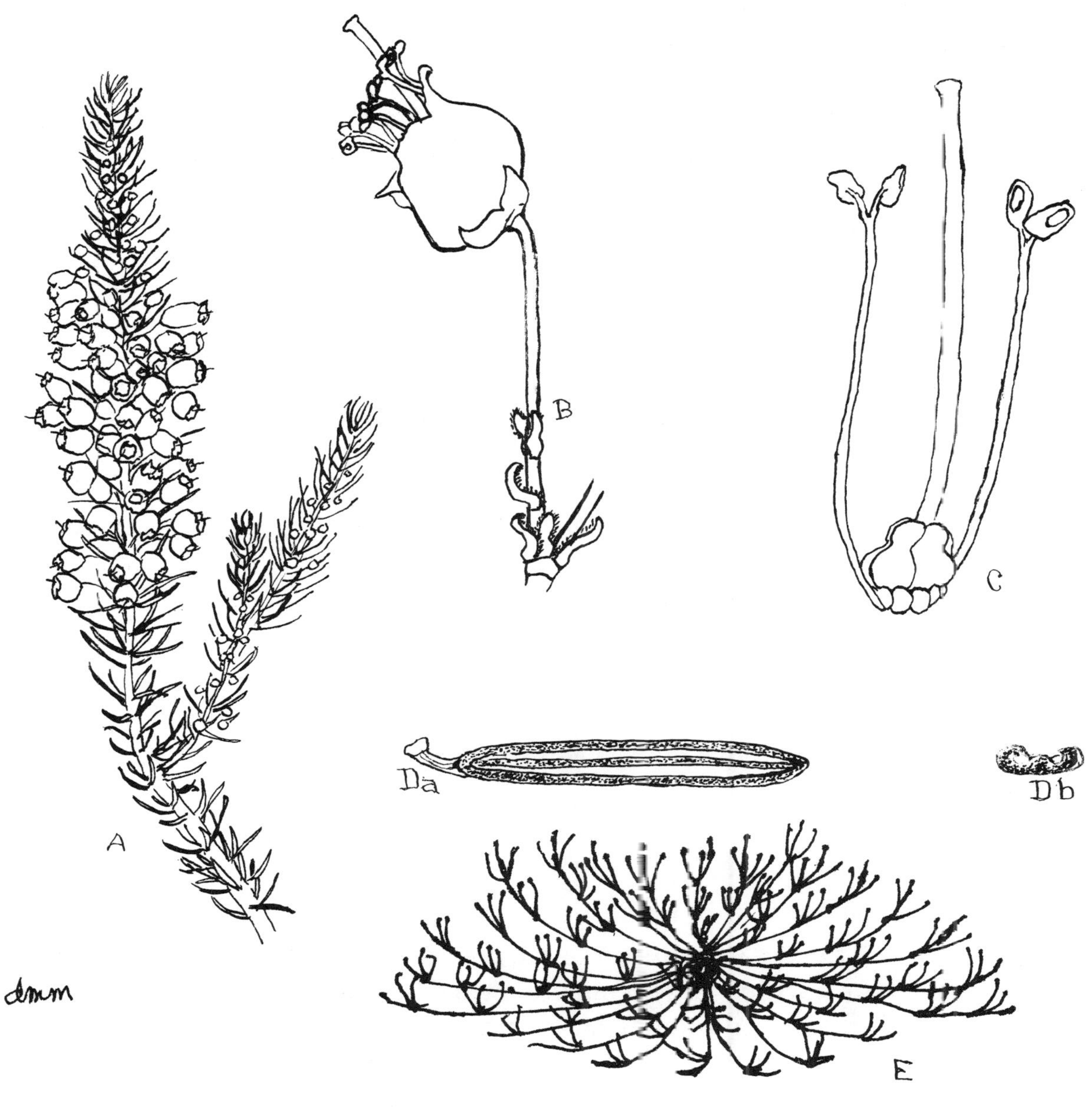

Erica vagans L. **'Lyonesse':** A, flowering stem 1X; B, flower 5X; C, pistil and 2 stamens 10X; Da, mature leaf beneath 5X; Db, leaf cross section 10X; E, branching habit of a mature *E. vagans* plant, up to 40 cm high and 135 cm diameter (16 X 54 in).

attractively clear. Spent flowers turn to shades of brown which vary from light to dark in accordance with the colors of the fresh flowers and may make a pleasing winter picture on a bank.

At Goonhilly Downs, in Cornwall, we saw it growing in an area of wet oozing mud, but also clambering over unmortared fieldstone walls with surely the sharpest possible drainage. However, that was in a very moist, misty atmosphere. In the summer dry spells of a more Mediterranean climate it does well enough with or without frequent soaking.

It can have its stems split by sharp cold. Dr. Munson(7) found in his heather trials in Ithaca, N.Y., that the few *E. vagans* plants in his trial plantings were more or less severely damaged by -5°F (-21°C), with occasional drops to -20°F (-29°C) for two or three hours, but none was killed outright.

Occasional spring trimming back of spent flower tips will keep the plants tidy. Too frequent sharp pruning may cause shorter flower spikes.

Besides *forma alba*, the common white, Yates in 1978 listed 32 cultivars, 22 of which were on the North American Cultivar List, 1983.(8) Numerous "finds" have been reported since, some of them of the recently popular golden-leaved variety. From experience with a limited list of "old stand-bys" we have noted the following according to flower colors:

<u>of the whites —</u>

'Lyonesse' 30 cm (12 in), with good spikes of sparkling white flowers, Aug.-Oct., and fresh green foliage. AGM 1969.

'Nana' 15 cm (6 in), with not many creamy white flowers but desirable where a spreading dwarf is needed.

'Valerie Proudley' 15 cm (6 in), is another few-flowered dwarf but with striking gold-green foliage. AM 1971.

Also, **'Cornish Cream'** was rated outstanding in the trials.(9)

<u>of the pinks —</u> There are numerous cultivars described as "pink," a word which is used to cover a wide range from a very pallid mauve-pink, e.g. 'Carnea', 'Pallida,' through lighter and darker clear pink and rose-pink, shading over to the purple end of the spectrum. Some writers describe the deeper of these shades as "glowing red". Perhaps there is a difference attributable to soil or situation; but *THE HEATHER SOCIETY COLOUR CHART* is of value to give a definite meaning to color names. Of the "pink" cultivars I have grown, the following can be fairly called pink and are all good garden plants:

'Birch Glow' 20 cm (8 in), deep pink, Aug.-Oct., bright green foliage.

'Diana Hornibrook' 25 cm (10 in), deep pink, early Aug.-Oct. AM 1967. Rated outstanding in the heather trials.(9)

'George Underwood' 30 cm (12 in), a slightly more lavender pink than the two above and less intense, Aug.-Oct.

'Miss Waterer' 35 cm (14 in), light pink, Aug.-Sept.

'Pyrenees Pink' 25 cm (10 in), medium dark lavender-pink, late Aug.-Oct.; dark green foliage. Rated outstanding.

'St. Keverne' 20 cm (8 in), clear medium light pink flowers terminate the branches, rather than intercalary, Aug.-Nov. AM 1914, AGM 1927, FCC 1971. As all the awards indicate, an old but still unbeaten cultivar.

<u>of the near-reds:</u>

'Mrs. D.F.Maxwell' 35 cm (14 in), cherry red, early Aug.-Oct. One of the taller of the vagans clan, with darker green foliage, this is among the best known of all heathers. The *HEATHER TRIALS*(9) did not report on it because they concluded their plants were not true to name, and this is probably a common occurrence. My original three plants, bought at the same nursery at the same time, bore flowers of three different shades of red, all acceptable; but if you have the true form, it is a winner. Numerous almost true seedlings have appeared here. AM 1925, AGM 1969, FCC 1970.

Also, **'Fiddlestone'** 30 cm (12 in), Aug.-Oct., long cerise flower spikes, color depending on growing conditions.(5) Rated outstanding in the heather trials.

References:

1) McClintock, David: *A GUIDE TO THE NAMING OF PLANTS*, 1980.

2) *FLORA EUROPAEA*, 1972.

3) Chopinet, R.: Les Bruyeres Rustiques, *PLANTES DES MONTAGNES*, Bul. de la Soc. des Amateurs de Jardins Alpins, 1967-68.

4) Magor, E. W. M.: *Riddles of the Irish Heaths*, *YEAR BOOK OF THE HEATHER SOCIETY,* 1981.

5) Yates, Geoffrey: *POCKET GUIDE TO HEATHER GARDENING*, 1978.

6) McClintock, David: *Iter Hispanicum Ericaceum*, *YEAR BOOK OF THE HEATHER SOCIETY*, 1983.

7) Munson, R. H.: *Heather Hardiness Trials, preliminary report*, noted in *HEATHER NEWS*, No. 11, Sept. 1980, p.5.

8) *Heathers in North American Gardens*, *HEATHER NEWS*, No. 21, Mar., 1983, p. 2.

9) The Heather Society: *HEATHER TRIALS* 1971-75.

ERICA X VEITCHII Bean

This hybrid between two Tree Heaths, the originally introduced form of *E. arborea* and *E. lusitanica*, appeared by chance as a seed plant in the nursery of R. Veitch, at Exeter, Devon in the 1890s. The nursery originally assumed it was a form of *E. arborea*, which in general it more or less resembles. Then in 1905, after it had been given an Award of Merit when shown by the nursery at a Royal Horticultural Society early spring show, W. J. Bean, distinguished horticulturist at Kew Gardens, examined the plant more closely and was persuaded of its hybrid origin.(1)

The confusion of identification later in North America, probably came about from the fact that information sources available to most of us made the distinction between the hybrid and its parents seem deceptively simple. The most quoted criteria were that if a tree heath 1)without the bright pink flower bud color of *lusitanica* and 2)with light green leaves had 3)a mixture of branched and simple new growth hairs and 4)a pink stigma, then it was *x veitchii*. Actually, there is a great variation in leaf color and others of these criteria in plants of *E. arborea* and/or *arborea alpina*, and they all seem to have some simple hairs mixed with the branched ones on their new growth. In Britain, where the original, bona fide plant of *E. x veitchii* could be seen at Kew Gardens, the distinction is much easier, because it is true that once one knows that the one plant is *x veitchii*, the other *arborea*, the appearance of the two plants is decidedly different. At the Royal Horticultural Society's garden at Wisley, the two are/were planted side by side, making the difference all the more apparent.

Maj. Gen. Turpin, Chairman of The Heather Society, published a more detailed differentiation in The Heather Society *YEAR BOOK* for 1979(2) but we still felt on somewhat shaky ground until Stuart Fraser, Lebanon, OR, sent us a photo copy of W. J. Bean's original publication of the hybrid *x veitchii* in *THE GARDENER'S CHRONICLE* for 1905.(1)

In his one-paragraph description accompanying the illustrations, Bean mentions the differences in the anther appendages (*lusitanica* much longer, *arborea* very short, *x veitchii* somewhat short), and in the pollen grains. Of the latter he says they "differ slightly in the two parent species, whilst those in the hybrid are unlike those of either progenitor." Making this distinction requires microscopic examination of the pollen. The illustrative drawing with this article shows rough drawings of the three kinds of pollen grain, from plants in my garden. (NOTE: Viable ericaceous pollen grains are normally tetrads, i.e., in four parts, but as most commonly seen under a two-dimensional enlargement (rather than by scanning microscope), they often appear as three-part bodies, with one part out of sight behind the others. We have kindly been supplied with pollen grain size and other data by Mr. A. W. Jones.(3) His data confirm our own rough observations. No effort is made here to give exact enlargement

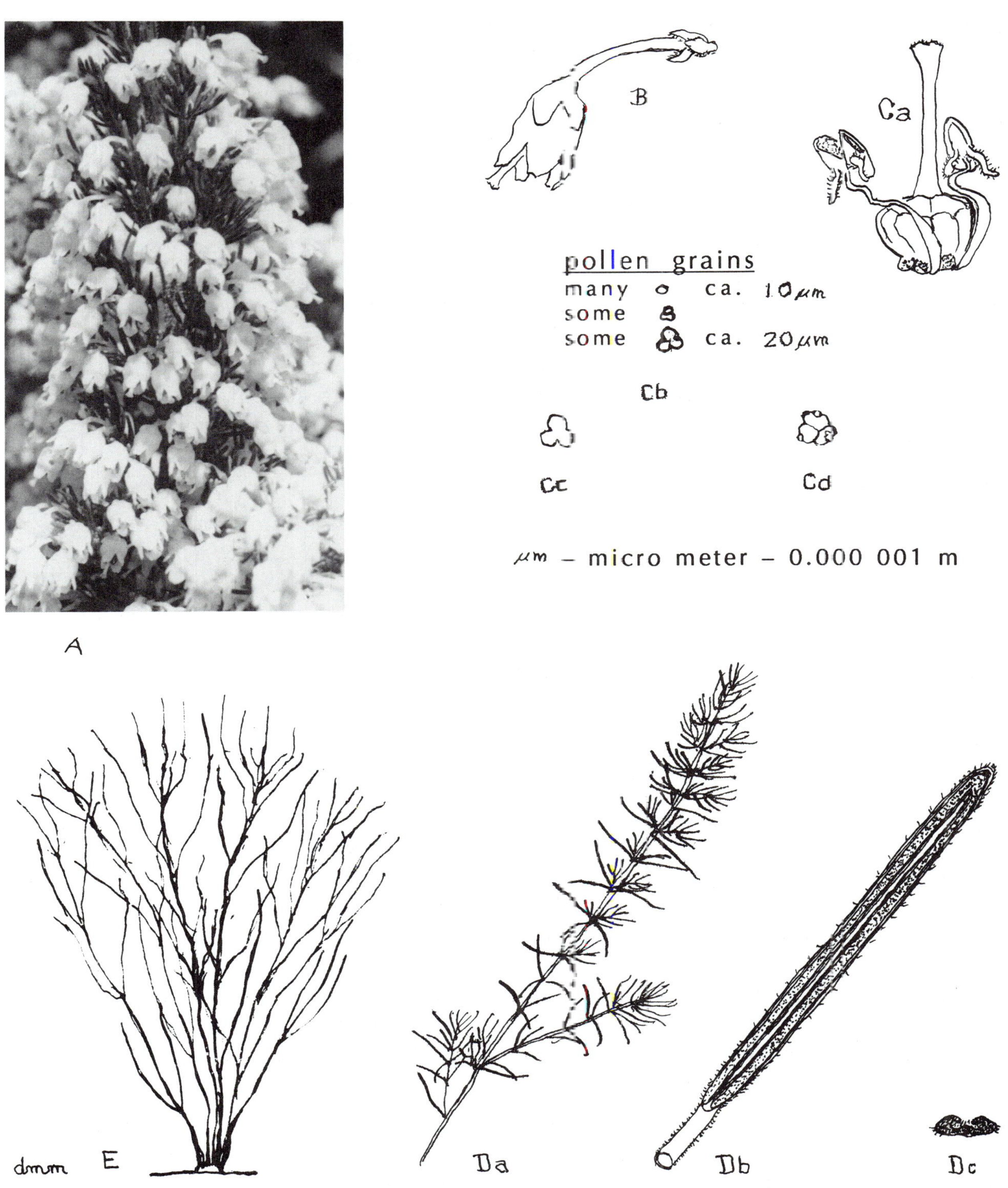

Erica x veitchii Bean **'Exeter':** A, flowering branches; B, flower 5X; Ca, pistil and 2 stamens 10X; Cb, pollen grains *x veitchii*; Cc, *arborea*; Cd, *lusitanica*; Da, leaf habit 1X; Db, leaf beneath 10X; Dc, leaf cross section 20X; E, plant habit. Note: stems all rise from single very short trunk.

figures for the accompanying pollen drawings, but only to show their relative sizes and shapes. It can be observed that there are some normal appearing pollen grains from the *x veitchii*. (If, as some have thought, *E. x veitchii* is actually a heather hybrid which is fertile, that would suggest a closer relationship between its parents than there is between the parents of other heather hybrids.(4))

According to the presently accepted rules for the naming of plants, whenever a hybrid is brought into cultivation and propagated it needs a cultivar name.(5) Every plant resulting from a cross between *E. arborea* and *E. lusitanica* would be known as *E. x veitchii*; but only the descendants of that first plant which appeared in R. Veitch's nursery at Exeter have the clone name 'Exeter'. Other plants resulting from seed from the same cross fertilization will have different characteristics (just as a family of children of the same parents differ from each other) and each has its own clone name. Only plants vegetatively propagated from a particular cultivar will have the same cultivar name.

My plant, presumed to be *E. x veitchii* **'Exeter,'** happens to be planted in a close group with some *E. arborea alpina* of about the same age (now 22 years from four-inch pots). Once we know the plant is *E. x veitchii* 'Exeter,' it is apparent that it is a little smaller, more compact with less gangly spreading branches, and neater looking, with lighter green new foliage in mid-July and with slightly lighter brown spent flowers. Like those of its *arborea* parent, the flowers of *x veitchii*, when fresh, are fragrant.

	E. arborea	*E. x veitchii* 'Exeter'
height	ca. 4 m. (13 ft)	ca. 3 m. (10 ft)
width	to ca. 3 m. (10 ft)	to ca. 2 m. (6.3 ft)
foliage	various, but usually darker	yellowish green

'Gold Tips' is said to be taller and more upright than 'Exeter' and with attractive new foliage, pale golden yellow with orange tips. I was given cuttings of this variety in 1971 and grew one on to about .8 m (2.6 ft) when it was killed by 11°F (-12°C) in December 1978. It is interesting to note that this heath, raised and introduced by the old firm of Maxwell & Beale, Wimborne, Dorset, was traded for 35 or 40 years as "*E. arborea* 'Gold Tips'" before being identified as a hybrid in the late 1970s. Maj. Gen. Turpin(2) says it is taller and more upright than 'Exeter' and its flowers are slightly smaller than those of *E. lusitanica*. Yates(6) reports it to be poor flowering.

'Pink Joy' is also best described by Maj. Gen. Turpin. It appeared at a Dutch nursery, from *E. arborea* seed and was first distributed in 1969. Yates(6, 7) describes it as having pink flower buds which open to white flowers [the color would have been inherited from *E. lusitanica*].

Besides these named varieties of *E. x veitchii*, other more recently mentioned(8) plants include one at the Royal Horticultural Society's garden at

Wisley which is taller [over 10 ft (3 m)] and hardier than 'Exeter,' having survived the severe freeze there of the winter of 1978-79, which killed 'Exeter.'

References:

1) Bean, W. J.: *ERICA VEITCHII x, GARDENER'S CHRONICLE*, 1905, Ser. 3, Vol. 37, p. 138, figs. 97-100.
2) Turpin, P. G.: *The Tree Heaths* 'Gold Tips' and 'Pink Joy,' *YEAR BOOK OF THE HEATHER SOCIETY*, 1979.
3) Jones, A. W.: personal communication, Dec. 1982.
4) Lawrence, G. H. M.: *TAXONOMY OF VASCULAR PLANTS*, 1951.
5) McClintock, David: *GUIDE TO THE NAMING OF PLANTS*, 1980.
6) Yates, Geoffrey: *POCKET GUIDE TO HEATHER GARDENING*, 1978.
7) Yates, Geoffrey: *THE GARDENER'S BOOK OF HEATHERS*, 1985.
8) Turpin, P. G.: Heather Gardens, *YEAR BOOK OF THE HEATHER SOCIETY*, 1981.

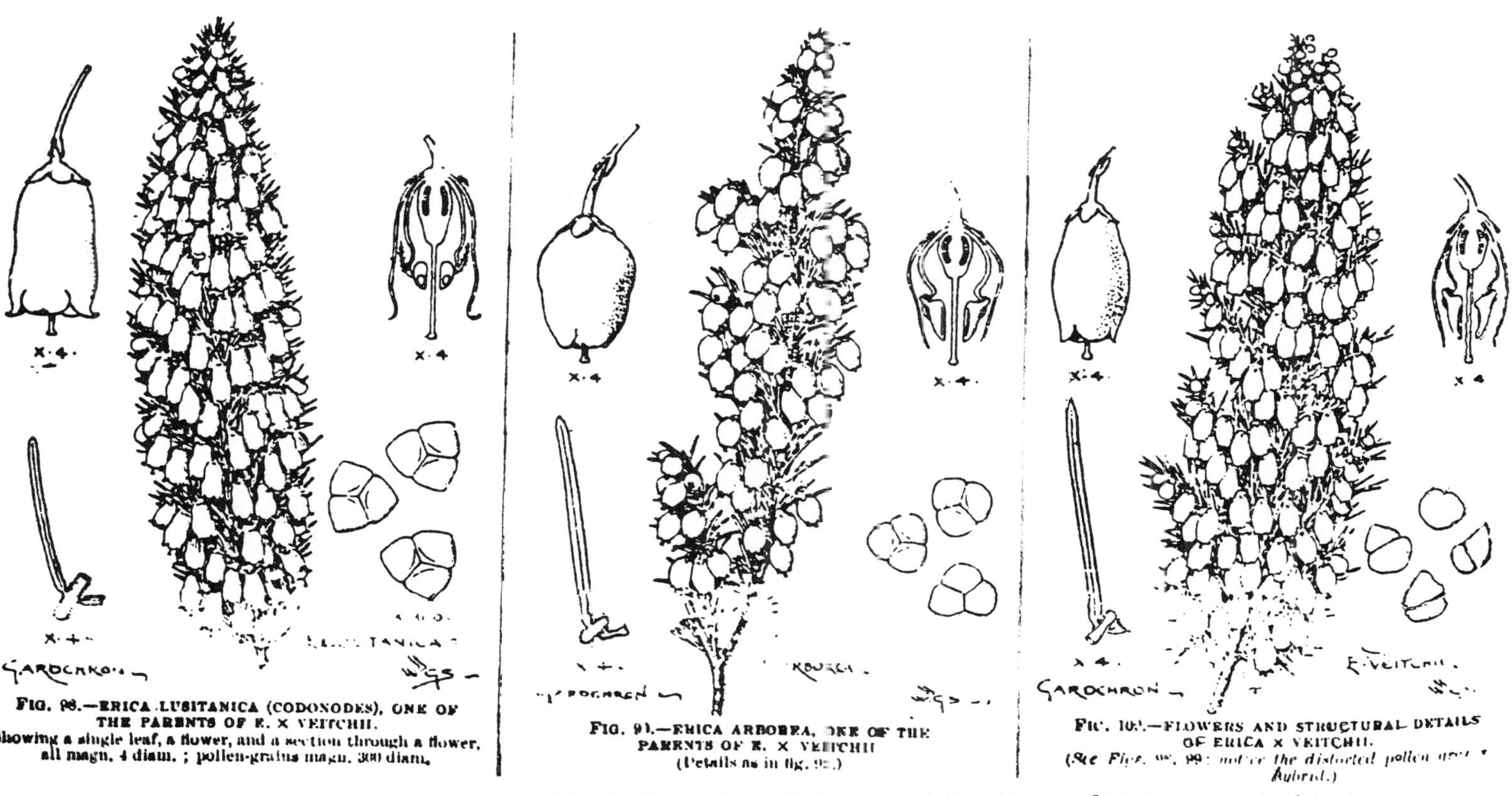

Illustration accompanying W. J. Bean's original publication of *Erica x veitchii*, in the *GARDENER'S CHRONICLE*, 1905. Ser. 3, Vol. 37, p. 138, figs. 97-100.

ERICA X WATSONII Benth.

(Erica ciliaris x Erica tetralix)(1) From a plant sale in autumn 1967 I brought home nine good, donated plants. All were tagged *E. x* 'Dawn' (i.e., *E. x watsonii* 'Dawn') and were planted out in one group. In December of the following year the garden suffered a damaging freeze of 9°F (-13°C) with no snow cover. A remarkable disparity soon became apparent in this planting, with three of the plants looking fine and six of them looking very sad. So then they got a more careful examination.

The sturdy three had 4 leaves per whorl, as do the forms of the hybrid, *E. x watsonii*; the sad six had 3 leaves per whorl, as does the species, *E. ciliaris.* Observation of the plants in the years since has shown that while both kinds *(ciliaris* and *x watsonii)* form similar low, broad mounds, with their low branches sweeping out along the ground before turning their tips up to display the flowers, the low branches of the hybrid 'Dawn' root down as they go making vigorous, intricately intertwined tops, and the branches of *ciliaris* do not root but keep themselves discrete. The hybrid cultivars have added attraction for their various shades of yellow to salmon to bronze new tip growth in the spring. The 3-leafers *(ciliaris)* had probably fooled their grower this time by also having bright new-growth tips in the spring.

E. x watsonii is a group of natural (found in the wild) hybrid cultivars. They have flowers which, some more and some less, resemble the bottle-shape bells of *ciliaris* and inflorescences which range in length between the longer ones of *ciliaris* and the shorter umbels of *tetralix*; but, like *tetralix*, their leaves are generally in whorls of 4 (or more).

The earliest of these hybrids to be reported was found and recognized as a hybrid near Truro, Cornwall, in 1839, by H. C. Watson, and their name memorializes the finder.(2) His plant, a very good one, now bears the cultivar name 'Truro.' Those added to the list in the first half of the twentieth century were found by members of the Wimborne nursery firm of Maxwell & Beale, in mild Dorset. D. F. Maxwell and P. S. Patrick who write so engagingly (but not with up-to-date nomenclature) about them made a number of the finds on their long walks over the Dorset moors.

An interesting note here is the comment of David Wilson, nurseryman of Sardis, B.C., Canada, who had been hybridizing heathers: He had assumed that because there are relatively few *x watsonii* cultivars in the trade, it would be difficult to obtain plants of this hybrid; but as it turned out he got hundreds.

Most of the hybrid cultivars available to us have fortunately inherited some of the hardiness of their parent *tetralix*. Their flowering seasons are very long, some from June to November. In an open winter around Puget Sound there are still a good many flowers on 'Dawn' and more on 'Gwen' even in January. In our experience, 'Dawn,' 'Gwen,' 'H. Maxwell' and 'Truro' are hard to beat for satis-

Erica x watsonii Benth. A, **'Dawn'**; AA, inflorescence 1X; AB, flower 5X; AC, pistil and 2 stamens 10X.

B, **'Gwen'**; BB, flower 5X; BC, pistil and 2 stamens 10X.

C, leaf; CA, leaf whorls 1X; CB, leaf beneath 10X; CC, leaf cross section 10X.

D, plant habits; DA, ground cover; DB, ascending.

factory performance of summer blooming in the garden.

The data given by Maxwell-Patrick vary from those given by Yates. Perhaps the differences are caused by their growing conditions/climates. The cultivars listed by Yates are:

'Ciliaris Hybrida' 20-23 cm (8-9 in). June/July to Oct/Nov. Of this variety Maxwell-Patrick says, "This was the first of my finds in this section; I named it without giving the subject sufficient thought. . . ." Flowers rosy pink/pale lilac pink. New spring growth bright yellow.

'Dawn' 20-23 cm. June/July-Oct/Nov. When I first observed the early spring new growth color, I assumed the cultivar name was chosen because of the sunrise colors; but it seems it was named for a daughter. Deservedly popular and rated good on all counts in the Heather Society Trials.(4)

'F. White' Of this one Maxwell-Patrick says, "I think of it as a self-conscious poor relation of the hybrids, and its white flowers are never without a blush." I have tried twice to have it, but without success. The Heather Trials rated it Good for flowers, Poor for garden worthiness.

'Gwen' A smaller version of 'Dawn' but with more lavender flowers and yellow spring new growth.

'H. Maxwell' June/July-Oct/Nov. 30-45 cm (12-18 in). Pink flowers. For me it has been less vigorous and less sturdy than the above two.

'Rachel' July-Oct. 25 cm (10 in). I have not seen it but Yates says it is almost identical to 'Dawn' but more vigorous.

'Truro' July-Oct. 15 cm. A more compact plant with inflorescences of similar color to 'Dawn' and seem just as large but more compact. Rated Good on all counts.

'Dorothy Metheny' Now on the list but I have not seen the garden cultivar—only the wild plant on Hartland Moor, from which it was propagated. It was found by Heather Society members on an afternoon's walk, in September, 1979. Its flowers resemble those of 'F. White,' but the plant is said to have a much better garden constitution.

References:

1) McClintock, David: *GUIDE TO THE NAMING OF PLANTS*, 1980.

2) Maxwell, D.F. & Patrick, P.S.: *THE ENGLISH HEATHER GARDEN*, 1966.

3) Yates, Geoffrey: *POCKET GUIDE TO HEATHER GARDENING*, 1978.

4) The Heather Society: *HEATHER TRIALS*, 1971-75.

ERICA X WILLIAMSII Druce

(Erica vagans x Erica tetralix) On the Lizard Peninsula, which juts out from the south coast of Cornwall into the western end of the English Channel, great masses of *E. vagans* grow intermixed with *E. cinerea, E. tetralix and Calluna vulgaris.* In the botanical order of things, *E. tetralix* and *E. vagans* are considered not very closely related. Nevertheless, though relatively rare, their hybrid progeny, *E. x williamsii*, are known to have been discovered on the Lizard four or more times: in 1860 when it was noted but not introduced(1); in 1910 when P. D. Williams, noted horticulturist and nephew of that first finder, found it nestling against his garden wall at St. Keverne, and introduced the cultivar now named 'P.D.Williams'(2); in 1924 by Mr. Williams' daughter; and about 1940, when Miss Gertrude Waterer, of Penzance found the ancestor of the plants now known as 'Gwavas,' near Gwavas farm.

The habit of *E. x w.* 'P. D. Williams' is dense, more erect and larger in spread than *E. tetralix* but not so high as many *E. vagans*. It lacks the low spreading and rooting branches of *vagans*. New-growth stems are slightly downy, but less so than those of *tetralix*. The leaves are close set in whorls of four and, with revolute margins, appear to be linear, somewhat resembling those of *tetralix* but with fewer hairs on apparent margins (*vagans* leaves lack marginal hairs); they are glabrous above and, with new leaves yellow in spring, have a fresh light yellow-green appearance, lacking the pubescence which gives *tetralix* varieties a more or less greyed look. The inflorescence somewhat resembles that of *E. vagans*. The three bracteoles on the pedicels are neither near the tops (like *tetralix*) nor near the base (like *vagans*). The sepals more resemble those of *tetralix* in shape but are less hairy. The campanulate corollas with erect lobes are proportionately narrower than those of *vagans*, but not pinched at the mouth like *tetralix*. The anthers are included (like *tetralix*) but unappendaged (like *vagans*). The exserted style has a broader stigma (like *tetralix*), but the ovary is hairy only on its upper half. In other words, the hybrid is midway between its accepted parents.

The flowers, a good warm lilac pink, have been scarce some of the twenty-four summers I have had it in the garden, and I have come to suspect that it flowers more freely when not pruned too much; so perhaps one could let it go every other year or so. My long-since mature plant is 40 cm high by 100 cm wide (16 X 40 in).

The only other *x williamsii* cultivar to date, 'Gwavas' is described by Yates(3) as a bit taller and with much paler flowers lacking the warmth of 'P.D.Williams'; but they are also larger.(4) Mr. Yates adds that both cultivars have inherited from *vagans* "tolerance of indifferent soil conditions"; and the *x williamsii* plants were among the few at Harlow Car(5) quite undamaged from the recent hard winters. U.B.C. Botanical Garden lists 'Gwavas' among its collection. And

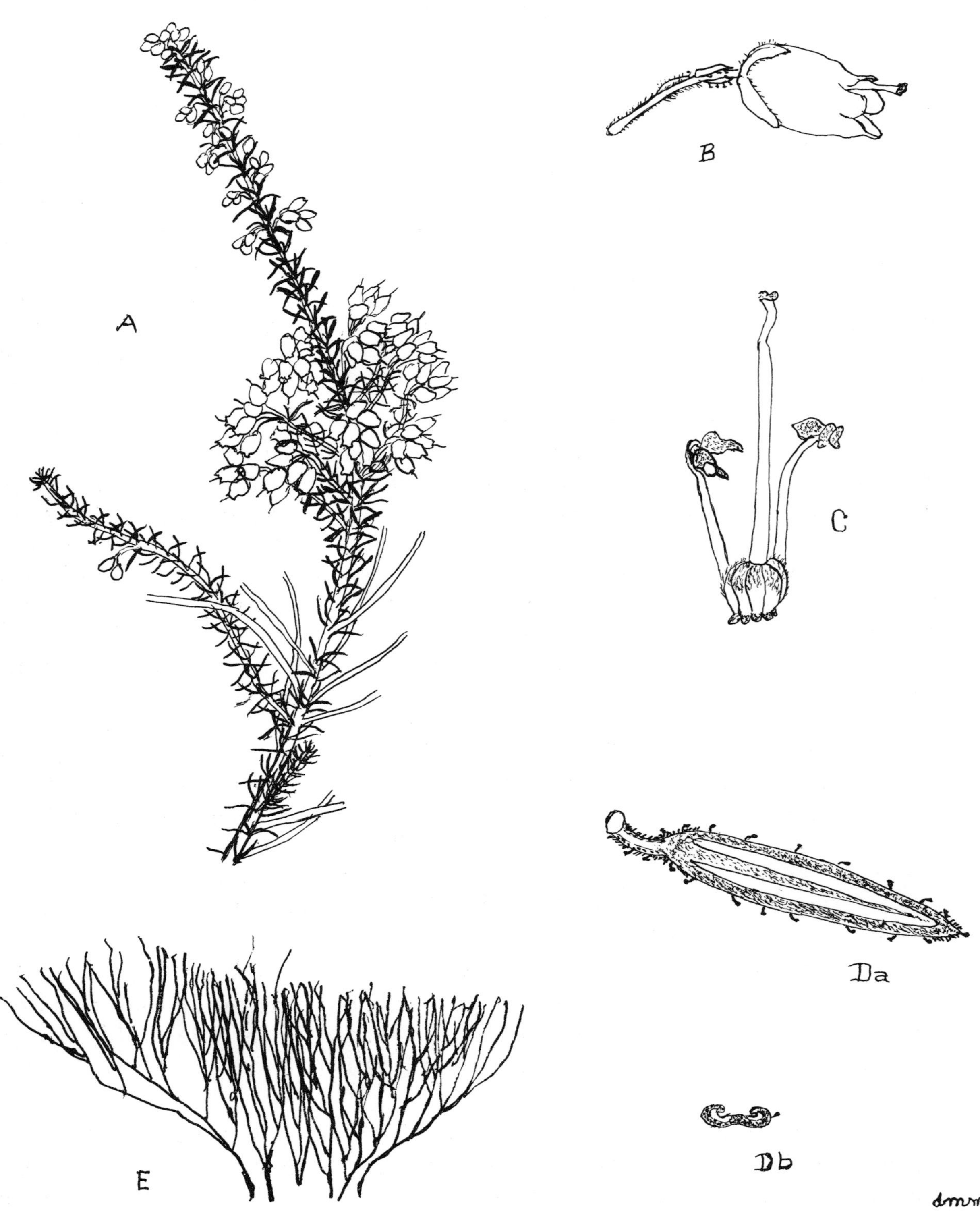

Erica x williamsii Druce **'P. D. Williams'**: A, flowering stem 1X; B, flower 5X; C, pistil and 2 stamens 10X; Da, leaf beneath 10X; Db, leaf cross section 10X; E, plant habit.

someone sent in to the *Heathers in North American Gardens*(6) list the name of "Gwavas Rubra," which is not to be found in Yates's list. Word (personal communication) from David McClintock is that another plant of this cross has been found, but seems not much different from what we already have.

The Harlow Car Trials Committee has rated both *x williamsii* cultivars Fair for amount of flower and Poor for garden worthiness. But I should not want to be without my 'P.D.Williams' with its fresh green foliage flecked all over with bright yellow and its warm rose flowers carried on into the autumn; and I must get a start of 'Gwavas'!

References:

1) McClintock, David: Notes on British Heaths, *YEAR BOOK OF THE HEATHER SOCIETY*, 1965.

2) Patrick, P. S.: Where have they come from?, *YEAR BOOK OF THE HEATHER SOCIETY*, 1964.

3) Yates, Geoffrey: *POCKET GUIDE TO HEATHER GARDENING*, 1978.

4) McClintock, David: Notes on British Heaths, *YEAR BOOK OF THE HEATHER SOCIETY*, 1965.

5) Eighme, Lloyd: Heathers in North American Gardens, *HEATHER NEWS*, No. 21, Mar. 1983.

6) The Heather Society: *HEATHER TRIALS*, 1971-75.

CASSIOPE D. Don

Arthur P. Dome

The genus *Cassiope* is a very interesting and desirable member of the Heath family *(Ericaceae)*, but unfortunately it cannot thrive under all garden growing conditions.

Cassiope species are found mostly in the Northern Hemisphere, usually in the higher altitudes or the more northern latitudes of North America, Japan, the Himalayas, Europe and the area of the North Pacific rim. It is often referred to as the "Mountain Heather," but it is not a "true heather."

These are dwarf evergreen shrubs that can form mats one inch (2.5 cm) high (e.g., *C. lycopodioides*), or can grow to 12 to 15 inches (30-37.5 cm) high e.g. *C. mertensiana*). Their foliage is very similar to that of *Calluna vulgaris*, the overlapping scale-like leaves being arranged in four rows and lying close to the stems. The color of the leaves can range from a grey-green to a rich green. Some species, such as *C. wardii*, have grey hairs along edges of the leaves, while most others are smooth, as with most forms of *C. mertensiana*.

They differ from the true heather, *Calluna vulgaris*, in dropping their lily-of-the-valley type blossoms from the stems after the pistils are no longer receptive to pollen.

Cassiope species are considered to be very hardy and capable of withstandng intense cold as long as they are dormant. Late frosts and below freezing weather after they have begun to grow and produce their blossoms can have a devastating effect on the plants. They do seem to be happier as well as produce more and larger blossoms when protected by a snow cover during periods of freezing weather. They should also have adequate moisture and protection during the winter time so the winds are less apt to dry them out.

Grown in cultivation they seem to do best when planted in a loose, lime-free, organic, peaty-type, well-drained soil that never dries out. They MUST have adequate moisture during the growing season.

As for location, they seem to do best out in the open or in a lightly shaded area. They MUST be protected from direct exposure to the hot afternoon sun, and the soil should never be allowed to get too warm. On hot days they really like being cooled off with the spray from a mist or fog nozzle. One should also avoid planting them in windy locations, especially if they can't be covered with snow during the winter time. Unfortunately, if they ever become stressed they can succumb to a root disease, if such a pathogen is present.

Cassiope plants need very little pruning or trimming except to keep them in bounds. But it is often desirable to cut off the tips of the new growth on newly transplanted rooted cuttings or seedlings. This is to induce branching and cause them to form more compact plants.

Cassiope plants do not transplant very well from the wild. It is best to get those plants propagated from cuttings, layers or seeds. Some species of *Cassiope* are so rare that you are lucky if you can even find a good seed source.

Cuttings are best taken in late summer as soon as the new wood is firm enough; but some gardeners have also rooted cuttings taken up to April. Some like a mixture of half coarse sand and half coarse peat. As far as rooting goes, some say it doesn't make any difference whether you have bottom heat or not; but with the heat they seem to start to grow a little sooner.

Most gardeners have developed their own media for starting such plants from seed; but many of them use a mixture of peat with more or less sand, or just straight peat.

It will be noted that two of the listed species have been reclassified as *Harrimanella*. This change has been made because of specific differences in plant characteristics:

Cassiope	*Harrimanella*
leaves opposite, scale-like	leaves, alternate, linear
imbricated	spreading

Following is a list of *Cassiope* species appearing in the literature. Some of these names could be synonyms, and some of the species may not be in cultivation:

Note:

For ***Cassiope abbreviata*** and ***C. dendrotricha*** see page 130-131.

Cassiope ericoides (Pall) D. Don (3,5,7)

This species is from Arctic Russia and not considered to be in cultivation. It is said to have fine foliage, like that of some heaths, finely fringed and bristly. The leaves are not very closely imbricated and have long reddish hairs on the margins and apices. The flowers are white and three-lobed.

Cassiope fastigiata D. Don (2,3,4,5,6,7)

From the Himalaya Mountains. An evergreen shrub with erect stems from 6 to 12 inches (15-30 cm) tall. The stems appear to be square, being covered with four rows of closely imbricated leaves, the margins of which are ciliate. It has single, white, bell-shaped flowers that come from the axils of the leaves and can be up to three-eighths inch (1 cm) across. There are two forms, one with red flower stems and calyx and the other with green. It usually blooms from April to early June, depending upon the location.

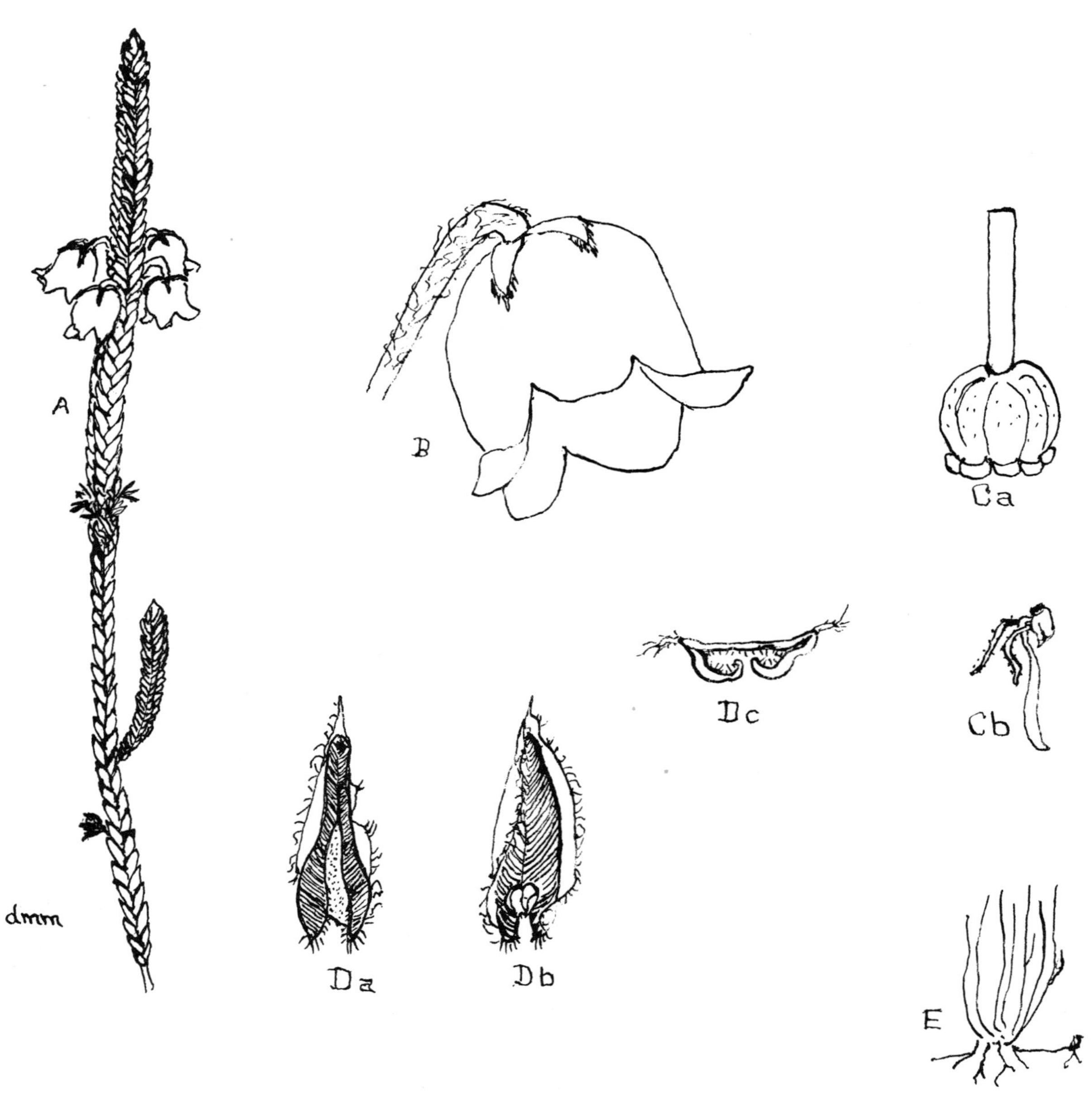

Cassiope fastigiata D. Don: A, flowering stem 1X; B, flower 5X; Ca, pistil 10X; Cb, stamen 10X (note pore opening at apex); Da, leaf, showing furrow on back 5X; Db, leaf (side facing stem) 5X; Dc, leaf cross section (furrowed outside below) 10X; E, plant habit.

Cassiope fastigiata L.S. 17451 (5)

Said to be a very fine dwarf form with exceptionally large flowers.

Cassiope hypnoides D. Don (1,2,3,4,5,7,8)

C. hypnoides has now been officially placed in the genus *Harrimanella* and may therefore be referred to as *Harrimanella hypnoides* Cov. It comes from the Arctic areas of America, Asia and Europe as well as the alpine areas of various mountain ranges. It is a tiny, prostrate, moss-like plant with small needle-like leaves spreading from the stems, and single, white, campanulate flowers, with red calyxes, borne on red flower stems at the ends of the branchlets. It blooms in April and May in most locations.

C. lycopodioides D. Don (1,2,3,4,5,6,7,8,9,11)

This species is from the alpine areas of the North Pacific rim from Washington around to the Aleutian Islands and Japan. It is a creeping evergreen shrub that may grow from one to three inches (2.5-7.5 cm) tall and can spread out into mats up to three feet (90 cm) across. It also has single, white, campanulate flowers that come from the axils of the leaves; and it usually blooms from May through June, depending upon location.

C. lycopodioides 'Beatrice Lilley' (3)

A more compact form considered to be one of the most desirable in the species, with single white flowers on one inch (2.5 cm) high scarlet flower stalks.

C. lycopodioides ssp. cristapilosa (11)

This species is said to be pretty much confined to the Queen Charlotte Islands (off the west coast of Central British Columbia) and differs from the type in that it has one to several conspicuously curled unicellular hairs up to 1.5 mm (1/16 in) long at the tip of each leaf. The tips of the leaves of the type form of *C. lycopodioides* are entirely glabrous. This subspecies is found in the alpine and subalpine areas of the Queen Charlottes. It has the typical prostrate habit of growth of the type form and has white flowers.

C. lycopodioides ssp. gracilis (10)

This is a delightful little form sent to Sallie Allen, of Seattle, Washington, by Dr. Tsuneshige Rokujo, of Tokyo, Japan. It is said to come from Mt. Daisetsu in the central part of Hokkaido Island. Prostrate plants about nine inches (23 cm) across hardly ever get over an inch and a half (3.8 cm) high. The branchlets are very slender, and happy plants really cover themselves with dainty little white blossoms in April to May.

C. lycopodioides **'Rigida'** (2,3,4,5,6,7)

Said by many authors to be the same as *C. lycopodioides* 'Major.' This form is said to be from Japan. It is a more robust grower than the type and larger in most of its parts. There seems to be a difference of opinion as to how floriferous it is. It produces its pendant white flowers April to May.

C. mertensiana G. Don (1,2,3,4,5,7,11,12)

This species can be found in alpine and subalpine areas from California up to Alaska. It has been reported growing along the shore of Star Lake in the Sierra Nevada Mountains of California. It can grow from six to fifteen inches (15-38 cm) tall, has dark green foliage and white, lily of the valley type blossoms. Some plants have green flower stems and calyx, while others have brown. It blooms April to May in lower elevation gardens and just after the snow leaves in its mountain habitats. It is often referred to as the "White Mountain Heather" by those who hike in the mountain regions of western North America.

C. mertensiana ssp. californica (1,5,12)

This form is found mostly in the Sierra Nevada regions. It is said to be a slightly superior form and does well in cultivation. I have seen it being offered for sale in the nursery trade in Washington. It seems to be a slower, more compact grower than the type. It also has white flowers.

C. mertensiana ssp. ciliolata (1,10)

This subspecies is found in the Mt. Eddy region of northwestern California. It is a much slower grower and more compact than the type. Under a hand lens one can see the edges of the leaves rimmed with fine hairs. It has white flowers that are a little smaller than those of the type.

C. mertensiana ssp. gracilis (1,5,7,8)

This subspecies is found in the mountains of northwestern America. It does not grow as tall as the type and the stems or branchlets are more slender than those of the type. It is very floriferous with large, white, bell-shaped flowers. I have seen this plant being offered for sale in gallon cans by some western Washington nurseries which propagated them from cuttings. It seems to be easier to grow as a garden plant than is the type.

C. mertensiana var. Mendenhall (10)

This is a very fine form found by Sallie Allen, of Seattle, Washington, while botanizing around the Mendenhall Glacier, near Juneau, Alaska. It is a fine robust grower with good rich green color to the foliage. It is covered with crisp, white flowers that seem to have a lot of substance. It is an improved form of *C. mertensiana* and definitely superior to it.

C. mertensiana pink form (1,10)

Sallie Allen mentions pink forms in her article that appears in "Alpines of the Americas," The Report of the First Interim International Rock Garden Plant Conference, 1976, page 43. I have obtained two plants of this form from Alan Smith, Victoria, B.C., Canada and they seem to be somewhat daintier growing plants than the type, with lighter green foliage. I have not as yet seen them in flower but have been told the color is a very light pink.

Cassiope mertensiana G. Don ***var. californica:*** A, flowering stem 1X; B, flower 5X; C, pistil and 2 stamens 10X; Da, leaf (side facing stem above) 5X; Db, leaf cross section (side facing stem above) 10X; E, plant habit.

Cassiope myosuroides W. W. Smith (3,5,7)

This species grows in upper Burma and western Yunnan, China and is considered not to be in cultivation at this time (1989). It has a mat-type habit of growth with large, white flowers on short stems.

Cassiope palpebrata W. W. Smith (3,5,7)

This species has been found in Burma and China but has as yet not been introduced into cultivation. It is said to be similar to *C. hypnoides (Harrimanella h.)*, being prostrate with the leaves spreading out at right angles to the stem. I have been unable to find out anything about the type of flowers it has.

Cassiope pectinata Stapf. (3,5)

This species is also found in the Burma-Tibet area. It has been very favorably described as one of the finest of the *Cassiope* genus, looking like an intermediate between *C. fastigiata* and *C. wardii*. It is said that its leaves are fringed with white hairs and that its blossoms are relatively large white bells.

Cassiope redowskii G. Don (5,7)

This species is found in Siberia and as yet is not known to be in cultivation. It has dark green foliage with darker margins and the bell-shaped flowers are four-lobed. It is considered to be of not much garden value.

Cassiope rigida Hort. (2,3,4,5,6,7)

Said to be a synonym of *C. lycopodioides* 'Rigida.'

Cassiope saximontana (1,4,5,7,8)

Said to be a form of *C. tetragona* D. Don.

Cassiope selaginoides Hook. (2,3,4,5,7)

This species comes from the Himalaya Mountains and western China. Different forms grow from two to ten inches (5-25 cm) tall. The foliage appears to be a little more slender than that of most *Cassiope* plants and is a dark green. It has white bell-shaped blossoms during April to May, depending on location.

***Cassiope selaginoides* L & S Form** (4,5)

A fine form collected by Ludlow, Sherriff and Elliott in southeast Tibet. It is a little, stiff, upright-growing plant from four to six inches (10-15 cm) high. Its white bell-shaped flowers seem to appear larger than normal because the plant is so small. It usually blooms April-May.

Cassiope selaginoides nana (4,7)

This is a form raised at Kew Gardens, London from seed sent from Darjeeling, northwest India. It is said to grow only one inch (2.5 cm) high.

Cassiope stelleriana DC. (1,2,3,4,5,7,8,11)

C. stelleriana has now been officially placed in the genus *Harrimanella,* and so may be referred to as *Harrimanella stelleriana* DC. It is native to the North

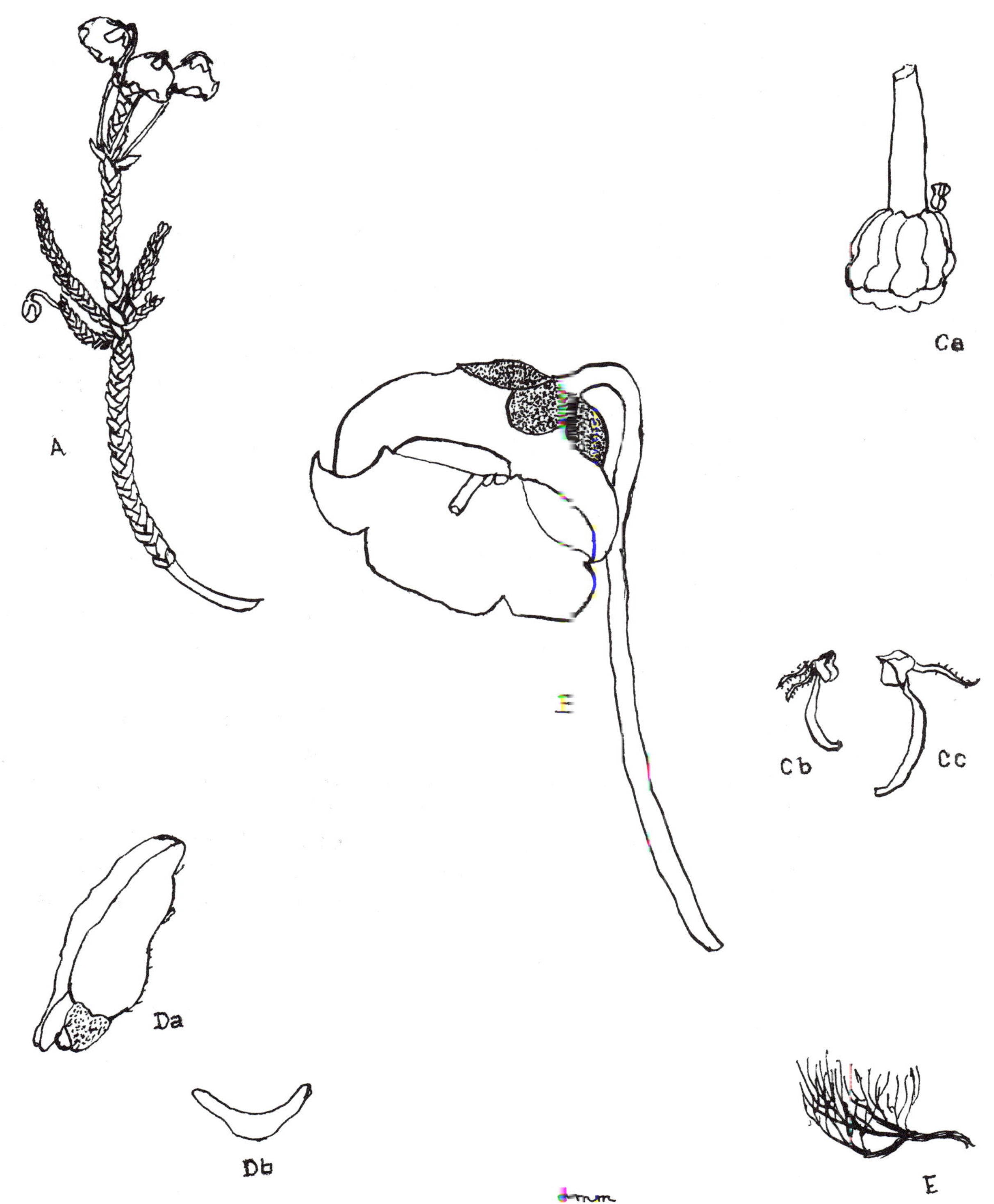

Cassiope selaginoides Hook: A, flowering stem 1X; B, flower 5X; Ca, pistil and 1 stamen 10X; Cb, 1 stamen 10X; Cc, stamen 15X; Da, leaf (side toward stem above) 10X; Db, leaf cross section (side toward stem above) 10X; E, plant habit.

Pacific regions from Washington, Canada and Alaska down into Japan. It very seldom gets over two to three inches (5-7.5 cm) high. Its leaves spread out at right angles to the stems rather than being appressed as in the other *Cassiope* species. It has single creamy-white flowers that appear at the tips of the branchlets, during April to May depending upon its location.

Cassiope tetragona D. Don (1,2,3,4,5,7,8)

C. tetragona grows in the Arctic and Sub-arctic regions of Siberia, Europe and North America, down into British Columbia, Washington and the Rocky Mountains. It has dark green foliage and a habit of growth very similar to *C. mertensiana*, with forms growing from four to ten inches (10- 25 cm) tall. The easiest way to tell the two apart is that *C. tetragona* has a groove or sunken mid-rib on the back of the leaf, while the back of the leaf of *C. mertensiana* has a ridge down the center. *C. tetragona* has white flowers which are sparsely produced along the stems of the new growth. It usually blooms during April to June, depending on location.

Cassiope tetragona ssp. saximontana (1,4,5,8)

C. tetragona ssp. saximontana is mostly confined to the higher elevations in the mountains of British Columbia, Washington and the Rockies. It does not grow as tall as the type and its white bell-shaped flowers are smaller and do not extend above the tips of the branchlets. It blooms during June.

Cassiope wardii Marquand (1,2,3,4,5,6,7)

C. wardii is truly one of the finest of the *Cassiope* genus. It is next to impossible to obtain one of these plants and if you can get one you find it is very difficult to make it happy. It comes from southeast Tibet. It grows to about eight inches (20 cm) tall and can spread from underground runners. Its leaves are about a quarter of an inch (6 mm) long and are rimmed with long silvery hairs which really add to the desirability of this plant. Its white, bell-shaped flowers are produced near the tips of the branchlets and usually appear during May.

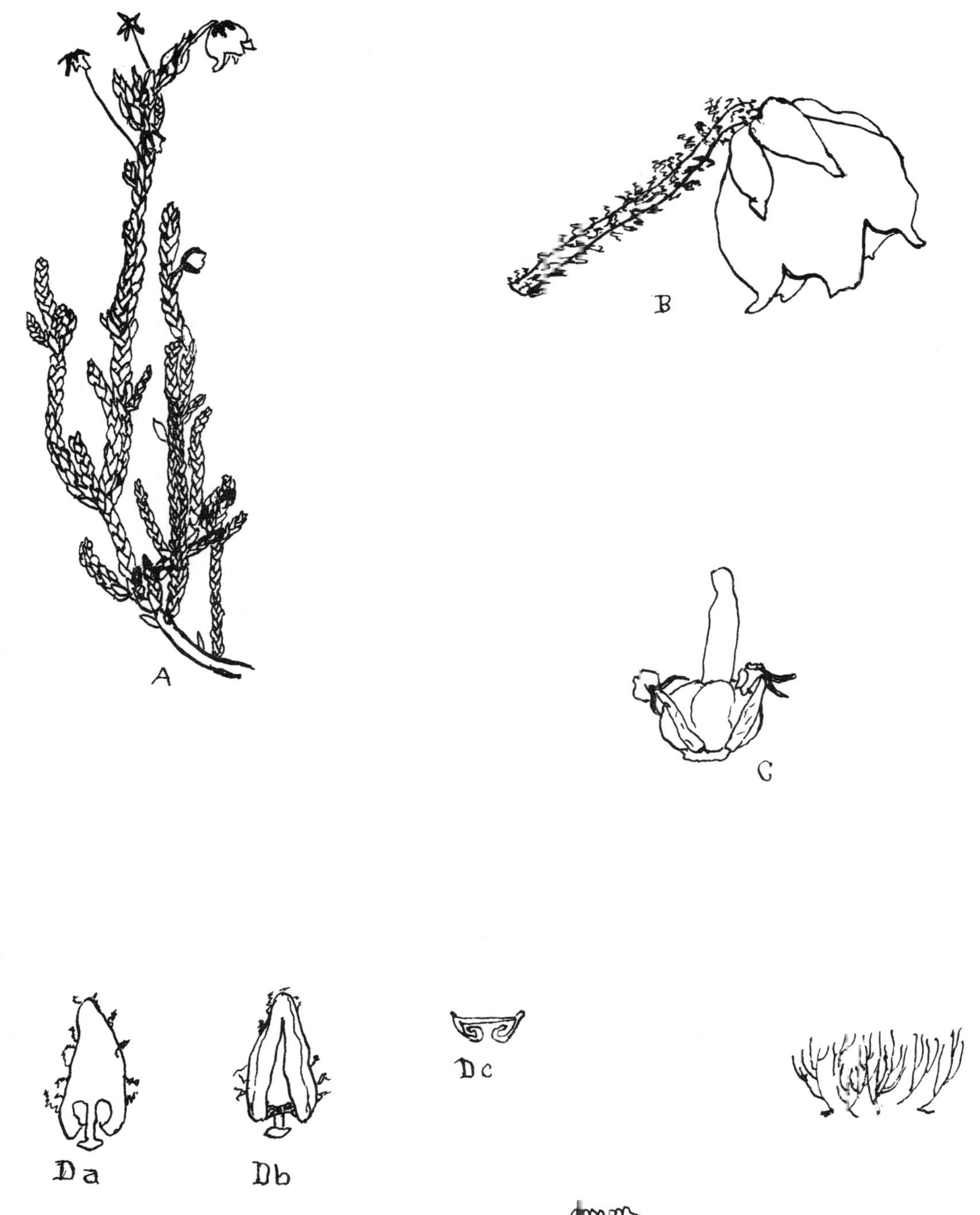

Cassiope tetragona (L.) D. Don ***var. saximontana***: A, flowering stem 1X; B, flower 5X; C, pistil and 2 (of 10) stamens 10X; Da, leaf (side toward stem) 5X; Db, leaf back (showing pronounced furrow) 5X; Dc, leaf cross section (furrowed back side below) 5X; E, plant habit.

The following two species descriptions appeared originally in Chinese, in ***ICONOGRAPHIA CORMOPHYTORUM SINICORUM, TOMUS III***, edited by Beijing Institute of Botany, Academia Sinica, and published in 1974 by Science Press, Beijing, People's Republic of China.

They were most kindly translated for this book by Judy Young, Seattle, July 1989.

Cassiope abbreviata Hand.-Mazz.

duanye yanxu—"short-leaved cliff-beard"

Plant 15-30 cm high; branches slender, dense, slanting outward or erect, many-branched, branchlets 5-10 cm long, bearing 4 dense rows of imbricate scale-like leaves, only 2-2.5 mm in diameter. Leaves subovate, 2.5-4 mm long, obtuse, dorsal surface protuberant, with one lengthwise groove about one-half the length of the leaf and far from the leaf apex. Flowers white, solitary, axillary, pendulous; pedicel about 3 mm long, densely hairy; calyx lobes 3 mm long, 2 mm broad, subovate, purplish-red, entire, with a slight, narrow membranaceous margin.

Occurs in northwest Sichuan. Grows at an altitude of about 3,800 m (12,500 ft) in alpine forests or in rhododendron thickets. This species resembles the "broom cliff-beard" *(saozhou yanxu)*, *[Cassiope fastigiata]* in the slender branches and the broad leaf margin which is finely ciliate and dry-membranaceous. However, the leaves [of *C. abbreviata*] are ovate and much shorter, the dorsal groove is short, only 1/2 to 2/3 the length of the leaf and far from the leaf apex, the dry membranaceous leaf margin is brown with shorter white ciliate hairs, and the calyx lobes are subovate and obtuse with a subentire narrow membranaceous margin.

Cassiope dendrotricha Hand.-Mazz.

jiemao yanxu, "eyelash cliff-beard"

Evergreen dwarf shrub, 15-30 cm high; branches erect, few-branched or unbranched, with four dense rows of obliquely spreading, contiguous leaves forming a 4-angled column, 5-6 mm in diameter. Leaves linear, stiff-coriaceous, 6-7 mm long, 1.2 mm broad at the lower part, mucronate, dorsal surface a keel-like protuberance, with 1 deep lengthwise groove nearly to leaf apex, margin not membranaceous but bearing from base to apex a single dense row of oblique reddish-brown bristles, to 1 mm long, more dense at the tip when young. Flowers solitary, axillary, pendulous, pedicel clad with long yellowish-brown downy hairs, about 1 mm long, in blooming period and later extending to 2.5 mm or more; calyx lobes 5, ovate-oblong, 3 mm long, entire, glabrous; corolla broadly campanulate, white, about 7 mm long, shallowly 5-lobed at the mouth. Capsule globose, 3 mm in diameter, wrapped within the calyx lobes.

Distributed in Yunnan and Sichuan. Grows in rock crevices beneath the forest at 3,400 meter (11,000 ft) elevation.

CASSIOPE HYBRIDS

There are some nice hybrids of these plants which, in some areas, are easier to obtain and easier to grow as garden plants than most of the species, when one favors their needs and tolerances.

***Cassiope x* 'Badenoch'** *(C. lycopodioides x C. fastigiata)* (4,6,7)

This is a loose-growing plant with an ascending habit. It grows to about six inches (15 cm) tall, and has grey-green foliage that turns a purplish-green during the winter months. It has numerous white, bell-shaped flowers usually blooming in May.

***Cassiope x* 'Bearsden'** *(C. fastigiata x C lycopodioides)* (3)

This plant is similar to *C. x* 'Badenoch' in growth, but the branchlets are much slenderer. It also produces an abundance of white bell-shaped flowers in May.

***Cassiope x* 'Edinburgh'** (*C. fastigiata x C. tetragona)* (2,3,4,5,7)

This is a compact, upright-growing plant that gets about twelve inches (30 cm) tall and has bright green foliage. The white, bell-shaped flowers are profusely produced on two-inch (5 cm) long racemes at the tips of the branchlets in April to May. This hybrid is one of the easier Cassiopes to obtain, and this is probably because of its being easier to grow. It is a natural hybrid that occurred at the Royal Botanic Garden, Edinburgh.

***Cassiope x* 'George Taylor'** *(C. wardii X C. fastigiata)* (3,4,6,7)

This is a very interesting plant that very closely resembles *C. wardii* and is much easier to obtain and grow. It is another natural hybrid that was found in the Himalayas. It grows about twelve inches (30 cm) tall, has dark green leaves about three-sixteenths inch (5 mm) long and rimmed with long, fine hairs. The white blossoms are very similar to those of *C. wardii* and are produced close to the stems toward the tips of the branchlets. It usually blooms in May.

***Cassiope x* 'Kathleen Dryden'** *(C. lycopodioides x C. fastigiata)* (3,7)

This plant has a few upright shoots that send out horizontal branchlets, which soon develop a mat-like appearance. It produces numerous white, urn-shaped flowers that hang perpendicularly to the branchlets.

***Cassiope x* 'Medusa'** *(C. fastigiata x C. lycopodioides)* (6,7)

This plant was described by Mr. S. E. Lilley as another very fine plant not yet in general cultivation. It is similar in growth to *C. lycopodioides* but less compact, and the branchlets are more curving. Among the interesting features of the plant are its white flowers produced on very red stems, and the calyx is equally red.

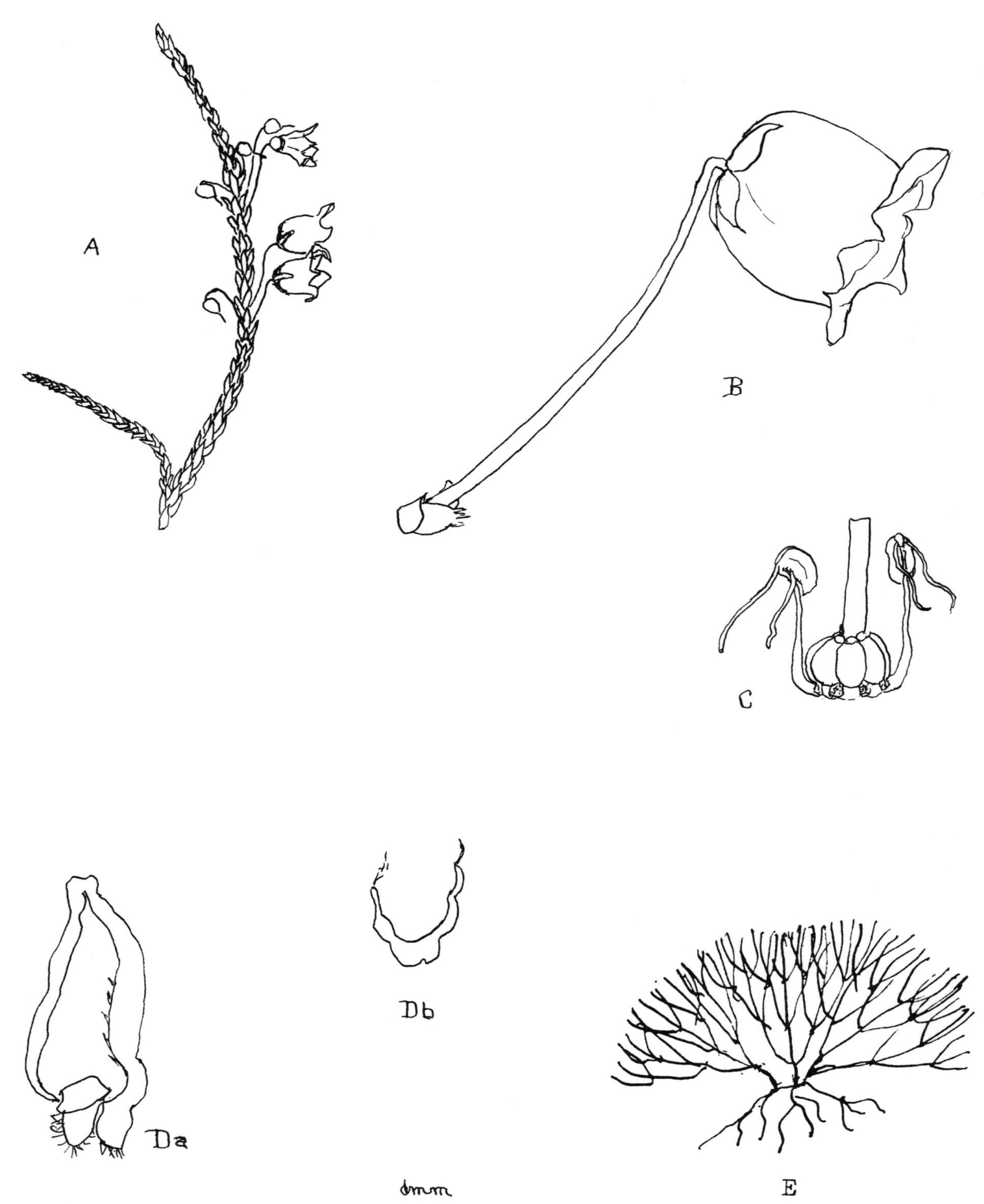

***Cassiope x* 'Randle Cooke'** *(fastigiata x lycopodioides)*: A, flowering stem 1X; B, flower 5X; C, pistil and 2 stamens 10X; Da, leaf (side facing stem) 10X; Db, leaf cross section (side facing stem above) 10X; E, plant habit.

***Cassiope x* 'Muirhead'** *(C. wardii x C. lycopodioides)* (2,3,4,5,6,7)

This plant seems to be a good garden plant and is one of the *Cassiope* hybrids that are more readily available in the Pacific Northwest. It is a semi-erect, much-branched plant that grows about six inches (15 cm) tall. The branchlets more closely resemble those of *C. lycopodioides*, and it produces its slightly larger, white, bell-shaped blossoms all along the branchlets during May.

***Cassiope x* 'Randle Cooke'** *(C. fastigiata x C. lycopodioides)* (3,4,6,7)

This plant grows about six inches (15 cm) tall with ascending growth and medium green foliage. The white flowers are produced at the ends of the branchlets and are a little larger than those of most *Cassiopes*, usually appearing April to May. This hybrid seems to do quite well in the home garden when its requirements are catered to.

This general descriptive list of *Cassiope* species and their hybrids is as complete as possible at this time, using reliable references and sources. Where there was a discrepancy of opinion among the authors referred to on a specific point, the opinion of the majority was used. It is suggested that those wishing for more information for taxonomic reasons, or for identification purposes refer to the appropriate references, a list of which follows:

References:

1) *ALPINES OF THE AMERICAS, ARGS* Report, 1976, pp. 42, 43, 215, 216, 278, 313.
2) Heath, Royton E.: *COLLECTORS' ALPINES*, 1983, pp. 236, 237, 238.
3) Ingwersen, William: *MANUAL OF ALPINE PLANTS*, 1978, pp. 111-113.
4) Bean, W. J.: *TREES & SHRUBS HARDY IN THE BRITISH ISLES*, Vol. 1, 1981, pp. 522-527.
5) Lilley, S. E.: *The Genus Cassiope, BULL. OF THE AGS*, Vol. 29, pp. 72-87.
6) Lilley, S. E.: *Cassiopes, JOUR. OF THE RHS*, Vol. 90, 1965, pp. 302-305.
7) Krussman, Gerd: *MANUAL OF CULTIVATED BROAD-LEAVED TREES & SHRUBS,* Vol. 1, 1985, pp. 289-291.
8) Szczawinski, A. F.: *THE HEATHER FAMILY OF BRITISH COLUMBIA*, 1962, pp. 37-47.
9) Ohwi, Jisaburo: *FLORA OF JAPAN*, 1984, p. 704.
10) Allen, Sallie, Seattle, Washington: personal communication.
11) Calder, James A. & Roy L. Taylor: *FLORA OF THE QUEEN CHARLOTTE ISLANDS*, Part 1, 1968, pp. 456-459.
12) Munz, Philip A.: *FLORA OF CALIFORNIA*, 1968, p. 414.
13) Beijing Institute of Botany, Academia Sinica: *ICONOGRAPHIA CORMOPHYTORUM SINICORUM*, Tomus III. Trans.

PHYLLODOCE Salisb.

When in the course of a Heather Program, in western Washington at least, the statement is made that there are no heathers native to North America, nearly invariably some mountain lover will ask, "How about our 'Mountain Heath' *(Phyllodoce)* and 'Mountain Heather' (*Cassiope*)?" The answer has to be that although these lovely plants belong to the same family, the *Ericaceae*, and are somewhat similar to "true heathers," *Calluna* and *Erica,* in habit, foliage and flower, they differ in botanical characters. Notably, their flowers are deciduous, i.e., when they are spent, have been pollinated, the bells fall to the ground instead of remaining on the stems to turn brown, as do those of the true heathers.

We are aware that there may be those among us and elsewhere who will object to our adopting the genera *Phyllodoce* and *Cassiope* as perhaps stepchildren. In the past, all or some species of the genus *Phyllodoce* have been referred to the genera *Andromeda, Bryanthus, Erica* or *Menziesia*. They are now (one hopes) firmly established in their own genus. British heather writers have sometimes been tempted to include *P. caerulea*, a rare native of Great Britain, but in the end have eliminated it because, though charming, it is not a heather.

On just the horticultural plane, we remember that before the International Botanical Congress of 1969 gave charge of their cultivar naming to the Heather Society, there were those who objected to including *Daboecia* as a heather (its bells are deciduous), not to mention that Balkan foreigner, *Bruckenthalia*, both now official members of the heather group, along with *Andromeda* which a lot of us still don't think of as a "heather." Botanically, *Cassiope* and *Phyllodoce* probably never will achieve that official status; but since the non-botanists among us look at them and think "heather," and because quite a few of us delight in and grow at least some of them, we take the liberty of welcoming them, if not into our homes, at least into our gardens.

It should be emphasized that plants dug up from the wild (which will possibly be illegal) are, in any case, most likely to expire. Grow them from seed or cuttings.

It is true that the "Mountain Heaths" and "Mountain Heathers" at low elevations in the Temperate Zone require different growing conditions from those suitable for our true heathers. In the cool mountains where they are frequently bathed by passing clouds they bask in full sunlight, but at nearer sea level in temperate latitudes, virtually all agree that they need to have the protection of high part-shade to help them retain enough moisture,—a situation which is of course anathema to the true heathers. But being natives of higher latitudes (far north) at lower elevations and increasing mountain heights farther south (up to 12,000 ft for *P. breweri* in the Sierra Nevada of California)(1), they are, to varying degrees, cold-hardy. If you can suit their tastes in food (plenty of peat in a lime-free humus) and beverages (constant moisture but good drainage at the roots), and make them comfortable with moisture retaining half-buried small rocks over their feet, they will reward you with their charming flowers which, if perhaps not so numerous as in their mountain homes, are still a sufficient reward to any gardener. One beautifully flowering plant of *Phyllodoce empetriformis* I once saw had been planted on the high-shaded west side of a Seattle home, where a slightly leaky hose faucet occasionally dripped on the earth around it, esthetically not an ideal situation. Krussman(2), with the Continental point of view, recommends "some winter protection advisable, but otherwise totally hardy. Gorgeous in flower."

Phyllodoce species may be propagated by seed, cuttings (soft tips taken in July or August, or half-ripened older wood with a heel)(3), or layers.

Phyllodoce is a circumboreal genus, various species found in Europe, Asia and North America. It was identified by *Linnaceus* in mid-18th Century, but originally lumped with other *ericaceous* genera as species of *Andromeda*, and underwent a string of name changes in the next fifty years until it got its present name from R. A. Salisbury in 1806.

The generally referred to authoritative description of the genus *Phyllodoce*, by Fred Stoker(4), was published in 1942 in a British journal. The *Phyllodoce* species are small evergreen much-branched shrubs with crowded small leaves whose recurved margins give them a needle-like appearance. They are arranged alternately on the stems and are virtually without petioles. The flowers are campanulate or ovoid bells (except *P. breweri*, in which they are shallow bowls), hanging from the tips of pedicels which elongate as the seeds ripen in the capsules.

Stoker identified ten species, but botanists since his time have reclassified his *P. intermedia* as the hybrid *P. x intermedia*, and his *P.* "pseudoempetriformis" as a form of *P. x intermedia*. The list now includes *PP. aleutica, alpina, breweri, caerulea, empetriformis, glanduliflora, nipponica, tsugifolia* and the hybrid *x intermedia*.

Plants in near sea level gardens flower in spring (April-May). At home in the mountains their flowering is observed progressively later (July-August) as they occur at higher altitudes.

Phyllodoce aleutica. (Not illustrated) Mostly erect branches, 15-20 cm high (6-8 in); leaves .7-1.4 cm long and 1.5-2 mm wide, bright green above and yellowish beneath; flowers nodding in terminal heads of 6-12; the corolla globose-urceolate, pinched at the mouth, .7 cm long, its color varies through chartreuse green to yellowish to whitish; calyx about two-thirds as long as the corolla; stamens and style included. A native of W. Alaska, the Aleutian Islands,

Sakhalin, the Kuriles and N. Japan, it flowers in April-May. ". . . a pretty plant, though scarcely equal in beauty to *P. breweri, P. nipponica or P. x intermedia.*"(5)

P. alpina. (Not illustrated) I have not seen this plant but those who have describe it as small, erect or prostrate, 6-14 cm (2.5-5.5 in) high, with small, dense leaves and an umbel-like inflorescence of elliptic-ovoid, bluish flowers. It is a native of Japan and not very commonly grown. At this time some horticulturists (W. J. Bean, J. B. A. Dekker) consider *P. alpina* to be a natural hybrid between *P. nipponica* and *P. aleutica*.

P. breweri. (Illustrated) A lax to erect plant [Munz(1) calls it semi-procumbent], it is 10-30 cm (4-12in) high, with leaves 6-15 mm long. It differs markedly from other *Phyllodoce* species in having its flowers on 12 mm pedicels in leafy racemes with wide open, shallow bowl corollas 1.0-1.5 cm across when fully expanded. The flower color can range from rose-purple to pink and is enhanced by the bowlful of ten exserted pink stamens with dark purple anthers and the even longer-exserted pink style. The same plant has been in a semi-shaded spot low on my rocky slope, through all vicissitudes of weather, since 1961. According to Rehder's(6) estimate it may be rated USDA Zone 6b-7a.

P. caerula (L.) Bab (Illustrated) Another plant that has been on our "alpine" slope for 25 years, it is a low (12-22 cm) (5-9 in) bushy evergreen shrub with crowded, linear, revolute leaves and terminal umbels of semi-nodding pinkish-purple flowers on 2.5-3 cm (1-1 3/16 in) long, brown-red slender pedicels. The accompanying drawing from a plant in our lowland garden was made at the end of March.

It has been suggested that Linnaeus selected the specific epithet, *caerulea*, because the dried flowers of pressed specimens become bluish. But Barry Starling(7) wrote, "In Linnaeus' homeland I found, just across the border in Norway, the form of *Phyllodoce caerulea* that the 'father of botany' would have known and, though not caerulean blue, it was closer to blue than to any other basic colour of the spectrum." The calyx is brown-red. W. J. Bean(5) mentions that a form from Japan with red-purple flowers had been exhibited in England.

This is another circumpolar species occurring in eastern North America as far south as Alberta, Maine, and New Hampshire(6). As mentioned earlier it also occurs in the Scottish Highlands and Bean adds that this species fares better in cooler, moister Scotland than in Southern England. Like the others, it needs plenty of peat. For hardiness it is rated Zone I.

P. empetriformis (Sm.) D. Don (Illustrated) is a western North America representative of the genus. It occurs on montane to alpine rocky slopes from Alaska to California, where Munz says it reaches from 5,000 to 9,000 ft (1,500-2,800 m), in the Olympic and Cascade Mountains, east to Alberta, and in the Rockies south to Colorado and west to Idaho (8).

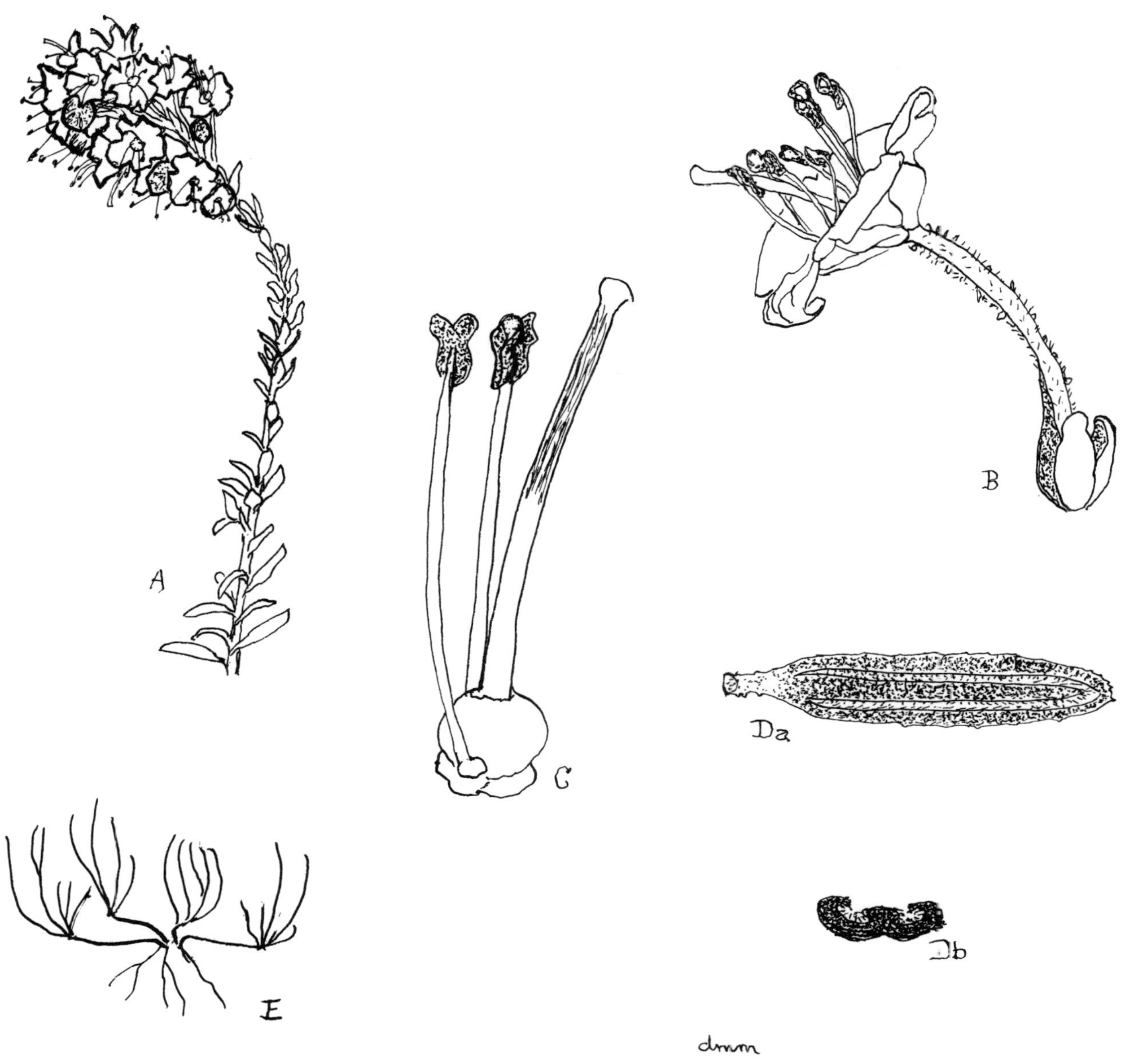

Phyllodece breweri (Gray) Heller: A, flowering branch 1X; B, flower 5X; C, pistil and 2 of the stamens 10X; Da, leaf beneath 5X; Db, leaf cross section 10X; E, plant habit.

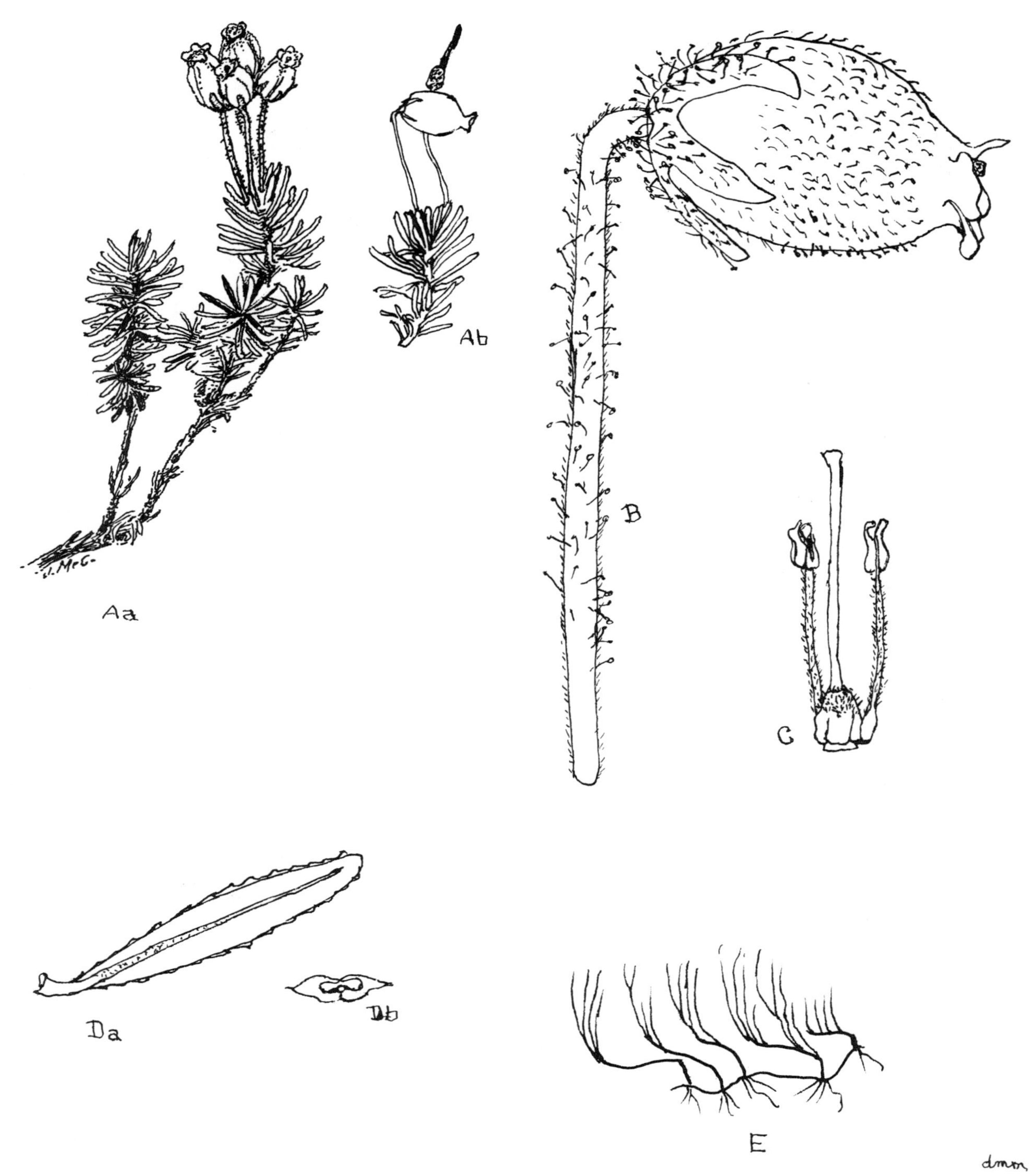

Phyllodoce caerulea (L.) Bab.: Aa, flowering branch 1X [drawn by Jean McConnell]; Ab, flower and spent flower with corolla dropped off 1X; B, flower 5X; C, pistil and 2 of the stamens 5X; Da, leaf beneath 5X; Db, leaf cross section 10X; E, plant habit.

In the mountains it is a low, much-branched shrub, its erect branches to 35-40 cm (14-16 in) tall but probably less in gardens; leaves linear or linear-oblong, revolute, to 15 mm (1/2 in) long and 1.5 mm wide. Its flowers, which may be few or many, wave on 2 cm (3/4 in) long pedicels and have rose pink open-bell corollas up to 8 mm (5/16 in) long and with recurved lobes. The stamens with their reddish anthers are included, but the style exserted(9). The accompanying drawing was made from a sea-level garden plant at the end of April and we have photographed it in the Cascades in July and August. - Rehder rated it the equivalent of USDA Zone 6a.

As Stoker(4) observed, the plant growing in Britain under this name since perhaps early 19th C. is actually one of its hybrids, *P. x intermedia*. Stoker added that after so long a time the mistake would be difficult to correct; and indeed Sallie Allen, Seattle, who has long been an expert on this genus and grows all of them except *P. alpina*, did observe the mistake still in evidence there within the last few years.

The Knights have *P. empetriformis* on their nursery list, but I must confess to having had it come and go in my garden, probably from insufficient water. Most plants that don't like it here I can do without; but with *P. empetriformis* I keep trying. Sallie says it's easy! And Lloyd Eighme(10) reported that he had it "well established" in his garden at Lyman, WA.

P. glanduliflora (Hook.) Coville (note: flower only illustrated) is the other *Phyllodoce* species native of the Northwest. It occurs on montane and alpine slopes from Alaska south to Oregon, in the Olympics and Cascades in Washington, east to the Canadian Rockies and south to Wyoming and Idaho.(8)

Adam Szczawinski(9), who spent much time plant hunting in the mountains of British Columbia, described *P. glanduliflora* as matted but with rather erect branches to 35 cm (14 in) tall. Its leaves are rather densely crowded. It is a glandular-puberulent plant with stems (when young), leaves, flower pedicels, calyxes and corollas glandular-hairy. Flowers are one to a few in a cluster on 3 cm long (1 3/16 in) pedicels, the corollas 5-8 mm long (1/4-5/16 in), narrowly urn-shape but with spreading lobes, are more than half enclosed by the hairy calyxes and yellowish (Hitchcock(8), another field botanist, says "dirty yellowish") to greenish-white. Krussman(2) says they are fragrant.

I had it from 1963 to 1978 when it expired.

P. x intermedia, denominates a group of hybrids with characteristics intermediate between the parents. Of this hybrid, Dr. Szczawinski(9) wrote, "It is a well-known fact that *P. glanduliflora* and *P. empetriformis* often hybridize, resulting in very striking intermediate forms which differ chiefly in the more elongated paler pink or purple corollas and the narrower acute sepals. Such hybrids occur only in areas where both parent plants are present . . ." [I.e., the hybrids are not able to maintain themselves independently because they do not

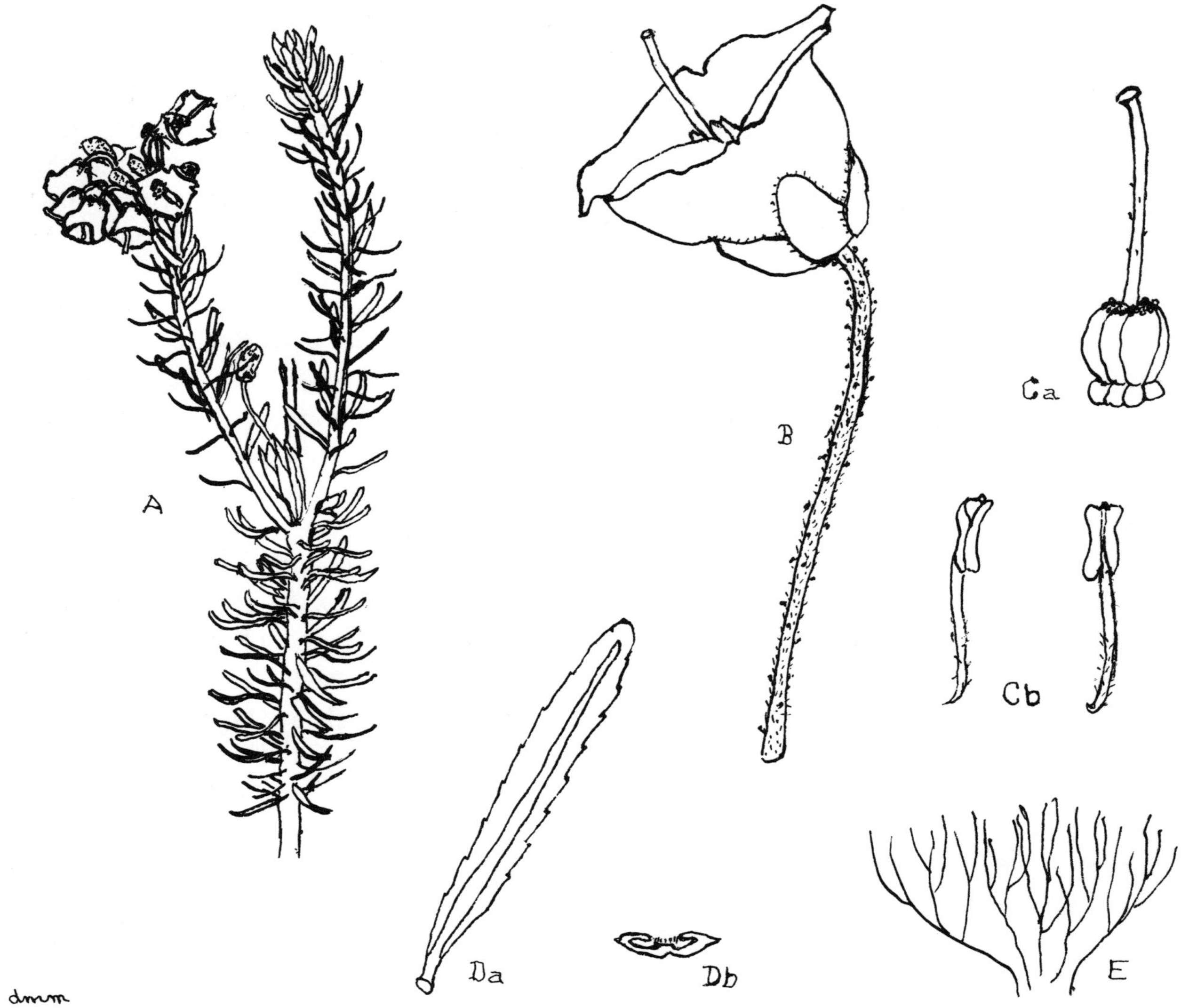

Phyllodoce empetriformis (Sm.) D. Don: A, flowering branch 1X; B, flower 5X; Ca, pistil 10X; Cb, stamens 10X; Da, leaf beneath 5X; Db, leaf cross section 10X; E, plant habit.

P. aleutica ***P. x intermedia*** ***P. glanduliflora*** **X5**

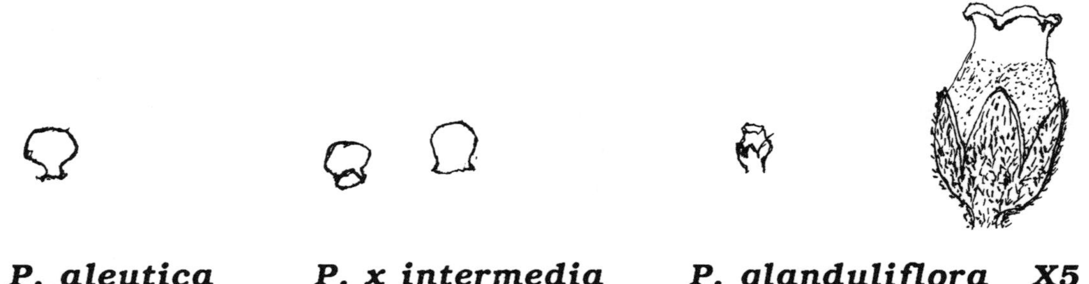

develop fertile seed. They may be of differing forms and would be known as a hybrid swarm.(11)] Szczawinski wrote, "I have seen this striking hybrid growing in great abundance, particularly in the Northwest in the Haines Cut-Off [northwest corner of British Columbia]. There are several horticultural forms of this hybrid, and I consider them as perhaps the nicest representatives of the Heather Family."—In his definitive article, in 1940, the American taxonomist, W.H. Camp(12), wrote, "There is no one description which will fit them all." Several of these forms are distributed under cultivar names: 'Fred Stoker' has light purple corollas; 'Drummondii' dark purple; J.B.A. Dekker(13) mentions a *x intermedia* with white flowers which he is naming 'Anna Barbara'; and Lloyd Eighme is growing a plant with pinkish-yellow flowers from the Cascades of Washington.

P. nipponica Makino (Illustrated), as its name tells us, is a native of Japan. It is a compact shrub 10-15 cm high (4-6 in), with erect branches and compact linear leaves .5-1.2 cm long. The white flowers which are about .85 cm long with somewhat greater width are a bit larger than those of the other *Phyllodoce* species except *P. breweri*. The illustration here is of the form ***amabilis***, another 25-year resident of our garden, which may be slightly smaller in all parts than the type. It also differs from the type in having a charming touch of red color—red pedicels, red sepals, rich crimson anthers and a pink tinge on the corolla lobes.(4) W.J. Bean(5) apparently described this form as the type, but in any case called it "this delightful little shrub." Rehder rates it the equivalent of USDA Zone 6.

P. tsugifolia Nakai (Not illustrated) Stoker(4) explains that the original description of this species was written in Japanese and so was not available to him. He wrote his description of the species from the illustration accompanying the Japanese text, which showed the leaves to be linear, the pedicels 5 times the length of the corollas and pubescent on their distal one-thirds only. The corollas were shown as ovoid, slightly contracted at the mouth and the lobes bent outward rather than recurved. He also said he doubted if it was in cultivation in Britain at that time (1940). There is very little else in the literature about this species. But Sallie Allen, Seattle, who actually grows it says it is easily distinguished by having very small white bells with a pinkish tinge.

Phyllodoce nipponica Mak. var. ***amabilis***: A, flowering stem 1X; B, flower 5X; C, pistil and 2 of the stamens 10X; Da, leaf beneath 5X; Db, leaf cross section 10X; E, plant habit.

References:

1) Munz, Philip A. with David W. Keck: *A CALIFORNIA FLORA*, 1968-73.

2) Krussman, Gerd: *MANUAL OF CULTIVATED BROAD-LEAVED TREES & SHRUBS*, 1985.

3) Hills, L. D.: *THE PROPAGATION OF ALPINES*, 1959, p. 350.

4) Stoker, Fred: *The Genus Phyllodoce*, *NEW FLORA AND SILVA*, Vol. XII, Spring 1942, pp. 30-42.

5) Bean, W. J.: *TREES AND SHRUBS HARDY IN THE BRITISH ISLES*, rev. 1976.

6) Rehder, Alfred: *MANUAL OF CULTIVATED TREES AND SHRUBS*, 2nd ed., rev. 1956.

7) Starling, Barry: *HORTICULTURE NORTHWEST*, No. 18, Spring 1982, p. 1.

8) Hitchcock, C. Leo & Arthur Cronquist: *FLORA OF THE PACIFIC NORTH-WEST*, 1973.

9) Szczawinski, Adam F.: *THE HEATHER FAMILY OF BRITISH COLUMBIA*, 1962.

10) Eighme, Lloyd: *HEATHER NEWS*, No. 20, Dec. 1982, p. 4.

11) Royal Horticultural Society: *DICTIONARY OF GARDENING*, 1962.

12) Camp, Wendell Holmes: *Phyllodoce Hybrids*, *NEW FLORA AND SILVA*, Vol. XII, Autumn, 1940, pp. 207-211.

13) Dekker, J. B. A.: *ERICULTURA*, No. 51, May-June 1986.

Phyllodoce empetriformis in the Cascades David Metheny

X PHYLLIOPSIS HILLIERI Cullen & Lancaster

The first plant of this hybrid appeared as a chance seedling at Hillier's nursery, Romsey, Hampshire, England, where it was noticed in 1960. Fortunately it was preserved. It was at first assumed to be an attractive form of *Kalmiopsis leachiana*, but later observers thought it somewhat resembled *Phyllodoce breweri*.

Eventually, specimens of the plant were sent to Dr. James Cullen at the Royal Botanic Garden, Edinburgh, and Dr. Cullen reported it as a presumed new hybrid between *Phyllodoce breweri* and *Kalmiopsis leachiana*. It was named ***X Phylliopsis hillieri*** and given the cultivar name **'Pinocchio,'** to distinguish it from later possible clones which might have the same two genera as parents. Barry Starling, nurseryman of Essex, England, acquired plants of this stock in 1971, grew them on in his nursery and when one of them flowered very well, in April-May, 1976 exhibited it at a Royal Horticultural Society show where it was judged worth of an Award of Merit.

X Phylliopsis hillieri **'Pinocchio'** is an evergreen shrub of ascending-erect habit, the height so far achieved in gardens not over 30 cm (12 in). Its leaves are alternate on the stems, crowded, more or less oblong-obovate in shape, 15-20 mm (5/8-3/4 in) long and 6-8 mm (1/4-5/16 in) wide, margins slightly revolute, shiny dark green above and lighter with a brownish-yellow indumentum beneath. The many-flowered inflorescence is a lengthened raceme with fresh red-purple flowers gradually opening out toward the tip. Both leaves and flowers differ in some respects from both parents.

The parents of this hybrid are both rated in the hardiness zone to withstand +5 to -5°F (-15 to -20°C) and my little plant of *X P. h.* 'Pinocchio' was unharmed by the 7°F (-14°C) to which it was subjected in February 1989. This hybrid's actual ability to withstand cold will only be determined by trial in a range of climates.

It is a very attractive little shrub. My young plant in its second year of flowering had achieved a height of 18 cm (7 in) and a spread of 30 cm (12 in). Its flowers appeared in April-May and again in July and August. They are bright purplish-pink, approximately heliotrope-magenta on the Heather Society Colour Chart. As with *X Phyllothamnus erectus*, some shade is advised for it, and it seems to do happily, protected from the west sun by a deciduous azalea. We have had a series of very dry summers but the *X P. h.* 'Pinocchio' seems not to have suffered unduly from the drought. It seems fair to assume that it might have grown faster with more moisture.

Roy Lancaster, in his 1977 article (cf. References, below), included remarks by Barry Starling on his own experience with growing the two plants of *X Phylliopsis* 'Pinocchio' he had acquired from Hillier's nursery in 1971. He wrote that he "decapitated one rather straggly plant." The other was planted out

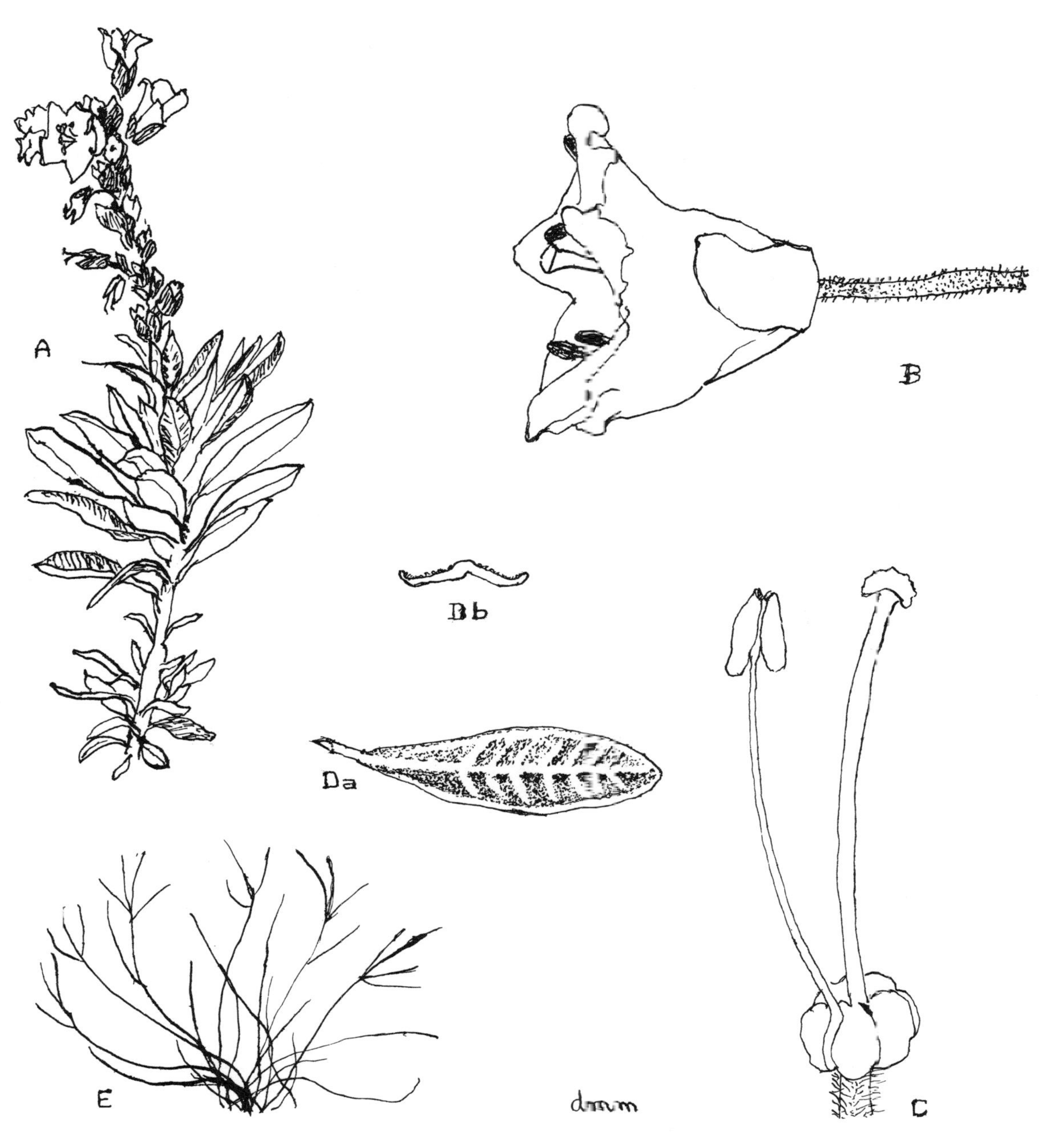

***X Phylliopsis hillieri* 'Pinocchio':** A, inflorescence 1X; B, flower 5X; C, pistil & 1 of the 8 stamens 10X; Da, leaf beneath 2X; Db, leaf cross section 3X; E, plant habit.

"where it thrived in peaty, well drained soil, in partial sun, on the rock garden, conditions which admirably suit *Kalmiopsis leachiana.*" It flowered spasmodically throughout the year the first few years and then in 1976 gave a full and colorful display during late April and early May. He adds that, "Even the drought of the last two years [in Essex, southeast England] has had no adverse effects"; in this bigeneric hybrid we have a dwarf shrub which will thrive and flower freely in a relatively dry garden.

Starling's "decapitated" plant was potted and grown in an alpine house during winters, then plunged outside after flowering, which takes place about three weeks earlier than with the open-ground plant. It was this plant which received the A.M. in 1976.

He recommends pruning the flowering shoots well back after flowering to maintain a shapely plant.

This hybrid develops no seed from self pollination but Barry Starling says that back crosses with *Kalmiopsis leachiana* and crosses with *Phyllodoce empetriformis* have yielded seedlings. If a flowering plant is cut well back after flowering, by July it will have developed new shoots which will be right for cuttings, which root readily in a peat/sand mixture. Pinching the rooted cuttings back when potting them will encourage bushy growth.

***X Phylliopsis hillieri* 'Coppelia.'** Following the introduction of *X P. hillieri* 'Pinocchio,' Barry Starling undertook the deliberate hybridization of another *X Phylliopsis hillieri.* This time he chose *Phyllodoce empetriformis* (rather than *P. breweri*) as the seed parent and treated it with pollen from *Kalmiopsis leachiana umpqua form.* Twelve seedlings resulted from the cross, of which four were very vigorous. The first flowers on these plants appeared in 1982. As reported in the *BULLETIN OF THE ALPINE GARDEN SOCIETY*, the flowers were said to be the same shape as those of *Phyllodoce empetriformis* but larger and have proved to be borne far more prolifically in cultivation than are those of the *Phyllodoce* parent. Three of the four seedlings were lavender-pink flowered; the plant considered to be the best of the lot was rose-pink flowered, and it is this plant which now bears the cultivar name 'Coppelia'. The black-and-white photograph accompanying the *A.G.S. BULLETIN* report shows 'Coppelia' to be a more spreading, lax-branched plant than is 'Pinocchio' with numerous rather lax, 20-flowered racemes at the branch tips. At the time of the report (1983) the original plant, after six years, was 8 in (20 cm) tall and 16 in (40 cm) in diameter, and had "shrugged off" some cold winters both in England and in Washington State. Like its cousin, 'Pinocchio', it requires part shade and acid, cool, moist but well-drained conditions in the peat or rock garden. It was given the R.H.S. Award of Merit in 1982.

References:

Lancaster, Roy: *Phylliopsis*, *THE GARDEN, JOUR. R.H.S.*, Vol. 102, 1977, pp. 380-382 [Includes article by Barry Starling.]

Anon: *BULLETIN OF THE ALPINE GARDEN SOCIETY*, Dec. 1982, p. 302.

Lancaster, Roy: *Award Plants 1982*, *THE GARDEN, JOUR. OF THE R.H.S.*, Vol. 108, pt. 2, Feb. 1983, p. 66.

Krussman, Gerd: *MANUAL OF CULTIVATED BROAD-LEAVED TREES & SHRUBS*, 1985.

X PHYLLOTHAMNUS ERECTUS (Lindl.) Schneid.

(Phyllodoce empetriformis X Rhodothamnus chamaecistus)

Of this small hybrid plant, John Lindley, co-author of *PAXTON'S FLOWER GARDEN*, a beautifully illustrated set of three volumes published 1850-1853, wrote, "Whatever its origin it is certainly one of the most lovely plants that our gardens know." Over a hundred years later, the authors of *ERICACEOUS PLANTS FOR NORTHWEST GARDENS* commented briefly, "Choice; rare; easier in cultivation than Rhodothamnus." On it the Royal Horticultural Society bestowed its Award of Merit in 1964, and First Class Certificate in 1969.

Like so many of our valued garden plants, this one has endured a succession of name changes. Lindley first reported it as an erect *Bryanthus*, and others hazarded other opinions before the presently accepted name was decided on. It is now fairly generally considered to have been a chance cross (about 1845, on the Edinburgh nursery of Messrs. Cunningham and Fraser) between the above-named species (the X before its name indicating that it is a hybrid of the two distinct genera). *X P. erectus* is the only known cultivar of this parentage.

Perhaps part, at least, of the cause for its scarcity in gardens where it would succeed if tried, is that in introducing it Lindley stated that it is impossible to keep such plants "in health in open ground in ordinary places in London." And later another author shoved it further into the background by adding that it is short-lived, "lasting hardly more than eight years in the garden."

We have no idea in what conditions these writers had tried to grow *X Phyllothamnus erectus*, but we can certainly affirm that our plant, acquired in 1963 and planted out with some peat added to the sandy soil at its roots, under the deciduous shade of an old apple tree, has stoutly remained with us, suffering whatever neglect came its way and temperatures as low as 7°F (-14°C) ever since. It must have acid soil and good drainage. The past drought-ridden summers it has had virtually no water at all. Perhaps it will not flower very well next spring, but this autumn it looks its same uncomplaining self. It appears to be as scarce in the Seattle vicinity as elsewhere; but one friend who probably acquired the species at the same time and from the same source as mine tells me that her plant, placed in peaty part-shade (in a colder garden) and also treated to neglect is equally thriving.

X P. erectus grows to a height of about 30 cm (12 in) and my plant has gradually achieved a diameter of 45 cm (18 in). Its crowded leaves resemble those of *Phyllodoce*. They are up to 15 mm (5/8 in) long and 3 mm (1/8 in) wide. Their margins are slightly revolute. They are said to be remotely toothed, but the teeth can be seen only by close examination with a lens. They are furnished beneath with short fine hairs, except the midrib which is raised and glabrous. The rosy-pink flowers (pink not only in the petals but also the stamens) are

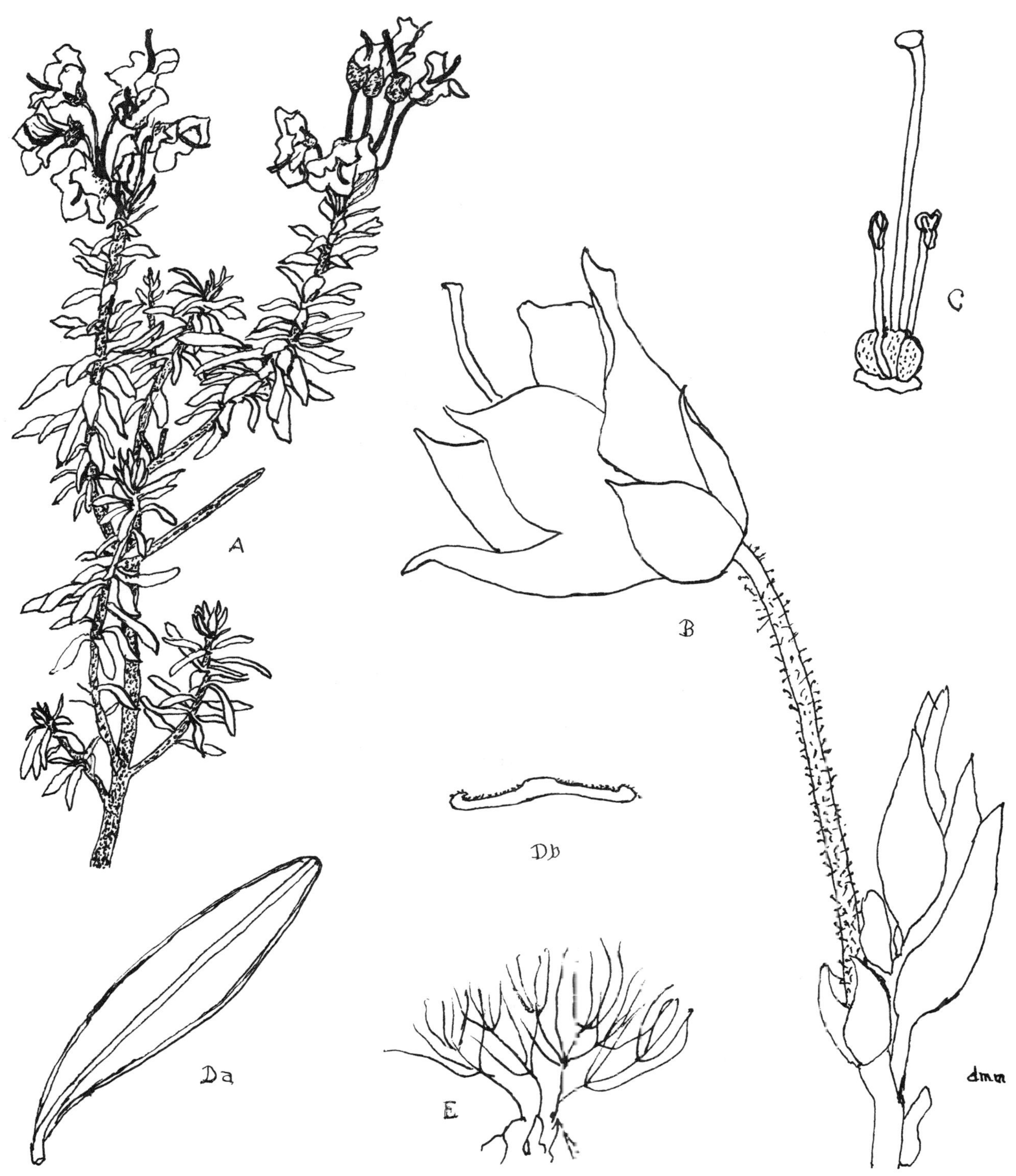

X *Phyllothamnus erectus* Schneid. *(Phyllodoce empetriformis x Rhodothamnus chamaecistus)*: A, flowering branch 1X; B, flower 5X; C, pistil and 2 of the stamens 5X; Da, leaf beneath 5X; Db, leaf cross section (under side at the top) 10X; E, plant habit.

Above is a copy of the beautiful colored illustration in *PAXTON'S FLOWER GARDEN*, edition of 1882. The plant, which John Lindley originally called *Bryanthus erectus*, The Upright Bryanth, is the one we now know as *X Phyllothamnus erectus* Schneid.

inverted cone- rather than bell-shape (thus more resembling those of its *Rhodothamnus* parent) and appear in April in my garden.

It is fairly readily propagated from cuttings of half-ripe wood, in July here.

Rehder gives it a hardiness rating of Zone V, equal to USDA Zone 6a.

References:

Bean, W.J.: *TREES AND SHRUBS HARDY IN THE BRITISH ISLES*, Rev. 1976.

Griffith, Anna N.: *COLLINS GUIDE TO ALPINES,* 1964.

HILLIERS' *MANUAL OF TREES & SHRUBS*, 1975.

Hills, L.D.: *THE PROPAGATION OF ALPINES*, 1959.

Krussmann, Gerd: *MANUAL OF CULTIVATED BROAD-LEAVED TREES AND SHRUBS*, 1985.

Lindley, John: *PAXTON'S FLOWER GARDEN*, Rev. 1882.

Rehder, Alfred: *MANUAL OF CULTIVATED TREES AND SHRUBS*, 1956.

Royal Horticultural Society: *DICTIONARY OF GARDENING*, 1984.

SANDERS' ENCYCLOPAEDIA OF GARDENING, Rev. 1958.

PROPAGATION

Alice and Bob Knight

Introduction. Most heaths and heathers are very easy to propagate and some even propagate themselves by seed or self-layering. Plants can also be propagated by tissue culture or by cuttings. Vegetative reproduction, or cuttings, is easy, inexpensive and a very reliable way to increase cultivars quickly and to insure true clones. There are many different opinions on best methods, timing, cutting size and rooting media. Most heaths and heathers root easily, so one should not be afraid to experiment or use a method best suited to individual needs.

When to take cuttings. Some commercial growers take cuttings as early as June and others successfully put in cuttings during fall or winter months. It is quite probable that, with care, some cuttings could be rooted almost any month of the year.

Erica carnea* and *Erica x darleyensis cuttings can be taken as early as June when new growth is sufficiently hardened to allow lower leaves to be stripped without breaking the tender stems. This timing enables one to get cuttings prior to flower bud set. Removal of buds on a cutting (to direct the plant's strength to more rapid vegetative growth rather than flowering) is often advised; however, even budded cuttings do root.

Although they strike roots well, there are some disadvantages to taking summer cuttings. They will require extra care in that they must be watered more frequently. An automatic mist system and bottom heat are definite advantages. Protection from direct sun during summer months will also be necessary in most areas.

***Calluna vulgaris* cuttings** seem to root almost any time of the year. Most commercial growers prefer taking these in early spring or late fall when there is sufficient new growth above flowering stalks to get a one and one-half to three-inch cutting from new wood.

Size of cuttings. A poll of commercial growers may find cutting sizes varied from one-half inch to four or five inches, depending on species and how rooted cuttings will be used. Larger cuttings are often taken if, soon after rooting, they will be grown on in the ground or large containers. Smaller cuttings, when rooted, are often transplanted into small pots and grown on for a season or more prior to being transplanted into the ground. Tiny half-inch cuttings may be all one can get from a dwarf *Calluna* or a newly acquired plant. Although it is possible to root larger or smaller size cuttings, most commercial growers prefer cuttings between one and one-half and three inches in length for most *Erica* and *Calluna* varieties. Tree heath cuttings are usually three to four inches in length.

The larger cuttings develop more quickly into salable-size plants.

Where to cut. Tip cuttings (new growth at the tip of a stem) are usually preferred, but second or third cuttings down the stem or even side shoots can be rooted. Half-ripe, unflowered cuttings are generally best. It is important to take cuttings from healthy, disease-free plants with no abnormalities.

Preparation. Leaves on the lower one-third of a cutting (the section to be inserted into the medium) are usually stripped prior to insertion to encourage rooting. Roots will spring from the leaf scars. Although cuttings should only be taken from healthy, disease-free plants, some growers also guard against disease by dipping cuttings in a weak chlorox solution or other plant sterilant.

Containers. A variety of containers can be used for rooting. Commercial growers usually stick cuttings into wooden or plastic flats which may each hold several hundred cuttings. A home gardener could use any container at least three inches deep—a clay or plastic pot, a small box, seed tray or even a discarded pan with holes for drainage. All containers should be carefully cleaned to minimize disease. Good drainage is very important; it is also important never to allow cuttings to dry out.

Cutting media, rooting and care. Heathers will root in many different media. A coarse builder's or concrete sand works well and provides the necessary good drainage. Some prefer using straight perlite, vermiculite, ground pumice or a mixture of peat with any one of these. Cuttings can also be rooted in commercial potting soil or well-drained regular garden soil. Highly alkaline soil is not suitable and alkaline water should not be used to keep cuttings moist.

Rooting hormones are sometimes used on heather cuttings, but most feel this is unnecessary. A few larger cuttings, or cultivars which are more difficult to root may benefit from being dipped into a rooting solution prior to insertion into media. Several rooting hormone compounds are on the market and one should carefully read and follow directions prior to using.

Inserting. There are several methods for inserting the cuttings into the media, which should be dampened and firmed prior to use. Some simply stick cuttings vertically, others insert at a slight angle. Some firm cuttings by pressing them into the medium while others simply water well to anchor the cuttings, in which case care must be taken not to wash out smaller cuttings.

Cuttings can be stuck quite close together if they will be potted soon after they are rooted. Heather roots are fine and do not penetrate deeply; so, if they are to remain in the cutting media for an extended period, roots may intertwine and be hard to separate without damage. Closeness also depends on the size of cuttings. One-half inch apart is considered good spacing for a one and one-half to three inch cutting. Larger cuttings will require more space.

Labeling. Labeling cuttings is very important. It is easy to forget or improperly guess a cultivar name at transplanting time if not labeled. A soft pencil and white plastic label is good. Writing the name on both sides of the label is even better. Other markers may not be waterproof or may fade in the sunlight. Pots and flats can be assigned numbers and this additional record kept as an extra guarantee.

Where to keep flats. Mist units are very good, but not essential. Cuttings can be rooted in a greenhouse, a small greenhouse-like structure (such as under plastic or glass) or on a kitchen window sill where there is a moist environment. Good ventilation is important. Cuttings kept too wet can mold or damp off. If an enclosed container is used, it should be partially uncovered to allow air circulation.

Covering summer or fall cuttings with two to four layers of damp newspaper for the first three to seven days is often helpful. Paper can be placed directly on cuttings and sprinkled lightly several times a day. This will keep foliage damp and seems to be beneficial in getting cuttings off to a better start. Cuttings which will be rooted during winter or early spring may not need to be covered.

If **bottom heat** is available, root temperatures are usually kept about 10°F (6°C) warmer than the surrounding air. Air temperatures of 60°-70°F (15°-21°C) are ideal for rooting, but this is not critical. Cuttings can be rooted at higher or lower temperatures if properly cared for.

Cuttings take various amounts of time to root. With bottom heat, some will root in two weeks and others may take up to three months. Bottom heat becomes a distinct advantage or even a necessity when taking cuttings after a plant has become dormant. *Erica carnea* cuttings taken in June often root in four to eight weeks without bottom heat. *Erica cinerea* may take six to ten weeks. Younger material usually roots more quickly. Cuttings taken in late fall or those placed in cold frames may not root until the following spring.

Fungicides are sometimes used to control mold or damping off. High humidity and low air temperature plus poor ventilation encourage rot, but if cuttings are well cared for and ventilation is good, fungicides may not be needed.

CARE AFTER ROOTING

Rooted cuttings can be over-wintered in cold frames, a cool greenhouse or even an outdoor protected area where temperatures are fairly moderate. If time and weather permit, rooted cuttings can be transplanted into pots for storage or for growing on. In some areas, it may be possible to transplant hardened off rooted cuttings directly into the ground. It is often, however, difficult to keep these small plants watered and weeded as they grow. Cuttings grown on for a few months in pots usually have a better survival rate and a good-sized plant will develop in a relatively short time.

Pots can be partially submerged in sand, soil or sawdust or grouped closely in a cold frame or protected area until planted in spring. Good ventilation and regular watering are necessities and some protection from direct sun may also be necessary. Rooted cuttings can be root-pruned if necessary and are often top-pruned to encourage branching. Cutting or pinching the ends off each branch and gently shaping the plant should be done prior to planting.

OTHER PROPAGATION METHODS

Layering. Many lower-growing heaths and heathers propagate themselves by layering. Deliberate layering can be done almost any time of the year and is often a quick method of propagating during the spring growing season. Branches can be secured, either at ground level or in a shallow trench, with bent wire loops or small stones. The portion of the stem to be layered is covered with a peat-sand mixture or existing soil, with the tip protruding. Another method is to remove leaves and make a small notch in the plant stem before burying. The tips of the shoot are always bent up more or less erect and can be fastened to a stake to be kept in position if necessary. It is important to keep the layered area moist at all times.

When the layered portion shows signs of good new growth, it can be severed from the parent plant; but it is best not to move it to a new site until it is growing quite vigorously. A disadvantage of layering is that it often takes several seasons' growth before the new plant can be pruned enough to be nicely shaped. Layering is also impractical on a commercial basis when many plants must be produced quickly.

Seed. Although heaths and heathers often propagate themselves by seed, this method is not recommended because cultivars do not always come true. The only way one can be positive of producing an actual clone is by vegetative reproduction. Seed is also hard to obtain and loses its viability quickly.

Tissue culture. Cloning by tissue culture is possible but is not widely practiced at this time because heaths and heathers can be propagated so easily and quickly from cuttings.

CULTIVATION

Alice and Bob Knight

Planting Season. In many parts of the world container-grown heathers can be planted almost any time of the year. Early fall planting, when soil is still warm, encourages prompt root growth and plants are quite well established before temperatures become extreme. Early spring planting is better than late spring when plants may dry out before rooting in.

Sun/Shade. Heathers are best in full sun, but most cultivars can tolerate partial shade. Plants in shade will not bloom well and tend to get "leggy". In areas where summers are long and hot, a planting site in filtered shade can be an advantage. Some varieties, particularly golden-foliaged *Callunas*, sunburn easily and do better if protected from hot midday sun. This cooler location may also reduce the need to water so frequently and could also reduce the risk of diseases caused by humid conditions.

Soil. Heaths and heathers are tolerant of a wide range of soil although various species have different pH preferences. In general, heaths and heathers can be divided into three groups: 1)lime lovers and those tolerant of lime; 2)those that are neutral tolerant with slight acceptance of alkalinity and complete acceptance of acid soil; and 3)those which must have acid soil.

Species tolerant of some lime include: *Daboecia cantabrica* and many of the *Erica* species such as *E. arborea, E. australis, E. carnea, E. x darleyensis, E. erigena, E. lusitanica, E. manipuliflora, E. multiflora, E. terminalis, E. umbellata* and *E. x veitchii*.

Species which require acid soil include: *Calluna vulgaris, Daboecia azorica, D. x scotica, Erica ciliaris, E. cinerea, E. mackaiana, E. tetralix, E. scoparia, E. x watsonii* and *E. x williamsii*. *E. vagans* does well in neutral soil.

Soil can usually be amended to adjust the pH and to improve heavy soil. Sand, vermiculite or perlite will improve drainage. Adding moist peatmoss in the planting hole is also often a good idea. Both heaths and heathers need a well-drained soil which will also hold moisture without becoming stagnant. A few species such as *Erica tetralix* and *Daboecia cantabrica* can tolerate poorer drainage; however, a well-drained site is always best. Planting areas are sometimes mounded into berms to improve drainage or for landscape interest.

Selecting and Planting. When selecting heaths and heathers for planting, always look for healthy plants which are bushy but not leggy. Roots should be moist as they come from the pots. It is often a good idea to submerse the potted plants in a bucket of water just prior to planting to be sure a plant has enough moisture to survive any transplant shock.

If possible, the entire bed should be worked up prior to planting. Prepare a hole at least twice the size of the plant root ball. Partially fill the hole with compost or top soil and possibly some moist peat moss if soil is poor, or to improve drainage. Heathers have relatively shallow roots which may have to be loosened prior to planting. Lightly scoring the rootball with a sharp object in two or three places may be necessary if plant has been in its pot long enough to be rootbound. **Never plant heathers too deeply.** Foliage should be resting on, or barely above the soil. Gently firm the plant into position and water well.

Spacing of plants depends on space available and landscape effect desired. Plantings in groups of three or more of the same variety is often very desirable. This gives a better display of color as plants merge together.

CARE

Water! Heaths and heathers are generally considered easy care plants; however, extra attention when planting and during the first season is very important for getting plants well established. Never allow plants to dry out! This is by far the most common reason for losses - particularly with new plants. Water deeply at least once a week during hot weather and even more often if newly planted.

Remove weeds carefully and be very careful with weed killers, if used. If plants are mulched, keep mulch away from stem and crown of the plant. Heathers have shallow roots and can easily be smothered. Holding mulching material back to the edge of the plant foliage allows roots to breathe and does not rob the plant or nutrients.

PROTECTION

Winter protection of some or all varieties of heather may be necessary in some areas. Where less than 0°F (-18°C) temperatures are common, particularly if they occur prior to snow cover, mulching is necessary. Evergreen boughs, straw or other material can be used to protect the plants prior to snow cover. Protection from drying winds is also a good idea. Some gardeners report that anti-dessicant sprays are helpful. Snow cover, of course, is very beneficial in seeing plants through a cold winter.

In areas where heat is a problem, planting heathers in filtered shade is often helpful. Close attention to watering is also important and plants must be watered deeply to insure that roots are not drying out. Once rootballs dry out, heathers seldom can be saved. Even though heaths and heathers may take some extra care in areas where they are not commonly grown they are worth the effort!

FERTILIZATION

Fertilization of heaths and heathers is a subject of much controversy. Heaths and heathers, once established, may not need as much care as some other plants; however, light applications of rhododendron-type fertilizers in early spring are usually helpful.

Fertilizer should not be applied to the foliage and should be kept at least two inches from the stem of the plant. Granular types with slow release are usually best. Fertilizer should be washed into the soil and washed off the foliage immediately. Over-feeding can cause too much soft growth and reduce flowering. Heathers doing well may not need annual or semi-annual applications of fertilizer.

Some heathers also benefit from application of iron if foliage turns pale from chlorosis. A light feeding of acid fertilizer or iron sulphate usually corrects a chlorotic condition.

PRUNING

Not all heathers require pruning on a regular schedule, especially the low-growing, winter-blooming cultivars. Pruning does usually increase the life of a plant, encourage fresh new growth and improve flowering. Pruning is also necessary to remove winter damage and to control size and shape of plants. Old flowered wood does not bloom again, so old blooms and straggly growth should be removed in the fall or early spring before new growth begins and the next season's flower buds are set.

It is necessary to prune most *Calluna vulgaris* cultivars each year after flowering. *Callunas* do not sprout from wood more than three years old, so it is advantageous to prune all upright cultivars annually. Compact and dwarf varieties should be pruned as needed to be kept attractive.

Summer-flowering hybrids have better early spring foliage color and flower well if sheared at least every other season. Tree heaths can be kept bushy and attractive by removing about one-third of the previous year's growth each spring after flowering. Keeping tree heaths bushy reduces the chance of branches breaking during winter storms.

Most *Erica carnea* and *E. x darleyensis* cultivars do not need annual pruning. They can be cut back to insure compactness or to be confined to an area, but usually continue to bloom each season with only an occasional pruning at two to three year intervals.

PESTS AND DISEASES

Alice and Bob Knight

Heaths and heathers are relatively free from both pests and diseases. Burrowing animals sometimes cause damage by undermining roots. This may not kill the plants, but can make it difficult to keep the roots sufficiently moist. Heathers can be damaged by urine from dogs and other pets. Some damage can be inflicted by rabbits and deer if other vegetation is not available. Heather does not seem to be a favorite for most grazing animals.

Established plantings which are well tended are usually quite disease free and most plant losses can be traced to cultural problems rather than disease.

However, some diseases have been reported: Scattered and sporadic outbreaks of *Phytophthora cinnamomi* have caused damage to heathers. This is a common root disease spread by water in wet and warm conditions. If caught early, it is not always fatal and can be controlled with chemical fungicides.

Root weavil and *Rhizoctonia*, a lower stem rot, are also sometimes found in heather plantings but have not been found with any regularity in home gardens.

HEATHER FLOWER COLORS —
HEATHERS FOR THE GARDEN

Alice and Bob Knight

Heaths and heathers are increasingly more widely used in both home and commercial landscaping in much of North America. They are easy-care evergreen shrubs which, in appropriate climate zones, can be used for all-year garden color. In many locations, with careful planning, one can have varieties in bloom every month of the year — a unique attribute. They vary from prostrate or low, spreading ground-covers to upright tree heaths and from small cushions to sizable bushes. Their foliage colors include many shades of green, grey, gold and bronze; their flower colors range from white to almost black in shades of pink, red and purple.

Considerable effort has been expended by The Heather Society and the Royal Horticultural Society, both based in Great Britain, to describe heather colors by standardized names. Sixteen color names have been selected to describe heather blooms. Color numbers and names designated by The Heather Society are as follows:

H1 Amethyst (violet or violet purple)
H2 Mauve (pale pinkish-purple)
H3 Lavender (light bluish-purple)
H4 Lilac (light purple)
H5 Ruby (clear red)
H6 Cerise (bright pinkish-red)
H7 Rose pink
H8 Pink
H9 Beetroot (dark purplish-crimson)
H10 Purple
H11 Lilac Pink
H12 Heliotrope
H13 Crimson
H14 Magenta (purplish-red)
H15 Salmon (yellowish-pink)
H16 Shell Pink (beige-pink)

HYBRIDIZING HEATHERS

To one concerned with the behavior of plant (or animal) cells, a hybrid is an individual which has been produced when an egg cell is united with an unlike sperm cell. There are three kinds of hybrids: 1)**intergeneric**—an individual whose parents are of two different genera, e.g., *X Phyllothamnus (Phyllodoce x Rhodothamnus)*—note the X before the name of the hybrid progeny; 2)**inter-specific**—an individual whose parents are of the same genus but of two different species, e.g., *Erica x darleyensis (E. erigena x E. carnea)*; 3)**intras-pecific**—an individual seed plant whose parents are of the same species, by far the commonest, e.g., the many cultivars, varieties of *Calluna vulgaris, Erica carnea*, etc. If given cultivar names, the names are capitalized and given in single quotes, e.g., *Calluna vulgaris* 'Aurea,' *Erica carnea* 'King George.'

Hybrids generally have been observed to share certain characters. 1)Often, in the description of a hybrid, will be found the phrase "midway between the parents," in plant habit, leaves, reproductive organs, etc., or it will be said to have inherited some characters from each parent, e.g., *E. x darleyensis* grows taller than *E. carnea*, less tall than *E. erigena*; is hardier than *E. erigena*, less hardy than *E. carnea*, etc.

2)Often a hybrid plant is observed to partake of the character of "hybrid vigor". An example is *E. x darleyensis* 'Darley Dale,' my original plant of which was planted in autumn 1936 in a wedge between large hillside boulders, persists there despite vagaries of weather and other hazards, is about 40cm (16in) high and 120cm (4ft) in diameter, thick with lively stems, and invariably flowers for half the year. It is a more vigorous growing plant than either of its parents.

3)Interspecific and intergeneric hybrids of European heathers, have so far not been observed to produce much, if any, viable seed. It is therefore probable that each new such plant of a particular cross must have been separately generated from a new cross of the same parents and will, to some extent, like individual children of the same human family, be supplied with its own set of inherited characters.

In the case of other species than hardy heathers, if the plants which are crossed are closely enough related, hybrid progeny may bear viable seeds, or may not. When different species in the same genus of orchid are crossed, viable seed is usually produced; but not with sweet peas. Up to this time no viable seed has been found in the hybrid hardy heathers

The history of intentionally hybridizing heathers is relatively recent. The first issue of the *YEAR BOOK OF THE HEATHER SOCIETY*, dated 1963 and edited by Mr. P. S. Patrick carried a Questions and Answers section. The first question printed was, "Can heaths be hybridized by humans?" The answer, signed with the initials of Mr. D. F. Maxwell, was, "The short answer is yes

. . . ," but adding the caution that heather flowers are tiny to deal with, the implication being that their small size makes them difficult to work with. In any case, we have not seen reports of serious attempts to hybridize heathers having been made up to that time.

By the early 20th century, five different *Erica* plants found in the wild or in gardens had been assumed to be hybrids. Their parentage was deduced partly from the plant populations in which they had appeared and more definitely on microscopic examination of their reproductive organs.

They were: ***Erica x watsonii*** (Benth. 1839) Bean. (*E. tetralix x E. ciliaris*, found growing wild in 1831.) ***E. x stuartii*** E.F. Linton 1902. (*E. tetralix x E. mackaiana,* found growing wild in 1846, the mystery of its parentage was not finally untangled until 1975 when Dutch nurseryman, Rinus Zwijnenburg noticed a reversion to what had been called *E. x praegeri*, on a plant of *E. x stuartii.* The earlier name, *E. x stuartii,* is the correct name for the whole group.) ***E. x williamsii*** Druce 1911. (*E. tetralix x E. vagans*, found in the wild, in 1860.) ***E. x veitchii*** Bean, 1905. (*E. arborea x E. lusitanica*, found in the Veitch nursery before 1900.) ***E. x darleyensis*** Bean 1914. (*E. erigena x E. carnea*, found about 1890 at James Smith & Son nursery at Darley Dale, Derbyshire.) Most recent find, ***Daboecia x scotica*** McClintock 1978. (*D. azorica x D. cantabrica*, found by the late Mr. William Buchanan in his Glasgow garden in the late 1950s.)

In 1972, intrepid Mrs. Anne Parris, who gardened at Usk, north of Cardiff, Wales and had a long row of well established plants of *E. x darleyensis*, had been wondering if she could perhaps confirm that hybrid's assumed parents by effecting a cross of them. After having taken necessary precautions to rule out stray pollen, she dusted the flowering stems of an *E. erigena* with pollen from an *E. carnea*, obtained seed and succeeded in raising plants which had the habit of her *E. x darleyensis* 'Darley Dale', were considerably taller and bushier than *E. carnea*, but lacked the erect "tree heath" habit of *E. erigena*. In other words, she had a new *E. x darleyensis.* She reported her procedure and findings in the *YEAR BOOK OF THE HEATHER SOC.* in 1976, 1978 and 1980. She then moved to Australia, but the heather hybridizers were off and running.

In the *YEAR BOOK*, 1985, David McClintock reported the work of Kurt Kramer with intraspecific crosses of *E. carnea* cultivars, at Edewecht-Suddorf, in northern West Germany. He has produced many plants with particularly fine new flower colors.—Also in that same issue, Dr. John Griffiths, who had begun experiments in 1981, reviewed the so far published hybrids and described in detail his method of procedure in hybridizing heathers in his Yorkshire garden. In the 1987 *YEAR BOOK*, *Hybridisation of the Hardy Ericas, Part 2*, he was able to report some of his results from the earlier experiments. For the 1989 *YEAR BOOK*, Mr. H. M. J. Blum wrote the account of the September 1988 Annual Conference of the Heather Society. He reported Dr. Griffiths' talk on *Further Progress on Experiments in Heather Hybridisation*, and mentioned his own hope that crosses of European and Cape Heaths would bring many good new plants. David Wilson, Sardis, B.C., reported his experiments with hybridizing several species of heather in *HEATHER NEWS*, in 1986 and 1987.

References:

Huxley, A. J.: Hybrid, *GARDEN TERMS SIMPLIFIED*, 1962, p. 49.

Lawrence, G. H. M.: *TAXONOMY OF VASCULAR PLANTS*, 1951, pp. 174-176.

Northen, Henry T. & Rebecca T.: *THE SECRET OF THE GREEN THUMB*, 1954, pp. 224-234. Technique illustrated.

Hartmann, H. T., W. J. Flocker, A. M. Kofranek: *PLANT SCIENCE*, 1981, p. 76.

YEAR BOOK OF THE HEATHER SOCIETY, 1963, p. 30.

McClintock, David: *GUIDE TO THE NAMING OF PLANTS*, 1980.

Parris, Mrs. Anne: *Preliminary note on a cross between Erica erigena and E. carnea, YR. BK. OF THE HEATHER SOC.*, 1976.

Parris, Mrs. A.: *Further note on a cross between Erica erigena and E. carnea, YR. BK. OF THE HEATHER SOC.*, 1977.

Parris, Mrs. A.: *Further Notes on E. x darleyensis induced Hybrids, YR. BK. OF THE HEATHER SOC.*, 1980.

Jones, A. W.: *Sharp eyes help to solve the mystery of Erica 'Stuartii', YR. BK. OF THE HEATHER SOC.*, 1979.

McClintock, D.: *Kurt Kramer's New Carneas, YR. BK. OF THE HEATHER SOC.*, 1985.

Crewe-Brown, J. E.: *Some Efforts at Hybridisation of South African Ericas, YR. BK. OF THE HEATHER SOC.*, 1985.

Griffiths, John: *Hybridisation of the Hardy Ericas, YR. BK. OF THE HEATHER SOC.*, 1985.

Griffiths, J.: *Hybridisation of the hardy Ericas, Part 2, YR. BK. OF THE HEATHER SOC.*, 1987.

Blum, H. M. J.: *Annual Conference, Gregynog, September 1988, Further Progress on Experiments in Heather Hybridisation, YR. BK. OF THE HEATHER SOC.*, 1989, pp. 8-10.

Wilson, David: *Summary of My Efforts at Heather Hybridizing, HEATHER NEWS*, No. 36, Dec. 1986.

Wilson, D.: *A further report on my efforts at hybridizing heathers, HEATHER NEWS*, No. 40, Dec. 1987.

Mycorrhizal Associations of Heathers

Donald A. M. Mackay*

Introduction

One of the particular pleasures of heather gardening is the knowledge that one is dealing with a plant not far removed from the wild. The great majority of heather cultivars are clonal reproductions of chance discoveries on moor or heath, preserving the genetic make-up of some freak form or variation that was at one time sufficiently in concert with its native environment to grow to discoverable size.

It is also pleasing to know that part of the ecological equation of survival in the wilderness are heather's fungal partners, the mycorrhizae; and it is reasonable to wonder whether fungal symbiosis can also be used to advantage in raising heathers in our own gardens. The answer, as with all matters of soil microbiology, is exceedingly complex. Before speculating about a possible answer it is necessary first to review at least some of the bacterial and fungal functions in soil.

Microbial Associations in Soil

Soil contains enormous numbers of bacteria, fungi, protozoa and other microscopic life forms intimately interconnected by both competitive and cooperative processes. The net result for any complex organic tissue of plant or animal origin present in the soil is its breaking down into fragments assimilable by microbial life-forms and plant roots. Dead organic tissue can be broken down by saprophytic microorganisms; live tissue also can be attacked and killed by pathogenic organisms, initiating the decay process for the saprophytes which follow.

In undisturbed soil there are gradients of moisture, oxygen, nitrogen, carbon dioxide and other gases. There are also likely to be nutrient, temperature and acidity gradients, as well as of decayed plant matter, for example, leaf litter slowly becoming humus. In time, the bacteria and fungi will arrange themselves along those gradients, each in its optimum niche in proximity to suitable other microorganisms whose specialized growth conditions and nutrient requirements are met by the breakdown products of immediate neighbors.

A plant root entering such soil becomes a major disturbance to the existing balance. By introducing air and carbon dioxide where there was none, or creating volatiles from its growth process, it can produce feedstock for certain microorganisms, or even stimulate fungal spores into germination.

The root itself, being rich in water and nutrients—notably the sugars syn-

---

*Information provided by Donald A.M. Mackay, President, Applied Microbiology, Inc., Brooklyn, NY, Public Health Research Institute, New York City.

thesized in the leaves and translocated to the roots for their growth and nutritional function—becomes the target of hungry microbes, some of which live off root exudates; some of these may be pathogens which try to invade the root and destroy it.

The microbial population in the cylindrical space within a few millimeters of the root, a space called the rhizosphere, is perhaps a hundred times denser with microbes than is the surrounding soil. Many microbes site themselves in the surface plane between the root and the soil, the rhizoplane, or may content themselves with life in the rhizosphere. Microorganisms already present in the soil when the root tip came to them can grow rapidly or their spores may germinate; others may migrate to the new nutrient sources. In any case, as far as root infections are concerned, the successful microorganism is the one which either quickly enough establishes a permanent colony of critical size, or creates a successful infection in a susceptible host, thus warding off later arriving microorganisms.

The Discovery of Mycorrhizae

Many plants are equipped, at their root tips, with root hairs which derive nourishment from the soil. (Heathers, however, among other plants, have fine hair roots, but no root hairs.) Many years ago it was noted that in certain forests, especially of oak and beech, characteristic mushrooms grew amidst the leaf litter. Under the litter it was found that tips of tree roots near the surface were invested by a sheath of mycelial tissue (mushroom "spawn"). This fungus sheath was found only at the root tips, replacing the root hairs, extending as the root extended, and usurping the nourishment-deriving function of root hairs. This fungus was called a mycorrhiza, a fungus root; and specifically an ecto-mycorrhiza because, except for a network of fungal threads penetrating a short way between the cells of the cortex, it stayed outside the root. The relationship between mycorrhiza and root was thought to be symbiotic—the fungus getting translocated sugar nutrients directly from the root, the tree being shielded from more aggressive disease-causing microorganisms and also supplied with more efficient means of obtaining water and minerals (especially phosphorus) from the soil.

A more recent view is that the relationship may be parasitic, rather than symbiotic, as the plant may have to work harder at photosynthesis to replace the sugar diverted to the mycorrhizae. However, the picture is unclear since extra plant growth might result solely from hormone-like substances released by the mycorrhizae. In general, the formation of mycorrhizae is not a property of one particular fungus, but of a group of fungi. It has long been noted to occur with a very wide range of fungal families and probably is an association likely to be found, or needed, only in sterile and undisturbed soil.

Though the first mycorrhizae were noted nearly 100 years ago, several additional kinds of mycorrhizae have been described as science and microscopic techniques have progressed. In fact, only within about the last 20 years have vesicular-arbuscular mycorrhizae (VAM) been described and their important function in nutrition of cereal grasses in tropical soils been realized. The current division of mycorrhizae into ecto, endo, ectendo and VAM types reflects only the progress of observation of the fungal penetration into the root. Because we can give something a name, we catalog it; we think we know it, its place, its function, but the truth may defy ready discovery.

Identification of the fungal partner in mycorrhizal associations is particularly difficult because standard microbiological identification depends heavily upon use of selective growth media, which can distinguish one microorganism in the presence of hundreds of others, though not always its significance to the phenomenon under study. But the growth and fruiting characteristics of mycorrhizal fungi are so greatly altered by the association with the root as to make standard identification tests even more uncertain. It was early realized that under experimental conditions so many different fungi from very different genera and families could form mycorrhizal associations with forest trees that the concept of a special symbiosis was in jeopardy. Even today it is still difficult to know which fungus (or fungi) actually are the important partners in nature, and whether joint fungal and bacterial relationships may be involved in some kinds of plants.

Practical use of mycorrhizal association has been achieved in silviculture by inoculation of spruce seedlings with fungi to assure even growth of closely spaced trees in order to suppress wasteful side branches. But even here this practice is useful only for certain trees, and may require altered forest management techniques such as thinning and intermediate harvesting to realize the benefits.

Much research is current in VAM inoculation of grasses, trying to improve cereal production in underdeveloped countries. But results are disappointing as the VAM naturally present in tropical soils rapidly displace the high-yielding bioengineered strains used for seedling inoculation.

Under practical application may also come such advice as to use soil from under rhododendrons to help establish heathers in the garden, or to strike cuttings in; but this advice seems more founded in general belief in the potential importance of mycorrhizae to heathers than in actual demonstration of particular benefit.

There is no doubt that both the orchid and erica families are prone to mycorrhizal associations. These are probably necessary for growth of orchid seedlings (which may, however, be as often killed as aided by them) and for the obviously saprophytic members of the Ericaceae such as the chlorophyll-free Indian pipe *(Monotropa uniflora)*. However, it has taken extensive work to unravel the special need for mycorrhizae on heather in moorland. Mycorrhizae may be needed not only for their fungal enzymes necessary to get nutrients from recalcitrant sources in peat, but for overcoming the several factors in peat generally hostile to plant growth and for functioning in water-logged soils where free fungi are usually inoperative.

Ericoidal Mycorrhizae

The entire Heath Family (Ericaceae) is known to be predisposed to fungal partners and the names ericoidal mycorrhizae, or ectendo (half-in, half-out) mycorrhizae have been coined to specify the association. Since heather seeds in the wild are naturally contaminated with fungi, it was at one time thought that such contamination was necessary in order for them to germinate and grow well; but this does not seem to hold true, though it may be that the association is an asset to certain plants on certain soils under certain conditions. Undoubtedly all plants must have fungi and bacteria in proximity to their roots; but in the nursery, with use of sterilized soil composts, rooting hormones and fertilizers, there is no need to invoke mycorrhizal benefits. In the garden, there is soil disturbance even if there is no deliberately added fertilizer and so mycorrhizae may not be needed, or able to establish even if they were.

Both bacterial and fungal associations are clearly evolutionary developments which have allowed such plants as heathers to survive in very nutrient-limited conditions such as found on Scottish peat moors or Dutch sand dunes. The microbial partners are likely to be different in different conditions in the wild. It would be surprising to find the same fungal partner for heather in sand at sea level, in pure peat at 3,000 feet in Scotland and in the stony 8,000 foot height of a Swiss alp, because of both the edaphic and climatic components of the ecology.

Heathers can be valued all the more for their versatility in the wild, but it is doubtful whether their potential for fungal symbiosis gets much use in the average garden. They are likely to be contaminated with fungi in any case as all plants are but, in the garden, benefit may lie more in the deterrence of later, would-be pathogenic fungi. However, as Terry L. Underhill (*HEATHS AND HEATHERS*, 1971) points out, one using mycorrhizae-bearing wild heath soil for seed germination will very likely find it produces an unsought batch of wild heathers along with the intended crop.

The mycorrhizal association may well keep a heather barely alive under harsh conditions in poor soil, but its nutritional contribution has to be judged remembering that the same plant that was dwarf on a mountain top may reach full size in a garden, or cuttings taken from it will grow normally in sterilized soil.

Role of Ericoidal Mycorrhizae in Moorland Heather

In recent years there has been a continuing study under D. J. Read (Sheffield University, U.K.) of ericoidal mycorrhizae, with particular emphasis on understanding the conditions favorable to calluna growth on moorland. In contrast with nearly all other studies of mycorrhizae in which the plant root is found capable of being colonized by one or more of a wide range of fungal families, there does seem to be a highly specific relationship operating on heather-dominated moors. A symbiotic fungus *(Hymenoscyphus ericae)* has been determined to have a key role in permitting or promoting calluna growth in peaty soil, which is often characterized by 1)high levels of soluble aluminum and iron salts in the acid soil, 2)periodic water-logging, and 3)the high phenolic acid content of the leaf litter on the soil surface produced by the dominant calluna. This soil surface is phytotoxic (poisonous to plants) not only to competitive species but even to germination of calluna seeds.

The fungus isolated, though itself inhibited by high concentrations of some phenolic acids produced in leaf litter, seems able to prevent the root-shortening effect of the aluminum salts especially notable in acid, periodically water-logged soil. This can result in mycorrhizal roots being up to four times longer than uninfected roots in such soil conditions. Conversely, the fungus seems to increase iron pickup from acid soil, which improves plant growth while protecting the plant from the toxic effects of excess iron.

Perhaps even more importantly, the germination and growth of heather seed in leaf litter containing phytotoxic levels of the phenolic acids derived from lignin breakdown seems to be strongly aided by the endophyte fungus, both in assimilating the phenolic acids which cause inhibition of germination, and in overcoming the subsequent toxicity to the seedlings.

The Sheffield group has also looked at competitive effects in moorland, especially with grasses and sedges. While growth of sheep's fescue *(Festuca ovina)*, a common moorland grass, is strongly inhibited by just the phenolic acids found in leaf litter, this effect is magnified in the presence of heather roots, with particularly dramatic effects obtained when the heather root is mycorrhizal. However, the ericoidal mycorrhiza needs oxygen, and the anoxia of permanently water-logged soils gives a strong competitive advantage over heather to plants like the sedges (Cyperaceae) which have internal air transport systems in their roots. Also, fatty acids like acetic acid which build up in water-logged soil can exert their own phytotoxic effects; but the ericoidal fungus can utilize them as carbon sources, thus exerting a protective detoxifying effect - as with the phenolic acids—permitting calluna growth in wet peaty soils.

Heather on moorland thus seems to be dependent on mycorrhizae, at least for its shallow roots which will be in the drier surface soil layer richest in the inhibiting phenolic acids. The benefits of the mycorrhizal function are seen in 1)reducing competition from grasses, 2)reducing the toxic effect of aluminum in acid, water-logged soil, 3)increasing the pickup of beneficial iron levels, and 4)permitting germination of heather seeds in phytotoxic soil. Removal of inhibiting fatty acids in wet acid soil may be another factor, but it is possible other kinds of fungi could break down these acids acting as free-ranging organisms, not necessarily as endophytes or highly localized symbionts of heather roots. A fungus may have a life of its own if the association with a heather root is not mandatory.

Gardeners have to decide for themselves 1)whether long periods of waterlogging in peaty soils are the norm for their own heather plants, 2)whether they have grown heathers long enough to have created an undisturbed, unique soil surface from leaf litter, and 3)whether natural germination of seedlings is of any import to their heather growing plans.

If you are growing heather in soil in which no other plant will grow you can be fairly sure the success of heathers lies in the presence of detoxifying mycorrhizae on their roots. But the significance of mycorrhizae in the normal garden is much harder to assess.

Conclusion

In sum, mycorrhizal associations are almost certainly the key to understanding the ecology of heather on heaths and moors. We can also guess that mycorrhizae have a protective function against pathogens, but may be affected by air pollution, toxic metals, acid rain, sheep droppings, liming, fertilizer run-offs and the other factors blamed, rightly or wrongly, for the loss of wild heath in Britain. However, the importance of mycorrhizae in the garden is still unknown.

If the gardener is prepared to put down a mulch of shredded wild heather or, more realistically, a thick layer of shredded bark that will eventually undergo fungal decay, it might be possible to recreate the natural cycle by which 1)fungi on living leaves predispose the fungi decomposing the leaf litter, which 2)predispose the fungi able to form mycorrhizae on roots with which they come in contact, and 3)eventually to colonize the entire plant and restart the cycle. But then cultivation, chemical fertilizers, herbicides and pesticides will have to be foresworn and regarded as practices likely to have deleterious consequences on the fungal symbiont being cultivated along with the heather. There is always the possibility that if mycorrhizae become too important as partners to the plant, that is the plant becomes dependent on the mycorrhizae, their loss or reduction through summer drought, winter freeze, or chemical or biochemical events subsequent to fertilizer or fungicide usage will bode poorly for the plant's survival.

CULTIVARS AVAILABLE IN NORTH AMERICAN HEATHER NURSERIES 1990

BRUCKENTHALIA spiculifolia

CALLUNA vulgaris
Aberdeen
Alba Carlton
Alba Elata
Alba Jae
Alba Minor
Alba Plena
Alba Pumila
Alba Rigida
Allegro
Alportii
Alys Sutcliffe
Anthony Davis
Applecross
Arran Gold
August Beauty
Aurea
Autumn Glow

Barbara Fleur
Barnett Anley
Battle of Arnhem
Beoley Crimson
Beoley Gold
Bess Junior
Blazeaway
Bonfire Brilliance
Boreray
Boskoop
Bradford
Branchy Anne
Brightness
Bronze Beauty

Caerketton White
Caleb Threlkeld
Calf of Man
Californian Midge
Carole Chapman
Citronella
Clare Carpet
Con Brio
Corbett's Red
Corbett's White
County Wicklow
Cramond
Crispa
Cuprea
C.W. Nix

Dainty Bess
Darkness
Dark Star
Darleyensis
David Eason
Devon
Drum Rae
Durfordii

Eckart Miebner
Edith Godbolt
E.F. Brown
E. Hoare
Elegantissima
Walter Ingwersen
Elkstone
Ellie Barbour
Else Frye
Elsie Purnell
Emerald Jock

Fairy
Finale
Findling
Firebreak
Firefly
Flamingo
Foxhollow Wanderer
Foxii Nana
Fred J. Chapple

Glenfiddich
Gnome Pink
Golden Carpet
Golden Feather
Gold Haze
Gold Kup
Goldsworth Crimson
Goldsworth Crimson Variety
Green Cardinal
Green Corduroy
Guinea Gold

Haitje's Herbstfeuer
Hamlet Green
Hammondii Aureifolia
Hammondii Rubrifolia
H.E. Beale
Hibernica
Hiemalis
Hirsuta Typica
Hoyer Hagen
Hugh Nicholson
Humpty Dumpty

Inshriach Bronze

Jan
Jan Dekker
Japanese White
J.H. Hamilton
Jimmy Dyce
Joan Sparkes
John F. Letts
Johnson's Variety
Joy Vanstone
Juno

Karin Blum
Kerstin
Kinlochruel
Kirby White
Kit Hill
Kuphaldtii
Kynance

Long White
Lyle's Late White
Lyndon Proudley

Macdonald of Glencoe
Mair's Variety
Marion Blum
Martha Hermann
Mayfair
Minima (Smith's)
Minioxabach
Molecule
Mousehole
Mrs. Pat
Mrs. Ronald Gray
Mullion
Multicolor

***CALLUNA VULGARIS*, continued**

My Dream

Nana
Nana Compacta
Naturpark

Orange Queen
Oxabach

Penhale
Penny Bun
Peter Sparkes
Pink Tips
Platt's Surprise
Prizewinner
Pygmaea
Pyramidalis

Radnor
Ralph Purnell
Red Carpet
Red Favorite
Red Haze
Red Wings
Robert Chapman
Roma
Rosalind
Rosea
Ross Hutton
Rubra
Rubrum
Ruby Slinger

Sally Anne Proudley
Saskia
Schurig's Sensation
Serlei
Serlei Aurea
Serlei Grandiflora
Serlei Purpurea
Sesam
Silver King
Silver Knight
Silver Queen
Silver Rose
Silver Spire
Sir John Charrington
Sister Anne
Soay
Spitfire
Spring Cream
Spring Torch

October White
Old Gold
Orange Carpet
St. Nick
Sunrise
Sunset

Tenuis
Tib
Tom Thumb
Tomentosa
Torulosa
Tricolorifolia

Underwoodii

Valorian
Velvet Dome
Velvet Fascination

Westerlin
Westphalia
White Knight
White Lawn
White Mite
Wickwar Flame
Winter Chocolate

DABOECIA* *azorica

DABOECIA* *cantabrica

Alba
Atropurpurea
Cinderella
Mrs. W.V. Manning
Praegerae
Rubra

DABOECIA* x *scotica

Jack Drake
William Buchanan
William Buchanan Gold

ERICA andevalensis

ERICA arborea

Alpina
Estrella Gold

ERICA australis (wild form), Mr. Robert, Riverslea

***ERICA carnea* (herbacea)** (wild form)

Adrian Duncan
Alan Coates
Anne Sparkes
Atrorubra
Aurea
Barry Sellers
Carnea
Ceclia M. Beale
December Red
Eilen Porter
Foxhollow
Foxhollow Fairy
Gracilis
Heathwood
James Backhouse
King George
Leslie Sparkes
Loughrigg
March Seedling
Mrs. Sam Doncaster
Myretoun Ruby
Pink Spangles
Pirbright Rose
Porter's Red
Praecox Rubra
Prince of Wales
R.B. Cooke
Rubnteppich
Ruby Glow
Sherwoodii
Sherwood's Early Red
Snow Queen
Springwood Pink
Springwood White
Startler
Vivellii
Westwood Yellow
Winter Beauty

ERICA ciliaris
Aurea
Corfe Castle
David McClintock
Maweana
Mrs. C.H. Gill
Stoborough
Wych

ERICA cinerea
Alba
Alba Minor
Apple Blossom
Atropurpurea
Atrorubens
Atrosanguinea
C.D. Eason
Cevennes
Cindy
Coccinea
Colligan Bridge
Constance
Eden Valley
Foxhollow Mahogany
Frances
Golden Drop
Golden Hue
Golden Sport
G. Osmond
Hookstone Lavender
Joyce Burfitt
Knap Hill Pink
Lilacina
Mrs. Ford
Pink Ice
Plummer's Seedling
Providence
P.S. Patrick
Purple Beauty
Pygmaea
Rosabella
Rose Queen
Rosea
Rozanne Waterer
Ruby
Splendens
Velvet Night
Vivienne Patricia
Violaceae
Windlebrooke

ERICA x darleyensis
Ada S. Collins
Arthur Johnson
Darley Dale
Furzey
George Rendall
Ghost Hills
Jack Brummage
Jenny Porter
J.W. Porter
Margaret Porter
Silberschmelze
(= Alba)

ERICA erigena
Brightness
Golden Lady
Irish Dusk
Maxima
Superba
W.T. Rackliff

ERICA lusitanica (wild form)
George Hunt

ERICA mackaiana
Plena
Dr. Ronald Gray

ERICA maderensis

ERICA manipuliflora

ERICA multiflora

ERICA scoparia Lionel Woolner

ERICA x stuartii (praegeri) Irish Lemon

ERICA terminalis

ERICA tetralix
Alba
Alba Mollis
Con Underwood
Daphne Underwood
Darleyensis
George Fraser
Gratis
Helma
Ken Underwood
L.E. Underwood
Mollis
Pink Glow
Pink Star
Rosea
Rubra
Swedish Yellow

ERICA umbellata

ERICA vagans
Alba
Birch Glow
Carnea
George Underwood
Lyonesse
Miss Waterer
Mrs. D.F. Maxwell
Mrs. S. Donaldson
Nana
Pyrenees Pink
St. Keverne
Valerie Proudley
Yellow John

ERICA x veitchii Exeter

ERICA x watsonii
Dawn
Dorothy Metheny
Gwen
H. Maxwell
Truro

ERICA x williamsii	Gwavas	P.D. Williams

RELATED PLANT CULTIVARS IN N. AMERICAN HEATHER NURSERIES

***CASSIOPE* Species**	**Forms**	**Hybrids**
fastigiata	lycopodioides	x 'Badenoch'
lycopodioides	'Beatrice Lilly'	x 'Bearsden'
selaginoides	l. ssp. gracilis	x 'Edinburgh'
stelleriana	l. 'Upright'	x 'Flora Slack'
	mertensiana	x 'Randle Cooke'
	m. ssp. californica	
	m. ssp. ciliolata	
	m. ssp. gracilis	

***PHYLLODOCE* Species**	**Hybrids**
aleutica (Bassetti)	x 'Drummondii'
aleutica (Berry)	x 'Fred Stoker'
breweri	*x intermedia*
empetriformis	x 'Barry Starling'

THE WHY OF PLANT NAMES

For gardeners, it is convenient to have our plants known by universally agreed-upon names, so that if we admire a plant and would like to acquire one like it for our garden, we know exactly what to ask for—in any part of the world.

Our own family and given names somewhat identify who we are. Some people study family genealogies. Taxonomic botanists (taxonomists) are those who might be said to do similar studies for plants, and the task they set themselves is a difficult one because they may try to go back to the first beginnings of the Vegetable Kingdom billions of years ago. We gardeners can usually skip their *Divisions, Classes, and Orders* and need only concern ourselves with the more recent derivation of our plants. For practical purposes we need to know:

Family: Ericaceae, the family of which our heathers are members—along with rhododendrons, blueberries and cranberries, bearberry, etc.—is an acid soil family. The Family names are capitalized and, except in the cases of Compositae and 7 others, family names end in -aceae. (But recently the names of these 8 families have been changed to conform, e.g. for Compositae now use Asteraceae, etc.)

Genus: *Erica*, the genus (generic) name of the heaths, is from the ancient Greek name for heaths; *Calluna*, the genus name of the so-called "Scotch Heather," is derived from the Greek word meaning to clean or adorn. *Daboecia*, St. Dabeoc's Heath, in N. America sometimes called "Irish Bell Heather." Note italics and capital initial for generic names.

Species: E.g., *cinerea* (from the Latin for ash-colored) is the species name (specific epithet) for the Scottish Heath *(Erica cinerea)*. The species name is spelled with a lower case initial and, with the genus name, the most important for identifying a plant. These names are customarily either in italics or underlined.

Cultivar (derived from "Cultivated Variety"): 'H. E. Beale,' a name honoring one of the proprietors of the nursery firm which introduced this particular kind of Scotch Heather, is its cultivar name. As heathers do not "come true" from seed, the only way to get an exact duplicate of a desirable heather cultivar is by vegetative reproduction (cuttings, layering, tissue culture). Cultivar names are spelled with capital initials and are given in single quotes. When we ask for a plant of *Calluna vulgaris* 'H. E. Beale,' there should be no mistaking what kind we have in mind, wherever in the world we are.

In determining what should be the scientific name of a plant, taxonomists, since and before the time of Linnaeus [1707-1778], have relied heavily on the characters of the reproductive parts (the flowers and seed-bearing structures) of vascular (with veins for transporting the sap) plants, the so-called Higher Plants, to serve as criteria of particular significance in their classification.

This book is an effort to make plain to lay gardeners enough of the flowers and seed-bearing structures of their heathers to enable them to identify their species. With this information and perhaps a 10-power magnifying glass, it is hoped that anyone will be able to determine the species names of their plants.

Heather Cousins

COROLLA GAMOPETALOUS

COROLLA DECIDUOUS

Tribe: RHODODENDREAE Spreng. Fruit a septicidal capsule; corolla sometimes of separate petals.		Tribe: ANDROMEDEAE Drude. Fruit a loculicidal capsule; calyx dry, small.	
PHYLLODOCE	DABOECIA	CASSIOPE	ANDROMEDA
— — — — — — — — — — — — — — Low evergreen shrubs: — — — — — — — — — — — — — —			
prostrate or ascending		buds minute	subterete branches, winter buds small with 2 outer scales
Leaves: alternate, crowded, linear, revolute, usually serrulate	alternate, entire, subsessile	scale-like and imbricated in 4 rows or linear	short-petioled, narrow, entire
Flowers: in terminal umbels, nodding on slender pedicels	in terminal racemes on current year's growth	solitary, axillary or terminal,nodding, usually 5-merous	nodding, in terminal umbels
Calyx: 4-6-parted, small, persistent	small, 4-parted	small, 4-5-parted, with ovate, imbricate lobes	small, 5-lobed
Corolla: urceolate or campanulate, 4-6-lobed	campanulate-urceolate, with 4 short recurved lobes	campanulate, 4-5-lobed or cleft	globose-urceolate, with 5 short recurved lobes
Stamens: 8-12; anthers oblong, opening by a large pore	8, included; anthers with apical pores	8-10, filaments short; anthers with recurved awns on back, opening by apical pores	10, included; anthers with 2 slender ascending awns, opening by apical pores
Style: slender		short	
Capsule: globose to ovoid, 4-6-valved; many seeded	4-valved; seeds small, globose-ovoid, verruculose	globose, 4-5-celled, loculicidal; seeds minute, wingless, smooth	subglobose, 5-valved, loculicidal, the sutures not thickened; seeds oval, smooth

Heather Cousins

COROLLA GAMOPETALOUS

COROLLA PERSISTENT

Tribe: ERICEAE Drude Corolla persistent; fruit a septicidal, rarely loculicidal capsule. Evergreen shrubs with opposite or whorled, small needle-shaped or scale-like leaves.

	CALLUNA	ERICA	BRUCKENTHALIA
	Low evergreen shrubs		
Winter buds:	minute with small scales	minute	
Leaves:	scale-like, opposite, 4-ranked, sessile, keeled	usually whorled, short-petioled, small, usually strongly revolute, linear	alternate or in whorls of 4, linear
Flowers:	in terminal spikes	terminal or axillary, often in terminal spikes, umbels, racemes or panicles	4-merous, in short terminal, dense spikes
Calyx:	4-parted, colored, with 4 small bractlets at base, longer than corolla, persistent	free, 4-parted, shorter than corolla	4-lobed to about the middle, lobes denticulate, colored tube about as long as lobe, about half as long as corolla
Corolla:	campanulate,	campanulate, tubular, or ventricose, lobes usually 4, very short	campanulate, deeply 4-lobed
Stamens:	8, shorter than corolla; anthers with 2 reflexed appendages on back	8, filaments slender anthers with or without appendages	8, included; filaments connate at base and adnate to corolla; anthers ellipsoid, attached at base to filament, opening by oblong terminal pores; disk rudimentary
Style:	slender, about as long as calyx	slender	exserted
Capsule:	4-valved, septicidal, included in persistent perianth, few-seeded	subglobose, 4-valved, loculicidal, enclosed in persistent corolla; seeds many, minute	subglobose, 4-valved, loculicidal, enclosed in persistent calyx

from Rehder, Alfred: *Manual of Cultivated Trees and Shrubs.* 1956

BIBLIOGRAPHY

Allen, Sallie: personal communication.

ALPINES OF THE AMERICAS, ARGS REPORT, 1976.

Anon: *Pentapera sicula, JR. ROYAL HORT. SOC.*, Vol. 76, p.332.

Anon: *P. sicula*, BUL. *ALPINE GDN. SOC.*, Vol. 19, p. 337.

Anon: *P. sicula, BUL. A.G.S.*, Vol. 20, p. 344.

Anon: *P. sicula, JR. R.H.S.*, Vol. 77, p. 423.

Anon: *P. sicula, List of Plant Awards, BUL. A.G.S.*, Vol. 23, p.89.

Anon: *X Phylliopsis hillieri, BUL. A.G.S.*, Vol. 50, No. 4, p. 302.

Baker, H.S. & E.G.H. Oliver: *ERICAS IN SOUTHERN AFRICA*, ca. 1968.

Bean, W.J.: *TREES & SHRUBS HARDY IN THE BRITISH ISLES*, 1973.

Bean, W.J.: *Erica x veitchii, GARDENER'S CHRONICLE*, 1905.

Beijerinck, W.S: *CALLUNA, A MONOGRAPH ON THE SCOTCH HEATHER*, 1940.

Beijing Institute of Botany, Academia Sinica: *ICONOGRAPHIA CORMOPHYTORUM SINICORUM*, Tomus III, trans. by Judy Young.

Blum, H.M.J.: *ERICULTURA*, Feb. 1988.

Cabezudo, B. & J. Rivera: *Erica andevalensis, LAGASCALIA*, No. 2, 1980.

Calder, James A. & Roy L. Taylor: *FLORA OF THE QUEEN CHARLOTTE ISLANDS*, Pt. 1, 1968.

Camp, Wendell Holmes: *Phyllodoce Hybrids, NEW FLORA AND SILVA*, Vol. 12, Autumn 1940.

Chapple, Fred J.: *THE HEATHER GARDEN*, 1964 ed.

Chopinet, R.: *Les Bruyeres Rustique, PLANTES DES MONTAGNES*, Bul. de la Soc. de Jardins Alpin, 1967-68.

Copeland, Harold W.: *Heaths & Heathers, AMERICAN HORTICULTURAL MAGAZINE*, 46/2, 1967.

Davidson, James: *Heathers, JR. OF THE SCOTTISH ROCK GARDEN CLUB*, No. 28, April, 1961.

Davis, P.H.: *A journey in southwest Anatolia, JR. R.H.S.*, Vol. 74, pp. 155-164, 1949.

Davis, P.H.: *FLORA OF TURKEY AND THE EAST AEGAEAN ISLANDS*, Vol. VI, Edinburgh, 1978.

Eighme, Lloyd: *Heather in North American Gardens, HEATHER NEWS*, No. 21, 1983.

Elliott, J.G.: *Pot Luck, BUL. A.G.S.*, Vol. 26, p. 170, pp. 276-277, 1958.

Elliott, Roy: *From Alpine House to Scree Frame, BUL. A.G.S.*, Vol. 26, p. 5.

ENCYCLOPAEDIA BRITANNICA, 11th ed., 1911.

Everett, T.H.: *Pentapera, N.Y. BOT. GDN. ENCYCLOP. OF HORT.*, 1981.

FLORA EUROPAEA, 1972 ed.

Fraga, M.I.: *Notes on the Morphology and Distribution of Erica and Calluna in Galicia, North-Western Spain, GLASRA*, No. 7, 1984, *Contributions from the Nat. Bot. Gdn.*, Glasnevin, Dublin.

Fraser, Stuart: *Calluna vulgaris, HEATHER NEWS*, No. 9, Mar. 1980.

Fraser, Stuart: *Heathers in the Pacific Northwest, YR.BK.H.SOC.*, 1983.

Gilman, Arthur: *Native plants of Vermont, BUL. AM. ROCK GDN. SOC.*, Vol. 43, No.

4, Fall 1985.
Gleason, Henry A. & Arthur Cronquist: *THE NATURAL GEOGRAPHY OF PLANTS*, 1964.
Good, Ronald: *THE GEOGRAPHY OF THE FLOWERING PLANTS*, 1964.
Gray, Violet: *Erica multiflora, YR. BK. OF THE H. SOC.*, 1970.
Griffith, Anna N.: *COLLINS GUIDE TO ALPINES*, 1964.
Griffiths, John: *Hybridisation of the Hardy Ericas, YR.BK.H.SOC.*, 1985.
Griffiths, J.: *Hybridisation of the Hardy Ericas*, Pt. 2, *YR.BK.H.S.*, 1987.
Hayworth-Booth, Michael: *THE FLOWERING SHRUB GARDEN TODAY*, 1961.
Heath, Royton: *Pentapera sicula, SHRUBS FOR THE ROCK GARDEN AND ALPINE HOUSE*, 1954, pp. 135-136.
HEATHER NEWS, JR. of the N. Amer. Heather Soc., 1978 et seq.
The Heather Soc.: *YEAR BOOKS*, 1963 et seq.
The Heather Soc.: *QUARTERLY BULS.*, 1963 et seq.
The Heather Soc.: *HEATHER TRIALS*, 1971-1975.
The Heather Soc.: *HEATHER CULTURE* leaflets, 1982.
Heawood, Edw.: Ruwenzori, *ENCYCLOPAEDIA BRITANNICA*, 1911.
Hillier & Sons: *HILLIERS' MANUAL OF TREES & SHRUBS*, rev.1974.
Hills, L.D.: *THE PROPAGATION OF ALPINES*, 1959.
Hitchcock C. Leo & Arthur Cronquist: *FLORA OF THE PACIFIC NORTHWEST*, 1973.
Hulme, J.K.: *The Heather Garden at Ness, JR. OF THE SCOTTISH ROCK GARDEN CLUB*, No. 43, Sept. 1968.
Huxley, A.J.: *GARDEN TERMS SIMPLIFIED*, 1962.
Ingwersen, Wm.: *MANUAL OF ALPINE PLANTS*, 1978.
Johnson, A.T.: *THE HARDY HEATHS*, 1928.
Jones, A.W.: personal communications to 1989.
Jones, A.W.: *Sharp eyes help to solve the mystery of Erica 'Stuartii', YR.BK.H.S.*, 1979.
Jones, A.W.: *Notes on Erica manipuliflora, E. vagans and their hybrids, YR.BK.H.S.*, 1987.
Jones, A.W.: *Erica manipuliflora* (Salisb.) *in Yugoslavia*, October, 1988, *YR.BK.H.S.*, 1989.
Joyner, P.L.: *Erica manipuliflora, YR.BK.H.S.*, 1980.
Julian, T.A.: *Winter Damage at Harlow Car, YR.BK.H.S.*, 1980.
Julian, T.A.: *Damage at Harlow Car During the Winter of 1982, YR.BK.H.S.*, 1983.
Knight, F.P.: *The Heather Garden, REPORT OF THE 3RD INTERNATIONAL ROCK GARDEN PLANT CONFERENCE*, 1961.
Knight, F.P.: *Heaths & Heathers, WISLEY HANDBOOK No. 3*, 1976.
Krussman, Gerd: *MANUAL OF CULTIVATED BROAD-LEAVED TREES & SHRUBS*, 1985.
Lambie, David & Betty: *HEATHERS, A GUIDE TO DESIGNING A HEATHER GARDEN*, ca. 1986.
Lancaster, Roy: *Phylliopsis, THE GARDEN, JR.R.H.S.*, Vol. 102, 1977.
Lancaster, Roy: *Award Plants 1982, THE GARDEN, JR.R.H.S.*, Vol. 108, Feb. 1983.
Lawrence, G.H.M.: *TAXONOMY OF VASCULAR PLANTS*, 1951.
Letts, John F.: *HARDY HEATHS & HEATHERS AND THE HEATHER GARDEN*,

1966.
Lilley, S.E.: *Cassiopes, JR.R.H.S.*, Vol. 90, 1965, pp. 302-305.
Lindley, John: *PAXTON'S FLOWER GARDEN*, 1882.
Magor, E.W.M.: *Riddles of the Irish Heaths, YR.BK.H.S.*, 1981.
Manning, L.S.: *Heaths & Heathers and Their Culture in California, CAL. HORT., JR. OF THE CAL. HORT. SOC.*, XXVI/1, 1965.
Maxwell, D. Fyfe: *THE LOW ROAD*, 1927.
Maxwell, D.F. & P.S. Patrick: *THE ENGLISH HEATHER GARDEN,* 1966.
McClintock, David: personal communications to 1989.
McClintock, D.: *Species of Heather in Great Britain, YR.BK.H.S.*, 1964.
McClintock, D.: *Notes on British Heaths, YR.BK.H.S.*, 1965.
McClintock, D.: *St. Dabeoc's heaths and their hybrids, THE GARDEN, JR.R.H.S.*, Mar. 1978.
McClintock, D.: *The Status of and Correct Name for Erica x stuartii, WATSONIA*, Vol. 12, No. 3, Feb. 1979.
McClintock, D.: *A Day in my Heather Garden, THE GARDEN, JR.R.H.S.*, May 1980.
McClintock, D.: *A GUIDE TO THE NAMING OF PLANTS,* 2nd ed., 1980.
McClintock, D.: *Erica sicula, YR.BK.H.S.*, 1980.
McClintock, D.: *A Double Form of Daboecia cantabrica, YR.BK. H.S.*, 1982.
McClintock, D.: *Iter Hispanicum Ericaceum, YR.BK.H.S.*, 1983.
McClintock, D.: *Daboecias with erect flowers, YR.BK.H.S.*, 1984.
McClintock, D.: *The Heathers of Europe and Adjacent Areas, BOT. JR. OF THE LINNEAN SOC.*, 101: 1989, pp. 279-289.
Mulligan, Brian O.: *WOODY PLANTS OF THE UNIV. OF WASH. ARBORETUM*, 1977.
Munson, R.H.: *Heaths and Heathers Cultivated in North America, BAILEYA*, Vol. 22, No. 3, Feb. 1984.
Munson, R.H.: *The Daboecia Species-Hybrid Complex. The Scanning Electron Microscope and Cultivar Identification. Chemical Means of Cultivar Identification. BAILEYA*, Vol. 22, No. 4, Jan. 1985.
Munz, Philip A. with David W. Keck: *A CALIFORNIA FLORA*, 1968- 1973.
Nederlandse Heidevereniging: *ERICULTURA*, No.40, 1980 and No. 61, 1986.
Nelson, E.C.: *Dabeoc—A Saint and his Heather, YR.BK.H.S.*, 1984.
Nelson, E.C. and M.I. Fraga: *Studies in Erica mackaiana Bab.,* II*: Distribution in northern Spain, GLASRA*, No. 7, 1982.
Nelson, E.C. & David McClintock: *Two new wild white-flowered heathers (Erica andevalensis and E. mackaiana) from Spain, GLASRA*, No. 7, 1982.
Northen, Henry T. & Rebecca: *THE SECRET OF THE GREEN THUMB*, 1954.
Ohwi, Jisaburo: *FLORA OF JAPAN*, 1984.
Parris, Anne A.: *Notes on a cross between Erica erigena and E. carnea, YR.BK.H.S.*, 1976-77-78-80.
Patrick, Leslie B.: *Making a Garden in Argyll, YR.BK.H.S.*, 1974.
Platt, J.: *New Acquisitions, YR.BK.H.S.*, annual reports, 1977 et seq.
Polunin, Oleg & Anthony Huxley: *FLOWERS OF THE MEDITERRANEAN*, 1966.
Polunin, O. & B.E. Smythies: *FLOWERS OF SOUTHWEST EUROPE*, 1973.

Proudley, Brian & Valerie: *HEATHERS IN COLOUR*, 1974.
Rehder, Alfred: *MANUAL OF CULTIVATED TREES & SHRUBS*, 1956.
Richards, D.A.: *Daboecia cantabrica at home, YR.BK.H.S.*,1970.
Richards, D.A.: *Mostly Erica maderensis and Daboecia azorica, YR.BK.H.S.*, 1976.
Ripley, D.: *Some Plants of Southern Europe, Bul.A.G.S.*, Vol. 5, p. 69.
Royal Horticultural Soc.: *COLOUR CHART*, 1966.
Royal Horticultural Soc.: *DICTIONARY OF GARDENING*, 1962.
Seymour, F.C.: *THE FLORA OF NEW ENGLAND*, 1969.
Sheat, W.G.: *PROPAGATION OF TREES, SHRUBS & CONIFERS*, 1953.
Singe, Patrick: *IN SEARCH OF FLOWERS*, 1985.
Small, David: personal communications.
Small, D.: *Champagne in Connemara, BUL. H. S.*, Autumn, 1983.
Smith, A.W.: *A GARDENER'S BOOK OF PLANT NAMES*, 1963.
Stevens, P.F.: *Ericaceae, FLORA OF TURKEY AND THE EAST AEGAEAN ISLANDS*, (P.H. Davis)
Stoker, Fred: *The Genus Phyllodoce, NEW FLORA & SILVA*, Vol. 12, Spring, 1942.
Stoker, F.: *Pentapera sicula, R.H.S. DICT. OF GARDENING*, 1962, 1984.
Street, Harold: *Living with Lime, YR.BK.H.S.*, 1979.
Szczawinski, Adam: *THE HEATHER FAMILY OF BRITISH COLUMBIA*, 1962.
Turpin, P.G.: personal communications.
Turpin, P.G.: *The Tree Heaths,* 'Gold Tips' *and* 'Pink Joy,' *YR.BK.H.S.*, 1979.
Turpin, P.G.: *Heather Gardens, YR.BK.H.S.*, 1981.
Underhill, Terry L.: *HEATHS & HEATHERS*, 1971.
van de Laar, Harry: *THE HEATHER GARDEN* (English ed.), 1978.
Webb, D.A.: *AN IRISH FLORA*, 1953.
Webb, D.A. & E.M. Rix: *Ericaceae, FLORA EUROPAEA*, 1972.
Webster, Norman: *Hardy Heathers, JR. SCOTTISH ROCK GARDEN CLUB*. No. 18, 1956.
Wilder, Louise Beebe: *THE GARDEN IN COLOR*, 1937.
Wilson, Ken: *The Botanical Garden, The Univ. of British Columbia, YR.BK.H.S.*, 1975.
Woolner, Lionel R.: *Erica scoparia, YR.BK.H.S.*, 1974.
Yates, Geoffrey: *Dwarf & Prostrate Heaths & Heathers, JR.A.G.S.*, No. 162, 1970.
Yates, G.: *THE GARDENER'S BOOK OF HEATHERS*, 1985.
Yates, G.: *POCKET GUIDE TO HEATHER GARDENING*, 1978.

GLOSSARY

Numbers refer to illustrations, pp. 185-186.

abortive: imperfectly developed; defective; barren.
acicular: needle-shaped. (1)
acute: coming to a sharp point. (2)
adnate: fused with unlike parts.
adpressed: lying flat against.
adventitious: growing elsewhere than in the usual place.
A.G.M.: Award of Garden Merit (Royal Horticultural Soc.)
alternate: growing not opposite or whorled but from different sides of the stem at different heights. (3)
A.M.: Award of Merit (Royal Horticultural Soc.)
anther: the pollen-bearing part of the stamen. (27b)
anthesis: when the flower is opening and can be pollinated.
apiculate: terminated in a short sharp point. (4)
appendage: an attached subsidiary part; a sort of tail attached to an anther. (27d)
ascending: rising obliquely and curving upward. (5)
auricle: an ear-shaped, leaf-like structure at the base of some leaves or petals. (19d)
biotype: a race typical of a genus; a group of biologically similar genera.
bract: a much reduced leaf, particularly those associated with a flower or inflorescence, or at the base of a leaf (26a)
bracteole: a secondary bract. (25b)
calcifuge: unable to tolerate calcareous soils.
calyx: the outer whorl of a flower, composed of the sepals. (25c)
campanulate: bell-shaped.
capitate: in a dense cluster; with a head, as the stigma of *Erica arborea*.
capsule: a dry fruit composed of chambers bearing several seeds.
cilia: fine hairs. (24b)
clone: a group of individuals resulting from vegetative propagation (e.g., by cuttings) and therefore presumably identical to the parent.
conical: cone-shape in outline.
corolla: the inner, usually conspicuous, whorl of a flower; in *Erica, Daboecia* species, for example, the bell. (25e)
cultivar: a contraction of 'cultivated variety'. A cultivar name is indicated by single quotes ' ' and capital initial(s); e.g., *Calluna vulgaris* 'Aurea'.
deciduous: dropping off of the plant at the end of one season.
decumbent: reclining just above but not on the ground, and with the ends rising. (6)
disjunct: plant population whose geographical location is separated by a wide geographical area from others of its same kind.
disc: structure from which the pistil and stamens rise. (27j)
divergent: spreading broadly.
elliptical: oval, but narrowed to rounded ends. (7)

endemic: a plant variety limited in its distribution to a (usually restricted) geographical area.
entire: without teeth or divisions.
erect: rising vertically.
exserted: protruding beyond the mouth of the corolla. (25g)
f.: forma, form, variety.
Family: a subdivision of an Order as determined by some authoritative botanist; e.g., the Family of Ericaceae, the Heath Family, is one member of the Order of Ericales.
fascicle: leaves or flowers gathered together in bundles. (8)
fastigiate: with erect branches.
F.C.C.: First Class Certificate, the highest plant award of the Royal Horticultural Soc.
filament: the stalk of the stamen. (27e)
5-parted: with the sepals and/or other flower parts in 5 divisions.
fruit: the seed-bearing organ of a flower.
gamopetalous: with the petals of the flower united, at least at the base. (25e)
genera: plural of genus.
genotype: a type plant or population, as determined by genetic characters; the type species of a genus.
genus (pl. genera): a unit of a plant Family; e.g., the genera *Andromeda, Bruckenthalia, Calluna, Daboecia, Erica, Cassiope, Phyllodoce* are members of the Ericaceae Family.
glabrous: lacking any kind of hairy vestiture.
gland-tipped: terminating in a gland-like body; e.g.,some hairs. (9, 24b)
glandular: bearing gland-like appendages.
heath: see p. 2.
Hort.: abbreviation of 'horticulture', used to identify the source of a cultivar name.
hybrid: a plant derived from female and male parents of different cultivars, species or more rarely genera.
imbricate: overlapping, as shingles on a roof, cf. *Calluna* illustration, p. 13, Db, *Cassiope fastigiata*, p. 122, A.
included: not protruding, e.g., stamens not protruding beyond mouth of corolla, as in *Daboecia cantabrica*, p. 21.
inflorescence: the flowering part of the plant. (16, 17, 18)
intercalary: indicating growth which takes place elsewhere than at the growing point.
internode: the area of a stem between two nodes or growing points.
layer: propagation by burying part of a still-attached, more or less horizontal branch under the soil until it develops roots.
loculicidal: opening of a fruit on the back, more or less midway between the partitions.
margin: the outside edge. (19a, 21a, 22a, 23a)
-merous: 3-merous, 4-merous, 5-merous, etc.: refers to the number of parts of the reproductive organs, e.g. petals, sepals, etc.
moor: see p. 4.
mucronate: (24a)
new-growth: normal young growth in its first season.
North American list, 1983: as published in North American Heather Society's *HEATHER*

NEWS, Mar. 1983.
obconical: inversely conical.
oblong-lanceolate: (10)
obtuse: blunt. (11)
ovary: the seed-bearing structure of a flower. (27i)
ovate: a flat surface which is egg-shaped in outline. (12)
ovoid: with the appearance of an egg-shaped solid body.
panicle: a branching type of inflorescence. (16)
patent (pay-tent): spreading horizontally. (13)
pedicel: the stalk of one flower. (16b, 17b, 18b, 25a)
peduncle: the stalk of a flower cluster, or what remains of one. (16c, 17c, 18c)
perianth: the corolla and calyx taken together.
persistent: remaining on the plant; not deciduous.
petaloid: resembling a petal.
petiole: the stalk of a leaf. (23c)
pistil: the female organ of a flower, consisting of the ovary, style and stigma. (27f)
procumbent: lying on the ground, but not rooting. (14)
puberulent or puberulous: with very small, scarcely visible hairs.
pubescent: downy, covered with short, soft hairs.
pulverulent: finely powdery.
raceme: a simple, elongated inflorescence with stalked flowers. (17)
Rehder rating: hardiness zone rating as stated in Alfred Rehder's *MANUAL OF CULTIVATED TREES AND SHRUBS*, 1926 et seq.
repent: creeping on the surface and rooting at the nodes. (15)
revolute: with margin rolled back toward the lower side. (21a, 22a, 23b)
rhizomatous: with rhizomes, i.e. underground stems or rootstocks, usually horizontally-growing.
saccate: shaped like a pouch.
scarious: thin and dry looking.
secund: with flowers appearing to grow on just one side of a stem, as with *E. x darleyensis* 'Darley Dale', p. 57, A.
sepal: a segment of the calyx. (25d)
septicidal: opening along the partition lines.
serrate: with a saw-toothed margin, the teeth pointing forward.
serrulate: serrate with very small teeth.
sessile: sitting, without a stalk, as a leaf without a petiole. (24c)
sp.: abbreviation for species (singular).
species: (sing. or pl.) a subdivision of a plant Family as determined by its botanical characters.
sport: a gene change occurring on a part of a plant which when propagated by cutting will develop into a plant showing the character of the original atypical part; e.g., a persisting stem of golden foliage on a generally green-leaved plant.
spp.: abbreviation indicating the plural of species; more than one species.
ssp.: subspecies, a division of a given species.
stamen: the male organ of a flower, consisting of the filament and the pollen-bearing